lonely planet

Ecuador & the Galápagos Islands

Regis St Louis
Lucy Burningham, Aimée Dowl
Michael Grosberg

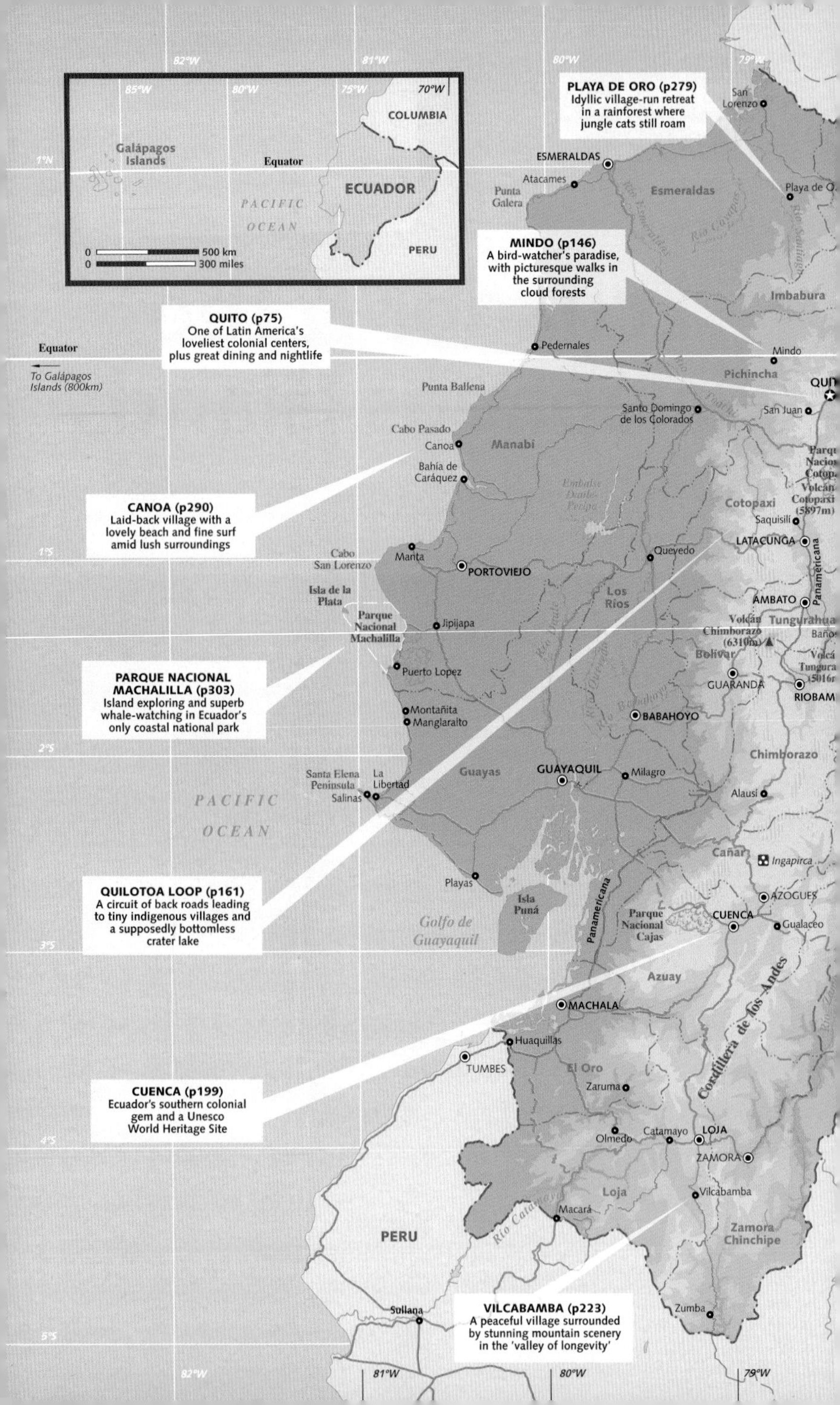
PLAYA DE ORO (p279)
Idyllic village-run retreat in a rainforest where jungle cats still roam
MINDO (p146)
A bird-watcher's paradise, with picturesque walks in the surrounding cloud forests
QUITO (p75)
One of Latin America's loveliest colonial centers, plus great dining and nightlife
CANOA (p290)
Laid-back village with a lovely beach and fine surf amid lush surroundings
PARQUE NACIONAL MACHALILLA (p303)
Island exploring and superb whale-watching in Ecuador's only coastal national park
QUILOTOA LOOP (p161)
A circuit of back roads leading to tiny indigenous villages and a supposedly bottomless crater lake
CUENCA (p199)
Ecuador's southern colonial gem and a Unesco World Heritage Site
VILCABAMBA (p223)
A peaceful village surrounded by stunning mountain scenery in the 'valley of longevity'
COLUMBIA
Galápagos Islands
Equator
ECUADOR
PACIFIC OCEAN
PERU
0 500 km
0 300 miles
85°W
80°W
75°W
70°W
82°W
81°W
80°W
79°W
1°N
1°S
2°S
3°S
4°S
5°S
Equator
To Galápagos Islands (800km)
San Lorenzo
ESMERALDAS
Atacames
Punta Galera
Esmeraldas
Playa de Oro
Río Esmeraldas
Río Cayapas
Río Santiago
Imbabura
Pedernales
Mindo
Pichincha
Punta Ballena
Santo Domingo de los Colorados
San Juan
Cabo Pasado
Canoa
Manabi
Bahía de Caráquez
Embalse Daule Peripa
Parque Nacional Cotopaxi
Volcán Cotopaxi (5897m)
Cotopaxi
Saquisilí
LATACUNGA
Panamericana
Cabo San Lorenzo
Manta
PORTOVIEJO
Quevedo
Isla de la Plata
Parque Nacional Machalilla
Los Ríos
AMBATO
Jipijapa
Volcán Chimborazo (6310m)
Tungurahua
Baños
Volcán Tungurahua (5016m)
Bolívar
Puerto Lopez
GUARANDA
RIOBAMBA
Montañita
Manglaralto
BABAHOYO
Chimborazo
Santa Elena Peninsula
La Libertad
Salinas
Guayas
GUAYAQUIL
Milagro
Alausí
PACIFIC OCEAN
Cañar
Ingapirca
Playas
AZOGUES
Isla Puná
Panamericana
Parque Nacional Cajas
CUENCA
Gualaceo
Golfo de Guayaquil
Azuay
Cordillera de los Andes
MACHALA
Huaquillas
TUMBES
El Oro
Zaruma
Olmedo
Catamayo
LOJA
ZAMORA
Loja
Vilcabamba
Macará
Río Catamayo
PERU
Zamora Chinchipe
Zumba
Sullana

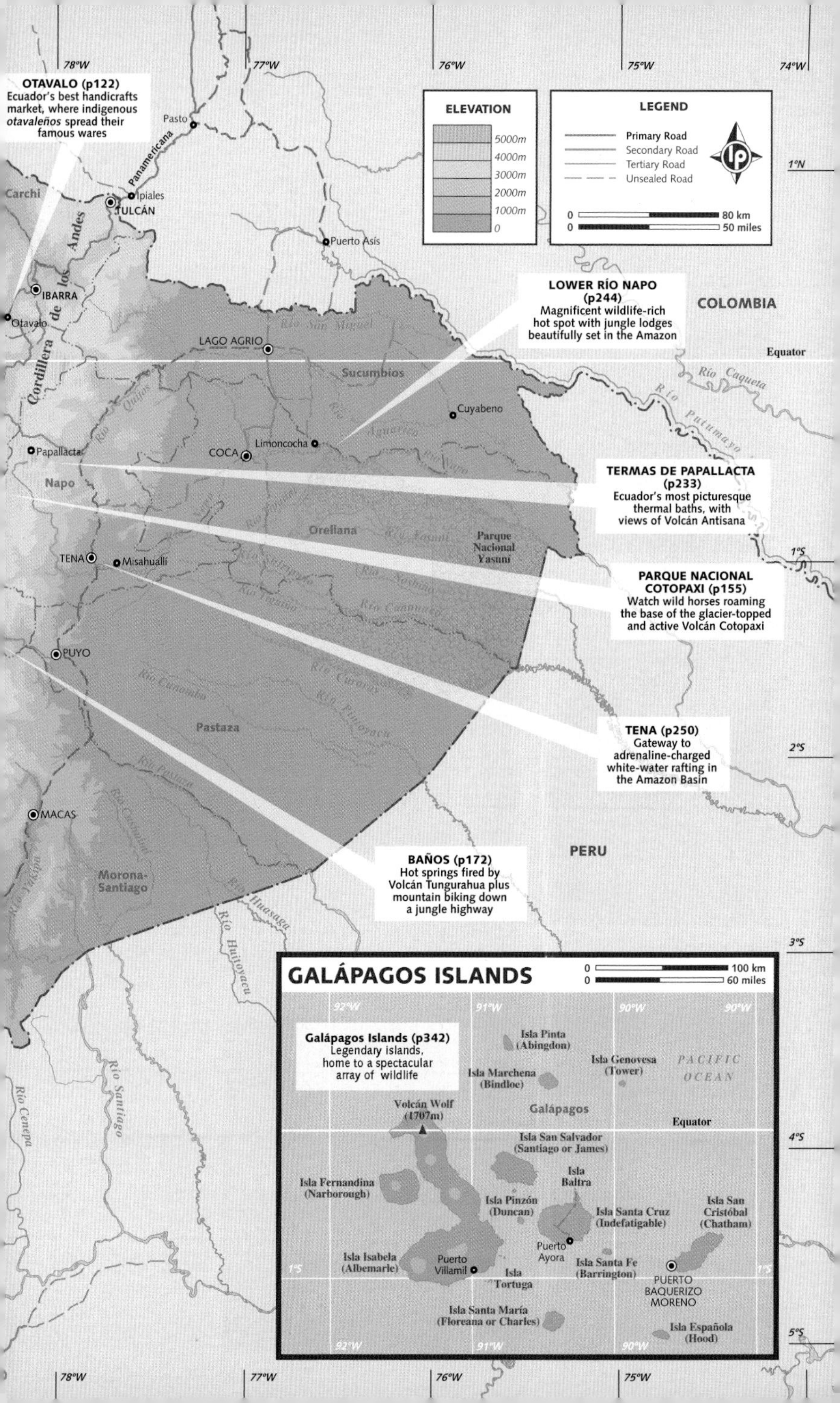
OTAVALO (p122)
Ecuador's best handicrafts market, where indigenous *otavaleños* spread their famous wares
LOWER RÍO NAPO (p244)
Magnificent wildlife-rich hot spot with jungle lodges beautifully set in the Amazon
TERMAS DE PAPALLACTA (p233)
Ecuador's most picturesque thermal baths, with views of Volcán Antisana
PARQUE NACIONAL COTOPAXI (p155)
Watch wild horses roaming the base of the glacier-topped and active Volcán Cotopaxi
TENA (p250)
Gateway to adrenaline-charged white-water rafting in the Amazon Basin
BAÑOS (p172)
Hot springs fired by Volcán Tungurahua plus mountain biking down a jungle highway
ELEVATION
5000m
4000m
3000m
2000m
1000m
0
LEGEND
Primary Road
Secondary Road
Tertiary Road
Unsealed Road
0 80 km
0 50 miles
78°W
77°W
76°W
75°W
74°W
1°N
Equator
1°S
2°S
3°S
4°S
5°S
COLOMBIA
PERU
Pasto
Panamericana
Ipiales
TULCÁN
Carchi
Cordillera de los Andes
IBARRA
Otavalo
Puerto Asís
LAGO AGRIO
Río San Miguel
Sucumbíos
Río Caquetá
Río Putumayo
Cuyabeno
Río Aguarico
Limoncocha
COCA
Río Napo
Río Quijos
Papallacta
Napo
Orellana
Río Yasuní
Parque Nacional Yasuní
TENA
Misahuallí
Río Tiputini
Río Nashiño
Río Curaray
Río Conambo
Río Pintoyacu
Pastaza
PUYO
Río Pastaza
MACAS
Río Cushuimi
Morona-Santiago
Río Yakipa
Río Huasaga
Río Huitoyacu
Río Santiago
Río Cenepa
GALÁPAGOS ISLANDS
0 100 km
0 60 miles
92°W
91°W
90°W
Galápagos Islands (p342)
Legendary islands, home to a spectacular array of wildlife
Isla Pinta (Abingdon)
Isla Genovesa (Tower)
PACIFIC OCEAN
Isla Marchena (Bindloe)
Galápagos
Volcán Wolf (1707m)
Equator
Isla San Salvador (Santiago or James)
Isla Fernandina (Narborough)
Isla Baltra
Isla Pinzón (Duncan)
Isla Santa Cruz (Indefatigable)
Isla San Cristóbal (Chatham)
Puerto Ayora
Isla Isabela (Albemarle)
Puerto Villamil
Isla Tortuga
Isla Santa Fe (Barrington)
PUERTO BAQUERIZO MORENO
1°S
Isla Santa María (Floreana or Charles)
Isla Española (Hood)

On the Road

REGIS ST LOUIS
Coordinating Author
In the afternoon I made the descent into Pululahua (p116) – which is always shrouded in mist after about midday. I would later meet some fascinating people in the village, including the 90-year-old and strong-as-an-ox Don Miguel and an engineer from Quito who's fallen hard for the volcanic Garden of Eden.

LUCY BURNINGHAM During my first spear-throwing lesson, my guide Delfin demonstrated how to propel the heavy weapon into an imaginary animal. I followed his lead in the sweltering heat outside the home of a village healer, on the edge of a cocoa plantation. Alas, my throws always fell short.

AIMÉE DOWL High in the Cordillera del Cóndor, downstream from Cabañas Yanquam (p222), and hundreds of kilometers from the sea, my Shuar guide pointed out petrified fossils of giant shells. I was checking them out while the blackwater Río Nangaritza tried to steal away with our boat.

MICHAEL GROSBERG
Waiting for a giant tortoise to poke its head out can be a long wait. Five minutes or so after squatting down, this one could only get so far.

For full author biographies see p416

Ecuador Highlights

It's the second-smallest country in South America, but Ecuador packs a punch. In one day you can drive from the Amazon Basin across glaciated Andean volcanoes, down through tropical cloud forest and sputter into the sunset for a dinner of ceviche on the Pacific Coast, where – yes indeed – the water is warm. The greatest challenge is just deciding where to begin. Shopping for hand-woven wool sweaters at a bustling indigenous market? Braving the hair-raising descent of El Nariz del Diablo (The Devil's Nose) on a rickety train? Spotting howler monkeys in the jungle canopy? Here, a selection of Lonely Planet authors and staff share their most memorable experiences.

ALFREDO MAIQUEZ

1 QUITO

I've visited scores of colonial cities all across Latin America, but strolling the old cobblestone streets of Quito's old town (p79) reminds me that nowhere else quite compares.

Regis St Louis, Lonely Planet Author

RALPH HOPKINS

2 GALÁPAGOS ISLANDS

Watching wildlife on the islands (p65) is a fascinating journey back through the millennia. It's easy to imagine Darwin's amazement at catching sight of giant tortoises lumbering over the volcanic landscape.

Regis St Louis, Lonely Planet Author

OTAVALO

At the market town of Otavalo (p122), the modern world comes crashing up against the old in a sensory assault of color, smell and sound. Under the cloud-covered shadow of the Imbabura volcanic peak, virtually the whole town is transformed into a street market. From the spectacularly colorful, locally woven textiles to the carved wooden trinkets; from the food vendors selling hot snacks from hand-woven baskets to the watercolorists from the Peruvian school painting and selling their scenes of local folklore. The well-heeled day-trippers from Quito rub shoulders with the local merchants, whose diverse ethnic origins are identifiable to those in the know by their distinctive traditional dress.

Neil Manders, Lonely Planet Staff

3

RICHARD I'AN

AIMÉE D

4 VOLCÁN COTOPAXI

The all-night climb to the summit of Volcán Cotopaxi (p155) is rewarded with extraordinary views of the surrounding plains, Volcán Sangay puffing plumes of smoke, and at least a dozen other peaks. When you peer down, you see a steaming black hole of a crater and get a strong whiff of sulfur.

Aimée Dowl, Lonely Planet Author

BRENT WINEBRENNER

SEEING A CONDOR

I was descending from the craggy summit of Volcán Rumiñahui (p152). As I was looking out over the plain an Andean condor, with his unmistakable white collar, soared up over a ridge, riding the thermals on enormous outstretched wings.

Aimée Dowl, Lonely Planet Author

6

JASON EDWARDS

5

RAINFOREST WALKS

In the jungle (p234), good guides move quietly and patiently, using all their senses to track wildlife. A creaky branch, a parade of leaf-cutter ants or a ripple in the blackwater speaks to them, and usually translates into a glimpse of something special.

Lucy Burningham, Lonely Planet Author

ALICE GRULICH-JONES

7

CUENCA

Cuenca (p199) was by far my favorite spot: a quaint colonial mountain town with stone streets lined with colorful buildings. We stayed there as a base for our camping foray into Parque Nacional Cajas, which was gloriously remote and untrammeled by visitors.

Christina Tunnah, Lonely Planet Staff

AIMÉE DOWL

8 GETTING HEALED AT LATACUNGA'S MAMÁ NEGRA FESTIVAL

Nobody gets to just watch the Mamá Negra festival (p158). As soon as the *huacos* (witches) saw me they ran over and started chanting and pretending to poke me with deer antlers. It wasn't over until I got the full ritual, which involved spitting *aguardiente* (sugarcane alcohol) all over my body.

Aimée Dowl, Lonely Planet Author

9 UNWINDING ON THE PACIFIC COAST

Ecuador's Pacific coast (p303) may not have the white-sand beaches of the Caribbean, but it has some marvelous places to unwind, take in a bit of surf and enjoy the charming pace of village life.

Regis St Louis, Lonely Planet Author

RYAN

GRANT DIX

10 THE RUINS AT INGAPIRCA

An amazing thing about Ecuador's best-preserved Inca ruins at Ingapirca (p196), besides the structure itself, is that local Cañari people still use it – to meet, to stage festivals, to graze their llamas and sheep. These ruins are not big as those at Machu Picchu in Peru, but they certainly have some local soul.

Aimée Dowl, Lonely Planet Author

Contents

Regional Map Contents

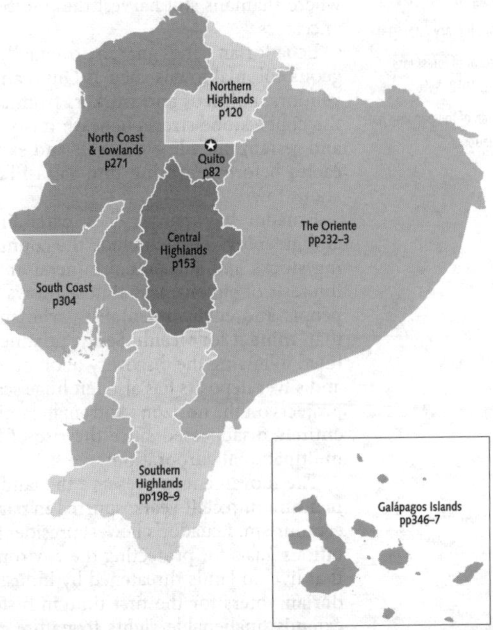

Destination Ecuador & the Galápagos Islands

This small Andean nation towers above most other countries when it comes to natural and cultural wonders. Amazonian rainforest, Andean peaks, premontane cloud forests and the Galápagos Islands set the stage for Ecuador's spectacular biodiversity. Wildlife-watching is just one way to enjoy its riches, with dozens of animal and plant species found nowhere else on earth. On even a short Ecuadorian adventure, it's possible to photograph monkeys from jungle canopy towers, swim with sea lions in the Pacific and admire dozens of Ecuador's 1600 bird species in misty forests.

Ecuador's blend of lush forested landscapes and volcanic scenery also provides a spectacular backdrop to adrenaline-charged adventures – from white-water rafting on Class V rivers to climbing 5000m-high volcanoes. There's magnificent hiking along old Inca trails, surfing on tight breaks off the west coast and diving amid dramatic underwater scenery.

The incredibly varied geography of Ecuador is matched only by its cultural diversity. Over a dozen indigenous peoples live here, each contributing to the rich and complicated notion of Ecuadorian identity. There are highland villages renowned for their colorful textiles, coastal Afro-Ecuadorian towns where days end with meals of fresh seafood enjoyed with memorable sunsets, and remote settlements in the Amazon where shamans still harvest the traditional rainforest medicines of their ancestors.

Ecuadorian cities march to equally alluring rhythms. By day, gorgeous colonial towns such as Quito and Cuenca teem with life, as street vendors, politicos and workers from all parts of the country mingle on the cobblestone streets beneath misty Andean skies. At night, the cafés and restaurants fill with locals and expats alike dining on regional delicacies before venturing into salsa-filled bars and nightclubs scattered about town.

Ecuador has many riches, extending well beyond its cities, people and greenery. These include the country's agricultural abundance, fishing stocks and substantial mineral and oil reserves. Until recently, the interests of big business almost always trumped the voices of indigenous people and environmentalists, who sought to preserve the land rather than mine it for wealth. Sadly, pristine swaths of the Amazon were polluted following the discovery of oil in the 1960s. Mining for gold, copper and silver deposits has also left huge scars on the countryside, with more projects on the horizon. And small family-run farms of the lowlands have entirely disappeared since the rise of large-scale plantations owned by multinational corporations.

The movement to preserve the land, however, has been gaining momentum in recent years, spurred in part by the increasing earnings from ecotourism. Ecuador's newest president, Rafael Correa, has set some ambitious goals for protecting the environment and the indigenous groups that live on lands threatened by industrial development. In 2008, Ecuadorian voters for the first time in history approved a constitution that extends 'inalienable rights to nature.' The ground-breaking document

FAST FACTS

Population: 14 million

GDP per capita: $7700

GDP growth rate: 3.4%

Minimum wage: $200 per month

Inflation rate: 8.6%

Unemployment rate: 8.7%

Number of internet users: 1.5 million

Adult literacy rate: 91%

Percent of forest loss since 1950: 54%

Origin of the panama hat: Ecuador

took a pronounced shift to the left on other issues as well, expanding indigenous rights and social-welfare policies and allowing civil unions for gay couples.

At the time of research, Correa enjoyed very high approval ratings. Meanwhile, he's earned critics on both sides of politics. Those on the right say the economic losses will be too high if Correa attempts to implement his socially progressive agenda, while those on the left feel his radical discourse is mere window dressing. The next few years will be pivotal to the young president – and for the many millions of Ecuadorians whose future is at stake.

Getting Started

Ecuador's great strengths are its astounding natural and cultural diversity coupled with its relatively small size. Although Ecuador is largely an uncomplicated country to travel around without a lot of planning, some places will require a bit of pre-trip legwork. This is particularly true of excursions to the Galápagos Islands, which you can arrange in your home country (the priciest option) or with tour companies in Quito (better value, but may require a few days or longer to schedule). You'll also want to book in advance for a jungle lodge if you're planning to include this in your itinerary, and you'll want to inquire with guides if you have any particular ambitions – climbing Cotopaxi or rafting the Upper Napo, for instance.

Travel in Ecuador accommodates a range of budgets. Those willing to rough it a bit will have the entire country open to them, with dizzying bus rides, hard-to-reach jungle destinations, long canoe rides and mystery market food all part of the equatorial experience. Those looking for high-end comfort will find it in heritage towns like Quito and Cuenca, the better haciendas in the highlands, some Amazon lodges and aboard the luxury boats cruising the Galápagos.

Travelers seeking a bit of balance between the two worlds – with a fair dose of adventure, good restaurants and memorable overnights, all at excellent prices – will find it all in Ecuador.

WHEN TO GO

Ecuador is a year-round destination. Each region – the Andes, the Pacific coast, the Oriente and the Galápagos – has its optimal visiting season (details are given in respective chapters). In terms of weather there are only two real seasons, the rainy season and the dry season, but there are significant variations between the geographical regions, and temperature is often a factor of altitude. Even during the rainy season, most days are sunny until the afternoon.

For more details on the weather, see Climate Charts (p380) in the Directory.

The highland dry season is June to the end of September. In the Oriente it rains during most months but August and December through March are usually the driest. Both seasons have advantages and disadvantages (see p231).

In the Galápagos, wildlife can be viewed year-round. If you're at all prone to sea sickness, avoid the rough seas from July to October. The dry season (June to December) is also cool and often misty. Also, see p349.

On the coast, the wet season (roughly January to May) sees sunny days with daily afternoon downpours, but it's the best beach weather. The dry season (roughly June to December) is cooler and usually overcast.

Tourist high seasons throughout Ecuador coincide with European, North American and Ecuadorian vacation periods, roughly mid-December through January and June through August. During this time accommodation rates are highest, and reservations at more popular lodging options are advised.

Accommodations can be hard to find during local festivals, so reserve in advance if you plan to arrive during a town celebration. Dates for these are provided in respective destination sections.

COSTS & MONEY

Costs in Ecuador have risen since the official currency was changed to the US dollar (see p33), but it's still affordable. Budget travelers can get by on $20 per day, staying in the cheapest hotels, eating *almuerzos* (set lunches), cooking their own food and taking buses rather than taxis. Raise the ante to around $40 per day, and you can stay in modest but comfortable hotels, take cab rides when you're feeling lazy, eat in better restaurants, visit museums, go out at night and

DON'T LEAVE HOME WITHOUT...

- A waterproof, windproof jacket – it will rain and the wind will blow (especially in the highlands)
- Ear plugs – often essential for sleeping
- A universal sink plug – a must for hand-washing clothes
- The proper vaccinations (see p402)
- Travel insurance (see p383)
- Dental floss – sews your clothes, laces your shoes and more!
- Duct tape (make your own mini-roll around a pencil stub or a lighter)
- A hat, sunglasses and sunscreen
- A pocket flashlight (torch)
- A travel alarm clock
- A Swiss Army–style pocket knife (but don't forget to pack it in your checked baggage)
- Ziplock bags
- A few meters of cord (makes great clothesline)
- Insect repellent (containing 30% DEET)
- Photocopies of your passport and essential travel documents
- A good novel for those long bus rides (p397)

cover the occasional $10 national park fee. Spending $50 to $70 per day will allow you to sleep and eat in style, plus partake in plenty of nightlife.

Things get expensive when you start adding tours (climbing, mountain-biking, bird-watching and other tours cost $35 to $80 per day), staying at jungle lodges or haciendas and – priciest of all – visiting the Galápagos Islands.

TRAVELING RESPONSIBLY

Tourist numbers have increased significantly in recent years, and tourism is the country's fourth-largest source of revenue. Undeniably, visitors have an impact on the country, which can be positive or negative depending on a number of factors. The best way to make sure your money goes to the right people is to support local businesses, such as small family-run restaurants and guesthouses rather than foreign-owned places. If you plan to study Spanish in Ecuador (and it's a great place to learn), try to choose a school that invests a portion of its profits in the community. And consider living with a local family.

Just by staying in a lodge in the Amazon, you can help to preserve the rainforest. In the face of increasing deforestation, more and more lodges are creating their own reserves simply to ensure their guests will have some wildlife to observe during their visit. Be sure to ask what the lodge is doing for the environment before booking a reservation.

Support local artisans by buying locally made handicrafts and artwork, and try to buy at the source. Keep an eye out for illegal artifacts such as pre-Columbian pieces, mounted insects, items made from endangered animals, or jewelry made from sea turtle or black coral, and avoid buying them.

What you eat also affects the environment. Shrimp farms, in particular, have caused widespread destruction of mangroves and coastal ecosystems. Try to limit your intake when in Ecuador.

What you leave behind is also something to consider. Take home your plastics and batteries when you leave, as Ecuador has no means of processing these things.

HOW MUCH?

Bus travel per hour about $1

Set lunch $2-3.50

Short cab ride in Quito $2

Private language class per hour $5-7

One-way mainland flight $60-90

When signing up for a package tour or expedition, whether it's a Galápagos tour or a rafting or climbing trip, be sure to ask lots of questions before committing. In order to minimize the impact of your visit, you'll want to choose an outfit that's sensitive to the local ecology and its resident communities. Guides shouldn't hunt, cut trees for bonfires, harass wildlife, or litter, and they should support in some way the communities they visit. Try to find out if outfits use indigenous or local guides.

TOP PICKS

OUTDOOR ADVENTURES

Ecuador's combination of tropical rainforest, snow-covered peaks and wild coastline makes for some superb adventures. For more on the array of adrenaline-fueled activities see p61.

- Snorkeling with marine life, followed by wildlife-watching in the Galápagos (p342)
- White-water rafting the Upper Napo river (p250) amid the rainforests
- Bird-watching in the cloud forests around Mindo (p147)
- Hiking the spectacular multiday Quilotoa loop (p161), stopping at Andean villages en route
- Scaling the 6300m-high Volcán Chimborazo (p184), Ecuador's highest peak
- Mountain biking the 61km 'ruta de las cascadas' (the highway of the waterfalls) from Baños to Puyo (p179)
- Surfing great breaks off Montañita (p311) and Mompiche (p289)
- Whale-watching on a cruise from Puerto López (p307)
- Exploring the Amazonian rainforest with naturalist guides at one of the lower Río Napo's jungle lodges (p244)

TRADITIONAL MARKETS

Ecuador's traditional markets are surely one of the country's highlights, and offer the chance to experience Ecuador's unique indigenous culture up close. Plus, you never know what treasures you might find.

- Otavalo on Saturday (p122)
- Riobamba on Saturday (p187)
- Latacunga on Tuesday and Saturday (p158)
- Guamote on Thursday (p192)
- Ambato on Monday (p167)
- Saquisilí on Thursday (p166)
- Gualaceo and Chordeleg on Sunday (p212)
- Saraguro on Sunday (p214)
- Zumbahua on Saturday (p163)

PARKS & RESERVES

For nature lovers, Ecuador is a paradise. Each and every one of the country's protected areas offers something different, but the following are the pick of the lot.

- Galápagos Islands (p342)
- Parque Nacional Yasuní (p248)
- Reserva Producción Faunística Cuyabeno (p240)
- Parque Nacional Podocarpus (p219)
- Parque Nacional Cotopaxi (p155)
- Parque Nacional Machalilla (p303)
- Parque Nacional Cajas (p211)
- Reserva Ecológica de Manglares Cayapas Mataje (p277)
- Reserva Ecológica Cotacachi-Cayapas (p277)
- Volcán Chimborazo (p184)

There are many ways for visitors to play a positive role in Ecuador, not least of which is volunteering. See p389 for a few ideas on how to get involved.

TRAVEL LITERATURE

If there's one book that nails Ecuadorian culture on the head, it's the eloquent and humorous *Living Poor,* written by Moritz Thomsen as a 48-year-old Peace Corps volunteer on the Ecuadorian coast during the 1960s.

Joe Kane's *Savages* (1995) is a compelling account of life on the *other* side of the Andes, an eye-opening (and sometimes hilarious) look at how the oil industry affects the indigenous Huaoranis and the rainforest.

More recently, Judy Blakenship's *Cañar: A Year in the Highlands of Ecuador* (2005) gives an in-depth portrait of life in an Andean village, complete with processions, traditional weddings, healing ceremonies and harvests. Blakenship's photographs accompany the text.

As for the Galápagos, no list of books is complete without Kurt Vonnegut's whimsical 1985 novel *Galápagos,* in which vacationers are stranded on the islands and become the progenitors for a strange new twist in human evolution.

The Panama Hat Trail (1986), by Tom Miller, is a fascinating book about the author's search for that most quintessential and misnamed of Ecuadorian products, the panama hat.

Robert Whitaker's *The Mapmaker's Wife: A True Tale of Love, Murder and Survival in the Amazon* (2004) is a gripping reconstruction of Isabela Godin's horrific 18th-century journey from the Andes to the Amazon. Godin was the wife of a scientist on La Condamine's equatorial mission.

In *Floreana* (1961), Margaret Wittmer tells her bizarre (and true) story of living off the land in the Galápagos with her eccentric husband. Murder, struggle and vegetarianism all come into play.

Finally, British climber Edward Whymper's *Travels Amongst the Great Andes of the Equator* is a climbing classic. Although published in 1892, it reads as beautifully today as any in the genre.

INTERNET RESOURCES

For websites on volunteering, Ecuadorian newspapers and embassies and consulates, see the Directory chapter. Websites for specific towns and regional attractions are given throughout this book.

The Best of Ecuador (www.thebestofecuador.com) Packed with information on just about everything you can think of.

Ecuador (www.ecuador.com) Overview site giving a condensed portrait of the country.

Ecuador Explorer (www.ecuadorexplorer.com) General travel and tour information and good classifieds.

Ecuaworld (www.ecuaworld.com) General information site jam-packed with everything from volcano elevations to hacienda reviews.

Latin American Network Information Center (http://lanic.utexas.edu/la/ecuador) Scores of useful links about everything Ecuadorian.

Lonely Planet (www.lonelyplanet.com) Find succinct summaries on traveling to most places on earth; postcards from other travelers; and the Thorn Tree bulletin board, where you can ask questions before you go or dispense advice when you get back.

Events Calendar

Ecuador's festivals, especially indigenous fiestas in the highlands, are worth planning a trip around. Each city, town and village has its local celebrations, which feature a generous dose of fireworks, alcohol, music and dancing. Many outwardly Catholic fiestas are indigenous celebrations at their core.

For national public holidays, see p383.

JANUARY

NAPO RIVER FESTIVAL mid-Jan

Organized by the Fundacion Río Napo, this event (p250) features aquatic antics like a kayak rodeo, a dugout canoe race, arts and crafts events, and indigenous music and dancing. It's held in Tena and Puerto Misahualli.

FEBRUARY–APRIL

CARNAVAL Feb/Mar

Held during the last few days before Lent, Carnaval is celebrated with water fights – sometimes dousing passersby with all manner of suspect liquids. Guaranda is famous for its Carnaval (p182), with dances and parades.

FRUIT & FLOWER FESTIVAL late Feb-early Mar

Held in Ambato (p168), the Fiesta de Frutas y Flores features fruit and flower shows, bullfights, parades and late-night dancing in the streets.

SEMANA SANTA Mar/Apr

Beginning the week before Easter Sunday, Semana Santa (Holy Week) is celebrated with religious processions throughout Ecuador. The Good Friday procession in Quito (p97), with its purple-robed penitents, is particularly colorful.

FOUNDING DAY, CUENCA Apr 12

The anniversary of Cuenca's founding is one of the city's biggest events, which locals celebrate by staging parades and lighting up elaborate fireworks-laced floats, which crackle and pop all day and night (p205).

INDEPENDENCE BATTLE OF TAPI Apr 21

Riobamba's biggest night out revolves around the historic 1822 battle. Expect an agricultural fair, with the usual highland events: street parades, dancing and plenty of traditional food and drink (p189).

MAY–JUNE

CHONTA FESTIVAL last week of May

In Macas (p263) the Chonta Festival is the most important Shuar celebration of the year. It culminates in a dance to help ferment the *chicha* (a corn drink).

CORPUS CHRISTI 9th Thurs after Easter

This religious feast day combines with a traditional harvest fiesta in many highland towns, and features processions and street dancing. Particularly good fests are in Cuenca (p205) and Salasaca (p171).

INTI RAYMI Jun 21-29

This millennia-old indigenous celebration of the summer solstice and harvest is celebrated throughout the northern highlands, including Otavalo (p125), where it is combined with celebrations of St John the Baptist (June 24) and Sts Peter & Paul (June 29).

JULY

CANTON FOUNDING DAY, SANTO DOMINGO 1st week of Jul

Santo Domingo de los Colorados (p273) becomes the center for country fairs and agricultural fests in the surrounding countryside.

FOUNDING OF GUAYAQUIL Jul 24-25

Make your way to Guayaquil for this wild celebration (p327) on the nights leading up to the anniversary of the city's founding (July 25). Combining this with the national holiday of July 24, the city closes down and parties hard.

AUGUST–SEPTEMBER

LA VIRGEN DEL CISNE Aug 15

In the southern highlands, thousands of pilgrims take part each year in the extraordinary 70km procession to Loja carrying the Virgen del Cisne (Virgin of the Swan) to Loja (p227).

FIESTA DEL YAMOR Sep 1-15

Imbabura province's biggest festival (p125) celebrates the fall equinox and Colla Raimi (festival of the moon) with bullfights, dancing, cockfights, partying, feasts and lots of *yamor* (a nonalcoholic corn drink made with seven types of corn).

FEIRA MUNDIAL DEL BANANO 3rd week of Sept

Machala celebrates its favorite yellow fruit (p335) with the usual revelry. One of the biggest events is a beauty pageant to select the Reina del Banano (the Banana Queen).

FIESTA DE LA MAMÁ NEGRA Sep 23-24

Latacunga hosts one of the highland's most famous celebrations (p158), in honor of the La Virgen de las Mercedes. La Mamá Negra, played by a man dressed as a black woman, pays tribute to the 19th-century liberation of African slaves.

OCTOBER–NOVEMBER

INDEPENDENCE DAY & DÍA DE LA RAZA Oct 9 & 12

These two big fests in Guayaquil (p327) combine to create a long holiday full of cultural events, parades and bigger-than-usual crowds on the Malecón.

INDEPENDENCE OF LOJA Nov 18

Locals let their hair down in the week surrounding Loja's Independence Day (p216). Revelry fills the streets for up to a week of big parades and cultural events.

DECEMBER

FOUNDING OF QUITO 1st week of Dec

Quito's biggest bash is a much-anticipated event, with bullfights, parades and street dances throughout the first week of December (p97).

CANTON FOUNDING DAY, BAÑOS Dec 16

The annual Baños festival (p176) features processions, fireworks, music and a great deal of street dancing and drinking.

PASE DEL NIÑO Dec 24

Cuenca hosts one of Ecuador's most spectacular parades, which lasts from morning until the afternoon of Christmas Eve (p205).

END-OF-YEAR CELEBRATIONS Dec 28-31

Parades and dances starting on December 28 culminate in the burning of life-size effigies in the streets on New Year's Eve, plus fireworks. It's biggest in Guayaquil and Quito.

Itineraries
CLASSIC ROUTES

BEST OF ECUADOR
Three Weeks / Andes, Galápagos & Amazon

Colonial treasures, volcanic peaks, cloud forests, rainforests and astounding wildlife are all on the menu of this action-packed journey around Ecuador. Begin the trip in **Quito's old town** (p79), spending a few days soaking up this magnificent World Heritage site. Fly to the **Galápagos** (p342) to enjoy a six-day cruise around the islands. Head back to Quito, change planes and journey to the **Oriente** (p230) to get a taste of the Amazon. Return to Quito and head north to **Otavalo** (p122) for the Saturday market, which is one of South America's biggest. Return to Quito and head west to the cloud forests around **Mindo** (p146), one of Ecuador's best destinations for bird-watching.

Head south for a stay in one of the splendid haciendas around **Parque Nacional Cotopaxi** (p155), which are great bases for hiking, horseback riding and summit attempts of the volcano. Return to Quito for a round-trip flight to **Cuenca** (p199), the colonial gem of the south. If time allows take day trips to stunning **Parque Nacional Cajas** (p211) and the fascinating Inca site of **Ingapirca** (p196).

This itinerary will take you from the historic streets of Ecuador's capital to the wildlife-watching paradise of the Galápagos, then to the rainforest and back into the Andean highlands, all in about three weeks.

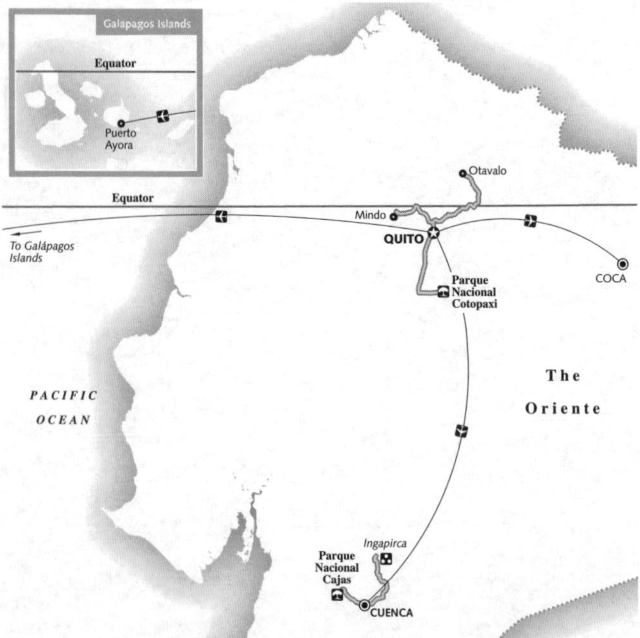

EXPLORING THE ANDES

Two to Three Weeks / Otavalo to Vilcabamba

Begin with a few days in **Quito** (p75), where you can acclimatize to the altitude while exploring one of South America's most fascinating capitals. Head south for a night or two in a historic hacienda on the flanks of **Volcán Cotopaxi** (p156), where you can horseback ride, hike and climb to your heart's content. Travel south to **Latacunga** (p157) and journey into the mountainous landscape of the **Quilotoa Loop** (p161) for two to four days. There you can explore indigenous villages and market towns amid striking Andean scenery. Head south to the delightful subtropical town of **Baños** (p172), where you can soak in the thermal baths and take a fabulous downhill bike ride to **Puyo** (p179) in the Oriente. After Baños, move on to **Riobamba** (p186) and do some high-adrenaline mountain biking or hiking around **Volcán Chimborazo** (p184). Continue south to the marvelous colonial city of **Cuenca** (p199), either via the famous **Nariz del Diablo** (p193) train ride or the **Inca trail to Ingapirca** (p196). After exploring Cuenca for a couple of days, wind your way south to **Loja** (p214) and the laid-back village of **Vilcabamba** (p223), where you could easily spend a few days hiking and relaxing. Be sure to take at least a one-day hike in **Parque Nacional Podocarpus** (p219) before flying from Loja back to Quito. Then treat yourself to a few relaxing days hiking and bird-watching in the cloud forests of the **western Andean slopes** (p145). Because you were thinking smart, you saved the **Otavalo market** (p122) for last, so the only place you have to lug all those beautiful ponchos and weavings is to Quito and onto the airplane.

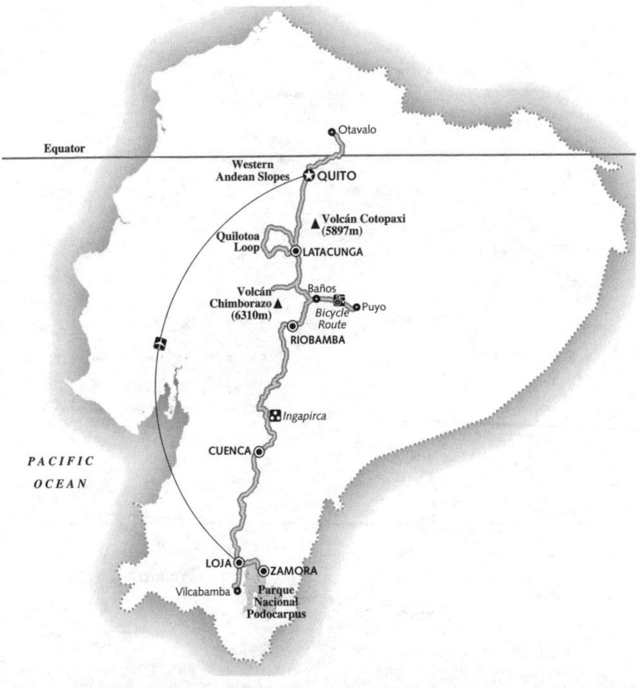

You'll traverse some 1050km of hair-raising, roller-coaster roads on a journey from Quito through the central highlands toward Vilcabamba, just north of the Peruvian border. You'll see Ecuador's astounding peaks, scenic roads and fascinating indigenous markets.

ROADS LESS TRAVELED

MARIMBAS & MANGROVES Two to Three Weeks / The Northern Coast

Ecuador's northernmost coastal region is a land of giant mangroves, Afro-Ecuadorian culture, incredible biodiversity, extreme poverty and serious off-the-beaten-track travel. The rewards are great for those adventurous enough to undertake the journey. From **Quito** (p75), travel north to **Ibarra** (p135), and then northwest along the windy road to **San Lorenzo** (p275). From there, explore the rarely visited mangroves and forested islands of **Reserva Ecológica de Manglares Cayapas Mataje** (p277), home to some of the world's tallest mangroves. Head back to San Lorenzo, then make your way to **Borbón** (p278) for a fascinating journey up the jungle-lined Río Cayapas. Spend the night in **San Miguel** (p279) and return to Borbón. From there continue on to Selva Alegre for another boat ride, this time along the Río Santiago to the wildlife reserve of **Playa de Oro** (p279). This must-see jungle lodge is beautifully set among the western reaches of **Reserva Ecológica Cotacachi-Cayapas** (p279), well worth a couple of days' exploration. After the jungle trip, head to **Esmeraldas** (p281), and change buses for the short trip along the coast to **Same** (p287), a tranquil spot overlooking a beautiful beach. While in the area, check out the fishing village of **Tonchigüe** (p287), pretty **Súa** (p286) and nightlife-loving beach town of **Atacames** (p284). Return to Quito, stopping en route at **Santo Domingo de los Colorados** (p272) for a visit to the indigenous **Tsáchilas community** (p273).

The largely Afro-Ecuadorian north coast has a magic all of its own. Traveling some 1100km by bus, boat and pickup truck, you will experience a side of Ecuador few tourists see – a world of giant mangroves, hidden fishing villages and hard-to-reach jungle reserves.

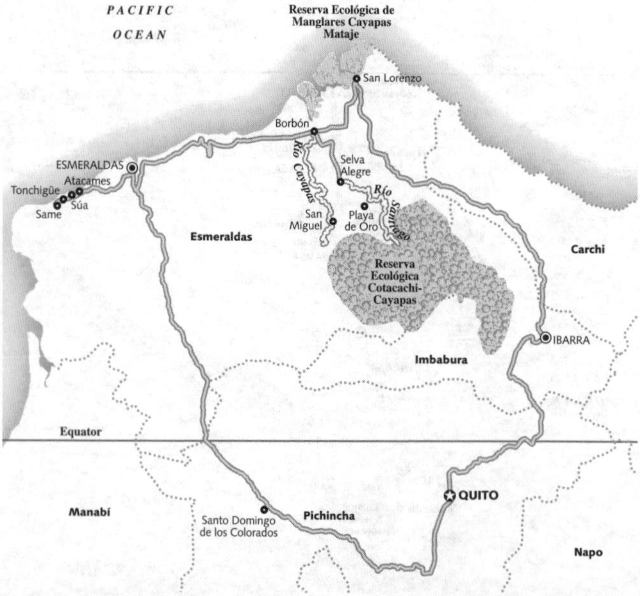

SOUTHERN ECUADOR — Two to Three Weeks / Guaranda to Puyango

Start off in **Guaranda** (p182), where you can catch a ride up to **Salinas** (p184), a charming country village famed for its cheeses, woolly sweaters and other goods. Stay overnight in the village before heading to **Riobamba** (p186) and continuing on to the fascinating Thursday market at **Guamote** (p192). Veer east into **Parque Nacional Sangay** (p180), a setting of magnificent volcanoes and diverse flora and fauna. Stop in Atillo for a couple of days of spectacular hiking around the crystalline **Lagunas de Atillo** (p182). From Atillo continue downhill to **Macas** (p263), a friendly town bathed in the siesta-inducing tropical humidity of the southern Oriente. In Macas hire a guide for a cultural tour to an indigenous Shuar community, or walk (without a guide) to the village of **Sevilla** (p266). You can also hire a guide in Macas to take you down the Río Santiago to the **Cueva de los Tayos** (p266), the cave home of Ecuador's mysterious oil birds. After a few days in Macas, travel south through **Sucúa** (p267), and the wee town of **Limón** (p267) and stop in whatever jungle village piques your interest. After a day in **Gualaquiza** (p267), continue south through the rainforest to **Zamora** (p221), where you can explore **Parque Nacional Podocarpus** (p219). After a day or two climb back into the Andes to **Loja** (p214), where you'll rejoin the tourist trail. Take a breather (and treat yourself to a massage) in laid-back **Vilcabamba** (p223), and then work your way down the western side of the Andes to **Catacocha** (p227). Spend a day here then make your way to **Puyango** (p338) to visit one of South America's largest petrified forests, before winding your way back to Cuenca.

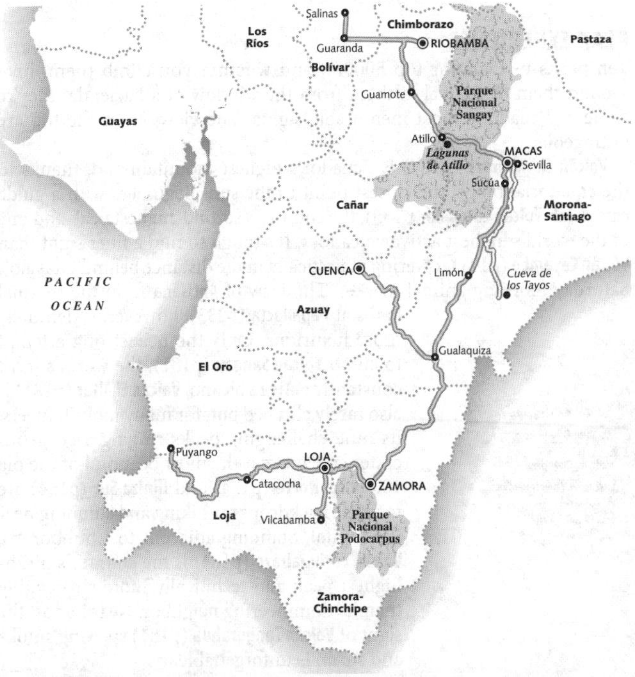

This 800km journey takes you through the southern reaches of Parque Nacional Sangay and into the little-visited reaches of the southern Oriente. You'll pass through tiny jungle towns and plenty of Andean scenery.

TAILORED TRIPS

SURF & SUN

Ecuador's charming coastal villages and attractive beaches draw a wide mix of travelers. The best spots on the north coast are **Mompiche** (p289), with its reliably good surf, and laid-back **Canoa** (p290), whose pretty beach is backed by forested cliffs. Travelers wanting to get off the beaten path might head for **Muisne** (p288) and its long comely stretch of palm-lined beach.

Next up, check out the **Ruta del Sol** (Route of the Sun; p303), the length of beautiful Ecuadorian coastline stretching from Parque Nacional Machalilla in the north down to Ballenita in the south. Spectacular **Los Frailes Beach** (p305), protected inside **Parque Nacional Machalilla** (p303), is a paradise. The bayside village of **Puerto López** (p307) is the perfect base for exploring the park. Divers should stop at **Salango** (p310) for some underwater adventures. South of here it's beach after beach, with the best lodging to be found at **Ayampe** (p311).

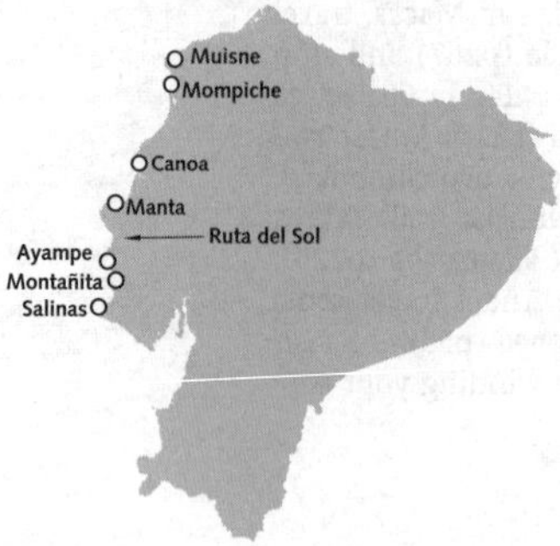

At last you arrive **Montañita** (p311) – its surf and laid-back vibe have made it famous. For the classic upperclass Ecuadorian experience, visit **Salinas** (p184), the country's most famous resort.

PEAK EXPERIENCE

Ten peaks in Ecuador top 5000m, and whether you climb them, hike around them or marvel at them from the window of a hacienda, they're some of Ecuador's most memorable sights. The views from the top are outrageous.

Volcán Chimborazo (p184) is Ecuador's highest mountain and, thanks to the equatorial bulge, the closest point to the sun. Beginners with a guide can climb **Volcán Cotopaxi** (p155), the country's second-highest peak and one of the world's highest active volcanoes. It's tough to find a finer sight than **Volcán Cayambe** (p121) towering majestically in the distance behind Otavalo's Saturday morning animal market. The view of **Antisana** from the thermal baths at **Papallacta** (p233), however, is definitely more luxurious. Only the headstrong attempt to climb **Volcán Sangay** (p181), the world's most constantly active volcano. **Volcán El Altar** (p181) is also rarely climbed but, for many mountaineers, its nine challenging peaks ringing a gorgeous crater lake make it the most beautiful of the big 10. **Iliniza Norte** (p154) and **Iliniza Sur** (p154) are majestic backdrops for hiking and climbing near the capital. Standing adjacent to Chimborazo, **Volcán Carihuairazo** (p184) is the country's ninth-highest peak and technically more challenging than its domineering neighbor. Near Baños, the sight of **Volcán Tungurahua** (p181) spewing smoke and steam is unforgettable.

AMAZONIAN ADVENTURE

The Amazon is one of the world's most biologically diverse regions. For adventurers and wildlife lovers, there's much to discover in Amazonian Ecuador, from indigenous reserves to jungle lodges with an incredible array of plant and animal life. Meet indigenous Achuar at the **Kapawi Ecolodge** (p265), a culturally and ecologically sensitive reserve in a remote part of the Amazon. The **Reserva Producción Faunística Cuyabeno** (p240) is a unique flooded forest, home to astounding bird and aquatic life – including pink river dolphins. In **Coca** (p241) you can hire local guides to take you into indigenous Huaorani territory. The jungle lodges along the **lower Río Napo** (p244) offer superb wildlife-watching on hikes, canoe rides or climbs to the top of the jungle canopy. One of the Oriente's gems is the **Parque Nacional Yasuní** (p248), a Unesco-declared biosphere reserve with 500 bird species and vast stretches of wetlands, swamps, lakes, rivers and tropical rainforest. For a piranha feast, head to **Laguna Pañacocha** (p247), a picturesque blackwater lake backed by cloud and dry forests. A tough trip into remote jungle is found inside the **Parque Nacional Sumaco-Galeras** (p249). Here you can walk (hire a guide in Huamaní) the tortuous route up 3732m-high Volcán Sumaco. For less strain, journey to the end of the road in **Misahuallí** (p254), a good place to take in Oriente village life.

CULINARY HIGHWAY

Ecuador's culinary wonders are little known outside the country's borders, but an endless bounty of satisfying meals awaits the curious and hungry explorer. The coast is justly famous for its seafood, with the *encocados* (coconut and seafood stews) of **Esmeraldas** (p281) among Ecuador's top dishes. The province of Manabí is also famed for fresh seafood, including great ceviches; fishing capital **Manta** (p296) is a good place to look. **Latacunga** (p157) serves delightful *chugchucara,* a pork lover's dream. The southern highlands have some decadent recipes, and they are many (p217). **Loja** (p214) is a good place to try *cuy* (roast guinea pig), *humitas* (corn dumplings), tamales and other regional specialties. Guayas province offers a good culinary mix. For delicious cheeses, dried mushrooms and artisanal chocolate visit **Salinas** (p184), where village-run co-ops produce the town's famous products. Head to **Playas** (p316) for its celebrated fresh-cooked crab, and don't neglect **Guayaquil** (p318) for its *seco de chiva* (goat stew) and *encebollado* (seafood, yuca and onion soup). Tasty bites from the Oriente include *ayampacos* (chicken, beef or fish steamed in *bijao* leaves), served in **Macas** (p263). If you're around during Semana Santa (Holy Week), don't miss Ecuador's famous *fanesca* soup. **Cuenca** (p199) serves some of the country's best. Other festival dishes include *yamor* (a complex corn drink) served appropriately at Otavalo's **Fiesta de Yamor** (p125) and Macas' **Chonta festival** (p263), where you can sample authentically made *chicha* (saliva-fermented corn beverage).

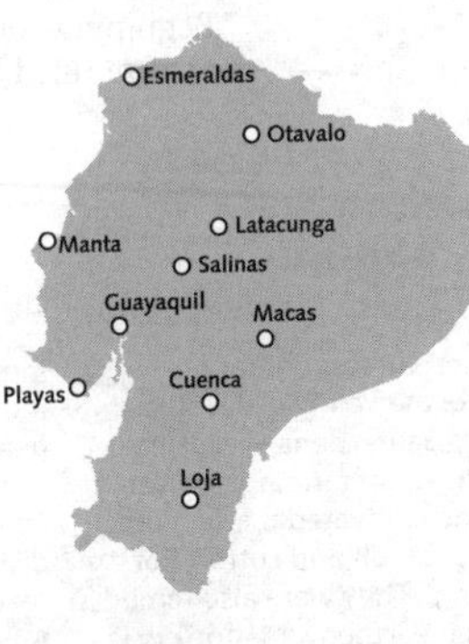

History

The land of fire and ice certainly has a tumultuous history. Since becoming an independent nation in 1830, Ecuador has gone through nearly 100 changes in government and 20 constitutions – the most recent drafted in 2008. Fueling the Andean nation's volatility are rivalries both internal (conservative, church-backed Quito versus liberal, secular Guayaquil) and external (border disputes with Peru).

Ecuador's varied peoples have seen the rise and fall of leaders great and small, who have left a mixed legacy in this Andean nation. For scholars, the unsung heroes of Ecuadorian history are its resilient indigenous groups, descendents of some of the great cultures that once flourished in the Americas.

EARLY CULTURES

Although the majority of indigenous people today live in the highlands and the Oriente, in pre-Spanish (and pre-Inca) times the coastline supported the densest concentration of peoples. The coastal cultures of La Tolita, Bahía, Manta, Valdivia and Machalilla are paramount to Ecuadorian identity, their importance in many ways even eclipsing the Inca, who didn't arrive in present-day Ecuador until a half century before the Spanish.

The majority of Ecuador's earliest cultures developed along the southern coast, not in the Andes.

It's now generally accepted that Ecuador was populated by people migrating west from Brazil, who were drawn to the habitable landscapes along the shore. Ecuador's first permanent sedentary culture was the Valdivia, which developed along the Santa Elena Peninsula from nearly 6000 years ago. One of the oldest settled cultures in the Americas, the Valdivia are famous for their finely wrought pottery, particularly the 'Venus of Valdivia.' These were feminine ceramic figurines with exaggerated breasts and genitalia, depicted in various stages of pregnancy and childbirth. They were likely used in fertility rituals. Quito's Museo del Banco Central (p87) and the Museo Guayasamín (p92) both have outstanding examples of these.

While the Valdivia was the first of Ecuador's settled cultures, the Chorrera was the most widespread and influential of the groups that appeared during this so-called Formative Period (4000 BC to 300 BC). Both the Chorrera and the Machalilla culture (which inhabited southern Manabí and the Santa Elena Peninsula from 1500 BC to 800 BC) are known for the practice of skull deformation. As a form of status, they used stones to slowly elongate and flatten their craniums, and they often removed two front teeth to further enhance their appearance.

Beginning sometime around 600 BC, societies became more stratified: they were ruled by an elite caste of shamans and elite merchants who con-

TIMELINE

3500 BC

Ecuador's first sedentary culture, the Valdivia, develops around Santa Elena Peninsula. They lived off farming and fishing, and cultivated maize, yuca, beans, squash and cotton (for clothing). They were also famed for their earthenware pottery.

600 BC

Indigenous societies become more stratified. Tribes are headed by an elite caste of shamans and merchants who conduct highly valued long-distance maritime trade – reaching as far north as Central America.

AD 800

Different cultures begin to merge, creating larger and more hierarchical societies. The emergent powers include the Manteños, the Huancavilcas and the Caras on the coast; and the Quitus, Puruhá and Cañari of the Sierra.

ducted highly valued long-distance trade. These included the Bahía, Jama-Coaque, Guangala and La Tolita cultures on the coast and the Panzaleo in the highlands. It is likely the Panzaleo was the first culture to practice the technique of *tzantza* (shrinking heads) for which the Shuar of the southern Oriente are much more famous (they practiced it until the mid-20th century). Cuenca's Museo del Banco Central 'Pumapungo' (p204) houses five of what are likely the most impressively displayed *tzantza* in the country – just in case you're interested.

Slowly, beginning probably around AD 800, cultures became integrated into larger, more hierarchical societies. These included the Manteños, the Huancavilcas and the Caras on the coast; the Quitus (from which the city of Quito takes its name) of the northern highlands; the Puruhá of the central highlands; and the Cañari of the area around present-day Cuenca. Around the end of the 1st century AD, the expansionist Caras of the coast conquered the peaceful Quitus of the highlands and the combined cultures became collectively known as the Quitu-Caras, or the Shyris. They were the dominant force in the Ecuadorian highlands until about the 1300s, when the Puruhá of the central highlands became increasingly powerful. The third important culture was the Cañari, further south. These were the cultures the Inca encountered when it began its expansion into the north.

At the height of its empire, the Inca ruled more than 12 million people across some 1 million sq km.

THE INCA EMPIRE

Until the early 15th century, the Inca Empire was concentrated around Cuzco in Peru. That changed dramatically during the rule of Pachacuti Inca Yupanqui, whose expansionist policies set into motion the creation of the vast Inca Empire, Tahuantinsuyo, meaning 'Land of the Four Quarters' in Quechua. By the time the Inca reached Ecuador they were under the rule of Tupac Yupanqui, Pachacuti's successor, and were met with fierce resistance.

The Cañari put up a resolute defense against the Inca, and it took some years for Tupac Yupanqui to subdue them and turn his attention to the north, where he was met with even greater resistance. At one point, the Cañari drove the invading army all the way back to Saraguro. When they were finally overcome, the Inca massacred thousands of Caras and dumped them into a lake near Otavalo, which supposedly turned the waters red and gave the lake its name, Laguna Yaguarcocha (Lake of Blood; p136).

The subjugation of the north took many years, during which the Inca Tupac fathered a son with a Cañari princess. The son, Huayna Capac, grew up in Ecuador and succeeded his father to the Inca throne. He spent years traveling throughout his empire, from Bolivia to Ecuador, constantly suppressing uprisings from all sides. Wherever possible, he strengthened his position by marriage and in the process produced two sons: Atahualpa, who grew up in Quito, and Huáscar, who was raised in Cuzco.

Valverde's Gold: In Search of the Last Great Inca Treasure, by Mark Honigsbaum describes the author's elusive search for the room of buried gold originally intended as part of the ransom for Inca emperor Atahualpa.

1463

The Inca, under the leadership of Pachacuti Inca Yupanqui, begin the conquest of Ecuador. His son Tupac leads the attack, facing down surprising resistance along the way.

1500

Tupac's son Huayna Capac overcomes the tribes of the Cañari (around modern-day Cuenca); the Cara (in the north); and the Quitu (around modern-day Quito). Ecuador becomes part of the vast Inca Empire.

1526

Inca ruler Huayna Capac dies suddenly (probably from smallpox or measles) and leaves the Inca Empire to his two sons, Atahualpa and Huáscar. A bitter power struggle ensues.

LIFE UNDER THE INCA

The Inca arrived in Ecuador a short time before the Spanish conquistadors overthrew them, but they had a lasting effect on the indigenous peoples of the area. Agriculture, social organization and land ownership saw pronounced changes. The Inca introduced new crops, including cocoa, sweet potatoes and peanuts, and new farming methods using llamas and irrigation. Private land ownership was abolished, with land collectively held by the *ayllu,* newly established agrarian communities. Each family was allotted a small plot of arable land within the *ayllu*. The state and high priests also held sizeable plots of land, upon which the emperor's subjects labored as part of their required public service.

The Inca state was highly organized. It introduced the Quechua language, levied taxes and built an extensive network of roads (later used with disastrous success by the horse-riding conquistadors). A system of runners relayed messages, allowing important news to travel hundreds of miles a day. The Incas spread their religion, whose pantheon of gods included Inti (the sun god) and Viracocha (the creator god). Local populations were required to worship the sun god, but their native beliefs were tolerated.

The economy was entirely based on farming, with maize and potatoes chief among the crops. They also raised *cuy* (guinea pigs), ducks, dogs, and llamas and alpacas, whose wool was spun for clothes. Cotton was also grown.

The Inca for their part grew quite fond of Ecuador. Emperor Huayna Capac made Quito a secondary capital of the Inca Empire and lived there until his death in 1527. Locals were largely left alone as long they paid tribute and acknowledged his divinity. Those who opposed him were exiled to far reaches of the kingdom, with other colonists brought in to take their place. This forced migration of peoples also helped to spread Quechua, the language of the empire.

When Huayna Capac died in 1526 he left his empire not to one son, as was traditional, but to two. Thus the Inca Empire was divided for the first time – an event that fatefully coincided with the mystifying appearance of a group of bearded men on horseback in present-day Esmeraldas province. They were the first Spaniards in Ecuador, led south by the pilot Bartolomé Ruiz de Andrade on an exploratory mission for Francisco Pizarro, who remained, for the time being, further north.

Meanwhile, the rivalry between Huayna Capac's two sons worsened, and the Inca nation broke into civil war. After several years of fighting, Atahualpa finally defeated Huáscar near Ambato and was thus the sole ruler of the weakened and still-divided Inca Empire when Pizarro arrived in 1532 with plans to conquer the Incas.

THE SPANISH CONQUEST

Pizarro's advance was rapid and dramatic. His horseback-riding, armor-wearing, cannon-firing conquistadors were believed to be godlike, and although they were few in number, they spread terror among the local people.

1532

Spanish conquistador Francisco Pizarro arrives with a band of 180 men in present-day Ecuador. Hearing of the fabled riches of the Incas he plans to conquer and plunder the country for the Spanish crown.

1533

The Inca ruler Atahualpa is killed by the Spanish, effectively decapitating the Inca Empire. Pizarro heads south to Cuzco (in present-day Peru) and plunders the once great capital of Tahuantinsuyo.

1563

The Spanish crown declares Ecuador the Audiencia de Quito, shifting political administration away from Lima, Peru. The territory extends far beyond today's borders from Cali (Colombia) in the north to Paita (Peru) in the south.

In late 1532, a summit meeting was arranged between Pizarro and Atahualpa. Although Atahualpa was prepared to negotiate with the Spaniards, Pizarro had other ideas. When the Inca arrived at the prearranged meeting place (Cajamarca, in Peru) on November 16, the conquistadors captured him and massacred most of his poorly armed guards.

Atahualpa was held for ransom, and incalculable quantities of gold, silver and other valuables poured into Cajamarca. Instead of being released when the ransom was paid, however, the Inca was put through a sham trial and sentenced to death. Atahualpa was charged with incest (marrying one's sister was traditional in the Inca culture), polygamy, worship of false gods and crimes against the king, and he was executed on August 29, 1533. His death effectively brought the Inca Empire to an end.

Inca ruler Huayna Capac had a third son, Manco Capac. He was the last Inca ruler and staged one of the greatest revolts against the Spanish. He was killed by a Spaniard whose life he had saved.

When Atahualpa was executed, his war-general Rumiñahui was supposedly on his way to Cajamarca with large quantities of gold and treasure as ransom for the Inca. Legend has it that, upon hearing of Atahualpa's death, Rumiñahui stashed the treasure in the impenetrable mountains of present-day Parque Nacional Llanganates (p171); it has never been found.

The general then continued to fight against the Spaniards for two more years. The general was so fierce that according to legend he dealt with a Spanish collaborator (and possible heir to Atahualpa's throne) by murdering him, breaking all the bones in his body to bits, extracting them through a hole, and stretching the body – with head and appendages intact – into a drum. By the time Pizarro's lieutenant, Sebastián de Benalcázar, had finally battled his way to Quito in late 1534, he found the city razed to the ground by Rumiñahui, who preferred to destroy the city rather than leave it in the hands of the conquistadors. Quito was refounded on December 6, 1534, and Rumiñahui was finally captured, tortured and executed in January 1535.

John Hemming's outstanding *The Conquest of the Incas* is one of the best descriptions of Francisco Pizarro's conquest of the Inca Empire. Although mostly about Peru, it has several sections on Ecuador.

Despite the Inca's short presence in Ecuador (just over 100 years), they left a indelible mark on the country. Quechua (now Quichua in Ecuador) was imposed on the population and is still spoken today by a quarter of all Ecuadorians. The Inca built a vast system of roads that connected Cuzco in the south with Quito in the north, and part of the 'royal highway' – the Inca trail to Ingapirca – can still be hiked today. Ingapirca itself (p196) is Ecuador's most important Inca archaeological site and has splendid examples of the Inca's mortarless stonework.

THE COLONIAL ERA

From 1535, the colonial era proceeded with no major uprisings by indigenous Ecuadorians. Francisco Pizarro made his brother Gonzalo the governor of Quito in 1540.

During the first centuries of colonial rule, Lima, Peru, was the seat of Ecuador's political administration. Originally a *gobernación* (province), in 1563 Ecuador became the Audiencia de Quito (a more important political

1600

The Quito School (Escuela Quiteña) emerges, with indigenous artists and artisans producing some of the finest religious art in the Americas. Masterful and syncretic works are produced over the next 150 years.

1600s

The use of the *encomienda* is widespread throughout the Spanish colonies: settlers are granted land, along with its inhabitants and resources – a system of virtual slavery of the indigenous.

1690

An epidemic of smallpox and diphtheria rages throughout Ecuador, killing one-third of the population. The native population (estimated at one million at the time of conquest) declines dramatically.

THE MYTHICAL AMAZON

One of the most significant events of the early colonial period was the epic journey of Francisco de Orellana along the Río Napo. Orellana set off in December 1541 to search for food to bring relief to a hungry contingent of Gonzalo Pizarro's men following a rigorous crossing of the Cordillera Oriental. Once Orellana caught sight of the lush promise of dense jungle lining the riverbanks, however, he quickly abandoned his original mission and set off in search of gold. These were the days when Spanish conquistadors spoke of legendary lost cities of gold, and Orellana was obsessed with finding El Dorado. 'Having eaten our shoes and saddles boiled with a few herbs,' Orellana wrote, 'we set out to reach the Kingdom of Gold.' It was a grueling journey that would leave half of his comrades dead.

On June 5, 1542, some five months after setting sail, Orellana's boats reached a large village decorated with carvings of 'fierce lions' (probably jaguars). One of the villagers said that the carvings represented the tribe's mistress and their ruler. When his boat later came under ferocious attack (following several raids by his own men on other riverside settlements), Orellana was convinced that female warriors were leading the onslaught. He later named the river after the Amazons, the mythical all-female warriors of ancient Greece. By the time he reached the Atlantic Ocean – some eight months after he began – he had given up his quest for gold. He became the first European to travel the length of the Amazon River, a feat not to be repeated for another 100 years. The event is still commemorated in Ecuador during the annual Aniversario del Descubrimiento del Río Amazonas (Discovery of the Amazon River), celebrated on February 12.

division), which in 1739 was transferred from the viceroyalty of Peru to the viceroyalty of Colombia (then known as Nueva Grenada).

Ecuador remained a peaceful colony throughout this period, and agriculture and the arts flourished. New products such as cattle and bananas were introduced from Europe, which remain important in Ecuador today. Churches and monasteries were constructed atop every sacred indigenous site and were decorated with unique carvings and paintings that blended Spanish and indigenous artistic influences. This so-called Escuela Quiteña (Quito School of Art), still admired by visitors today, left an indelible stamp on the colonial buildings of the time and Ecuador's unique art history.

For deep insight into colonial life and intrigue during one of Ecuador's most tumultuous times, pick up John Leddy Phelan's *The Kingdom of Quito in the Seventeenth Century: Bureaucratic Politics in the Spanish Empire.*

Life was comfortable for the ruling colonialists, but the indigenous people (and later the mestizos, people of mixed Spanish and indigenous descent) were treated abysmally under their rule. A system of forced labor was not only tolerated but encouraged, and by the 18th century there were several indigenous uprisings against the Spanish ruling classes. Social unrest, as well as the introduction of cocoa and sugar plantations in the northwest, prompted landowners to import African slave laborers. Much of the rich Afro-Ecuadorian culture found in Esmeraldas province today is a legacy of this period.

1736

A French scientific mission arrives in Ecuador, bringing Europe's best minds to Quito. They carry out research and share Enlightenment ideals (nationalism, individualism and self-destiny), which will figure critically in the early independence drive.

1767

King Charles III expels the Jesuits from the Spanish Empire. Missions in the Oriente are abandoned, while some of colonial Ecuador's best schools and haciendas fall into decline following the loss of essential staff.

1790

Following a century of economic mismanagement by Spain and declining demand for textiles, the Ecuadorian economy suffers a severe depression. Its cities are in ruins, with the elite reduced to poverty.

INDEPENDENCE

The first serious attempt to liberate Ecuador from Spanish rule was by a partisan group led by Juan Pío Montúfar on August 10, 1809. The group managed to take Quito and install a government, which lasted only 24 days before royalist troops (loyal to Spain) regained control.

Independence was finally achieved by Simón Bolívar, the Venezuelan liberator who marched southward from Caracas, freed Colombia in 1819 and supported the people of Guayaquil when they claimed independence on October 9, 1820. It took almost two years before Ecuador was entirely liberated from Spanish rule. The decisive battle was fought on May 24, 1822, when one of Bolívar's finest officers, Mariscal (Field Marshal) Antonio José de Sucre, defeated the royalists at the Battle of Pichincha and took Quito. This battle is commemorated at a stunningly situated monument (p85) on the flanks of Volcán Pichincha, overlooking the capital.

Bolívar's idealistic dream was to form a united South America, and he began by amalgamating Venezuela, Colombia and Ecuador into the independent nation of Gran Colombia. This lasted only eight years, with Ecuador becoming fully independent in 1830. In the same year, a treaty was signed with Peru, drawing up a boundary between the two nations; this boundary is the one shown on all Ecuadorian maps prior to 1999. The border had been redrawn in 1942 after a war between Ecuador and Peru, but was not officially acknowledged by Ecuadorian authorities until a peace treaty was signed with Peru in late 1998.

Written in the 16th century, Bartolomé de las Casas' *A Short Account of the Destruction of the Indies* is a searing, and readable account of the Spaniards' abuse of the native population during colonization.

POLITICAL DEVELOPMENT

Following independence from Spain, Ecuador's history unfolded with unbridled political warfare between liberals and conservatives. The turmoil frequently escalated to violence. In 1875, the church-backed, conservative dictator President García Moreno (who attempted to make Catholicism a requisite for citizenship) was hacked to death with a machete outside Quito's presidential palace. In 1912 liberal President Eloy Alfaro, who attempted to undo much of García Moreno's legacy, was murdered and burned by a conservative mob in Quito. Rivalries between these factions continue to this day, albeit less violently. Quito remains the main center for the church-backed conservatives, while Guayaquil stands, as it has for centuries, on the side of more liberal and sometimes socialist beliefs. The rivalry has even seeped into everyday life (see p36).

Throughout much of the 20th century, Ecuador's political sphere remained volatile, though the country never experienced the bloodshed or brutal military dictatorships suffered by other Latin American countries. That's not to say the military never took the reins of power, with the 20th century seeing almost as many periods of military rule as civilian rule. One president, José María Velasco Ibarra, was elected five times between 1934 and 1972 and was

O Hugo Benavides' *Making Ecuadorian Histories: Four Centuries of Defining Power* is an excellent if scholarly exploration of nation-building, gender, race and sexuality as it relates to the corridors of power inside Ecuador.

1791

Eugenio de Santa Cruz y Espejo, a famed intellectual and early independence advocate, becomes director of the 'patriotic society,' an organization aimed at civic improvement. His writings land him in prison, where he dies in 1795.

1809

The first serious attempt to liberate Ecuador from Spanish rule is led by a partisan group. They take Quito and install a government, which lasts only 24 days before Spanish loyalist troops regain control.

1822

Two years after Guayaquil declares emancipation from Spain, António Jose de Sucre, one of Simón Bolívar's finest officers, defeats Spanish royalists at the Battle of Pichincha. Ecuador becomes part of Gran Colombia.

ousted by the military before he could complete any one of his terms. Ibarra wasn't alone: in the 10 years between 1930 and 1940, 17 different presidents took a shot at leading Ecuador, not one of whom completed a term.

In 1955 Ecuadorian officials seized two US fishing boats, charging them with fishing inside the 200-nautical-mile limit claimed by Ecuador as territorial seas under its sovereignty. It was the opening salvo in what was later known as 'the tuna wars.'

YELLOW GOLD TO BLACK GOLD

Until the 1970s, Ecuador was the archetypal 'banana republic,' and the fruit was the country's single most important export. In fact, Ecuador exported more bananas than any country in the world. Although bananas are a staple of the country's economy today, they ceased being Ecuador's sole export after the discovery of oil in the Oriente in 1967. By 1973, oil exports had risen to first place, and by the early 1980s they accounted for well over half of total export earnings. Oil undoubtedly boosted the economy, though politicians from the left, allied with indigenous-rights groups, say much of the largesse remained in the hands of a few controlling interests with little benefit to the many. The statistics support this claim, with the majority of the rural population at an equal – or lower – living standard than they experienced in the 1970s.

After oil was discovered, Ecuador began to borrow money, with the belief that profits from oil exports would enable the country to repay its foreign debts. But this proved impossible in the mid-1980s due to the sharp decline in Ecuador's oil exports; world oil prices slumped in 1986, and in 1987 a disastrous earthquake wiped out about 40km of oil pipeline, severely damaging both the environment and the economy. The discovery of oil also opened up vast tracts of Ecuador's Amazon Basin to exploration, affecting both the rainforest and the local indigenous tribes – some of whom had never before encountered outsiders.

Ecuador continues to rely on oil as its economic mainstay, but reserves are not as large as had been anticipated. Overreliance on oil revenues has also wreaked havoc on the economy when the world price of oil collapses (as it did most recently in 2008).

Mike Tidwell's *Amazon Stranger: Rainforest Chief Battles Big Oil*, is a great read, although the Cofan village chief on whom the book is based, Randy Borman, says to take it with a pinch of salt.

RETURN TO DEMOCRACY

Ecuador's return to democracy began in 1979, when President Jaime Roldos Aguilera was elected. But he died in a mysterious airplane crash (conspiracy theorists point fingers at US constituents with interests in Ecuadorian oil) in 1981, and his term of office was completed by his vice president, Osvaldo Hurtado Larrea.

The 1980s and early '90s were a continuing struggle between conservatives and liberals, with a few corruption scandals that weakened public confidence in the ruling elites. The contenders in the 1996 election were two firebrand politicians from Guayaquil, both known for their brashness. The man who won, Abdala Bucaram, was nicknamed 'El Loco' (The Madman) for his fiery, curse-laden style of oration and his penchant for

1830

Ecuador leaves Gran Colombia and becomes an independent nation. A group of Quito notables draws up a constitution, placing General Flores in charge of military and political matters. He remains a dominant figure for 15 years.

1851

Amid one of Ecuador's most turbulent times, General José Maria Urbina frees the nation's slaves. His successor, General Francisco Robles, puts an end to 300 years of required annual payments by the indigenous.

1859

The highly controversial García Moreno comes to power. Decried by political opponents as a dictator, he nevertheless makes vital contributions in education, public welfare and economic development. He is assassinated in 1875.

BORDER BUDDIES

Despite fighting three wars in the 20th century over disputed border territories, relations between Ecuador and Peru remain warm – at least for the moment. Following a peace treaty signed in 1998, both Peru and Ecuador have met the accord's US$1.5 billion investment goals to build roads and health centers in the border zone. Removing the thousands of land mines along the frontier is also a major concern for the two nations, as mines have claimed the lives of more than 100 people since the end of the 1995 conflict. In 2008 both nations agreed to finance the remainder of the demining project, estimated at US$30 million.

performing at rock concerts as part of his campaign. Bucaram promised cheap public housing, lower prices for food staples and free medicine; but instead he promptly devalued Ecuador's currency, the sucre, and increased living costs, and was often spotted carousing in nightclubs by Quito residents.

Former president Abdala Bucaram (aka The Madman) recorded a CD titled *A Madman in Love*.

Within a few months, massive strikes led by trade unions and the Confederation of Indigenous Nationalities of Ecuador (Conaie) paralyzed the country. Congress declared Bucaram 'mentally unfit' and terminated his presidency, and Bucaram fled to Panama.

After Bucaram was ousted, his vice president, Rosalía Arteaga, became Ecuador's first female president, albeit for fewer than two days. Congress voted overwhelmingly to replace her with Fabián Alarcón, the head of congress. He led the government until 1998, when *quiteño* Jamil Mahuad of the Popular Democracy party was elected president.

Mahuad had his political savvy put to the test. The effects of a nasty El Niño weather pattern and the sagging oil market of 1997–98 sent the economy into a tailspin in 1999, the same year that shrimp exports dropped by 80% following devastating shrimp diseases. The sucre depreciated from about 6000 per US dollar at the start of 1999 to about 25,000 by January 2000. When inflation topped 60% – making Ecuador's the worst in Latin America – the embattled president took drastic measures: he pinned Ecuador's economic survival on dollarization, a process whereby Ecuador's unstable national currency would be replaced by the US dollar.

DOLLARIZATION

Approximately 40% of Ecuador's national income goes to the richest 5% of the population.

Dollarization has been used successfully in a few other economically hard-hit countries, including nearby Panama (where the US dollar is called a balboa), but when President Mahuad declared his plan to dump the national currency, the country erupted in strikes, protests and road closures. On January 21, 2000, marches shut down the capital, and protesters took over the legislative palace, forcing Mahuad to resign.

1890

Cacao drives the economy, with production up from 6.5 million kilograms in 1852 to 18 million in 1890. Ecuador's exports grow in value from US$1 million to US$10 million over the same period.

1895

José Eloy Alfaro Delgado takes power. A champion of liberalism from the lower classes, he strips the Church of power and promulgates civil rights: legalizing civil marriage and divorce, and establishing freedom of speech and religion.

1920

Economic problems cripple Ecuador. A fungal disease and decline in world demand destroy the cacao industry. The working class protests skyrocketing inflation and declining living conditions, but strikes are brutally suppressed.

BREAKING NEW GROUND

In a nationwide referendum held in September 2008, 65% of Ecuadorians voted in favor of changing the constitution. In a country that has seen 19 other constitutions drafted in its 180-year history (the previous one in 1998), this may not seem like news. And yet the 444-page document contains many bold new initiatives, which if carried out could alter the nature of Ecuadorian society.

Among its most important tenets: it prohibits discrimination, increases spending on health care and the poor, allows civil unions for gay couples, and gives more rights to indigenous groups. It also focuses on the environment, requiring the government to avoid actions that would destroy ecosystems or drive species to extinction – the first such measure of its kind according to Ecuadorian officials.

Critics of the new constitution say the government will be unable to meet its new obligations owing to a lack of resources. Others say it is a move to the left in reducing the power of big business and the land-owning elite. Opponents also cite the expanded powers of the president, with added control over the economy as well as the oil and mining industries. It also allows the president to dissolve congress within the first three years of its four-year term.

Most agree that it is a historic document, and President Rafael Correa has already put some of its provisions into effect. The constitution allows that some foreign loans could be declared illegitimate and not have to be paid – which is exactly what happened in December 2008, when Correa announced that Ecuador was defaulting on billions of dollars of so-called illegitimate foreign debt. Whether the president can deliver the goods on other matters in Ecuador's ambitious new constitution remains the million-dollar question.

For an insider's take on the USA's role in Ecuador's acceptance of foreign aid that was used to fund lucrative contracts to US development companies, pick up a copy of John Perkin's *Confessions of an Economic Hitman*.

The protesters were lead by Antonio Vargas, Colonel Lucio Gutiérrez and former supreme court president Carlos Solorzano, who then formed a brief ruling triumvirate. Two days later – and largely due to the international pressure that followed Latin America's first military coup in two decades – the triumvirate turned the presidency over to Vice President Gustavo Noboa.

Noboa went ahead with dollarization, and in September 2000 the US dollar became the official currency. Although only one year earlier 6000 sucres bought one dollar, people were forced to exchange their sucres at the dramatically inflated year 2000 rate of 25,000 to $1. Their losses were severe.

THE 21ST CENTURY

Along with dollarizing the economy, Noboa also implemented austerity measures to obtain US$2 billion in aid from the International Monetary Fund (IMF) and other international lenders. At the end of 2000, gas and cooking-fuel prices sky-rocketed (largely because of dollarization) and the new year saw frequent strikes and protests by unions and indigenous

1930s

Following a period of reform in the late 1920s (including pensions for state workers), the Ecuadorian economy crashes. World demand for cacao dissolves, unemployment soars and political instability rocks the government.

1941

Tensions rise over disputed Amazon territories, and Peru invades Ecuador with 13,000 troops. Argentina, Brazil, Chile and the US broker a peace accord. Ecuador cedes more than half its territories, but doesn't acknowledge its new borders.

1948

Galo Plaza is elected president, marking an era of progress and prosperity. He slows inflation, balances the budget and invests in schools, roads and other infrastructure. Ecuador sees a boom in the banana industry.

groups. The economy finally stabilized, and Noboa left office on somewhat favorable terms.

President Noboa was succeeded in 2002 by former coup leader Lucio Gutiérrez, whose populist agenda and promises to end government corruption won him the crucial electoral support of Ecuador's indigenous population. But shortly after taking office, Gutiérrez began backing down from his commitment to radical reform and instead began implementing IMF austerity measures to finance the country's massive debt. Gutiérrez also tossed out almost the entire supreme court. His adversaries claim that he purged the court to rid it of his rivals and to allow himself to change the constitution in order to drop corruption charges on his former ally, ex-president Bucaram. Protests erupted in the capital, and in 2005 congress voted overwhelmingly to remove Gutiérrez (the third Ecuadorian president ousted in eight years), replacing him with Vice President Alfredo Palacio.

A political newcomer who referred to himself as a 'simple doctor,' Palacio soon turned his attention to the social problems his predecessor had abandoned. In order to fund health and education programs and kick-start the economy, Palacio announced he would redirect oil profits earmarked for paying the foreign debt. An essential partner in this endeavor was Rafael Correa, a US-educated economist, whom Palacio appointed as his finance minister. Correa focused on poverty reduction and on reshaping Ecuador's economy by moving away from a heavy reliance on US trade. Correa was skeptical of signing a free-trade agreement with the US, looking instead to cultivate relationships with other Latin American countries. However, he didn't stick around long. When the World Bank denied the government a loan, he resigned.

Stay up to date with the Council of the Americas (http://coa.counciloftheamericas.org/resources.php), which houses a conservative-leaning collection of recent news items on Ecuador – and practically every other Latin American country.

Despite his brief stint as finance minister, Correa's work earned him many admirers, who carried him to power in the 2006 presidential election. Correa describes himself as a humanist, a fervent Catholic of the left and a proponent of 21st-century socialism. Since taking the reins, he's focused on social welfare. One of his biggest targets is the oil industry: he's called for increased taxes on oil revenue to be spent on the Ecuadorian poor, and has accused foreign oil companies operating in Ecuador of failing to meet current environmental regulations.

He also criticized his predecessor Mahuad for adopting the US dollar as the national currency, and suggests Ecuador will return to the sucre when economically feasible. Supporters applaud Correa's attention to the poor and his focus on economic reform; they also voted in favor of his sweeping changes to the constitution (see the boxed text, opposite). Meanwhile, critics describe Correa as an aspiring Hugo Chávez, Venezuela's controversial left-wing president, who has nationalized major industries such as telecommunications, and has the possibility of serving as president for life (following a Venezuelan referendum removing term limits for public officials).

1970s

Following the discovery of oil in the Oriente, Ecuador undergoes profound changes. The government budget, exports and per-capita income increase 500%. Industrial development progresses, and a small middle class begins to emerge.

2000

Facing spiraling inflation, contracting GDP and default on external debts, Ecuador dumps the sucre (the national currency) for the US dollar. The economy makes a modest recovery, although numerous Ecuadorians slip below the poverty line.

2008

In a nationwide referendum, Ecuadorians vote to change the constitution. The new document expands the powers of the president while increasing spending on social welfare and enshrining rights for indigenous people and the environment.

The Culture

Ecuador's famous diversity extends well beyond geography. The country's varied cultures – from indigenous groups and *serranos* (people from the mountains) to Afro-Ecuadorians and *costeños* (people from the coast)– have all contributed to Ecuador's complicated soul. This is the historic birthplace of the renowned Escuela Quiteña, one of colonial Latin America's most important art schools, and its contributions are evident in dozens of architecturally dazzling buildings in its most important cities. Meanwhile, the rich textile traditions of ancient cultures live on in humble communities across the nation. Ecuador's musical output is small but impressive, with deep roots in folklore, *pasillo* (Ecuador's national music) and marimba.

THE NATIONAL PSYCHE

Most Ecuadorians have three things in common: pride in the natural beauty of their country; disdain for the seemingly endless crop of politicians who fail to deliver on their promises; and the presence of a relative in another country (some 1.5 million people – over 10% of the population – have left Ecuador in search of work elsewhere).

From there the communal psyche blurs, and attitude becomes a matter of altitude. *Serranos* and *costeños* can spend hours telling you what makes them different (ie better) than the other. Largely rooted in the historic rivalry between conservative *quiteños* (people from Quito) and more liberal *guayaquileños* (people from Guayaquil), *serranos* call people from the coast *monos* (monkeys) and say they're lazy and would rather party than keep their cities clean. *Costeños,* on the other hand, say *serranos* are uptight and elitist, and that they pepper their interactions with shallow formalities. They jokingly refer to highlanders as *'serranos que comen papas con guzanos'* (hill people that eat potatoes with worms). Of course, *costeños* still speak longingly of the cool evenings of the highlands, and *serranos* pour down to the coast in droves for vacations, and everyone mixes everything up on the beach in peace.

Abya Yala Net/Native Web (www.abyayala.nativeweb.org) provides a good introduction and general overview of Ecuador's indigenous cultures.

LIFESTYLE

How an Ecuadorian lives is a matter of geography, ethnicity and class. A poor indigenous family that cultivates the thin soil of a steep highland plot lives very differently from a coastal fishing family living in the mangroves of Esmeraldas province, or a family living in the slums of Guayaquil. An indigenous Saraguro family that tends communally owned cattle in the southern highlands leads a dramatically different life than an upper-class *quiteño* family with two maids, a new computer and a Mercedes in the garage. As a visitor you might find yourself surrounded by middle-class folks in a city such as Ambato or Cuenca, or you may find yourself spending a night in a humble shack with an indigenous family near Laguna Quilotoa.

There is simply no better book on highland indigenous dress than Ann P Rowe's *Costume and Identity in Highland Ecuador*. It's available at bookshops in Quito if you can't find it online.

But one hard fact is certain: an estimated 40% of Ecuadorians live below the poverty line. For many Ecuadorians, paying for cooking fuel and putting food on the table are constant concerns. But, as most first-time visitors are often astounded to experience, even the poorest Ecuadorians exude an openness, generosity and joie de vivre not always seen in richer countries. Fiestas are celebrated with particular fervor, which may mean sleepless nights for neighbors as the nearby birthday bash or soccer celebration rages on early into the morning.

SOCIAL GRACES

Greetings are important to Ecuadorians, especially in the highland areas. Strangers conducting business will, at the very least, exchange a cordial '*¿Buenos días, cómo está?*' (Good morning, how are you?) before launching into whatever they are doing. Male friends and casual acquaintances meeting one another in the street shake hands at both the beginning and the end of even a short meeting. Women will kiss one another on the cheek in greeting and in farewell. Men often kiss women decorously on the cheek as well, except in a business setting, where a handshake is deemed more appropriate. Close male friends hug one another in the traditional *abrazo* (hug). Indigenous people, on the other hand, rarely kiss, and their handshakes, when they're offered, are a light touch rather than a firm grip. In all situations, politeness is a valued habit.

Personal space is a fully different concept for Ecuadorians than it is for North Americans and Europeans. Conversations tend to take place face to face; streets and market places can get as packed as a fruit crate; standing in line becomes a game of bump-and-nudge; and homes have little individual space. Noise is a part of life: giant speakers blast *cumbia* (dance music originally from Colombia, similar to salsa) from massive storefront speakers, and guests staying in cheaper hotel rooms crank up their TVs so loud that the barber across the street can follow the soccer match.

Spitting and even urinating in public are commonplace, particularly in the lower socioeconomic classes; however, burping in public is considered the absolute height of bad manners by everyone.

The near mythologized idea of a better life elsewhere also plays a role in Ecuadorian society. The steady flow of emigration has winnowed indigenous communities throughout the highlands, as people abandon traditional lives and customs to migrate either to the city or to another country. *Turismo comunitario* (community tourism) projects, such as those in and around Cuenca (p205), Salinas (p184) and Tena (p252), have sprung up in recent years and offer the visitor an excellent way to help contribute to an economic alternative to emigration.

Michael Handelsman's *Culture and Customs of Ecuador* is an excellent resource for understanding the nation's rich multiculturalism. In addition to addressing culture and social customs, he discusses religion, literature, art, cinema and media.

ECONOMY

Petroleum plays a major role in Ecuador's economy, accounting for more than half the country's export earnings and 25% of public-sector revenues. Other major industries include mining, agriculture (seafood, bananas, flowers, coffee, cacao, sugar, tropical fruits, corn and livestock), food processing, wood products, textiles, chemicals and pharmaceuticals.

Overreliance on petroleum has wreaked havoc on the economy in past years. In 1999 and 2000 Ecuador suffered a dire economic crisis, with GDP contracting by more than 6% and poverty increasing significantly. The banking system also collapsed and Ecuador defaulted on its external debts. Dollarization (adopting the US dollar as currency) helped to stabilize the economy and bring positive growth, with GDP expanding 5.5% from 2002 to 2006 (its highest five-year expansion in 25 years). The poverty rate also declined, though it still remains high today at 38%.

In recent times Ecuador's president Rafael Correa, who is a US-trained economist, announced that spending on social services would take priority over debt servicing. The collapse of oil prices in 2007 and 2008, however, left the government unable to pay for its ambitious reforms or provide the much needed investment in infrastructure and industry. The global recession that began in 2008 has also affected Ecuador, and Correa announced that the government would take strict measures to avoid a 1999-style economic collapse. Measures included recovering unpaid back taxes owed by large companies (estimated at $1.2 billion), adding steep tariffs to unnecessary imports, and regulating the banking sector. Correa has snubbed the International Monetary Fund (IMF) and pulled out of free-trade negotiations with the US, although the US remains Ecuador's largest market by far (accounting for 42% of Ecuador's exports).

Money sent home from emigrants (one million of whom live and work in the US) contributes substantially to the Ecuadorian economy: an estimated $2 billion is sent home each year. Economists fears that these funds too will dwindle as the global recession continues.

POPULATION

Ecuador has the highest population density of any South American nation – about 49 people per square kilometer. Despite this, the country still feels incredibly wild, mainly because around 60% of the population lives in urban areas (and this most likely means Quito or Guayaquil).

The Amazon's indigenous Cofán are one of the most traditional cultures in all of Ecuador. Ironically, it's one of the few indigenous groups with its very own website! See www.cofan.org.

About 25% of the population is indigenous (living largely in rural areas), and the majority of these are Quichua (called Quechua in Peru) and speak Quichua as their first language. Another 65% of the population is mestizo (people of mixed indigenous and European decent). Except in towns with sizeable indigenous populations such as Otavalo, mestizos own and work in the vast majority of businesses; they are the people with whom travelers have most of their day-to-day contact. Some 3% of the population is Afro-Ecuadorian, the majority whom live in the province of Esmeraldas (in northwestern Ecuador) and the Valle de Chota in the northern highlands. About 6% of the population is of pure European descent, and a small but growing number of people are of Asian descent. The western-lowlands town of Quevedo has a substantial Asian-Ecuadorian population (and is likely the best place to pick up an authentic plate of Chinese food).

The majority of Ecuador's *indígenas* (indigenous people) live in the highlands, and they have distinctive differences in dress depending on their region. Someone familiar with highland dress can tell exactly where an indigenous person is from by the color of their poncho or by the shape of their hat. Some of the best-known highland groups include the Otavaleños, the Salasacas, the Cañaris and the Saraguros.

SPORTS

Soccer

Pablo Mogrovejo's documentary film *Ecuador vs el resto del mundo* (Ecuador versus the Rest of the World) takes a look at the country's participation in the 2002 World Cup and its significance to ordinary Ecuadorians.

The national sport is *fútbol* (soccer), which is played in every city, town, village and outpost in the country. Major-league games are played in Quito and Guayaquil on Saturday afternoons and Sunday mornings, and if you have a chance, they're a spectacle well worth attending. People in Ecuador, as throughout Latin America, can be extremely passionate about soccer, and going to a game is usually exciting to say the least. When Ecuador qualified for the World Cup in 2005, the nation celebrated just as it did when the team qualified for the first time ever in 2002. The partying began before the game ended and continued until the next morning. Even in small towns, giant speakers were dragged out onto the street or set up in central plazas, and people danced, drank and sang into the wee hours.

Bullfighting & Cockfighting

As throughout most of Latin America, bullfighting and cockfighting are popular in Ecuador. The main bullfighting season is during the first week in December, when bullfighters of international stature may arrive in Quito from Mexico and Spain. The professional bullfight consists of various *toreros* (bullfighters) angering the bull before he is killed by a sword thrust to the neck.

THE INDIGENOUS OF ECUADOR

Ecuador's vibrant indigenous population is made up of some 3.5 million people, roughly 25% of Ecuadorians. There are more than a dozen distinct groups in Ecuador, speaking some 20 different languages.

The country's largest indigenous ethnic group, the Quichua, are one part of a total Andean population of 11 million (scattered across Peru, Ecuador, Colombia and even Chile and Argentina). In Ecuador, the Quichua live in both the Sierra and the Amazon, and vary considerably in customs and lifestyles. Those in the mountains subsist on small plots of farmland, raising sheep and cattle, and their fine textiles and weavings are an essential source of income.

One of the best-known groups within the Quichua community are the Otavaleños. Like other indigenous groups, they have a unique dress that sets them apart from other groups. For men, this consists of a blue poncho, a fedora, white calf-length socks, and a *shimba* (a long braid that hangs down nearly to the waist). Wearing the hair in this fashion probably dates back to pre-Inca times, and is an established and deeply rooted tradition. The women's dress may be the closest to Inca costume worn anywhere in the Andes. White blouses, blue skirts, shawls and jewelry are all part of the way of outwardly expressing their ethnicity.

Short in stature (men average 1.5m or about 5ft in height), the Huaorani are an Amazonian tribe living between the Río Napo and the Río Curaray in the Oriente. They number no more than 4000 and remain one of Ecuador's most isolated indigenous groups. They have a reputation for being warriors, defending their territory against outsiders, whether they be rival tribes or encroaching oil developers. They have a complex cosmology – making no distinction between the physical and spiritual worlds – and an intimate understanding of the rainforest in cultivating medicine, poisons for defense and hallucinogens for spiritual rites. Some still refer to them as the Auca, which means 'savage' in Quichua – a name which the Huaorani, not surprisingly, find extremely offensive.

Until the 1950s the Shuar living in the Amazonian lowlands were a seminomadic society of male hunters and female gardeners. As a means of preserving their culture and lands, the Shuar (which today number 40,000) formed the first ethnic federation in Ecuadorian Amazonia in 1964. They are one of the most studied Amazonian groups, and were once feared as 'headhunters.' In the 19th century they were famous for the elaborate process of *tsantsa,* shrinking the heads of slain opponents. Shuar believed the *muisak* (soul) of the victim remained inside the head and that keeping the *tsantsa* would bring the warrior good fortune and please the spirits of his ancestors.

The Chachi originally lived in Ecuador's highlands, but fled to the Pacific coast (in present-day Esmeraldas province) in the wake of Inca and Spanish conquests. Boasting a population of around 4000, they live in homes made of palm fronds, travel by canoe through a watery landscape and cultivate cocoa and tropical fruits. They are highly skilled artisans, particularly known for their hammocks.

Straddling the Ecuador-Colombia border in the northeast, the Cofan number about 1500, half of whom live in Ecuador. Like other Amazonian groups they have seen a significant loss and degradation of their environment, largely due to oil drilling. Fortunately, in recent years they have waged a successful campaign for land rights, and are presently in control of 4000 sq km of rainforest (a seemingly large number, but only a fraction of the 30,000 sq km originally belonging to the group).

By contrast, the *pueblo* (small town) bullfight is a largely bloodless event, although the contest plays out much the same way, with the tormenting of the bull the essential feature of both events. Small-town bullfights often end with a game of 'bull soccer' in which (usually drunk) volunteers leave the relative safety of the stands, enter the ring in two teams of five and do their best to tease the bull into chasing them through the opponents' goal posts.

Animal rights groups, including the World Society for the Protection of Animals, object to bullfights. In 2007 the town of Baños declared itself 'antibullfighting', becoming the first city in Latin America to speak out against the event.

Cockfighting is popular nationwide, and most towns of any size will have a *coliseo de gallos* (cockfighting arena). Each event lasts anywhere from 30 seconds to five minutes as two roosters, with metal spikes implanted on their claws, fight to the death. Most tourists avoid these arenas. The sport has a long and important history throughout Latin America, and the country's most famous gamecock trainers have even been prominently featured in *El Comercio,* the nation's most important newspaper. Gambling is a key component of the cockfight.

Other Sports

The only locally played sport even remotely approaching soccer's popularity is volleyball, known colloquially as 'Ecua-volley,' but even it is played with a soccer ball. A much rarer ballgame is a sort of paddleball called *pelota de guante,* where players hit a rubber ball with large, spiked paddles. Occasionally in the highlands you'll spot people playing a game similar to the French game of *boules* or *petanque,* which involves tossing steel balls the size of baseballs along an impromptu dirt court.

Ecuadorian mountaineer Ivan Vallejo is one of the world's top mountain climbers, having summitted all 14 of the world's 8000m peaks (including Everest) without the use of supplemental oxygen.

RELIGION

As with most Latin American countries, Ecuador's predominant religion is Roman Catholicism. About 95% of the population is Catholic, and the Church is still considered an important part of Ecuadorian society. For many, however, attending Sunday services is a low priority – though on holidays and feast days the churches are packed.

For indigenous Ecuadorians, Catholicism is often only a veneer laid over millennia-old indigenous beliefs and practices. Ecuador's many religious festivals are perfect examples of this. The summer equinox of Inti Raymi, celebrated around Otavalo, coincides with the Catholic celebration of St John, and Corpus Cristi celebrations coincide with indigenous harvest festivals throughout the highlands. The Catholic church in Saraguro is another obvious illustration: corn stalks and woven corn husks decorate the entrance, and the Inca commandments *'Ama killa, ama llulla, ama shua'* (Do not be lazy, do not lie, do not steal) hang over the altar inside.

WOMEN IN ECUADOR

On paper, women in Ecuador have almost identical rights to those enjoyed by women in the USA, France or Canada. Constitutionally, women are equal to men in all spheres of public and private life. In reality, however, things are different.

Women occupy a large part of the workforce, and as a traveler to Ecuador you'll encounter just as many women in the workplace as you will men. Yet a huge of number of working women suffer discrimination in the form of sexual harassment (which ranges from mild but ever present to severe), lower wages and difficulty in advancing to positions of real power. Indigenous and Afro-Ecuadorian women experience a harsh form of double discrimination in a society dominated by mestizos and men.

Life can be particularly tough for women in the highlands, as many are expected to raise the children (and families here are often quite large – five to nine children is not uncommon) while still contributing to the family's income. The social safety net is often nonexistent, leaving women to struggle on their own; even the presence of a doctor when a woman goes into labor is a rarity. In recent years a few grassroots organizations have appeared, providing women with education and training, helping with family life and providing microloans to start up small businesses (Mama Cuchara, p214, run by an indigenous women's association, is one such organization).

In 1929 Ecuador became the first Latin American nation to grant equal voting rights to women. Today approximately 25% of Ecuador's government positions are held by women, though only a handful of these are high decision-making positions. On the flipside, women (especially indigenous and poor women) have played a huge role in politics at the grassroots level. Women have stood on the frontline of countless protests and political movements.

ARTS

Music

Most people are familiar with traditional Andean *folklórica* (folk music) without even knowing it: Simon and Garfunkel's version of 'El Cóndor Pasa (If I Could)' was a classic Andean tune long before the popular duo got their hands on it. Hearing it day in and day out (as is quite possible in certain market towns) may induce insanity, but its distinctive and even haunting sound is characteristic of Andean folk music. *Folklórica's* definitive instrument is the *rondador* (bamboo panpipe). Other traditional instruments include the *quena* and *pingullo* (large and small bamboo flutes) and the *charango,* a mandolin-like instrument with five double strings and a sounding box that was originally made with an armadillo shell.

Although most people associate Ecuador with *folklórica,* the country's true national music is the *pasillo,* which is rooted in the waltz. Its most famous voice was Julio Jaramillo (known affectionately as 'JJ'; 1935–78), a handsome singer from Guayaquil whose emotive singing popularized the genre throughout Latin America.

For profiles of Ecuador's music scene, including folk and rock bands, visit www.goecuador.com/magazine/ecuador-mp3-music.html. You can even listen to MP3s of featured groups.

Northwest Ecuador, particularly Esmeraldas province, is famous for its marimba music, which is historically the music of Ecuador's Afro-Ecuadorian population. Today it's becoming increasingly difficult to hear live because of the increased popularity of salsa and other musical forms in the Afro-Ecuadorian community. One name to look out for is Afro-Ecuadorian dance and music group Azúcar. Its choral arrangements feature African-style rhythms alongside the marimba and *cunucos* (rustic congas).

Ecuador's rock scene is small but growing, with a number of original bands breaking new ground. Esto es Eso is a talented US-Ecuadorian duo blending hip-hop, pop, rock and reggae, along with *pasillo* and other traditional sounds (see the boxed text, p80). Of any band destined for crossover success in North American and Europe, Esto es Eso is it.

Sudakaya, a young band that hails from Ambato, is mostly known for reggae, though it also blends other Afro-Latin rhythms such as ska and calypso with bossa nova and samba. Rocola Bacalao is a top performer in the Quito scene, playing a mix of ska, punk, merengue and other sounds, with irreverent lyrics and a good sense of humor. The percussion band Tomback (which takes its name from an Iranian hand-drum) is a youthful nine-member group playing progressive rock as well as rap and jazz laced with heavy beats. Ecuador also has its share of Latin pop artists, with teen-idol voices such as Fausto Miño filling the airwaves.

If there's one inescapable music in this Andean country, it's *cumbia,* whose rhythm resembles that of a trotting three-legged horse. Originally from Colombia, Ecuadorian *cumbia* has a rawer (almost amateur), melancholic sound, and is dominated by the electronic keyboard. Bus drivers love the stuff, perhaps because it so strangely complements those back-road journeys through the Andes (and hopefully it keeps them awake at the wheel).

A nightclub favorite is Caribbean-born *reggaetón* (a blend of Puerto Rican *bomba,* dancehall and hip-hop) with its grinding melodies and racy lyrics.

Architecture

When it comes to colonial architecture, two cities stand high above the rest: Quito and Cuenca. Both have historical centers that are so stunning, each has been declared a Unesco World Heritage site (Quito in 1978 and Cuenca in 1999). Quito's churches are some of the richest, most spectacular colonial buildings in all of South America. Bearing testament to the fact that Spain was under the rule of the Moors for centuries, many of Quito's churches have striking Moorish (Arabic) influences known as *mudéjar*. Many of Quito's churches were built atop sacred indigenous sights, adding yet another layer to the cultural mix. The overall appearance of the city's colonial churches is overpoweringly ornamental and almost cloyingly opulent.

By contrast, the houses of the middle and upper classes during the colonial period were elegant and simple, often consisting of rooms with verandas around a central courtyard, with whitewashed walls and red-tile roofs. Many houses had two stories, and the upper floors had ornate wooden balconies with intricately carved balustrades. Cuenca is the true exemplar of these.

Painting & Sculpture

Ecuador's most significant artistic contribution is the Quito School of Art (see the boxed text, opposite), which reached its zenith between 1600 and 1765. The Quito School died out following independence, largely because the style was associated with the Spanish regime. The 19th century brought the Republican period – favorite subjects were heroes of the revolution, florid landscapes and important members of the new republic's high society.

The 20th century saw the rise of the *indigenista* (indigenous-led) movement, whose unifying theme was the oppression and burdens of Ecuador's indigenous inhabitants. The pioneer of the *indigenista* movement was Camilo Egas (1899–1962), who, along with painter Eduardo Kingman (1913–98), placed Ecuadorian modern art on the international map. The country's most famous *indigenista* painter, however, is Oswaldo Guayasamín (1919–99), whose evocative and haunting works tackle such themes as torture, poverty and loss. His pieces hang in galleries all over the world, although the best place to see his work is in Quito (p92).

> The indigenous painting technique known as *tigua* receives colorful treatment in Jean G Colvin's beautiful bilingual coffee-table book *Arte de Tigua.*

The best places to see the work of Ecuador's contemporary artists are at Quito's Museo del Banco Central (p87) and in commercial art galleries (p111).

No discussion of Ecuadorian painting is complete without mentioning *tigua,* an intricate, colorful painting style generally depicting Andean indigenous groups. The art form's major progenitor is the internationally known Alfredo Toaquiza. For more information, see p166.

Crafts

In Ecuador, as in much of Latin America, there is a bridge between 'fine arts' and *artesanía* (crafts). Literally this means 'artisanship' and refers to textile crafts ranging from finely woven ponchos to hammocks, panama hats, basketwork, leatherwork, jewelry, woodcarving and ceramics. For a more detailed discussion of these items, see p385.

> For an in-depth look at the Otavalo weaving industry and the region's 'indigenous middle class,' read Rudi Colloredo-Mansfeld's *The Native Leisure Class: Consumption and Cultural Creativity in the Andes.*

Literature

Ecuador has several notable literary figures, although none have become household names outside the country. Juan Montalvo (1832–89) was a prolific essayist from Ambato who frequently attacked the dictatorial political

THE QUITO SCHOOL OF ART

As the Spanish colonized present-day Ecuador, religious conversion became the key to subduing the indigenous population and remaking the New World in a likeness of the Old. The most successful tool for conversion was art, whose story-telling power and visual representations had long served the Catholic Church for gaining believers. At first, sculptures and paintings were imported from Spain, but from the mid-16th century the Church set up guilds and workshops to train a local base of indigenous artisans. From these workshops blossomed one of the most important artistic genres in Latin America: the Escuela Quiteña (Quito School of Art).

The beauty of the Escuela Quiteña is its fascinating blend of indigenous concepts and styles and European art forms. The beliefs and artistic heritages of the artisans crept into their work. If you look closely at paintings in Quito's many religious museums and churches, you'll see many non-European themes: Christ eating a plate of *cuy* (roast guinea pig), or the 12 apostles dining on *humitas* (a type of corn dumpling). Religious figures are often depicted with darker skin or stouter builds that reflect indigenous Ecuadorian body types. Inside churches, sun motifs and planetary symbols appear on ceilings that are decorated in what appear to be simply Moorish patterns.

The Escuela Quiteña became renowned for its mastery of the realistic. By the 18th century, artisans were using glass eyes and real hair and eyelashes in their sculptures. They added moving joints, inserted tiny mirrors into the mouth to mimic saliva, and became known for their mastery of polychrome painting (the use of multiple colors). Some sculptures, particularly those of the 18th-century carver Manuel Chili (nicknamed 'Caspicara'), are so realistic they almost seem to be alive. Notable painters of the Escuela Quiteña include Miguel de Santiago, whose huge canvases grace the walls of Quito's Monastery of San Agustín; Manuel Samaniego; Nicolás Goríbar; and Bernardo Rodríguez.

After Quito gained independence from Spain in 1822, the religious art of the Escuela Quiteña lost both its potency and necessity. Today, Caspicara's work can be seen in Quito's Monastery of San Francisco (p84) and the Museo del Banco Central (p87).

figures of his time. His best-known work is the book *Siete tratados* (Seven Treatises; 1882), which includes a comparison between Simón Bolívar and George Washington. Juan León Mera (1832–94), also from Ambato, is famous for his novel *Cumandá* (1891), which describes indigenous life in the 19th century.

Perhaps the most notable Ecuadorian writer of the 20th century is *quiteño* Jorge Icaza (1906–79), who was profoundly influenced by the *indigenista* movement. His most famous novel, *Huasipungo* (1934; translated as *The Villagers* in 1973) is a brutal story about indigenous Ecuadorians, the seizure of their land and the savage massacre of those who protested.

A good introduction to Ecuadorian literature is *Diez Cuentistas Ecuatorianos* (1990), an anthology of short stories by 10 Ecuadorian writers born in the 1940s. The stories are written in Spanish with English translations.

Gustavo Guayasamin's documentary *Hieleros del Chimborazo* (Icemen of Chimborazo; 1980) is a fascinating portrayal of the men who hacked ice from the glaciers of Chimborazo to sell in highland markets. Available online.

Cinema

One of Ecuador's first internationally applauded directors was Sebastián Cordero. His 1998 film *Ratas, ratones, rateros* tells the story of a *quiteño* kid whose ex-convict cousin drags him into a life of street crime. This movie offers a glimpse into the capital's dark side – one that you're not likely to see otherwise. Cordero's more recent *Crónicas* (Chronicles), from 2004, takes place in the city of Babahoyo in Los Ríos province. The narrative revolves around a warped deal between a serial killer and a Miami reporter.

Camilo Luzuriaga is another influential Ecuadorian filmmaker. His *Cara o cruz* (Heads or Tails; 2004) tells the story of two sisters who reunite in Quito after a 25-year separation. Luzuriaga made his name internationally with his film *Entre Marx y una mujer desnuda* (Between Marx and a Naked Woman; 1996), which portrays a group of young communist intellectuals in Quito, whose idealism dissipates beneath the inescapable realities of Ecuadorian corruption and bureaucracy.

One filmmaker breaking barriers is Tania Hermida. Her 2006 film *Qué tan lejos* (How much further?), which she wrote and directed, is a sweet road movie about two young women on a quiet and unexpected journey of self-discovery in the highlands. It's beautifully shot in the Andean countryside.

Food & Drink

Ecuadorian cuisine benefits from the country's rich geographic diversity, with tropical fruits, fresh seafood and classic recipes from the *campo* (countryside) all contributing to the bounty of the Andean table. Many dishes have evolved over the years, blending Spanish and indigenous influences. And while it's little known outside the country's borders, Ecuadorian cooking offers some outstanding opportunities for gustatory exploration, with coast, mountain and forest all offering quite distinct and rewarding dining experiences.

STAPLES & SPECIALTIES

Altitude and geography play a sizable role in Ecuadorian cooking, with highland restaurants serving quite different dishes to those you'll see in places along the coast. There are also specialties found only in particular regions. Cities like Quito and Guayaquil, however, benefit from immigrants who've arrived from all parts of the country (and from abroad); here you can enjoy the widest variety of regional, ethnic and international dishes.

The International Potato Center (www.cipotato.org) has identified over 4000 varieties of potato in the Andes, the birthplace of the world's potatoes.

Although the cost of food has risen substantially in recent years, Ecuador's restaurants still represent excellent value for most foreign visitors. *Almuerzos* (set lunches) run about $2 to $3 at inexpensive restaurants, and midrange dinner spots charge around $5 to $9 for a main.

Highlands

It's impossible to consider food from the highlands without discussing the once highly revered crop, *maíz* (corn). In its numerous varieties, corn has been the staple of the Andean diet for a millennium, and today it forms the basis of countless highland specialties. Kernels are toasted into *tostada* (toasted corn), popped into *cangil* (popcorn), boiled and treated to make *mote* (hominy) and milled into cornmeal. The latter is flavored or filled and wrapped in corn husks or dark green *achira* leaves and steamed. The results are some of the tastiest treats in the highlands, including tamales

ECUADOR'S TOP RESTAURANTS BY REGION

- **Quito** Feast on delectable ceviche and seafood at **Cevichería Manolo** (p106), in Quito's lively new town.
- **Northern highlands** Enjoy decadent dining befitting a royal at **Hostería La Mirage** (p132), a magnificent estate outside of Otavalo.
- **Central highlands** Visit long-time favorite **Chugchucarras La Mamá Negra** (p160) for Latacunga's classic pork dish.
- **Southern highlands** Taste heavenly highland delicacies *quimbolitos, humitas, empanadas de verde* and *tamales lojanos* at **El Tamal Lojano** (p218).
- **Oriente** Try award-winning Oriente dishes at **El Jardín** (p261), a handsomely set bistro with gardens overlooking the river.
- **North coast & lowlands** Eat outstanding seafood at **Seaflower** (p287), right near the beach at Same.
- **South coast** Experience the delicious changing menu while whale-watching from the deck of **Hosteria Farallón Dillon** (p314) in Ballenita, just north of Santa Elena.
- **Galápagos Islands** Dine on fantastic seafood at Puerto Ayora's **Angermeyer Point** (p361).

(similar to Mexican tamales), *humitas* (lightly sweetened corn dumplings) and *quimbolitos* (sweeter, more cakelike corn dumplings).

Potatoes, of course, originated in the Andes, and are another important highland staple. Besides a vast array of tiny colorful potatoes, you'll find creations such as *llapingachos,* fried potato-and-cheese pancakes that are often served as a side dish with fried eggs. Quinoa is an extremely protein-rich grain that forms a staple of the highland indigenous diet and has made its way into contemporary dishes throughout Ecuador.

For a fascinating look at Ecuador's favorite highland dish, pick up *The Guinea Pig: Healing, Food and Ritual in the Andes,* which goes beyond food in talking about folk medicine and religious practices in various Andean societies.

The highlands' most famous *plato típico* (typical dish) – one that visitors either love or hate to spot in the highland markets – is *cuy* (roasted guinea pig). *Cuy* is an indigenous specialty that dates back to Inca times and is supposedly high in protein and low in cholesterol. They're usually roasted whole on spits, and the sight of the little paws and teeth sticking out can be a bit unnerving, but for meat eaters it's well worth sampling. Cuenca (p199) and Loja (p214) are both good places to try it.

Another eye-catching specialty is whole roasted pig. Known as *hornado* (literally, 'roasted'), this is one of the highland's most popular dishes. In the markets, the juicy meat is pulled right off the golden-brown carcass when you order it. *Hornado* is almost as popular as *fritada,* fried chunks of pork that are almost invariably served with *mote.* Latacunga (p160) has a famous take on this dish known as the *chugchucara,* which, aside from elevating your cholesterol into the stratosphere, makes for a great weekend event.

Quinoa has been a staple of Andean food for thousands of years. This grain grows at altitudes of up to 4000m and is classified by the UN as a 'supercrop' due to its extremely high protein content. The Inca called it 'mother grain.'

As throughout Ecuador, soups are an extremely important part of the highland diet and come in countless varieties, including *caldos* (brothy soups), *sopas* (thicker broth-based soups), *locros* (creamier and generally heartier soups), *sancochos* (stewlike soups) and *secos* (stews that are usually served over rice). *Locro de papa* is a satisfyingly smooth potato soup served with avocado and cheese.

The Coast

The coast is where Ecuadorian food really shines. The entire coast is blessed with culinary riches, and it's easy to eat delicious, healthy food there. Manabí cooking in particular rates among the country's best, and it is a big reason so many Ecuadorian expats long for home.

BANANA REPUBLIC

Bananas play a vital role in Ecuador. They keep the economy humming along: Ecuador is still the world's largest banana exporter (to the tune of 7 million tons a year). This high-calorie, potassium-rich food plays an essential role in the diet of many Ecuadorians. Bananas are even a part of pop culture. In the coastal city of Machala, the prettiest girls in town compete to become *la Reina del Banano* (the banana queen).

You'll come across bananas in many shapes and forms while traveling here, and it never hurts to know your *chifles* from your *patacones*. Here's an introduction to the varied world of Ecuador's famous fruit.

Plátanos are plantains, *verdes* are green plantains and *maduros* are ripe, yellow plantains. *Guineos* are the yellow sweet bananas that most foreigners are familiar with.

OK, now let's take 'em apart: *chifles* are thinly sliced *guineos* fried into crisps, while *patacones* are thickly sliced, smashed *verdes* fried into chewy fritters. *Maduros* are often sliced lengthwise, fried and served whole as a side dish. In the Oriente, *plátanos con queso* are green plantains split lengthwise, filled with cheese and grilled. Loja is famous for its *empanadas de verde* (empanadas made with plantain dough), while the coast is known for its *bolas de verde* (balls of mashed plantains with cheese).

The staple of coastal cuisine, of course, is seafood, with the great fruits of the sea arriving fresh from the fishing boat at ports across the country. The most widely found seafood dish is *corvina,* which literally means 'sea bass,' but is usually just whatever white fish happens to be available that day. When it's really *corvina,* it's worth seeking out.

Ceviche is superb in Ecuador. This delicious dish consists of uncooked seafood marinated in lemon juice and seasoned with thinly sliced onion and herbs. It's served cold and, on a hot afternoon, goes down divinely with popcorn and a cold beer. Ceviche is prepared with *pescado* (fish), *concha* (shellfish), *camarones* (shrimp), *calamares* (squid), or some combination (*mixto*). Only shrimp is cooked before being marinated. Improperly prepared ceviche can make you sick (and even spread cholera), but careful restaurants in Ecuador are aware of this and make ceviche under sanitary conditions.

Esmeraldas province, which has a large Afro-Ecuadorian population, is home to some interesting African-influenced specialties including the downright sublime *encocado,* shrimp or fish cooked in a rich, spiced coconut sauce. Guayas province, and especially the town of Playas (p316), is famous for its crab, which is cooked whole and served in piles as big as your appetite, along with a wooden hammer for cracking open the shells. It's one of the most pleasurable (and messy!) culinary experiences in the country. Guayas is also famous for its *seco de chivo* (goat stew), an Ecuadorian classic. If you're not keen on goat, look for *seco de pollo,* the same dish made with chicken.

Although it's in Spanish, André Obiol's *Aromas Colores y Sabores de un Nuevo Ecuador* is worth picking up for its beautiful images – particularly on Ecuador's fruits and vegetables.

Plantains and bananas (see the boxed text, opposite) play a huge role in coastal cooking. One tasty and intriguing dish is *sopa de bolas de verde,* a thick peanut-based soup with seasoned, mashed-plantain balls floating in it. And as you're busing along the northern coast, kids often board the bus selling *corviche* (a delicious plantain dumpling stuffed with seafood or shrimp) from big baskets dangling from their arms.

Seafood soups are often outstanding. One of the most popular (and an extremely cheap way to fill the belly) is *encebollado,* a brothy seafood and onion soup poured over yuca and served with *chifles* (fried banana chips) and popcorn. It's usually eaten in the morning or for lunch. Another fabulous soup is *sopa marinera,* a fine broth – which can range from clear to thick and peanuty – loaded with fish, shellfish, shrimp and sometimes crab.

The Oriente

Food from the Oriente plays a less prominent role in the nation's cuisine. Some typical Oriente dishes include simple yuca- and plantain-based dishes; river fish (including piranha and catfish); the pulpy fruit of the chonta palm; and hunted jungle animals, including *guanta* (agouti, a rabbit-sized rodent), turtle and occasionally monkey. Most of these foods are not part of travelers' everyday dining experience in the Oriente, however, although you will encounter some unusual foods. *Pan de yucca* (yuca bread) is sold all over the Oriente. *Ayampacos* are a southern Oriente specialty consisting of chicken, beef or fish wrapped in *bijao* leaves and cooked on a grill. They're particularly popular in Macas (p263). Also look out for dishes cooked with *ishpingo,* a type of cinnamon native to the Oriente. On the off chance that monkey or turtle (or any other rainforest animal) is offered to you during a trip in the Oriente, decline – hunting these animals is threatening their existence.

DRINKS

Ecuador offers plenty of tempting libations, from fresh-squeezed tropical fruit juices to steaming cups of *canelazo* (Ecuador's answer to the hot toddy). Unless your drink maker uses purified water, it's best to order

TASTY TRAVEL – WE DARE YOU

Perhaps even more fun than choking down exotic food is telling your friends about it afterwards. Rest assured, you'll find some good story fodder in Ecuador.

- *Cuy* – you can't leave without trying roast guinea pig!
- *Yaguarlocro* – with floating chunks of blood sausage, this potato-based soup is a classic.
- *Guatita* – tripe in a seasoned peanut sauce with avocado. When it's good, it's great.
- *Caldo de tronquit* – bull-penis soup…go on, give it a try.
- *Caldo de pata* – another classic, cow-hoof soup is…well…you decide.
- Lemon ants – have your jungle guide point out some of these and eat 'em up. They taste just like lemon!

cocktails and soft drinks *sin hielo* (without ice). For more on special drinks that are whipped up for fiestas, see Celebrations (opposite).

Nonalcoholic Drinks

Ecuadorian juices are as exotic as the country's tropical fruit trees, and are highly recommended to sate your thirst. Most juices are either *puro* (with no water) or made with *agua purificada* (boiled or bottled water), although you may want to avoid juices from roadside stands or cheap restaurants, where the water quality is questionable. The most common juices are *mora* (blackberry), *naranja* (orange), *toronja* (grapefruit), *piña* (pineapple), *maracuyá* (passion fruit), *sandía* (watermelon), *naranjilla* (a local fruit that tastes like a bitter orange) and papaya. But plenty of exotic flavors appear, like tomatillo (tree tomato) juice, so a bit of exploration is essential.

The nonalcoholic beverage *yamor* is made from seven varieties of corn, and is consumed in great quantities during Otavalo's Fiesta de Yamor (p125).

Almost as tasty as juices are *batidos* (fruit shakes), usually made with fruit, milk and sugar. One flavor to look out for is *taxo*, a type of passion fruit that goes especially well with milk. Another fruit best enjoyed in a *batido* is *borojó*. Found mostly in the north, it not only tastes unlike anything else but reportedly increases blood flow to the sexual organs.

Chicha (a fermented corn or yuca drink) is a traditional indigenous beverage still widely consumed. *Chicha de maíz* (corn *chicha*) is the highland variety, while *chicha de yuca* (yuca *chicha*) features more prominently in the Oriente (although both varieties are found there). Traditionally, the yuca variety was made by women who masticated the yuca and spit it into pots, where it was left to ferment with the help of enzymes from the saliva. Today it's rarely made this way, although a few traditional indigenous communities still follow the old-fashioned recipe – particularly during festivals (see p266). It's definitely an unusual (some would say acquired) taste well worth sampling.

Coffee is available everywhere, but is generally disappointing as the best beans are earmarked for export. *Café con leche* (coffee with milk) simply equates to instant coffee powder stirred into a cup of hot milk. *Café negro* is black coffee. *Té* (tea) is served black with lemon and sugar unless you order *té de hierbas* (herbal tea).

Alcoholic Drinks

As throughout Latin America, *cerveza* (beer) is of the light pilsner type – in fact, the national beer is called Pilsener and it's rivaled only by Club, the beer of choice on the coast. Both are light and refreshing, and go down beautifully in the hot equatorial sunshine. Wines come mostly from Chile and Argentina, though high-end restaurants stock a range of European (and some Californian) vintages.

As for the strong stuff, the local firewater is *aguardiente* (sugarcane alcohol), which promises a serious hangover to the unwary. Brands such as Cristal from Cuenca are now marketing their drinks to a younger crowd, offering slicker labeling and variations such as Cristal Limón (lemon Cristal) or mixed-down versions such as 'Sexy Apple,' 'Fashion Orange' and 'Extreme Wild.' Rum is widely available, and locally made brands range from truly bad to quite good. Ron San Miguel is a respectable label to seek out.

An old Ecuadorian adage affirms that *'Chocolate sin queso es como amor sin besos'* (chocolate without cheese is like love without kisses).

CELEBRATIONS

Food and feasting are an important part of many Ecuadorian celebrations, but two annual events really stand out: Semana Santa (Holy Week) and Finados, or Día de los Difuntos (Day of the Dead). During the week leading up to Good Friday, Ecuadorians feast on a hearty soup called *fanesca.* The best *fanesca* is made with salt cod and at least a dozen types of grains and flavored with a wild array of ingredients. According to nearly everyone who's tasted it, *fanesca* is the best of all Ecuadorian soups, but you'll have to time your visit to try it. Its origins are unclear, but its ingredients adhere to a blend of Catholic and indigenous beliefs: fish, to avoid the no-meat rule of Lent, and grains to celebrate the early harvest. Preparing it is an extremely labor-intensive process.

During the weeks leading up to Finados (celebrated November 2) bakeries start selling the delightful *guaguas de pan,* loaves of bread shaped and decorated to look like babies. *Guaguas de pan* are invariably accompanied by a cup of *colada morada,* a sweet, thick beverage of cornmeal, blackberries and other fruits. On November 2, people take both to the cemetery to eat with their deceased loved ones in a tradition rooted in pre-Hispanic rituals.

Of course, no fiesta is complete without a little *canelazo* – a shot of *aguardiente* livened up with a dose of hot, fresh fruit cider. During any nighttime festival it's likely you'll see someone selling shots of it in little plastic cups. Don't miss it!

WHERE TO EAT & DRINK

The *restaurante* is where you'll often eat when you eat out. A *comedore* is a cheap restaurant and may offer a more authentic experience both in terms of food and atmosphere. *Cevicherías* are ceviche restaurants, and *parrillas* are steak houses. For fresh-baked goods, head to the nearest *panaderia* (bakery). Nearly every city in Ecuador has a *chifa* (Chinese restaurant), offering an alternative to standard Ecuadorian fare.

One of the best cookbooks for traditional Ecuadorian recipes remains Michelle Fried's Spanish-language bestseller *Comidas del Ecuador,* available at Libri Mundi in Quito (p77).

A handful of places serve *desayuno* (breakfast), complete with *huevos* (eggs) and *tostadas* (toast), although you're more likely to encounter Ecuadorian dishes like chicken and lentils or whatever meat-and-grains dish is on the menu. Places that cater to tourists, however (ie every third building in the Mariscal, p104), often prepare hearty American-style breakfasts (pancakes, omelets etc).

Ecuadorians are family-oriented folks, so dragging the kids to all but the fanciest restaurants is generally not a problem. Obviously, solo travelers can eat wherever they please, but they'll most likely find conversation at cheap *comedores,* where Ecuadorians often dine alone as well.

For a primer on Ecuadorian cooking, pick up *The Ecuador Cookbook* (Buchanan and Franco), featuring vegetarian versions of classic dishes as well as seafood recipes. Available at Libri Mundi in Quito (p77).

Quick Eats

Street foods and market fare are two of the great culinary experiences of Latin America, and Ecuador is no exception. The primary concern, of course, is hygiene, so always follow the tried-and-true rule – if it's busy, it's probably fine. The exception – and it's a serious one – is the water problem. Even when a stand is busy, if the salad is soaked with tap water, or the glasses pulled from a dirty tub, you'll probably get sick whether the locals do or not. Exercise caution, but by all means explore (and you may want to give yourself a week or so for your belly to adjust before diving in).

Piping hot *tostada* (toasted corn) is sold in tiny bags from streetside vendors. With a little onion and spices thrown on top, it's a favorite highland snack.

Whether you like it or not, you'll definitely be inundated with street fare while on the buses. Keep an eye out for what's on sale – it's often a great way to try regional food. As a bus passes through Latacunga, women board selling biscuits called *allullas*. In Esmeraldas, children jump on selling *corviche*, and near San Miguel de Salcedo ice-cream vendors bombard the buses with shouts of '*¡Helados!*' (Ice cream!).

VEGETARIANS & VEGANS

In the big cities vegetarians can eat quite well. In rural areas things can be a little more complicated, as the range of offerings dwindles considerably. But memorize this: *arroz con menestra* (rice with lentils or beans). It'll come in handy. Almost every restaurant serves *arroz* or *menestra* as a side dish, but for vegetarians and vegans it can be a delicious main course (at least the first dozen or so times you eat it), especially with some *verduras* (vegetables) ordered as well. *Pizzerías* and *chifas* are both great for vegetarians. Note that asking the wait staff if something contains *carne* (meat), and receiving the answer '*No*' may simply mean it doesn't have red meat or pork. *Pollo* (chicken) is rarely considered *carne*, so be specific. Buying fruits and veggies in the market is an excellent way to get a wholesome, meatless lunch.

Banana trees (and Ecuador has millions of them) are not trees at all – because their trunks have no wood tissue, they're technically herbs!

HABITS & CUSTOMS

In Ecuador, lunch is the big event of the day, and it's not uncommon for locals to linger for several hours over their midday meal. For working-class families, dinner is a more sedate affair and may simply consist of leftovers from lunch.

Table manners are fairly straightforward. It's customary not to eat with one's hands (and this includes pizza). It's also considered polite to keep one's hands exposed on the table. Smoking is allowed almost anywhere. Splitting checks at restaurants is considered rude. If you invite someone out to dinner, you should offer to pay.

When dining out, breakfast is eaten between 8am and 10am, and only market and bus-terminal cafés open before 8am. Lunch is served between noon and 2pm. Dinner starts as early as 5pm, although most Ecuadorians dine between 6pm and 8pm, which is when you should dine if you want a lively meal. For standard opening hours, see p379.

At restaurants it's common to leave a small tip (around 10%), assuming *servicio* (service) wasn't included on the bill.

DOS & DON'TS

Do...

- tip 10% if *servicio* (service) isn't included in the bill
- exercise patience when ordering something that's not on the menu
- approach eating with an adventurous attitude!
- insist on paying if you invite someone to dine with you

Don't...

- eat with your hands
- drink tap water
- eat hunted animals during rainforest tours (or any time)

EAT YOUR WORDS

Useful Phrases

Do you have a menu in English?
¿Tienen una carta en inglés? — *tye*·nen oon·a *kar*·ta en een·*gles*

What do you recommend?
¿Qué me recomienda? — ke me re·ko·*myen*·da

Do you have any vegetarian dishes?
¿Tienen algún plato vegetariano? — *tye*·nen al·*goon pla*·to ve·khe·ta·*rya*·no

I'd like the set lunch/dinner, please.
Quisiera el almuerzo/la merienda, por favor. — kee·*sye*·ra el al·*mwer*·so/la me·*ryen*·da por fa·*vor*

The bill (check), please.
La cuenta, por favor. — la *kwen*·ta por fa·*vor*

Food Glossary

a la brasa	a la *bra*·sa	grilled
aguardiente	a·gwar·dyen·te	sugarcane alcohol
almuerzo	al·mwer·so	inexpensive set-lunch menu
arroz	a·*roz*	rice
arvejas	ar·ve·khas	peas
batido	ba·tee·do	fruit shake
caldo	*kal*·do	clear soup
camarones	ka·ma·*ro*·nes	shrimp
canelazo	ka·ne·la·zo	*aguardiente* livened up with a dose of hot, fresh fruit cider
cangil	kan·khil	popcorn
cangrejo	kan·gre·kho	crab
carne	*kar*·ne	meat, usually beef
ceviche	se·vee·che	seafood that is 'cooked' by marinating it in lemon juice
chifa	chee·fa	Chinese restaurant
chifles	chee·fles	crispy fried bananas
chivo	chee·vo	goat
churrasco	choo·*ras*·ko	dish of fried beef, rice, fried egg, avocado and potatoes
comedore	ko·me·do·res	cheap restaurant
concha	kon·cha	shellfish
corvina	kor·vee·na	sea bass
cuy	koy	roast guinea pig
encebollado	en·se·bo·la·do	seafood, yuca and onion soup garnished with *chifles*
guatita	gwa·tee·ta	a tripe and potato stew in a seasoned, peanut-based sauce
helados de paila	e·*la*·dos de *pai*·la	ice cream handmade in large copper bowls
huevos	*hwe*·vos	eggs; *huevos fritos* are fried eggs and *huevos revueltos* are scrambled. Order them *bien cocido* (well cooked) if you don't like them runny.
jugo	khoo·go	juice
legumbres	le·goom·bres	pulse vegetables
lentejas	len·te·khas	lentils
llapingachos	lya·pin·ga·chos	fried pancakes of mashed potatoes with cheese
maitos	mai·tos	fish cooked in palm leaves
mantequilla	man·te·kee·lya	butter
menestra	me·ne·stra	mixed grains or beans
merienda	me·*ryen*·da	inexpensive set-dinner menu
mermelada	mer·me·la·da	jam
mistela	mi·ste·la	an anise-flavored liqueur

mote	mo·te	hominy, served with fried pork, toasted corn and hot sauce
pan	pan	bread
patacones	pa·ta·ko·nes	sliced then mashed and fried plantains
pescado	pes·*ka*·do	fish
plátanos	pla·ta·nos	plantains
pollo	*po*·lyo	chicken
postre	*pos*·tre	dessert
seco	se·ko	stew
tallarines	ta·lya·ree·nes	noodles
tortillas de maíz	tor·tee·lyas de ma·ees	fried corn pancakes
tostada	tos·ta·da	toast
trucha	troo·cha	trout
verdes	ver·des	literally 'greens' but refers to green plantains
verduras	ver·*doo*·ras	vegetables

Environment

THE LAND

Ecuador straddles the equator on the Pacific coast of South America, and is bordered by Colombia to the north and Peru to the south and east. Despite its small size Ecuador is one of the world's most varied countries, making it possible to experience astonishingly different landscapes in a single day.

At 283,560 sq km, Ecuador is about the size of New Zealand or the US state of Nevada, and it's somewhat larger than the UK. The country is divided into three regions. The dramatic Andean mountain range runs roughly north to south and splits the country into the western coastal lowlands and the eastern jungles of the upper Amazon Basin, known as the Oriente. The Andes (known in Ecuador as the highlands) stretch high above the landscape, with Volcán Chimborazo, Ecuador's highest peak, topping out at 6310m.

The Doldrums was the name sailors gave to the windless belt around the equator. It is caused by intense heating along the equator, causing air to rise rather than blow, spelling disaster for sailing ships.

The central highlands contain two somewhat parallel volcanic mountain ranges, each about 400km long. The valley nestled between them was appropriately dubbed 'the Avenue of the Volcanoes' by the German explorer Alexander von Humboldt, who visited the country in 1802. Quito lies within this valley and, at 2850m, is the world's second-highest national capital, second only to La Paz, Bolivia. The central highlands are also home to countless towns and tiny villages well known for their indigenous markets and fiestas. This region has the highest population density in the country.

The western coastal lowlands were once heavily forested, but encroaching agriculture has meant the replacement of forest with fruit plantations, and the clear-cutting of mangroves for shrimp farming. The beaches are blessed with warm water year-round and provide decent surfing, but are not as pretty as the beaches of the Caribbean.

Thanks to the earth's equatorial bulge, the summit of Volcán Cotopaxi (p155) is the furthest point from the center of the earth and the closest to the sun.

The eastern lowlands of the Oriente still retain much of their virgin rainforest, but colonization and oil drilling have damaged this delicate habitat. The population of the Oriente has more than tripled since the late 1970s.

Ecuador also owns the Galápagos Islands, which are on the equator about 1000km west of the mainland.

WILDLIFE

Ecologists have labeled Ecuador one of the world's 'megadiversity hotspots.' The tiny nation is one of the most species-rich countries on the planet. Ecuador's astounding biodiversity is due to the great number of habitats within its borders, with dramatically different fauna in the Andes, the tropical rainforests, the coastal regions and the numerous transitional zones. The result is a wealth of habitats, ecosystems and wildlife.

Animals

For more detailed information about the wildlife of the Galápagos Islands, see p65.

While in Ecuador, keep your eyes peeled for wildlife photographers Pete Oxford and Reneé Bish's two outstanding photography books, *Amazon Images* and *Ecuador*.

BIRDS

Bird-watchers from all over the world flock to Ecuador for one simple reason: the country is home to nearly 1600 species, twice the number found in the continents of Europe and North America combined. It's impossible to give a precise number because formerly unobserved species are often reported, and very occasionally a new species is discovered – an incredibly rare event in the world of birds. Bird-watching is outstanding year-round and every part of the country offers unique habitats. For more information, see p61.

Hummingbirds beat their wings up to 80 times per second in a figure-eight pattern that allows them to hover in place or even to fly backward.

Ecuador's emblematic bird is the Andean condor, whose 3m wingspan makes it one of the largest flying birds in the world. In 1880, the British mountaineer Edward Whymper noted that he commonly saw a dozen condors on the wing at the same time. Today there are only a few hundred pairs left in the Ecuadorian highlands, so sighting one is a thrilling experience. Another majestic highland bird is the carunculated caracara, a large member of the falcon family with bright-orange facial skin, a yellowish bill, and white-on-black wings and body. The bird is often seen in the *páramo* (high Andean grasslands) of Parque Nacional Cotopaxi (p155).

For many visitors, the diminutive hummingbirds found throughout Ecuador are the most delightful birds to observe. About 120 species have been recorded in Ecuador, and their exquisite beauty is matched by extravagant names such as green-tailed goldenthroat, spangled coquette, fawn-breasted brilliant and amethyst-throated sunangel.

MAMMALS

Some 300 species of mammals have been recorded in Ecuador. These range from monkeys in the Amazonian lowlands to the rare Andean spectacled bear in the highlands.

For many, the most amusing mammals to spy upon are monkeys. Ecuadorian species include howler monkeys, spider monkeys, woolly monkeys, titi monkeys, capuchin monkeys, squirrel monkeys, tamarins and marmosets. The best places to see them in their natural habitat include Reserva Producción Faunística Cuyabeno (p240) and Parque Nacional Yasuní (p248) in the Amazonian lowlands, and the rarely visited lowlands sector of Reserva Ecológica Cotacachi-Cayapas (p133), near the coast. A group of marvelously mischievous capuchin monkeys has taken over the central plaza in the Oriente town of Misahuallí (p254), where you're guaranteed an up-close (and sometimes too personal) experience. In the Oriente you may hear howler monkeys well before you see them; the males' eerie roars carry great distances and can sound like anything from a baby crying to wind moaning through the trees.

Other tropical specialties include two species of sloth: the diurnal three-toed sloth and the nocturnal two-toed sloth. It's very possible to spot the former while hiking in the Amazon. They are usually found hanging motionless from tree limbs or progressing at a painfully slow speed along a branch toward a particularly succulent bunch of leaves, which are their primary food source.

There are far fewer species of mammal in the highlands than in the lowlands, but include commonly seen deer and rabbits and the more rarely sighted Andean fox. One of the icons of the Andes is the llama, which is domesticated and used primarily as a pack animal. Its wild relative, the lovely vicuña, has been reintroduced to the Chimborazo area (p184) – you're almost guaranteed to see them as you drive, bus or walk through the park.

Other possible mammal sightings include anteaters, armadillos, agoutis (large rodents), capybaras (even larger rodents, some weighing up to 65kg), peccaries (wild pigs) and otters. River dolphins are occasionally sighted in Amazonian tributaries. Other exotic mammals, such as ocelots, jaguars, tapirs, pumas and the Andean spectacled bear, are very rarely seen.

INSECTS

Many thousands of insect species have been recorded in Ecuador; undoubtedly, tens of thousands more remain undiscovered.

Butterflies are among the first insects that the visitor to the tropics notices – there are some 4500 species in Ecuador. Perhaps the most dazzling is the morpho, with its 15cm wingspan and electric-blue upper wings. They lazily flap and glide along tropical rivers in a shimmering display.

Ants are a delightful diversion in the forest. Nearly any walk through a tropical forest will allow the observer to study many different types. Particularly interesting are the leaf-cutter ants, which can be seen marching in columns along the forest floor carrying pieces of leaf like little sails above their heads. The leaf segments are taken into the ants' underground colony where they rot into a mulch, which produces a fungus that feeds the ants.

Caterpillars are masters of disguise, some mimicking twigs, others the head of a viper, even a pile of bird droppings – all in the name of defense.

AMPHIBIANS & REPTILES

The majority of Ecuador's approximately 460 species of amphibian are frogs. There are tree frogs that spend their entire lives in trees and lay their eggs in water trapped inside bromeliads (a type of epiphytic plant). The ominously named poison-dart frog is among the most brightly colored species of frog anywhere. Its colors run the spectrum from bright red-orange with jet-black spots to neon green with black wavy lines. Some poison-dart frogs have skin glands exuding toxins that can cause paralysis and death in animals, including humans.

Of Ecuador's reptiles, four really make an impression on visitors. Three of them – the land tortoise, the land iguana and the marine iguana – live in the Galápagos and are easy to see. The fourth is the caiman, which inhabits lagoons in the Oriente. With a little patience and a good canoe guide, you'll spot these spooky creatures as well.

Snakes, which are much talked about but seldom seen, make up a large portion of Ecuador's reptiles. They usually slither away into the undergrowth at the sound of approaching humans, so only a few fortunate visitors get to see them. Perhaps Ecuador's most feared snake is the fer-de-lance, which is extremely poisonous. Visitors are rarely bitten, but it is wise to take precautions. If you do see a snake, keep a respectful distance, and avoid provoking the reptile.

FISH

Most visitors encounter fish in the Galápagos, but there is also a vast number in the Amazon. Recent inventories counted some 2500 species in the whole Amazon Basin, and roughly a thousand of these are found in Ecuador. Some are fearsome: the electric eel can produce shocks of 600V; a school of piranhas can devour a large injured animal in minutes; stingrays can deliver a crippling zap; and the tiny candirú catfish can swim up the human urethra and become lodged there by erecting its sharp spines. Despite these horror stories, most Amazonian rivers are safe to swim in. Just follow the locals: shuffle your feet as you enter the water to scare off the bottom-dwelling stingrays; wear a bathing suit to avoid having a candirú swim up your urethra; and don't swim with open, bleeding cuts or in areas where fish are being cleaned, because piranhas are attracted to blood and guts.

Thanks to their ability to metabolize stored fat, Galápagos tortoises can go for more than a year without food or water.

Plants

Some 25,000 species of vascular plants reside in Ecuador (compared to 17,000 species in North America), and new species are being discovered every year. Most plants in Ecuador are unique to their habitat, and the following are Ecuador's primary habitats.

With decent color photos and good illustrations, John Kricher's *A Neotropical Companion* is a comprehensive guide to America's tropical ecosystems.

PÁRAMO

Above the cloud forests lie the Andes' high-altitude grasslands and scrublands, known as the *páramo*. The *páramo* is characterized by a harsh climate, high levels of ultraviolet light and wet, peaty soils. It is an extremely

TROPICAL CLOUD FORESTS

One of Ecuador's most enchanting habitats is the tropical cloud forest. These moist environments are found at higher elevations and earn their name from the clouds they trap (and help create), which drench the forest in a fine mist. This continual moisture allows particularly delicate forms of plant life to survive. Dense, small-leaved canopies and moss-covered branches set the scene for a host of plant life within, including orchids, ferns and bromeliads. The dense vegetation at all levels of this forest gives it a mysterious and delicate fairy-tale appearance. Some people find it even more beautiful than the rainforest since many of the plants grow closer to the forest floor. This creates a far more luxuriant environment where the diverse fauna thrives – and remains easier to spot.

specialized habitat unique to the neotropics (tropical America) and is found only in the area between the highlands of Costa Rica and northern Peru.

The *páramo* is dominated by cushion plants, hard grasses and small herbaceous plants that have adapted well to the harsh highland environment. Most plants up here are small and compact and grow close to the ground. An exception is the giant *Espeletia,* one of the *páramo*'s strangest sights. These bizarre-looking plants stand as high as a person, and have earned the local nickname *frailejones* (gray friars). They are an unmistakable feature of the northern Ecuadorian *páramo,* particularly in the El Ángel region (p140).

The *páramo* is also characterized by dense thickets of small trees, often of the *Polylepis* species, which along with Himalayan pines are the tallest-growing trees in the world. They were once extensive, but fire and grazing have pushed them back into small pockets.

RAINFORESTS

The Oriente is Ecuador's slice of the Amazon, the greatest rainforest habitat in the world. It is home to an astounding variety of plants and animals, located in much denser concentrations than in temperate forests.

Regardless of your science background (or lack of it), the entertaining and highly readable classic *Tropical Nature,* by Adrian Forsyth and Kenneth Miyata, is an excellent read before or during any trip to the rainforest.

Lianas (thick dangling vines) hang from high in the canopy, and the massive roots of strangler figs engulf other trees, slowly choking them of light and life. Spread across the forest floor are the buttressed roots of tropical hardwoods, which are sometimes so massive you can just about disappear inside their weblike supports. Equally impressive are the forest's giant leaves, which are thick and waxy and have pointed 'drip tips,' which facilitate water runoff during downpours.

Much of the rainforest's plant and animal life is up in the canopy rather than on the forest floor, which can appear surprisingly empty to the first-time visitor. If you're staying in a jungle lodge, find out if it has a canopy tower; climbing into the canopy provides spectacular views.

MANGROVE SWAMPS

Mangroves are trees that have evolved with the remarkable ability to grow in salt water. The red mangrove is the most common in Ecuador and, like other mangroves, it has a broadly spreading system of intertwining stilt roots to support the tree in the unstable soils of the shoreline. These roots trap sediments and build up rich organic soil, which creates a protected habitat for many plants and fish, as well as mollusks, crustaceans and other invertebrates. The branches provide nesting areas for seabirds, such as pelicans and frigate birds. Extensive mangrove areas on Ecuador's coastline have been cleared for shrimp farms, and most are now found in the far northern and southern coastal regions. For more information, see p278. The tallest mangroves in the world are inside the Reserva Ecológica de Manglares Cayapas Mataje (p277).

TROPICAL DRY FORESTS

This fascinating habitat is fast disappearing and is found primarily in the hot coastal areas near Parque Nacional Machalilla (p303) and in southwest Loja Province en route to Macará (p228). Its definitive plant species is the majestic bottle-trunk ceiba (also known as kapok), a glorious tree with a massively bulging trunk and seasonal white flowers that dangle like lightbulbs from the bare branches.

THE GALÁPAGOS ISLANDS

The Galápagos Islands support surprisingly diverse plant species within distinctive vegetation zones that begin at the shoreline and end in the highlands. The shorelines of the main islands host low mangroves with bright-green leaves, while slightly higher arid zones are characterized by the islands' evocative cacti, including forests of the giant prickly pear. Trees such as the ghostly palo santo, the paloverde and spiny acacia are also found here. As you move higher, a transition zone supports perennial herbs, smaller shrubs and lichens, and the vegetation becomes increasingly varied and thick. This zone gives way to humid cloud forest with a closed canopy dominated by scalesia, bromeliads, ferns, mosses and orchids. The highest elevations are home to the unique Galápagos tree fern, which grows up to 3m high.

NATIONAL PARKS & RESERVES

Ecuador's first *parque nacional* (national park) was the Galápagos, formed in 1959. Today Ecuador has more than 30 government-protected parks and reserves (of which nine carry the title of 'national park') as well as numerous privately administered nature reserves. A total of 18% of the country lies within protected areas. Yet despite their protected status, many of these areas continue to be susceptible to oil drilling, logging, mining, ranching and colonization.

Many parks are inhabited by indigenous groups, whose connection to the area long precedes modern park or reserve status. In the case of the Oriente parks, the indigenous maintain traditional hunting rights, which also affect the ecology. The question of how to protect the national parks from damage by heavy industry (oil, timber and mining) while recognizing the rights of indigenous peoples – all in the context of keeping the nation financially solvent – remains one of the hot-button topics in Ecuador.

National-park entrance fees vary, but are usually a one-time fee valid for one week. Fees range from $10 in the highlands to $20 in the lowlands and $100 on the Galápagos Islands. Most national parks have little tourist infrastructure.

For a list of the country's national parks, see p58. Other important reserves are shown on the map (p59). All of Ecuador's parks can be visited year-round, and the best time to visit will depend on your interests (climbers may chose different seasons than hikers). Here, the 'best time to visit' is generally defined as the most comfortable.

The best general guide to the history, geology and plant and animal life of the Galápagos Islands is the highly recommended *Galápagos: A Natural History*, by Michael H Jackson.

ENVIRONMENTAL ISSUES

According to ecologists, Ecuador has the highest deforestation rate and the worst environmental record in South America. Deforestation is Ecuador's most severe environmental problem. In the highlands, almost all of the natural forest cover has disappeared and only a few pockets remain, mainly in private nature reserves. Along the coast, once-plentiful mangrove forests

NATIONAL PARKS

Name of Park	Features	Activities	Best Time to Visit
Cajas (p211)	*páramo,* lakes, small *Polylepis*, forests	hiking, fishing, bird-watching	year-round
Cotopaxi (p155)	*páramo,* Volcán Cotopaxi: Andean condor, deer, rabbits	hiking, climbing	year-round
Galápagos (p342)	volcanically formed islands: seabirds, iguanas, turtles, rich underwater life	wildlife-watching, snorkeling, diving	Nov-Jun
Llanganates (p171)	*páramo,* cloud forest, lowland forest: deer, tapir, jaguars, spectacled bears	hiking	year-round (access difficult)
Machalilla (p303)	coastal dry forest, beaches, islands: whales, seabirds, monkeys, reptiles	hiking, wildlife-watching	year-round
Podocarpus (p219)	*páramo,* cloud forest, tropical humid forest: spectacled bear, tapir, deer, birds	hiking, bird-watching	year-round
Sumaco-Galeras (p231)	Volcán Sumaco, subtropical and cloud forest	off-trail hiking	year-round (access difficult)
Sangay (p180 and p265)	volcanoes, *páramo,* cloud forest, lowland forest: spectacled bears, tapirs, pumas, ocelots	hiking, climbing	year-round
Yasuní (p248)	rainforest, rivers, lagoons: monkeys, birds, sloths, jaguars, pumas, tapirs	hiking, wildlife-watching	year-round

have all but vanished, too. These forests harbor a great diversity of marine and shore life, but they have been removed to make artificial ponds in which shrimp are grown for export (see p278).

About 95% of the forests of the western slopes and lowlands have become agricultural land, mostly banana plantations. These forests were host to more species than almost anywhere on the planet, many of them endemic. Scientists suggest that countless species have likely become extinct even before they were identified, and in recent years a small preservation movement has taken root.

For an explanation of why 30,000 Ecuadorians are locked in a class-action lawsuit against oil giant Chevron Texaco, check out Chevron Toxico (www.chevrontoxico.com).

Although much of the rainforest in the Ecuadorian Amazon still stands, it is seriously threatened by fragmentation. The main threats to the rainforest are logging, cattle ranching and oil extraction. The discovery of oil has brought with it roads and new settlements, and rainforest clearing has increased exponentially.

Equally destructive to the environment is mining, which has the potential to wreak as much havoc on the southern Amazon as oil has on the north. Among the most serious concerns is contamination of groundwater and nearby rivers with chemicals used for processing minerals and ore. Highly elevated levels of mercury, manganese and lead – posing significant health risks – were found in inhabitants living near the mining regions near the Puyango River basin. Mining is also a serious problem in the highlands, although effective NGOs have sprung up to halt new projects.

Clearly, these issues are tightly linked with Ecuador's economy. Oil, minerals, bananas and shrimp are some of the nation's top exports. Industry advocates claim the cost of abandoning these revenue sources is too high for a small developing country to shoulder. Environmentalists, on the other hand, claim the government has given free rein to big industry,

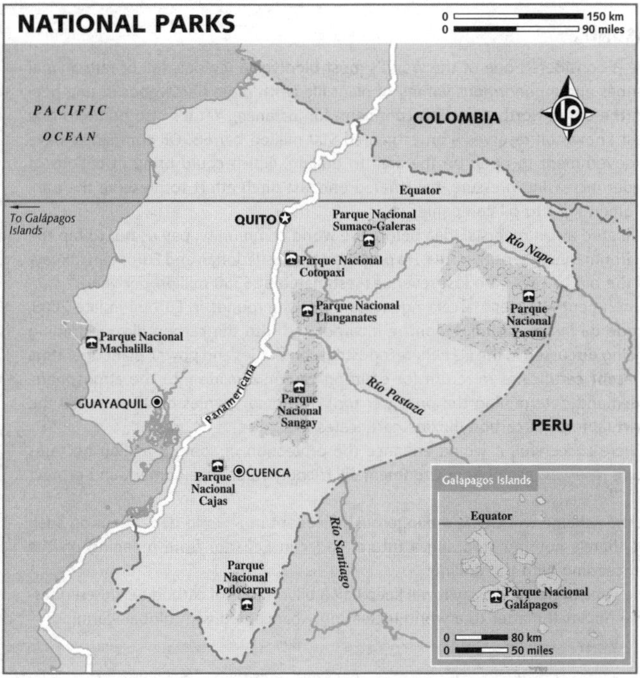

which has resulted in at times catastrophic damage to the local ecology. One of Ecuador's biggest environmental lawsuits was still in limbo at the time of research – namely the $27 billion class-action lawsuit brought against Chevron Texaco for dumping 18 billion gallons of toxic waste in the Amazon and abandoning 900 waste pits (see p239).

The rainforest's indigenous inhabitants – who depend on the rivers for drinking water and food – are also dramatically affected. Oil residues, oil treatment chemicals, erosion and fertilizers all contaminate the rivers, killing fish and rendering formerly potable water undrinkable. Past Ecuadorian governments have actively supported oil exploration. The current administration, however, has tried to find a balance between development and preservation, even floating some radical ideas before the world community (p60).

For more information on the controversial scheme to keep the Yasuní reserve oil in the ground, visit www.sosyasuni.org.

Environmental Groups

The environment has usually taken a backseat to financial considerations in Ecuador's history, largely owing to the government's lack of financial resources to commit to effective conservation programs. Various international conservation agencies have provided much-needed expertise and economic support, and ecotourism projects have largely had a positive effect on habitat protection.

Ecuador's biggest environmental NGO is Fundación Natura (see p117), which has created and manages several nature reserves throughout the country. On a grassroots level, local conservation groups have blossomed since the late 1980s. Groups on the coast are particularly concerned with defending the mangrove forests, while those in the Amazon region

Defending Our Rainforest: A Guide to Community-Based Ecotourism in the Ecuadorian Amazon, by Rolf Wesche, is a recommended read covering just what its title says it does.

DRILLING IN YASUNÍ?

The Yasuní reserve is considered one of the world's most biodiverse regions, full of rare animal species, isolated tribes and an enormous variety of plant life (with more hardwoods in one hectare than found in the entire North American continent, for instance). Yet it's also home to one of Ecuador's largest known oil reserves – an estimated 900 million barrels. Oil companies have long lobbied the government to open up the area to drilling, which could bring in billions of dollars. Correa, under increasing pressure, has offered one last-ditch effort to preserve the park before giving the green light to oil companies.

In 2008 Correa floated a controversial idea before the world community: pay us not to tap the reserves in this environmentally sensitive area. He proposed that Ecuadorian and European taxpayers each foot half the bill to cover the lost revenues (estimated at $350 million per year).

Ecuadorian Environment Minister Marcela Aguiñaga made the rounds in Europe in late 2008, proposing that crude oil in the Yasuní region be incorporated into the carbon-dioxide trading system currently being discussed in the EU (where industrial companies and power-plant operators are required to present certificates in return for emitting carbon dioxide into the atmosphere, with supply and demand determining the price per ton). These companies could then sell the Yasuní oil in the virtual form of carbon-dioxide certificates.

If the scheme were successful, it would enhance the protection of some 5 million hectares of Ecuadorian nature reserves, promote environmentally friendly rural development and protect indigenous tribes.

Critics say that the scheme will create a dangerous precedent in a world dependent on such reserves, and that there's nothing stopping a future leader in Ecuador from reneging on the agreement and proceeding with the drilling.

Advocates of the controversial plan say it will keep half a billion tons of carbon dioxide sequestered in the earth – no small matter to a world increasingly concerned with global warming.

focus not only on the environment but also on the protection of the rights of indigenous inhabitants. In the past decade, the organizations that are protecting the fast-diminishing and unique forests on the western Andean slopes, particularly in the Mindo area (p146), have become increasingly important.

Indigenous organizations have also played a role in environmental protection. Their struggle to secure land rights, particularly in the Amazon regions, has helped to preserve the tropical forests in that area.

In the Galápagos Islands, the **Galápagos Conservancy** (formerly the Charles Darwin Foundation; www.galapagos.org) is a long-established and tireless protector of the archipelago. Conservation, scientific research and the education of both locals and international visitors are among its main goals.

Ecuador Outdoors

Ecuador's diverse geography provides the backdrop to an astounding range of adventure, and its compact size makes it possible to combine a number of diverse activities in a short time. You can go bird-watching in misty cloud forests on the Andean slopes, plot multiday treks through lush national parks, climb the peaks of the country's towering volcanoes, and snorkel with giant manta rays, turtles and sea lions off the Galápagos Islands. There's also some excellent surfing and mountain biking, along with world-class rafting.

BIRD-WATCHING

Ecuador has few rivals when it comes to bird-watching. Nowhere else in the world has such incredible avian diversity been crammed into such a small country. Some 1600 different species have been spotted in Ecuador, with a number of unique species on both the mainland and in the Galápagos. Scope is one of the biggest challenges for bird-watchers – with rainforest, cloud forest and islands all offering their allure.

One highly recommended place to start the exploration is just north of Quito. The cloud forests around **Mindo** (p147) and **Tandayapa** (p145) are a bird-watcher's paradise. During the Audubon Society's Christmas Bird Count, over several hundred species are typically spotted in a single day. Highlights include the Andean cock-of-the-rock, scaled fruiteater and golden-headed and crested quetzals. (For a complete list check out www.tandayapa.com.) Mindo itself boasts over 400 recorded bird species and has become a major bird-watching center, with excellent guides and lodges in the area. In the same area is the 700-hectare **Reserva Bellavista** (p146), which has 8km of well-marked trails – along which some 320 bird species have been recorded.

In two outstanding volumes, Robert Ridgely's *The Birds of Ecuador* is the only bird-watching guide covering the entire country. The first volume has more details for the serious bird-watcher, while the second has great pictures and descriptions.

Another excellent destination is the lower **Río Napo** (p244) region of the Amazon, where over 500 bird species have been logged. Some of Ecuador's best jungle lodges are in this area, some with their own canopy towers and biologist guides. These make an excellent base for exploring the jungle and lush waterways of this biodiverse region.

The **Galápagos Islands** (p342) is another mecca for bird-watchers. Although the number of species isn't jaw-dropping (a modest 58 species have been recorded in the archipelago), the uniqueness of the birds here is truly staggering. Some 28 species are endemic to the islands, and the birds here have evolved in extraordinary ways. Isla Santa Cruz boasts the highest bird count overall, and it's a good place to begin the quest to find the 13 species of Darwin's finches. Various large species are easily seen around Puerto Ayora harbor, including blue-footed boobies, magnificent frigate birds and herons.

For more information about the colorful birdlife in Ecuador see p53 and p66.

HIKING

The opportunities for hiking are practically limitless. Stunning scenery is a guarantee no matter where you go, with snow-covered peaks, misty cloud forests and verdant lowland jungle setting the stage for hiking and wildlife-watching. An excellent resource for hikers is *Trekking in Ecuador* by Robert and Daisy Kunstaetter.

Most of the best independent hiking is in the national parks. One of the most popular destinations for exploring is the 33,400-hectare **Parque Nacional Cotopaxi** (p155). The snowcapped peak of the active Volcán Cotopaxi is Ecuador's second-highest point (5897m), and there a number of great day hikes in the surrounding countryside, or you can plan a hike all the way around the volcano (allow a week).

For an introduction to the captivating scenery of the southern highlands, plan a visit to the **Parque Nacional Cajas** (p212). Amid the picturesque *páramo* (high-altitude Andean grasslands), there are a number of trails (some better signed than others), which take in great views of pretty alpine lakes. Be prepared for rain (the driest months are August to January).

Ecuador's southernmost park, the **Parque Nacional Podocarpus** (p219) spreads across lush tropical lowlands and chilly, mountainous highlands. It offers several memorable hikes including a day hike through cloud forest and a multiday hike to Andean lakes.

The country's only coastal national park is the 40,000-hectare **Parque Nacional Machalilla** (p305), with trails through tropical dry forest as well as cloud forest. The park also includes Isla de la Plata, which has several loop hiking trails and has been called 'the poor man's Galápagos' on account of its wildlife, which includes red-footed boobies.

Ingapirca (which means 'Wall of the Inca') was built toward the end of the 15th century and boasts some of the Incas' finest mortarless stonework. The main structure may have been used as a solar observatory.

Another rewarding hike in Ecuador takes in the mountain lakes of **Lagunas de Mojanda** (p129) just outside of Otavalo. For shorter walks, a good base is the tranquil mountain town of **Vilcabamba** (p223), which offers pleasant walks through countryside amid stunning alpine scenery. There's equally bucolic walks through hilly terrain outside of the hot-springs town of **Baños** (p175 and p176). **Mindo** (p146) and elsewhere along the western Andean slopes is the gateway to enchanting hikes through cloud forests. For a fascinating journey along part of the royal road that linked Cuzco (Peru) to Quito, take the Inca trail to the archaeological site of **Ingapirca** (p196); it's a popular 40km hike that most travelers do in three days (see the boxed text, p197).

Topographical maps are available from the Instituto Geográfico Militar (p76), located in Quito. Also pick up a copy of Lonely Planet's *Trekking in the Central Andes.*

HORSEBACK RIDING

Ecuador has some great horseback-riding opportunities, especially in the highlands. Unfortunately, many of the horses used in tourist hikes are not properly looked after, and several travelers have written to say that their horses were old, overworked and underfed. There are, however, some agencies that do take proper care of their animals, and they're worth seeking out, even though they charge more for tours. Budget rides usually entail a poorly maintained animal that won't be better for the wear following a day's journey. Haciendas throughout the highlands generally use good horses and offer some of the best opportunities for horseback riding. **Vilcabamba** (p223) offers some fine rides in the surrounding mountains. Trips range from a few hours to three days. **Baños** (p176) is also a good place to sign up for a casual half- or full-day ride. These two towns are among the best places to set up horseback rides if you're not staying at a hacienda.

Until 10,000 years ago, the horse's wild ancestor flourished throughout the Americas, and even migrated across the land bridge to Asia. Then, the species vanished from the Americas, probably through overhunting and climate change.

Another great place for riding is inside the **Reserva Geobotánica Pululahua** (p116) near Quito. Located inside a volcanic crater, this reserve boasts cloud forests and a fascinating microclimate. You can arrange day-long or even multiday horseback rides from there.

An expensive but fully reputable company is **RideAndes** (www.rideandes.com). It offers day tours, multiday tours and custom-made tours for both experienced and inexperienced riders. One of its most popular excursions is the seven-day hike around Volcán Cotopaxi. Horses and guides are top-notch.

ALTERNATIVE ADVENTURES

Ecuador has much more than volcanoes and rainforests up her sleeve. Wondrous caves, pretty rivers and the fortuitous proximity of the continental shelf all create opportunities for some uncommon adventures.

- **Caving:** Located on the eastern slopes of the Andes, the **Cueva de los Tayos** (Cave of the Oil Birds, p266) provides a fascinating wonderland for cave lovers. The entrance is located within rainforest at the bottom of a valley – but it's no easy entrance. The journey starts with a 70m drop into the caves – from which you could then spend a week (or a lifetime?) exploring the stalactite- and stalagmite-filled caverns. A guide is recommended.
- **Tubing:** While some prefer kayaks and rafts, in **Mindo** (p147) there's nothing quite equal to the joy of gliding down the fern-lined Río Mindo, bottom securely planted in a rubber inner tube. If all this sounds overly bucolic, keep in mind this is white water (and all the livelier in the rainy season), and helmets and life jackets are essential.
- **Whale-watching: Puerto López** (p307) is considered the epicenter of whale breeding grounds, with an annual population of humpback whales of around 400. Numerous boat operators ply the waters in search of the magnificent mammals, with excellent sighting opportunities from June to September (July and August are peak months).
- **Puenting:** In **Baños** (p173), visitors with a rock-solid life-insurance policy might consider the freefall excitement called *puenting* (think bungee jumping without the bounce). It roughly translates as 'bridging' but it's really leaping, then swinging pendulum-style on a rope tethered to two bridges.
- **Sportfishing:** Some 13km offshore from **Salinas** (p315) the continental shelf drops off, providing an ideal setting for deep-water fishing. Swordfish, sailfish, tuna, dorado and black marlin all frequent the waters, with the best fishing from September to December. Salinas is the place to charter a boat.

MOUNTAINEERING

The towering Andes sweeping through Ecuador set the stage for serious adventure. The country has 10 peaks over 5000m, eight of which are in the central highlands (p151). This is where you'll find Ecuador's most impressive summits. Keep in mind that many of Ecuador's most impressive peaks are volcanoes, and their status can change quickly. Some are climbable one year and not the next. Those looking to climb a peak where no equipment is required might consider **Volcán Imbabura** (4609m) (p139) in the northern highlands. It's a good, challenging and highly rewarding climb just outside of Ibarra.

Ecuador's highest peak is **Volcán Chimborazo** (p185), an extinct volcano that tops out at 6310m. It's a relatively straightforward climb for experienced climbers, but the usual ice-climbing gear is essential. From the climbing refuge, most climbers take the Normal Route, which takes eight to 10 hours to the summit and two to four on the return. There are some excellent guides leading tours up Chimborazo. Riobamba is the best place for arranging a guided hike, hiring equipment and unwinding when the climb is done.

Cotopaxi, which means 'neck of the moon' in Quichua, is one of the world's highest volcanoes (5897m). There have been some 50 recorded eruptions since 1738.

The active volcano **Cotopaxi** (p155) is the country's second-highest peak, and is a popular goal for serious climbers. Like Chimborazo, Cotopaxi can be climbed in one long day from the climbers refuge, but sane people allow for two days. Climbers must acclimatize for several days before attempting an ascent. Lodges in and around Cotopaxi (p156) are great for acclimatization.

The **Ilinizas** (p154) also offer excellent climbing. The jagged sawtooth peak of Iliniza Sur (5248m) is Ecuador's sixth-highest peak and one of the country's most difficult climbs. It's suitable only for experienced climbers. Iliniza

Norte (5126m), on the other hand, is a rough scramble and can be climbed by acclimatized, experienced hikers. It's the country's eighth-highest peak. The small village of El Chaupi is a good base for acclimatizing climbers and hikers, with a handful of simple but pleasant guesthouses.

A remote and beautiful region with three 5000m peaks is inside the **Parque Nacional Sangay** (p180). The long-extinct volcano **El Altar** (5319m) (p181) is widely considered the most beautiful and most technical of Ecuador's mountains. December to March is the best time to visit this area. In July and August El Altar is frequently socked in with clouds.

For the lowdown on rock climbing in Ecuador, visit Mono Dedo (www.monodedo.com) and have a go on its climbing wall in Quito (see p111).

Mountaineers will require standard snow and ice gear: a rope, crampons, ice axe, high-altitude sun protection and cold-weather clothing as a minimum. Unless you are very experienced, hiring a guide from Quito (p96) or Riobamba (p189) is recommended. The weather can turn bad quickly in the Andes, and even experienced climbers have been killed. Several agencies offer both rental gear and guides: very roughly expect to pay $60 to $80 per person per day to climb a major peak. The best guides have a card accrediting them to the Ecuadorian Mountain Guides Association (ASEGUIM).

You can climb year-round, but the best months are considered to be June to August and December to February.

MOUNTAIN BIKING

Mountain biking has grown increasingly popular, especially the adrenaline-charged downhills on the flanks of Cotopaxi and Chimborazo. The best mountain-biking operators (with the best bikes, guides and equipment) can be found in Quito (p93) and Riobamba (p189).

Every year intrepid souls undertake the 26,000km Alaska-to-Argentina journey by bicycle. The youngest solo rider was 18-year-old Emmanuel Gentinetta (www.bikeitsolo.com). One whole family even attempted it, setting off on a 2½-year trek in 2008 (www.familyonbikes.org).

Baños is also awash in midrange mountain bikes, thanks to the popular and excellent downhill ride (by road) to Puyo. Nicknamed 'La Ruta de las Cascadas' (Highway of the Waterfalls), it follows the Río Pastaza canyon, dropping steadily from the highlands town of Baños at 1800m to the jungle settlement of Puyo at 950m. It's a 61km ride to the end, with some refreshing dips in waterfalls along the way. For complete details on the ride see p179.

If you're doing any serious cycling on your own, bring all your own gear and replacement parts, as specialty parts are only available in Quito or, if you're lucky, from one of the operators in Riobamba or Baños. Also remember the very real threat of dehydration; in Ecuador you're either riding at altitude or in the extreme heat of the lowlands, so always carry plenty of water.

DIVING & SNORKELING

The Galápagos Islands are one of the world's great dive destinations, offering opportunities to see dramatic underwater wildlife: hammerhead and other sharks, a variety of rays (occasionally a manta ray will appear), turtles, penguins, sea lions, moray eels, sea horses, huge numbers of fish of many kinds and, if you're very lucky, dolphins or even whales. The conditions here, however, are difficult for beginners, with strong currents and cold water temperatures. There are four dive operators based in **Puerto Ayora** (p357). Experienced divers can opt for a week's tour aboard a dive-dedicated boat stopping at the aquatic hot spots around the archipelago. Those looking for less commitment can usually hook up with a diving boat for a day or two if arranged in advance.

If you lack an underwater camera, it's worth buying a disposable one before snorkeling in the Galápagos. Penguins, sea lions and many fish are so tame that even an amateur can get decent underwater snapshots.

Diving has also become popular out of the coastal town of **Puerto López** (p307). The sea bottom here is a mix of rock with coral reef patches and sand. Aquatic life includes angelfish, trumpet fish, puffer fish, morays, parrot fish, manta rays, guitar rays and white-tip sharks. The occasional sea turtle is also spotted.

(Continued on page 73)

GALÁPAGOS WILDLIFE GUIDE

Ecuador's famed archipelago was known to early explorers as Las Islas Encantadas (The Enchanted Isles). Although the name has changed, the Galápagos have lost none of their power to captivate. This remote, seemingly barren chain of volcanic islands is home to an astounding variety of wildlife – including many species found nowhere else on earth. It remains one of the world's best places for interacting with animals in the wild at such close range, both above and below the sea.

1

Birds

Like other Galápagos fauna, bird species have followed an extraordinary evolutionary path, which visitors can observe in the flightless cormorant, the Galápagos penguin (the world's only tropical penguin), the comical blue-footed booby and the surprising Darwin's finch – made famous by the great naturalist himself.

2

❶ Swallow-Tailed Gull

Often touted as the world's only nocturnal gull species, the endemic swallow-tailed gull sometimes follows boats at night, emitting peculiar clicking calls that are thought to be a form of echolocation.

❷ Galápagos Hawk

A generalist hunter, the endemic Galápagos hawk preys on creatures as small as insects and as large as small goats. Galápagos hawks practice polyandrous breeding, whereby a female mates with several males who help incubate and raise the chicks.

❸ Blue-Footed Booby

The blue-footed booby is one of four booby species on the islands. During courtship it picks up its bright-blue feet in a slow, dignified fashion and then grows more animated, bowing, wing-spreading and sky-pointing in an enchanting, if rather clownish, display.

❹ Frigate Birds

The two species of frigate bird are dazzling fliers, riding high on thermals above coastal cliffs. Also known as man-o'-war birds, frigate birds sometimes harass smaller seabirds into dropping or regurgitating their catch and then swoop to catch the booty in midair.

❺ Flightless Cormorant

Apart from penguins, the flightless cormorant is the only flightless seabird in the world, and it is endemic to the Galápagos. When an ancestral population colonized this predator-free archipelago the birds eventually lost the need for flight. About 700 pairs remain.

❻ Galápagos Penguin

Long ago, a population of penguins followed the cool Humboldt Current up from Antarctica and settled in the Galápagos. Today the Galápagos penguin is the most northerly penguin in the world and the only species that lives in the tropics.

❼ Waved Albatross

The waved albatross is helpless in calm weather, relying utterly on southeast trade winds to transport it to feeding areas. The archipelago's largest bird (weighing 5kg, with a 2.4m wingspan) is the only albatross species that breeds at the equator.

❽ Darwin's Finches

All of the islands' finches are believed to be descendents of a common ancestor. Upon arrival in the archipelago, it found a host of vacant ecological niches and evolved into 13 unusual species, including the tool-using woodpecker finch and the blood-sucking vampire finch.

❾ Mockingbirds

Fearless parties of mockingbirds are often the first birds to investigate visitors at beach landings, and are famous for poking around in bags and perching on hats. Recognizable by their down-curved bill, these thrush-sized birds are actually fine songsters.

1

Reptiles

The Galápagos Islands have one of the most fascinating collections of reptiles found anywhere in the world. Giant, prehistoric-looking tortoises and fearsome-looking land iguanas are easily observed and photographed on terra firma, while snorkelers can glimpse the bizarre seagoing iguana and graceful sea turtles in their native element.

2

❶ Giant Tortoise
The archipelago's most famous reptile is the giant tortoise, or Galápagos ('saddle' in Spanish), after which the islands are named. Ancestral tortoises probably drifted to the islands on their journey back from South America. They can live for several hundred years.

❷ Marine Iguana
The remarkable marine iguana is the world's only seagoing lizard, and is common on the rocky shores of all the Galápagos islands. Its size and coloration vary between islands, with the largest specimens growing up to 1.5m.

❸ Galápagos Land Iguana
Despite their large size and fearsome appearance, land iguanas are harmless vegetarians that thrive on succulent opuntias (pear cactuses). Mature males weigh up to 13kg and grow to 1m; they are territorial, engaging in head-butting contests to defend their terrain.

❹ Lava Lizards
Tortoises and iguanas may be more famous, but the most commonly seen reptiles on the islands are the various species of lava lizard, which are frequently seen scurrying across rocks or even perched on the backs of iguanas.

❺ Green Sea Turtle
Adult green sea turtles are huge: they can reach 150kg in weight and 1m in length. They can be seen readily surfacing for air at many anchorages in calm water and are often encountered underwater by snorkelers.

Marine Life

The archipelago is home to a startling array of marine life. There are many thousands of aquatic species in all shapes and sizes, including 25 species of dolphin and whale, and 400 species of fish. Most famous of all are the Galápagos sea lion and the Galápagos fur seal.

1 Sally Lightfoot Crab

This abundant marine animal is blessed with spectacular coloration. Sally Lightfoot crabs (named by English seafarers) adorn the rocks on every island and are extremely agile. They can jump from rock to rock and even appear to walk on water.

2 Galápagos Fur Seal

More introverted than its sea lion cousin, the endemic Galápagos fur seal has a dense, luxuriant, insulating layer of fur. Although it was nearly hunted to extinction in the 19th century, it has made a remarkable comeback and numbers some 30,000 animals.

3 Galápagos Sea Lion

Nearly everyone's favorite island mammal is the widespread Galápagos sea lion, which numbers about 50,000 and is found on every island. These delightful animals often lounge about on sandy beaches and will often swim with snorkelers and bathers.

4 Tropical Fish

Over 400 fish species have been recorded in Galápagos waters, including some 50 endemic species. Snorkeling here is simply spectacular, among commonly sighted species such as blue-eyed damselfish, white-banded angelfish, yellow-tailed surgeonfish, Moorish idols, blue parrotfish and concentric puffers.

5 Bottlenose Dolphin

The most commonly sighted cetacean in Galápagos waters is the bottlenose dolphin, which has a playful and inquisitive nature. They typically feed cooperatively in pods of 20 to 30 individuals and have a varied diet, diving up to 500m offshore.

6 Killer Whale

Truly spectacular to see in the wild, the killer whale is actually a species of dolphin. It is a ferocious hunter (but no threat to humans), traveling at up to 55km per hour, while preying on fish or other whales.

7 Manta Ray

Of 15 species of ray inhabiting Galápagos waters, the magnificent manta ray is the largest of the bunch – and one of the world's largest fish. Some giants reportedly stretch 9m across the 'wings', although 4m adults are more common.

Habitats

The entire archipelago is volcanic in origin, with the main islands just the tips of vast submarine volcanoes. In the relatively short span of geological time since the islands were formed, they have been transformed from sterile lava flows into complex vegetation communities with many unique species.

1 Coastline

Thousands of kilometers of coastline surround the Galápagos Islands, nourishing dynamic and diverse ecosystems. Ever-eroding lava flows make up the rocky shoreline, providing habitat for sea lions, marine iguanas and Sally Lightfoot crabs.

2 Arid Zone

Poor volcanic soils cover much of the islands, with bristling cacti towering above the surrounding vegetation. Despite the challenging environment, diverse species thrive here, including the endemic lava cactus, which takes root in the cracks in barren lava flows.

3 Highlands Zone

The high peaks of several islands have eroded into rich volcanic soil, supporting dense vegetation. Fascinating species flourish here, like the 15m-high scalesia (tree daisy), whose trunk and branches are covered in epiphytes: dripping mosses, ferns, orchids and bromeliads.

4 Ocean

Highly productive currents bathe the islands in a year-round supply of nutrients. Plankton drift on the sunlit surface, sustaining fish, their predators further up the food chain and some of the world's largest animals – the great whales.

(Continued from page 64)

When it comes to snorkeling, the Galápagos is the place to head. The rich marine life here doesn't often require great depths to access. Baby sea lions swim up to snorkelers and sate their curiosity with a good look, various species of rays slowly undulate by, and penguins dart past in a stream of bubbles. The hundreds of species of fish are spectacularly colorful, and the round, flapping shapes of sea turtles gliding by is truly an awe-inspiring sight. For a glimpse of what lies below the surface see p70.

You may be able to buy a mask and snorkel in sporting-goods stores in Quito or Guayaquil, and they can sometimes be borrowed or rented in the Galápagos, but you're better off bringing a mask from home to ensure a good fit. The water temperature is around 22°C (72°F) from January to April and about 18°C (64°F) during the rest of the year, so consider bringing a spring-suit (shorty) with you, too.

WHITE-WATER RUSH

Both in terms of white water and scenery, Ecuador boasts world-class river rafting and kayaking year-round. Some of the country's rivers offer up to 100km of continuous Class III to Class IV white water before flattening out to flow toward the Pacific on one side of the Andes and into the Amazon Basin on the other.

Ecuador's reputation as a white-water destination par excellence was solidified in 2005 when the IRF World Rafting Championship was held on the Río Quijos, a spectacular Class IV to V river amid stunning scenery on the eastern slopes of the Andes, not far from the town of **El Chaco** (p236). El Chaco, incidentally, is a great place for arranging a rafting trip along the spectacular Quijos. Wherever you go, the best time for rafting is from October to February.

In the Oriente, the town of **Tena** (p250) has become Ecuador's de facto white-water capital. Near it, the upper Río Napo (Class III) and the feisty Río Misahuallí (Class IV) are the country's best-known rivers, after the Quijos. The Misahuallí is best during the dry months of October through March and does not lack for excitement (it even has a portage around a waterfall). The most popular river for rafters of all levels is along the Jatunyacu, where rafters tackle a 25km stretch of Class III white water. There are several other Class IV and V runs around Tena as well, making the town a great base for kayakers.

Further south, the Río Upano (Class IV to IV+) near **Macas** (see p263) is excellent for multiday trips and outrageous jungle scenery, including the spectacular stretch along the Namangosa Gorge, where more than a dozen waterfalls plummet into the river. The Upano is best from about September to February.

On the western slopes of the Andes, about 2½ hours west of Quito, the Río Blanco (Class III to IV), is a year-round possibility and a favorite day trip from the capital, with wildest conditions from February to about June. There is approximately 200km of maneuverable white water here, including the challenging Upper Blanco. Also called 'The Long Run,' this stretch consists of 47km of nonstop rapids, which are completed in a little over four hours (making it one of the world's longest one-day trips). There are several Class II to III runs suitable for complete beginners and families near Quito as well. See p96 for rafting operators in the capital.

The Río Pastaza and Río Patate are two of the country's most popular rivers thanks to their proximity to the tourist mecca of Baños (see p176), but the Patate unfortunately remains very polluted.

Kayakers regularly bring their own boats to Ecuador (those eager to get some experience under their belts can sign up for a white-water kayaking course with agencies in Tena, Baños or Quito). Most rafters usually sign on with a local operator. Even beginners can enjoy the activity, as rafts are captained by seasoned and qualified experts. Ecuador's river-guide association is called Asociación de Guías de Aguas Rapidas del Ecuador (AGAR; Ecuadorian White-Water Guides Association). Only reputable companies are listed in this book. When shopping around for an outfit, make sure they have decent life jackets, professional guides, first-aid kits and throw bags. Some outfitters also offer wet-suit rental on several of the longer runs (recommended).

SURFING

Ecuador isn't a huge surf destination, but it has some excellent breaks if you know where to go. Surf season is generally November through April, with peak months in January and February. Localism is generally minimal, with Ecuadorians and foreigners mixing it up pretty peacefully.

Two excellent online resources for surfers are Wannasurf (www.wannasurf.com) and Wavehunters (www.wavehunters.com); both provide comprehensive sections on Ecuador.

The classic mainland break is **Montañita** (p311), a fast, powerful reef-break that can cough up some of the mainland's best barrels. The break is best from December to May, when swells of 2m to 3m are common. It also has some tolerable beach-breaks nearby. Near Muisne, in Esmeraldas province, **Mompiche** (p289) is a world-class left point-break offering rides of up to 500m on top days. **Canoa** (p290) is a fun spot for left and right beach-breaks, if only because the town here is a great little hangout and the beach is beautiful.

There are dozens of other good breaks – including left and right beach, reef- and point-breaks – along the mainland coast that are beyond the scope of this book. The great majority of them are south of Manta (p296) and most are hidden and require tapping local resources. For information's sake, the best place to start is Montañita.

In the Galápagos, Isla San Cristóbal is home to three world-class reef-breaks, all near the town of **Puerto Baquerizo Moreno** (p365). They're extremely fast, however, and manageable only for experienced surfers. The high price of getting there keeps the crowds down. The optimal surf season on the islands is from December to May.

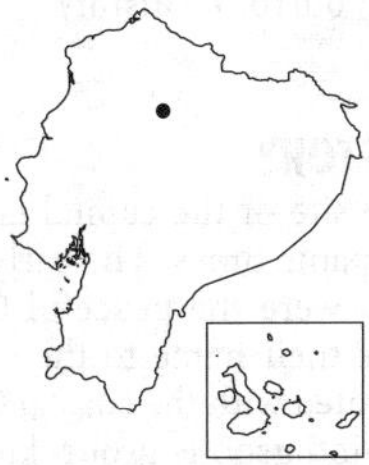

Quito

High in the Andes, amid dramatic, mist-covered peaks, Quito is a beautifully located city packed with historical monuments and architectural treasures. It's Ecuador's most dynamic city, with a vibrant civic scene and a fascinating collection of neighborhoods. Dining, drinking and merrymaking are all part of the equatorial experience in the world's second-highest capital.

Quito's jewel is its historic center, or 'old town' as it's often called. A Unesco World Heritage site, this handsomely restored neighborhood blooms with 17th-century facades, picturesque plazas and magnificent churches that blend Spanish, Moorish and indigenous elements. It's also home to the presidential palace, which presides over the animated streets full of people from all walks of society mingling throughout the day.

Just north of the old town lies the aptly named 'new town,' a modern and bustling collection of neighborhoods, intersected by noisy avenues and sprinkled with high-rises. The magnet for travelers is the Mariscal Sucre, a condensed area of guesthouses, travel agencies, diverse eateries and a pulsing nightlife scene. This is indeed 'gringolandia' as some locals describe the area, though plenty of *quiteños* (Quito residents) frequent the bars and restaurants here.

Quito is an alluring city for wanderers, where a day's saunter can lead past little-explored cobblestone lanes through lively markets and shops, and on up into hilly neighborhoods where breathtaking views lurk around every corner. Not surprisingly, the capital is a popular place to enroll in a Spanish school and stay for a while – perhaps far longer than planned, as more than a few captivated expats can attest. For many – foreigners and locals alike – Quito is the heart and soul of Ecuador.

HIGHLIGHTS

- Explore the picturesque streets of **old town** (p79), its cobblestones crisscrossing one of Latin America's finest colonial centers.
- Pay homage to Guayasamín, one of Ecuador's greatest painters, at the fascinating **Capilla del Hombre** (p92).
- Discover the vastness of Ecuador's cultural treasures at the **Museo del Banco Central** (p87), housing the country's finest collection of pre-Colombian and colonial art.
- Journey north to learn about the thousand-year-old civilization well acquainted with the true equator at the **Museo de la Cultura Solar** (p115).
- Join the revelry in the animated bar scene of the **Mariscal** (p108).

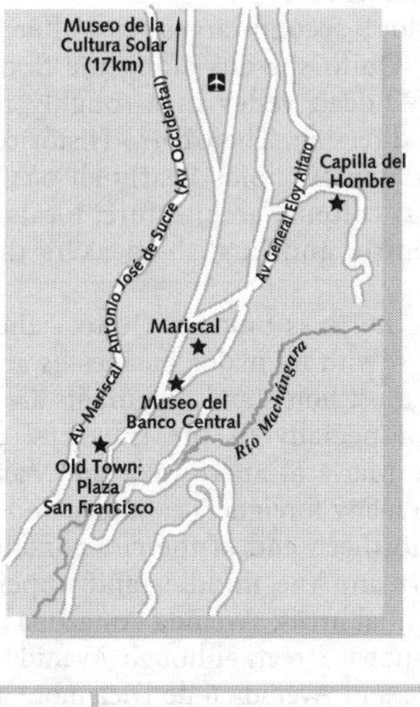

TELEPHONE CODE: 02	POPULATION: 1.5 MILLION	AREA: 324 SQ KM

HISTORY

The site of the capital city dates from pre-Hispanic times. The early inhabitants of the area were the peaceful Quitu people, who gave their name to the city. The Quitus integrated with the coastal Caras, giving rise to the indigenous group known as the Shyris. Around AD 1300, the Shyris joined with the Puruhás through marriage, and their descendants fought against the Incas in the late 15th century.

By the time the Spanish arrived in Ecuador in 1526, Quito was a major Inca city. Rather than allowing it to fall into the hands of the Spanish conquerors, Rumiñahui, a general of Atahualpa, razed the city shortly before their arrival. There are no Inca remains. The present capital was founded atop the ruins by Spanish lieutenant Sebastián de Benalcázar on December 6, 1534. Many colonial-era buildings survive in the old town.

CLIMATE

High in the mountains but near the equator, Quito enjoys mild days and cool nights most of the year. Evening temperatures of 7°C and daytime temperatures of 25°C are common. Seasonal variations are slight, with a rainy season running from October to May (April is often the wettest month) and drier, slightly warmer months running from June to September.

ORIENTATION

Ecuador's second-largest city after Guayaquil, Quito spreads along the floor of a high Andean valley in a roughly north–south direction. The Centro Histórico (historical center) holds nearly all of Quito's famous colonial architecture; locals call it El Centro, and English-speakers the 'old town.'

The north is modern Quito – the 'new town' – with all major businesses and services. Most hotels and restaurants are found here, especially in the travelers' ghetto of the Mariscal Sucre (aka the Mariscal), where many foreigners eat, sleep and drink. The northern end of the city contains the airport and the middle- and upper-class residential areas. Avenida Amazonas is the best-known street, although Avenida 10 de Agosto and Avenida 6 de Diciembre are the most-important thoroughfares.

The far south of Quito consists mainly of working-class residential areas. Few travelers venture here – it's unsafe and there are few sights.

The surrounding hills and peaks make orienting yourself easy: Cruz Loma and the flanks of Volcán Pichincha are the massive mountains to the west of the city. If you stand facing them, north will be to your right; to the south looms the giant hilltop statue of La Virgen de Quito.

The bus terminal is directly south of the old town, about a 10-minute walk from the Plaza Grande. The best way into town from the airport is by taxi (see p113).

Quito's streets are usually one-way: Calles Guayaquil and Venezuela head into the old town, and Calles García Moreno and Flores head out.

Maps

The tourist office distributes free, useful maps with scenic highlights. For something more in-depth, you can purchase the indexed *Quito Distrito Metropolitano* ($6) published by Prodoguias. It's sold at the main tourist office and in some pharmacies.

Excellent topographical maps ($2 each) and various tourist-highlight maps are available in the map-sales room at the **Instituto Geográfico Militar** (IGM; Map pp88-9; ☎ 254-5090; ⏲ 8am-4pm Mon-Thu, 7am-12:30pm Fri), located on top of a hill southeast of Parque El Ejido. There are no buses, so you have to either walk or take a taxi, and you'll need to leave your passport at the gate. Aside from the giant map of Quito for sale, city maps are limited.

ADDRESSES IN QUITO

A few years ago, Quito changed to a new address system based on 'N,' 'S,' 'W' and 'E' quadrants. An old address might be Avenida Amazonas 433, while the new one would be Avenida Amazonas N22-62; the numbers bear no relation to each other. Most buildings now display the new address, but some show the old address, and some have both. In other words, it can be extremely confusing. Both are used in this chapter, depending on the information received from each business. Taxi drivers find places based on cross streets.

QUITO IN…

Two Days

Start your day off in the **old town** (p79) with a cuppa at **El Cafeto** (p104). From there, stroll the picturesque streets, taking in **La Compañía de Jesús** (p83), the **Museo de la Ciudad** (p84) and **Plaza San Francisco** (p84). In the evening, drink or dine at the magical rooftop setting of **Vista Hermosa** (p103).

On day two, ride the **teleféricQo** (p85) up to Cruz Loma. Visit the **Capilla del Hombre** and nearby **Museo Guayasamín** (p92), before heading to the Mariscal for souvenir shopping at **Galería Latina** (p110) and coffee at **Kallari** (p107). Close the night with dinner and drinks at **El Pobre Diablo** (p108).

Four Days

Follow the two-day itinerary, then on your third day add an excursion to **La Mitad del Mundo** (p114), possibly overnighting inside the nearby volcanic crater (p116). On the last day, visit the **Museo del Banco Central** (p87), and then see the orchids at the **Jardín Botánico** (p92). That evening, join the salsa-loving crowds at **Seseribó** (p109).

INFORMATION

Bookstores

Abya Yala Bookstore (Map pp88-9; ☎ 250-6247; www.abyayala.org; cnr Av 12 de Octubre 1430 Wilson; 🕑 8am-7pm Mon-Fri, to 5pm Sat & Sun) Outstanding selection of books on indigenous culture and anthropology (in Spanish).

Confederate Books (Map p90; ☎ 252-7890; Calama 410; 🕑 10am-6pm Mon-Sat) Ecuador's largest selection of second-hand books in English and several other languages.

English Bookstore (Map p90; ☎ 254-3996; Calama 217; 🕑 10am-6.30pm Mon-Sat) Good selection of used books in English.

Libri Mundi (Map p90; ☎ 223-4791; www.librimundi.com, in Spanish; Mera 851; 🕑 8:30am-7:30pm Mon-Fri, 9am-2pm & 3-6pm Sat) Quito's best bookstore, with a good selection of titles in English, German, French and Spanish. Lonely Planet guides available.

Libro Express (Map p90; ☎ 254-8113; Av Amazonas 816 btwn Wilson & Veintimilla; 🕑 9:30am-7:30pm Mon-Fri, 10am-6pm Sat) Good for maps, magazines, Lonely Planet guides and Ecuador-related books.

Paldeia Books (Map pp88-9; ☎ 223-2417; Leonidas Plaza N21-262; 🕑 9:30am-8pm Mon-Fri, 10am-noon Sat) Small shop selling new and used titles in Spanish, English, German and French.

Cultural Centers

Alianza Francesa (Map pp88-9; ☎ 224-9345/50; Av Eloy Alfaro N32-468) French cultural center near Belgica and Av 6 de Diciembre.

Asociación Humboldt (Map pp88-9; ☎ 254-8480; Vancouver E5-54 at Polonia) German cultural center.

Casa Cultural Afro-Ecuatoriano (Map p90; ☎ 222-0227; Av 6 de Diciembre Oe123-58; 🕑 10am-8pm Mon-Tue & Thu-Fri, to 5pm Wed) A good information source for black Ecuadorian culture and events in Quito.

Centro Cultural Metropolitano The hub of cultural events in the old town (see p80).

Centro Cultural Mexicano (Map pp88-9; ☎ 256-1548; cultural@embamex.org.ec; Orellana 473; 🕑 10am-1pm & 3:30-5:30pm Mon-Fri) Features great monthly exhibits of Mexican artists.

Emergency

Ambulance (☎ 131)

Emergency (☎ 911)

Fire (☎ 102)

Police (☎ 101)

Internet Access

The Mariscal area (along J Calama) is packed with internet cafés, many with inexpensive international calling rates. Most charge $0.75 to $1 per hour:

Friends Web Café (Map p90; Calama E6-19; 🕑 7:30am-10:30pm Mon-Fri, 8am-10:30pm Sat & Sun) Cozy internet café with tasty juices and snacks.

La Sala (Map p90; cnr Calama & Reina Victoria; 🕑 8am-midnight) Buzzy net café, where you can enjoy decent coffee, dessert and snacks over email or inexpensive international calls.

Monkeys (Map p90; Mera N24-200, 2nd fl; 8am-11pm) Popular, traveler-recommended internet café.

Papaya Net (Map p90; Calama 413 at Mera; 🕑 7:30am-1am) The most-popular internet café in the Mariscal, with good music, drinks and snacks.

Papaya Net Old Town (Map p86; Chile Oe4-56, Palacio Arzobispal; 🕑 8am-2am) The old town's best cyber spot, with a great location facing Plaza Grande.

Internet Resources

Corporación Metropolitana de Turismo (www.quito.com.ec)
Gay Guide to Quito (http://gayquitoec.tripod.com)
Municipal website (www.quito.gov.ec, in Spanish)

Laundry

There are no laundries in the old town. Most hotels will wash and dry your clothes, but this is expensive. The following wash and dry clothes within 24 hours (often within five), charging between $0.75 and $1 per kilo:

Lavanderia (Map p90; Foch Es-43)
Opera de Jabón (Map p90; ☎ 254-3995; Pinto 325 near Mera)
Sun City Laundry (Map p90; ☎ 255-3066; cnr Mera & Foch)
Wash & Go (Map p90; ☎ 223-0993; Pinto 340, btwn Mera & Reina Victoria)

Medical Services

The following individual doctors have been recommended, many of whom have offices in the Centro Meditropoli (Map p82) near the Hospital Metropolitano.

Clínica de la Mujer (Map p82; ☎ 245-8000; Av Amazonas 4826 & Calle de Villarroel) A private clinic specializing in women's medical problems.
Clínica Pichincha (Map p90; ☎ 286-2680; 6ta Transversal & Av El Progreso) Does lab analysis for parasites, dysentery etc.
Dr Alfredo Jijon (Map p82; ☎ 245-6359, 246-6314; Centro Meditropoli, office 215, Mariana de Jesús & Av Occidental) Gynecologist.
Dr John Rosenberg (Map p90; ☎ 252-1104, ext 310, 222-7777, 09-973-9734, pager ☎ 222-7777; Foch 476) Internist specializing in tropical medicine; speaks English and German, makes house calls and is available for emergencies nearly anytime.
Dr Jorge Cobo Avedaño (Map p82; ☎ 225-6589, 246-3361, ext 222; Centro Meditropoli, office 004) English-speaking dentist.
Dr José A Pitarque (Map p82; ☎ 226-8173; Centro Meditropoli, office 211) English-speaking ophthalmologist.
Dr Silvia Altamirano (☎ 244-4119; Av Amazonas 2689 & Av de la República) Orthodontist and dentist; excellent. Near Parque La Carolina.
Fybeca new town (Map pp88-9; ☎ 222-4263; Av 6 de Deciembre 2077); old town (Map p86; ☎ 228-2281; Guayaquil N9-01) Pharmacy
Hospital Metropolitano (Map p82; ☎ 226-1520, 226-9030, emergency ☎ 226-5020; Mariana de Jesús & Av Occidental) The best hospital in town.
Hospital Voz Andes (Map p82; ☎ 226-2142; cnr Villalengua Oe2-37 & Av 10 de Agosto) American-run hospital with an outpatient department and emergency room near the Iñaquito trolley stop.

Money

There are several banks and a few *casas de cambio* (currency-exchange bureaus) in the new town, along Avenida Amazonas between Avenida Patria and Orellana, and there are dozens of banks throughout town. Banks listed here have ATMs and change traveler's checks. If you need to change money on a Sunday, head to the Producambios at the airport: the *casa de cambio* in the international arrival area is open for all flight arrivals.

American Express (Map p90; ☎ 256-0488; Av Amazonas 329, 5th fl; 🕑 8:30am-5pm Mon-Fri) Sells Amex traveler's checks to Amex card-holders only. Also replaces lost or stolen checks.
Banco de Guayaquil Av Amazonas (Map p90; ☎ 256-4324; Av Amazonas N22-147 at Veintimilla); Colón (Map p90; Colón at Reina Victoria)
Banco del Pacífico new town (Map pp88-9; ☎ 250-1218; 12 de Octubre & Cordero); old town (Map p86; ☎ 228-8138; cnr Guayaquil & Chile)
Banco del Pichincha (Map p86; ☎ 258-4149; Guayaquil btwn Olmedo & Manabí)
MasterCard (Map p82; ☎ 226-2770; Naciones Unidas 8771 at De Los Shyris)
Producambios airport (Map p82; 🕑 6am-9pm); Mariscal (☎ 256-3900; Av Amazonas 350; 🕑 8:30am-6pm Mon-Fri, 9am-2pm Sat)
Servicio Cambios (Venezuela N5-15; 🕑 9am-6pm Mon-Fri, to 1pm Sat)
Visa (Map p82; ☎ 245-9303; De Los Shyris 3147)
Western Union Av de la República (Map pp88-9; ☎ 256-5059; Av de la República 433); Colón (Map pp88-9; ☎ 290-1505; Av Colón 1333) For money transfers from abroad.

Post

You can mail a package up to 2kg from any post office. Packages exceeding 2kg must be mailed from the **branch post office** (Map p90; ☎ 250-8890; cnr Av Cristóbal Colón & Reina Victoria) in the Mariscal or from the parcel post office (see below).

Central post office (Map p86; ☎ 228-2175; Espejo 935) In the old town; this is where you pick up your *lista de correos* (general delivery) mail. See p385 for more information.
DHL (Map pp88-9; ☎ 290-1505; Av Colón 1333 at Foch; 🕑 8am-7pm Mon-Fri, 9am-5pm Sat)
Parcel post office (Map pp88-9; ☎ 252-1730; Ulloa 273) If you are mailing a package over 2kg, use this post office, near Dávalos.

'PostOffice' (Map pp88-9; ☎ 290-9209; cnr Av Amazonas & María; 🕑 9:30am-5pm Mon-Fri) Private company offering FedEx, UPS and other international courier services.

Telephone

For international calls, it's much cheaper to call from an internet café (p77).

Andinatel Mera (Map p90; ☎ 290 2756; Mera 741 at Baquedano); new town (Map pp88-9; ☎ 297-7100; Eloy Alfaro 333 near 9 de Octubre); old town (Map p86; ☎ 261 2112; Benalcázar btwn Mejia & Chile); Reina Victoria (Map p90; near Calama) The main office is in the new town.

Tourist Information

South American Explorers (SAE; Map pp88-9; ☎ 222-5228; www.saexplorers.org; Washington 311 & Plaza Gutiérrez; 🕑 9:30am-5pm Mon-Wed & Fri, to 6pm Thu, to noon Sat) For more information on this travelers' organization, see p388.

Tourist Office (Corporación Metropolitana de Turismo; www.quito.com.ec); airport Map p82; ☎ 330-0163; Mariscal Map p90; ☎ 255-1566; Cordero btwn Diego de Almagro & Reina Victoria; 🕑 9am-5pm Mon-Fri); old town (Map p86; ☎ 228-1904; cnr Venezuela & Espejo, Plaza Grande; 🕑 9am-8pm Mon-Sat, 10am-6pm Sun) The old-town branch is well located and helpful for general questions, directions and maps; a selection of handicrafts is on sale. There's also a branch at Museo del Banco Central (see p87).

Travel Agencies

Ecuadorian Tours (Map p90; ☎ 256-0488; www.ecuadoriantours.com; Av Amazonas 329) This is a good, all-purpose travel agency near Washington.

Metropolitan Touring (Map p90; ☎ 250-6650/1/2; www.metropolitan-touring.com; Av Amazonas N20-39 near 18 de Septiembre) Ecuador's biggest travel agency.

DANGERS & ANNOYANCES

Quito has its share of robberies and petty crime, though the city's dangers can largely be avoided by taking a few precautions.

The area with the most hotels, restaurants and nightlife, the Mariscal Sucre, is well worth visiting, but it remains a target for muggers and pickpockets. Although the neighborhood has seen some improvement in recent years, it's still wise to take a taxi after about 9pm – even if you have only a few blocks to walk. Sunday, when no one else is around, is also a dodgy time to wander the empty streets of the Mariscal.

The old town, once more dangerous than the Mariscal, has been cleaned up and is now safe as late as 10pm during the week and until around midnight on Friday and Saturday. It's well lit and the city has taken a keen interest in keeping it safe. After dark, do not stray south of Plaza Santo Domingo, east of Plaza San Francisco or north of the Church of La Merced.

> **ANDEAN HIGH**
>
> Did the hotel stairs make you breathless? Is your head spinning or achy? Having trouble sleeping? If so, you're probably suffering the mild symptoms of altitude sickness, which will disappear after a day or two. Quito's elevation of about 2850m can certainly have this effect if you've just arrived from sea level. To minimize symptoms, take things easy upon arrival, eat light and lay off the smokes and alcohol. For alleviating symptoms, some swear by the benefits of *te de coca* (coca-leaf tea), which some cafés, such as Tianguez (p103), have on hand.

The trolley system is plagued with pickpockets – keep an eye out while riding, and avoid taking it during rush hour.

The steps of García Moreno, heading from Ambato to the top of El Panecillo, are potentially dangerous, with continued reports of muggings. Take a taxi to the top and flag another to return.

If you get robbed, file a police report at the **police station** Mariscal (Map p90; cnr Reina Victoria & Roca); old town (Map p86; cnr Mideros & Cuenca) between 9am and noon, particularly if you wish to make an insurance claim.

SIGHTS

Justly, Quito's old town deserves much attention: it's one of the most spectacular colonial centers in the Americas, with an impressive array of churches, historic squares and intriguing museums, amid all the hustle and bustle of the city's colorful civic life.

Old Town

With its narrow streets, restored colonial architecture and lively plazas, Quito's Centro Histórico (aka the old town) is a marvel to wander. Built centuries ago by indigenous artisans and laborers, Quito's churches, convents, chapels and monasteries are cast in legend and steeped in history. It's a bustling area, full of yelling street vendors, ambling pedestrians, tooting taxis, belching buses and

THE HOT NEW SOUND FROM ECUADOR

When Luís Villamarín of Quito and Max Epstein, an expat from Los Angeles, California, first met back in 2006, little did the pair realize they were on the verge of something big. The two formed Esto Es Eso, combining traditional Ecuadorian sounds such as *pasillo* (a kind of romantic guitar-based music) with a dizzying blend of hip-hop, beatbox, rock and reggae. In the process of playful experimentation, they created a new genre of music called *pasillo-hop*.

The pair sings in both Spanish and English, reaching a core of Spanish-speaking Anglophiles and English-speaking Latinos stretching from South America to the United States. Three of Esto Es Eso's singles have been smash hits on Ecuadorian radio, and the group has been featured in *Rolling Stone's* Latin edition.

How did you two meet?

Luís: I was making this album. I wanted to find an international sound. My cousin told me about this gringo rapping really fast – in English. Bring him to me, I said [laughs]. He came to my studio, and he started doing what he does really good. Shocking really.

Max: He had a song in Spanish called 'Mala'; 'maybe you could rap over that,' he told me. I had some lyrics in my head, and we started jamming.

Luís: 'But we're not jamming, we're creating a movement,' I told Max. 'We're about to create a Latin American bilingual musical movement.' I'd never heard anything like it – that mix of Spanish and English. It was amazing to share this experience. The most amazing thing that happened to me – aside from the birth of my daughter. Sorry, Max [laughs].

whistle-blowing policemen trying to direct traffic in the narrow one-way streets. The area is magical and one in which the more you look, the more you find.

Churches are open every day (usually until 6pm) but are crowded with worshippers on Sunday. They regularly close between 1pm and 3pm for lunch.

PLAZA GRANDE

The heart of the old town is the Plaza Grande (Map p86; formally known as Plaza de la Independencia), a picturesque, palm-fringed square surrounded by historic buildings. The austere, white building on the plaza's northwest side (between Chile and Espejo), with the national flag flying atop, is the **Palacio del Gobierno** (Presidential Palace; Map p86; García Moreno; guided tours 10am, 11.30am, 1pm, 2.30pm & 4pm). Visitors can enter by guided tours (in Spanish and sometimes English), which offer a glimpse of the brilliantly hued mosaic depicting Francisco de Orellana's descent of the Amazon. You'll also peer in a few of the staterooms. The president carries out business in this building, so sightseeing is limited to rooms not currently in use. On Monday, the changing of the guards takes place on the plaza at 11am.

On the plaza's southwest side stands Quito's **cathedral** (Map p86; admission $1.50; 9.30am-4pm Mon-Sat, services 7am Sat & Sun). Although not the most ornate of the old town's churches, its interior has some fascinating religious works from artists of the Quito School (see p43). Don't miss the painting of the Last Supper, with Christ and disciples feasting on *cuy* (roast guinea pig), *chicha* (a fermented corn drink) and *humitas* (similar to tamales). The Nativity painting includes a llama and a horse peering over the newborn Jesus. You'll also see the ornate tomb of Mariscal Sucre, the leading figure of Quito's independence. Behind the main altar is a plaque showing where President Gabriel García Moreno died on August 6, 1875. He was slashed with a machete outside the Palacio del Gobierno and was carried, dying, to the cathedral. Admission includes a free guided tour in Spanish.

On the northeast side of the plaza, the **Palacio Arzobispal** (Archbishop's Palace; Map p86; Chile) is now a colonnaded row of small shops and restaurants, located between García Moreno and Venezuela.

Just off the plaza, the outstanding **Centro Cultural Metropolitano** (Map p86; 295-0272; www.centrocultural-quito.com; cnr García Moreno & Espejo; admission free; 9am-5pm Tue-Sun, patio to 7:30pm) houses several temporary art exhibits, an intriguing museum, two rooftop terraces and a pleasant café on the interior patio.

What are some of your musical influences?
Luís: My heart says that romantic songs from Ecuador – *pasillo* – this is the greatest music in the world. My father used to play that a lot – and Pink Floyd. **You've played a number of shows around the country. What has been your favorite?**
Max: Our best show was probably playing in the Plaza de San Francisco, during the Founding of Ecuador holiday (First Shout of Independence, on August 10). There must have been 10,000 people in the audience. That was maybe our most epic show.

What's next for Esto es Eso?
Luís: I have a feeling in my heart. I would like to be a part of this amazing movement. There are a lot of talented guys doing amazing things. The doors of the music world are closed right now for Ecuadorian musicians. We're trying to open them.

Max: We just want to go around the world making music.

Some of the pair's favorite nightspots in Quito:

- **Pobre Diablo** (p109) Good, cutting-edge music. The best place for jazz, playing something different. Gives young musicians a chance – particularly on Wednesday and Thursday.
- **Ananké** (p108) Hosts lesser-known jazz or funk bands. It has criteria about who plays here.
- **El Aguijón** (p109) Good place for dancing and music. Cool owner plays popular American hits. Very representative of Quito, the mix of people.
- **Blues** (p109) One of the only places in town open late. Plays '70s hits and DJs. Great late-night parties.

The beautifully restored building, which you can wander freely, is rich in history, supposedly the pre-Hispanic site of one of Atahualpa's palaces. A Jesuit school from 1597 to 1767, it became a *cuartel* (army barracks) after their expulsion in the late 1700s. In 1809, royalist forces held a group of revolutionaries here and gruesomely murdered them a year later. Get a glimpse of Quito's early colonial history (and some rather lifelike wax figures) in the on-site **Museo Alberto Mena Caamaño** (admission $1.50; 9am-4.30pm Tue-Sun).

NORTH OF PLAZA GRANDE

Two blocks northwest of the Plaza Grande, you'll find **La Merced** (Map p86; cnr Cuenca & Chile; admission free; 7am-noon & 2-5pm), constructed between 1700 and 1742. At 47m, its tower is the highest in colonial Quito. Legend has it that the tower, the only unblessed part of the church, is possessed by the devil. Supposedly the only person strong enough to resist the devil was a black bell-ringer named Ceferino, and no one has dared enter the tower since he died in 1810. Hence the clock stands still and the bell hangs unrung.

Myth aside, La Merced has a wealth of fascinating art including paintings that show volcanoes erupting over the church roofs of colonial Quito and the capital covered with ashes.

One block to the northeast is the excellent **Museo de Arte Colonial** (Map p86; ☎ 221-2297; Mejía Oe6-132, cnr Cuenca). In a restored 17th-century building, the museum houses what many consider to be Ecuador's best collection of colonial art. On display are famous sculptures and paintings of the Quito School including the works of Miguel de Santiago, Manuel Chili (the indigenous artist known as Caspicara) and Bernardo de Legarda. The museum was closed indefinitely for restoration at time of research.

Several blocks east, inside a beautifully restored colonial home, the **Museo Camilo Egas** (Map p86; ☎ 257-2012; Venezuela 1302, cnr Esmeraldas; admission $0.50; 9.30am-5pm Tue-Fri, 10am-4pm Sat & Sun) houses a small but iconic collection of painter Camilo Egas' work. Egas was Ecuador's first *indigenista* (indigenous movement) painter, and his paintings of indigenous people – idealistic as they are – are stunning.

High on a hill in the northeastern part of the old town stands the Gothic **Basílica del Voto Nacional** (Map p86; ☎ 258-3891; cnr Venezuela & Carchi; tower admission $2; 9am-5pm), built over several decades beginning in 1926. Rather than gargoyles, however, turtles and iguanas protrude from the church's side. The highlight is the basilica's **towers**, which you can climb if you have the nerve – the

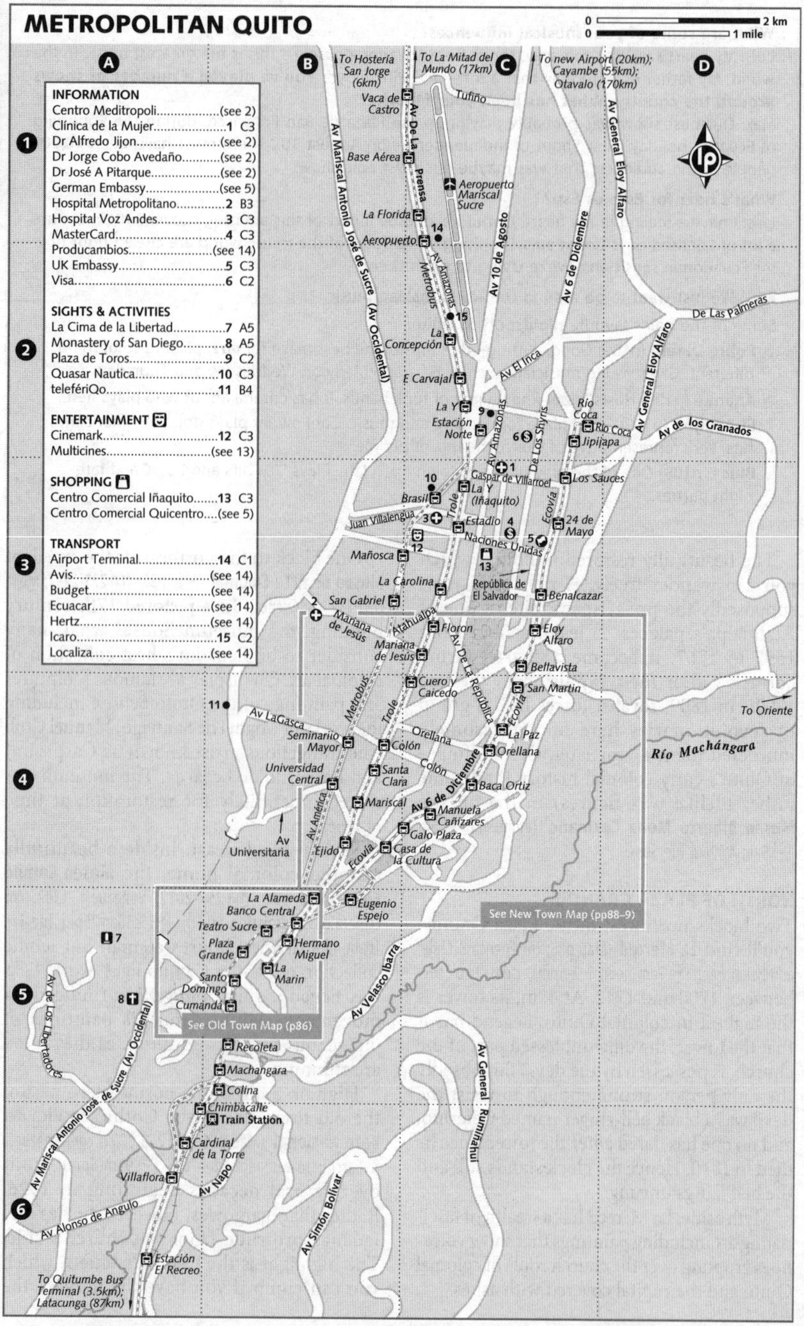
METROPOLITAN QUITO
0 2 km
0 1 mile
A
B
C
D
1
2
3
4
5
6
INFORMATION
Centro Meditropoli....(see 2)
Clínica de la Mujer....1 C3
Dr Alfredo Jijon....(see 2)
Dr Jorge Cobo Avedaño....(see 2)
Dr José A Pitarque....(see 2)
German Embassy....(see 5)
Hospital Metropolitano....2 B3
Hospital Voz Andes....3 C3
MasterCard....4 C3
Producambios....(see 14)
UK Embassy....5 C3
Visa....6 C2
SIGHTS & ACTIVITIES
La Cima de la Libertad....7 A5
Monastery of San Diego....8 A5
Plaza de Toros....9 C2
Quasar Nautica....10 C3
teleférIQo....11 B4
ENTERTAINMENT
Cinemark....12 C3
Multicines....(see 13)
SHOPPING
Centro Comercial Iñaquito....13 C3
Centro Comercial Quicentro....(see 5)
TRANSPORT
Airport Terminal....14 C1
Avis....(see 14)
Budget....(see 14)
Ecuacar....(see 14)
Hertz....(see 14)
Icaro....15 C2
Localiza....(see 14)
To Hostería San Jorge (6km)
To La Mitad del Mundo (17km)
To new Airport (20km); Cayambe (55km); Otavalo (170km)
Tufiño
Vaca de Castro
Base Aérea
La Florida
Aeropuerto
Aeropuerto Mariscal Sucre
Av De La Prensa
Av Amazonas
Metrobus
Av 10 de Agosto
Av 6 de Diciembre
Av General Eloy Alfaro
Av Mariscal Antonio José de Sucre (Av Occidental)
De Las Palmeras
La Concepción
E Carvajal
Av El Inca
La Y
Estación Norte
Río Coca
Jipijapa
Av de los Granados
De Los Shyris
Gaspar de Villarroel
La Y (Iñaquito)
Los Sauces
Brasil
Juan Villalengua
Estadio
Naciones Unidas
24 de Mayo
Ecovía
Trole
Mañosca
La Carolina
República de El Salvador
Benalcazar
San Gabriel
Mariana de Jesús
Atahualpa
Floron
Eloy Alfaro
Av De La República
Bellavista
Cuero y Caicedo
San Martin
To Oriente
Av LaGasca
Orellana
La Paz
Río Machángara
Seminario Mayor
Colón
Universidad Central
Santa Clara
Baca Ortiz
Mariscal
Manuela Cañizares
Av América
Av Universitaria
Ejido
Galo Plaza
Casa de la Cultura
La Alameda
Banco Central
Eugenio Espejo
See New Town Map (pp88–9)
Teatro Sucre
Plaza Grande
Hermano Miguel
La Marin
Santo Domingo
Cumandá
See Old Town Map (p86)
Av Velasco Ibarra
Av de Los Libertadores
Recoleta
Machangara
Colina
Chimbacalle
Train Station
Cardinal de la Torre
Villaflora
Av Napo
Av General Rumiñahui
Av Alonso de Angulo
Av Simón Bolívar
Estación El Recreo
To Quitumbe Bus Terminal (3.5km); Latacunga (87km)

ascent requires crossing a rickety wooden plank inside the main roof and climbing steep stairs and ladders to the top. You can also climb the spiral staircase and three sets of ladders into and above the clock tower. There's a patio café just outside the church and a snack bar on the tower's 4th floor.

EAST OF PLAZA GRANDE

Two blocks from the Plaza Grande, the **Monastery of San Agustín** (Map p86; Chile & Guayaquil; admission free) is another fine example of 17th-century architecture. Many of the heroes of the battles for Ecuador's independence are buried here, and it is the site of the signing of Ecuador's declaration of independence on August 10, 1809.

Due south of San Agustín stands the **Monastery of Santa Catalina** (Map p86; Espejo 779 at Flores; admission $1.50; 8:30am-5pm Mon-Fri, to 12:30pm Sat), a fully functioning convent and monastery that opened to the public in 2005. Since its founding in 1592, entering nuns have spent five cloistered years in solitary cells. To this day, the 21 nuns inside have only one hour to talk to each other or watch TV. But they make all sorts of natural products (shampoos, wine, hand cream, elixirs and more), which you can purchase from a rotating door that keeps the nuns hidden.

A free tour (in Spanish) of the monastery's museum takes in 18th-century religious paintings, some of which are downright gruesome. At the end of the tour, you'll get a shot of the nun's rather tasty wine. Supposedly, secret underground tunnels connect Santa Catalina to the church of Santo Domingo three blocks away.

Further northeast, at the junction of Calles Guayaquil and Manabí, is the tiny **Plaza del Teatro**, where you'll find the exquisitely restored **Teatro Sucre** (p109). Built in 1878, it stages Quito's best theater, dance and music performances.

CALLES GARCÍA MORENO & SUCRE

Beside the cathedral on García Moreno stands the 17th-century **Church of El Sagrario** (Map p86; García Moreno; admission free; 6am-noon & 3-6pm), originally intended as the main chapel of the cathedral but now a separate church.

Around the corner, on Calle Sucre, is Ecuador's most ornate church, **La Compañía de Jesús** (Map p86; admission $2; 9:30am-5.30pm Mon-Fri, to 4.30pm Sat), capped by green-and-gold domes visible from Plaza San Francisco one block away. The marvelously gilded Jesuit church was begun in 1605 and not completed for another 160 years. Free guided tours in English or Spanish highlight the church's unique features including its Moorish elements, perfect symmetry (right down to the trompe l'oeil staircase at the rear), symbolic elements (bright-red walls a reminder of Christ's blood) and its syncretism (Ecuadorian plants and indigenous faces hidden along the pillars). *Quiteños* proudly call it the most beautiful church in the country and it's easy to see why.

A block-and-a-half southeast of La Compañía is the beautifully restored **Casa de Sucre** (Map p86; ☎ 295-2860; cnr Venezuela 573 & Sucre; admission $1; 9am-5.30pm Mon-Fri, 10am-5.30pm Sat), the former home of Mariscal Antonio José de Sucre, the hero of Ecuadorian independence, and now a small museum full of early-19th-century furniture.

Back on Calle García Moreno, just southwest of Calle Sucre, you'll find the **Casa Museo María Augusta Urrutía** (Map p86; ☎ 258-0107; García Moreno N2-60; admission $2; 10am-5.30pm Tue-Sun). Of Quito's house museums, this is the one not to miss: it's a splendidly preserved, 19th-century house, once the home of the city's best-loved philanthropist, María Augusta Urrutía, and sprinkled with period furnishings, stained-glass windows, European artwork and a lush courtyard. Free guided tours are in Spanish and English.

La Ronda

One of the most recent areas to undergo restoration in the old town is the handsome street known as 'La Ronda' (Map p86). This narrow lane is lined with picture-book 17th-century buildings, with placards along the walls describing (in Spanish) some of the street's history and the artists, writers and political figures who once resided here. A new crop of restaurants and shops has opened in recent years, though La Ronda remains a delightfully local and unpretentious affair. The street is at its liveliest on Friday and Saturday nights, when *canelazo* (*aguardiente* – sugarcane alcohol – with hot cider and cinnamon) vendors keep everyone nice and cozy and live music spills out of restaurant windows.

south, the **Arco de la Reina** (Map p86; o at Rocafuerte), a massive arch built th century to give shelter to church-go, spans García Moreno. On one side, the **Museo de la Ciudad** (Map p86; ☎ 295-3643; www.museociudadquito.gov.ec, in Spanish; cnr García Moreno & Rocafuerte; admission $2; ⌚ 9:30am-5:30pm Tue-Sun) occupies the beautifully restored San Juan de Dios hospital (built in 1563, it functioned as a hospital until 1973). The museum depicts Quito's daily life through the centuries, with displays including dioramas, model indigenous homes and colonial kitchens. Guides are available in Spanish, English, French or German ($4).

On the other side of the arch stands the **Monasterio de Carmen Alto** (Map p86; ☎ 228-2320; cnr García Moreno & Rocafuerte; ⌚ 8am-4pm). Inside this fully functioning convent, cloistered nuns stay busy producing some of Quito's tastiest traditional sweets. Top picks include the *limones desamargados* (literally 'de-soured lemons'), made by hollowing out tiny lemons and filling them with a sweetened-milk concoction. Purchase them through a revolving contraption, which keeps the nuns hidden, or at the shop next door, where you can also buy traditional baked goods, aromatic waters for nerves and insomnia, bee pollen, honey and bottles of full-strength *mistela* (anise-flavored liqueur).

PLAZA & MONASTERY OF SAN FRANCISCO

Walking from the old town's narrow colonial streets into the open **Plaza San Francisco** reveals one of the finest sights in all of Ecuador: a sweeping cobblestone plaza backed by the mountainous backdrop of Volcán Pichincha, and the long, whitewashed walls and twin bell towers of Ecuador's oldest church, the (Map p86; Cuenca at Sucre; admission free; ⌚ 7-11am daily, 3-6pm Mon-Thu).

Construction of the monastery, the city's largest colonial structure, began only a few weeks after the founding of Quito in 1534, but the building was not finished for another 70 years. The founder was the Franciscan missionary Joedco Ricke, credited with being the first man to sow wheat in Ecuador. He is commemorated by a **statue** at the far right of the raised terrace in front of the church.

Although much of the church has been rebuilt because of earthquake damage, some is original. The **chapel of Señor Jesús del Gran Poder**, to the right of the main altar, has original tile work. The **main altar** itself is a spectacular example of baroque carving, while much of the roof shows Moorish influences.

To the right of the main entrance is the **Museo Franciscano** (☎ 295-2911; www.museofranciscano.com, in Spanish; admission $2; ⌚ 9am-1pm & 2-6pm Mon-Sat, 9am-noon Sun), which contains some of the church's finest artwork including paintings, sculpture and 16th-century furniture. Some of the furniture is fantastically wrought and inlaid with thousands of pieces of mother-of-pearl. The admission fee includes a guided tour in English or Spanish. Good guides will point out *mudejar* (Moorish) representations of the eight planets revolving around the sun in the ceiling, and will explain how the light shines through the rear window during the solstices, lighting up the main altar. They'll also demonstrate an odd confessional technique, where two people standing in separate corners can hear each other while whispering into the walls.

To the left of the monastery stands the **Capilla de Cantuña** (Cantuña Chapel), which houses a small art collection from the Quito School. It's also shrouded in one of Quito's most famous legends, that of the indigenous builder Cantuña, who supposedly sold his soul so the devil would help him complete the church on time. But just before midnight of the day of his deadline, Cantuña removed a single stone from the structure, meaning the church was never completed. He duped the devil and saved his soul.

PLAZA & CHURCH OF SANTO DOMINGO

Plaza Santo Domingo, near the southwest end of Calle Guayaquil, is a regular haunt for street performers. Crowds of neighborhood *quiteños* fill the plaza to watch pouting clowns and half-cocked magicians do their stuff. The plaza is beautiful in the evening, when the domes of the 17th-century **Church of Santo Domingo** (Map p86; cnr Flores & Rocafuerte; admission free; ⌚ 7am-1pm & 4:30-7:30pm), on the southeast side of the plaza, are floodlit.

In front of the church stands a **statue of Mariscal Sucre**, depicting the marshal pointing toward La Cima de la Libertad (opposite), where he won the decisive battle for independence on May 24, 1822.

A fabulous Gothiclike altar dominates the inside of the church; the original wooden floor was only recently replaced. An exquisite **statue**

of the Virgen del Rosario, a gift from King Charles V of Spain and one of the church's main showpieces, resides in an ornately carved, baroque-style side chapel. Construction of the church began in 1581 and continued until 1650.

EL PANECILLO

The small, ever-present hill to the south of the old town is called **El Panecillo** (the Little Bread Loaf) and is a major Quito landmark. It is topped by a huge statue of **La Virgen de Quito** (Virgin of Quito), with a crown of stars, angelic wings and a chained dragon atop the world. *Quiteños* proudly claim she is the only Madonna in the world depicted with wings.

From the summit, there are marvelous **views** of the sprawling city and the surrounding volcanoes. The best time for volcano views (particularly in the rainy season) is early morning, before the clouds roll in. Definitely don't climb the stairs at the end of Calle García Moreno on the way to the statue – they're unsafe due to muggings. A taxi from the old town costs about $4, and you can hail one at the top for the trip back to town.

Around the Old Town

MONASTERY OF SAN DIEGO

Northwest of El Panecillo, this beautiful 17th-century **monastery** (Map p82; ☎ 295-4026; Calicuchima 117 & Farfán; admission $2; 🕑 9:30am-12:30pm & 2:30-5:30pm) sits in a quiet courtyard behind thick walls above the old town. The only way inside is by tour, which, although it's recited with the enthusiasm of a mass in Latin, is worth suffering through to see the wealth of colonial art inside. There are outstanding works from both the Quito and Cusco schools including one of Quito's finest pulpits, carved by the notable indigenous woodcarver Juan Bautista Menacho.

There's also a fascinating 18th-century painting by Miguel de Santiago of the Last Supper. The oddest piece of work here is an **unidentified painting by Hieronymus Bosch**, titled *Passage from this Life to Eternity*: no one can explain how it got here. At the end of the tour, you can climb narrow stairs to the bell tower and walk along the rooftop.

LA CIMA DE LA LIBERTAD

Further up the flanks of Volcán Pichincha, one of the finest views of the city can be had from **La Cima de la Libertad** (Map p82; ☎ 228-8733; Av de los Libertadores s/n; admission $1; 🕑 8:30am-4:30pm Tue-Fri, 9am-1:30pm Sat & Sun). This monument was built at the site of the Batalla de Pichincha (Battle of Pichincha), the decisive battle in the struggle for independence from Spain, which was led by Mariscal Antonio José de Sucre on May 24, 1822.

There is also a rather soporific military museum housing a collection of military artifacts and a shrine to an unknown soldier. Don't miss the tiled mural by Eduardo Kingman, which hangs above the building.

The best way here is by taxi.

PARQUE ITCHIMBIA

High on a hill east of the old town, this grassy park boasts magnificent views of the city. It's the perfect spot to spread out a picnic lunch, soak up the sun and take in the unobstructed 360-degree views.

The park's centerpiece is the **Centro Cultural Itchimbia** (Map p86; ☎ 295-0272), a large glass-and-iron building, modeled after the city's original Mercado Santa Clara, that hosts regular art exhibits and cultural events. The park has cycling paths and walking paths too.

Buses signed 'Pintado' go here from the Centro Histórico, or you can walk up (east) Elizalde, from where signed stairways lead to the park.

TelefériQo

For spectacular views over Quito's mountainous landscape, hop aboard the **telefériQo** (Map p82; ☎ 250-0900; Av Occidental near Av La Gasca; adult/express lane $4/7; 🕑 9.45am-9pm Mon-Thu, 9am-midnight Fri & Sat), a multimillion-dollar sky tram that takes passengers on a 2.5km ride up the flanks of Volcán Pichincha to the top of Cruz Loma. Once you're at the top (a mere 4100m), you can hike to the summit of Rucu Pichincha (4680m), an approximately three-hour hike for fit walkers; see p93 and p118. Don't attempt the hike to Rucu Pichincha until you've acclimatized in Quito for a couple days.

To get here, either take a taxi (about $3 from the Mariscal) or take one of the telefériQo shuttles ($1), which depart about every 30 minutes from the Trole's Estación Norte stop, the Río Coca stop of the Ecovía line and Plaza La Marín parking area in the old town.

On weekends the wait can be long and tedious; either pay the $7 express-line fee, or (even better) come on a weekday. Try to visit in the morning, when the views here are best; the clouds usually roll in by noon.

OLD TOWN

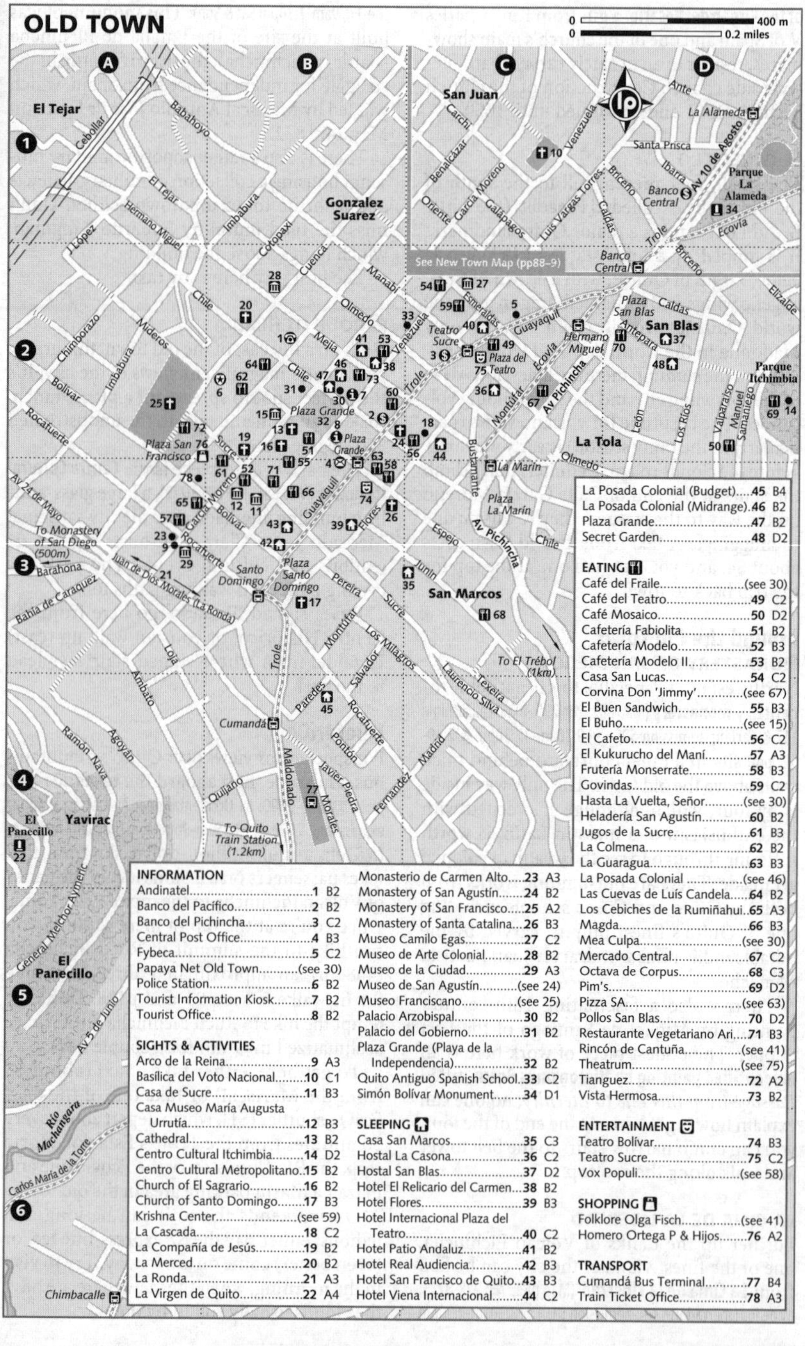

INFORMATION
- Andinatel.......................1 B2
- Banco del Pacífico.......................2 B2
- Banco del Pichincha.......................3 C2
- Central Post Office.......................4 B3
- Fybeca.......................5 C2
- Papaya Net Old Town.......................(see 30)
- Police Station.......................6 B2
- Tourist Information Kiosk.......................7 B2
- Tourist Office.......................8 B2

SIGHTS & ACTIVITIES
- Arco de la Reina.......................9 A3
- Basílica del Voto Nacional.......................10 C1
- Casa de Sucre.......................11 B3
- Casa Museo María Augusta Urrutia.......................12 B3
- Cathedral.......................13 B2
- Centro Cultural Itchimbia.......................14 D2
- Centro Cultural Metropolitano.......................15 B2
- Church of El Sagrario.......................16 B2
- Church of Santo Domingo.......................17 B3
- Krishna Center.......................(see 59)
- La Cascada.......................18 C2
- La Compañía de Jesús.......................19 B2
- La Merced.......................20 B2
- La Ronda.......................21 A3
- La Virgen de Quito.......................22 A4
- Monasterio de Carmen Alto.......................23 A3
- Monastery of San Agustín.......................24 B2
- Monastery of San Francisco.......................25 A2
- Monastery of Santa Catalina.......................26 B3
- Museo Camilo Egas.......................27 C2
- Museo de Arte Colonial.......................28 B2
- Museo de la Ciudad.......................29 A3
- Museo de San Agustín.......................(see 24)
- Museo Franciscano.......................(see 25)
- Palacio Arzobispal.......................30 B2
- Palacio del Gobierno.......................31 B2
- Plaza Grande (Playa de la Independencia).......................32 B2
- Quito Antiguo Spanish School.......................33 C2
- Simón Bolívar Monument.......................34 D1

SLEEPING
- Casa San Marcos.......................35 C3
- Hostal La Casona.......................36 C2
- Hostal San Blas.......................37 D2
- Hotel El Relicario del Carmen.......................38 B2
- Hotel Flores.......................39 B3
- Hotel Internacional Plaza del Teatro.......................40 C2
- Hotel Patio Andaluz.......................41 B2
- Hotel Real Audiencia.......................42 B3
- Hotel San Francisco de Quito.......................43 B3
- Hotel Viena Internacional.......................44 C2
- La Posada Colonial (Budget).......................45 B4
- La Posada Colonial (Midrange).......................46 B2
- Plaza Grande.......................47 B2
- Secret Garden.......................48 D2

EATING
- Café del Fraile.......................(see 30)
- Café del Teatro.......................49 C2
- Café Mosaico.......................50 D2
- Cafetería Fabiolita.......................51 B2
- Cafetería Modelo.......................52 B3
- Cafetería Modelo II.......................53 B2
- Casa San Lucas.......................54 C2
- Corvina Don 'Jimmy'.......................(see 67)
- El Buen Sandwich.......................55 B3
- El Buho.......................(see 15)
- El Cafeto.......................56 C2
- El Kukurucho del Maní.......................57 A3
- Frutería Monserrate.......................58 B3
- Govindas.......................59 C2
- Hasta La Vuelta, Señor.......................(see 30)
- Heladería San Agustín.......................60 B2
- Jugos de la Sucre.......................61 B3
- La Colmena.......................62 B2
- La Guaragua.......................63 B3
- La Posada Colonial.......................(see 46)
- Las Cuevas de Luís Candela.......................64 B2
- Los Cebiches de la Rumiñahui.......................65 A3
- Magda.......................66 B3
- Mea Culpa.......................(see 30)
- Mercado Central.......................67 C2
- Octava de Corpus.......................68 C3
- Pim's.......................69 D2
- Pizza SA.......................(see 63)
- Pollos San Blas.......................70 D2
- Restaurante Vegetariano Ari.......................71 B3
- Rincón de Cantuña.......................(see 41)
- Theatrum.......................(see 75)
- Tianguez.......................72 A2
- Vista Hermosa.......................73 B2

ENTERTAINMENT
- Teatro Bolívar.......................74 B3
- Teatro Sucre.......................75 C2
- Vox Populi.......................(see 58)

SHOPPING
- Folklore Olga Fisch.......................(see 41)
- Homero Ortega P & Hijos.......................76 A2

TRANSPORT
- Cumandá Bus Terminal.......................77 B4
- Train Ticket Office.......................78 A3

New Town

PARQUES LA ALAMEDA & EL EJIDO

From the northeast edge of the old town, the long, triangular **Parque La Alameda** begins its grassy crawl toward the new town. At the southern apex of the park stands the **Simón Bolívar monument**; toward the middle of the park are **statues** of the members of the 1736–44 French Académie des Sciences expedition that surveyed Ecuador and made the equatorial measurements that gave rise to the metric system.

Nearby, the **Quito Observatory** (Map pp88-9; ☎ 257-0765; admission $1; 🕑 8am-noon & 3-5pm Mon-Fri, 8am-noon Sat), opened by President García Moreno in 1864, is the oldest observatory on the continent. It opens for stargazing on only the clearest nights – call ahead to confirm if the weather looks promising.

Northeast of La Alameda, the pleasant, tree-filled **Parque El Ejido** is the biggest park in downtown Quito, a popular spot for impromptu games of soccer and volleyball. The north end of the park teems with activity on weekends, when **open-air art shows** are held along Avenida Patria. Just inside the north end of the park, artisans and crafts vendors set up stalls and turn the sidewalks into Quito's largest handicrafts market.

Between Parque Alameda and Parque El Ejido is the **legislative palace** (Map pp88-9; Montalvo near Av 6 de Diciembre), the equivalent of the houses of parliament or congress. A huge frieze depicting the history of Ecuador spans the north side of the building.

CASA DE LA CULTURA ECUATORIANA

Located across from Parque El Ejido, this circular, glass-plated, landmark building houses a movie theater, an auditorium and one of the country's most important museums, the **Museo del Banco Central** (Map pp88-9; ☎ 222-3258; cnr Av Patria & Av 12 de Octubre; admission $2; 🕑 9am-5pm Tue-Fri, 10am-4pm Sat & Sun). It showcases the country's largest collection of Ecuadorian art, from beautifully displayed pre-Hispanic and colonial religious art to 20th-century paintings and sculpture.

A walk through the museum usually begins in the **Sala de Arqueología**, where moody tribal music drones over a marvelous display of more than 1000 ceramic pieces dating from 12,000 BC to AD 1534. The mazelike exhibit begins with arrowheads from Ecuador's first nomadic hunter-gatherers, then continues with the Valdivia culture (Ecuador's first settled agriculturalists) and ends with the Inca. En route are magnificent pieces including 'whistle bottles' from the Chorrea culture, figures showing skull deformation practiced by the Machalilla culture, wild Asian-looking serpent bowls from the Jama-Coaque, ceramic representations of *tzantzas* (shrunken heads), 'coin axes' from the Milagro-Quevedo culture and the famous ceremonial stone chairs of the Manteños.

The second room is the **Sala de Oro** (Gold Room), which, among other magnificent pre-Hispanic gold pieces, displays the radiating, golden sun mask that is the symbol of the Banco Central. Upstairs, the **Sala de Arte Colonial** (Colonial Art Room) showcases masterful works from the Quito School of Art including several pieces by Ecuador's most famous indigenous sculptor Manuel Chili (Caspicara).

Finally, the **Sala de Arte Contemporáneo** (Contemporary Art Room) boasts a large collection of contemporary, modern and 19th-century Ecuadorian art. The exhibits include canvases by some of Ecuador's most famous artists including the likes of Oswaldo Guayasamín, Eduardo Kingman and Camilo Egas.

AVENIDA AMAZONAS

A solitary stone archway at the north end of Parque El Ejido marks the beginning of **Avenida Amazona**. This is modern Quito's showpiece street, rolling as far north as the airport, although the strip with which you're likely to become most familiar lies between Parque El Ejido and the busy Avenida Cristóbal Colón. It's the main artery of the **Mariscal Sucre** area, lined with modern hotels, souvenir stores, travel agencies, banks and restaurants. There's plenty of room for pedestrians, and the outdoor restaurants near the intersection of Vicente Ramón Roca are favorite spots to enjoy espresso, newspapers, sandwiches and ice-cold Pilsener, Ecuador's national beer.

MARISCAL SUCRE & AROUND

'Gringolandia,' as some refer to the Mariscal Sucre, is the epicenter of Quito's tourist infrastructure, with scores of tour agencies, guesthouses, restaurants and souvenir shops. Two worthwhile museums are located just south of the Mariscal.

NEW TOWN

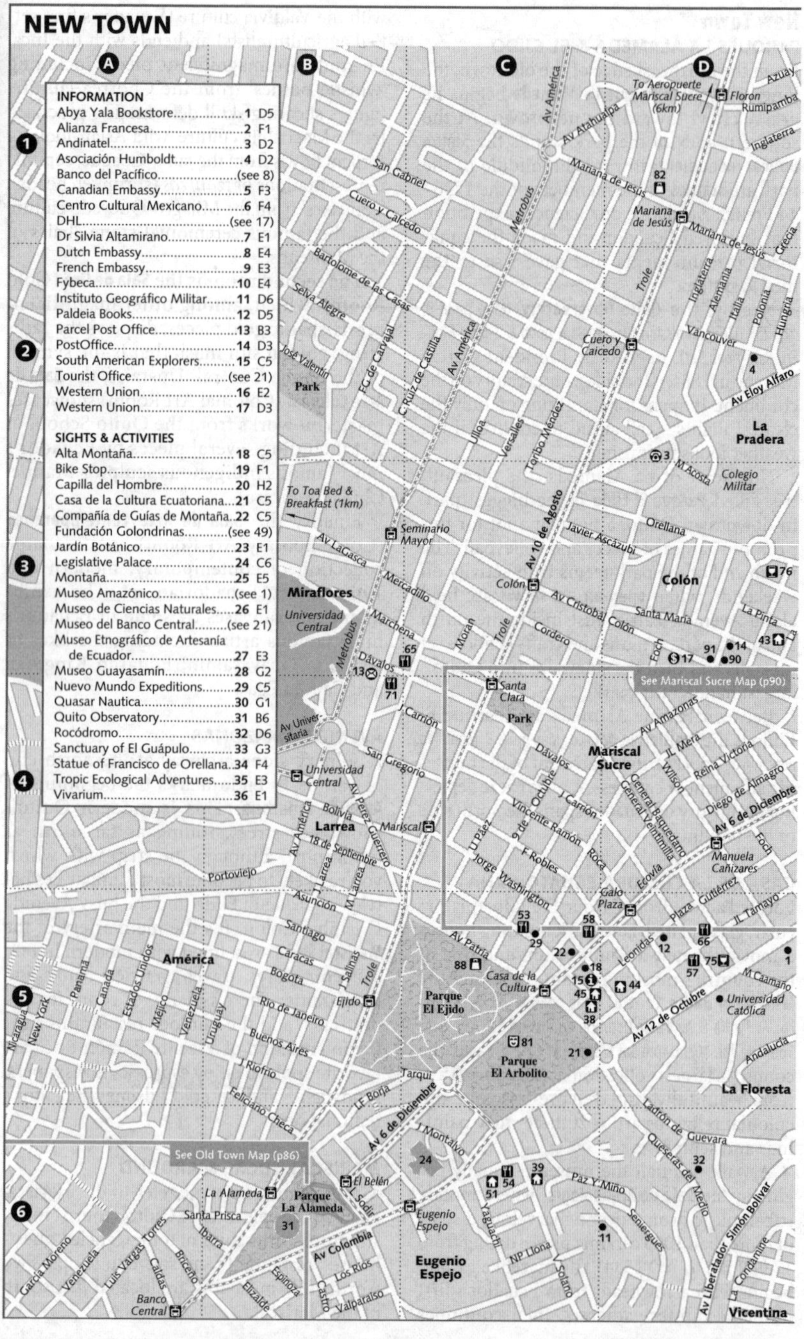
INFORMATION
Abya Yala Bookstore 1 D5
Alianza Francesa 2 F1
Andinatel 3 D2
Asociación Humboldt 4 D2
Banco del Pacífico (see 8)
Canadian Embassy 5 F3
Centro Cultural Mexicano 6 F4
DHL (see 17)
Dr Silvia Altamirano 7 E1
Dutch Embassy 8 E4
French Embassy 9 E3
Fybeca 10 E4
Instituto Geográfico Militar 11 D6
Paldeia Books 12 D5
Parcel Post Office 13 B3
PostOffice 14 D3
South American Explorers 15 C5
Tourist Office (see 21)
Western Union 16 E2
Western Union 17 D3
SIGHTS & ACTIVITIES
Alta Montaña 18 C5
Bike Stop 19 F1
Capilla del Hombre 20 H2
Casa de la Cultura Ecuatoriana 21 C5
Compañía de Guías de Montaña 22 C5
Fundación Golondrinas (see 49)
Jardín Botánico 23 E1
Legislative Palace 24 C6
Montaña 25 E5
Museo Amazónico (see 1)
Museo de Ciencias Naturales 26 E1
Museo del Banco Central (see 21)
Museo Etnográfico de Artesanía de Ecuador 27 E3
Museo Guayasamín 28 G2
Nuevo Mundo Expeditions 29 C5
Quasar Nautica 30 G1
Quito Observatory 31 B6
Rocódromo 32 D6
Sanctuary of El Guápulo 33 G3
Statue of Francisco de Orellana 34 F4
Tropic Ecological Adventures 35 E3
Vivarium 36 E1
To Aeropuerte Mariscal Sucre (6km)
To Toa Bed & Breakfast (1km)
See Mariscal Sucre Map (p90)
See Old Town Map (p86)
La Pradera
Colegio Militar
Colón
Miraflores
Universidad Central
Mariscal Sucre
Larrea
América
Parque El Ejido
Parque El Arbolito
La Floresta
Parque La Alameda
Eugenio Espejo
Vicentina
Av 10 de Agosto
Av América
Av 6 de Diciembre
Av 12 de Octubre
Av Patria
Av Eloy Alfaro
Av Amazonas
Av Colombia
Av Libertador Simón Bolívar

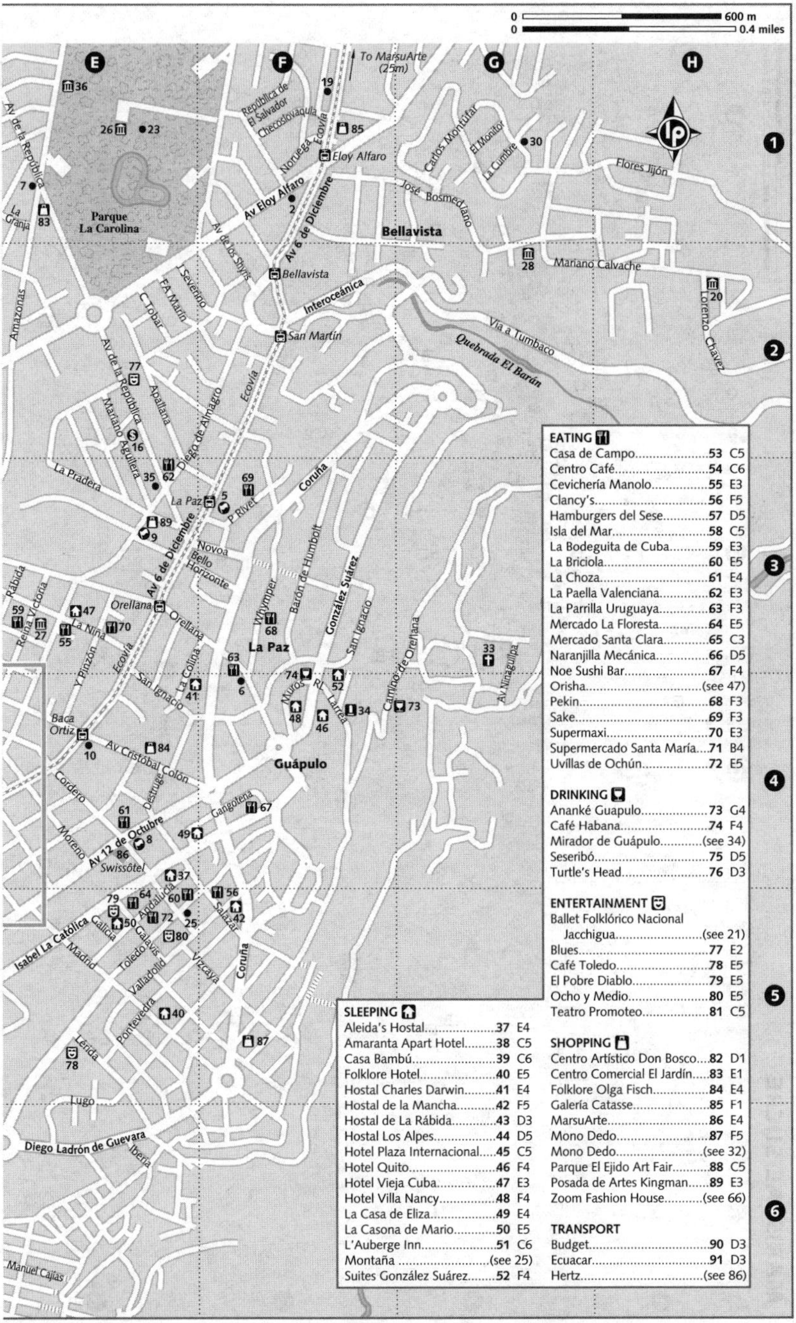

EATING

Casa de Campo......53 C5
Centro Café......54 C6
Cevichería Manolo......55 E3
Clancy's......56 F5
Hamburgers del Sese......57 D5
Isla del Mar......58 C5
La Bodeguita de Cuba......59 E3
La Briciola......60 E5
La Choza......61 E4
La Paella Valenciana......62 E3
La Parrilla Uruguaya......63 F3
Mercado La Floresta......64 E5
Mercado Santa Clara......65 C3
Naranjilla Mecánica......66 D5
Noe Sushi Bar......67 F4
Orisha......(see 47)
Pekin......68 F3
Sake......69 F3
Supermaxi......70 E3
Supermercado Santa María......71 B4
Uvíllas de Ochún......72 E5

DRINKING

Ananké Guapulo......73 G4
Café Habana......74 F4
Mirador de Guápulo......(see 34)
Seseribó......75 D5
Turtle's Head......76 D3

ENTERTAINMENT

Ballet Folklórico Nacional Jacchigua......(see 21)
Blues......77 E2
Café Toledo......78 E5
El Pobre Diablo......79 E5
Ocho y Medio......80 E5
Teatro Promoteo......81 C5

SHOPPING

Centro Artístico Don Bosco......82 D1
Centro Comercial El Jardín......83 E1
Folklore Olga Fisch......84 E4
Galería Catasse......85 F1
MarsuArte......86 E4
Mono Dedo......87 F5
Mono Dedo......(see 32)
Parque El Ejido Art Fair......88 C5
Posada de Artes Kingman......89 E3
Zoom Fashion House......(see 66)

TRANSPORT

Budget......90 D3
Ecuacar......91 D3
Hertz......(see 86)

SLEEPING

Aleida's Hostal......37 E4
Amaranta Apart Hotel......38 C5
Casa Bambú......39 C6
Folklore Hotel......40 E5
Hostal Charles Darwin......41 E4
Hostal de la Mancha......42 F5
Hostal de La Rábida......43 D3
Hostal Los Alpes......44 D5
Hotel Plaza Internacional......45 C5
Hotel Quito......46 F4
Hotel Vieja Cuba......47 E3
Hotel Villa Nancy......48 F4
La Casa de Eliza......49 E4
La Casona de Mario......50 E5
L'Auberge Inn......51 C6
Montaña......(see 25)
Suites González Suárez......52 F4

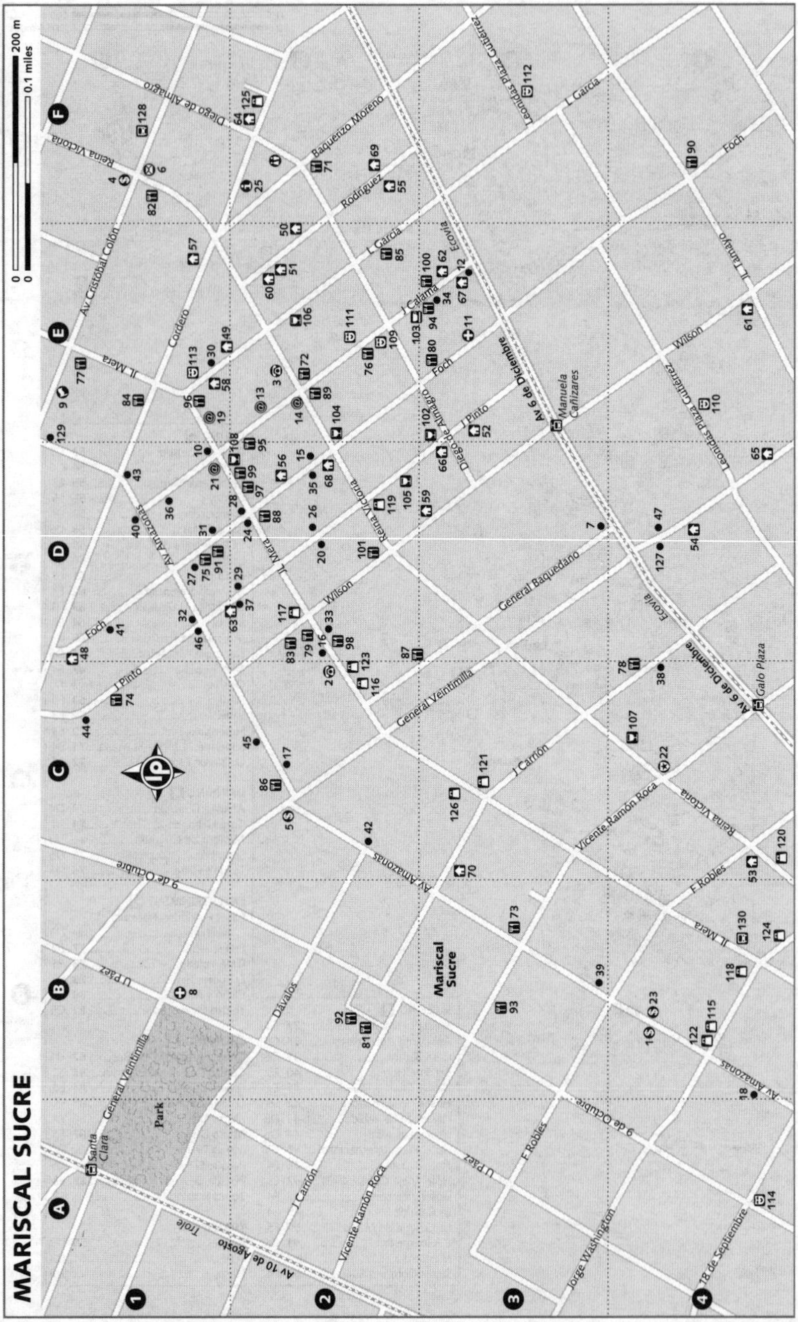
MARISCAL SUCRE
0 200 m
0 0.1 miles
Park
Mariscal Sucre
Santa Clara
Manuela Cañizares
Galo Plaza
Av 10 de Agosto
Trole
General Veintimilla
U Páez
9 de Octubre
Av Amazonas
JL Mera
Reina Victoria
Diego de Almagro
Leonidas Plaza Gutiérrez
Av 6 de Diciembre
Ecovía
Av Cristóbal Colón
Cordero
Baquerizo Moreno
Rodríguez
L García
J Calama
Foch
J Pinto
Wilson
General Baquedano
J Carrión
Vicente Ramón Roca
F Robles
Dávalos
Jorge Washington
18 de Septiembre
JL Tamayo

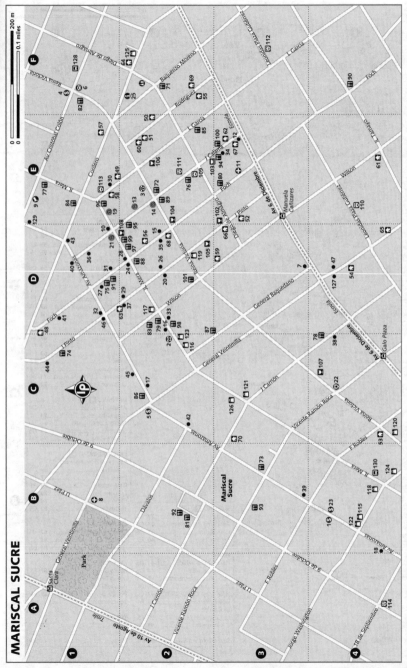

INFORMATION
- American Express ... 1 B4
- Andinatel ... 2 C2
- Andinatel ... 3 E2
- Banco de Guayaquil ... 4 F1
- Banco de Guayaquil ... 5 C2
- Branch Post Office ... 6 F1
- Casa Cultural Afro-Ecuatoriano ... 7 D3
- Clínica Pichincha ... 8 B1
- Colombian Embassy ... 9 E1
- Confederate Books ... 10 D1
- Dr John Rosenberg ... 11 E3
- Ecuadorian Tours ... (see 1)
- English Bookstore ... 12 E3
- Friends Web Café ... 13 E2
- La Sala ... 14 E2
- Lavandería ... 15 D2
- Libri Mundi ... 16 D2
- Libro Express ... 17 C2
- Metropolitan Touring ... 18 B4
- Monkeys ... 19 E1
- Opera de Jabón ... 20 D2
- Papaya Net ... 21 D1
- Police Station ... 22 C4
- Producambios ... 23 B4
- Sun City Laundry ... 24 D2
- Tourist Office ... 25 F2
- Wash & Go ... 26 D2

SIGHTS & ACTIVITIES
- Academia Salsa & Merengue ... 27 D1
- Biking Dutchman ... 28 D2
- Dracaena ... 29 D2
- Ecole Idiomas ... 30 E1
- Enchanted Expeditions ... 31 D1
- Eos Ecuador ... 32 D1
- Green Planet ... 33 D2
- Guayasamín Spanish School ... 34 E3
- Gulliver ... (see 108)
- Happy Gringo ... 35 D2
- Moggely Climbing ... 36 D1
- Neotropic Turis ... 37 D2
- Pichincha Spanish School ... 38 C4
- Rainforestur ... 39 B3
- Ritmo Tropical ... 40 D1
- River People ... (see 31)
- Safari Tours ... 41 D1
- San Francisco Language Institute ... 42 C2
- Sangay Touring ... 43 D1
- Sierra Nevada Expeditions ... 44 C1
- Surtrek ... 45 C2
- World Bike ... 46 D1
- Yacu Amu Rafting/Ríos Ecuador ... (see 31)
- Yanapuma Language School ... 47 D4

SLEEPING
- Albergue El Taxo ... 48 D1
- Alberto's House ... 49 E1
- Antinea Apart Hotel ... 50 E2
- Backpacker's Inn ... 51 E2
- Blue House ... 52 E3
- Café Cultura ... 53 C4
- Casa Helbling ... 54 D4
- Casa Kanela ... 55 F2
- Crossroads ... 56 D2
- El Cafecito ... 57 E1
- El Centro del Mundo ... 58 E1
- El Vagabundo ... 59 D3
- Hostal El Arupo ... 60 E2
- Hostal Fuente de Piedra ... 61 E4
- Hostal Jardín del Sol ... 62 E3
- Hostal Nassau ... 63 D2
- Hotel Sebastián ... 64 F2
- Hotel Sierra Madre ... 65 D4
- Huaukí ... 66 D3
- La Casa Sol ... 67 E3
- Nü House ... 68 D2
- Posada del Maple ... 69 F2
- Sakti ... 70 C3

EATING
- Aladdin's ... 71 F2
- Boca del Lobo ... 72 E2
- Café Amazonas ... 73 B3
- Café Colibri ... 74 C1
- Café Mango Tree ... 75 D1
- Canoa Manabita ... 76 E2
- Chandani Tandoori ... 77 E1
- Chifa Mayflower ... 78 C4
- El Cafecito ... (see 57)
- El Español ... 79 D2
- El Maple ... 80 E3
- El Puerto Callao ... 81 B2
- Hassan's Café ... 82 F1
- Kallari ... 83 D2
- La Canoa ... 84 E1
- La Crêperie ... 85 E2
- Las Redes ... 86 C2
- Le Arcate ... 87 D2
- Magic Bean ... 88 D2
- Mama Clorinda ... 89 E2
- Mare Nostrum ... 90 F4
- Red Hot Chili Peppers ... 91 D1
- Restaurante Manantial ... 92 B2
- Rincón de Francia ... 93 B3
- Ristorante Pizzeria Milano ... 94 E3
- Siam ... 95 D2
- Su Cebiche ... 96 E1
- Texas Ranch ... 97 D2
- Tio Billy's ... 98 D2
- Tomato ... 99 D2
- Uncle Ho's ... 100 E3
- Yanuna ... 101 D2

DRINKING
- Ananké ... 102 E3
- Coffee & Toffee ... 103 E2
- Coffee Tree ... 104 E2
- Finn McCool's ... 105 D2
- Kilkenny ... 106 E2
- La Reina Victoria ... 107 C4
- Zócalo ... 108 D2

ENTERTAINMENT
- Bungalow 6 ... 109 E2
- Café Libro ... 110 E4
- El Aguijón ... 111 E2
- Humanizarte ... 112 F3
- Mayo 68 ... 113 E1
- Patio de Comedías ... 114 A4

SHOPPING
- Ag ... (see 121)
- Arte Sacra ... 115 B4
- Centro Artesanal ... 116 C2
- Cholo Machine ... 117 D2
- El Aborigen ... 118 B4
- Explorer ... 119 D2
- Galería Beltrán ... 120 C4
- Galería Latina ... (see 16)
- La Bodega ... 121 C3
- Latino Americana ... 122 B4
- Mele Sport ... 123 C2
- Mercado Artesanal La Mariscal ... 124 B4
- Productos Andinos ... 125 F2
- Rosy Revelo ... 126 C3

TRANSPORT
- Localiza ... 127 D4
- Panamericana ... 128 F1
- TAME ... 129 E1
- Transportes Ecuador ... 130 B4

Above Abya Yala bookstore (p77), the **Museo Amazónico** (☎ 256-2663; Av 12 de Octubre 1436; admission $2; 9am-12:30pm & 2-5.30pm Mon-Fri) is run by the Salesian Mission and houses an impressive display of indigenous artifacts collected by the missionaries in the Oriente. It's not huge, but it's an interesting exhibit, especially if you plan to head to the jungle.

Just north of the Mariscal, the small but worthwhile **Museo Etnográfico de Artesanía de Ecuador** (Map pp88-9; ☎ 223-0609; www.sinchisacha.org; Reina Victoria N26-166 & La Niña; admission $3; 9.30am-5:30pm Mon-Sat, 10.30am-4.30pm Sun) exhibits the artwork, clothing and utensils of Ecuador's indigenous people, with special emphasis on the peoples of the Oriente. It's run by the outstanding Fundación Sinchi Sacha (see p103 and p110), and there's a pleasant café on-site.

PARQUE LA CAROLINA

North of the Mariscal lies the giant **Parque La Carolina**. On weekends it fills with families who come out for paddleboats, soccer and volleyball games, and exercise along the bike paths.

The park's newest addition is the **Jardín Botánico** (Map pp88-9; ☎ 246-3197; admission $3.50; 9am-5pm). With more than 300 plant and tree species from around Ecuador and an outstanding *orquideario* (orchid greenhouse) featuring nearly 1000 orchid species, it's well worth the admission price. An ethno-botanical garden is also in the works.

To further acquaint yourself with Ecuador's flora and fauna, head next door to the curious natural-history museum, the **Museo de Ciencias Naturales** (Map pp88-9; ☎ 244-9824; Rumipamba s/n, Parque La Carolina; admission $2; 8:30am-1pm & 1:45-4:30pm Mon-Fri). Contemplating the thousands of dead insects and arachnids on display is a good way to rile your nerves before a trip to the Oriente.

Nearby, you can provide further fodder for your jungle fears with a visit to the **Vivarium** (Map pp88-9; ☎ 227-1799; www.vivarium.org.ec, in Spanish; Av Amazonas 3008 at Rumipamba; admission $2.50; 9:30am-5:30pm Tue-Sun), home to 87 live reptiles and amphibians including poisonous snakes, boa constrictors, iguanas, turtles, frogs and tortoises. It's a herpetological research and education center, and the staff periodically gives close demonstrations with one of the snakes.

MUSEO GUAYASAMÍN & THE CAPILLA DEL HOMBRE

In the former home of world-famous painter Oswaldo Guayasamín (1919–99), this wonderful **museum** (Map pp88-9; ☎ 246-5265; Bosmediano 543; admission $2; 10am-5pm Mon-Fri) houses the most complete collection of his work. Guayasamín was also an avid collector, and the museum displays his outstanding collection of more than 4500 pre-Colombian ceramic, bone and metal pieces from throughout Ecuador. The pieces are arranged by theme – bowls, fertility figurines, burial masks etc – rather than by era or cultural group, and the result is one of the most beautifully displayed archaeological collections in the country.

The museum also houses Guayasamín's collection of religious art including a crucifix by the famous indigenous carver Caspicara, and a tiny crucifix with a pendulum heart inside that ticks against the chest cavity when touched (or breathed on, according to the caretaker).

If you're moved to take something home with you, there's a jewelry store, a T-shirt store and a gallery with original prints.

A few blocks away stands one of the most important works of art in South America, Guayasamín's **Capilla del Hombre** (Chapel of Man; Map pp88-9; ☎ 244-6455; www.guayasamin.com; Mariano Calvache at Lorenzo Chávez; admission $3, with purchase of entry to Museo Guayasamín $2; 10am-5pm Tue-Sun). The fruit of Guayasamín's greatest vision, this giant monument-cum-museum is a tribute to humankind, to the suffering of Latin America's indigenous poor and to the undying hope for something better. It's a moving place and the tours (in English, French and Spanish, included in the price) are highly recommended. They usually leave upon request during opening hours.

Mirroring the Inca cultural reverence of the number 'three,' the chapel is broken architecturally and thematically into three: there are three levels to the chapel, the windows are 3 sq meters and each tile around the *capilla* is 30 sq cm. The exhibits adhere to precolonial, colonial and contemporary themes and follow the three stages of Guayasamín's career.

The collection itself, which has numerous murals, is superb. One of the most impressive works is *Los Mutilados,* a meditation on the Spanish Civil War; Guayasamín studied Da Vinci for eight years and did 470 sketches to get it right.

The other masterwork is the *El condor y el toro* mural, which represents the forced fight between a condor and a bull during *Yaguar raimi* (blood festival). During the festival, a condor was tied to the bull's neck – if the condor won, it prophesied a good harvest.

The museum and chapel are in the residential district of Bellavista, northeast of downtown. You can walk uphill, or take a bus along Avenida 6 de Diciembre to Avenida Eloy Alfaro and then a Bellavista bus up the hill. A taxi costs about $2.

Guápulo

If you follow Avenida 12 de Octubre up the hill from the Mariscal, you'll reach the Hotel Quito at the top. Behind the hotel, stairs lead steeply down the other side of the hill to the historic neighborhood of Guápulo. The views all the way down here are magnificent, ramshackle houses stand interspersed among colonial whitewashed homes with terra-cotta-tile roofs, and the odd Bohemian café makes for a welcome break.

At the bottom of the hill stands the neighborhood's centerpiece, the **Sanctuary of El Guápulo** (Map pp88-9; 9am-6pm, sometimes closed for lunch), a beautiful church built between 1644 and 1693. It has an excellent collection of Quito School art and sculpture, and a stunning 18th-century pulpit carved by master wood-carver Juan Bautista Menacho.

The best views of Guápulo are from the lookout behind the Hotel Quito, next to the **statue of Francisco de Orellana** (Map pp88-9; Calle Larrea) near González Suárez. The statue depicts Francisco de Orellana looking down into the valley, marking the beginning of his epic journey from Quito to the Atlantic – the first descent of the Amazon by a European.

ACTIVITIES

Those seeking a bit more adventure can spend the day rock climbing, hiking and cycling – all within city limits.

Climbing

Climbers can get a serious fix at the **Rocódromo** (Map pp88-9; ☎ 250-8463; Queseras del Medio s/n; admission $2; 8am-8pm Mon-Fri, to 6pm Sat & Sun), a 25m-high climbing facility across from the Estadio Rumiñahui. There are more than a dozen routes (some as hard as class 5.12, or 7C on the French scale) on the three main walls, a four-face bouldering structure and a rock building. Shoes, ropes, harnesses, chalk bags and carabiners are all available for rental. If you rent equipment, the staff will belay you.

The Rocódromo is walking distance from the Mariscal.

Montaña (Map pp88-9; ☎ 2238-954; mountain_refugeecuador@yahoo.com; Cordero E12-141 at Toledo; 10am-10pm Mon-Wed, to midnight Thu & Fri, 3-10pm Sat) is a meeting place for climbers from Quito. It's a useful source of nonbiased information (no one's trying to sell anything but a cup of coffee) and a good place to meet local climbers. Trips are sometimes arranged and everyone's included. The owner sets up slide shows or chats on weekend evenings.

For information on climbing operators, see p79.

Cycling

Every other Sunday, the entire length of Avenida Amazonas and most of the old town closes to cars, as loads of pedalers take to the street for the bimonthly **ciclopaseo**. The entire ride (some 10km), which you can cycle part or all of, stretches from the airport, through the old town and into the southern reaches of Quito. Visit www.ciclopolis.ec for more info (in Spanish).

Local mountain-biking companies rent bikes and offer excellent tours including one-day rides through the *páramo* (Andean grasslands) of Parque Nacional Cotopaxi, as well as down-hill descents, trips incorporating a stop at Papallacta hot springs, and two-day trips to Cotopaxi and Chimborazo and to Cotopaxi and Laguna Quilotoa. Single-day trips cost about $50, not including park-entrance fees. Compare prices and trips at the following operators: **Biking Dutchman** (Map p90; ☎ 256-8323; www.bikingdutchman.com; Foch 714 at Mera) is Ecuador's pioneer mountain-biking operator, has good bikes and guides and an outstanding reputation, while **Arie's Bike Company** (☎ 238-0802; www.ariesbikecompany.com) has received great reports from readers.

For high-quality parts and bikes by makers including KHS, Marin and Manitou, stop by **Bike Stop** (Map pp88-9; ☎ 225-5404; www.bikestopecuador.com, in Spanish; Av 6 de Diciembre N34-55 at Checoslovaquia; 10am-7pm Mon-Fri, 9:30am-1:30pm Sat). It's also a good source of information.

Hiking

Quito's new teleféricQo (p85) takes passengers up to Cruz Loma (4100m), from where you can hike to the top of jagged Rucu Pichincha (about 4680m). Beyond the rise of Cruz Loma, and past a barbed-wire fence that no one seems to pay any attention to, trails lead to Rucu Pichincha – it's approximately three hours to the top, and some scrambling is required. Don't attempt this hike if you've just arrived in Quito – allow a couple of days to acclimatize.

Before the teleféricQo went in, climbing Rucu Pichincha was dangerous due to armed robberies. There have been attacks in recent years, and it's well worth assessing the security situation from local authorities, including SAE (p79), before heading out.

Soaking

After a long day's hike, **La Cascada** (Map p86; ☎ 295-8200; Flores 41-47; admission $6; 10am-8pm) may ease your weary limbs. The tiny bathhouse has a small pool, a sauna and a hot tub.

Yoga

For Hatha yoga classes, stop by the friendly **Krishna center** (Map p86; ☎ 296-6844; Esmeraldas 853; per class/month $5/40), with the excellent Govindas restaurant (p104) on-site. Classes are currently held on Monday, Wednesday and Friday from 5 to 6pm. Inquire about yoga tours and holistic retreats.

Other excellent places to take a class:

Centro Alternativo de Arte Shakti (Rafael Larrea 1050 y Camino de Orellana; per class $5) Located in Guápulo, behind the Hotel Quito.

Yoga Studio Sadhana (☎ 290-7606; Whymper 31-128 y Paul Rivet Quito; per class $15)

OLD TOWN WALKING TOUR

This meandering 3.5km walk takes in some of the historic sights of the old town before moving north through various green spaces into the new town, leaving you on the edge of the Mariscal. Weekdays are the liveliest time to wander the streets. You might consider timing your visit to catch the changing of the guards on the Plaza Grande, currently held on Monday around 11am. While Sunday is a pleasant day to stroll the old town, which is then closed to traffic, it can be unsafe to wander through the new town, because it's deserted.

The photogenic **Plaza Grande** (**1**; p80) is a good starting point. After checking out the **Palacio del Gobierno** (**2**; p80) and the **cathedral** (**3**; p80), continue southwest on García Moreno and turn right on Sucre to see **La Compañía de Jesús** (**4**; p83). From here, walk one block northwest along Sucre to the impressive **Plaza and Monastery of San Francisco** (**5**; p84).

From the plaza, backtrack to García Moreno and then head southwest (right) for three blocks, under the arch at Rocafuerte, to the **Museo de la Ciudad** (**6**; p84). If you continue past the museum on García Moreno, you'll hit the historic street Juan de Dios Morales, also known as **La Ronda** (**7**; p83), with colonial balconied houses that are some of Quito's oldest. From La Ronda, walk up to Calle Guayaquil and turn northeast (left), and you'll pass the **Church and Plaza of Santo Domingo** (**8**; p84) on your right.

From the Plaza Santo Domingo, head north along Calle Flores to the attractive Plaza del Teatro. Here, you can stop for a drink or a snack at an outdoor table of the nicely positioned **Café del Teatro** (**9**; p103). From here, walk north to Calle Esmeraldas and turn left, then turn right at Venezuela and continue north to the looming **Basílica del Voto Nacional** (**10**; p81). Climb to the top of the clock tower for superb views over the old town (daredevils can opt for the ascent up the bell tower). From the church, walk east along Calle Caldas to busy Calle Guayaquil. Have a glimpse of the pretty **Plaza San Blas (11)** before continuing on to the impressive **Simón Bolívar monument** (**12**; p87) inside the **Parque La Alameda** (**13**; p87). Just ahead, you'll spot the **Quito Observatory** (**14**; p87).

> **WALK FACTS**
> **Start:** Plaza Grande
> **End:** Avenida Amazonas
> **Distance:** 3.5km
> **Duration:** Four hours

As you leave the park, continue north on Avenida 6 de Diciembre. After three blocks, you'll pass the modern **legislative palace** (Legislative Congress Building; **15**; p87) on your right. Continuing on Avenida 6 de Diciembre takes you past the popular **Parque El Ejido** (**16**; p87) on your left, and the huge, circular, mirror-walled **Casa de la Cultura Ecuatoriana** (**17**; p87) on your right.

Turn left past the Casa de la Cultura and walk three blocks along Avenida Patria, with Parque El Ejido to your left, until you reach the small, stone arch marking the beginning of Quito's most famous modern street, **Avenida Amazonas (18)**. From here, it's a short stroll to many excellent eateries in the Mariscal (p104).

COURSES

Dance

Learn to dance salsa, or you'll spend a lot of time shoegazing anytime you hit one of Ecuador's *salsotecas* (salsa clubs). Most schools also offer merengue (a ballroom dance originating from Haiti), *cumbia* (a dance originally from Colombia, similar to salsa) and other Latin American dances.

The following schools are excellent:

Academia Salsa & Merengue (Map p90; ☎ 222-0427; Foch E4-256; 🕒 10am-8pm Mon-Fri) Run by Sylvia Garcia, a pro dancer with 20 years experience, this place offers private/group (per hour $6/5) lessons in a wide variety of styles.

Casa Cultural Afro-Ecuatoriano (p77) Offers salsa and other classes for $5/45 (per hour/12 classes).

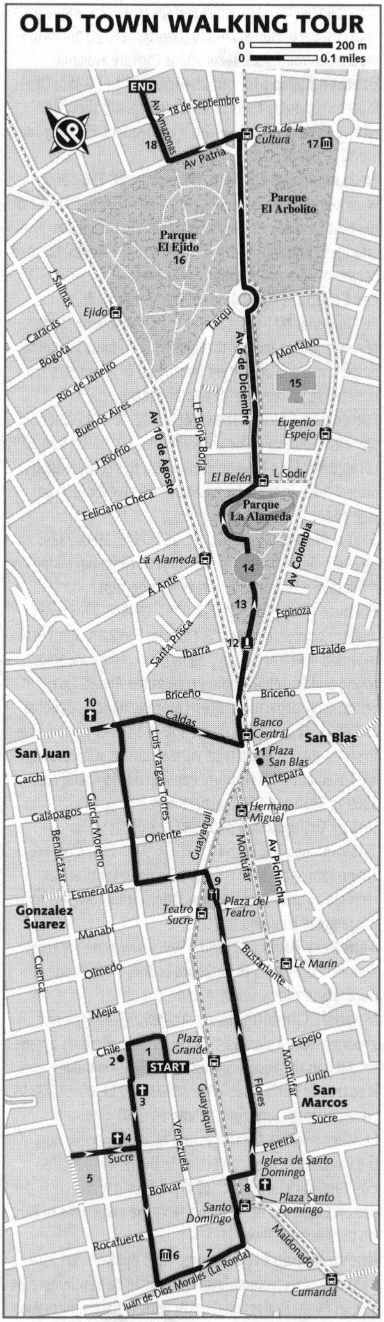

Ritmo Tropical (Map p90; ☎ 255 7094; ritmotropical5@hotmail.com; Av Amazonas N24-155 at Calama; 🕑 9am-8pm Mon-Fri) Lessons cost $5/4.50 per hour (private/group). Offers capoeira too.

Language

Studying Spanish is the perfect excuse for a prolonged stay in Quito. There are more than 80 Spanish schools, many offering private and group classes, homestays with local families, organized activities and volunteer opportunities. Courses can last anywhere from a couple of days to months or more. Visit a few schools before committing. Private lessons cost from $6 to $9 per hour, and some charge an inscription fee (usually around $20).

Ecole Idiomas (Map p90; ☎ 223-1592; info@ecotravel-ecuador.com; García E6-15 near Mera) Volunteer projects available.

Guayasamín Spanish School (Map p90; ☎ 254-4210; www.guayasaminschool.com; Calama E8-54 near Av 6 de Diciembre) Ecuadorian owned, and carries lots of reader recommendations.

Pichincha Spanish School (Map p90; ☎ 222-0478; www.pichinchaspanishschool.com; Carrión 437) This small school receives good reviews, with both morning and evening classes and family stays.

Quito Antiguo Spanish School (Map p86; ☎ 295-7023; Venezuela 1129) The old town's only language school offers a wide range of study options, learning-while-traveling programs, volunteer opportunities and homestays. Approximately 20% of profits are donated to social projects.

San Francisco Language Institute (Map p90; ☎ 252-1306; www.sanfranciscospanish.com; Av Amazonas 662, cnr of Dávalos, 2nd fl, Office 201) Pricey (per hour $9, plus $50 inscription fee) but gets high recommendations.

Yanapuma Language School (Map p90; ☎ 254-6709; www.yanapuma.org; Veintimilla E8-125, 2nd fl) Excellent foundation-run school with opportunities to study while traveling or volunteering, both in Quito and remote villages in the jungle, the coast and the mountains.

QUITO FOR CHILDREN

Keeping the kiddos happy in Quito might require a bit of effort, but there's definitely plenty to do. **Parque La Carolina** (p91) has loads of fun stuff: after taking them to one of the playgrounds or pedaling them around the lake in a paddleboat, walk them through the natural-history museum or (even better) the **Vivarium**, where the snakes, turtles and lizards will surely interest and/or frighten them. Another museum that will likely go over well is the **Museo Amazónico** (p91).

Puppet shows are usually held on Sunday in the Plaza Grande, and occasionally staged at Centro Cultural Itchimbia and other theaters; browse the entertainment listings for the word *'títeres'* (puppets).

There's a sparkling new **theme park**, complete with bumper cars and other rides, at the telefériQo (p85).

Tourist-oriented babysitting services are impossible to find in Quito unless you're staying at one of the city's top-end hotels, in which case the hotel will arrange for a sitter.

TOURS

Conventional travel agencies (p79) offer all sorts of standard tours to places such as Mitad del Mundo, Pululahua, Cayambe rose plantations and more.

City Tours

The Corporación Metropolitana de Turismo offers four different **cultural walks** (paseos culturales; adults/children under 12 $10/5; ⌚ morning & afternoon departures Tue-Sun) in the old town with friendly cop-cum-tourist guides. They depart from the tourist office inside the Palacio Arzobispal.

Outside Quito

Quito is one of the easiest places in Ecuador to arrange a guided tour, be it a Galápagos cruise, climbing trip or jungle tour. Tours, of course, can also be arranged in towns closer to the destination (especially in Riobamba, Baños and Tena), which is sometimes better value. But many find Quito the most convenient. Also see p234 for more information. For mountain-biking tours near Quito, see p93.

Many tour companies that operate in the Oriente or Gálapagos (or anywhere in the country for that matter) have offices in Quito; these are included as follows, but receive more detailed treatment (including prices) in the respective regional chapters.

Alta Montaña (Map pp88-9; ☎ 252-4422, 09-422-9483; Washington 8-20) Owner Ivan Rojas has been on the Ecuadorian mountain scene for years and is an invaluable resource for expeditionists. Courses, guide recommendations and equipment rental are available.

Compañía de Guías de Montaña (Map pp88-9; ☎ 290-1551, 255-6210; www.companiadeguias.com; Washington 425 at Av 6 de Diciembre) A top-notch mountain-climbing operator, with guides who are all Asociación Ecuatoriana de Guías de Montaña (ASEGUIM ; Ecuadorian Association of Mountain Guides) instructors and speak several languages. Trips cost per person $224/330 (two/three days) not including park entrance fees. Tailor-made trips are available.

Dracaena (Map p90; ☎ 254-6590; Pinto E4-453) Offers four- to eight-day tours of Cuyabeno (p240) that have received excellent reviews from our readers. Five-day tours are $200 per person.

Enchanted Expeditions (Map p90; ☎ 256-9960; www.enchantedexpeditions.com; Foch 769) Runs some of the best (and priciest) small boats in the Galápagos. Also arranges excursions to the Oriente and the Andes. Located between Mera and Avenida Amazonas.

Eos Ecuador (☎ 601-3560; www.eosecuador.travel; Av Amazonas N24-66 at Pinto) Eos offers a wide range of conventional and off-the-beaten-path tours including jungle tours and adventure hikes. Half of the profits are donated to sustainable-development projects.

Fundación Golondrinas (Map pp88-9; ☎ 222-6602; www.ecuadorexplorer.com/golondrinas; Católica N24-679) Located inside La Casa de Eliza (p99), this conservation project hikes in the *páramo* and forests west of Tulcán (see p141).

Green Planet (Map p90; ☎ 252-0570; Mera 2384; ⌚ 9am-6pm) Offers a good range of climbing, hiking and mountain-biking trips and river-rafting trips.

Gulliver (Map p90; ☎ 252-9297, 09-946-2265; www.gulliver.com.ec; cnr Mera & Calama; ⌚ 8am-8pm) Well-regarded operator offering hiking, climbing, mountain-biking and horseback-riding trips in the Andes. Excellent prices, daily departures; does Cotopaxi, Ilinizas, Quilotoa and more. Most day trips cost $30 to $45 per person. Five- to seven-day Cotopaxi trips with acclimatization programs are based out of its Hostería PapaGayo (p154) and cost $360 to $450 and $500 respectively.

Happy Gringo (Map p90; ☎ 222-0031; www.happygringo.com; Foch E6-12; ⌚ 9am-7pm Mon-Fri, 10am-4pm Sat & Sun) A fairly new operator that has received numerous recommendations from travelers for its full range of trips and tours.

Kem Pery Tours (☎ 250-5599; www.kempery.com) Kem Pery does trips to Bataburo Lodge, on the edge of Huaorani territory. See also p244.

Moggely Climbing (Map p90; ☎ 255-4984; www.moggely.com; Calama E4-54) Reputable climbing operator, long in the business, uses only ASEGUIM guides.

Neotropic Turis (Map p90; ☎ 252-1212, 09-980-3395; www.neotropicturis.com; J Pinto E4-340) Between Avenida Amazonas and Mera, Neotropic runs the wonderful Cuyabeno Lodge in the Reserva Producción Faunística Cuyabeno (p241). A four-day trip costs per person $200 to $288. Also available are excursions to Peru via the Marañon River.

Nuevo Mundo Expeditions (Map pp88-9; ☎ 250-9431; www.nuevomundotravel.com; 18 de Septiembre E4-161, at Mera) Professional outfit with strong conservation interests, top-end prices and top-end tours and guides. Organizes Galápagos tours, four- to five-day Río Napo cruises aboard its comfy *Manatee Amazon Explorer* (see p244) and Andean hiking and ethnobotanical trips.

Quasar Nautica (Map p82; ☎ 244-6996; www.quasarnautica.com; Brasil 293 near Granda Centeno, Edificio IACA, 2nd fl) Offers expensive but excellent luxury yacht trips in the Galápagos.

Rainforestur (Map p90; ☎ 223-9822; www.rainforestur.com; Av Amazonas 420 near Robles) Offers well-received rafting trips on the Río Pastaza near Baños, and trips to Cuyabeno and elsewhere (see p172). Also offers hiking and indigenous market tours in the Quito area.

River People (Map p90; ☎ 290 6639; www.riverpeopleraftingecuador.com; Foch 746) Family-run, affable and highly professional white-water rafting outfit. Trips start in Tena but go to a variety of rivers.

Safari Tours (Map p90; ☎ 255-2505; Foch E4-132; 🕑 9am-7pm) Excellent reputation and long in the business. Offers all range of tours and trips, from volcano climbs and jungle trips to local jeep tours and personalized off-the-beaten-track expeditions. It's also a great place to arrange Galápagos trips.

Sangay Touring (Map p90; ☎ 255-0176/80; www.sangay.com; cnr Av Amazonas N24-196 & Cordero) Offers a variety of standardized day tours including jeep trips, hiking excursions and visits to cloud forests and volcanoes. Rates range from $25 to $75 per person. Also arranges economically priced Galápagos tours.

Sierra Nevada Expeditions (Map p90; ☎ 255-3658; www.hotelsierranevada.com; J Pinto 637) Near Cordero and long in the business, Sierra Nevada offers climbing and river-rafting trips. Owner Freddy Ramirez is well established and a very reputable mountain guide.

Surtrek (Map p90; ☎ 223-1534, 250-0530; www.surtrek.com, www.galapagosyachts.com; Av Amazonas 897) Top-end company with years of experience in hiking and climbing. Personalized tours available. Prices average $130 to $160 per day. Also offers unique 'island hopping' Galápagos tours, where you sleep on different islands rather than aboard a cruise ship.

Tropic Ecological Adventures (Map pp88-9; ☎ 222-5907; www.tropiceco.com; Av de la República E7-320) Long-time agency offering numerous three- to six-day tours to the Oriente, Andes and cloud forest. It sells other operators' tours, but it's a good way to compare some of the best on offer, and rates are good.

Yacu Amu Rafting/Ríos Ecuador (Map p90; ☎ 223-6844; www.yacuamu.com; Foch 746) Excellent river-rafting operator with daily departures to the Río Toachi and Río Blanco and several other Class III–IV options. Located between Mera and Avenida Amazonas, rates start around $75 per person. Other trips range from two to eight days. There is also a four-day kayaking school. Owner Steve Nomchong has competed and worked as a judge and safety inspector on the international circuit, so you're in good hands. He now owns Ríos Ecuador (p252), based in Tena.

FESTIVALS & EVENTS

As throughout Ecuador, people celebrate **New Year's Eve** by burning elaborate, life-sized puppets in the streets at midnight, launching explosives into the sky and otherwise throwing general public safety to the wind. It's a great time to be here.

Carnaval, held the weekend before Ash Wednesday (a changing date in February), is celebrated by intense water fights – no one is spared (careful with your camera if it isn't waterproof!).

Colorful religious processions are held during **Semana Santa** (Easter Week), the most spectacular being the procession of *cucuruchos* (penitents wearing purple robes and inverted cone masks) on Good Friday.

By far the biggest event of the year is the **founding of Quito festival**, held in early December (see below).

SLEEPING

Most travelers tend to stay in the Mariscal, which has an impressive assortment of guesthouses plus international restaurants, internet cafés, adventure outfitters and nightlife. Visitors seeking a more traditional side of Quito book a room in the old town, which, while lacking in Thai restaurants and expat

FIESTAS DE QUITO

Quito's biggest annual event commemorates the founding of the city by the Spanish on December 6. The festivities, however, start much earlier. In late November, Quito chooses a queen, and the evenings are dominated by colorful *chivas* (open-topped buses) maneuvering through the streets, packed with dancing revelers. On the week leading up to the big day, bullfights are held at the **Plaza de Toros** (Map p82) and flamenco dancing is staged throughout town as *quiteños* connect with their Spanish roots. Momentum builds as the day draws near, with nightly street parties erupting as DJs and popular local bands taking to open-air stages set up all over town. Quito comes to a near standstill on December 5, when everyone comes out to party.

bars, offers unrivaled beauty and historic streets that make for some great exploring.

The quiet and increasingly artsy new-town neighborhood of La Floresta is a pleasant (and safer) alternative to the Mariscal, and it's only a few blocks away.

The rather hazily defined area between the old and new towns (southeast of Parque El Ejido, near the Instituto Geográfico Militar) has a nontouristy feel and is a 10- to 15-minute walk from both the old town and the Mariscal (it's technically part of the new town).

The area around Guápulo and Hotel Quito, also in the new town, doesn't boast much selection, but it's an interesting area. Guápulo is wonderful at night (and during the day) and the area has a more local, nontouristy feel.

Old Town

The hotels between Plaza Santo Domingo and the bus terminal are some of the cheapest, but it's a dodgy area after about 7pm.

BUDGET

Hostal San Blas (Map p86; ☎ 228-1434; Caldas 121, Plaza San Blas; s/d from $6/8) This friendly, family-run hotel on the attractive Plaza San Blas is a good deal if you don't mind small rooms. Rooms are dark (windows open onto a small interior patio) but clean and cute.

La Posada Colonial (Map p86; ☎ 228-2859; Paredes 188; r per person with shared/private bathroom $6/8) Although a bit close to the bus terminal, this family-run place is still one of the old town's best value accommodations. Beds are saggy, but it's extremely well kept and totally secure. Rooms are bright and cheerful with wood floors and the staff is great.

Hostal La Casona (Map p86; ☎ 257-0626; Manabí Oe1-59; s/d $8/10) This family-run place has a dimly lit interior patio watched over by three floors of small rooms with low ceilings and wide, plank floors. It's the sort of place that has plenty of things (low doorways, strangely placed TV mounts) to hit your head upon.

Hotel Flores (Map p86; ☎ 228-0435; Flores 355; s/d $10/15) Decent and efficient option for cheap, safe lodging in the old town. Rooms have tiled floors and beamed ceilings, and open onto an interior courtyard. Friendly service.

Secret Garden (Map p86; ☎ 295-6704; www.secretgardenquito.com; Antepara E4-60; dm/d with shared bathroom $8/20) Owned by an Ecuadorian/Australian couple, this popular hostel has a party vibe and attracts a mix of young backpackers. The rooms are basic, livened up by artwork in the halls and a 5th-floor terrace with sublime views. There's an all-you-can-eat breakfast ($3.50), nightly dinners ($5 to $8), Spanish lessons, travel information and lots of activities.

MIDRANGE

Hotel Internacional Plaza del Teatro (Map p86; ☎ 295-9462; Guayaquil N8-75; s/d $12/24) Across from the Plaza del Teatro, this grand old dame has seen better days, but offers good value for its clean, carpeted rooms, some of which have balconies. Off-street rooms lack balconies and character, but are quieter.

Hotel Viena Internacional (Map p86; ☎ 295-4860; www.hotelvienaint.com; Flores 600; s/d with bathroom $15/30) Though the '70s-style grapevine wallpaper can bug your eyes out, the spotless rooms, top-notch service and cheerful interior patio make this the best hotel deal in the old town. Rooms have hardwood floors, TVs, hot water and good showers. Those with balconies are a bit noisy, but the breeze is nice.

Hotel San Francisco de Quito (Map p86; ☎ 228-7758; www.sanfranciscodequito.com.ec; Sucre Oe3-17; s/d $14/38, s/d mini-apartments with kitchenettes $28/44) This historic converted house boasts spotless rooms with telephone, TV and constant hot water (some even have lofts). Because it's a colonial building, most rooms lack windows, but double doors open onto a lovely balcony over a pretty interior courtyard. It's very popular, so reserve well in advance.

La Posada Colonial (Map p86; ☎ 228-0282; posadacolonial@yahoo.com; García Moreno 1160; s/d/tr/ste $26/36/61/71) The eight rooms at the pleasant Posada Colonial boast classic decor, tall ceilings, wood floors and sizeable windows (a rarity in old colonial houses). The enormous corner suite has huge windows and scenic old-town views. There are several restaurants on-site. Don't confuse this with a budget hotel of the same name near the bus station. It's between Mejia and Chile.

Hotel Real Audiencia (Map p86; ☎ 295-2711; www.realaudiencia.com; Bolívar 220; s/d $30/48; 💻) The Real Audiencia offers nondescript but nicely kept rooms with wi-fi. Most rooms are carpeted and many have views. The service is friendly and attentive, and the price includes breakfast in the top-floor restaurant with its great views.

TOP END

Hotel El Relicario del Carmen (Map p86; ☎ 228-9120; hotelrelicarmo@andinanet.net; Venezuela 10-41; s/d with breakfast $75/97) This delightful guesthouse is set in a converted colonial mansion sprinkled with colorful paintings and stained-glass windows. Rooms are even sweeter, with polished-wood floors and beamed ceilings (but small bathrooms); most face onto an interior courtyard.

our pick **Casa San Marcos** (Map p86; ☎ 228-1811; casasanmarcos@yahoo.com; Junín 655; d $80-150) Yet another beautifully restored colonial mansion, Casa San Marcos has just four rooms, all of which are exquisitely set with antique furnishings, heritage artwork on the walls, and tall ceilings. All rooms are bright and have windows. There's also an art gallery and antiques shop here, and an elegant terrace café is in the works.

Hotel Patio Andaluz (Map p86; ☎ 228-0830; www.hotelpatioandaluz.com; García Moreno N6-52; d $250; 💻) Inside a remodeled 16th-century home, the plush rooms of this elegant hotel open onto interior wooden-floor balconies. Beautiful woodwork fills the rooms and common areas, service is top-notch and a peaceful air pervades the place.

Plaza Grande (Map p86; ☎ 251-0777; www.plazagrandequito.com; cnr García Moreno & Chile; ste from $500; 💻) Quito's finest hotel offers gorgeously decorated rooms (all suites) with carved-wood details, chandeliers and marble bathrooms with Jacuzzi tubs. Some rooms have small balconies. There's a small spa, several restaurants (including one in the wine cellar) and impeccable service.

New Town

BUDGET

Casa Bambú (Map pp88-9; ☎ 222-6738; Solano E5-27; dm/s/d with shared bathroom $5/7/10, d with private bathroom $20; 💻) This gem of a place has bright and airy rooms, a wee garden, a giant rooftop terrace, a guest kitchen, a book exchange, laundry facilities and outstanding views from the hammocks on the roof. It's worth the uphill hike to get there.

El Centro del Mundo (Map p90; ☎ 222-9050; www.centrodelmundo.net; García E7-26; dm/s $6/8) A magnet among young backpackers, this popular French-Canadian–owned hostel has brightly painted rooms, a guest kitchen and traveler-friendly ambience.

La Casa de Eliza (Map pp88-9; ☎ 222-6602; manteca@uio.satnet.net; Isabel La Católica N24-679; dm/d $6/12) Although this old favorite is definitely showing its age, it's still a friendly, homespun place. It occupies a converted house with a big guest kitchen, a sociable common area, a small book exchange and simple rooms.

Hostal Nassau (Map p90; ☎ 256-5724; www.nassauhostal.com; Pinto E4-342; s/d with shared bathroom $7/10, with private bathroom $10/14) A good cheapie option popular with travelers, Nassau offers a range of rooms. Rooms with private bathrooms are clean and bright, while rooms without are dark and somewhat dismal.

Backpacker's Inn (Map p90; ☎ 250-9669; www.backpackersinn.net; Rodriguez 245; dm/s/d from $6/8/13; 💻) Overlooking a peaceful street, this well-located hostel has a laid-back vibe with just a handful of simple rooms – all with decent light and wood floors.

Albergue El Taxo (Map p90; ☎/fax 222-5593; Foch E4-116; s/d with shared bathroom $7/14, with private bathroom $8/16) Friendly and modest, El Taxo occupies a converted '70s house with pleasant, colorful rooms, most of which have shared bathrooms. The no-frills common area has a fireplace (rarely fired up) and the guest kitchen is well kept.

Montaña (Map pp88-9; ☎ 223-8954; mountain_refugeecuador@yahoo.com; Cordero E12-141 at Toledo; dm/s/d $7/9/15) Opened in 2004 by an avid local climber, Montaña has a welcoming vibe and is an excellent choice for climbers and hikers on a budget. It's a great place to hook up with local altitude freaks. With one double, two singles, a triple and a quad, it only sleeps 11.

El Cafecito (Map p90; ☎ 223-4862; www.cafecito.net; Cordero E6-43; dm $7, s/d with shared bathroom $10/15, d with private bathroom $25) Over the excellent café of the same name (p107), this is an eternally popular budget choice, and for good reason. Rooms are clean, the place has a mellow vibe and the café with outdoor seating serves great breakfasts.

L'Auberge Inn (Map pp88-9; ☎ 255-2912; www.ioda.net/auberge-inn; Av Colombia N12-200; s/d with shared bathroom $8/16, with private bathroom $11/19) This clean, cheerful inn boasts a good traveler vibe with agencies on hand for arranging hikes and other adventure trips. It has spotless rooms, a small garden area, a common room with a fireplace, a pool table and a decent in-house restaurant.

Posada del Maple (Map p90; ☎ 254-4507; www.posadadelmaple.com; Rodriguez E8-49; dm $8, s/d with shared bathroom $15/19, with private bathroom $25/29) Maple is a friendly place with clean but dated rooms, comfy lounge areas and outdoor space. It's well liked by many travelers.

Huaukí (Map p90; ☎ 290-4286; www.hostalhuauki.com; Pinto E7-82; dm/d from $6/20) Opened by a Japanese expat, this sleek new hostel offers small but clean colorful rooms with wood floors. The restaurant with draped fabrics is a popular traveler hangout, with Japanese and vegetarian fare.

Blue House (Map p90; ☎ 222-3480; www.bluehousequito.com; Pinto E8-24; dm/d $8/20) New in 2008, this friendly guesthouse has six pleasant rooms with wood floors in a converted house on a quiet street. There's a grassy yard in front for barbecues, a comfy lounge with fireplace and a kitchen for guest use.

La Casona de Mario (Map pp88-9; ☎ 254-4036; www.casonademario.com; Andalucía N24-115; r per person $10) In a lovely old house, La Casona de Mario is outstanding value with homey rooms, shared spotless bathrooms, a garden, a TV lounge and a guest kitchen.

Sakti (☎ 252-0466; Carrión 641; s/d $12/20) Located behind a vegetarian restaurant, Sakti offers a handful of clean, simple rooms with a grassy courtyard in front.

El Vagabundo (Map p90; ☎ 222-6376; www.exploringecuador.com/vagabundo; Wilson E7-45; r per person $14) 'The Vagabond' offers clean but dull rooms, which amount to a fairly good deal thanks in large part to its friendly owners and the attached pizzeria.

Magic Bean (Map p90; ☎ 256-6181; Foch E5-08; dm/s/d $10/25/30) Better known for its lively restaurant (p108), the Magic Bean offers clean, spruce lodging. The downside is the noise from the restaurant, meaning little rest for light sleepers.

MIDRANGE

Casa Helbling (Map p90; ☎ 222-6013; www.casahelbling.de; General Veintimilla 531; s/d with shared bathroom $14/20, with private bathroom $22/30; 💻) In a homey, colonial-style house in the Mariscal, Casa Helbling is clean, relaxed and friendly; and it has a guest kitchen, laundry facilities and plenty of common areas for chilling out.

Crossroads (Map p90; ☎ 223-4735; www.crossroadshostal.com; Foch E5-23; dm $8-9, s/d with shared bathroom $15/23, with private bathroom $23/30) A popular guesthouse among travelers despite the worn but bright rooms in need of a good scrub. It's set in a big converted house with kitchen, patio and lounge areas. Has wi-fi access.

Aleida's Hostal (Map pp88-9; ☎ 223-4570; www.aleidashostal.com.ec; Andalucía 559; s/d with shared bathroom 13/26, with private bathroom $18/36) This friendly, three-story guesthouse in La Floresta is family run and has a very spacious feel with lots of light, huge rooms; high, wooden ceilings; and hardwood floors. The owner welcomes guests with a shot of *punta* (homemade firewater). Breakfast is available for $2 to $4 extra.

Folklore Hotel (Map pp88-9; ☎ 255-4621; www.folklorehotel.com; Madrid 868; s/d with breakfast $19/29) Near Pontevedra, this delightfully converted house in La Floresta has spacious, colorful rooms with blue-and-yellow–checkered bedspreads that match the house's paintjob. It has a small garden and a welcoming, family feel.

Casa Kanela (Map p90; ☎ 254-6162; www.casakanela.mamey.org; Rodriguez 147; dm/s/d/tr with breakfast $12/19/30/36; 💻) An excellent new addition to Mariscal, Kanela offers minimalist but stylish rooms in a pleasant converted house on pretty Rodriguez. It's a friendly, welcoming place.

Hostal El Arupo (Map p90; ☎ 255-7543; www.hostalelarupo.com; Rodríguez E7-22; s/d with breakfast $25/33) One of several good guesthouse/hostels on the quietest street in the Mariscal, El Arupo is a spotless and homey converted house with a lovely little front patio. Rooms are a bit dark, but the beds are firm and there's an immaculate communal kitchen.

Hostal Jardín del Sol (Map p90; ☎ 223-0941; www.hostaljardindelsol.com; Calama E8-29; s/d $25/37) Located on a quiet street, but near all the action, Jardín del Sol is a good-value spot with clean, comfortable, unfussy rooms, some of which open onto shared verandas.

Hotel Plaza Internacional (Map pp88-9; ☎ 252-4530; www.hotelplazainternacional.com; Leonidas Plaza 150; s/d $28/38) Inside a large colonial mansion, this converted guesthouse offers bright rooms with stucco walls and friendly service. Some rooms are bigger than others and the best have wood floors and balconies.

Toa Bed & Breakfast (Map pp88-9; ☎ 222-4241; www.hostaltoa.ec; F Lizarazu N23-209 near La Gasca; s/d $35/42) Although slightly out of the way (about a 15-minute walk from the Mariscal), Toa is a wonderful B&B with cheery, comfy rooms adorned with handicrafts, a common area with a fireplace, a big communal table and a spotless kitchen. There's a sunny back patio and a fully equipped apartment to boot.

Hostal Charles Darwin (Map pp88-9; ☎ 223-4323; www.chdarwin.com; Colina 304; s/d incl breakfast $31/43; 💻) This intimate hotel sits on a quiet street and has 12 comfortable rooms with carpeting and homey furnishings. Extras include a small garden, kitchen facilities and laundry service. Needless to say, the owners are Darwin fanatics.

Hostal de la Mancha (Map pp88-9; ☎ 322-8334; www.hostaldelamancha.com.ec; Vallodolid N24-562; s/d with breakfast $40/45) Set in a sleek, modern, five-story building, this is a comfortable if somewhat bland midrange option. The clean rooms feature a mint color scheme with dark-green carpeting, good mattresses and huge windows, and there's wi-fi access.

Hostal Fuente de Piedra (Map p90; ☎ 252-5314; www.ecuahotel.com; Wilson 211; s/d incl breakfast $39/46; 🖳) This solid, midrange option has a good assortment of rooms in a dapper colonial house. Rooms have wood or terra-cotta tile floors, and all have sizable windows (with great views in some). There's a pleasant outdoor patio, which doubles as a restaurant, and wi-fi access.

Hotel Sierra Madre (Map p90; ☎ 250-5687; www.hotelsierramadre.com; Veintimilla 464; s/d from $39/49) In a handsomely restored colonial building, the Sierra Madre is an inviting Ecuadorian-Belgian–run place. Rooms vary in size but most have wood floors, excellent beds and a warm color scheme, while the best quarters have vaulted ceilings and verandas. There's a popular restaurant below.

Hotel Los Alpes (Map pp88-9; ☎ 256-1110; www.hotellosalpes.com; Tamayo 233; s/d/tr with breakfast $49/59/69; 🖳) A touch over the top in the design department, Los Alpes has wild wallpaper, decorative plates and gilded knickknacks that somehow don't detract from the overall alpine charm of the place. Accommodation ranges from spacious, airy quarters with wood floors to smaller, cabin-style rooms with carpeting. Very friendly.

Hotel Villa Nancy (Map pp88-9; ☎ 255-0839; www.hotelvillanancy.com; Muros 146; s/d/tr $41/61/76; 🖳) In a well-to-do residential neighborhood, this large, pretty house with wooden shutters provides an elegant but unpretentious stay. The rooms have sponge-painted walls, big windows, framed artwork and a trim, neat design. There's a sundeck, sauna, small garden and a living room with old black-and-white photos of Quito.

Antinea Apart Hotel (Map p90; ☎ 250-6838; www.hotelantinea.com; Rodríguez E8-20; s/d from $52/62; 🖳) One of Quito's finest boutique hotels, this warmly remodeled mansion is the place to treat yourself. Persian rugs, beautiful art, ceramics, gold-framed mirrors, black porcelain in the bathrooms and great attention to detail give it a deliciously luxurious atmosphere. The priciest rooms have fireplaces.

La Casa Sol (Map p90; ☎ 223-0798; www.lacasasol.com; Calama E8-66; s/d with breakfast $44/69; 🖳) This friendly traveler favorite has a warm, inviting lobby with a colonial color scheme and cheerfully painted rooms that face onto an interior courtyard. There are nice touches throughout, as well as artwork and photos lining the corridors and in the rooms.

Suites González Suárez (Map pp88-9; ☎ 223-2003, 222-4417; www.hotelgonzalezsuarez.com; cnr San Ignacio 2750 & González Suárez; s/d from $60/70; 🖳) This sophisticated little hillside hotel has plush rooms with pine-colored carpeting, cheery yellow walls and outstanding views over Guápulo. Some rooms have balconies and all have excellent beds and tasteful furnishings. Buffet breakfast and airport pickup are included, and there's wi-fi access.

Hotel Vieja Cuba (Map pp88-9; ☎ 290-6729; viejacuba@andinanet.net; Almagro 1212; s/d $56/73) This stunning boutique hotel, masterfully designed in a crisp, colonial Cuban theme, has refreshing rooms and a colorful flair. Two rooms have fireplaces, and the wood floors throughout are polished to a sheen.

Hotel Sebastián (Map p90; ☎ 222-2400; hotelsebastian.com; Diego de Almagro 822; s/d $60/74; 🖳) Many of the Sebastián's 50 good-sized rooms have balconies and some have great views. The rooms all feature cable TV, direct-dial phones, room service, desks and attractive furnishings. There is a cozy bar with a fireplace.

TOP END

Hostal de La Rábida (Map pp88-9; ☎ 222-2169; www.hostalrabida.com; La Rábida 227; s/d $61/76) This option occupies a lovely converted house with an immaculate white-wall interior and fresh, carpeted rooms. There's a tiny bar-lounge and a restaurant serving delicacies such as *filet chateaubriand* (thick steak) and crêpe suzette – for guests only.

Café Cultura (Map p90; ☎ 222-4271; www.cafecultura.com; Robles 513; s/d/tr $79/99/109) This atmospheric boutique hotel is set in a converted mansion with a garden, crackling fireplaces and handsome, mural-filled bedrooms all adding to the charm. Reservations recommended.

Hotel Quito (Map pp88-9; ☎ 254-4600; www.hotelquito.com; González Suárez N27-142; s/d/ste from $100/110/140; 🖳 🏊) A Quito landmark, this huge, 215-room hotel is high on the hill above Guápulo. Its

APARTMENTS & HOMESTAYS

Visitors wanting to stay for a longer time may want to rent a room, apartment or suite with a kitchen. Many apartments require a one-month minimum stay, although we've listed some here that can be rented daily or weekly as well. South American Explorers (SAE) has a notice board full of shared-housing advertisements (see p79), and it also keeps lists of locals interested in hosting travelers; if you are taking Spanish courses, inquire at your school. Prices average between $5 and $15 per person per day, and sometimes include meals and laundry service. English is not always spoken.

Hotel San Francisco de Quito (Map p86; ☎ 228-7758; hsfquito@andinanet.net;Sucre Oe3-17; s/d/tr $18/25/45) This charming old-timer has a few modern apartments over its hotel (p98) in the old town.

Amaranta Apart Hotel (Map pp88-9; ☎ 254-3619; www.aparthotelamaranta.com; Leonidas Plaza Gutiérrez N20-32; d $41, apt $61-81; 💻) Amaranta offers small, simply furnished rooms as well as two different types of apartments. Low-end apartments are spacious and bright but minimally furnished, while the best quarters are quite comfortable with balconies and fully stocked kitchens. Breakfast is included.

Alberto's House (Map p90; ☎ 222-4603; www.albertoshouse.com; García 545; r per week/month from $70/180) Alberto's has facilities that include shared hot showers, a laundry room, kitchen privileges, a TV lounge, a pool table and a garden with a barbecue area. It's popular with volunteers thanks to its welcoming, communal spirit. Rooms are private with shared bathroom (it's a house, after all).

heyday was in the '60s, as its minimalist design makes clear, but it still attracts handfuls of business and leisure travelers. Some of the bland rooms offer superb views. The services are extensive, with a bar, a restaurant, a swimming pool and a casino all on hand.

Nü House (Map p90; ☎ 255-7845; www.nuhousehotels.com; Foch E6-12; s/d/ste $145/160/250) This new boutique hotel offers a touch of stylish modernism in a Scandinavian-style, wood-and-glass building rising over the Mariscal. Its 57 rooms are set with dark-wood floors, huge windows, lovely bathrooms tiled with river stones and an overly dramatic color scheme (red-velvet curtains). There's a spa in the works.

EATING

Quito's rich and varied restaurant scene offers a fine mix of traditional fare and ethnic and international eateries. All budgets and tastes are catered for, and you'll find everything from ubermodern sushi restaurants to classic Andean cooking served in a landmark colonial dining room, alongside good options for vegetarians, pizza lovers and those simply seeking a good café on a drizzly afternoon.

Many restaurants close on Sunday. For more on Ecuadorian cuisine, see p45.

Old Town

The historical center is where you'll find Quito's most traditional eateries, some of which have been honing family recipes for generations.

ECUADORIAN

Cafetería Fabiolita (El Buen Sanduche; Map p86; ☎ 228-4268; Espejo Oe4-17; sandwiches $1, secos de chivo $2.50; ⏲ 9am-6pm) For more than 40 years, Fabiola Flores and her daughter Margarita have been serving up the city's favorite *secos de chivo*, in this immaculate little shop beneath the cathedral, still the most authentic place to try this dish (9am to 11am only). Its famous *sanduches de pernil* even humble city politicians.

Mercado Central (Map p86; Pichincha; full meals $1-3; ⏲ 8am-4pm, to 3pm Sun) For stall after stall of some of Quito's most traditional (and cheapest) foods, head straight to the Mercado Central, between Esmeraldas and Manabí, where you'll find everything from *locro de papa* (potato soup with cheese and avocado) and seafood, to *yaguarlocro* (blood-sausage soup) and *fritada* (fried pork). Fruits and veggies are available too.

El Buen Sandwich (Map p86; Venezuela N3-49; mains $1-3; ⏲ 11am-3pm Mon-Sat) Secreted inside a shopping gallery, the unassuming El Buen Sandwich has just three things on the menu: *secos de chivo* (goat stew; one of Ecuador's most traditional dishes), ceviche and *sanduches de pernil* (ham sandwiches). All are quite good, and the garrulous owner has many talents – his artwork fills the restaurant.

La Colmena (Map p86; ☎ 228-4823; Benalcázar 619; lunch $2.50-3; ⏲ 9am-7:30pm, to 5pm Sun) For 50 years, the Vaca Meza family has been serving one of Ecuador's favorite dishes, *guatita*, a tripe-and-potato stew in a seasoned, peanut-based sauce. Whether you can stomach tripe or not, it's well worth sampling the original at this old-town landmark.

La Guaragua (Map p86; ☎ 257-2552; Espejo Oe2-40; mains $2-6; ⏰ 10am-9pm Mon-Thu, to 11pm Fri-Sun) Near Guayaquil, the tables are a bit office-like, but the food is excellent at this new café-restaurant including imaginative salads and delicious appetizers such as *tortillas de quinoa* (quinoa patties) and empanadas.

Tianguez (Map p86; Plaza San Francisco; mains $3-5; ⏰ 10am-6pm Mon & Tue, to 11.30pm Wed-Sun) Tucked into the stone arches beneath the Monastery of San Francisco, this Bohemian-style café prepares tasty appetizers (tamales, soups) as well as heartier mains. Tables on the plaza are perfect for an evening *canelazo* or an afternoon *te de coca* (coca-leaf tea).

Café del Fraile (Map p86; ☎ 251-0113; Chile Oe4-22, Palacio Arzobispal, 2nd fl; mains $5-8; ⏰ 10am-midnight Mon-Sat, noon-10pm Sun) Country-rustic charm (cast-iron lanterns, wood-beam ceiling) and balcony seating set the stage for a tasty selection of grilled dishes, sandwiches and cocktails. Recent favorites include vegetable soup, *truta a la plancha* (grilled trout) and corvina.

Hasta La Vuelta, Señor (Map p86; ☎ 258-0887; Chile Oe4-22, Palacio Arzobispal, 3rd fl; mains $6-10; ⏰ 11am-11pm Mon-Sat, to 8pm Sun) Ecuadorian cuisine is prepared with panache at this excellent restaurant with balcony seating. Reliable favorites include ceviche, *secos de chivo*, tilapia and sea bass.

Vista Hermosa (Map p86; ☎ 295-1401; Mejia 453, 5th fl; mains $6-10; ⏰ 1pm-2am Mon-Sat, noon-9pm Sun) A much-loved newcomer to El Centro, Vista Hermosa (Beautiful View) delivers the goods with a magnificent 360-degree panorama over the old town from its rooftop terrace. Live music on Wednesday to Saturday (from 9pm onwards) adds to the magic. Bring a jacket and arrive early to beat the crowds.

Las Cuevas de Luís Candela (Map p86; ☎ 228-7710; Benalcázar 713 & Chile; mains $6-10; ⏰ 10am-11pm) Built in the vaulted cellar of an old-time building, this atmospheric and windowless Spanish/Ecuadorian restaurant has been around since 1963. Bullfighting greats Manolo and Manolete both ate here.

Café Mosaico (Map p86; ☎ 254-2871; Samaniego N8-95; mains $9-12; ⏰ 11am-11pm) Near Antepara, Itchimbia, the drinks here are pricey, but the views over the city are unrivaled. Mosaico is a must for an evening cocktail, when it's at its liveliest, or an early afternoon coffee, when you'll likely have the balcony and those views all to yourself.

INTERNATIONAL

Frutería Monserrate (Map p86; ☎ 258-3408; Espejo Oe2-12; mains $2-3.50; ⏰ 8am-7.30pm Mon-Fri, 9am-6.30pm Sat & Sun) A looming ceiling, brick walls and concrete pillars give an industrial feel to this popular and casual eatery. A mix of travelers and locals stop in for the filling breakfasts and giant fruit salads, though empanadas and ceviche are also among the offerings.

Café del Teatro (Map p86; ☎ 228-9079; Plaza del Teatro; mains $2.50-8; ⏰ 10am-7pm) Grab a table on the plaza and enjoy a drink with great views of the Teatro Sucre. Inside, you'll find a stylish, multilevel café-restaurant with chefs whipping up corvina with shrimp sauce, ribs, steak and other comfort food, as well as sandwiches and lighter fare. It stays open later when events are on at the theatre.

El Buho (Map p86; ☎ 228-9877; cnr García Moreno & Espejo; mains $4-8; ⏰ 11am-7pm Mon-Wed, to 9pm Fri & Sat, noon-5pm Sun) Inside the Centro Cultural Metropolitano (p80), El Buho serves a small selection of sandwiches, salads, burgers and ceviches. The café tables on the patio are also a pleasant spot for coffee and dessert.

Mea Culpa (Map p86; ☎ 295-1190; Chile Oe4-22, Palacio Arzobispal; mains $9-20; ⏰ 12:30-3:30pm & 7-11pm Mon-Sat, noon-5pm Sun) An over-the-top Mediterranean menu and a strictly enforced dress code (no jeans, shorts or sneakers) make this one of the old town's premier restaurants. The views and romantic setting reportedly dwarf the food, but it remains a favorite with the well-heeled crowd. Reservations essential.

Theatrum (Map p86; ☎ 257-1011; www.theatrum.com.ec; Manabí N8-131; mains $10-15; ⏰ 12:30-4pm Mon-Fri, 7-11pm daily) On the 2nd floor of the historic Teatro Sucre, creatively concocted and extravagantly presented prix-fixe meals are served to a well-heeled crowd before the show downstairs. It's one of the city's most elegant dining rooms.

Octava de Corpus (Map p86; ☎ 295-2989; Junín E2-167; mains $12-15; ⏰ 12.30-3pm & 7-11pm Mon-Sat) For a completely different dining experience, head to this little-known restaurant hidden inside a colonial home on lovely Junín. Artwork covers every surface of the place, and there's a homey lounge with an enormous wine cellar featuring more than 230 vintages from both the new and old world. The menu features classic meat and seafood (all grilled or steamed). Free transport is provided with a reservation (which is recommended).

Rincón de Cantuña (Map p86; ☎ 228-0830; García Moreno N6-52; mains $12-17; 7am-10:30pm) Inside the Hotel Patio Andaluz (p99), this upscale restaurant serves both gourmet Spanish and Ecuadorian fare to a foreign clientele.

GRILLS

Pollos San Blas (Map p86; cnr Av Pichincha & Anteparra; mains $2-3.50; 11am-6pm) Near the pretty Plaza San Blas, this popular and casual spot is a great place for piping hot plates of roast chicken.

SEAFOOD

Corvina Don 'Jimmy' (Map p86; Mercado Central; Pichincha; mains $2-4; 8am-4pm, to 3pm Sun) Open since 1953, this is the Mercado Central's most famous stall, serving huge portions of corvina (sea bass) – ask for it with rice if you don't want it over a big bowl of ceviche. Everyone from governors to diplomats has eaten here.

Los Cebiches de la Rumiñahui (Map p86; ☎ 228-5239; cnr García Moreno & Bolívar; mains $5-7; 10am-5pm) In a recently restored colonial building, this casual but inviting newcomer serves tasty ceviche and seafood dishes.

ITALIAN

Pizza SA (Map p86; ☎ 258-8858; Espejo Oe2-46; mains $3-5; 11am-11pm Mon-Sat, to 9pm Sun) On a lane filled with restaurants facing the Teatro Bolívar, this casual spot with s sidewalk seating bakes up delicious, individually sized thin-crust pizzas. You can also enjoy sandwiches, salads and calzones.

VEGETARIAN

Govindas (Map p86; ☎ 296-6844; Esmeraldas 853; mains $1.50; 8am-4pm Mon-Sat) Proudly serving 100% vegetarian cuisine, the Krishnas here whip up tasty, fresh lunch plates from a changing menu, plus yogurt and granola, juices and sweets.

Restaurante Vegetariano Ari (Map p86; ☎ 258-5888; Sucre Oe4-48; mains $2-3.50; 8am-5pm Mon-Sat) Hidden on the 2nd floor of a commercial center, Ari is a colorful, if boxy, space serving a small selection of daily vegetarian specials such as vegetarian frittata, as well as juices and fruit salad.

CAFÉS & SNACKBARS

Opened in 1950, **Cafetería Modelo** (Map p86; cnr Sucre & García Moreno; 8am-8pm) is one of the city's oldest cafés and a great spot to try traditional snacks such as *empanadas de verde* (plantain empanadas filled with cheese), *quimbolitos* (a sweet cake steamed in a leaf), tamales and *humitas*. There's another version, **Cafetería Modelo II** (Map p86; Venezuela N6-19; 8am-8pm Mon-Sat, to 6pm Sun), offering the same trappings of old-world style (plus live music some weekend nights) on Venezuela.

Jugos de la Sucre (Map p86; Sucre Oe5-53; drinks $0.50-0.75; 7.30am-6pm) For a freshly squeezed serving of vitamins, this popular juice stand is hard to beat. Try passion fruit, orange or a dozen other flavors.

El Cafeto (Map p86; Chile 930 & Flores, Convento de San Agustín; coffee $0.90-2; 8am-7.30pm Mon-Sat, to noon Sun) This cozy and welcoming Ecuadorian-owned coffee shop serves coffee made from 100% organic Ecuadorian beans. Espressos and cappuccinos are excellent, and small breakfasts and snacks are available.

Casa San Lucas (Map p86; ☎ 295-0923; cnr Venezuela & Esmeraldas; drinks $1-2; 11am-5pm Tue-Fri, 10.30am-4pm Sat & Sun) Enjoy coffee or a cold drink in the sitting room of this beautifully preserved but underutilized colonial house. It also houses a small gallery with temporary exhibitions.

Heladería San Agustín (Map p86; ☎ 228-5082; Guayaquil 1053; ice cream $1.20; 9am-6pm Mon-Fri, to 4pm Sat, 10am-3pm Sun) The Alvarez Andino family has been making *helados de paila* (ice cream handmade in big copper bowls) since 1858, making this Quito's oldest ice-cream parlor and an absolute must for ice-cream fans. Made with real fruit juices, they're more akin to sorbets.

El Kukurucho del Maní (Map p86; Rocafuerte Oe5-02 at García Moreno; snacks $0.25-0.50; 7am-7pm Mon-Sat, 8am-6pm Sun) This delightful snack stand cooks up kilos of nuts, corn kernels and *coquitos* (coconut sweets) in a giant copper kettle.

SELF-CATERING

Magda (Map p86; Venezuela N3-62; 8.30am-7pm Mon-Sat, 9am-5pm Sun) A conveniently located and well-stocked supermarket.

New Town

The city's best restaurants spread across the rolling avenues of the new town, with an excellent assortment of classic and nouveau fare. This is the place to go for ceviche, Japanese, Thai, Tex-Mex and Italian.

ECUADORIAN

Casa de Campo (Map pp88-9; ☎ 222-7388; 18 de Septiembre E4-147; mains $3-6; 🕑 7am-8pm Mon-Fri, 8am-6pm Sat & Sun) Bamboo walls and a thatched roof set the stage for hearty dishes from field and coast. Simple but tasty favorites include grilled fish, seafood rice and grilled pork chops.

La Canoa (Map p90; ☎ 250-1419; Cordero E4-375; mains $4-8; 🕑 24hr) Near Mera, this highly regarded restaurant from Guayaquil is your best opportunity to try Ecuadorian delicacies without emptying your wallet: there's *sopa de verde* (plantain soup), *caldo de manguera* (tripe soup that's said to be an aphrodisiac), *bandera* (a mixed seafood plate) and other treats.

La Choza (Map pp88-9; ☎ 223-0839; Av 12 de Octubre N24-551; mains $5-10; 🕑 noon-4pm & 7-10pm Mon-Fri, to 4pm Sat & Sun) Delicious Ecuadorian food served in colorful, elegant surroundings.

Mama Clorinda (Map p90; ☎ 254-4362; Reina Victoria 1144; mains $6-9; 🕑 11am-10pm Mon-Sat) This modest, friendly restaurant serves tasty national specialties to a mostly foreign clientele. Try the *llapingachos* (cornmeal cakes) with steak.

Pim's (Map p86; ☎ 322-8410; Iquique; mains $6-9; 🕑 noon-10pm Mon-Sat, to 6pm Sun) Inside the Parque Itchimbia, this new outpost of the Pim's chain offers fantastic views over the city. Enjoy tasty traditional Ecuadorian fare, plus sandwiches and cocktails in the elegant, if somewhat stuffy, dining room, or on the outside patio.

INTERNATIONAL

La Crêperie (Map p90; ☎ 222-6274; Garcia; mains $3-5; 🕑 5pm-midnight Mon-Sat) Just off the beaten path, La Crêperie has a spacious, handsomely dark-wood dining room lined with black-and-white photos of old Hollywood stars. Tasty savories and desserts fill up the menu. English is spoken.

Yanuna (Map p90; ☎ 223-9283; Wilson E6-35; mains $4-6; 🕑 noon-midnight) This colorful, Bohemian bistro serves a huge variety of global fare including Indian Tahli, Greek salads, Vietnamese *pho*, Peruvian ceviche and lots of vegetarian options. There's a loungelike deck overlooking the street and world beats to match the eclectic fare.

Naranjilla Mecánica (Map pp88-9; 🕑 252-6468; Tamayo N22-43; mains $6-10; 🕑 noon-midnight Mon-Fri, 8pm-midnight Sat) This self-consciously hip restaurant attracts a fun, mixed crowd gathering over inventive salads, tasty sandwiches and satisfying mains such as grilled haddock with capers. The menu comes in hardback, comic-book form and the decor is Bohemian chic, with an enclosed patio in back that gets swelteringly hot on sunny days.

Boca del Lobo (Map p90; ☎ 254-5500; Calama 284; mains $6-12; 🕑 5pm-2am) Beneath the soundtrack of ambient grooves, a mix of stylish Ecuadorians and neatly dressed foreigners mingle over raclette, crepes, open-faced sandwiches, baked desserts and sugary sweet cocktails. The ambience is pure kitsch, with colored-glass globes, empty birdcages and psychedelic paintings.

Clancy's (Map pp88-9; ☎ 255-4525; cnr Salazar & Toledo; mains $10-15; 🕑 noon-midnight) In a peacefully set, vine-covered house in Floresta, Clancy's aims for classic European bistro decor and a wide-ranging menu of pizzas, risotto dishes, sandwiches and grilled meats and fish.

La Paella Valenciana (Map pp88-9; ☎ 222-8681; Diego de Almagro 1727; mains $10-24; 🕑 noon-3pm Mon-Sun & 7-9:30pm Mon-Sat) Serves knockout Spanish seafood plates including excellent paella. Portions are gigantic.

Rincón de Francia (Map p90; ☎ 222-5053; Vicente Ramón Roca 779; dinner for 2 $40-80) For decades, this has been one of Quito's best-known French restaurants. A full meal will cost at least $20, twice that if you dip into the wine.

GRILLS

Texas Ranch (Map p90; ☎ 290-6199; Mera 1140; mains $4-7; 🕑 1pm-midnight) Texas Ranch serves up whopping burgers (that's the Texas part) and Argentine-style grilled meats.

La Parrilla Uruguaya (Map pp88-9; ☎ 223-1139; cnr Av Orellana & Whymper; mains $10-15; 🕑 noon-4pm & 7-10pm) This elegantly set dining room has a trim, contemporary design that takes nothing away from the delicious cuts of sizzling grilled beef. There's a decent wine list and live tango on Tuesday and Thursday nights.

SEAFOOD

Isla del Mar (pp88-9; Av 6 de Diciembre at Jorge Washington; mains $2.50-6; 🕑 7:30am-5pm Mon-Fri, to 4pm Sat & Sun) It doesn't look like much, but this hole-in-the-wall restaurant serves knockout ceviche and seafood dishes at rock-bottom prices. It's owned by a family from Manabí, the land containing arguably Ecuador's best food.

Canoa Manabita (Map p90; ☎ 256-3349; Calama 247; mains $4-6; 🕑 lunch Tue-Sun) This casual and unassuming place is extremely popular with locals (and virtually unknown to many tourists, despite its Mariscal location). Mouth-watering servings of ceviche and seafood plates bring in the crowds.

Cevichería Manolo (Map pp88-9; ☎ 256-9254; cnr Almagro & La Niña; mains $4-6; 8am-5pm or 6pm) Join the locals at this excellent and affordable seafood restaurant, with several types of Ecuadorian and Peruvian ceviches on the menu, plus great seafood dishes including *camarones al ajillo* (shrimp in garlic sauce) and *sopa marinera* (mixed-seafood soup).

Su Cebiche (Map p90; ☎ 252-6380; Mera N24-200; mains $4-7; 9am-5pm) This slick little lunchtime joint serves excellent coastal specialties. Try the *sopa marinera* or one of seven types of ceviches.

Las Redes (Map p90; ☎ 252-5691; Av Amazonas 845; mains $6-16; noon-10pm Mon-Sat) One of the city's best *cevicherías* (ceviche restaurants), Las Redes has a small, cozy dining room decorated with fish nets and stained glass. Friendly staff bring around favorites such as the highly satisfying *gran ceviche mixto* (mixed ceviche).

Mare Nostrum (Map p90; ☎ 223-7236, 252-8686; cnr Foch 172 & Tamayo; mains $10-17; noon-10pm Tue-Sat) In a Gothic, castlelike building complete with knights in armor on the walls and giant wood tables and chairs, Mare Nostrum serves exquisite seafood dishes with both Spanish and Ecuadorian influences.

ITALIAN

Le Arcate (Map p90; ☎ 223-7659; General Baquedano 358; mains $4-6; 12:30-3pm & 6-11pm Mon-Sat, noon-4pm Sun) This Mariscal favorite bakes more than 50 kinds of pizza (likely the best around) in a wood-fired oven, and serves reasonably priced lasagna, steak and seafood. It's a great place.

Tomato (Map p90; ☎ 290-6201; Mera N24-148; mains $4-7; noon-2am) The pizzas aren't Quito's best, but that doesn't stop travelers and a few locals from packing this festive but low-key place most nights. Pizzas by the slice, fat calzones, lunch specials and plenty of cold draft beer bring them in.

Ristorante Pizzeria Milano (Map p90; ☎ 252-8181; Calama E8-40; mains $5-7; noon-3pm & 5-10pm Mon-Sat) Cozy spot with outdoor tables, delicious thin-crust pizzas and the usual Italian temptations including pastas, risottos and gnocchi.

La Briciola (Map pp88-9; ☎ 254-7138; Toledo 1255; mains $6-10; 12:30-3pm & 7:30-11pm Mon-Sat) This longtime favorite has an outstanding and varied menu. The portions are large and the wine is fairly priced. Make a reservation if you hope to eat before 9:30pm.

VEGETARIAN

Restaurante Manantial (Map p90; ☎ 222-7569; 9 de Octubre N22-25; mains $1-3; 8am-6pm Sun-Fri) Run by a sweet old vegan soul, Manantial is a simple, unfussy spot serving healthy, carefully prepared dishes such as veggie burgers, tofu sandwiches, soups of the day and juices (try the filling *aguacatado* – blended soy milk, avocado and plantain).

El Maple (Map p90; ☎ 290-0000; Foch btwn Diego de Almagro & Av 6 de Deciembre; mains $3-5; noon-9pm) This well-loved restaurant serves excellent organic vegetarian food. The four-course set lunches ($2.80) are a steal, and the juices are tops.

LATIN AMERICAN

La Bodeguita de Cuba (Map pp88-9; ☎ 254-2476; Reina Victoria 1721; mains $3-5; noon-4pm & 7-10pm Tue-Fri, noon-midnight Sat & Sun) With its wooden tables and graffiti-covered walls, this is a great place for Cuban food and fun. Live bands perform from time to time, and there's outdoor seating.

Red Hot Chili Peppers (Map p90; ☎ 255-7575; Foch E4-314; mains $4-6; noon-10:30pm Mon-Sat) Think fajitas – the rest of the menu is good, but doesn't quite measure up to that sizzling plate of chicken or beef. Wash 'em down with smooth piña coladas.

Orisha (Map pp88-9; ☎ 252-0738; Diego de Almagro 1212; mains $4-7; noon-3pm & 7-10pm Mon-Sat) This is a cozy little Cuban restaurant with Yoruba crafts adorning the walls and excellent food on the menu.

El Puerto Callao (Map p90; 9 de Octubre 591; mains $5-8; 11am-10pm) Overlooking a small plaza, this cozy slightly upscale restaurant serves a good mix of classic Peruvian staples. Start with the *pulpo al olivo* (marinated octopus and olives) or *papa rellena* (mashed potatoes stuffed with seasoned ground beef) before moving on to ceviche, grilled shrimp or seafood with rice.

ASIAN & INDIAN

Chandani Tandoori (Map p90; ☎ 222-1053; Mera 1333; mains $3-5; 11am-10pm Mon-Sat, to 3.30pm Sun) Bouncy Bollywood hits and sizzling platters of tikka masala make up the soundtrack to this good, inexpensive Indian restaurant. Other tasty menu items in this minimalist place include curry, vindaloo and korma.

Uncle Ho's (Map p90; Calama E8-29; mains $3-6; ⌚ noon-10.30pm Mon-Sat) Sleek and slender, Uncle Ho's whips up tasty bowls of *pho* (noodle soup), sea bass with chili and lime over rice noodles, glazed spare ribs and other Vietnamese hits. Eat at the counter or grab an outdoor table on the quiet street in front.

Chifa Mayflower (Map p90; ☎ 254-0510; Carrión 442; meals $3-6; ⌚ 11am-11pm) Celebrity chef Martin Yan, believe it or not, called this busy Chinese restaurant the best in town (check out his autographed photo by the door), and whether you agree or not, it's definitely a great deal. Lots of veggie options.

Siam (Map p90; ☎ 223-9404; Calama E5-10, 2nd fl; mains $5-8; ⌚ 1pm-midnight Mon-Fri, to 11pm Sat & Sun) Siam cooks up delicious Thai food, served in a cozy upstairs dining room amid Eastern art and relaxing music.

Pekin (Map pp88-9; ☎ 223-5273; Whymper N28-42; mains $5-9; ⌚ noon-3pm & 7-10:30pm Mon-Sat, to 8:30pm Sun) Pekin has a slightly conservative air, but the owners are friendly and the food is good.

Sake (Map pp88-9; ☎ 252-4818; Rivet N30-166; dinner for 2 $50-80; ⌚ 12:30-3pm & 6:30-11pm Mon-Sat, 6:30-9pm Sun) This is Quito's premier sushi restaurant, a trendy, upscale place with outstanding food. Reservations are a must on weekends.

Noe Sushi Bar (Map pp88-9; ☎ 322-7378; Isabel La Católica N24-827; dinner for 2 $50-80; ⌚ 12.30-4pm & 6.30-10pm) This stylish, Zen-like restaurant offers tender, fresh sushi and sashimi, teppanyaki, Kobe beef and a range of other Japanese delicacies.

MIDDLE EASTERN

Aladdin's (Map p90; ☎ 222-9435; cnr Diego de Almagro & Baquerizo Moreno; mains $2-4; ⌚ 10:30am-11pm, to 1am Fri & Sat) This extremely popular souk-themed restaurant serves great falafel and *shawarma* sandwiches, as well as main courses. Giant hookahs attract the hipsters.

Hassan's Cafe (Map p90; ☎ 223-2564; Reina Victoria; mains $2-6; ⌚ 9:30am-8pm Mon-Sat) Lebanese food – *shawarmas,* hummus, kebabs, stuffed eggplant, veggie plates – is good, fresh and cheap at this 10-table restaurant near Colón.

CAFÉS & SNACKBARS

Café Amazonas (Map p90; cnr Av Amazonas & Roca; mains $2-5; ⌚ 7am-10pm Mon-Fri, to 7pm Sat & Sun) A Quito classic, this popular café attracts a mix of old-timers and upstarts to its smoke-filled interior. There's good people-watching at the outdoor tables.

Coffee & Toffee (Map p90; ☎ 254-3821; Calama; ⌚ 24hr) Equal parts café and lounge, Coffee & Toffee is a mellow and inviting place, with warmly lit brick walls, an open kitchen and a pleasant top-floor terrace. Locals and expats alike enjoy the wi-fi and the 24-hour service.

Café Colibri (Map p90; ☎ 256-4011; Pinto 619; mains $2-5; ⌚ 8am-6.30pm) This German-owned café is a great spot for breakfasts, crepes (savory and sweet), sandwiches and coffee. Big windows, skylights and a gardenlike front patio create an airy ambience.

El Cafecito (Map p90; Cordero 1124; mains $2-5; ⌚ 8am-11pm). On the ground floor of the popular guesthouse of the same name, this charming café and restaurant serves tasty, inexpensive dishes and snacks all day long. On a warm day, dine in the pleasant garden in front. Delicious breakfasts.

Kallari (Map p90; ☎ 223-6009; www.kallari.com; Wilson E4-266; breakfast/lunch $2/2.50; ⌚ 9am-5pm Mon-Fri, to 1pm Sun) This Quichua coop serves up some delicious, healthy breakfasts and lunches, and stocks its famous chocolate bars. For lunch, try the guacamole sandwich and the grilled plantain with cheese.

El Español (Map p90; ☎ 255-3995; cnr Mera & Wilson; mains $3-6; ⌚ 8am-9pm Mon-Fri, 8:30am-6pm Sat & Sun) This delightful Spanish delicatessen stocks a range of old-world provisions including olives, prosciutto, goat's cheese, wine and other picnic fare, as well as sandwiches made to order.

Centro Café (Map pp88-9; ☎ 223-6548; www.centro-café.com; Av Colombia 1222; mains $3-6; ⌚ 8am-9pm) This small, red-walled café serves set lunches ($3) as well as tapas, snacks and drinks. Live jazz, blues and bossa nova livens up the space on Thursday and Friday.

Uvíllas de Ochún (Map pp88-9; ☎ 322-8658; Andalucía N24-234; mains $3-5; ⌚ 1-9pm Mon-Fri) Ochún, the Yoruban goddess of love, wealth and happiness watches over this friendly, colorfully decorated café (that's her in the corner). In addition to smooth Cuban coffee and strong Cuban rum, visitors can sample tasty snacks, sandwiches, pizzas and light fare. The artwork on the walls is for sale.

Café Mango Tree (Map p90; ☎ 229-0249; Foch E4-310; mains $3-6; ⌚ 12.30-10pm) A pleasant café with an interior patio strung with hanging plants. In addition to coffee and smoothies, you'll find veggie plates, fajitas, lasagna, waffles, crepes, salads and other bistro fare.

Magic Bean (Map p90; ☎ 256-6181; Foch E5-08; mains $4-8; ⏰ 7am-10pm) Long the epicenter of the Mariscal, the Magic Bean serves a variety of well-prepared breakfasts, lunches, juices and snacks for the ever-present crowd of hungry travelers.

FAST FOOD

Hamburgers del Sese (Map pp88-9; cnr Tamayo & Carrión; mains $2-3; ⏰ lunch) One of many student hangouts in the area, Sese serves some of Quito's best burgers (including veggie burgers) – chow down inside or on the rooftop patio. For more cheap meals, head to the restaurants along Carrión between Tamayo and Av 12 de Octubre.

Tio Billy's (Map p90; ☎ 252-7479; Mera N23-78; mains $3-5; ⏰ noon-2am Mon-Sat) This tiny expat-owned spot has earned a local following for its tasty square burgers. Outdoor tables and kitschy decor set the scene.

SELF-CATERING

Mercado Santa Clara (Map pp88-9; cnr Dávalos & Versalles; ⏰ 8am-5pm) This is the main produce market in the new town. Besides an outstanding produce selection, there are cheap food stalls.

Supermercado Santa María (Map pp88-9; cnr Dávalos & Versalles; ⏰ 8:30am-8pm Mon-Sat, 9am-6pm Sun) Huge supermarket conveniently across from Mercado Santa Clara.

Supermaxi (Map pp88-9; cnr La Niña & Pinzón; ⏰ daily) Biggest and best supermarket near the Mariscal.

Mercado La Floresta (Map pp88-9; cnr Galavis & Andalucía; ⏰ 8am-5pm Fri) A small but delightful fruit market set in the peaceful Floresta neighborhood.

DRINKING & ENTERTAINMENT

Most of the *farra* (nightlife) in Quito is concentrated in and around the Mariscal, where the line between 'bar' and 'dance club' is blurry indeed. Mariscal bars, for better or worse, are generally raucous and notorious for 'gringo hunting,' when locals of both sexes flirt it up with the tourists (which can be annoying or enjoyable, depending on your state of mind). Bars with dancing often charge admission, which usually includes a drink. Remember to always take a cab home if you're out in the Mariscal at night (see p79).

For something far more relaxed, sans the pickup scene, head to La Floresta or Guápulo, where drinking is a more cerebral affair.

For movie listings and other events, check the local newspapers *El Comercio* and *Hoy*, or pick up a copy of *Quito Cultura*, a monthly cultural mag available free from the tourist offices.

Bars

Finn McCool's (Map p90; Pinto 251; ⏰ 5pm-2am) Proudly flying the green, white and orange, this Irish-owned bar is the current favorite among expats (and a growing number of locals) for its friendly, welcoming vibe, quiz nights (currently Tuesday) and pool, darts and table football. The classic wood-lined bar is also a good place to dig into fish and chips, shepherd's pie, burgers and other pub grub.

Coffee Tree (Map p90; ☎ 252-6957; cnr Reina Victoria & Foch; ⏰ 24hr) A good place to start the night off is this outdoor bar anchoring lively Reina Victoria. There's great people-watching from the tables on the plaza (and numerous other eating/drinking spots nearby). It also roasts its own coffee.

La Reina Victoria (Map p90; ☎ 222-3369; Reina Victoria 530; ⏰ 5pm-midnight Mon-Sat) This longtime expat watering hole is a cozy spot for a drink, with a fireplace, dartboard, bumper pool, and Anglo pub ambience. There's also decent pub fare including pizzas and fish and chips. Happy hour runs from 5pm to 7pm.

Mirador de Guápulo (Map pp88-9; ☎ 256-0364; Larrea & Pasaje Stübel; ⏰ 4pm-12:30am) This cozy café-cum-bar sits on the cliffside overlooking Guápulo. The views are unbeatable, and the snacks – mostly Ecuadorian specialties – are tasty. There's live music Wednesday through Saturday nights, with a cover charge of $5.

Ananké Guápulo (Map pp88-9; Orellana 781; ⏰ 6pm-late) This cozy bar-pizzeria sits perched on the hillside in Guápulo. It has a wee terrace (complete with fireplace) and several good nooks for secreting away with a cocktail and a friend.

Ananké (Map p90; cnr Almagro & Pinto) The newest branch of Ananké (see above) brings Bohemian style to the Mariscal. In addition to the tasty wood-fired pizzas, Ananké hosts an excellent lineup of musical talent including jazz, salsa, ska, funk, cumbia and reggae. Even if there's nothing on, the outdoor courtyard is an idyllic spot for an evening drink.

Café Habana (Map pp88-9; ☎ 290-0344; Calle Muros 243; ⏰ noon till late) Newly inaugurated in 2008, this dark-wood tavern offers live music (Cuban son, salsa) Thursday through Saturday nights, served alongside traditional Cuban fare.

Zócalo (Map p90; ☎ 223-3929; cnr Mera & Calama; noon-1am) Zócalo is a popular, buzzy place, with a prime, 2nd-floor location, situated right in the hub of the Mariscal Sucre. The atmosphere is fun and the food (snacks, Mexican-style dishes etc) is decent.

English and Irish pubs have long been the rave in Quito, and most serve food. The most popular include the following:

Kilkenny (Map p90; ☎ 290-1476; Garcia E7-36; until late) Rockin' Irish bar, with live music on Saturday nights from 8pm.

Turtle's Head (Map pp88-9; ☎ 256-5544; La Niña 626) Raucous spot with decent beer and food.

Nightclubs

Hitting the dance floor of one of Quito's *salsotecas* is a must. If you don't know how to salsa, try a few classes first (see p94).

Bungalow 6 (Map p90; cnr Calama & Almagro; admission $5; 7pm-3am Wed-Sat) The favorite Mariscal dance spot among foreigners, Bungalow 6 plays a good mix of beats – salsa, reggae and British and North American hits. The small but lively dance floor, good drink specials and popular events nights (including as Ladies night on Wednesday) always attract a festive crowd. Arrive early to avoid being turned away.

El Aguijón (Map p90; Calama E7-35; admission $5; 9pm-3am Tue-Sat) This excellent and unpretentious nightclub in the Mariscal attracts a good ratio of 20-something locals and foreigners. The space is open and somewhat industrial, with video art playing on a large screen above the dance floor. DJs spin a little of everything on weekends, with live bands on Thursday and salsa on Wednesday.

Seseribó (Map pp88-9; ☎ 256-3598; Veintimilla & Av 12 de Octubre, Edificio Girón; admission $5-10; 9pm-2am Thu-Sat) Quito's best *salsoteca* is a must-stop for salsa fans. The music is tops, the atmosphere is superb and the dancing is first-rate. Devoted *salseros* (salsa dancers) turn up on Thursday, which makes it a great night to go.

Blues (Map pp88-9; 222-3206; www.bluesestodo.com; Av República 476; admission $7-15; 10pm-6am Thu-Sat) Quito's only late-night club, Blues is the place party-goers head at 3am. DJs spin electronica and rock (with live rock bands playing on Thursday nights) to a style-conscious *quiteño* crowd. Well-respected international DJs spin here, and depending on the night, Blues can be great fun (sometimes the DJs and crowd disappoint).

Mayo 68 (Map p90; García 662) This popular salsa club is small and conveniently located in the Mariscal, and has a local following.

Live Music

our pick **El Pobre Diablo** (Map pp88-9; ☎ 223-5194; www.elpobrediablo.com; Católica E12-06; noon-3pm & 7pm-2am Mon-Sat) Locals and expats rate El Pobre Diablo as one of Quito's best places to hear live music. It's a friendly, laid-back place with a well-curated selection of talent (jazz, blues, world music, experimental sounds) performing most nights. It's also a great place to dine, with delectable fusion fare, a solid cocktail menu and a great vibe.

Café Libro (Map p90; ☎ 223-4265; www.cafelibro.com; Leonidas Plaza Guitierrez N23-56; admission $3-5; noon-2pm & 5pm-midnight Mon-Fri, 6pm-midnight Sat) Live music, poetry slams, contemporary dance, tango, jazz and other performances draw an artsy and intellectual crowd to this handsomely set Bohemian venue.

Café Toledo (Map pp88-9; ☎ 255-8086; cnr Lérida E12-12 & Toledo; admission $5) Small, mellow place for live music.

Theater & Dance

Teatro Sucre (Map p86; ☎ 228-2136; www.teatrosucre.com, in Spanish; Manabí N8-131; admission $5-20; ticket office 10am-1pm & 2-6pm) Recently restored and now standing gloriously over the Plaza del Teatro, this is the city's most historical theater. Performances range from jazz and classical music to ballet, modern dance and opera.

Teatro Bolívar (Map p86; ☎ 258-2486/7; www.teatrobolivar.org; Espejo) Likely the city's most illustrious theater and definitely one of its most important, the Bolívar is currently undergoing restoration work after a fire nearly burnt it to the ground. Performances and tours are still given, everything from theatrical works to international tango-electronica gigs. It's situated between Flores and Guayaquil.

Humanizarte (Map p90; ☎ 222-6116; www.humanizarte.com; Leonidas Plaza Gutiérrez N24-226; 5:30pm Wed) This excellent theater and dance group presents Andean dance performances. You can either call or check the website for other performances.

Ballet Folklórico Nacional Jacchigua (Map pp88-9; ☎ 295-2025; www.jacchigua.com, in Spanish; cnr Avs Patria & 12 de Octubre; admission $25) This folkloric ballet is as touristy as it is spectacular. It is presented daily at the Teatro Demetrio Agilera at the Casa de la Cultura Ecuatoriana (p87), and is quite a show. Contact any travel agency or upper-end hotel for tickets, or buy them at the door or online.

Teatro Prometeo (Map pp88-9; ☎ 222-6116; Av 6 de Diciembre 794) Affiliated with the Casa de La Cultura Ecuatoriana (p87), this inexpensive venue often has modern-dance performances and other shows that non-Spanish speakers can enjoy.

Patio de Comedías (Map p90; ☎ 256-1902; 18 de Septiembre 457) Presents plays and performances Thursday through Sunday nights, usually at 8pm.

Cinemas

Most Quito cinemas show popular English-language films with Spanish subtitles.

Ocho y Medio (Map pp88-9; ☎ 290-4720/21/22; www.ochoymedio.net, in Spanish; Valladolid N24-353 & Vizcaya; café 11am-10:30pm) This Floresta film house shows great art films (often in English) and has occasional dance, theater and live music. There's a small café attached.

The most recent Hollywood blockbusters are shown at **Cinemark** (Map p82; ☎ 226-0301; www.cinemark.com.ec, in Spanish; Naciones Unidas & Av América; admission $4) and **Multicines** (Map p82; ☎ 225-9677; www.multicines.com.ec, in Spanish; Centro Comercial Iñaquito; admission $4), both multiscreen, state-of-the-art cinemas.

SHOPPING

Arts & Crafts

There are loads of excellent crafts stores in the new town along and near Avenida Amazonas. If buying from street stalls, you should bargain; in the fancier stores, prices are normally fixed, although bargaining is not out of the question. Note that souvenirs are a little cheaper outside Quito, if you have the time and inclination to search them out.

Arte Sacra (Map p90; ☎ 254-7572; Washington E4-141) This tiny shop has a lovely collection of high-quality crafts: colorful masks, hand-painted picture frames, linen, glassware and even chocolate liqueur and honey.

La Bodega (Map p90; ☎ 222-5844; Mera N22-24) In business for 30-odd years, La Bodega stocks a wide and wonderful range of high-quality crafts, both old and new.

Latino Americana (Map p90; ☎ 254-7572; Av Amazonas N21-20) Boasts a huge selection of handicrafts, plus panama hats, ceramics, jewelry and alpaca wear. Check the quality carefully.

Ag (Map p90; ☎ 255-0276; Mera N22-24) Ag's selection of rare, handmade silver jewelry from throughout South America is outstanding. There are also antiques including rarities such as *vaca loca* (crazy cow) costumes, perfect for your next indigenous party.

Mercado Artesanal La Mariscal (Jorge Washington btwn Mera & Reina Victoria) Half a city block filled with crafts stalls (and the usual hippie bracelets, ponchos and even a couple of body piercing stalls), with good prices and mixed quality. It's great for souvenirs.

Folklore Olga Fisch new town (Map pp88-9; ☎ 254-1315; Colón 260); old town (Map p86; García Moreno N6-52, Hotel Patio Andaluz) The store of legendary designer Olga Fisch (who died in 1991), this is the place to go for the very best and most expensive crafts in town. Fisch was a Hungarian artist who immigrated to Ecuador in 1939 and worked with indigenous artists melding traditional crafts with fine art – her unique designs are stunning.

Productos Andinos (Map p90; ☎ 222-4565; Urbina 111) This sweet artisans' cooperative is crammed with reasonably priced crafts.

Galería Latina (Map p90; ☎ 254-0380; Mera N23-69) This well-stocked handicrafts shop offers an excellent selection of high-quality items: tagua carvings, colorful Andean weavings, textiles, jewelry, sweaters and handmade items from across Latin America.

Centro Artesanal (Map p90; ☎ 254-8235; Mera E5-11) This excellent shop is known for canvases painted by local Indian artists.

Tianguez (Map p86; Plaza San Francisco) Attached to the eponymous café (p103), Tianguez is a member of the Fair Trade Organization and sells outstanding crafts from throughout Ecuador.

El Aborigen (Map p90; ☎ 250-8953; Washington 614) More like an arts-and-crafts supermarket! Huge selection and good prices, too.

Centro Artístico Don Bosco (Map pp88-9; ☎ 252-7105; Mariana de Jesús Oe1-92) Near Calle 10 de Agosto, this is the retail outlet for a cooperative of woodworkers from throughout the highlands, formed to give people an alternative to immigrating to cities, so it's an excellent cause. It has mostly furniture, but beautiful boxes, frames and wall hangings too.

Clothing

Zoom Fashion House (Map pp88-9; ☎ 252-6468; Tamayo N22-43; noon-midnight Mon-Fri, 8pm-midnight Sat) Above the stylish restaurant-lounge

Naranjilla Mecánica (p105), Zoom is a trim little men's and women's boutique selling eye-catching urban and beachwear from both Dutch and Ecuadorian designers.

Cholo Machine (Map p90; ☎ 222-6407; www.cholomachine.com, in Spanish; Wilson 712 at Mera) Pop into this hipster boutique for a look at some eye-catching graphic T-shirts by local urban designer Cholo Machine.

Homero Ortega P & Hijos (Map p86; ☎ 295-3337; www.genuinepanamahat.com; Benalcazar N2-52; 9.30am-6.30pm Mon-Fri, to 1.30pm Sat) One of Ecuador's biggest sellers of Ecuadorian straw hats (aka panama hats), offering a small but versatile selection of its famous Cuenca brand.

Galleries

Quito's gallery scene is pretty limited, with just a handful of places exhibiting and selling local work. The most popular place to purchase paintings is **Parque El Ejido Art Fair** (Map pp88-9; Avs Patria & Amazonas; 9am-dusk Sat & Sun) during the weekend art fair. The work here consists mostly of imitations of established Ecuadorian artists, but it's cheap and colorful. Also pop into La Bodega (opposite), which usually has some excellent art on hand.

Posada de Artes Kingman (Map pp88-9; ☎ 222-2610; Diego de Almagro 1550 at Pradera) This small but well-stocked gallery is dedicated to the works of Ecuadorian painter Eduardo Kingman, the teacher and primary influence on the better-known artist Guayasamín. Prints, cards, T-shirts, etchings and jewelry line the walls and shelves.

Rosy Revelo (Map p90; ☎ 256-3022; www.rosyrevelo.com; Mera N22-37) Brilliantly hued canvases and tiny craftlike items adorn the walls of this colorful gallery. Ecuadorian artist Revelo has exhibited her abstract and intriguing pieces in galleries across the globe.

MarsuArte main gallery (Map pp88-9; ☎ 245-8616; www.marsuarte.com; Av 6 de Diciembre 4475 at Portugal); Swissôtel (Map pp88-9; ☎ 254 1283; Av 12 de Octubre 1820) This exclusive gallery isn't cheap, but it's one of the few in town where you can get a look at some of the country's most established artists.

Galería Catasse (Map pp88-9; ☎ 224-0538; Av 6 de Diciembre at Checoslovaquia) Chilean-born painter Carlos Tapia Catasse is one of Quito's premier (if not mainstream) contemporary artists. Galería Catasse is worth a visit if you're an art hound.

Galería Beltrán (Map p90; ☎ 222-1732; Reina Victoria 326) With more than 30 years in the art business, this art gallery sells paintings by well-known Ecuadorian artists.

Outdoor Supplies

Mono Dedo La Floresta (Map pp88-9; ☎ 222-9584; www.monodedo.com, in Spanish; Rafael Leon Larrea N24-36; 11am-7pm Mon-Fri, 9.30am-1.30pm Sat); Rocódromo (Map pp88-9; Queseras del Medio s/n; 11am-7:30pm Mon-Fri, 9:30am-5pm Sat & Sun) Outstanding climbing store with rock and ice gear, clothing, tents, bags and more. The Rocódromo (p93) branch has more gear.

Mele Sport (Map p90; ☎ 222-6290; Mera N22-44) Stocks good-quality climbing, rafting and other gear for outdoor adventures. Small climbing wall in front.

Explorer (Map p90; ☎ 255-0911; Reina Victoria 928) Another shop that sells and rents camping and mountaineering equipment.

Shopping Centers

Centros comerciales (shopping malls) are nearly identical to their North American counterparts, and sell international brands. Most stores are closed Sunday, but the following malls are open every day from about 10am to 8:30pm. They all have fast-food restaurants inside.

Centro Comercial El Jardín (Map pp88-9; ☎ 298-0300; Av Amazonas & Av de la República)

Centro Comercial Iñaquito (Map p82; CCI; ☎ 225-9444; Av Amazonas & Naciones Unidas)

Centro Comercial Quicentro (Map p82; ☎ 246-4512; Av 6 de Diciembre & Naciones Unidas)

GETTING THERE & AWAY

Air

As this book went to press, the construction of a new, larger airport, 25km east of the city center, was well underway. It's scheduled to open in 2010, although project delays are likely. Visit www.quiport.com for the latest info. Quito's current airport, **Aeropuerto Mariscal Sucre** (Map p82; ☎ 294-4900; www.quitoairport.com, in Spanish; Av Amazonas at Av de la Prensa) serves all international and domestic flights in and out of the capital. It's located about 10km north of downtown – see p113 for bus and taxi information on getting there. For domestic and international flight and airline information, see p391 and p395. The following are Ecuador's principal domestic airlines, with the widest choice of routes provided by TAME:

AeroGal (☎ 225-7301, 225-8086/7; Av Amazonas 7797) Near the airport.

Icaro (Map p82; ☎ 245-0928, 245-1499; www.icaro.com.ec, in Spanish; Palora 124 at Av Amazonas) Across from the airport runway.
TAME (Map p90; ☎ 250-9375/6/7/8, 290-9900; Av Amazonas 1354 at Colón)

Bus

Quito's main bus terminal is the **Cumandá Bus Terminal** (Map p86; Maldonado at Javier Piedra), just south of Plaza Santo Domingo in the old town. It can be reached by walking down the steps from Maldonado, or by taking the Trole (see opposite) to the Cumandá stop. After 6pm you should take a taxi, as this is an unsafe area at night. Don't take the Trole if you're loaded with luggage; it's notorious for pickpockets.

Several new terminals are scheduled to open at some point in the future (city officials couldn't pin down a date at the time of research). **Terminal Quitumbe** (Av Cóndor Ñan, near Av Mariscal Antonio José de Sucre), located 5km southwest of the old town, will handle destinations south of Quito. Terminal Carapungo, located in the north of the city, will service northern Ecuador. Check with the tourist office for the latest information on the terminals – and where your particular bus will depart from – before heading to the bus station.

BUSES FROM QUITO

Destination	Cost ($)	Duration (hr)
Ambato	2	2½
Atacames	9	7
Bahía de Caráquez	9	8
Baños	3.50	3
Coca	9	9 (via Loreto)
Cuenca	10	10-12
Esmeraldas	9	5-6
Guayaquil	7	8
Huaquillas	10	12
Ibarra	2.50	2½
Lago Agrio	7	7-8
Latacunga	1.50	2
Loja	15	14-15
Machala	9	10
Manta	8	8-9
Otavalo	2	2¼
Portoviejo	9	9
Puerto López	12	12
Puyo	5	5½
Riobamba	4	4
San Lorenzo	6	6½
Santo Domingo	2.50	3
Tena	6	5-6
Tulcán	5	5

Approximate fares and travel times are shown in the boxed table (left). There are daily departures for each destination and several departures per day to most of them, as well as numerous buses per hour to popular places such as Ambato or Otavalo. There is a $0.20 departure tax from the bus terminal.

For comfortable buses to Guayaquil from the new town, travel with **Panamericana** (Map p90; ☎ 255-3690, 255-1839; Av Colón btwn Reina Victoria & Diego de Almagro), or **Transportes Ecuador** (Map p90; ☎ 222-5315; Mera N21-44). Panamericana also has long-distance buses to other towns, including Machala, Loja, Cuenca, Manta and Esmeraldas.

A few buses leave from other places for some destinations in the Pichincha province. **Cooperativa Flor de Valle/Cayambe** (☎ 252-7495) goes daily to Mindo from Quito's Terminal Terrestre La Ofelia, reachable by taking the Metrobus line to the last stop. See p149 for departure times.

Car

Car rental in Quito, as with elsewhere in Ecuador, is expensive – taxis and buses are much cheaper and more convenient than renting a car. Rental vehicles are useful for visiting some out-of-the-way areas that don't have frequent bus connections (in which case, renting a more expensive 4WD vehicle is a good idea). See p399 for more car-rental information.

Alternatively, contact Ivan Segovia at **Edivanet** (☎ 264-6460, 09-379-1889, 09-824-5152), who will drive you anywhere in the country (provided there are roads) in a van for up to 10 people. The cost is about $60 per day, plus the price of his hotel room. Split with a group, it's quite affordable.

Car-rental companies:
Avis (☎ 244-0270) At the airport.
Budget (www.budget-ec.com, in Spanish); airport (p82; ☎ 224-0763, 245-9052; Av Amazonas at Av de la Prensa); Amazonas (pp88-9; ☎ 223-7026; cnr Avs Amazonas & Av Cristobal Colón)
Ecuacar airport (p82; ☎ 224-7298; Av Amazonas at Av de la Prensa); Av Cristóbal Colón (pp88-9; ☎ 252-9781, 254-0000; Av Colón 1280 near Av Amazonas)
Hertz airport (☎ 225-4257; Av Amazonas at Av de la Prensa); Swissôtel (☎ 256-9130; Av 12 de Octubre 1820)
Localiza (☎ 250-5974, 250-5986; Av 6 de Diciembre 1570 near Wilson)

Train

Although most of Ecuador's train system is in shambles, you can still ride the rails if you're determined. A weekend tourist train normally heads south from Quito for about 3½ hours to the Area Nacional de Recreación El Boliche, adjoining Parque Nacional Cotopaxi (p155). The line was out of commission at the time of research; ask at the tourist office or train ticket office for the latest info.

The **Quito train station** (Map p86; ☎ 265-6142; Sincholagua & Vicente Maldonado) is about 2km south of the old town. Buy tickets in advance at the **train ticket office** (Map p86; ☎ 258-2921; Bolívar 443; 🕑 8am-4:30pm Mon-Fri). The trains are old-fashioned with primitive bathroom facilities (part of the fun), and many passengers ride on the roof.

GETTING AROUND

To/From the Airport

Quito's new airport is scheduled to open in 2010; visit www.quiport.com to check if it's operational before you depart. The old airport is at the north end of Avenida Amazonas, about 10km north of the old town. Many of the northbound buses on Avenidas 10 de Agosto and Amazonas go there (look for *Aeropuerto* and *Quito Norte* placards). If you're going from the airport into town, you will find bus stops on Avenida 10 de Agosto, about 150m away from the terminal's front entrance.

A taxi is the best way to get into town. A new voucher system from the airport offers fixed rates – current charges are $6 into the new town and $8 to the old town. To save a couple of dollars, catch a cab just outside the airport on either side of Avenida Amazonas.

Car

Driving in Quito can be a hectic experience, especially in the old town. Remember, most streets are one-way, and on Sunday the streets in the old town are closed to traffic. Leaving your car (or a rental car) on the street overnight is asking to have it stolen. There are private garages throughout town where you can park overnight for around $10; inquire at your hotel for the nearest.

Public Transportation

BUS

Local buses all cost $0.25 – pay as you board. They are safe and convenient, but watch your bags and pockets on crowded buses. There are various types, each identified by color: the blue *Bus Tipos* are the most common and allow standing, while the red *ejecutivo* buses don't allow standing and are therefore less crowded, but are more infrequent.

Buses have destination placards in their windows (not route numbers), and drivers will (usually) gladly tell you which bus to take if you flag the wrong one.

TROLE, ECOVÍA & METROBUS

Quito has three electric bus routes: the Trole, the Ecovía and the Metrobus. Each runs north–south along one of Quito's three main thoroughfares, and each has designated stations and car-free lanes, making them speedy and efficient. As the fastest form of public transport, they're also crowded and notorious for pickpockets. Because of this, it's not recommended to use the Trole when traveling to or from the airport. They run about every 10 minutes from 6am to 12:30am (more often in rush hours) and the fare is $0.25.

The Trole runs along Maldonado and Avenida 10 de Agosto. It terminates at the Quitumbe bus terminal, 5km southwest of the old town. In the old town, southbound trolleys take the west route along Guayaquil, while northbound trolleys take the east route along Montúfar and Pichincha.

The Ecovía runs along Avenida 6 de Diciembre, between Río Coca in the north and La Marin in the south.

The Metrobus route runs along Avenida América from the Universidad Central del Ecuador (northeast of Parque El Ejido) to north of the airport.

Taxi

Cabs are all yellow and have red 'taxi' stickers in the window. Usually there are plenty available, but rush hour, Sundays and rainy days can leave you waiting 10 minutes for an empty cab. A few taxi companies include **Rodan Taxi** (☎ 248-5888), **City Taxi** (☎ 253-3333) and **Occidentaxi** (☎ 249-2222).

Cabs are legally required to use their *taxi-metros* (meters), and most drivers do; many however charge a flat rate of $2 between the old and new towns, about $0.25 to $0.50 more than if the meter was on. When a driver tells you the meter is broken, flag down another cab.

Late at night and on Sunday, drivers will ask for a higher fare, but it should never be more than twice the metered rate.

The minimum fare is $1. Short journeys will start at that and climb to about $4 for a longer trip. You can also hire a cab for about $8 per hour, which is a great way to see outer city sites. If you bargain hard and don't plan on going very far, you could hire a cab for a day for about $60.

AROUND QUITO

☎ 02

Quito makes a great base for exploring the striking geography and biodiversity of the region, with a number of excellent day trips from the capital. As well as the destinations covered in this section, Otavalo (p122) can be visited on a long day trip from Quito. The train ride to El Boliche recreation area in Parque Nacional Cotopaxi also makes for a spectacular outing (see p155), as do the magnificent hot springs of Termas de Papallacta (p233).

Getting There & Away

Destinations in this section can all be reached by public bus in less than two hours. Taxis are an option if you have between $30 and $60 to spare. Travel agencies in Quito (p79) also offer day trips to most of the places covered here.

LA MITAD DEL MUNDO

Ecuador's biggest claim to fame (and name) is its location right on the equator. **La Mitad del Mundo** (The Middle of the World City; admission $2; 9am-6pm Mon-Fri, to 7pm Sat & Sun) is the place where Charles-Marie de La Condamine made the measurements in 1736 showing that this was indeed the equatorial line. His expedition's measurements gave rise to the metric system and proved that the world is not perfectly round, but that it bulges at the equator. Despite the touristy nature of the equator monument that now sits here, there is simply no excuse to come this far and not see it. You just have to get into the spirit of things.

Sundays are busy with *quiteño* families, but if you don't mind the crowds they can be great days to visit because of the live music on the outdoor stage between 1pm and 6pm. Listening to a nine-piece salsa band rip up the equatorial line beneath the bright Andean sunshine can be quite an experience.

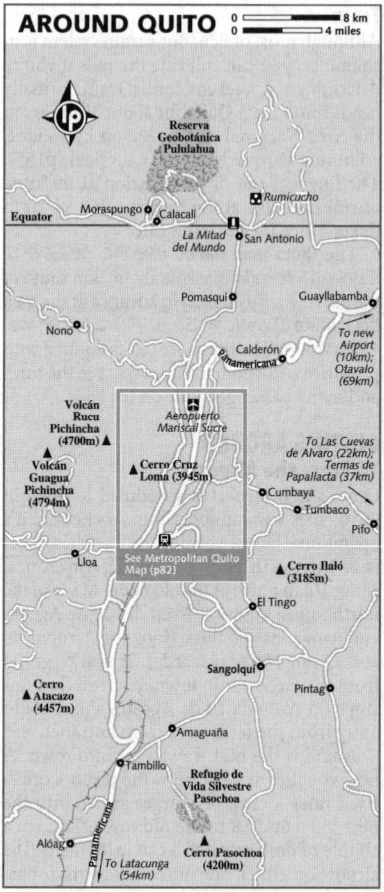

At the center of La Mitad del Mundo stands a 30m-high, stone trapezoidal **monument** (admission $3) topped by a brass globe. It is the centerpiece of the park, containing a viewing platform and an ethnographic museum, which provides a good introduction to the indigenous groups of Ecuador through dioramas, clothing displays and photographs.

Also at La Mitad del Mundo is an impressive 1:200 scale model of colonial Quito, housed in the **Museo del Quito en Miniatura** (admission $2; 9am-5:30pm). A light show takes you from dawn in the miniature city to late at night. Nearby, the **planetarium** (admission $2; 9am-5:30pm) presents a variety of astronomy shows. Of course, there are plenty of gift shops selling postcards and cheap souvenirs.

MYSTERIES FROM MIDDLE EARTH

The idea of standing with one foot in each hemisphere is an intriguing one, and the closer you get to the equator, the more you hear about the equator's mysterious energy. But what is fact and what is fiction?

There's no point in starting softly, so let's debunk the biggest one first. La Mitad del Mundo is not on the equator – but it's close. Global Positioning System (GPS) devices show that it's only about 240m off the mark. And no one who sees the photos of you straddling the equator has to know this, right?

Another tough one to swallow is the myth of the flushing toilet. One of the highlights of the Museo Solar Inti Ñan is the demonstration of water draining counterclockwise north of the equator and clockwise 3m away, south of the equator. Researchers claim it's a crock. The Coriolos Force – which causes weather systems to veer right in the northern hemisphere and left in the southern hemisphere – has no effect on small bodies of water like those in a sink or a toilet. Draining water spins the way it does due to plumbing, eddies in the water, the shape of the basin and other factors.

How about some truth: you do weigh less on the equator. This is due to greater centrifugal force on the equator than at the poles. But the difference between here and at the poles is only about 0.3%, not the approximately 1.5% to 2% the scales at the monument imply.

It is true that the spring and autumn equinoxes are the only days when the sun shines directly overhead at the equator. In fact, that's what defines an equinox. But that doesn't mean the days and night are equal in length, as many would have you believe – this happens just before the spring equinox and just after the autumn equinox, and the day depends on where you are on the planet.

More fascinating than any of the hoaxes perpetuated by Inti Ñan and Ciudad Mitad del Mundo, however, is the fact that the true equator (0.00 degrees according to GPS readings) resides on a sacred indigenous site constructed more than 1000 years ago. The name of the site is Catequilla, and visitors can learn more about this mysterious place in the Museo de la Cultura Solar (below).

Calima Tours (☎ 239-4796/7), located inside the complex, arranges short hikes ($8 per person) around the crater rim of nearby Pululahua. It's a good price, considering it includes the $5 park entrance fee. It also goes to Rumicucho archaeological site (p116).

Just outside, a few steps east of La Mitad del Mundo complex, is the one-room **Museo de la Cultura Solar** (www.quitsato.org; donations accepted; 9:30am-5:30pm). Here, visitors can learn about the real site of the equator, which happens to be on a hill called Catequilla visible across the highway. Zero degrees latitude lies on an old indigenous site that was only discovered by researchers in the late 1990s. Little is known of the 1000-year-old culture, aside from their magnificent equatorial and solar calculations. More sights are still being discovered all over the country, which astoundingly coincide with other equinoctial points. The informational museum is run by the Quitsato scientific research center. This is also a good place to inquire about hikes to the real equator, with tours led by indigenous guides (around $25 per person).

Continue east, a few hundred meters from La Mitad del Mundo, to the amusing **Museo Solar Inti Ñan** (☎ 239-5122; adult/child under 12 $2/1; 9:30am-5:30pm), supposedly (but again not actually) the site of the true equator. More interesting than the official complex next door, it's a meandering outdoor exhibition with fascinating exhibits of astronomical geography and explanations of the importance of Ecuador's geographical location. One of the highlights is the 'solar chronometer,' a unique instrument made in 1865 that shows precise astronomical and conventional time, as well as the month, day and season – all by using the rays of the sun. The real reason to come, of course, is for the water and energy demonstrations, but you'll have to decide for yourself if it's just a smoke-and-mirrors funhouse.

Getting There & Away

La Mitad del Mundo is 22km north of Quito, near the village of San Antonio. From Quito, take the Metrobus ($0.25) north to the last stop, Ofelia station. From there, transfer to the Mitad del Mundo bus – they're clearly marked, and they currently leave from the far-right platform as you roll up. The transfer costs an additional $0.15 (pay on the bus), and the entire trip takes one to 1½ hours. The bus drops you right in front of the entrance.

RUMICUCHO

About 3.5km northwest of La Mitad del Mundo, this small, pre-Columbian **archaeological site** (admission $1; 9am-3pm Mon-Fri, 8am-4pm Sat & Sun) was built around 500 BC by the Quitu-Cara culture and used principally as a ceremonial site during the equinoxes. The site is officially open during the hours listed above, but you can walk in at anytime. It's not Ecuador's most impressive site, but there are good views of Quito in the distance, and there probably won't be anyone else around. Walk all the way through – the best views are from the side furthest from the entrance.

Taxis to Rumicucho are available in San Antonio (the town near La Mitad del Mundo) – the round-trip fare, including waiting time, is between $5 and $8.

RESERVA GEOBOTÁNICA PULULAHUA

This 3383-hectare reserve lies about 4km northwest of La Mitad del Mundo. The most interesting part of the reserve is the **volcanic crater** of the extinct Pululahua. This was apparently formed in ancient times, when the cone of the volcano collapsed, leaving a huge crater some 400m deep and 5km across. The crater's flat and fertile bottom is used for agriculture. Within the crater there are two small cones, the larger Loma Pondoña (2975m) and the smaller Loma El Chivo.

The crater is open to the west side, through which moisture-laden winds from the Pacific Ocean blow dramatically. It is sometimes difficult to see the crater because of the swirling clouds and mist. The moist winds, combined with the crater's steep walls, create a variety of microclimates and the vegetation on the fertile volcanic slopes is both rampant and diverse. Because the walls are much too steep to farm, the vegetation grows undisturbed and protected. There are many flowers and a variety of bird species.

The crater can be entered on foot by a steep trail from the **Mirador de Ventanillas** viewpoint on its southeast side (easily reached by bus from La Mitad del Mundo). The steep trail is the best way to see the birds and plants, because most of the flat bottom is farmed. There is also an unpaved road on the southwest side via Moraspungo.

In the colorful village of Calacalí, the (much smaller) **original equatorial monument** can be seen; it was moved there after being replaced by the enlarged replica now at La Mitad del Mundo.

Information

The official entrance fee for the reserve is $5, which you must pay before you hike down into the crater or as you enter by car via Moraspungo; there are no charges for viewing from the Ventanillas viewpoint. See p115 for information on inexpensive tours.

Sleeping & Eating

Pululahua Hostel (☎ 09-946-6636; www.pululahuahostal.com; dm per person $12, cabañas $24-36) This ecologically friendly guesthouse, which opened fairly recently, is located inside the crater. Pululahua Hostel offers a handful of simple, comfortable rooms in a pristine setting. The owners cook tasty meals (mains $2 to $4) using ingredients from their organic farm whenever possible. Guests can use the Jacuzzi, hire bikes ($3 per hour) or horses ($8 per hour), and you can volunteer to work on the farm with (two-week minimum commitment). English and German are spoken.

El Crater (☎ 243-9254, 09-981-1653; d from $100) Near the Ventanillas viewpoint, El Crater offers a touch of luxury in its 12 suites. Rooms are nicely outfitted with king-sized beds and loads of amenities, and all have superb views over the volcanic crater. The restaurant onsite, currently open on weekends only, serves good food to outstanding views.

Getting There & Away

From La Mitad del Mundo, a paved road continues to the village of Calacalí, about 7.5km away. There are occasional buses from San Antonio to Calacalí, particularly on weekends. About 4km beyond La Mitad del Mundo on the road to Calacalí is the first paved road to the right. Ask the driver to drop you off there. About 1km along this road, there is a small parking area at the viewpoint.

Alternatively, continue on the road to Calacalí for 3km, which brings you to a sign for Moraspungo to the right. From the turnoff, it's 3km to Moraspungo and about 12km more into the crater. You pay the entry fee of $5 per person at Moraspungo.

CALDERÓN

This village is about 10km northeast of Quito on the Panamericana (not the road to La Mitad del Mundo). Calderón is a famous center of unique Ecuadorian folk art: the people make bread-dough decorations, ranging from small statuettes to colorful Christmas tree ornaments such as stars, parrots, Santas, tortoises, candles and tropical fish. The ornaments make practical gifts as they are small, unusual and cheap (buy a handful for $2). These decorative figures are inedible – preservatives are added so that they'll last many years. There are many stores selling the crafts on the main street.

From Quito, take an *interparroquial* bus from Plaza La Marín in the old town, or the intersection of Avenida Cristóbal Colón and Avenida América in the new town.

GUAYLLABAMBA & AROUND

If you follow the Panamericana another 15km beyond Calderón you will hit **Guayllabamba**, a small town set in a fertile river valley of the same name that is famous for its produce. Try to stop off at the roadside stands selling enormous avocados and bumpy green *chirimoya,* a fruit whose creamy center is slightly tart and pure ecstasy.

About 3km before you reach Guayllabamba, you'll pass the **Quito Zoo** (☎ 236-8900, 236-8898; admission $3; ⏰ 9am-5pm Tue-Sun). There are a few African and Asian species but the highlight is the Ecuadorian animals including the rare Andean spectacled bear and Galápagos turtles. Buses from Quito's Plaza Italia to Guayllabamba make the trip.

Some 3km beyond Guayllabamba, the road forks, and both routes end at Cayambe (p121). About 10km along the right fork, you pass a turnoff that leads back to Quito via **El Quinche**, whose impressive church and Virgin of El Quinche draws crowds from Quito during its November festival. The road passes through countryside and tiny hamlets to the town of **Pifo**. The road will eventually lead you back to Quito via the town of **Tumbaco**.

SANGOLQUÍ

Sangolquí's bustling Sunday-morning market is Quito's nearest indigenous market. The market actually runs all week (though to a much smaller extent), with the second-biggest day on Thursday. Sunday is the best day to visit. Local buses head here from Plaza La Marín in Quito's old town. Sangolquí is about 20km southeast of Quito's old town.

Situated 2.5km southwest of Sangolquí, on the road to Amaguaña, **Hostería La Carriona** (☎ 233-1974, 233-2004; www.lacarriona.com; s/d $86/98; 🍴) is a 200-year-old colonial hacienda that is a delightful place to stay. The old architecture is fronted by a cobbled courtyard and is surrounded by flower-filled gardens. It also has a pool, sauna, steam bath, Jacuzzi, games area and a large restaurant. The 30 units vary distinctly in character, from the cozy rural rooms to lavish suites. It is a 30-minute drive from Quito.

REFUGIO DE VIDA SILVESTRE PASOCHOA

This small but beautiful **wildlife reserve** (admission $7; ⏰ dawn-dusk) stands on the northern flanks of the extinct Pasochoa volcano, at elevations between 2900m and 4200m. It has one of the central valley's last remaining stands of humid Andean forest, with more than 100 species of birds. The luxuriant forest contains a wide range of highland trees and shrubs including the Podocarpaceae, the Ecuadorian Andes' only native conifer (the pines seen elsewhere are introduced). Orchids, bromeliads, ferns, lichens and other epiphytic plants also contribute to the beauty.

There are several trails, from easy half-hour loops to fairly strenuous all-day hikes. The shorter trails are self-guided; guides are available for the longer walks. One trail, which takes about eight hours, leads out of the reserve and to the summit of Pasochoa (4200m). The park ranger will give you a small trail map. **Fundación Natura** (☎ 254-7399; Moreno Bellido E6-167) in Quito, between Avenidas Amazonas and Mariana de Jesús, has trail maps and information and can make overnight reservations.

Overnight **camping** (per person $3) is permitted in designated areas. There are latrines, picnic areas, barbecue grills and water. There is also a simple **shelter** (dm $5) with 20 bunk beds, hot showers and kitchen facilities; bring your own sleeping bag. On weekends, when the place is usually crowded with locals, a small restaurant is open; otherwise, bring your own food.

Getting There & Away

This is the tricky part. Refugio de Vida Silvestre Pasochoa lies about 30km south of Quito. Buses leave from Plaza La Marín in

Quito's old town about twice an hour for the village of Amaguaña ($1, one hour). Ask the driver to let you off near Parque El Ejido. From the church nearby, there is a signed cobblestone road to the reserve, which is about 7km away. Walking is the only option. Alternatively, you can go all the way into Amaguaña (about 1km beyond El Ejido) and hire a truck to the reserve's entrance and information center for about $10 (the truck can take several people).

VOLCÁN PICHINCHA

Quito's closest volcano is Pichincha, looming over the western side of the city. The volcano has two main summits – the closer, dormant **Rucu Pichincha** (4680m) and the higher **Guagua Pichincha** (4794m), which is currently very active and is monitored by volcanologists. A major eruption in 1660 covered Quito in 40cm of ash; there were three minor eruptions in the 19th century. A few puffs of smoke occurred in 1981, but in 1999 the volcano rumbled into serious action, coughing up an 18km-high mushroom cloud and blanketing the city in ash.

Climbing either of the summits is strenuous but technically straightforward, and no special equipment is required. Rucu Pichincha is now easily climbed from the top of the teleféríQo.

Climbing the smoking Guagua Pichincha is a longer trip. It is accessible from the village of Lloa, located southeast of Quito. From the village, it's about eight hours by foot to the **refugio** (hikers refuge; dm $5). It is then a further short but strenuous hike from the *refugio* to the summit. Reaching the summit will take you two days if you walk from Lloa. There are numerous agencies in Quito (Safari Tours is a good one, p97) that offer this as a day trip from town.

Dangers & Annoyances

Before the teleféríQo was built, Rucu Pichincha was plagued with crime. Things were safer for a while, but unfortunately there have been several armed robberies recently along the main trail. The teleféríQo management is aware of this problem and it's hoped that they and the Ecuadorian police will beef up security. Hikers are advised to check with SAE (p79) for an update on conditions before heading out. As for Guagua Pichincha, stay up to date on the volcano's activity either by dropping into SAE or checking the website of the **Instituo Geofísico** (www.igepn .edu.ec).

Northern Highlands

As the spine of the Andes bends north from Quito, volcanic peaks punctuate valleys blanketed by green farm plots, flower farms and fields of sugarcane. Most visitors arrive on the Panamericana (Pan-American Hwy), the same route the Incas traversed, and head to Otavalo's vibrant outdoor market.

But the behind-the-scenes action takes place in tiny outlying villages, where artisans produce various crafts using the same methods as their ancestors did: weaving wool on handlooms and chiseling chunks of walnut trees into intricate figurines.

These highlands hold more hints of the past, from old colonial haciendas-cum-luxury lodges to indigenous shamans who turn off televisions to perform ancient rituals. Strong indigenous cultures, Afro-Ecuadorian communities, colonial descendants and mestizos (people of mixed indigenous and Spanish descent) all inhabit this place.

Adventurers come to conquer the ice-blue glaciers on Volcán Cayambe, the country's third-highest volcano, and hike through the uninhabited, misty *páramo* (high-altitude Andean grasslands) in the north before soaking in steaming thermal baths.

High-altitude landscapes surrender to the steamy lowlands to the west, a rich transition zone where coffee plantations flourish in places such as the Intag Valley (Valle Intag). Further south, the cloud forests of Mindo harbor hundreds of bird species, a rich destination for bird-watchers and weekenders alike.

HIGHLIGHTS

- Browse a dazzling array of goods in Otavalo's colorful **crafts market** (p122).
- Hike into the cloud forests around **Mindo** (p147) to glimpse hundreds of bird species.
- Ride through the countryside on horseback starting from a historic **colonial hacienda** (p130) on the outskirts of San Pablo del Lago, near Otavalo.
- Drink the fermented corn drink *chicha de yamor*, during the **Fiesta del Yamor** (p125).
- Summit the massive, glacier-covered **Volcán Cayambe** (p121)
- Wander among the artfully sculpted topiaries in **Tulcán's cemetery** (p142).

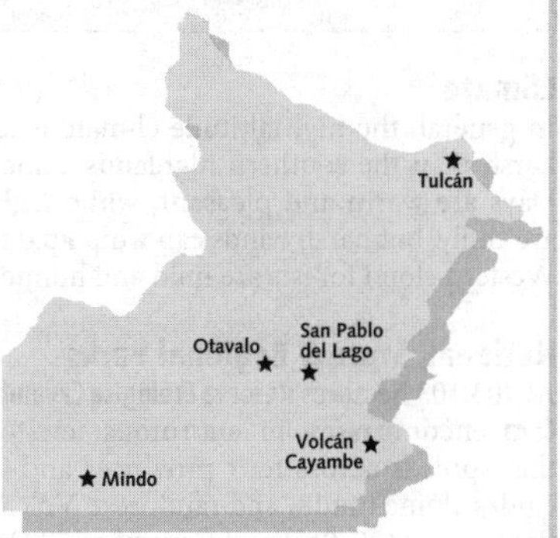

- AVERAGE TEMP IN TULCÁN: 10°C (50°F)
- RAINIEST MONTHS IN TULCÁN: OCT & NOV

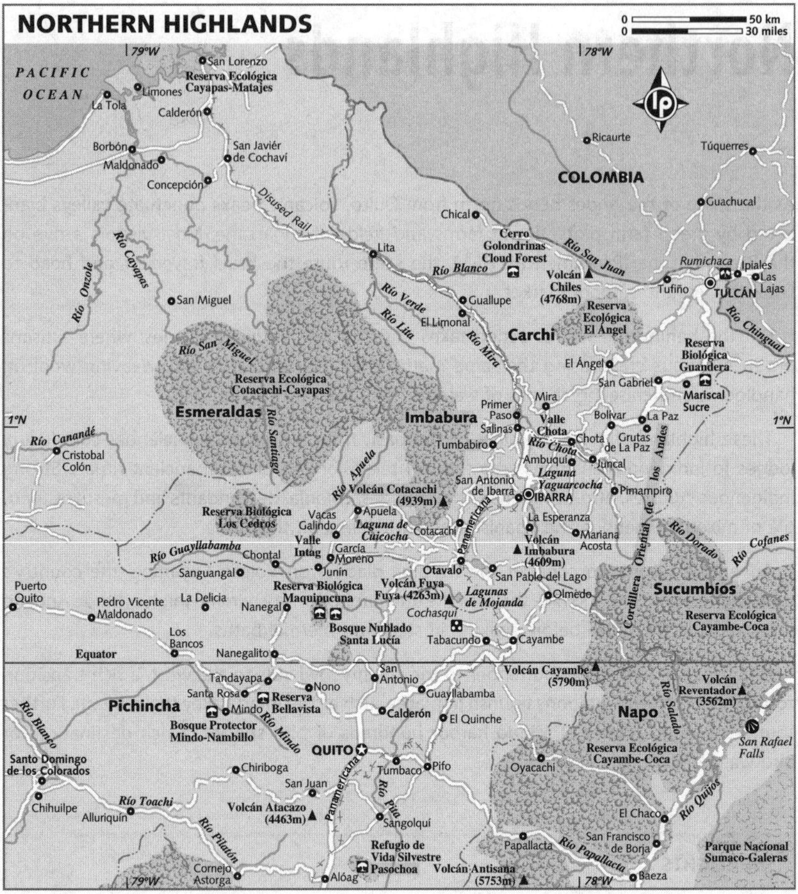

Climate

In general, the high-altitude climate is less harsh than the southern highlands climate. Days are warm and pleasant, while nights are chilly, but harsh winds can whip up dust. Western cloud forests are mild and humid.

National, State & Regional Parks

At 403,103 hectares **Reserva Ecológica Cayambe-Coca** encompasses an enormous territory that spreads across four provinces and includes alpine tundra and rainforest. Volcáns Reventador (3562m) and Cayambe (5790m) sit within its bounds. Also straddling the rainforest is 204,420-hectare **Reserva Ecológica Cotacachi-Cayapas**; its most accessible point is Cotacachi. The comparatively tiny 15,715-hectare **Reserva Ecológica El Ángel** is a *páramo* treasure harboring condors and foxes and the rare, hairy-leaved *frailejones* (gray friars; local name for the *Espeletia* plant).

Dangers & Annoyances

The border between Ecuador and Colombia can be dangerous; hire guides when venturing into the outdoors there and only attempt border crossings at Tulcán (see p144).

Getting There & Around

Buses from Quito run frequently to most towns and cities in the region, with Otavalo getting most of the tourist traffic. Shuttles to Otavalo leave from most Quito hotels as well.

Buses are common and main roads are well maintained, but a reliable road does not connect the Intag Valley with the cloud forests to the south. A 4WD can come in handy if you're venturing off the Panamericana.

The only public airport is in Tulcán.

COCHASQUÍ ARCHAEOLOGICAL SITE

A searing, shadeless site requires an imaginative mind to conjure up images of the ancient Cara civilization (see p26) living among the pillowy mounds that remain. Much here has been whittled away by the elements and left untouched by archaeologists. Even so, it's worth a visit.

The grass-covered, rounded pyramids and mounds, some of which date to AD 900, are thought to have been a military stronghold and religious center. Local Spanish-speaking guides provide tours of the open-air **museum and site** (admission $3; 8am-5pm Mon-Fri, to 6pm Sat & Sun). Guides earn little and would be well thanked with a tip.

There is no public transportation. Some buses take the Tabacundo road between Quito and Otavalo and can drop you off at the turnoff. From there, a cobbled road climbs 9km to the site. Try to grab a lift from Cochasquí workers and guides arriving around 9am. Taxis from nearby Cayambe charge about $10 per hour for the service.

CAYAMBE

☎ 02 / pop 36,453

The snow-dusted peak of Cayambe looms over the rolling farmland surrounding the town of the same name, 64km north of Quito along the Panamericana. The region is considered Ecuador's flower capital (see the boxed text, p123). Enormous white tents packed with rows of blooms blanket the hillsides.

Most buses between Quito and Otavalo can drop you in Cayambe. In town, buses head north and south along Natalia Jarrin; taxis are on the Parque Central. Rows of shops, banks and a supermarket make Cayambe feel large and commercially important. Pyramids of *bizcochos,* salty, dry breadsticks, are stacked in every bakery next to creamy cuts of locally made white cheese. The **tourism office** (☎ 236-0052; www.municipiocayambe.gov.ec; cnr Teran & Sucre) can provide information about visiting the archaeological sites on Cayambe's outskirts.

About 2km north of town on the Panamericana you'll find **Las Cabañas de Nápoles** (☎ 236 1388; s/d $20/40), where you can stay in comfortable brick cabins and try local cheese at the popular restaurant.

In town, try **El Refugio Hotel** (☎ 236-3700, 09-803-7514; cnr Teran & 10 de Agosto; s/d $10/12), where a narrow stairwell leads to small but cheery rooms, some of which have televisions. The friendly owner can help arrange hikes into the mountains.

Grab a sandwich or leafy salad at **Aroma Cafetería** (cnr Bolívar & Rocafuerte; lunches $2; 7am-9pm, closed Wed) alongside office workers on coffee breaks, but save room for a satisfying slab of cake. Next door, CoffeeNet provides reliable internet access.

CAYAMBE TO OYACACHI

☎ 06

On a clear day, the road north from Cayambe to Ibarra, which passes through the village of Olmedo, provides excellent views. Heading south, you'll encounter the little village of Oyachi, known for its indulgent community-run **hot springs** (admission $2). Some basic hostels and camping by permission are your options for overnighting.

On the road to Oyacachi, **Hacienda Guachala** (☎ 236-3042/2426; www.guachala.com; s/d $40/54;) dates back to 1580, making it the oldest hacienda in Ecuador. The sprawling property features whitewashed rooms, a sunny stone courtyard anchored by an old fountain, horse stables and a restaurant. Seven kilometers south of Cayambe, it's a great base for visiting the hot springs, hiking or horseback riding.

A popular **hike** from Oyacachi goes through the Reserva Ecológica Cayambe-Coca to Papallacta (see p231) and takes two to three days, depending on conditions.

VOLCÁN CAYAMBE

At 5790m, the extinct Volcán Cayambe is Ecuador's third-highest peak and is the highest point in the world through which the equator directly passes – at 4600m on the south side. There is a **climbing refuge** (per person $20), but you need a 4WD to reach it. The seven-hour climb is more difficult than the more frequently ascended Cotopaxi (p155). **Safari Tours** (Map p90; ☎ in Quito 222-0426; admin@safari.com.ec; Foch E4-132 & Cordero, Quito) offers a three-day glacier school and guided trips to the summit, as does **World Bike** (☎ in Quito 290-6639; info@bikeclimbecuador.com; Pinto E4-358 & Amazonas, Quito). Guide services average $80 per day and most do not include the $10 park entrance fee.

THOSE RANDY PEAKS

As if it wasn't enough that all Spanish nouns have a gender, apparently volcanoes do too. The locals refer to Volcán Imbabura (4609m) as Taita (Daddy) Imbabura and Volcán Cotacachi (4939m) as Mama Cotacachi. These two extinct volcanoes can be seen from Otavalo on clear days: the massive bulk of Taita to the east and the sharper, jagged peak of Mama to the northwest. When it rains in Otavalo, they say that Taita Imbabura is pissing in the valley. Another legend suggests that when Mama Cotacachi awakes with a fresh covering of snow, Taita Imbabura has paid her a conjugal visit. What happens when snow falls on Imbabura? Or when drought dries the valleys? You'll have to ask a local.

OTAVALO

☎ 06 / pop 43,122 / elevation 2550m

For hundreds of years, Otavalo has hosted one of the most important markets in the Andes, a weekly fiesta that celebrates the gods of commerce. In the colorful open-air marketplace, vendors hawk everything from handmade crafts to slyly disguised imports. The tradition of swapping money for goods here stretches back to pre-Incan times, when traders would emerge from the jungle on foot, ready to conduct business.

These days the market has morphed into a broader cultural crossroads – a place where packs of tourists from around the globe roam alongside Ecuadorians on a shared hunt for bargains. Visitors feel welcome here. For its size, the town has an abundance of lodging and restaurants.

Otavaleños are known for their exquisite weavings (see the boxed text p132), and have been exploited for their textile-making skills by the Incas, Spanish and eventually, Ecuadorians. Life improved for many of the *indígena* (indigenous) people after the Agrarian Reform of 1964, which abolished the long-standing tradition of serfdom and permitted local land ownership. Still, many villagers struggle to profit from their crafts. That said, *otavaleños* are the wealthiest and most commercially successful *indígena* people in Ecuador, an honorable achievement that has allowed many to live in relative comfort.

The *indígena* people wear traditional clothing and take extreme pride in their appearance. Women wear white blouses embroidered with flowers, long wool skirts, *fachalinas* (headcloths), woven belts, canvas sandals and strands of beads. Men wear felt hats, blue ponchos and calf-length pants, and braid their hair in one long strand.

Otavalo has become a must-see destination for most tourists who visit the country, but don't let its popularity keep you away. Instead, witness – and let your pocketbook participate in – one of the most successful entrepreneurial stories in the Andes. But don't stop there. To truly appreciate the handcrafted items, visit nearby villages to see artisans at work.

Information

Banco del Pacífico (cnr Bolívar & Moreno) Has an ATM and changes traveler's checks.

Banco del Pichincha (Bolívar, btwn Moreno & Piedrahita) Changes traveler's checks and has an ATM.

Book Market (Roca; ⏲ Mon-Sat) The place to buy, sell and trade books in English, German, French and other languages. Between Moreno and Montalvo.

C@ffé Net (☎ 292-0193; Sucre near Colón; per hr $1; ⏲ 8am-10pm Mon-Sat, 9am-9pm Sun)

Casa Turismo (☎ 292-7230; www.otavalo.gov.ec; cnr Quiroga & Jaramillo; ⏲ 8:30am-1pm & 2:30-6pm Mon-Fri, 9:30am-1pm Sat & Sun) Helpful staff. The building also houses art, photography and history exhibits.

Dr Leonardo Suarez (☎ 09-779-1206) Locally recommended doctor who speaks some English and makes house calls.

Hospital (☎ 292-0444/3566; Sucre) Some 400m northeast of downtown.

Police station (☎ 101; Av Luis Ponce de Leon) At the northeastern end of town. Authorized to process replacements for identity documents.

Post office (cnr Sucre & Salinas, 2nd fl)

Vaz Cambios (☎ 292-3500; cnr Jaramillo & Saona) Exchange house with good rates. Changes traveler's checks.

Sights

MARKETS

Every day, vendors hawk an astounding array of goods in the Plaza de Ponchos, the nucleus of the **crafts market**. But the real action happens on Saturday, official market day, when the market swells into adjacent roads. The aptly named Plaza de Ponchos offers mostly artisan crafts, in particular, woolen goods, such as tapestries, blankets, ponchos, belts, thick hooded sweaters, scarves, gloves, hats and furry alpaca rugs from other regions.

Otherwise, there are embroidered blouses, hammocks, carvings, beads, original paintings and struggling Guayasamín imitations, knit finger puppets, clay pipes, fake shrunken heads, woven mats and jewelry made from tagua nut (also known as vegetable ivory).

Sellers lure browsers with friendly smiles and chipper adjectives; *their* goods are softer, stronger, prettier, cheaper and better. The options can be dizzying, similar and yet different all at once. Take your time. Browse the tables and check out pricing at a few stalls. Bargaining is expected, especially with multiple purchases. Don't be shy about asking for a deal, but don't be ruthless either.

Food stalls set up at the northern end proffer vats of chicken or tripe soup roiling on portable stove tops; crispy whole fried fish; scraps of flop-eared suckling pigs served with *mote* (maize) kernels; and scoops of *chicha* (a fermented corn drink) from plastic buckets.

The daily **market** (cnr Jaramillo & Montalvo; 7am-1pm) is stuffed with everything from exotic highland fruits and baggies of ground spices to mops, weaving tools and bootleg CDs. On Saturdays, this market also explodes with even more raw foods. There's also an indoor 'food court,' a chance to belly up alongside locals and slurp soups.

Visitors who get up before the sun are rewarded with Saturday morning's **animal market** (6-10am). While you might have little use for screaming piglets or a lethargic cow, it's certainly worth visiting. Observe the subdued bargaining over a fresh *empanada de queso* (cheese turnover) from a hillside vendor. Cross the bridge at the end of Colón and follow the crowds to get to the market, which is a kilometer out of town, west of the Panamericana in the Viejo Colegio Agrícola.

Between June and August, arrive on Fridays to shop before tour groups choke the passageways. Make reservations for weekends, even in budget hotels, which fill up year-round. The market is not free of pickpockets. While shopping, leave valuables at the hotel and keep your money in a safe spot.

EL LECHERO

The **Lechero** is a famous magical tree outside of Otavalo known for its healing powers. It's worth the 4km walk if you want some fresh air, great views of town or a little magic. But be careful. Readers have reported some robberies. Taxis also visit the spot; ask the driver to wait if you don't want to walk back.

To get there take Piedrahita out of town going south. The road quickly steepens. Look for arrows painted along the way. Hike some unpaved switchbacks and go past a fragrant eucalyptus grove to the crest of a hill where you'll see a lone, stubby tree. You can continue north another 4.2km to get to Parque Condor.

A ROSE BY ANY OTHER NAME

Flower farms are considered to be the star industry of the highlands, employing 76,600 people in small communities with few other job opportunities. Ecuador exports one-third of roses grown annually to the US for Valentine's Day alone. The flower boom has brought prosperity to many Ecuadorians, but this has come at a cost to the environment and workers.

In order to grow plump, flawless roses in Ecuador's tropical climate, a number of growers use chemical pesticides and fungicides, some of which are listed as extremely or highly toxic by the World Health Organization. Not all farms provide safety equipment such as fumigation suits, which can lead to serious health consequences ranging from rashes to cancer. Many employees receive substandard wages, and sometimes work 70 to 80 hours a week. A 2005 study by the International Labor Rights Fund in 2005 found that over 55% of Ecuador's flower workers had been the victims of some kind of sexual harassment.

The German-based **Flower Label Program** (www.fairflowers.de) is working to reform the industry by rewarding flower producers that meet environmental and social standards with FLP-certification labels for their products. Equivalent US-based programs include **VeriFlora** (www.veriflora.com) and **TransFair USA** (www.transfairusa.org). To qualify for these schemes, farmers must use natural pesticides, such as chili and chamomile extract, and offer their workers fair wages and conditions.

With an increasing awareness of socially and environmentally conscious blooms, more consumers are shopping for the greenest flower, not the reddest rose.

OTAVALO

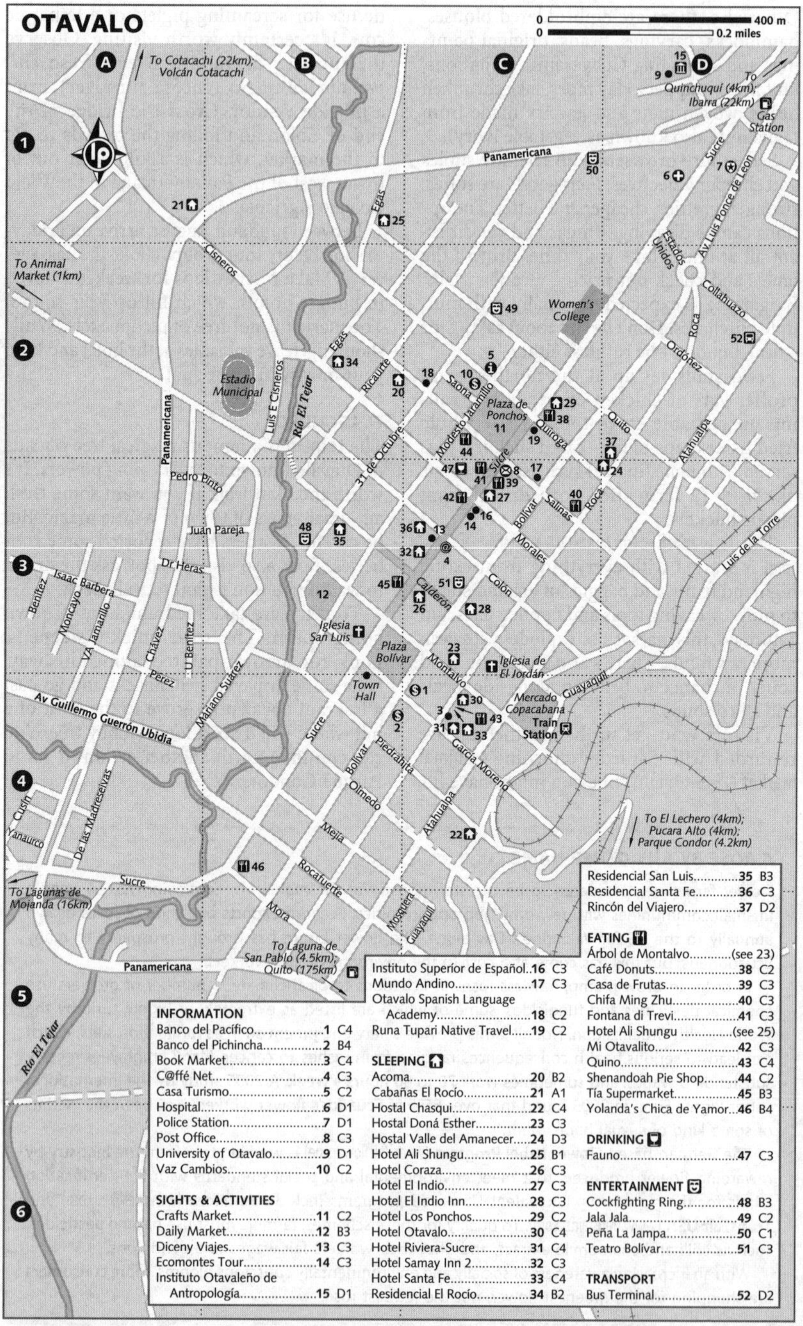

INFORMATION		
Banco del Pacífico	1	C4
Banco del Pichincha	2	B4
Book Market	3	C4
C@ffé Net	4	C3
Casa Turismo	5	C2
Hospital	6	D1
Police Station	7	D1
Post Office	8	C3
University of Otavalo	9	D1
Vaz Cambios	10	C2
SIGHTS & ACTIVITIES		
Crafts Market	11	C2
Daily Market	12	B3
Diceny Viajes	13	C3
Ecomontes Tour	14	C3
Instituto Otavaleño de Antropología	15	D1
Instituto Superior de Español	16	C3
Mundo Andino	17	C3
Otavalo Spanish Language Academy	18	C2
Runa Tupari Native Travel	19	C2
SLEEPING		
Acoma	20	B2
Cabañas El Rocío	21	A1
Hostal Chasqui	22	C4
Hostal Doná Esther	23	C3
Hostal Valle del Amanecer	24	D3
Hotel Ali Shungu	25	B1
Hotel Coraza	26	C3
Hotel El Indio	27	C3
Hotel El Indio Inn	28	C3
Hotel Los Ponchos	29	C2
Hotel Otavalo	30	C4
Hotel Riviera-Sucre	31	C4
Hotel Samay Inn 2	32	C3
Hotel Santa Fe	33	C4
Residencial El Rocío	34	B2
Residencial San Luis	35	B3
Residencial Santa Fe	36	C3
Rincón del Viajero	37	D2
EATING		
Árbol de Montalvo	(see 23)	
Café Donuts	38	C2
Casa de Frutas	39	C3
Chifa Ming Zhu	40	C3
Fontana di Trevi	41	C3
Hotel Ali Shungu	(see 25)	
Mi Otavalito	42	C3
Quino	43	C4
Shenandoah Pie Shop	44	C2
Tía Supermarket	45	B3
Yolanda's Chica de Yamor	46	B4
DRINKING		
Fauno	47	C3
ENTERTAINMENT		
Cockfighting Ring	48	B3
Jala Jala	49	C2
Peña La Jampa	50	C1
Teatro Bolívar	51	C3
TRANSPORT		
Bus Terminal	52	D2

PARQUE CONDOR

A Dutch-owned foundation that rehabilitates raptors, vultures and other birds of prey, **Parque Condor** (☎ 292-4429, 09-778-9353; www.parquecondor.org; admission $3; 9:30am-5pm Tue-Sun) offers a great opportunity to see an Andean condor up close, as well as eagles, owls, falcons and hawks. Don't miss the free flight demonstrations at 11:30am and 4:30pm. The center is perched on the steep hillside of Pucara Alto, 4km from town.

INSTITUTO OTAVELEÑO DE ANTROPOLOGÍA

The **Instituto Otavaleño de Antropología** (☎ 292-0461; admission free; 8:30am-noon & 2:30-6pm Tue-Fri, 8:30am-noon Sat) is packed with ancient artifacts from the region. It's located inside the University of Otavalo, one block north of Sucre and Panamericana.

Courses

Mundo Andino (☎ 292-1864; www.mandinospanishschool.com; cnr Salinas & Bolívar 4-04; lessons per hr $5) teaches classes Monday through Friday, arranges homestays with local families and organizes activities and long-term volunteer opportunities.

Instituto Superíor de Español (☎ 299-2424; www.instituto-superior.net; cnr Sucre & Morales; groups/individuals per hr $5.75/7) receives high marks from readers. It can also arrange family homestays.

Readers also recommend the **Otavalo Spanish Language Academy** (☎ 292-1404; www.otavalospanish.com; cnr 31 de Octubre & Salinas) for its volunteer programs and homestays.

Tours

Diceny Viajes (☎ 269-0787/0460, 09-705-4295; cnr Sucre 10-11 & Colón) Readers give kudos to this guide service run by native *otavaleña* Zulay Saravino (see the boxed text, p126), who helped start Otavalo's first tour agency. Knowledgeable, bilingual guides lead tours to various villages to learn about crafts, music and local traditions. Stay in guest rooms (rooms per night $14) in Zulay's own home in the small village of Quinchuquí.

Ecomontes Tour (☎ 292-6244; www.ecomontestour.com; cnr Sucre & Morales) Offers day trips on Saturdays and Wednesdays. Trips include visits to a *bizcocho* (biscuit) factory in Cayambe and the Peguche Falls.

Runa Tupari Native Travel (☎ 292-5985; www.runatupari.com; cnr Sucre & Quiroga) Renowned for its approach to community tourism, Runa Tupari has partnered with 44 indigenous, mestizo and Afro-Ecuadorian rural communities to offer sightseeing, hiking, horseback riding and biking trips. Rural homestays are $25 per night. Offbeat options include a bumpy 2000m mountain-bike descent into the Intag's tropical cloud forest, a round-trip 10-hour hike up 'Mama' Volcán Cotacachi (4939m) and some culinary adventuring (see the boxed text, p135). It also sells Intag coffee and local crafts.

Festivals & Events

Otavalo's best-known celebration, the **Fiesta del Yamor**, occurs during the first two weeks of September in honor of the fall harvest. An elected queen oversees processions, live music and dancing, fireworks displays and cockfights. Revelers consume copious amounts of *chicha de yamor*, seven varieties of corn slowly simmered together to produce this unusual nonalcoholic drink (longer-fermented versions are alcoholic). It's available only during fiesta time from Yolanda's Chicha de Yamor (p127).

June 24 is **St John the Baptist Day** (especially celebrated in its namesake suburb near the intersection of Cisneros and the Panamericana), known locally as La Fiesta de San Juan or its pagan name Inti Raymi. It is said that local *indígenas* live and die to celebrate this event, saving money year-long for costumes, food and drink. The festivities continue through June 29, the **Day of St Peter & St Paul**. Look for the bullfight in Otavalo and the boating regatta on Laguna de San Pablo, as well as celebrations in nearby Ilumán.

Some small surrounding villages still celebrate pre-Columbian rituals that can last up to two weeks. For dates and info, visit www.otavalo.gov.ec.

Sleeping

Otavalo's perennial popularity has created a good selection of well-priced accommodations. Make sure your bargain hotel has hot water and adequate bedcovers. Reserve in advance for the weekend rush.

BUDGET

Residencial El Rocío (☎ 292-4606; Morales 11-70; r per person with shared/private bathroom $5/6) Friendly, clean accommodations on the quieter side of downtown. Modest rooms vary in size, but all have hot water. A rooftop strewn with laundry lines offers great views of the hilltops. The family also owns Cabañas El Rocío (rooms per person $12), a comfortable garden escape in the San Juan neighborhood on the other side of the Panamericana.

OTAVALEÑA: ZULAY SARAVINO

The daughter of a weaving family, Zulay Saravino started the first tour agency in Otavalo in 1980. Two film professors from UCLA documented eight years of her life for *Zulay, Facing the 21st Century,* a documentary about the challenges facing an indigenous woman who lives abroad then returns home. Zulay lives in Quinchuquí, where she was born, and runs the Diceny Viajes tour agency (p125) in Otavalo.

How has Otavalo changed in the past few decades?

We have more infrastructure, including roads and houses, but now we want to adopt archetypes that are not ours, and in turn we are losing ourselves.

How do you feel when otavaleños choose not to wear traditional clothes?

It's sad to see young people not wearing these clothes, which are part of our identity and what differentiates us from other Ecuadorian cultures. Little by little, they lose their identification with the town and tradition. Personally, I feel too proud to abandon these clothes.

Do you feel the same when otavaleño men cut their trensas (braids of hair)?

Yes, when a man cuts the *trensa,* he loses his connection to our indigenous ethnic group. Many times, a man cuts his hair to avoid racism and become more accepted by modern society without thinking about the real meaning.

What don't most visitors understand about otavaleños?

Most of them think Otavaleños are primitive and underdeveloped, but when they arrive they see a city that's advancing. We are a developed, civilized people who are dedicated to our own businesses and don't depend on people who could exploit us.

When you returned to Otavalo after living in the US, did people treat you differently?

Yes. Many people could not accept that I had learned to be a totally independent woman. Despite the challenges of being woman in Otavalo, there is no challenge that can get in the way of the *otavaleña's* advancement within the developed world. For me, being an Otavaleña is a source of pride. Having transcultural experiences has not changed my identification as a native, something that makes me unique.

Hotel Los Ponchos (☎ 292-2035; www.hotellosponchos.com; Sucre 14-15 near Quito; r per person $10) This dated megamotel with a maze of clean tiled rooms with fuzzy animal bedspreads is good value. Stay streetside on the top floor for views of Volcán Cotacachi.

Hostal Valle del Amanecer (☎ 292-0990; www.hostalvalledelamanecer.com; cnr Roca & Quiroga; r per person incl breakfast with shared/private bathroom $9/11) The tropical-themed decor and pebbled courtyard saturated with hammocks creates a popular choice for travelers. Small rooms force guests into communal spaces and the on-site restaurant. Rent bicycles for $8 a day.

Rincón del Viajero (☎ 292-1741; www.rincondelviajero.org; Roca 11-07; r per person incl breakfast with shared/private bathroom $10/12) A great choice for its warm hospitality and homey, snug rooms. After artwork was stolen by guests, the owners had landscapes painted directly on the walls. English is spoken and there's a restaurant, TV lounge with fireplace, hot water and a rooftop terrace peppered with hammocks. Ask about camping facilities outside of town.

Hotel Samay Inn 2 (☎ 292-1826; samayinnhotel@hotmail.com; Sucre 1009 near Colon; r per person $10, incl breakfast $12) Located in the heart of the action, shady hallways lead to basic rooms with some welcome daylight. Balconies offer prime people-watching, but it's a noisy spot.

Hotel Santa Fe (☎ 292-3640; www.hotelsatafeotavalo.com; cnr Roca 7-34 & Moreno, r per person $13) Despite a forced freshness, understated Southwestern decor and friendly service create a decent place to spend a night. The first-floor restaurant serves breakfast and dinner.

Hotel El Indio (☎ 292-0060; Sucre 12-14, s/d $15/25) Remodeled under the hand of a sure, new owner, this hotel is a reliable option close to the Plaza de Ponchos. Large colorful rooms with glossy wood trim surround a small, open-air courtyard with tables and umbrellas. The restaurant serves lunch and dinner.

Hotel Riviera-Sucre (☎ 292-0241; www.rivierasucre.com; cnr Moreno 3-80 & Roca; s/d $15/26) This Belgian-owned hotel in a large, old home offers high-ceilinged rooms and endless nooks with a garden, fireplaces, courtyard hammocks, a library, laundry facilities, internet and a small café. But unreliable hot water can detract from the experience.

Hotel Coraza (☎ 292-1225; hotelcoraza@hotmail.com; cnr Sucre & Calderón; r per person incl breakfast $19) This large hotel appeals to a constant stream of Ecuadorian nationals. Spacious, carpeted rooms are set off with glass and mirrors and touches of kitsch. In addition to TV and telephone, there's a restaurant and laundry service.

Other reasonable and cheap spots include reader-recommended **Hostal Chasqui** (☎ 292-3199; cnr Piedrahita & Guayaquil; r per person $8), **Residencial San Luis** (☎ 292-5609; Calderón 6-02; r per person with shared/private bathroom $5/6) and **Residencial Santa Fe** (☎ 292-0171; Colon near Sucre; r per person $6).

MIDRANGE

Hostal Doña Esther (☎ 292-0739; www.otavalohotel.com; Montalvo 4-44; s/d $22/32) This small, Dutch-owned colonial-style hotel is cozy, with attractive rooms surrounding a courtyard ornamented with ceramics and ferns. The service is personable and there's an attached restaurant (see p128).

Hotel Otavalo (☎ 292-0416; Roca 5-04; s/d $22/37) A welcome, chipper colonial place decked out with polished hardwood floors and a bright covered courtyard. The high-ceilinged rooms tucked away from the street are some of the quietest in town. Time breakfast in the restaurant to avoid tour groups.

Acoma (☎ 292-6570; Salinas 7-57; s/d incl breakfast with shared bathroom $18/24, with private bathroom $24/37, ste $61) The decor in this modern Santa Fe–style hotel may make you crave chili stew and desert views. But who needs the Southwest when you've got beautiful cedar floors, mosaic tiles and skylights surrounding a sleek bar in Ecuador? A detached building in the back offers less luxury; small rooms with shared baths inspire main-building envy.

Hotel El Indio Inn (☎ 292-0922; Bolívar 9-04; s/d incl breakfast $32/47) A modern, generic hotel that caters to the business set with its large carpeted, no-nonsense rooms and highly professional staff. Not to be confused with the smaller, more-colorful Hotel El Indio (opposite).

Hotel Ali Shungu (☎ 292-0750; www.alishungu.com; cnr Egas & Quito; s/d $42/55, apt $110-165) This classic, which has long been one of Otavalo's best hotels, still reigns supreme. Heated rooms (a rarity here) decorated with Andean designs are tidy, with desks, tables and garden views. Large apartments are great for families. The sprawling garden patio offers views of Volcán Imbabura. Try the excellent restaurant (p128). The American owners have recently opened the Ali Shungu Mountaintop Lodge (rooms per person including breakfast a dinner $85) 5km outside of town.

Eating

Restaurants are plentiful, even if you're craving international fare.

Tía (Sucre near Calderón; 🕑 9am-8pm) Don't expect much meat or produce at this grocery store/supermarket, whose specialty is all things canned. But you will find an ATM here.

Shenandoah Pie Shop (Salinas 5-15; pie slices $1.30; 🕑 7:30am-9pm) Try a slice of these famous deep-dish pies à la mode. The *mora* (blackberry) pie is thick with fruit and perfectly tart yet sweet.

Café Donuts (cnr Sucre & Quiroga; 🕑 6am-10pm) Join the city's early risers, including the police force, for pastries topped with glazed fruits, basic breads and an extensive coffee drink list.

Casa de Frutas (Sucre near Salinas; mains $3-5; 🕑 8:30am-10pm) Located in an eclectic, disheveled courtyard, this spot serves satisfying granola and fruit bowls and omelets. Lunch includes stuffed avocados, soy burgers, juices and Intag coffee.

Chifa Ming Zhu (☎ 09-771-0381; cnr Roca & Salinas; mains $3-6) Tucked inside a colorful house, plates of steaming noodle dishes and gleaming vegetables draw crowds on weekends. Portions are huge.

Mi Otavalito (☎ 292-0176; Sucre 11-19; mains $3-6; 🕑 8am-11pm) Some of the best Ecuadorian dishes in town attract locals and tourists alike. Fresh ingredients shine in grilled meats, trout and hearty soups.

our pick **Yolanda's Chicha de Yamor** (green house at Sucre & Mora; meals $3-7; 🕑 late Aug–mid-Sep, during festival time) Yolanda Cabrera has become famous (see the clippings on the wall) for delicious local fare such as *tortillas de maiz* (corn tortillas), *mote* (hominy), *empanaditas* (Spanish pies) and the local favorite of *fritada* (fried pork). Of course, the real attraction is her *chicha de yamor* (see p125), which Yolanda stirs out back in large bubbling cauldrons over smoky fires.

Quino (☎ 292-4094; Roca near Montalvo; mains $5; ⏰ 10am-11pm) This popular locale with bright, citrus-colored walls and a homey atmosphere will satisfy your seafood cravings. Try the grilled fish or shrimp ceviche with lots of lime.

Fontana di Trevi (Sucre near Salinas; meals $5-6; ⏰ noon-11pm) Navigate a small, indoor mall to this second-floor pizza joint. While food can be slow in coming, it's worth the wait for a cheesy vegetarian pizza and richly layered lasagnas.

Árbol de Montalvo (☎ 292-0739; Montalvo 4-44; mains $5-8; ⏰ noon-10pm Fri-Sun, 6-9pm Mon-Thu) Make your way to the back of the Hostal Doña Esther (p127) for organic salads, seasonal vegetables and Mediterranean-inspired pastas.

Hotel Ali Shungu (☎ 292-0750; cnr Egas & Quito; meals $7-12; ⏰ 7:30am-8:30pm) Food with gourmet touches (and higher prices) is served up in a greenhouse-like setting decorated with Andean crafts. The menu caters to homesick visitors, with waffles in raspberry syrup, roast-beef sandwiches, curries, enchilada casserole and New York cheesecake all on offer. Check out the impressive jewelry case while you wait.

Drinking & Entertainment

Peñas are lively folk venues (bars or clubs with live music) common to the high Andes, and Otavalo has a few good ones. It's not a party town per se, but on weekend nights the disco scene can simmer into something sweaty and festive.

Peña La Jampa (☎ 292-7791; cnr 31 de Octubre & Panamericana; ⏰ 7pm-3am Fri & Sat) Offers a mix of live salsa, merengue, rock en español and *folklórica* (folk music).

Fauno (Morales btwn Bolívar & Sucre; ⏰ 2pm-3am daily) A slicker three-level club attracting the younger crowd with Latin rock on weekends.

Jala Jala (☎ 292-4081; www.jalajalaotavalo.com; cnr 31 de Octubre & Quito; ⏰ 7pm-3am Fri & Sat) One of the town's newer *peñas,* this elongated space gets busy in the wee hours.

Teatro Bolívar (Bolívar 9-03) This cinema presents two showings daily: one for kids and the other for Jean Claude Van Damme fans. It's between Calderón and Colón.

There's a weekly **cockfight** (31 de Octubre; admission $1; ⏰ 7pm Sat), which one local argues is not about the aggressive gamecocks but the passionate audience.

Getting There & Away

BUS

Buses depart from Quito's main terminal every 20 minutes or so and charge $2 for the two- to three-hour ride to Otavalo. Transportes Otavalo and Transportes Los Lagos both use Otavalo's bus terminal. The others drop passengers off on the Panamericana, from where they have to walk six to eight blocks to downtown.

From the terminals of Ibarra ($0.45, 35 minutes) and Tulcán ($3, three hours), buses leave for Otavalo every hour or so. Buses from Tulcán drop you on the Panamericana.

In Otavalo, the **main bus terminal** (Atahualpa) is at the northern end of town; you can take a taxi to most hotels for $1. From the terminal, Transportes Otavalo and Los Lagos leave for Quito and Ibarra every 10 minutes.

Transportos Otavalo, Los Lagos and Transportes 6 de Junio make the spectacular, hair-raising journey to the remote Intag Valley hamlets of Apuela ($3, 2½ hours) and García Moreno ($4, 3½ hours).

Old local buses, with fares roughly $1 per hour of travel, go south to San Pablo del Lago (20 minutes) and Araque (30 minutes). Cooperativa Imbaburapac has buses to Ilumán (30 minutes), Agato (1 hour), San Pablo del Lago (15 minutes), Ibarra (45 minutes) and Cayambe (45 minutes) every hour or so. The bus to Ibarra passes through small indigenous villages en route.

Transportes 6 de Junio goes to Cotacachi via the longer route (through Quiroga), and Transportes Cotacachi takes the shorter route ($0.25, 25 minutes) via the Panamericana.

For the villages of Calderón, Guayllabamba and Cayambe, take an Otavalo–Quito bus (most frequent on Saturday afternoons). The buses stop at the turnoff from the main road in Cayambe, which leaves a walk of several hundred meters into town.

TAXI

Taxis charge a minimum of $1 per ride and $10 per hour. **Taxi Los Lagos** (☎ 292-3203) takes six people at a time to Quito for $7.50 per person. Luggage costs $2 to $3 extra.

AROUND OTAVALO

☎ 06

Green checkered farmland creeps up the steep flanks of the mountains surrounding Otavalo, a rewarding combination for visitors seeking heart-pounding exercise and long views. Hikers shouldn't miss the spectacular Lagunas de Mojanda, southwest of Otavalo.

Hidden haciendas, once-grandiose epicenters of colonial society, woo anyone willing to step on the sprawling grounds. Then there's Ecuador's largest lake, Laguna de San Pablo, a more domesticated setting with paddleboats and groomed shoreline hotels. Each September an international swimming competition has competitors swimming 3800 cold meters across the lake. Visitors can reach all these places within a short bus or taxi ride from downtown Otavalo.

The Panamericana heads northeast out of Otavalo, passing by the indigenous villages of **Peguche**, **Agato** and **Ilumán**. Explore them by bus, taxi or with a tour. The villages southwest of Laguna de San Pablo manufacture fireworks, totora mats and other reed products. Other *otavaleño* villages are nearby. Consult the tourist agencies in Otavalo (p125), as tour prices are not much more than a long taxi rental.

Las Palmeras (☎ 292-2607; www.laspalmerasinn.com; s/d $50/60, ste $75-100) offers colorful cottages set in the rural hills. Meander the cobblestone pathways then try the neighbor's Hawaiian energy massages, rent a bike or go horseback riding with an expert trainer. Spanish lessons, laundry, internet and movies are available. Meals, including box lunches, cost extra. German and English are spoken.

Lagunas de Mojanda

A crumbling cobbled road leads high into the *páramo* to three turquoise lakes set like gemstones into the hills. Located 17km south of Otavalo, the area acquired protected status in 2002 and since has become a safer and better-protected destination. If you have come to camp, set up on the south side of the biggest lake, **Laguna Grande**, or in the basic stone refuge (bring a sleeping bag and food). The jagged peak of **Fuya Fuya**, an extinct volcano (4263m), looms nearby; be cautious on this hike and leave valuables behind. If you want to hoof it from the closest lodgings (listed below), bring lots of water. Taxis charge extra (about $17 each way plus $10 per hour to wait) for wear and tear. To save a few bucks, stay at a nearby inn and hike or taxi out early from Otavalo and hike back the same day. Runa Tupari Native Travel (p125) offers guided hikes that include transportation. For information about the lakes visit the **Mojanda Foundation/Pachamama Association** (☎ 292-2986; www.casamojanda.com/foundation.html) across from Casa Mojanda.

An extended scenic walk across the *páramo* will drop you into the archaeological site of Cochasquí, 20km due south. Bring a 1:50,000 topographical map of the Mojanda area, numbered ÑII-F1, 3994-III, available from the Instituto Geográfico Militar (IGM) in Quito (p76).

our pick **Casa Mojanda** (☎ 09-972-0890, 09-973-1737; www.casamojanda.com; s/d incl breakfast & dinner $110/150) Consummate relaxation can be found at this lovely inn, 4km south of Otavalo. It's on the road to Lagunas de Mojanda, with views of steep Andean farmland. Cheerful cottages are equipped with electric heaters and hot-water bathrooms; some have fireplaces. Slip into the outdoor Japanese-style hot tub after a long day of hiking. The grounds include horse stables, an organic garden, a library and mini-theatre. The American/Ecuadorian owners are active in local nature preservation and community projects and can help arrange tours and activities, including mountain biking, rafting and horseback riding. Rates include breakfast and dinner made from fresh garden ingredients, and a short, guided hike to waterfalls.

Visit **La Luna** (☎ 09-315-6082, 09-829-4913; www.hostallaluna.com; campsites $2.50, dm $6, r per person with shared/private bathroom $9/12) for a low-key, low-budget getaway with beautiful views. Located 4.5km south of Otavalo on the way to Lagunas de Mojanda, it's a great haven for hikers. Guests dine in the main house, where the fireplace games are the nexus of evening activity. Showers are hot and four of the doubles have a private bathroom and fireplace. The owners speak English and will arrange hikes (with lunchboxes) or Spanish lessons with advance notice. Walk an hour from town or grab a taxi for $4.

Laguna de San Pablo

A popular stop for weekenders who want to escape the hectic pace of Otavalo but stay within reach of the market. Houses, farms and the paved road encircling the lake are never far from sight, but great views of Volcán Imbabura (see the boxed text, p122) compensate.

Cabañas del Lago (☎ 291-8001/8108; www.cabanasdellago.com; r per night $67, cabañas $79) caters to families, with a *fútbol* field, minigolf, jet skis and *agua* (water) park on the east side of the

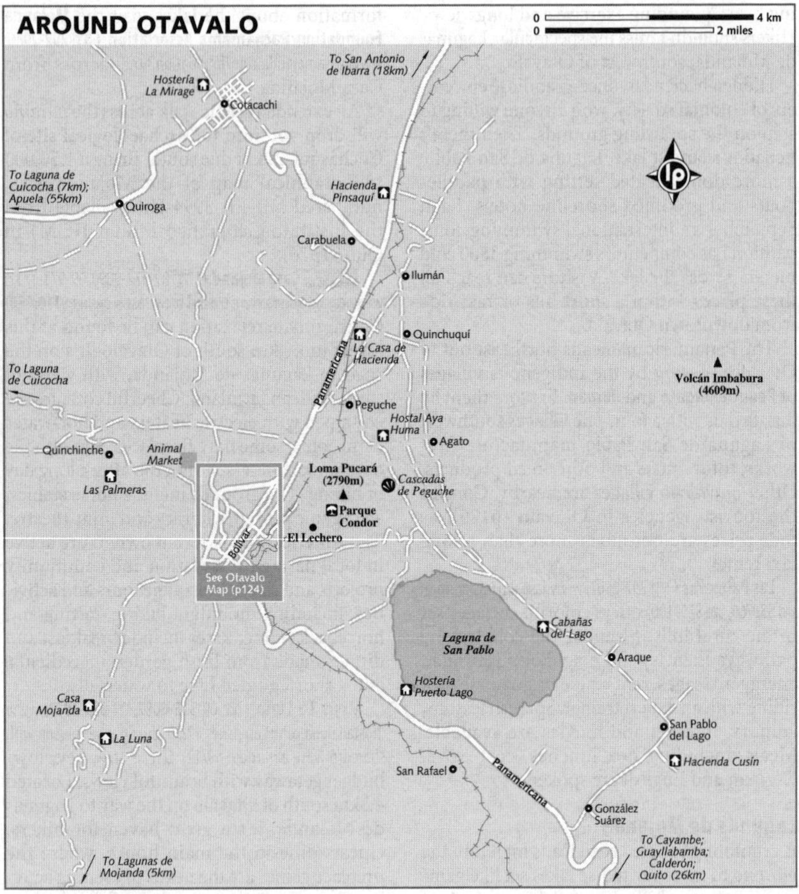

lake. Prim, postage stamp–sized cabins are overshadowed by the other amenities. The on-site restaurant fuels the fun.

Hacienda Cusín (☎ 291-8013/8316, 800-683-8148 in the US; www.haciendacusin.com; s/d $80/120) is a fairy-tale 17th-century hacienda. It's located on the southern outskirts of San Pablo del Lago, 10km from Otavalo. Tall cedar trees shade the garden paths linking the cottages and old buildings. Impressive carved wooden doors, oil paintings from Europe, and South American textiles and antiques create museum-like interiors. Guests can play squash, ride horses or mountain bikes, lounge in the reading library then cozy up to the bar where a roaring fire cuts the highland chill. There are two exclusive craft shops, including one run by the Andrango family from Agato (see opposite). The formal, proper dining room serves delicious meals. Packages offer everything from overnight horseback-riding expeditions and Spanish-language lessons to weaving courses. Book well in advance for weekends.

Hostería Puerto Lago (☎ 292-0920; www.puertolago.com; s/d/ste $60/75/95) is located just off the Panamericana 5km southeast of Otavalo. An immaculate, green lawn groomed by grazing llamas surrounds austere cabins that look out onto the lake. The popular, white-linen restaurant offers traditional cuisine on the waterfront, and guests can laze the day away in a paddleboat, kayak or on the tennis court.

North Along the Panamericana

Hacienda Pinsaquí (☎ 294-6116; www.haciendapinsaqui.com; s/d/ste incl breakfast $99/130/160) offers a taste of old-world Ecuador. Wooden-beamed ceilings, grand grounds and refined decor, including antique French washbasins and gaunt portraits, channel the past. Constructed in 1790, parts of this purebred hacienda survived the disastrous earthquake of 1857, and South American liberator Simón Bolívar used to stay here on his route north to Bogotá. Some of the 30 rooms and suites have Jacuzzis and fireplaces. Check out the chapel or the cozy low-lit bar, an ideal place to sip *canelazo* (aguardiente with hot cider and cinnamon) and hatch revolutionary plans. Guests can go horseback riding with a pick from the renowned stables. A stay includes breakfast; lunch and dinner cost $20 each. Located 5km north of Otavalo along the Panamericana.

Peguche

In this tiny weaving village, sheep traipse past clotheslines draped with dyed wool drying in the breeze. While electric looms occupy many homes here, it's the traditional, handmade products that deserve attention. Ask locals for directions to sites listed below.

Start at **Tejidos Mimahuasi**, the home of weavers José María Cotacachi and Luz María Fichabamba, who demonstrate various weaving processes. Then visit **Taller de Instrumentos Andimos-Nañda Mañachi**, where a family crafts traditional musical instruments including panpipes and *charangos,* 10-stringed mandolin-like instruments traditionally made from armadillo shells.

On the central plaza of Peguche, **El Gran Condor** (☎ 269-0161; www.artesaniaelgrancondor.com; 8am-7pm Mon-Fri, 11am-4pm Sun) is the place for textile fanatics who didn't find what they wanted in Otavalo. The shop sells high-quality textiles made locally, including sweaters, scarves and wall hangings. Call ahead to arrange for demonstrations of dyeing and weaving techniques.

From the abandoned railway line in Peguche, a trail leads about 2km southeast to the waterfalls **Cascadas de Peguche**. These falls are sacred to the locals and visitors should stay away during Inti Raymi (p125), June's festival of the sun, when men conduct ritual cleansing baths. Near the falls is a pre-Columbian archaeological site in poor condition.

Guests come to **Hostal Aya Huma** (☎ 269-0333; www.ayahuma.com; s/d with shared bathroom $4.50/8, with private bathroom $17/24) for a quiet village retreat. Rooms are basic but clean, and the café serves hearty breakfasts and good vegetarian food. If you're lucky there's live music.

Take in the spectacular valley view at **La Casa de Hacienda** (☎ 294-6336; www.casadehacienda.com; r per person incl breakfast s/d $35/25), a collection of secluded brick cabins with fireplaces and rocking chairs. The large window-walled restaurant serves *cuy asado* (roasted guinea pig) with advance notice. Located 1km north of Peguche.

Cooperativa Imbaburapac (Av Atahualpa or bus terminal) has some buses that go through Peguche en route to Agato.

Agato

Take a road uphill 2km east of Peguche to the **Tahuantinsuyo Weaving Workshop**, where master weaver Miguel Andrango demonstrates traditional weavings on old looms and sells his products on-site. The Andrango family runs an outlet at the Hacienda Cusín on weekends (see opposite).

Ilumán

Weavers work in this village off the Panamericana about 7km northeast of Otavalo. It is also famous for its shamans; the local shamans' association has around 120 members. Members advertise by scrawling their name in large letters on their homes. Feel free to try it out, but remember that cleansings, involving raw egg and spittle, can get messy. From Otavalo, take an Imbaburapac bus.

Cotacachi

☎ 06 / pop 10,492 / elevation 2560m

On any night in Cotacachi, you'll understand why Unesco benighted this town 'City of Peace.' *Otavaleños,* uninspired by the tranquility, say, *'Mil veces preso en Otavalo que suelto en Cotacachi,'* which translates roughly to, 'Prison in Otavalo is a thousand times better than being let loose in Cotacachi.' But that solitude has inspired a recent influx of foreigners, who are snatching up property. With Laguna de Cuicocha and Volcán Cotacachi close by, this mannered and mellow colonial town may some day give Otavalo a run for its money.

Town streets smell like the inside of a fine shoe store, the first hint of the leatherworking specialty. Men on bicycles creatively

A TIGHTLY WOVEN CULTURE

Behind the bountiful woolens stalls at the Otavalo market is a living, breathing industry with a culture unto itself. Small indigenous villages outside Otavalo are home to weaving families. The activity starts before dawn in many households. Weavers gather in a small dirt-floor room to do their swift, silent work. Production starts with washing, carding, spinning and dyeing the wool. Children play with yarn instead of Lego, practicing to one day join in.

Four thousand years ago, the ancestors of *otavaleño* weavers started using the backstrap loom, which can still be seen in some homes today. They sat on the cold ground, holding the loom between their bare feet, and interlaced threads to make complex and dazzling designs.

The tradition faces its own challenges as the use of electric looms continues to rise. And as trade beyond borders has shot up, so has the incursion of foreign products. Visitors who travel the length of the Andes begin to spot the same stuff everywhere and stop buying. Otavalo addressed this problem by placing stricter controls on goods sold in its market. These days 80% to 90% of the artistry sold is local. If you want to support the traditional industry, purchase handmade goods, even though their bulk is murder on the luggage.

transport stacks of hide, and stores lining 10 de Agosto sell everything from leather handbags and wallets to designer jackets. Sunday is market day.

For information about community tourism, horseback riding and hiking, go to the municipal tourism office in the **Casa de las Culturas** (☎ 291-5140; www.cotacachi.gov.ec; cnr Bolívar & 9 de Octubre; 9am-1pm & 3-7pm Mon-Fri, 9am-5pm Sat & Sun). The spacious building has an exhibit of Guayasamín paintings and a library/internet center. The friendly staff can help with emergencies, such as lost documents and theft.

The **Museo de las Culturas** (Moreno 13-41; admission $1; 9am-noon & 2-5pm Mon-Fri, 2-5pm Sat, 10am-1pm Sun), located in the neoclassical old municipal palace, presents the ethnohistory of the region, from 8500 BC through colonial and republican periods. Don't miss the costumes and photos from indigenous religious festivals.

SLEEPING & EATING

Hostal Tierra Mia (☎ 291-5873; cnr Bolívar & 10 de Agosto; r per person $7) While you may miss the sign on the street, the third floor houses a quiet, clean hotel. The rooms are small, especially the triples, but it's the best budget option in town.

our pick **El Mesón de las Flores** (☎ 291-5264; www.landofthesun.org; Moreno & Sucre; d incl breakfast $59) A quaint, historic colonial place, with an open courtyard draped with potted flowers. Rooms are cozy and comfortable, and balconies have views of the convent. The bar is well stocked and the courtyard restaurant (mains $4 to $8; open 7am to 8pm), which once functioned as horse stables, serves delicious food. Try the breakfast omelets, chicken in wine sauce or *locro de papas* (potato soup served with avocado and cheese). Guests get free international phone calls. Tours are available through guide Mauricio Bonilla, who works at the front desk. Proceeds from the hotel go to a nonprofit foundation that benefits indigenous people.

Hostería La Mirage (☎ 291-5237, 439-1486, 800-327-3573 in the US; www.mirage.com.ec; s & d $300, ste $350-800;) The unpaved entry road belies one of Ecuador's finest hotels. Part of the exclusive Relais & Chateaux association, La Mirage counts among its distinguished guests the Queen of Spain and enough Hollywood stars to warrant a regular paparazzi. Beyond the locked iron gates, peacocks stroll the green past white cupolas and columned entrances. The decor is Louis XIV–exquisite, with original paintings, canopy beds, flower bouquets and luxurious linens. If you can pull yourself away from your room, head to the rose petal–strewn indoor swimming pool and Jacuzzi. The attached spa is a throwback to Roman decadence, featuring treatments ranging from milk-and-rose-petal baths to shamanic cleansings in a stone-slab candlelit nook. Plain massages start at $35. Tennis, horseback riding, bird-watching and mountain biking are offered. Rates include dinner and breakfast. A leisurely meal at the restaurant (mains $14, prix-fixe dinners $35) guarantees a memorable experience in international fusion; think oxtail *consommé, cuy* off the bone, duck *à l'orange* and New Zealand lamb chops. For dessert, try the rose sherbet. The glassed-in restaurant fills up on Saturday with shoppers from the Otavalo market. Reservations are recommended for meals and accommodations.

La Marqueza (☎ 291-5488; cnr 10 de Agosto & Bolívar; mains $6-8; ⏲ 7:30am-9pm) A cavernous joint with a big-screen TV that caters to tourist groups. Serves typical Ecuadorian dishes in portions big enough to feed a busload.

El Leñador (☎ 291-5083; cnr Sucre 10-12 & Montalvo; mains $5-8; ⏲ 7am-10pm) An Argentine-style grill with fresh linen tablecloths and tasteful decor. Carnivores should order any beef dish (the delicious consequences of a leather-making society), which will arrive juicy and perfectly cooked to your specification.

GETTING THERE & AWAY

Cotacachi is west of the Panamericana and 15km north of Otavalo. From Otavalo's bus terminal, buses to Otavalo leave at least every hour ($0.25, 25 minutes). In Cotacachi, *camionetas* (pickups or light trucks) can be hired from the bus terminal by the market at the far end of town to take you to Laguna de Cuicocha ($12 round-trip, including half-hour waiting time). A more economical option is to take a Transportes Cotacachi bus (from Otavalo or Cotacachi) to Quiroga, where you can grab a taxi from the plaza.

RESERVA ECOLÓGICA COTACACHI-CAYAPAS

This **reserve** (lake admission $1, entire park $5) protects a huge swath of the western Andes. The range of altitudes, from Volcán Cotacachi to the coastal lowland rainforests, means an abundance of biodiversity. Travel from the highland to lowland areas of the reserve is nearly impossible – how's your bushwhacking? Most visitors either visit the lowlands from San Miguel on Río Cayapas (see p278) or the highlands around Laguna de Cuicocha, which are described here. From Cotacachi, just before arriving at Laguna de Cuicocha, a rangers' booth serves as the entrance to the reserve.

Sights

Head 18km west from Cotacachi and you'll come upon **Laguna de Cuicocha**, a still, dark lagoon cradled in a collapsed volcanic crater. Some 3km wide and 200m deep, the lagoon features two mounded islands that shot up in later eruptions. The islands look like the backs of two guinea pigs, hence the name: '*cuicocha*' means 'guinea pig lake' in Quichua. Hike the trail skirting the shore, where hummingbirds feed on bright flowers and the occasional condor circles over the glassy expanse. The trail begins near the reserve's entrance booth, a circuit of five or six hours. If the clouds clear, you'll see Volcán Cotacachi. Boats for hire ($2) make short trips around the islands. There have been robberies here in the past; never go alone and check the current situation with the local guards at the park entrance.

Sleeping & Eating

For clean rooms with lake views, stay in **Hosteria Cuicocha** (☎ 264-8040; www.cuicocha.org; s/d incl breakfast & dinner $40/70). The on-site restaurant (mains $3 to $7) is open to the public and serves good, basic meals such as grilled trout and empanadas.

Getting There & Away

A group can hire a taxi or pickup from Cotacachi for about $20; be sure to pay after returning so you don't get ditched. One-way fares by taxi or truck cost about $8 from Cotacachi. A two-day hike goes from Laguna de Cuicocha to Lagunas de Mojanda via a southern trail through the village of Ugshapungu. The 1:50,000 Otavalo map numbered ÑII-F1, 3994-IV is recommended from the IGM in Quito (p76).

INTAG VALLEY

Hang on for the dramatic descent into Intag. After chugging to dry and scrabbled heights, the road plunges downward only to crawl out of mountain gutters and climb again. Sometimes mudslides block this road, but drivers, who may cross themselves before embarking, seem to have an uncanny talent for its narrow dimensions and ghastly conditions. The valley is famous not only for its coffee, but its activism (see the boxed text, p135).

The **Andean Bear Conservation Project** (www.andeanbear.org; volunteers per month $600) trains volunteers as bear trackers. Hike through remote cloud forest to track the elusive spectacled bear, whose predilection for sweet corn is altering its wild behavior. Other jobs here include working with local farmers to replenish cornfields ravaged by bears (to discourage bear hunting) and maintaining trails. Volunteers can come for a week but a month is recommended.

Get off just before Santa Rosa for the two-hour walk into **Siempre Verde** (☎ 404-262-3032 in the US, ext 1486; www.siempreverde.org) a small community-run research station supporting tropical conservation education with excellent hiking and bird-watching. Students and researchers are welcome with prior arrangement.

An hour's walk from Santa Rosa you'll find the **Intag Cloud Forest Reserve** (☎ 264-8509; www.intagcloudforest.com; r per person incl all meals $40), a primary cloud forest reserve run by the founder of Defense and Ecological Conservation for Intag (DECOIN). Visitors in groups of eight or more stay in rustic cabins with solar-heated hot water and hike, bird-watch and eat vegetarian meals.

Apuela

☎ 06

The tiny town of Apuela hugs the Río Intag, which has carved a vast slit through the mountains as it roars toward the Pacific. On Sundays locals flood the center to play soccer and browse the market for provisions and blue jeans. Coffee addicts should visit Café Río Intag, a cooperative coffee factory. The beans are produced by **Asociación Río Intag** (☎ 264-8489; aacri@andinanet.net; near plaza), a group of local farmers and artists. It also sells handbags woven with agave fibers, soaps and crafts made by local women.

The office of **DECOIN** (☎ 664-8593 in Otavalo; www.decoin.org), a long-standing environmental organization that opposes mining in the region, is located uphill from the plaza.

Pradera Tropical (☎ 264-8557; cabins per person $4) has decent cabins near the school. Five kilometers outside of town, **Hostal el Cafetal de Intag** (☎ 292 0990 in Otavalo; www.hostalvalledelamanecer.com; r per person $5, cabins with private bathroom $20) offers good, basic brick and wood cabins and rooms in the main house.

You'll find a complex of tidy, four-person wood cabins called **Cabañas Río Grande** (☎ 264-8296; s/d $20/25) right next to some hot springs. It boasts the softest beds in town and also has a good restaurant, with meals starting at $4.50.

Nangulví thermal springs (☎ 264-8291; www.nangulvi.com; admission $1; 🕑 7:30am-9pm) has a cluster of cabins (rooms per person $8) and a restaurant with $2 set meals to maximize on-site soaking. Tucked between steep valley walls and surrounded by colorful gardens, these tiled pools next to the rushing Río Intag are a gorgeous place to unwind. Five hot pools range from 35°C (98°F) to 25°C (77°F), and there's one cold plunge pool, all of which fill up on weekends.

Pass through town to Cuellaje to reach **Finca San Antonio** (☎ 264-8627; www.intagtour.com; r per person $7). The farm houses guests in basic cabins or dorm rooms or arranges for stays with families. Meals cost extra, although there's a kitchen, if you want to bring your own food. Guests can pay extra for guided hikes, a visit to a nearby cheesemaker and trout fishing.

Transportos Otavalo, Los Lagos and Transportes 6 de Junio have buses from Otavalo ($3, 2½ hours) at least four times daily. Ask which buses continue to villages past Vacas Galindo to García Moreno and Junín. A few buses go as far as Limones then return to Otavalo. Some roads can become impassable during the rainy season.

Junín

☎ 06

Continue further into remote Andean hills on the road to Junín, taking in the view near the farming village of García Moreno, where a narrow ridge fringed with banana trees drops to hills rolling toward the horizon.

The highly recommended **Junín Community Reserve** (☎ 887-1860; www.junincloudforest.com; r per person incl 3 meals $30, volunteers $15) operates a three-story bamboo lodge that's popular with bird-watchers. Relax in a hammock on the terrace, peruse the orchid collection, then hike to waterfalls with attentive Spanish-speaking guides. Bunkrooms are plain but snug and vegetarian meals come with robust cups of Intag coffee.

The reserve offers a great opportunity to meet the locals, and visiting helps fund a program that develops sustainable income for the community without degrading the environment. The area is under considerable pressure to open up to copper mining but so far a cohesive grass-roots opposition has thwarted attempts. Volunteers can help by farming, doing biological research or teaching English and computer skills. Donations of used books for children are happily received.

Contact the center in advance to volunteer or visit. In the rainy season bus services are limited on the muddy roads; arrange for transportation or a guide with the reserve.

RESERVA BIOLÓGICA LOS CEDROS

This fantastic, remote reserve is set in 6400 hectares of primary forest contiguous with the Reserva Ecológica Cotacachi-Cayapas. It is one of the only access points to the Southern Chocó, a forest ecosystem considered to be one of the most diverse bioregions

DETOUR: INTAG VALLEY

In the rural Intag Valley, trees are weighted with tropical fruit and kids ride horses bridled with a scrap of rope – an unlikely hotbed of activism. And yet residents have successfully curbed copper mining (www.decoin.org), started a community newspaper (www.intagnewspaper.org) and organized coffee cooperatives.

Next up? The reintroduction of native crops to local farmers who've gradually stopped planting what's been grown in the Andes for hundreds, if not thousands, of years. The project aims to restore over 100 varieties of indigenous crops and medicinal plants, including tree tomatoes, hot peppers, root crops, seven species of potato, and quinoa.

The program aims to increase agro-biodiversity and maintain culinary traditions, and is run in part by the Union of Peasant and Indigenous Organizations of Cotacachi (UNORCAC). See, and taste, the results by staying at a rural, family-run lodge participating in the program. You'll eat meals alongside your indigenous hosts, who prepare dishes using ingredients grown in their gardens. Trips are run by Runa Tupari Native Travel in Otavalo (see p125).

on the planet. Living treasures include more than 240 species of birds, 400 types of orchids and more than 960 nocturnal moths.

Guests of **Los Cedros** (☎ 286-5176; www.reservaloscedros.org; r per person $50, scientists & students $30) arrive at the village of Chontal and undertake a rugged four- to six-hour hike through the Magdalena river valley into the Cordillera de la Plata. Contact the reserve in advance to arrange for a guide, pack animals and accommodations. Facilities include a scientific research station, dining and cooking facilities, accommodations in dorms or private rooms, hot water and electricity. The price includes all meals and guide services, but a three-night minimum stay is required. Volunteers are accepted ($450 per month, one month minimum).

A bus from Otavalo to Chontal should start running in late 2009 or early 2010. From Quito, **Transportes Minas** (☎ 06-286-8039) leaves the La Ofelia bus station and goes to Chontal (3½ hours) four times daily, starting at 6am. In Chontal, the reserve offers a mule train that leaves daily at 9:30am. Make other lodging arrangements in town through the **Comite de Turismo en Español** (☎ 09-764-3809).

SAN ANTONIO DE IBARRA

☎ 06

This small village near Ibarra specializes in woodcarvings. Artisans whittle cedar and walnut into Virgin Marys, Don Quixotes, chess sets, vases and nursing mothers. Craft stores crowd the Parque Central and line 27 de Noviembre. To see artists at work, wander off these streets and peek into the numerous workshops around town. The most renowned gallery is **Galería Luís Potosí** (☎ 293-2056; Parque Central; admission free; 🕑 8am-6pm). Potosí has achieved fame throughout Ecuador and abroad. Ask to see the workspace he shares with other woodworkers when you visit the gallery.

Hostal Los Nogales (☎ 293-2000; Sucre 3-64; r per person $6) is a quiet spot with basic rooms with small private bathrooms. The more modern **Hotel Ibiza** (Parque Central; r per person $12) offers cool, clean rooms with televisions and phones. Even so, most visitors spend their nights in Ibarra or Otavalo.

Buses from Ibarra ($0.18, 15 minutes) are frequent throughout the day. Get off at the main plaza. A taxi from town costs around $3.

IBARRA

☎ 06 / pop 151,146 / elevation 2225m

Packed with a large and bustling population, Ibarra feels appropriately cosmopolitan. Narrow corridors are lined with hip clothing stores and electronics. Despite its size, the city still feels connected to the surrounding mountains, especially when harsh winds scour everything with a bit of grit. The fast-growing capital of Imbabura province lies just 22km northeast of Otavalo.

It's the patient, observant visitor who reaps the rewards of spending time in *la ciudad blanca* (the white city). Beautiful palm-lined parks and plazas modestly reveal fine colonial architecture, and friendly residents are happy to share these pockets of peace with outsiders. After all, it's already a diverse place, with a population of students, mestizos, indigenous groups and Afro-Ecuadorians.

When the sun sets, action in Ibarra subsides, and on Sundays, only the rare newspaper stall, ice-cream shop, sweets kiosk and internet café opens for business. No matter – you can always satisfy your sweet tooth with the prevalent *arrope de mora* (thick blackberry syrup), *nogadas* (caramel nougat) and ice cream (see the boxed text, p139).

The town seems uninterested in courting tourists, so infrastructure is lacking. But the hotels fill up quickly during the last two weeks of September during Ibarra's annual fiesta, a lively event with food, music and dancing.

Orientation

Ibarra's old architecture and shady plazas sit north of the center. The area around Mercado Amazonas and Sánchez y Cifuentes are unsafe at night.

Information

Andinatel (Sucre 4-48)
Banco del Pacífico (☎ 295-7714; cnr Olmedo & Moncayo) The only place in town that changes traveler's checks. Has an ATM.
iTur Tourism Office (☎ 260-8489; www.imbaburaturismo.gov.ec; cnr Oviedo & Sucre; 🕑 8:30am-1pm & 2-5pm Mon-Fri) Staff can direct you to community tourism.
Metropolitan Touring (☎ 260-0626; Flores near Sucre; 🕑 9am-1pm & 3-6pm Mon-Fri) Reliable, all-purpose travel agency that handles international flights and local tours with English-speaking guides.
Post office (☎ 264-3135; Salinas 6-64)
Produbanco ATM (cnr Sucre & Flores)
Zonanet (☎ 225-8858; Moncayo 5-74; per hr $1; 🕑 8:30am-9pm) Internet access.

Sights & Activities

Find the **Parque La Merced**, also known as Peñaherrera, by locating an oversized statue of the Virgin atop the plaza's church. Built at the beginning of the 19th century, the main feature of the Church of La Merced is a gold leaf–covered altar with the Virgin of La Merced, patron saint of armed forces. The church holds a special mass in remembrance of the victims and survivors of the devastating 1868 earthquake.

The gorgeous palm-filled plaza of **Parque Pedro Moncayo** is dominated by the baroque-influenced **cathedral**. The altars are covered in gold leaf and Troya's paintings of the 12 apostles adorn the pillars. The park itself is named after native son Pedro Moncayo (1807–88), a journalist and diplomat.

At the north end of Bolívar you'll find the quaint **Parque Santo Domingo**. Behind this small park, the Dominican **Church of Santo Domingo** houses La Virgin del Rosarío, a painting by famous artist Diego de Robles, on its altar. The church also has a **museum of religious art** (admission $0.50; 🕑 9am-noon & 3-6pm Mon-Sat).

On the corner of Oviedo and Sucre, a tiled patch not bigger than a parking space is called **Plazoleta del Coco** by the locals. Here you'll find the tourist office. The **Centro Cultural** (☎ 264-4087; cnr Oviedo & Sucre; admission $1; 🕑 8:30am-6pm Mon-Fri, 10am-5pm Sat) houses an archaeology museum featuring prehistoric ceramics and gold artifacts from Pimampiro with signs in English. There's also a local historical archive and library.

Locals are fond of **Laguna Yaguarcocha**, a lake encircled by an auto racetrack 3km north of town on the Panamericana. Its name, 'blood lake,' was coined when the Incas defeated the Caras and dumped thousands of their bodies into the lake. Buzzing cars and boats, along with the litter, make it an unlikely destination for visitors seeking refuge in nature.

Nearby mountains serve as launching pads for **paragliding**. **Fly Ecuador** (☎ 295-3297; www.flyecuador.com.ec; cnr Oviedo 9-13 & Sánchez y Cifuentes) offers beginner courses and tandem flights.

Sleeping

While you'll find plenty of budget options in town (make sure there's hot water), the larger, pricier hotels are west of town, near the Panamericana. They're often booked in advance, particularly on weekends.

BUDGET

Hotel Imbabura (☎ 295-8522; Oviedo 9-33; r per person $7) This 100-year-old-plus colonial's revamped courtyard is filled with tables for the on-site restaurant and a popular bar. Rooms are spacious and neat with high ceilings, and communal bathrooms are clean. Can arrange for Spanish classes. Ask the talkative owner about his one-of-a-kind collection of mini-bottles.

Hostal El Retorno (☎ 295-7722; Moncayo 4-32; r per person with shared/private bathroom $7/8) A cheery little place with pint-sized beds and TVs that makes for a good bargain. Streetside rooms bring some rooms to life.

Hostal El Ejecutivo (☎ 295-6575; Bolívar 9-69; s/d $9/14; 💻) Old plaids dominate the ample rooms and lend a retro feel. Rooms have hot baths, telephone and TV. The 1st floor is a busy internet café.

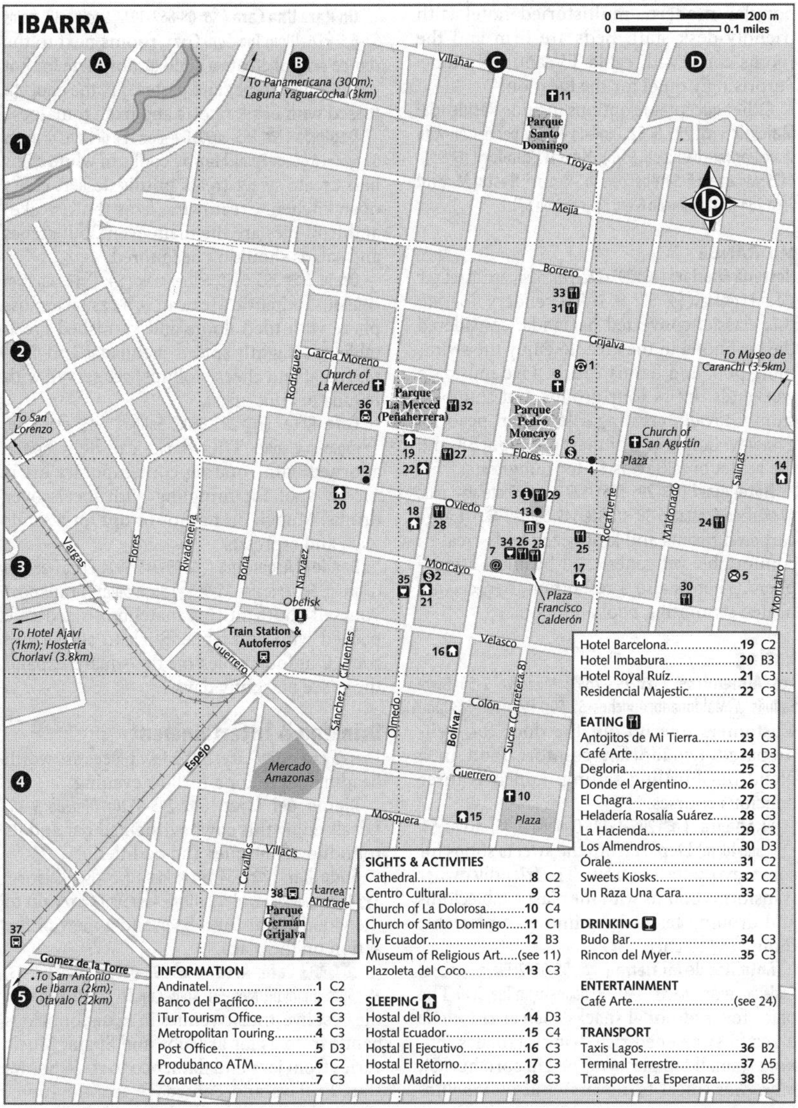

Hotel Barcelona (☎ 292-4740; Flores 8-51 btwn Olmedo & Sánchez y Cifuentes; r per person $10) Spacious rooms in this old colonial building circle a light, central courtyard with sunny paint. Ask for rooms that face the park for an inspiring view.

our pick **Hostal del Río** (☎ 261-1885, 09-080-0849; cnr Montalvo 4-55 & Flores; r per person $15) Fusing modern art deco with regional colonial style, this excellent option starts with a curved staircase leading to rooms with red hardwood floors, snug fluffy beds and bright accents. For pampering, ask for the rooms with Jacuzzis for $20 per night. Located in a quiet neighborhood a few blocks east of downtown.

Hotel Royal Ruíz (☎ 264-4644/53; hroyalruiz@yahoo.com; Olmedo 9-40; r per person incl breakfast $16) A popular modern, multistoried hotel with friendly desk staff. Beds are firm and the rooms come with cable TV and telephone. Surprisingly quiet for the location.

Other acceptable options include **Residencial Majestic** (☎ 295-0052; Olmedo 7-63; r per person with shared/private bathroom $3/6), **Hostal Ecuador** (☎ 295-6425; Mosquera 5-54; r per person $5) and **Hostal Madrid** (☎ 264-4918; Olmedo 8-69; r per person $7).

MIDRANGE

Hostería Chorlaví (☎ 293-2222; chorlavi@andinanet.net; s/d incl breakfast $45/50;) Weekenders flock to this classic, converted hacienda, considered the best hotel in the area, to enjoy the swimming pool and tennis courts. Live music on weekends draws tour groups and shoppers from Otavalo, creating a less-than-peaceful getaway. Lunch and dinners are about $8, and the buffet breakfast is $7 for nonguests.

Hotel Ajaví (☎ 295-5555/5221; www.hotelajavi.com; Av Maríano Acosta 16-38; s/d/ste $49/63/82;) Large carpeted rooms and king-sized beds create a comfortable yet generic, all-business atmosphere. There's also a restaurant, bar, casino, heated swimming pool and sauna.

Eating

Los Almendros (☎ 295-7631; Moncayo 2-56 btwn Salinas & Maldonado; lunches $2.50; noon-3:30pm) Customers line up out the door for well-prepared Ecuadorian comfort food in a bland but bustling setting. Lunch is three delicious courses.

El Chagra (☎ 295-4517; Olmedo 7-48; mains $3; 8am-10pm) Depart from the sweets shops for some savory stew or trout. The friendly owner transforms booths with the plastic tablecloths and droning telenovelas into a comfortable dining experience.

Antojitos de Mi Tierra (☎ 295-0592; Plaza Francisco Calderón, Sucre; snacks $1-3; noon-10pm Tue-Sun) The place for traditional snacks such as *chicha de arroz* (a sweetened rice drink), tamales, *humitas* (small tamales wrapped in corn husks), *morochos* (meat turnovers) and *quimbolitos* (corn dumplings steamed in corn husks or leaves). Owner Marta Jduregi is a well-known local historian and chef.

La Hacienda (☎ 09-502-8493; cnr Oviedo & Sucre; sandwiches $3; 8am-9pm) Pull up a hay-stuffed bench at this friendly, barn-themed deli. Baguette sandwiches are the specialty, but if you've got dining companions, try the multi-person tapas plates for an array of cheeses.

Un Raza Una Cara (☎ 08-862-3078; Sucre 3-37; mains $3-6; 6-10pm Tue-Sun) Cozy rooms next to the dance school create a good atmosphere for hot sandwiches, crepes and pastas. Try the gnocchi tossed with basil, ricotta and fresh tomatoes.

Degloria (☎ 295-0699; Oviedo 5-45; desserts or mains $3-6; 8:30am-8pm) Happy cooks in white chefs hats create sweet treats in this dessert café's open kitchen. Creamy *tres leche* (butter cake) and fruit pies are the main event, but crepes and salads shouldn't be ignored.

Órale (☎ 295-0850; Sucre; mains $4; 11am-8pm Mon-Sat) Authentic Mexican in a casual atmosphere with tiled floors and varnished green tabletops. Lightly spiced enchiladas and *flautas* (meat and cheese rollups) are served with tequila or fruit juices.

Café Arte (☎ 295-0806; Salinas 5-43; mains $6; 5pm-midnight) This dark, candlelit space adorned with rotating contemporary art is a cozy spot for mingling with locals over drinks. Munch on nachos or opt for a sandwich and espresso.

Donde el Argentino (☎ 09-945-9004; Plaza Francisco Calderón, Sucre; mains $5-9; noon-9pm) Transport yourself south in this matchbox-sized café packed with ambience. Stick to steaks and fries. Outdoor tables on the square expand the space on sunny days.

Drinking & Entertainment

Ibarra is a quiet city, but a few places are worth heading out to for a mellow evening.

Rincon del Myer (☎ 295-9520; Olmedo 9-35) Locals enjoy this cowboy-themed bar and its roundup of antiques and oddities.

Budo Bar (☎ 264-0034; Plaza Francisco Calderón; 4pm-midnight Wed-Sat, 10am-4pm Sun) Cozy up to the wooden bar for a beer and a view of the action on the plaza.

our pick **Café Arte** (☎ 295-0806; Salinas 5-43; 5pm-midnight Mon-Fri, 4pm-3am Fri & Sat) One of the best live-music venues in Ecuador brings bands from as far as Cuba and Spain. Music varies from jazz and flamenco to rock. Shows start Fridays and Saturdays around 10pm. Check the schedule for films, dance lessons, live concert recordings and art shows.

Getting There & Away

BUS

Ibarra's modern bus terminal, Terminal Terrestre, is located at the end of Avenida Teodoro Gomez de la Torre, near Espejo. You can grab a taxi to/from downtown for $1.

THE CONE OF ETERNAL YOUTH

Teenage boredom inspired Rosalía Suárez to invent ice creams in the kitchen back in 1897, when she was just 17. Her experimentation led to a discovery – the best ice cream had no cream at all. Rosalía decided to share the sweet treat, and her shop **Heladería Rosalía Suárez** (☎ 06-295-8722; Oviedo 7-82) has been a sensation for more than a century. *Helados de paila* are actually sorbets stirred with a wooden spoon in a large copper bowl (the *paila*) and cooled on a bed of straw and ice. The shop, now run by her grandson, claims the recipe requires pure juice from tropical fruits and egg whites. It's not entirely possible to imitate – ice from the first versions was brought down from the glacier of Volcán Imbabura, which has since disappeared.

Doña Rosalía lived until the age of 105, which speaks something to the restorative qualities of a good *helado*. It's a theory worth testing, anyway. *Guanábana* (similar to soursop) is the shop's most popular flavor. The tart *naranjilla* (known as lulo) and *maracuyá* (passion fruit) are also worth a lick.

The following (apart from Transportes La Esperanza) depart from here. For San Antonio de Ibarra, see right.

Aerotaxi (☎ 295-5200) Quito, Guayaquil ($9, 10 hours), Esmeraldas ($8, nine hours), Atacames ($9, nine hours) and San Lorenzo ($4, 3½ to four hours)
Cita Express (☎ 295-5627) Ambato ($5, five hours) via El Quinche
Expreso Baños Baños at 5am and 2:30pm ($6)
Expreso Turismo (☎ 295-5730) Tulcán ($2.50, 2 ½ hours) every 45 minutes and Quito ($2.50, 2½ hours)
Flota Imbabura (☎ 295-1094) Tulcán, Guayaquil ($10, 11 hours), Cuenca ($14, 12 hours) and Manta ($10, 12 hours)
Transportes Andina (☎ 295-0833) Quito ($2.50, 2½ hours) every 10 minutes, San Lorenzo and Santo Domingo ($4, six hours) every half-hour
Transportes del Valle Four trips daily to Chota Valley, Lago Agrio ($9, eight hours) and San Lorenzo
Transportes Espejo (☎ 295-9917) Quito, San Lorenzo and El Ángel ($1.25, 1½ hours) seven times a day
Transportes La Esperanza (Parque German Grijalva near Sánchez y Cifuentes) Goes to the village of La Esperanza ($0.22, 25 minutes)
Transportes Otavalo (☎ 295-2951) Otavalo ($0.45, 35 minutes)

TAXI

If you're rushing to Quito, try **Taxis Los Lagos** (☎ 295-5150; Flores 9-24). Six passengers can cram into a large taxi ($7.50, 2¼ hours). Luggage costs $2 to $3.

TRAIN

Since the road opened to the coastal town of San Lorenzo, the train service on the Ibarra–San Lorenzo line has been suspended. There are *autoferros* (buses mounted on a train chassis) as far as Primer Paso ($3.80 one-way, 1¾ hours), less than a quarter of the way from Ibarra to San Lorenzo. The short ride is now essentially a round-trip tourist attraction. Alternatively, you can get off at Primer Paso and wait for a passing bus to San Lorenzo.

The *autoferro* only leaves Ibarra with a minimum of 16 passengers. It leaves the train station at 8am on Friday, Saturday and Sunday. The return ride departs Primer Paso at 2pm. In tourist low season, cancelled departures are the norm. Call the **train station** (☎ 295-0390) for the latest info.

Getting Around

Catch a local bus to San Antonio de Ibarra ($0.18, 15 minutes) and other nearby towns on Sánchez y Cifuentes near Guerrero.

LA ESPERANZA

☎ 06

This picturesque village is set against the sloping flanks of Volcán Imbabura, 7km south of Ibarra. It's respite for the road-weary and the best spot to climb **Volcán Imbabura** (4609m). To climb the peak, start in the early morning and follow the escalating ridge 2000m to the summit, 8km southwest. The last stretch is a scramble over loose rock. If you're not experienced, hire a local guide. Allow for 10 hours round-trip. Those of middling ambition can try the easier three-hour climb to **Loma Cubilche** (3886m), a hill south of La Esperanza with lovely views.

our pick Rest up for your adventure at the affable **Casa Aida** (☎ 266-0221; www.casaaida.com; Calle Gallo Plaza; r per person $7). Brightly painted rooms are simple but clean and comfortable. Aida is a great source of local information and will make you feel at home with her famous hearty pancakes, box lunches and dinners. She can help arrange a guide for an Imbabura summit.

You can walk here from Ibarra, take one of the frequent buses ($0.22, 25 minutes) or get a taxi for about $5.

NORTH OF IBARRA

☎ 06

The smooth Panamericana snakes north, offering plenty of pavement to spandex-clad cyclists, who pound up this punishing route on weekends. Entering the **Río Chota valley** at 1565m, the road drops sharply. Round, dry hills covered with cacti surround a lush green valley floor fed by the chocolaty river. Within an hour's drive from Ibarra, the always-warm valley is within arm's reach for day trips.

Sugarcane thrives here, and the valley's inhabitants, Afro-Ecuadorians descended from 17th-century plantation slaves, grow and harvest the crop. Stop at any roadside stand for a juicy sugarcane stick. Farmers here also produce a variety of fruits, beans, yuca and tomatoes.

A token of the unique Afro-Andean culture is *bomba* music, a blend of driving African drums and plaintive highland notes. At bus stops and fruit stands, children dance to the beat in their heads. Fiestas and concerts are irregular, but are sometimes advertised in Ibarra.

Palm-lined hotels with swimming pools make **Ambuquí** a popular weekend destination for highlanders seeking warmth. At **Hosteria El Kibutz** (☎ 294-1141; www.hosteriaelkibutz.com; r per person incl breakfast $25;), bougainvillea, citrus trees and a green lawn surround two bright-blue pools. The collection of cabañas looks better from the outside, with a mishmash of decor and dated bedding.

A bit further north on the Panamericana, **Oasis** (☎ 294-1192; r per person weekdays/weekends $43/50;) offers a festive weekend atmosphere. Guests mingle around the swimming pools with aging waterslides, in the disco and lush gardens – all of which help mask that they're vacationing next to a highway. Cabañas are tidy and modern and all meals from the on-site restaurant are included. A day pass to the pools costs $8.

Next door, the basic **Aruba Hostería** (☎ 294-1146; r per person $12;) has helpful staff and a nice swimming pool. Along the road open-air eateries serve *sancocho* (stew).

Juncal, the breeding ground for the World Cup soccer team, is next up with its cluster of informal restaurants along the highway. This hot, dusty village is the turn off for the road to **Pimampiro**. Adventurers eager to chart new territory should come to this out-of-the-way village that sits perched on a steep hillside. **Hospedates Jose Alveiro** (☎ 293-7070; cnr Olmedo & Flores; r per person $5) welcomes guests with good, basic rooms and tiny, shared bathrooms. A block away on the main square, **El Forastero** (meals $3; 7am-8pm) offers hearty breakfasts and a good *seco* (meat in sauce) served with rice.

This area borders the backside of Reserva Ecológica Cayambe-Coca. Hikers should take a bus to the village of Mariana Acosta, where guides lead four-to-five-hour walks from Nueva America to **Laguna Puruhanta**, a peaceful lake ringed by high peaks. Hospedates Jose Alveiro (above) can arrange guide services.

Back on the Panamericana, the Carchi province marks a return to high Andean landscape and cooler temperatures. **Bolívar** is a large hill town known for its paleontological finds (acknowledged by a wooly mammoth statue next to the road). Off the main highway, you'll come to **Grutas de la Paz**, a grotto converted to a chapel whose famous Virgin sparkles under the stalactites. Nearby **thermal springs** (Thu-Sun) and **waterfalls** round out the attractions. Take a bus to the springs from Tulcán, or walk the 5km southeast of the Panamericana from La Paz on the road marked 'Las Grutas.'

About 38km south of Tulcán, the small town of **San Gabriel**, at an elevation of 2900m, has a couple of basic hotels. Five kilometers east is **Bosque de los Arreyanes** (8:30am-4:30pm), a lovely myrtle forest ideal for bird-watching. On-site camping is available.

The waterfalls **Las Cascadas de Paluz** are found on Río San Gabriel 3km to 4km north of San Gabriel (head north on Calle Bolívar and keep going). Mountain bikers recommend the three-hour ride from San Gabriel to El Ángel.

EL ÁNGEL

☎ 06

Tufts of ocher grasses ripple surrounding hillsides around the stark-still Andean village of El Ángel, the entry point to Páramos El Ángel, a misty wilderness favored by foxes and condors. It's part of the 16,000-hectare **Reserva Ecológica El Ángel** (admission $10), which includes *frailejones*, rare, otherworldly plants with fuzzy leaves and thick trunks. You can arrange *páramo* visits with Cerro Golondrinas (right) or with local hotels. The village springs to life with a Monday market.

Travelers recommend **Polylepis Lodge** (☎ 295-4900; www.polylepislodge.com, r per person incl 3 meals $70), located 14km outside of town. Sturdy huts have private bathroom, hot water and wood stoves or fireplaces. Activities include horseback and mountain-bike riding or hiking with native guides through the surrounding bosque (forest), where remnants of an ancient forest includes *Polylepis* trees, otherwise known as 'paper trees' for their thin, peeling bark.

El Ángel Hostería (☎ 297-7584; hwy & Av Espejo 1302; r per person $16) has snug high-ceilinged cabins with comfortable beds and modern bathrooms. The well-run *hostería* offers guided hikes to the reserve and city tours in English or German. It's a 10-minute walk to town.

Simple restaurants are found in town, including **Los Faroles** (☎ 297-7144; cnr Salinas & Grijalva), which also offers basic lodging for $6 per night. Transportes Espejo, on the main plaza, goes to Quito ($3.50, four hours) via Ibarra ($1.50, 1½ hours) every hour. Buses to Tulcán leave early in the morning. At the plaza you'll find shared taxis going to and from the Bolívar crossroads ($1), where frequent buses go north or south, and private 4WD vehicles can be rented for excursions into the reserve.

RESERVA BIOLÓGICA GUANDERA

This 1000-hectare, tropical, wet, montane forest reserve was founded in 1994 by Fundación Jatun Sacha (see p256). The reserve lies between 3100m and 3600m on a transitional ridge (forest to *páramo*) 11km east of San Gabriel. Projects include reforestation and finding alternatives to chemical-intensive potato production. Andean spectacled bears (rarely glimpsed), high-altitude parrots and toucans are among the attractions. Jatun Sacha operates a **refuge** (dm $15). Reservations are required and fees must be paid in advance at the **Jatun Sacha office** (☎ 02-331-7163 in Quito; www.jatunsacha.org; cnr Eugenio de Santillán N34-248 & Maurián, Urbanización Rumipamba) in Quito. Researchers and volunteers are welcome for a minimum two-week visit ($240).

From the village of San Gabriel it is 1½ hours on foot to the reserve, but the office can arrange a ride with prior notice.

RÍO BLANCO AREA

☎ 06

Ditch your highland woolen clothing for the twisty, scenic ride to the steamy tropic lowlands abutting the northern coast. Afro-Ecuadorian farmers tend crops of sugarcane, bananas and tropical fruits on the steep slopes of the 1000m valley.

Bospas Forest Farm (☎ 264-8692; www.bospas.org; r per person $17, volunteers per month $225) on the outskirts of **El Limonal**, is run by a friendly Ecuadorian/Belgian couple. Comfortable lodge accommodations are in a lush setting, a 15-minute walk from the bus. The food is wonderful (tending toward coastal specialties) and guided hikes are offered. Owner Piet enthusiastically imparts his knowledge of tropical plants and preservation. The farm promotes reforestation, organic pest-control and farming in this highly deforested area. Located 1½ hours from Ibarra.

Guallupe is the entry point to the **Cerro Golondrinas Project** (☎ 264-8679/62; www.fgolondrinas.org; 4-day packages per person $210), where the non-governmental organization (NGO) Fundación Golondrinas works locally to promote sustainable farming techniques and curb rampant deforestation. The project aims to conserve some of the remaining forests while improving local living standards and providing sustainable incomes. Its reserve occupies some 1600 hectares between Reserva Ecológica El Ángel and the Colombian border, in stunning habitats ranging from *páramo* to temperate and subtropical montane cloud forest. Depending on weather conditions, arrangements can be made to hike into the reserve via El Ángel.

Local hosts provide hospitality to visitors, volunteers and researchers. Four-day hikes or horseback-riding trips include all food, accommodations and guiding services. The best time to go is the dry season between June and September, although the *páramo* region may be visited anytime. A few readers have complained about the type of volunteer work they were asked to do, so clarify expectations ahead of time.

TULCÁN

☎ 06 / pop 63,163 / elevation 3000m

The busy highland city of Tulcán is the last Ecuadorian stop for visitors headed overland to Colombia. The high altitude creates a constant chill, even among the narrow streets packed with pedestrians and erratic taxis. This provincial capital of Carchi is a commercial center; the town used to attract Colombians bargain hunting with the Ecuadorian sucre (Ecuador's currency before dollarization), but these days, Colombian imports are the more coveted deals. The Sunday street market offers goods and clothing but few handicrafts.

Orientation

The town is a long strip with action primarily on Bolívar and Sucre. Most of the parallel streets house shops selling cheap sneakers and electronics. Take taxis from the bus station to downtown or to the border, but otherwise the city is walkable. Addresses are numbered in two different ways. To prevent confusion, the nearest intersections, rather than the numbers, are used here.

Information

Exchanging money (between US dollars and Colombian pesos) is slightly better in Tulcán than at the border. If the currency-exchange centers are closed, try the street moneychangers in front of the banks. They are associated and wear ID numbers you can record in case of later problems.

Andinatel (Olmedo near Junín) Branches at the bus terminal and the border.

Banco del Pichincha (cnr 10 de Agosto & Sucre) Changes currency and traveler's checks Monday to Friday. Has an ATM. Other banks are nearby.

Café Net (cnr Sucre & Boyacá; per hr $1; 🕑 8am-10pm) Internet access inside Wimpy restaurant (p144).

Clínica Metropolitana (cnr Sucre & Panamá; 🕑 24hr) A better hospital is in Ipiales, 2km north of the border.

Colombian Consulate (☎ 298-0559; Manabí 58-087; 🕑 8:30am-1pm & 2:30-3:30pm Mon-Fri)

iTur Tourist Information (☎ 298-5760; Cotopaxi; 🕑 8am-6pm Mon-Fri) At the cemetery entrance. Staff is friendly and helpful.

Post office (☎ 298-0552; Bolívar near Junín)

Sights & Activities

Tulcán is well known for its **cemetery**, a quiet modern burial site and topiary garden. A maze of cypress trees sculpted into bulbous, pre-Columbian totems, mythological figures, animals and geometric shapes lines graves and mausoleums ornamented with candles and plastic flowers. Bushes and hedges take shape as the son of the original topiary master and another artist trim the masterpieces, a fragrant undertaking.

On the weekends, behind the cemetery, locals play an Ecuadorian paddleball game called **pelota de guante**, which requires a soft ball and large, spiked paddles. Walk south from the cemetery one block to the mural-covered **Museo Arqueologico** (admission $0.50; 🕑 9am-4pm), which houses pre-Columbian artifacts, ceramics, and modern and contemporary art.

Hot springs are within reach for day trippers. Take a taxi to San Gabriel then bus to the lukewarm **La Paz thermal springs**. Or head to **Aguas Hediondas**, 6km west of Tufiño. These 'stinking waters' are hot, high-sulfur thermal baths. Many of the pools are on the Colombian side; you can cross the border on a day pass, but those who want to stay must enter via the Tulcán border crossing. Get there before 4pm when the springs take on extra stench; go on weekdays to avoid crowds. Mondays through Fridays, Cooperativa Transportes Norte can take you to the turnoff for the hot springs.

Beyond the baths on the main road, **Volcán Chiles** (4768m) offers a challenging six-hour summit on the border of Colombia. The peak offers spectacular views; locals say that on a clear day you can see the ocean. Take a bus or taxi to Tufiño and hire a guide (recommended) in the town's main square. Ask locally about the safety of travel in this remote border region due to the conflict in Colombia.

Sleeping

There's no shortage of hotels, but most fall short on charm. Hotels by the bus station are convenient for late arrivals, but slightly dodgy.

Hotel San Francisco (☎ 298-0760; Bolívar near Atahualpa; r per person $5) While comparisons with the Bay City are scant, this vertical hotel is one of the better options in town. Outer rooms are brighter and more airy than those next door at Hotel Azteca Internacional, and include hot water and TV.

Hotel Azteca Internacional (☎ 298-0481/1447; cnr Bolívar & Atahualpa; r per person $7) Dark-paneled, cavernous, carpeted rooms create a '70s feel. Beds are firm and there's TV and phone. The disco downstairs can either be a pro or con, depending on how loud you like your weekends.

Hotel Unicornio (☎ 298-0638; cnr Pichincha & Sucre; r per person $9) A variety of carpeted rooms of varying quality are conveniently located over a tasty Chinese restaurant (see p144). Rooms have TV and telephone, and those on the street can be loud. A new casino is in progress on the main floor.

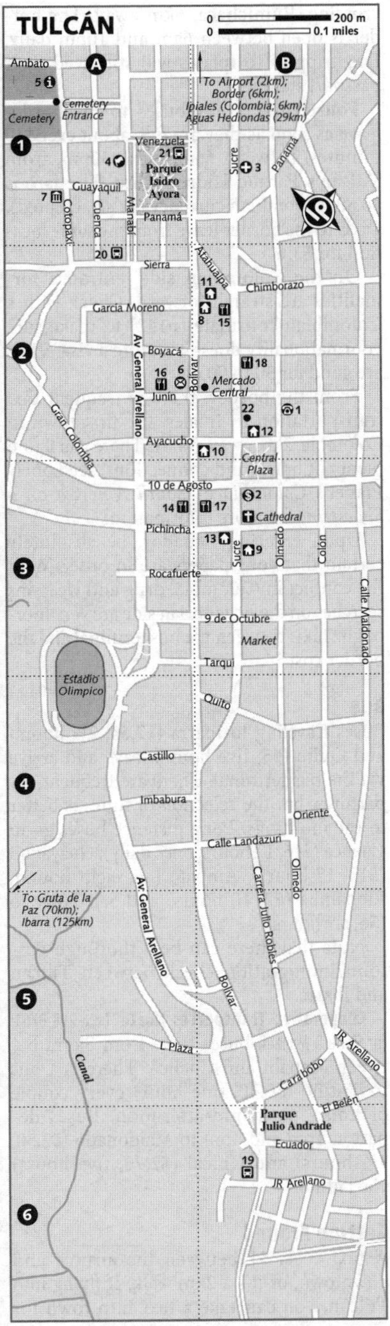

INFORMATION

Andinatel......1 B2
Banco del Pichincha......2 B3
Café Net......(see 18)
Clínica Metropolitana......3 B1
Colombian Consulate......4 A1
iTur Tourist Information......5 A1
Post Office......6 A2

SIGHTS & ACTIVITIES

Museo Arqueologico......7 A1

SLEEPING

Hotel Azteca Internacional......8 B2
Hotel Lumar......9 B3
Hotel Machado......10 B2
Hotel San Francisco......11 B2
Hotel Sara Espindola......12 B2
Hotel Unicornio......13 B3

EATING

Chifa Pack Choy......(see 13)
El Patio......14 A3
Mama Rosita......15 B2
San Francisco......16 A2
Tekila......17 B3
Wimpy......18 B2

ENTERTAINMENT

Crazy......(see 12)

TRANSPORT

Bus Terminal......19 B6
Cooperativa Transportes Norte......20 A2
Minibuses to Airport & Border......21 A1
TAME Office......22 B2

Hotel Lumar (☎ 298-0402/7137; Sucre near Pichincha; r per person $12) Don't judge Lumar by the plastic roses. This clean, modern hotel is a reliable choice, with a quiet lounge, soft beds and cable TV in every room. English is spoken here.

Hotel Machado (☎ 298-4221; cnr Ayacucho & Bolívar; r per person incl breakfast $20) Dated rooms come with cable TV and phone, and even though hot water can be spotty, it's a quiet and secure spot.

Hotel Sara Espindola (☎ 298-6209; cnr Sucre & Ayacucho; s/d $45/70) Considered the town's best hotel, this modern monolith is fraying around the edges. Still, well-furnished rooms and an eager staff aren't found elsewhere. There's an on-site disco (p144), sauna and restaurant, which serves typical dinners and buffets.

Eating

Tulcán's Colombian restaurants provide a welcome alternative to the Ecuadorian staples.

Mama Rosita (☎ 296-1192; Sucre, near Chimborazo; mains $1-3; 9am-7pm) Famous for its *fritada* and other *comida típica* (traditional Ecuadorian food). Excels at pork dishes.

Wimpy (☎ 298-3218; cnr Sucre & Boyacá; mains $2-3; 6:30am-11pm;) A popular greasy spoon serving burgers, hot dogs and fried chicken. There's an internet café (see Information, p142) upstairs.

Tekila (☎ 298-7248; Bolívar; mains $3-5; 9am-11pm) A cafeteria-style joint featuring Colombian food. Mild beef with fries and rice or *mondongo* (tripe stew) are the specialties. Don't get it confused with a nearby disco of the same name.

Chifa Pack Choy (☎ 298-0638; cnr Pichincha & Sucre; mains $3-5; noon-11:30pm) Beneath Hotel Unicornio (p142), this place serves the town's best Chinese food. Try the chop suey, which in honest fusion style, is served alongside a plate of *papas fritas* (french fries).

El Patio (☎ 298-4872; Bolívar near 10 de Agosto; mains $3-5; 8am-9pm Mon-Sat, to 6pm Sun) The dust has settled on the stables decor, but the Colombian food is delicious. Try the *bandeja paisa,* which includes no less than four fried foods (pork skins, sausage, egg and banana) plus rice, tender smoky beans and avocado. Portions are enormous and service is good.

San Francisco (☎ 298-0750; cnr Junín & Bolívar; mains $4-5; 9am-10pm). This new, modern restaurant is very popular. Check the chalkboard menu before you order at the counter for the reliable *plato del día* (daily special; $3.50). Don't miss the fresh berry desserts and ice creams.

By the border, there are plenty of snack stalls and fast-food carts.

Entertainment

Flashing strobes and blaring Latin pop inspire movement at **Crazy** (cnr Sucre & Ayacucho; 9pm-late Thu-Sat), the *discoteca* (discotheque) in Hotel Sara Espindola (p143).

Getting There & Away

AIR

The **airport** (☎ 298-2850) is 2km northeast of downtown. **TAME** (☎ 298-0675; Sucre near Junín; 8:30am-1pm & 3-6pm Mon-Fri) flies from Quito to Tulcán at 9pm Monday to Friday and Tulcán to Quito at 10am Monday to Friday. On Sunday, it flies from Quito to Tulcán at 3:30pm and Tulcán to Quito at 4:30pm. The $50 flight fills up fast.

BORDER CROSSINGS

Entering Colombia via the Panamericana north of Tulcán is currently the only recommended crossing. All formalities are taken care of at the Ecuador–Colombia border crossing, Rumichaca, 6km away. The border is open between 6am and 10pm daily. Day trippers to Ipiales will still need their passport stamped.

Fourteen-seat minibuses to the border leave as soon as they are full, about every 10 minutes, between 6am and 7:30pm, from Tulcán's Parque Isidro Ayora. The fare is $0.80 (Colombian currency is also accepted). Taxis to the border leave from the same location for $3.

On the Colombian side, entrance formalities are straightforward. Check with a Colombian consulate (p142) to make sure your nationality doesn't require a visa. Visas are good for 30 to 90 days.

From the border, there is frequent taxi transportation to Ipiales, the first town in Colombia, 2km away, for $1. There you'll find plenty of hotels and connections; see Lonely Planet's *Colombia* or *South America on a Shoestring* for more information.

Upon entering Ecuador, be absolutely certain that your papers are in order. With the conflict in Colombia, drug and weapons searches on the Ecuadorian side are very thorough. Taxis between the bus terminal and the border cost $4.

BUS

Buses traveling to Ibarra ($2.50, 2½ hours) and Quito ($5, five hours) leave and arrive via the bus terminal. There are frequent departures, but the selection of times is better in the mornings. Long-distance buses go to Cuenca ($16, 17 hours, once daily), Guayaquil ($13, 13 hours), Ambato ($6, eight hours), Riobamba ($7, 10 hours) and San Lorenzo ($6, six hours).

Note that there can be a thorough customs/immigration check between Tulcán and Ibarra.

Cooperativa Transportes Norte (☎ 298-0761; cnr Sierra & Manabí) buses leave from Sierra between Manabí and Cuenca. There is a bus to Tufiño ($0.40, one hour) every couple of hours until mid-afternoon. Buses depart at 1pm and 4pm to Maldonado ($2.50, 4½ hours) and Chical ($2.75, five hours) via Tufiño.

Getting Around

A taxi costs $1 between the airport and downtown, or it's a 2km walk. If flying into Tulcán, you can take a taxi into town for the same price. Shared taxis and minibuses heading to the border leave from the Parque Isidro Ayora.

The **bus terminal** (cnr JR Arellano & Bolívar) is inconveniently located 2.5km southwest of downtown. City buses ($0.20) run southwest from downtown along Bolívar and will deposit you at the terminal. To get downtown, take a taxi for $1 or cross the street in front of the terminal and catch the city bus.

WESTERN ANDEAN SLOPES

The old road to Santo Domingo wends atop dramatic drop-offs while descending through lush, misty cloud forests. Within just a few hours of Quito, visitors can experience some welcome climate shock in the cool, humid hills. The area is known for its bird-watching, but the landscape inspires mountain biking, horseback riding and hiking as well. Small villages, including Nanegalito and Nanegal, serve as gateways to remote lodges and reserves. In laidback Mindo, a high concentration of lodging and restaurants creates a welcome retreat. The region still feels remote, but the scene could change quickly with blooming development and mining companies jockeying for potential projects.

CLOUD FOREST LODGES

☎ 02

Tandayapa

Tandayapa Bird Lodge (☎ 244-7520, 09-923-1314, 409-515-0514 in the US; www.tandayapa.com; s/d incl 3 meals $109/185) is a serious bird-watcher's paradise, with highlights such as the Andean cock-of-the-rock, scaled fruiteater and golden-headed and crested quetzals. The lodge offers multilingual bird-watching guides, a comfortable lodge in the cloud forest, a canopy platform and a number of trails for day trips. Well-placed fruit feeders increase sightings from the lodge. Prices do not include bird guides or transport. From 32km into the journey from Quito, a road branches south to the town of Tandayapa, 6km away.

Santa Lucía

A foray into **Bosque Nublado Santa Lucía** (☎ 215-7242; www.santaluciaecuador.com; dm/r/cabin per person $25/50/60) inspires wonder. This is a trip for the adventurous. The rustic lodge, a steep one- to two-hour hike from the road (mules carry the luggage), rests on the tip of a peak with commanding 360-degree views of lush hills and valleys. Bird-watching and hiking opportunities are excellent. Rooms in the lodge are basic but comfortable with mostly twin beds, and there are shared bathrooms, composting toilets and solar-powered electricity. New cabañas with impressive views sleep two to three people and have private bathrooms. You'll get local flavor from the friendly administrator and chef, who cooks up excellent meals that include salad, potato pancakes and hearty soups. Prices include three meals a day.

The reserve is owned and run by a cooperative of 12 families who, looking for a more sustainable future, stopped farming *naranjilla* (tart tropical fruit) with pesticides to work with tourism and preservation. Considered one of the country's best examples of community tourism, Santa Lucía has won numerous awards for sustainability and reducing poverty. Volunteers are welcome.

A minimum stay of three days is recommended, with entry into the reserve and guide service for the first and last day included in the price. Certified guides from the local families speak basic English and know the scientific names for plants and birds. Transportation by 4WD from Nanegal to the base of the trail is $20 for the half-hour round-trip (for singles or groups); transportation from Quito is $70 one-way.

Reserva Biológica Maquipucuna

Preserving a large swath of the important Chocó-Andean bioregion, this 6000-hectare reserve offers opportunities for hiking, bird-watching and relaxing. Its territory covers a variety of premontane and montane cloud forests in the headwaters of Río Alambi at elevations ranging from 1200m to 2800m. The area, located about 80km northwest of Quito, is truly wonderful and holds a lodge and research station.

About 80% of the reserve is primary forest; the remainder is secondary growth. The reserve holds 370 species of birds, including 30 species of hummingbirds (a bird list is available); 240 species of butterflies; and 45 species of mammals including the spectacled bear. The nonprofit Fundación Maquipucuna administers the reserve, which it purchased in 1988.

Guests stay at a rustic **lodge** (www.maqui.org; r per person incl 3 meals with shared/private bathroom $45/65) with great deck views from the hammocks and tasty, healthy meals at the restaurant, which serves its own shade-grown coffee. In addition to a variety of lodge rooms, there's a family cabin with two bathrooms and a private deck. Day guests pay a $10 entry fee and can hire a guide for $25. Trails range from an easy 1km walk to a demanding 5.5km hike. The Fundación can arrange a private vehicle from Quito for $80. If you're driving, you'll need a 4WD for the 7km from the main road.

Get more information from **Fundación Maquipucuna** (☎ 02-250-7200 in Quito; info@maquipucuna.org; cnr Baquerizo E9-153 & Tamayo, La Floresta, Quito) or the **Chocó Andean Rainforest Corridor** (☎ 706-542-2968 in the US; Institute of Ecology, University of Georgia).

Reserva Bellavista

This 700-hectare reserve is in the same western Andean slopes as Maquipucuna at about 2000m above sea level. About 25% is primary forest and the rest has been selectively or completely logged, but is regenerating. Various conservation projects are under way. There are 8km of well-marked trails and the area is highly recommended by bird-watchers (320 species of birds have been recorded).

The main **lodge** (in Quito ☎ 02-211-6232, 02-223-2313; www.bellavistacloudforest.com; cnr Jorge Washington E7-23 & Reina Victoria; s/d incl 3 meals $83/142, dm $47) is a wooden geodesic dome with a jaw-dropping panoramic view. There's a library/restaurant/bar on the ground floor, over which are five small rooms topped by a two-story dormitory area with a shared bathroom, a restaurant and balcony. Light pours into these cozy rooms, but if you prefer privacy, larger private cabins are a short walk from the lodge. About a kilometer away is a research station with a kitchen and accommodations.

Guided hikes and horseback riding are offered, as well as multiday packages. Hiring a truck in Nanegalito (56km along on the road to Puerto Quito) is $15. Trucks are lined up on the left side where a small sign says 'Bellavista transport.'

MINDO

☎ 02 / pop 2500 / elevation 1250m

Just a 2½-hour drive from Quito, Mindo attracts serious bird-watchers, backpackers and weekenders seeking a retreat into nature. The tiny town, which sits in a green valley well off the main road, feels as laid-back as a costal surf spot. Friendly locals have created an impressive infrastructure for enjoying the cloud forest, including butterfly farms and orchid collections. Stay a few days and try horseback riding, mountain biking, hiking, bird-watching, tubing or hurtling down zip-lines – all means for exploring waterfalls, rivers and beautiful cloud forest.

The town does not have a bank, so bring necessary cash and traveler's checks. The nearest ATM is in Los Bancos (p149). The intersection where the main road meets the Mindo turnoff is commonly called the 'Y.'

Information

Amigos de la Naturaleza de Mindo (☎ 276-5463) is a local conservation organization with an office near Parque Central. It provides information about reserves, activities and hiking. The nearby **Bosque Protector Mindo-Nambillo**, 192,200 hectares of premontane cloud forest, is no longer open to visitors.

The **Mindo Cloudforest Foundation** (☎ 09-355-1949; www.mindocloudforest.org) operates two superb bird sanctuaries nearby: the **Milpe Bird Sanctuary**, a 155-acre reserve with a network of trails located 15km west from the 'Y,' and the **Río Silanche Sanctuary**. Entry is $6 per day or $10 for a three-day pass. This nonprofit place also produces shade-grown coffee, which converts cattle pasture into bird habitat.

Sights & Activities

Soar across a lush river basin on the **tarabita** (hand-powered cable car; Rd to Cascada de Nambillo; per person $2; ⏲ 8:30am-4pm, closed Mon), a perfectly safe wire basket on steel cables that glides 152m above the ground. On the other side, find a network of trails in the Bosque Protector Mindo-Nambillo. Hire a guide at the *tarabita* to visit the falls or follow the well-marked trails on your own. It's a 4km walk from town or you can take a taxi.

Halfway up the road to the *tarabita,* two dueling zipline companies compete for adrenaline seekers. Fly over the canopy in a harness attached to a cable strung above the trees, an activity that gets faster in the rain. The original company, **Mindo Canopy Adventure** (☎ 09-453-0624; www.mindocanopy.com; per person $15) has 13 different cables ranging from 70m to 400m in length. **Mindo Ropes & Canopy** (☎ 390-0454/31; www.mindoropescanopy.com; per person $15) offers a similar experience on 10 cables.

THE EARLY BIRD GETS…THE MATE

While most birds preen and strut to attract members of the opposite sex, the Andean cock-of-the-rock *(Rupicola peruvianus)* takes top prize for persistence.

Every day, rain or shine, male cocks-of-the-rock, with their bulbous coif of blood-red or orange feathers, gather at 6am and squawk loudly, dance on branches and dive and wrangle with each other, hoping to win some female attention. This all-male revue is called a 'lek' for any bird species. If they're lucky, a drab-brown female will dive into the crowd and choose a mate, but more often than not, females never show.

How can the plainer sex resist the impressive display? Maybe they're too busy single-parenting; alone, females build nests and care for their offspring while males remain focused on the daily possibility of mating.

Cock-of-the-rock leks are prevalent around Mindo. Witnessing the spectacle requires a predawn wakeup call.

Tubing ($5 per person with group of 4) is best in the rainy season, when the rapids on the Río Mindo get a little feisty. Places on Avenida Quito rent inner tubes; most mandate that you hire a guide for safety. If you want to pedal around the countryside, Efrain Silva guides and rents mountain bikes at **Bicistar** (per day $10). If you prefer riding horses, call **Miguel Patiño** (☎ 09-945-6862) for a guided ride. **La Isla** (☎ 09-327-2190; Av Quito) offers camping (sites per person $5) and canyoning ($20 per person), using harnesses and ropes to descend waterfalls.

Check out the blooms at **Armonía Orchid Garden** (☎ 390-0431; www.birdingmindo.com; admission $2; 🕑 7am-5pm), which boasts a collection of more than 200 orchids. Lodging is available.

Mindo has several butterfly farms. Visit **Mariposas de Mindo** (☎ 224-2712; www.mariposasdemindo.com; admission $3; 🕑 9am-4pm) in the warmest part of the day, around 11am, when butterflies are most active. It also has a restaurant and lodging.

If you're interested in the flirting behavior of the dashing crimson cock-of-the-rock, grab a local guide or inquire at your hostel about the **cock-of-the-rock lek** (see the boxed text, above).

Finally, perk up with a quick tour of **Vivero Mindo** (☎ 390-0445; admission free; 🕑 weekends only), a tiny organic coffee plantation that won 'Best Coffee in Ecuador' in a local competition. Coffee afterwards is free.

BIRD-WATCHING

With more than 400 species of birds recorded, Mindo has become a major center for bird-watchers. Locally there are many competent, professional guides. Although many speak only Spanish, guides still know the bird names in English and can easily guide non-Spanish speakers. Most charge between $70 and $200 per day.

Fernando Arias (☎ 09-442-1957; tntedoblef@yahoo.es) A knowledgeable bird-watcher who got his chops at El Monte.

Irman Arias (☎ 09-170-8720; www.mindobirdguide.com) An excellent local guide.

Marcelo Arias (of Rubby Hostal, p148; marceloguideofbirds@yahoo.com) Comes highly recommended by many readers.

Juan Carlos Calvachi (☎ 09-966-4503, 286-5213; calvachi@uio.satnet.net) A top guide from Quito who speaks perfect English; $200 per day for three people including transportation.

Danny Jumbo (☎ 09-328-0769) Comes recommended. Local, speaks English.

Nolberto Jumbo (☎ 08-563-8011) Experienced and knowledgeable.

Julia Patiño (☎ 390-0419, 08-616-2816; juliaguideofbird@yahoo.com) A vivacious, highly recommended guide. The first woman to guide in town.

Sandra Patiño (☎ 09-935-9363) Provides excellent guiding. Local and speaks English.

Javier Perez (☎ 09-490-5339; crisjapean@hotmail.com) A good local guide who speaks English.

Sleeping

The village has a few new, midrange options and plenty of basic accommodations; the fancier places are outside town. Don't be shy about asking locals directions since there are no street signs.

La Casa de Cecilia (☎ 390-0413, 09-334-5393; casadececilia@yahoo.com; r per person $6) Cecilia's warm reception spruces up this maze of bunk beds. You'll find an outdoor fireplace on the hammock deck and an open-air kitchen on the river. On nice days take advantage of the lovely swimming hole and sunbathing platform. Camping is $2. Ask about long-term discounts and work exchanges.

Rubby Hostal (☎ 09-340-6321, 09-193-1853; rubbyhostal@yahoo.com; r per person $6) Highly recommended for its clean, basic rooms and hearty breakfasts. Owner Marcelo is a known bird-watching guide.

Hospedaje el Rocío (☎ 390-0041; Rd to Nambillo; r per person $8, ste $25-40) A dark jungle hideout with colorful, cozy group spaces, hammocks looking out on the wild garden and stacks of old *National Geographic* magazines in the hall. Breakfasts get rave reviews.

Jardin de los Pájaros (☎ 09-422-7624; Barrío El Progreso; r per person incl breakfast $12;) This *hostal* lacks some finishing touches, but the carpeted rooms are ample and comfortable. Look down on the small, heated outdoor pool from the large, shaded deck.

Cabañas Armonía (☎ 390-0431, 09-943-5098; www.orchids-birding.com; per person incl breakfast $14) Tucked away in tousled, unkempt gardens, the accommodations here are in quiet, rustic cabins or dorm-style rooms in the main house. Attached is Armonía Orchid Garden (p147).

Caskaffesu (☎ 390-0400, 09-386-7154; caskaffesu@yahoo.com; s/d incl breakfast $15/20) Sunny and reliable, two stories of tidy rooms washed in color surround a small garden courtyard tucked behind the popular restaurant. English is spoken.

Dragonfly Inn (☎ 229-7507, 09-238-2189; www.dragonflyinn-mindo.com; s/d incl breakfast $20/35) A new structure on the main road with spotless wood-paneled rooms, comfy beds and a small garden where hummingbirds flit.

OUTSIDE OF TOWN

Quindepungo (☎ 390-0491, 09-954-7434; www.quindepungo.com.ec; r per person incl breakfast $20) A tilapia pond and prime spot on the Río Mindo help compensate for dark rooms and sagging beds. Still, it's one of the rare budget options outside of town.

El Carmelo Hosteria (☎ 02-222-4713 in Quito; www.mindo.com.ec; r per person incl breakfast $35;) A pleasant Ecuadorian-owned complex with cabins that sleep two to six people scattered among sparse vegetation. While the place feels less remote than you may like, the new treetop cabins are a unique take on cloud forest lodging. A giant pool area is suited to families and groups.

Mindo Gardens Lodge (in Quito ☎ 02-225-2488, 09-733-1092; www.mindogardens.com; d incl breakfast $65) Owned by an Ecuadorian hotel company, this place feels small and personal. Pathways wind through wooded gardens to a main lodge and cozy cabins. The dining room (meals $7) has patio seating and two-story cabins have bright bedspreads. The best rooms have river views. A trail on the property leads to the *tarabita*. The lodge can be reached by car or a 45-minute walk from town.

Séptimo Paraíso (in Quito ☎ 02-289-3160, 09-368-4417; www.septimoparaiso.com; r per person incl 3 meals $80) Elegant country-style rooms in a woodsy building make this Mindo's 'seventh heaven.' Covered pathways connect the excellent restaurant, Lo Chorrera (mains $8 to $13), to a heated pool and Jacuzzi. Restaurant patrons can peruse the wine cellar or play pool in the bar. The hotel recycles 95% of its waste and operates the Green Mindo Foundation, which conducts cloud forest research and bird counts, educates locals on conservation efforts, reforests old pastureland and oversees a 420-acre reserve. Just off the road into Mindo, 2km below the 'Y.'

Casa Divina (☎ 09-172-5874, 09-146-2112; www.mindocasadivina.com; s/d incl breakfast & dinner $83/145) Located 1km outside of town, two-story wooden cabins are still shiny and new against a quiet, forested hillside. Porches with hammocks provide comfortable roosts for bird-watching and short on-site trails expand the observation territory. The owners, a woodworker and baker, are gracious hosts at this family-friendly location.

our pick **El Monte Sustainable Lodge** (☎ 390-0402, 09-308-4675; www.ecuadorcloudforest.com; r per person incl 3 meals & activities $86) Run by a warmhearted and knowledgeable young American/Ecuadorian couple, El Monte is a lush retreat with three lovely, private riverside cabins. The aesthetic is contemporary and comfortable, with lots of wood and natural tones. Three cabins sleep up to four people and have hot showers and bathtubs. Located 4km south of Mindo along a winding dirt road, it's reached by a *tarabita* over the Río Mindo. The communal lodge has rustic, oversized furniture, fire pits, a library and some solar-powered electricity. The food is delicious and mostly vegetarian – candlelit dinners include pastas, empanadas, curries and salads from the organic garden. Guided activities include bird-watching, hiking and tubing, but guests can also wander the on-site trails or swim in the river-fed pool. Reserve ahead so the owners can arrange transport from Mindo. A two-night minimum is suggested. The owners are assisting a new Huaorani-owned tour in the Oriente (see p241).

Eating

Café El Monte (☎ 390-0402; mains $3-5; 🕒 10am-9pm Fri-Sun, 4-9pm Mon-Thu) Specializes in vegetarian plates. Good bets include the whole-wheat pizza with zucchini and tomatoes, veggie burger and burrito. The café is also popular for its homemade baked goods, garden salads and organic coffee.

El Quetzal (☎ 623-6805; www.elquetzaldemindo.com; Calle 9 de Octubre; mains $3-5; 🕒 10am-8:30pm) The coffee-roasting machine reveals the American owner's obsession with a good cup of joe. The menu includes a delicious *arroz con camarones* (rice with shrimp), sandwiches and *yuca frita con queso* (fried yuca with cheese). Try the bubbling cobblers or a cookie for dessert.

Fuera de Babylonia (☎ 09-475-7768; Calle los Ríos; mains $4-5; 🕒 7:30am-9:30pm) An earthy jungle ambience attracts the dreadlocked set in search of Bob Marley and *cerveza* (beer). Try the pastas, steamed trout or beet soup. Located one block off the plaza.

El Chef (☎ 390-0478; mains $4-7; 🕒 8am-8pm) A popular spot for set meals, this basic steakhouse sizzles. Try the *lomo a la piedra* (steak cooked on a 'stone') or a hearty burger.

our pick **Caskaffesu** (☎ 390-0400, 09-386-7154; caskaffesu@yahoo.com; mains $5-8) Fresh ingredients make everything – from the steamed tilapia to roasted chicken – delectable. Dine in the spacious dining room near the fireplace or on the shady streetside patio. The owner makes the brownies with two kinds of Ecuadorian chocolate. Don't pass up the real espresso drinks.

Getting There & Away

From Quito, **Cooperativa Flor de Valle** goes to Mindo ($2.50, 2½ hours) Monday to Friday at 8am and 3:45pm. On weekends buses leave at 7:20am, 8am and 3:45pm; on Saturday at 7:20am, 8am, 9am and 3:45pm, with an additional 1:45pm bus on Sunday. The cooperative is located in the new Terminal Terrestre Norte La Ofelia. The bus returns from Mindo to Quito daily at 6:30am and 2pm. On Saturday, buses depart at 6:30am, 2pm, 3:30pm and 5pm. Sunday buses depart at 6:30am, 2pm, 3pm, 4pm, 5pm and 6pm.

Cooperativa Kennedy, **Cooperativa San Pedro** and **Cooperativa Aloag** leave the Cumanda Terminal and don't go directly to Mindo, but can drop you at the top of the 'Y,' a five-hour ride.

Getting Around

A taxi cooperative runs from the plaza. Prices are higher than in other areas. A trip to the 'Y' costs $3, where a number of buses go to Quito, Santo Domingo or the coast. Drivers with private cars provide transport around town and to Quito ($50 one-way). Mindo resident Jairon Garzon (☎ 09-400-9485) is safe and attentive.

WEST OF MINDO

This beautiful and out-of-the-way route links Quito to the western lowlands and coast. The town of **Los Bancos** provides access to bird-watching in the **Milpe Sanctuary**. Heading west, the landscape changes quickly, from cool cloud forest to hotter, lush lowlands as the road drops and flattens near **Puerto Quito**. Soon after, you'll hit the main road between Santo Domingo de los Colorados and the north-coast port of Esmeraldas.

Pedro Vicente Maldonado

The village is a strip of squat cement buildings fringed by steamy, lowland jungle. At the far edge of town you'll find **Arashá Rainforest Resort & Spa** (☎ Quito 02-224-9881, 09-198-1668; www.arasharesort.com; s/d inclusive package $561/398;) nuzzling visitors in the lap of cloud forest luxury. The poshest spot on the western Andean slope, the resort is popular with nationals and families. Accommodations are in stilted thatched huts set among beautifully manicured grounds. In addition to bird-watching, hiking and wildlife-watching excursions, the resort offers an excellent spa, pool, disco, a kids' swimming area, minigolf and restaurant. Package rates include transport to and from Quito, three meals a day, a spa treatment and guided tours. The hotel is 3km outside of Pedro Vicente Maldonado, on the old road to Santo Domingo, and about 200m off the main road to Puerto Quito.

Puerto Quito

Not much goes on in Puerto Quito and that's the charm. It's a relaxing place to see birds and waterfalls and swim in lazy rivers. There are frequent buses from Quito's bus terminal and Santo Domingo. Downtown offers a few

NORTHERN HIGHLANDS

budget hostels, but better options are found outside town.

Hostal Cocoa (☎ 215-6233; r per person $10, incl 3 meals $18) is a quiet, family-run spot with a gorgeous setting on a tropical river bend. Rooms are basic, which draws guests outdoors to enjoy the hammocks. Packages can include visits to a waterfall and an organic fruit farm, or tubing and chocolate making. Located 2km outside of town; you can take a taxi there for $3.

Ítapoa Reserve (☎ 09-478-4992, 255-1569; r per person incl 3 meals $33) is a small pocket of primary and secondary forest with an old farmhouse where guests can stay. The owner Raul is an affable biologist who gives engaging presentations about flora and fauna – a wonderful introduction to cloud forests. Activities include tubing, making chocolate and tagua rings. English is spoken here. Volunteers are needed for native plant reintroduction. Call ahead for transport from town.

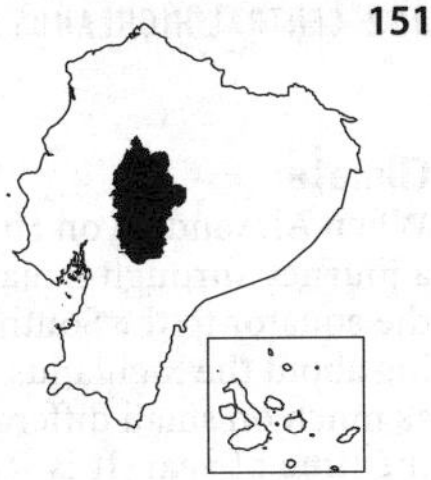

Central Highlands

When it comes to glaciered mountains and volcanoes, central highlanders have a monopoly that includes one of the *highest* active volcanoes anywhere, one of the *most* active volcanoes in the world, extinct craters topped up with incomparable, sulfur-blue lakes and enough snow-dusted minor peaks to fill the spaces in between.

Highlanders see these Quichua-named Andes – Cotopaxi, Rumiñahui, Quilotoa, Tungurahua, Chimborazo – as more than just beautiful views. The volcanoes send water and cool breezes, and some of them send the occasional lava flow, which inspires respect.

The folks who live in the folds of the mountains are a diverse lot – indigenous farmers who grow potatoes and corn, mestizo (of mixed Spanish and indigenous descent) artisans who fashion traditional crafts, old hacienda owners of Spanish descent and not a few gringos who can't seem to pull themselves away from the scenery.

Rich varieties of plants and animals are also at home among these living mountains including the world's largest and smallest birds, wide-winged condors soaring in the crisp azure sky and hummingbirds darting in and out of flowers.

If you could possibly tire of all this wondrous nature, head into colonial-era cities and the bustling villages, which erupt into riotously colorful markets at least once a week, when all the people come together to buy, sell and trade in the shadows of the peaks.

HIGHLIGHTS

- Bounce along the backcountry roads of the **Quilotoa loop** (p161), passing indigenous communities, arts-and-crafts villages and a supposedly bottomless crater lake.
- Get splashed by waterfalls as you plunge down the **Baños–Puyo** road (p179) on a mountain bike.
- Take the high road to **Salinas** (p184), a model of rural development against a sublime *páramo* (high-altitude Andean grassland) backdrop.
- Ride the rails down **La Nariz del Diablo** (p193), an unparalleled switchback descent down a sheer rock face.
- Hike beneath, around and up one of the world's highest active volcanoes in **Parque Nacional Cotopaxi** (p155).

- AVERAGE TEMP IN RIOBAMBA: 12°C (53°F)
- RAINIEST MONTH IN RIOBAMBA: MAR

Climate

When Alexander von Humboldt compared a journey through Ecuador to a trip from the equator to the South Pole, he was talking about the highlands. Weather depends as much on small differences in altitude as the time of year. It is wise to be prepared pretty much any time for wet and dry, warm and cold.

The highlands experience a dry season from about June to September and a dry spell during December to January – both are considered great times to visit. March to May is generally rainy, although on the eastern slopes of the Andes this period can be wetter (thanks to moisture rising up from the Amazon Basin) and can persist all the way to September.

National Parks

For such a small region, the central highlands have quite a collection of protected areas. All but **Parque Nacional Llanganates** (p171), which is truly a tough wilderness to crack open, have activities for everyone from leisurely day-trippers to hardcore hikers and climbers. **Parque Nacional Cotopaxi** (p155), one of the country's most visited national parks and a quick trip from Quito or Latacunga, is easily accessible. The **Reserva Ecológica Los Ilinizas** (p154) encompasses the two Ilinizas peaks, and stretches all the way to Laguna Quilotoa. Volcán Chimborazo is the centerpiece of the **Reserva de Producción Faunística Chimborazo** (p184), where roving harems of vicuña scamper across the *páramo* (high Andean grasslands). **Parque Nacional Sangay** (p180) is the region's largest park with terrain as varied as jungle and glaciated peaks.

Dangers & Annoyances

Theft of backpacks and other belongings on buses is common, especially on nighttime trips and journeys between Quito, Latacunga and Baños. If it can be avoided, do not carry valuables on day hikes, especially in areas commonly visited by tourists. Violent crime against travelers is rare.

Volcanic eruptions are a part of life in the central highlands. Outside of Baños, however, the most significant threat is ash fall, in which case you should stay indoors or wear a mask outdoors. Masks are for sale in hardware stores, although a damp handkerchief could do the trick as well.

Getting There & Around

Latacunga has an airport that is technically international, but so far has no passenger service. If Quito were fogged in, you could find yourself sitting on Latacunga's tarmac for a couple of hours. Buses, of course, go just about everywhere. The most important transportation hubs are Latacunga, Ambato, Baños, Riobamba and Guaranda.

MACHACHI & ALOASÍ

☎ 02

Machachi and Aloasí, about 35 kilometers south of Quito on opposite sides of the Panamericana, serve as gateways to nearby mountains and wilderness. The quiet hamlet of Aloasí (population 6855), on the west side of the highway, sits at the base of the long-extinct volcano El Corazón (4788m), or 'The Heart,' whose name comes from the shape formed by two canyons on its west side.

Aloasí will likely win greater attention when the Ferrocarril Transandino (Trans-Andean Railway; see p193) resumes services sometime in 2009 (details may be available at www.efe.gov.ec). Some confusion stems from the fact that the Machachi train station is located in Aloasí: most train riders once traveled through here to the big market town of Machachi.

The busy town of Machachi (population 12,470) on the east side of the highway sits at a close but respectful distance to the hulking, active Volcán Cotopaxi and just a stone's throw from Volcán Rumiñahui, making it a convenient access point to Parque Nacional Cotopaxi (p155). The pretty main square has piped-in organ music, and an important **Sunday market** spills all over the city. A boisterous festival celebrating *chagras* (Andean cowboys) rides into town every July 23.

Sleeping & Eating

La Estación de Machachi (☎ 230-9246; s/d $34-36/36-42) Despite its name, this dollhouse of a hotel, occupying a 19th-century renovated hacienda, is actually in Aloasí across from the Machachi train station. The pretty wooden stairs are rickety and the balconies sag, adding to La Estación's charm, but the beds are firm and the water is hot, making it comfortable. Several spacious rooms in the back courtyard have been built to match the house and have wood-burning stoves. The restaurant, festooned with farm-related antiques, serves breakfasts ($4 to $5) and other meals for $10.

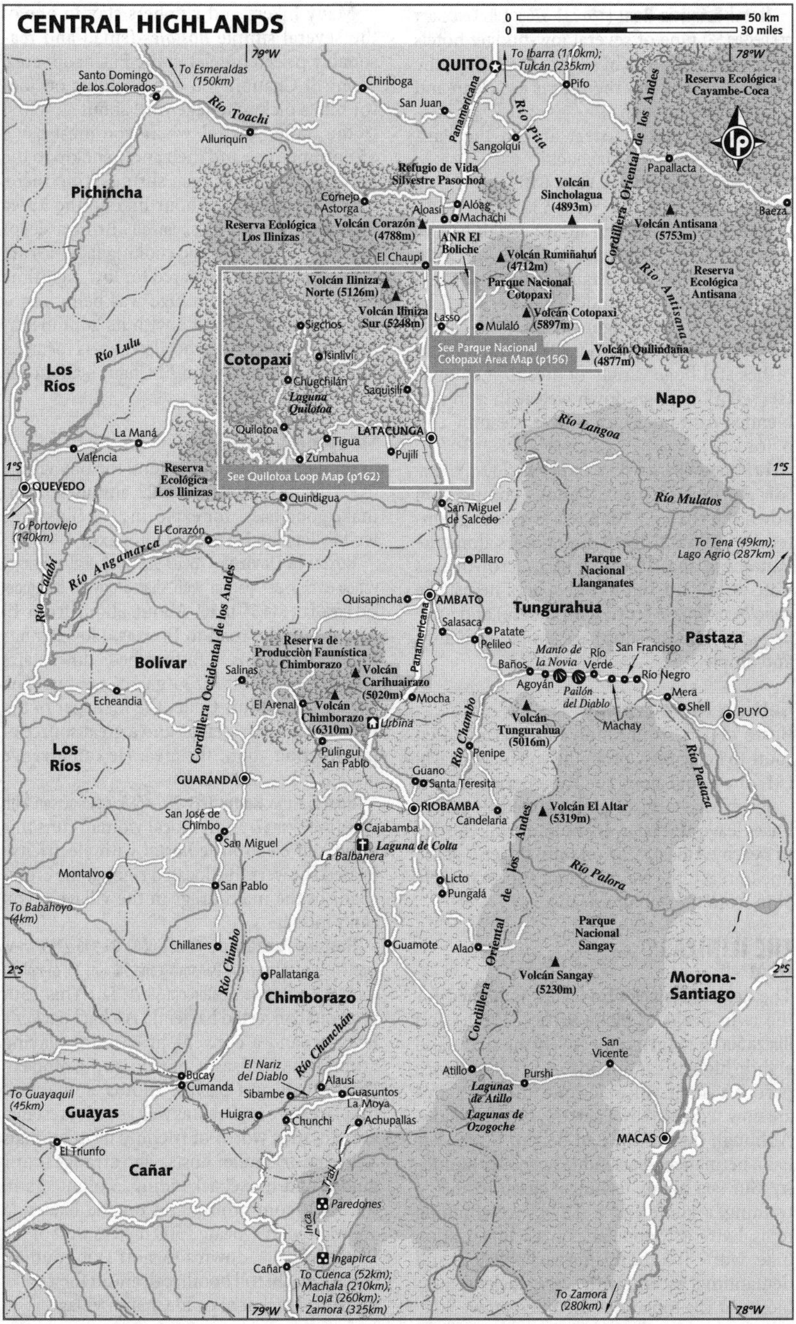
CENTRAL HIGHLANDS
0 50 km
0 30 miles
79°W
78°W
1°S
2°S
QUITO
To Ibarra (110km); Tulcán (235km)
To Esmeraldas (150km)
Santo Domingo de los Colorados
Río Toachi
Alluriquín
Chiriboga
San Juan
Panamericana
Pifo
Río Pita
Sangolquí
Reserva Ecológica Cayambe-Coca
Papallacta
Baeza
Cordillera Oriental de los Andes
Refugio de Vida Silvestre Pasochoa
Pichincha
Corneio Astorga
Aloasí
Alóag
Machachi
Volcán Sincholagua (4893m)
Volcán Antisana (5753m)
Reserva Ecológica Los Ilinizas
Volcán Corazón (4788m)
ANR El Boliche
El Chaupi
Volcán Rumiñahui (4712m)
Río Antisana
Reserva Ecológica Antisana
Volcán Iliniza Norte (5126m)
Parque Nacional Cotopaxi
Volcán Iliniza Sur (5248m)
Lasso
Volcán Cotopaxi (5897m)
Mulaló
Sigchos
See Parque Nacional Cotopaxi Area Map (p156)
Volcán Quilindaña (4877m)
Río Lulu
Isinliví
Cotopaxi
Los Ríos
Chugchilán
Laguna Quilotoa
Saquisilí
Napo
Río Langoa
Quilotoa
LATACUNGA
La Maná
Tigua
Valencia
Pujilí
Zumbahua
Reserva Ecológica Los Ilinizas
See Quilotoa Loop Map (p162)
QUEVEDO
Quindigua
San Miguel de Salcedo
Río Mulatos
To Portoviejo (140km)
El Corazón
Río Angamarca
Río Calabí
Píllaro
To Tena (49km); Lago Agrio (287km)
Parque Nacional Llanganates
Quisapincha
AMBATO
Tungurahua
Cordillera Occidental de los Andes
Salasaca
Patate
Pelileo
Pastaza
Reserva de Producciòn Faunística Chimborazo
Bolívar
Salinas
Volcán Carihuairazo (5020m)
Manto de la Novia
Río Verde
San Francisco
Baños
Río Negro
Agoyán
Pailón del Diablo
Mera
Echeandia
El Arenal
Volcán Chimborazo (6310m)
Mocha
Shell
PUYO
Urbina
Machay
Río Chambo
Volcán Tungurahua (5016m)
Los Ríos
Pulingui San Pablo
Penipe
Río Pastaza
GUARANDA
Guano
Santa Teresita
RIOBAMBA
Candelaria
Volcán El Altar (5319m)
San José de Chimbo
Cajabamba
San Miguel
Laguna de Colta
La Balbanera
Río Palora
Montalvo
Licto
Pungalá
San Pablo
To Babahoyo (4km)
Parque Nacional Sangay
Chillanes
Guamote
Alao
Río Chimbo
Pallatanga
Volcán Sangay (5230m)
Morona-Santiago
Chimborazo
Río Chanchán
San Vicente
Bucay
Cumanda
El Nariz del Diablo
Atillo
Purshi
To Guayaquil (45km)
Sibambe
Alausí
Guasuntos
La Moya
Lagunas de Atillo
Guayas
Huigra
Chunchi
Achupallas
Lagunas de Ozogoche
El Triunfo
MACAS
Cañar
Inca Trail
Paredones
Ingapirca
Cañar
To Cuenca (52km); Machala (210km); Loja (260km); Zamora (325km)
To Zamora (280km)

Hotel Estancia Real (☎ 231-5760; Luis Cordero; r per person $8) One of several low-budget hotels across from Machachi's Plaza Mayorista, the beds are lumpy but the rooms are clean and comfortable enough.

The best places to eat are on the Panamericana south of Machachi.

our pick **El Café de la Vaca** (☎ 231-5012; Panamericana Km 23; mains $3-8; 8am-5:30pm) On weekend afternoons, you will almost certainly have to wait to dine alongside carloads of Quito day-trippers at this restaurant painted like a black-and-white cowhide. They flock to 'The Cow Café' for its straight-off-the-farm cheese served with every order. The Ecuadorian dishes and huge variety of breakfast combos (served all day) go down well with a freshly blended fruit juice or a simple, steamin' cup o' Joe.

La Manuela (Panamericana Km 20; mains $3-8; 8am-5pm) An imitator of its famous competition down the road, La Manuela is a strong contender in the sit-down dining wars along the Panamericana. It won't be as crowded as Café de la Vaca, but its old-school items, like *choclo con queso* (corn with cheese) and *locro de papas* (potato soup) are simple, delicious and ample.

Getting There & Away

Buses depart from Quito's bus terminal en route to Latacunga, dropping you in Machachi ($1, one hour) along the Panamericana.

From Machachi, brightly painted old school buses leave at least every hour during the day to nearby Aloasí. Stay on until the end of the line to reach the train station, approximately 3km from the Panamericana.

THE ILINIZAS

☎ 02

The **Reserva Ecológica Los Ilinizas** is named for the twin peaks of **Iliniza Norte** (5126m) and **Iliniza Sur** (5248m), respectively the sixth- and eighth-highest mountains in Ecuador. Once part of a single volcanic cone, the two spires are now separated by a narrow, sloping saddle. Although they're close in height, Iliniza Sur has a permanent glacier due to greater humidity. Sur is a highly technical climb requiring training, a guide and a slew of ice-climbing tools. Extremely popular as an acclimatization hike, Norte is a more approachable, but still demanding, ascent, with scree, rocky scrambles near the top and sometimes snow.

Many hikers and climbers stay in one of the several simple *hostales* (small and reasonably priced hotels) in the El Chaupi area. From El Chaupi, you can continue on foot (or hire a pickup to take you) about 3km first to the staffed **Control**, where you must pay a $5 entrance fee, and then another 6km to the parking lot at La Virgen shrine. From there, it is a roughly three-hour hike to the **Nuevo Horizontes Refuge** (4650m; dm $10). Bring a sleeping bag and food (basic cooking facilities are available), and be prepared for low nighttime temperatures. This refuge was being renovated in 2009, so check with its administrator, Bladimir Gallo, who also owns Hostal La Llovizna (see below) in El Chaupi, about the current availability.

Sleeping & Eating

Several *hostales* in and around the tiny village of El Chaupi (population 1322, altitude 3311m) make good bases for exploring the Ilinizas as well as Parque Nacional Cotopaxi.

Hostal La Llovizna (☎ 09-969-9068; iliniza_blady@yahoo.com; r per person with shared/private bathroom incl breakfast $14.64/18.30) About 500m from El Chaupi on the road to Ilinizas, Llovizna has big, warm rooms with firm beds downstairs and cozy, hobbit-sized garret rooms. The owner is Bladimir Gallo, the manager of the Ilinizas climbers' refuge and a great source of information about the area. He can arrange guided hikes and climbs.

Hostal Nina Rumy (☎ 286-4688; r per person with shared bathroom $7) A nice local woman runs this basic and clean little *hostal* with electricity-heated showers. It's located right at the crossroads of the main drags in the village – you can't miss it.

Hostería PapaGayo (☎ 231-0002, 09-946-2269; www.hosteria-papagayo.com; Panamericana Sur Km 26; camping/dm $4/8, r with private bathroom $8-20;) This 150-year-old converted hacienda is a backpacker's favorite, and a convenient base for playing around the Ilinizas, Corazón and Cotopaxi. Dorm beds and private rooms, some with fireplaces, are available as well as a nice restaurant, an ark's worth of friendly farm animals and even-friendlier hosts, who arrange tours, guides and horseback riding. Volunteers in the local community and on the hacienda are wanted. It's located 500 meters west of the Panamericana, down a turnoff 1km south of the Machachi toll booth; call ahead for a pick-up from Machachi or El Chaupi village.

GETTING THERE & AWAY

Blue-and-white buses signed 'El Chaupi' ($0.25, 40 minutes) leave about every hour until dark from Amazonas at 11 de Noviembre in Machachi. From the Panamericana, a faded metal sign indicates the El Chaupi turnoff, about 6km south of Machachi – the cobbled road continues another 7km to El Chaupi. From El Chaupi, the road turns to dirt and continues another 9km to the Ilinizas parking area, identified by a small shrine to the Virgin. You can also hire a pickup in Machachi (ask around the plaza) to take you directly to the parking area for about $25.

PARQUE NACIONAL COTOPAXI

☎ 03

Although you can see Volcán Cotopaxi from several provinces, its majestic bulk and symmetrical cone take on entirely new dimensions within the bounds of its namesake national park. Covered in a draping glaciated skirt that gives way to sloping gold and green *páramo*, the flanks of Cotopaxi are home to wild horses, llamas, foxes, deer, Andean condor and the exceedingly rare spectacled bear.

Morning views are the best, making a stay in the park a desirable option. There's nothing like waking up to Cotopaxi during a crisp dawn, when you can appreciate the contours of the glacier and see the Yanasacha 'Forest,' which is not really a forest but a large, exposed rock face near the peak.

Zooming out to Cotopaxi from Quito or Latacunga for a day trip is also feasible. Hiking and mountain biking to pre-Columbian ruins around the area's lakes and along the park roads are activities that you can do with guides or on your own.

Bird-watching in the park is excellent. Keep your eyes peeled for the giant, soaring Andean condor and the Ecuadorian hillstar, one of the world's highest-altitude hummingbirds. Shorebirds and ducks are common visitors to Laguna Limpiopungo.

Infrastructure is better than in most Ecuadorian parks but still limited. *Ganados* (livestock) are raised here, and it is not unusual to see SUVs off-roading over bird nesting grounds or visitors toying with the wild horses. To deal with heavy deforestation, environmental groups have planted large stands of conifers – while these non-native trees have helped prevent erosion, they have only partially solved the problem of restoring habitat, and their symmetrical rows certainly are not as beautiful as Cotopaxi's native forests.

Among the hazards here are the serious threat of altitude sickness and bulls. These problems can be avoided, the first by acclimatizing in Quito for a couple days, the second by keeping your distance.

Information

The entrance fee ($10) does not include the overnight refuge fees or camping fees. The main entrance is officially open 7am to 3pm, but drivers can get *out* until about 6:30pm. Hikers can get in or out at anytime.

If you plan to take a guided tour or climb, you're best off doing so from Quito (p96), Latacunga (p159) or Riobamba (p189), which have the best climbing operators.

Sights & Activities

Laguna Limpiopungo is a shallow, reedy lake at the base of Rumiñahui that is home to local and migrating waterfowl. An easy-as-pie trail (one hour) circumnavigates the lake, but keep a safe distance from the bulls that like to sip at the shore. Several campsites in the lake area have fire pits and outstanding morning views of the mountains.

Mountain biking around the park's circuit of relatively flat, dirt roads is popular. The Biking Dutchman (see p93) transports riders up to the *refugio* (mountain refuge) parking lot, where you can peer up at the awesome glacier before bombing down the western slope of Cotopaxi. Helmets, lunch, and transfer from Quito are included.

Summit attempts can be arranged in Quito and Latacunga. Although the climb is not technical, it is physically demanding, freezing, and for some people, vertigo inducing. The ascent starts around midnight from **Refugio José Rivas** (4800m; dm $20), where you can cook and get a bunk (bring a sleeping bag and a padlock to store your gear). Even experienced, fit and acclimatized climbers only reach the summit at dawn about one of every two tries (no guarantees, baby!). The reward for those who make it to the top (on a clear day!) are awesome views of other mountains and a peek at the crater's smoking fumaroles.

Nine km into the park from Control Caspi (southern entrance), **Museo Nacional Mariscal Sucre** (admission free) explains the natural history of the area.

Sleeping

All of these lodgings in and around the park offer unique experiences and make convenient bases for exploring Cotopaxi. Most of them offer *cabalgatas* (horseback riding trips) for which they'll set you up, cowboy style, with a pair of llama-skin chaps and a poncho.

Albergue de Alta Montaña Paja Blanca (☎ 231-4234; adjacent to museum; per person incl breakfast $12.50) For the most budget conscious, the shared A-frames here have beds, fireplaces, and hot water, but no electricity at night. Next door, the restaurant of the same name serves good local trout and cold beers.

Cuello de Luna (☎ 09-970-0330, 02-290-5939; www.cuellodeluna.com; dm per person incl breakfast $15, s/d incl breakfast $23/34) The 'Neck of the Moon' is a convenient midrange option, located 1.5km down a turnoff across from the south entrance of Parque Nacional Cotopaxi. Dorm beds are available, and standard rooms have private bathrooms and wood stoves or fireplaces. Dinners ($7 to $10) are available.

Tambopaxi (☎ 222-0241/0242; r per person in main lodge $16, s/d in private structure $60/80) About 25km along the main road from the park's south entrance, this certified sustainable-tourism project is involved in wildlife conservation and watershed protection, and hires local workers. The rustic, stove-heated main lodge offers views of llamas and wild horses. In the morning, look through the telescope in the dining room to watch climbers push for Cotopaxi's summit. The dorm rooms have fluffy down comforters and outrageous views of Cotopaxi. A new, separate structure has private rooms.

El Porvenir (☎ 02-223-1806; www.volcanoland.com; r per person incl breakfast $25, full board & activities $89) Just 4km from the north entrance to the park, El Porvenir mixes the rustic comfort of an authentic hacienda experience with a strong ecological slant and tons of outdoors activities such as horseback riding and mountain biking. The setting, high in the *páramo* with nothing but views of Cotopaxi for company, is spectacular. A wood-burning fire keeps the cozy common area warm and the rooms are loaded with amenities. The hacienda is run by Tierra del Volcán (www.volcanoland.com), an excellent, eco-conscious company with two other haciendas. The owners provide jeep transportation to El Porvenir via a dirt road.

our pick **Hostería La Ciénega** (☎ 271-9052, in Quito 02-254-9126; www.hosterialacienega.com; s/d/ste $55/77/121) This 400-year-old hacienda has hosted some illustrious guests, including the French Geodesic Expedition, Alexander von Humboldt and Ecuadorian presidents. A hotel since 1982, it still has hacienda charm: a long, eucalyptus-lined drive, meter-thick walls and an old chapel. The modern annex is less attractive (but priced the same), so confirm that your reservation is in the original house. The restaurant/bar serves classic (but expensive) Ecuadorian fare, done very well. La Ciénega is 1.5km west of the Panamericana, about 2km south of the village of Lasso. Bus drivers will drop you at the sign, and you can walk from there.

Hacienda Yanahurco (☎ 02-244-5248 in Quito; www.haciendayanahurco.com; 2-day packages per person $250) A remote ranch on the southeast side of the park, Yanahurco has 12 comfortable rooms and private bathrooms. It affords the opportunity to see some of the rarer wildlife that has largely fled the western slope of Cotopaxi, as well as high-altitude cattle ranching. Rates include all meals, horseback riding, fishing, rain gear and rubber boots. Camping is also available.

Hacienda San Agustín de Callo (☎ 271-9160, in Quito 02-290-6157/8; www.incahacienda.com; s/d $278/425) This hacienda has seen a lot of history over the last five centuries. Originally an Incan fortress, it later served as an Augustinian monastery. The French Geodesic mission used it as a triangulation point to measure the equator in 1748, and Alexander von Humboldt stayed here in 1802 and climber Edward Whymper in 1880. The owner is the warm-hearted Mignon Plaza, the granddaughter of a former Ecuadorian president. The distinctive mortarless Incan stonework that forms many of the walls makes this hotel unique and mysterious; excavations and investigations by North American researchers are ongoing. The hacienda is also the site of indigenous celebrations around the solstices. All the rooms have at least two fireplaces, one in the bedroom and one in the bathroom. Rates include breakfast, dinner and guided activities such as fishing, hiking, mountain biking and two hours of horseback riding.

Getting There & Away

All of the haciendas provide transportation from Quito, often at an additional cost.

There are three entrances to the park. The main entrance, **Control Caspi**, is via a turnoff about 22km south of Machachi (or roughly 30km north of Latacunga). From the turnoff, it's 6km northwest over dirt roads to the control and another 9km to the museum. Any Quito–Latacunga bus will drop you at the turnoff.

It's possible to reach the park through the northern entrance, known as **Control Norte**, via Machachi, but you'll need to hire a pickup or 4x4 vehicle. The 21km route is now well signed and easy to follow.

The third, rarely used entrance is the turnoff road to Área Nacional de Recración El Boliche, about 16km south of Machachi. The road passes the Clirsen Satellite Tracking Station (once operated by NASA), about 2km from the Panamericana. Just beyond Clirsen is the Cotopaxi train station, where train service is scheduled to resume in 2009 (details may be available at www.efe.gov.ec). From here, the road is closed to vehicles but eventually reaches the unattended entrance to Cotopaxi.

On weekends, local tourists visit the park and there is a good chance of getting a lift from the turnoff to the main entrance and on to Laguna Limpiopungo. Midweek, the park is almost deserted and you'll probably end up walking if you don't arrange transportation.

From Latacunga, you can hire a pickup (about $40 to the refuge), but you should bargain and be specific if you want to go all the way to Refugio José Rivas. You can arrange for the pickup to return for you on a particular day for another $30 to $40, depending on the pickup location. It is almost an hour's walk uphill from the parking lot to the refuge (4800m), which looks as if it's only about a 10-minute stroll away.

LATACUNGA

☎ 03 / pop 87,417 / elevation 2800m

Many travelers end up passing through Latacunga, either to access the Quilotoa loop (p161), the Thursday morning market in Saquisilí (p166) or Parque Nacional Cotopaxi (p155). But for those who stick around, Latacunga also offers a quiet and congenial historic center that has partially survived several Cotopaxi eruptions. You'd never know that such a charming city lies behind the loud and polluted section that greets visitors on the Panamericana.

Cotopaxi volcano, which dominates the town on a clear day, erupted violently in 1742 and again in 1768, destroying much of the city both times. The indomitable (or foolhardy) survivors rebuilt, only to have an immense eruption in 1877 wreak havoc a third time. Not to be outdone by Mother Nature, the townspeople were compelled to try again, and they have been spared Cotopaxi's wrath ever since.

To celebrate this good luck and revel in their rich indigenous and Catholic history, the people of Latacunga put on one of the most famous and magnificent parties in all of Ecuador, the Mamá Negra festival (see the boxed text, below).

Information

Andinatel (Quevedo; 8am-10pm) Telephone center near Maldonado.
Banco de Guayaquil (Maldonado 7-20) Bank with ATM; changes traveler's checks.
Banco del Pichincha (Quito) Bank with ATM near Salcedo.
Captur (281-4968; Orellana btwn Echeverria and Guayaquil; 8am-noon, 2-6pm) Moderately helpful tourist information.
Discovery Net (280-6557; Salcedo 4-16; per hr $1; 8am-9:30pm Mon-Sat, noon Sun) Internet access.
Hospital (Hermanas Páez) Near 2 de Mayo.
Jovy Lavanderia and Café (Ordoñez & Rumiñahui; per kg $0.80; daily) Same-day laundry service.
Post office (Quevedo) Near Maldonado.
Tovarnet (Quito; per hr $1; 9am-9pm) Newer computers with fast internet; between Salcedo and Maldonado.

Sights & Activities

Latacunga's huge and completely untouristy **markets** are quite utilitarian, but that's what makes them interesting. You can see a mingling of Ecuadorian cultures (people from all over the country live and trade here), a tempting variety of foods and snacks, and a riot of fruits, baskets and pirated DVDs. The three sweeping market plazas around the intersection of Echevería and Amazonas are busy everyday, but especially on market days, Tuesday and Saturday.

The well-tended **Parque Vicente León** is a pretty, enclosed park surrounded by buildings from multiple periods. At the southeast corner of the plaza stands the republican-era **town hall**, topped by a pair of stone condors. On the south side stands the colonial-style **cathedral**; on an exterior wall to the left of the main entrance is an interesting descriptive mural of Cotopaxi erupting over the city. A 17th-century arcaded building houses the provincial government offices on the west side, and a few cement monstrosities of recent vintage line the north block.

CENTRAL HIGHLANDS

LATACUNGA'S MAMÁ NEGRA

One of the biggest celebrations in the highlands, the Mamá Negra (Black Mother) parade is a combination of Catholic, pre-Columbian and civic rituals that fill the streets of Latacunga with hundreds of costumed and dancing revelers.

At the head of it all is a statue of the Virgen de las Mercedes, Latacunga's protectress from volcanic eruptions. Believing that the relic has saved the city from Volcán Cotopaxi's wrath many times, people from Latacunga have great faith in her image. (Apparently they overlook the three times that the city *has* been destroyed by Cotopaxi.)

The Mamá Negra, represented by a local man dressed up as a black woman, is said to have been added to the festivities later on. According to one of several legends about him/her, a priest that wanted to earn favor by hosting the Virgin's procession failed to provide sufficiently grand quantities of food and drink, and during the night an apparition of a black woman berated his negligence. She terrified the priest and the rest of the town, so they introduced a new figure to the procession, that of the black mother astride a horse.

Politically incorrect as it might seem, Mamá Negra is an event loved by all. No one – especially foreign tourists! – can escape the *huacos* (witches), who execute a ritual *limpieza* (cleansing) by blowing smoke and *aguardiente* (sugarcane alcohol) on spectators. Most impressive are the *ashangueros*, the men who carry *ashangas*: whole roast pigs, flayed open and flanked by dozens of *cuy* (guinea pigs), chickens, bottles of liquor and cigarettes. The *ashangueros* stop now and then to rest while their friends ply them with more *aguardiente*.

Players representing *yumbos* (indigenous people from the Oriente), *loeros* (African slaves), *camisonas* (colonial-era Spanish women) and many more all have a role in this grand street theater. If you're in town, undoubtedly you will too.

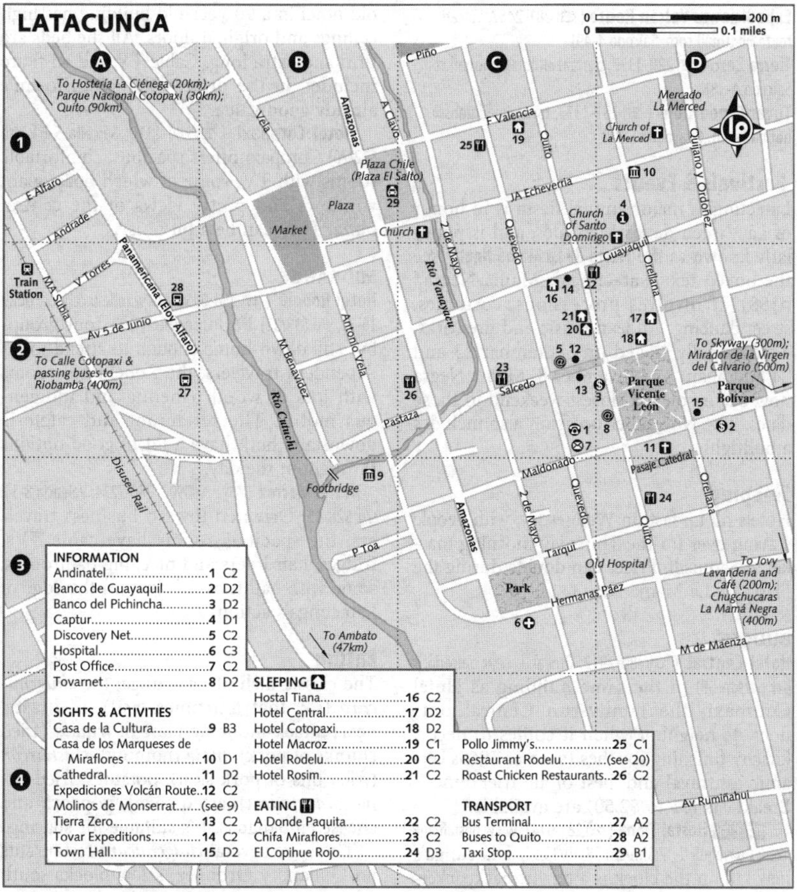

The **Casa de la Cultura** (☎ 281-3247; Vela 3-49; admission $1; ⌚ 8am-noon & 2-6pm Tue-Fri), built on the site of a former Jesuit watermill known as **Molinos de Monserrat**, houses a small ethnography and art museum. The stone steps above the river are a nice retreat from Latacunga's busy sidewalks.

The **Casa de los Marqueses de Miraflores** (Orellana & Echevería; admission free; ⌚ 8am-noon, 2pm-6pm Mon-Sat), an archaeological and religious museum in a surviving colonial-era mansion, covers the Mamá Negra festivals.

On a clear day, the **Mirador de la Virgen del Calvario** (Floreana at Oriente) lookout offers views of several distant volcanic peaks. Follow Maldonado up the stairs, go left on Oriente and follow it up to the statue of the Virgin.

Tours

A number of tour operators have sprung up in recent years, offering excursions to Volcán Cotopaxi (p155). Day trips cost around $50 per person, with the price depending on the size of your group and whether the $10 park entrance fee is included (usually it is not). Two-day climbing trips to Volcán Cotopaxi cost about $160 per person – make sure that your guide is qualified and motivated if you're attempting the summit. Excursions to Laguna Quilotoa and other mountains are also available. The following outfitters are all licensed by Ecuador's department of tourism and have received positive reports from Lonely Planet readers.

Expediciones Volcán Route (☎ 281-2452; volcan route@hotmail.com; Salcedo 4-49)
Tierra Zero (☎ 280-4327; tierraazultours@hotmail.com; Salcedo 4-38)
Tovar Expeditions (☎ 281-1333; tovarexpeditions@ hotmail.com; Guayaquil 5-38)

Festivals & Events

Latacunga's major annual fiesta is in honor of La Virgen de las Mercedes, and is popularly known as the **Fiesta de La Mamá Negra** (see the boxed text 'Latacunga's Mamá Negra,' p158). It involves processions, costumes, street dancing, Andean music and fireworks. Traditionally staged on September 23 and 24 and again on November 8, Mamá Negra now occurs on the closest weekend to those dates. The November occasion also includes a bullfight.

Sleeping

Hotels fill up fast on Wednesday, with people staying over for the Thursday-morning market at Saquisilí. Prices can double during the Fiesta de La Mamá Negra.

BUDGET

Hotel Central (☎ 280-2912; Orellana, near Salcedo; r per person $8) In the same building as Hotel Cotopaxi, the family-run Central outdoes its neighbor when it comes to decor, kitschy finishing touches (such as 1960s ceramic ashtrays) and, best of all, friendliness. Breakfasts ($1 to $2.50) are available.

our pick **Hostal Tiana** (☎ 281-0147; www.hostaltiana .com; Guayaquil 5-32; dm/s/d $8/10/13.50) Latacunga's new kid on the block is a terrific backpacker- and climber-oriented *hostal* situated in a century-old house with a pretty courtyard and some Mamá Negra history (ask about it). The shared and private accommodations are straightforward but exactly what the doctor ordered if you're coming in from the backcountry. If you're headed out, the big breakfast included in the price will get you off to a good start. A true wellspring of traveler's information and assistance, Tiana has a book exchange and can help with onward reservations and activities in Parque Nacional Cotopaxi and the Quilotoa loop. Luggage storage ($2) is available and Dutch, English and Spanish is spoken.

Hotel Rosim (☎ 280-2172, 281-3200; www.hotel rosim.com; Quito 16-49; r per person $11.20; 💻) With lots of emphasis on cleanliness, this 10-year-old hotel in a 90-year-old building has high ceilings and original floors. All the beds are firm and extra long. Cable TV and wi-fi are included in the price, enhancing Rosim's already good value.

Hotel Cotopaxi (☎ 280-1310; Salcedo 5-61; s/d $12/20) Cotopaxi offers spacious, comfortable rooms with TV, some of which boast giant windows and pretty views of the central plaza. They can be a bit noisy.

MIDRANGE

Hotel Rodelu (☎ 280-0956, www.rodelu.com.ec; Quito 16-31; s/d $18/32) Popular with the tour groups but still down-home enough to attend to independent travelers, the Rodelu has rooms with lots of wood paneling and indigenous motifs. The restaurant and cafeteria downstairs both have a lot of good options throughout the day.

Hotel Macroz (☎ 280-0907, 280-7274; Valencia 8-56; s/d $28/45) Oriented toward business travelers, the spacious rooms have cable TVs, fridges, hairdryers and nice, big bathrooms, some with bathtubs. It's just on the edge of Latacunga's action.

Eating

The classic dish of Latacunga, the *chugchucara* (say that ten times fast!), is a tasty, heart-attack-inducing plate of *fritada* (fried chunks of pork), *mote* (hominy), *chicharrón* (fried bits of pork skin), potatoes, fried banana, *tostado* (toasted corn), popcorn and cheese empanadas. It's suitable for sharing.

There are several *chugchucara* restaurants on Quijano y Ordoñez, a few blocks south of downtown – they're all family-friendly. **Chugchucaras La Mamá Negra** (☎ 280 5401; Quijano y Ordoñez 1-67; chugchucara $5.90; 🕑 10am-7pm Tue-Sun) is one of the best.

The Latacunga area is also famous for its *allullas* (pronounced 'azhiuzhias'), dry biscuits made of flour and pork fat, as well as its *queso de hoja,* unpasteurized cheese wrapped in banana leaves. Both are available along the Panamericana directly north of the main pedestrian bridge (Avenida 9 de Julio).

Pollo Jimmy's (☎ 280-1922; Quevedo 8-85; mains $2.25-2.50; 🕑 10am-10pm) Pop in for delicious rotisserie chicken served with rice, potatoes and chicken soup. The place stays busy for a reason. Near Valencia.

A Donde Paquita (Guayaquil & Quito; mains $2-4; 🕑 6:30am-8pm) Paquita serves the earliest breakfast in town and light fare and juices throughout the day.

El Copihue Rojo (☎ 280-1725; Quito 14-38; mains $3-5, almuerzos $2; ⏰ 12:30-3pm & 6-9pm Mon-Sat) If you're looking for a local recommendation, the Copihue Rojo is it. Their daily *almuerzo* (set-lunch) service is always busy, and meats and soups are popular with families during the dinner hour.

Chifa Miraflores (☎ 280 -9079; 2 de Mayo & Salcedo; mains $3-5; ⏰ 10am-9pm) When you tire of chicken and *chugchucaras*, or if you are a vegetarian, Miraflores makes mean stir-fries and other Chinese classics.

Restaurant Rodelu (☎ 280-0956; Quito 16-31; mains $4-7; ⏰ 7:15am-9:30pm Mon-Sat) In its namesake hotel, Rodelu also serves early breakfast as well as wood-oven, medium-crust pizzas, sandwiches and pasta.

Many cheap *leñadores* (wood-burning ovens) roast chicken along Amazonas between Salcedo and Guayaquil.

Entertainment

Latacunga is pretty quiet, but if you want to see what the local youth get up to on a weekend night, pop into **Skyway** (☎ 281-3016; Av Oriente 137 at Napo), where karaoke is free on Friday nights. Saturdays are all about the dance floors.

Getting There & Away

BUS

From Quito ($1.50, two hours), buses will drop you at the **bus terminal** (Panamericana) if Latacunga is their final destination. If you're taking a bus that's continuing to Ambato or Riobamba, it'll drop you on the corner of 5 de Junio and Cotopaxi, about five blocks west of the Panamericana and 10 minutes' walk to downtown. Buses to Quito ($1, one hour) and Ambato ($1, 45 minutes) leave from the bus terminal and 5 de Junio and Cotopaxi. For Riobamba, it's easiest to catch a passing southbound bus from the corner of 5 de Junio and Cotopaxi.

Interminably slow Quito-bound buses leave from the terminal, while faster long-distance buses can be flagged on the Panamericana near 5 de Junio.

Transportes Cotopaxi has hourly buses to Quevedo ($3.75, 5½ hours) in the western lowlands.

For buses to villages along the Quilotoa loop, see the boxed text 'Transport on the Quilotoa Loop,' p164.

TAXI

You can hire taxis and pickup trucks in Plaza Chile (also called Plaza El Salto) for visits to Parque Nacional Cotopaxi (a bargain at $40 round-trip to destinations well within the park, and $15 one-way to the Control Caspi entrance).

THE QUILOTOA LOOP

☎ 03

The Quilotoa loop is a bumpy, ring-shaped road that travels from the Panamericana far into the backcountry of Cotopaxi province. Along the way you'll encounter colorful indigenous markets, a crystal-blue lake that the local people believe has no bottom, a community of painters who are preserving the legends of the Andes and ancient trails that meander in the shadow of snow-capped volcanoes. Paradoxically, the isolation of the loop brings you into contact with lots of Quichua-speaking indigenous people and their centuries-old way of life.

Several villages offer lodgings and most travelers go from one place to the next by bus, hired truck or their own two feet. The hiking is fantastic, and although guides are inexpensive (and a good way to support the local economy), many *hostales* and inns have maps for solo wanderers.

Transportation is infrequent, so it takes some planning if your time is limited and it's wise to travel the loop with rain gear, water and plenty of snacks for long waits and hikes. It's worth spending at least two nights, but it's easy to get sucked in for days.

The loop is explained heading clockwise, starting in Latacunga and taking the southern route through Zumbahua, although traveling in reverse also works.

No buses go all the way around the loop. From Latacunga, they only travel as far as Chugchilán, either taking the southern

DETOUR: LATACUNGA TO QUEVEDO

The 110-km bus ride from Latacunga to Quevedo is one of the least-traveled and most spectacular bus routes joining the highlands with the western lowlands. The bus climbs to Zumbahua, at 3500m, and then plunges down to Quevedo at only 150m above sea level, losing an average of 30m of altitude per kilometer.

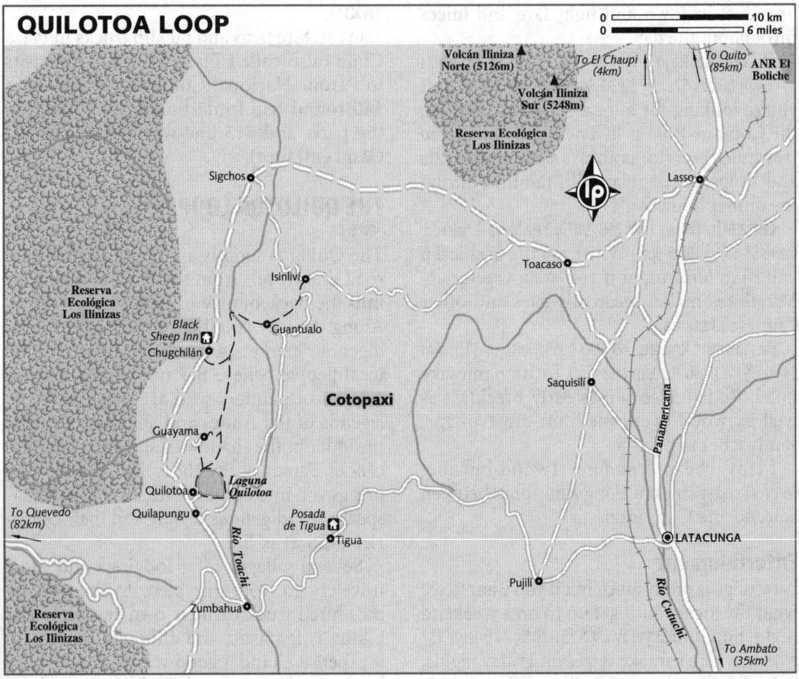

road through Zumbahua and Quilotoa or the northern road via Saquisilí and Sigchos. Tigua is served by regular buses passing between Latacunga and Quevedo. If you're more adventurous, catch a *lechero* (milk truck) or even ride on the roof of the bus (they go pretty darn slow). If speed is your need, hire a taxi in Latacunga, which starts around $60 (see the boxed text, pp164-5).

Tigua

pop 3000 / elevation 3500m

The first leg of the loop out of Latacunga climbs a comfortable, paved road into a golden patchwork of Andean landscape. On clear days, the views may include Cotopaxi, Rumiñahui and the Ilinizas; on any given day, you could see indigenous families walking the road and milk casks sitting out for the *lechero*.

Around Km 49 on the Latacunga–Zumbahua road, there's a signed turnoff to Tigua, a community of farmers and painters (but not a village proper) that's known for bright paintings of Andean life (see the boxed text, p166). Back up on the main road, at Km 53, you'll find the outstanding **Galería Tigua-Chimbacucho**, which sells the paintings as well as wooden masks at prices that are lower than those in Quito. One-of-a-kind pieces by Alfredo Toaquiza – whose father, Julio, was a progenitor of the artform – are available, and the artist himself may be hanging around. If the gallery is closed (which it usually is), poke around and ask for someone to open it (they will, happily). Paintings run from a few dollars to about $250.

Posada de Tigua (Hacienda Agrícola-Ganadera Tigua-Chimbacucho; www.laposadadetigua.com; ☎ 281-3682, 280-0454; Vía Latacunga-Zumbahua Km 49; r per person with breakfast & dinner $30) is part of a working dairy ranch. The farmhouse dates to the 1890s and is now a rustic and delightfully cozy inn. The rooms with meter-thick walls have modern bathrooms and hot water, and meals include cheese and yogurt made on the farm. Having lived among the local indigenous people most of their lives, the warm and helpful couple that owns the posada know the area well and have great stories to tell. They can set up horseback riding and guides. It's about 500m down the signed road to Tigua – tell the bus driver to drop you at the turnoff.

Zumbahua

pop 3000 / elevation 3800m

Some 15km southwest of Tigua, the small town of Zumbahua is surrounded by high bluffs and agricultural fields that soon give way to *páramo*. The village has a wonderfully authentic **Saturday market** that draws indigenous people from the mountains, who haul animals, produce, milk and more on llamas. Check out the men on the south side of the market, who use old Singer sewing machines to tailor clothes, and the cuddly *cuy* (guinea pig) trade is fun to watch.

There are a few small and very basic *residenciales* (cheap hotels) around the main plaza and side streets. They always fill up on Fridays when it could be hard to get a room.

Condor Matzi (☎ 281-4611; r per person $6) is in an old building with a wooden balcony that makes for great people-watching. It's a simple place but has handsome woodwork and Tigua paintings that give it a cheerful feel. If you don't want to stay, they'll watch your bags for $1 while you wander the market. Call ahead or ask at the store two doors down to be let in.

Hotel Quilotoa (r with shared/private bathroom $6/7), directly across the market plaza from Condor Matzi, is a modernish but simple and clean place run by a friendly Quichua woman. Only the private bathrooms have hot showers and there's a rooftop terrace for your viewing pleasure.

Quilotoa

pop 150 / elevation 3914m

About 14km north of Zumbahua, the famous volcanic-crater lake of **Laguna Quilotoa** (admission to crater & village per person $2) is a gasp-inducing sight. A lookout on the precipitous crater rim offers stunning views of the mirror-green lake 400m below and the snowcapped peaks of Cotopaxi and Iliniza Sur in the distance. When you ask the locals how deep it is, they inevitably say it has no bottom, which seems entirely plausible given its awesomeness (the geologists say 250m).

Fit walkers can hike the crater rim trail in about six hours; another path leads down to the water, where canoes and kayaks can be rented (per hour $5). The hike down takes about half an hour and over twice that to get back up (they also have donkeys that you can ride back up at $5 an hour). The alkaline lake water is not potable.

On the southwest side of the crater, the hamlet of Quilotoa has accommodations in ramshackle little places along the single road through town. Although extremely basic, they offer a unique chance to spend time with Quichua families and support indigenous businesses. Most have grass roofs typical of traditional homes in the *páramo*, and can be freezing at night (bring warm clothes and a sleeping bag if you plan on staying). The smaller places tend to be slightly more personal and homey, and they all have smoky fireplaces, communal sleeping areas and charge about $5 to $8 per person.

Princesa Toa (r per person incl two meals $8; 🕒 8am-8pm) is a community-run place, located across from the lake-viewing area. It also has a restaurant serving chicken-and-potato *almuerzos* ($2.50).

Hostal Cabañas Quilotoa (☎ 09-212-5962; r per person incl two meals $11.20), located about 200m toward the lake from the entrance to Quilotoa, is operated by the renowned and affable Tigua artist Humberto Latacunga. He has comfortable, two-story rooms with private bathrooms and hot showers.

Kirutwa (☎ in Quito 02-267-0926; mains $3-8; 🕒 8am-5pm) is a big, new, comparatively swanky restaurant right up on the crater rim. Offering classics like *locro de papa* (potato soup with cheese) and *choclo con queso* (corn on the cob with cheese), Kirutwa is run by a foundation that returns much of the revenue back to the local community.

Dozens of excellent Tigua painters live in Quilotoa and finding a place to buy their work involves little more than having your eyes open. Or, if you are hanging around the lookout for more than a few minutes, someone will bring the paintings to you.

Chugchilán

pop 100 / elevation 3200m

The dirt road winds down 22km of breathtaking scenery to Chugchilán, a tiny Andean village that has been greatly enriched by eco-tourism but which maintains its age-old ways. From here you can hike to nearby villages, visit a cooperatively run cheese factory (see the boxed text, p185) or ride horses

TRANSPORTATION ON THE QUILOTOA LOOP

Bus seats on the loop are in demand. Arrive a good 30 minutes to an hour early for departures, and then be prepared for the bus to run late. Rainy season can increase travel times.

Latacunga–Chugchilán (via Zumbahua, $2.50, three to four hours)
A Transportes Iliniza bus via Zumbahua departs from Latacunga every day at noon. It passes Zumbahua around 1:30pm, reaches Quilotoa around 2pm and arrives in Chugchilán around 3:30pm.

Chugchilán–Latacunga (via Zumbahua, $2.50, three to four hours)
Buses to Latacunga via Zumbahua leave Chugchilán Monday through Friday at 4am, passing Quilotoa around 5am, Zumbahua around 5:30am and arriving in Latacunga around 7:30am. On Saturday, this bus leaves at 3am and on Sunday at 6am, 9am and 10am.

Latacunga–Chugchilán (via Sigchos, $2.50, three to four hours)
Transportes Iliniza bus via Sigchos departs daily at 11:30am, passing Saquisilí just before noon and Sigchos around 2pm, arriving in Chugchilán around 3:30pm. This bus leaves Latacunga's bus terminal an hour earlier (10:30am) on Saturdays and only departs from Saquisilí Market on Thursdays.

Chugchilán–Latacunga (via Sigchos, $2.50, three to four hours)
Good morning! Buses leave Monday through Saturday at 3am, passing Sigchos around 4am, Saquisilí around 7am and arriving in Latacunga around 7:30am. On Sunday the service leaves at 4am and at noon, but you must switch buses in Sigchos. You can also return via Zumbahua (see above).

Latacunga–Zumbahua ($1.50, 1½ to two hours)
Transportes Cotopaxi buses bound for Quevedo depart hourly from Latacunga's bus terminal and drop passengers just above Zumbahua.

Zumbahua–Latacunga ($1.50, 1½ to two hours)
Transportes Cotopaxi buses return to Latacunga from Quevedo just as frequently.

Zumbahua–Quilotoa (30 minutes)
Trucks can be hired for $5 per person. The Latacunga–Chugchilán bus passes Zumbahua around1:30pm ($1).

into the nearby cloud forest. Three excellent places to stay on the northern edge of town set up well-priced horseback-riding trips, provide local hiking information and can help you arrange private transport in and out of the loop.

Hostal Cloud Forest (☎ 281-4808; www.hostalcloudforest.com; r per person incl breakfast & dinner with shared/private bathroom $12/15) The least expensive and simplest of Chugchilán's accommodations has wood-accented rooms, clean bathrooms and hot water. The nice Ecuadorian owners serve tasty meals, and guests can chill out in the fireplace-heated common area.

Hostal Mama Hilda (☎ 281-4814, in Quito 02-258-2957; r per person incl breakfast & dinner with shared/private bathroom $17/21) Mama Hilda is a real lady and she runs a tight but attractive and cozy ship right on the edge of 'downtown' Chugchilán. The brick-wall rooms have lofts, porches with hammocks and spotless bathrooms with hot water.

our pick **Black Sheep Inn** (☎ 281-4587; www.blacksheepinn.com; dm/s/d/tr/q per person with shared bathroom $32.50/65/50/45/40, s/d/tr/q with private bathroom $100/80/70/60; ⊠ 🖳) Honored time and again by international travel magazines and organizations for its sustainable-tourism practices, the Black Sheep Inn is one of Ecuador's most successful ecotourism projects. Owned by a friendly North American couple, the inn maintains organic vegetable gardens, pumps water with solar power, runs a community recycling project and employs local staff.

Quilotoa–Zumbahua (30 minutes)
Unless you want to take the 4am bus headed to Latacunga, you'll need to hire a truck to get to Zumbahua ($5 per person). On Sunday, however, the Latacunga-bound bus leaves Chugchilán at 6am, 9am and 10am, passing Quilotoa at 7am, 10am and 11am.

Quilotoa–Chugchilán (one hour)
To get from Quilotoa to Chugchilán take the Latacunga–Chugchilán bus between 2pm and 2:30pm ($1), or hire a truck for about $25.

Chugchilán–Quilotoa (one hour)
Again, unless you're dying to leave at 4am (on the bus to Latacunga), you'll need to hire a truck to get to Quilotoa ($25). Additionally on Wednesday there's a bus at 5am, Friday at 6am, and on Sunday buses depart Chugchilán at 6am, 9am and 10am ($1).

Chugchilán–Sigchos ($1, one hour)
A daily milk truck leaves Chugchilán between 8am and 9am, allowing you to avoid the 3am departure of the Chugchilán–Latacunga bus. Two other buses go to Sigchos on Thursday and Saturday afternoon. Sunday departures are at 4am, 5am and noon.

Sigchos–Chugchilán ($1, one hour)
Transportes Iliniza from Latacunga stops in Sigchos around 2pm, and the milk truck leaves Sigchos daily at 7am.

Sigchos–Latacunga ($2, two hours)
Buses from Sigchos to Latacunga depart daily at 3am, 4am, 5am, 6am, 7am, 2:30pm and 4:30pm from beside the church. Additional buses leave in the afternoon on Wednesday, Friday, Saturday and Sunday. Buses stop in Saquisilí on their way to Latacunga.

Latacunga–Sigchos ($2, two hours)
Transportes Nacional Saquisilí buses leave Latacunga's bus terminal at 9:30am, 10am, noon, 2pm, 4pm, 5pm and 6pm daily.

Saquisilí–Latacunga ($0.40, 20 minutes)
Buses depart Plaza Concordia in Saquisilí every 10 minutes.

Latacunga–Saquisilí ($0.40, 20 minutes)
Buses depart from Latacunga's bus terminal every 10 minutes.

No matter how wonderful these things are, the biggest attraction for many guests is the pooper. That's right, Black Sheep Inn's ecological composting toilets impress because they use no water, have no foul odors, overflow with flowers and have views that will make you want to linger (yes, that's right, you might want to hang out in the bathroom).

A three-story bunkhouse sleeps 10 and the private rooms, which sleep up to four, have lofts and wood-burning stoves. Free purified water, coffee and tea are available all day long and cold beer and snacks are always on hand. Outside there's a zip line, a wooden sauna ($10 extra per group) and the world's highest Frisbee-golf course. Rates include three delicious, wholesome vegetarian meals served family-style in the homey main cottage, and access to a recreation room/yoga studio with views of the Río Toachi canyon.

Sigchos

pop 2259 / elevation 2800m

From Chugchilán, it's a journey of 23 muddy, bumpy kilometers to the growing town of Sigchos. You'll likely stop here to catch a bus or while hiking from Chugchilán or Isinliví, otherwise it's not much of a destination.

Restaurant y Hotel La Posada (☎ 271-4224; cnr Galo Atiaga & Las Ilinizas; r per person $5) has private bathrooms and small but respectable rooms, plus a good restaurant downstairs (*almuerzos* $2; 6am to 9pm).

TIGUA PAINTINGS

One of Ecuador's homegrown art forms (and a worthy collector's item) is a style of painting called Tigua that originated near the shores of Laguna Quilotoa. The name comes from the small community of Tigua, where indigenous people had decorated drum skins for many generations. During the 1970s, Julio Toaquiza, a young indigenous man from the area, got the idea to turn those skins into canvases and paint colorful scenes from Quichua legends. The artist, who spent his days growing potatoes and tending llamas, depicted these legends against the beautiful Andean scenery where he lived. He painted the condor wooing a young girl and flying over the mountains in a red poncho, the 'bottomless' Quilotoa crater lake with spirits hovering over its waters and Volcán Cotopaxi, a sacred place that highland indigenous people called 'Taita' (Father).

Originally working with enamel paints and chicken-feather brushes, Toaquiza taught all of his children and neighbors how to paint. They began to incorporate new themes, such as Catholic processions, interiors of indigenous homes and even important political events. But over time, the enamel fumes took a toll on their health and the artists switched to acrylics and oils that only increased the vibrancy of the colors.

Toaquiza's art has brought fame to Tigua, and today more than three hundred painters are at work in the highlands with about twenty studios in Tigua itself. The pieces are exhibited at the community gallery/store in Tigua (see p162), in selected galleries in Quito and in exhibitions around the world.

The newer **Hostal San Miguel** (☎ 271-4193; cnr Amazonas & Juan Sagastivoelsa; r per person $5.50) has clean, tile-floor rooms and hot showers.

Isinliví

pop 3310 / elevation 2900m

Some 14km southeast of Sigchos and just off the Quilotoa loop, the beautiful village of Isinliví makes a good hike from either Sigchos or Chugchilán. A woodworking/cabinetry shop makes high-end furniture and locals can direct you to nearby *pucarás* (pre-Incan hill fortresses).

our pick **Llullu Llama** (Little Llama; ☎ 281-4790; www.llullullama; dm/r per person from $8/10) is an enchanting, old farmhouse with meter-thick adobe walls, colorful and comfortable rooms and a wood-burning stove. Breakfasts and dinners are available (including veggie options) for $3.50 to $6 per meal. Contact Hostal Tiana (p160) in Latacunga for additional information about Isinliví including reservations, or for the many volunteer opportunities available here.

A popular day hike is to the Monday-morning market at nearby Guantualo. A bus leaves Guantualo ($3.50, 3½ hours) at 1:30pm for Latacunga through Sigchos.

Vivero buses leave Latacunga's bus terminal for Isinliví ($3, three hours) at 1pm all days except Saturday, when it leaves at 11am, and Thursday, when it leaves from Saquisilí at 11am.

Saquisilí

pop 9296 / elevation 2940m

Until recently, the **Thursday-morning market** here was one of the most untouristy markets in the central highlands. Now backpackers and camera-wielding gringos shuttled in on tour buses roam among vendors and even a few *otavaleños* (people from Otavalo) selling their sweaters and weavings to tourists. Still, it's a mostly authentic market and a fascinating place to observe an array of material goods that constitute life in the highlands. The market is composed of eight plazas, which are like a bustling outdoor department store with mostly indigenous shoppers; there's a department for *cuy*, *esteras* (straw mats), *angarillas* (donkey saddles), *sastrería* (tailor services), *ollas* (pots) and hundreds, perhaps thousands, of other items.

Especially interesting is the **animal market**, a cacophonous affair with screaming pigs playing a major role. It starts before dawn and lies on the edge of the market – just follow all the folks with animals.

No restaurants here cater to tourists, but there's never a shortage of food at the market and in the side streets. Most travelers stay in Latacunga and jump on buses that start running at dawn ($.40, 20 minutes), but you can stay at **Hotel San Carlos** (☎ 272-1981; Bolívar & Sucre; s/d $7/12), a humble place on the main plaza that fills up quickly on Wednesday night. North of the cemetery, on Calle Chimborazo, the newer **Hostería Gilocarmelo** (☎ 272-1630; www.hosteriagilocarmelo.com; r per person incl breakfast $12;) has nice rooms around a garden with hummingbird feeders, a common room with a fireplace, sauna and fresh-trout dinners.

AMBATO

☎ 03 / pop 217,075 / elevation 2577m

As the Panamericana beelines from Latacunga to Ambato, buses fill up with vendors selling treats: *helados de Salcedo,* layered, fruit-based ice cream on a stick, or little bags of *fritada* with *mote* and *chochos* (lupine seeds). When you get to Ambato, the food fest continues with many local favorites, including *cuy* and especially *llapingachos* (fried potato and cheese pancakes), which you can buy in the market and restaurants.

The **Monday market** fills Ambato's central streets and plazas, and as a major hub in the flower trade, Ambato sometimes drips with roses, carnations and tropical varieties coming up from the coast.

Above town, there are fabulous views of the puffing Volcán Tungurahua (5016m), and Ambato's parks and quintas (historic country homes converted into parks) offer some respite from the bustle of downtown.

The city is proud of its cultural heritage and nicknames itself 'Tierra de Los Tres Juanes' (Land of the Three Juans), after the writers Juan Montalvo and Juan León Mera (p42), and lawyer/journalist Juan Benigno Malo. All three Juans are immortalized in Ambato's parks, museums and buildings.

In 1947, an earthquake destroyed Ambato, the capital of Tungurahua province, and a modern city was rebuilt.

Information

Andinatel (Castillo) Telephone center near Rocafuerte.
Banco de Guayaquil (cnr Mera & Sucre) Bank with an ATM.
Banco del Pacífico (cnr Lalama & Cevallos) Bank with an ATM.
Banco del Pichincha (Lalama near Sucre) Bank with ATM.
Post office (cnr Castillo & Bolívar)
Set-up Internet (Quito 4-29; per hr $1) Internet access.
TAME (☎ 282 6601/0322/2595; Bolívar 20-17) Airline office for flight reservations from other cities.
Tourist office (☎ 282-1800; www.ambato.com; Guayaquil & Rocafuerte; 8am-2pm & 3-5pm Mon-Fri)

Sights & Activities

LAS QUINTAS

Several famous *ambateños* (people from Ambato) had quintas that survived the earthquake. They were probably once considered countryside homes, but today they are right on the edge of this growing city.

La Quinta de Juan León Mera (☎ 282-0419; Av Los Capulíes; admission $1; 9am-5pm Tue-Sun) is set on the banks of the Río Ambato in the suburb of Atocha, about 2km northeast of downtown. The estate, built in 1874, has period furnishing and is set in the **Jardín Botánico La Liria** (admission $1; 9am-5pm Tue-Sun), a lush garden with more than 200 plant species and a trail down to the river. To get there by foot, walk northwest on Montalvo, cross the river and turn right on Capulíes.

Just on the north side of La Liria is the **Museo Histórico Martínez-Holguim** (admission $1; 9am-5pm Tue-Sun), another period quinta formerly owned by a famous mountain climber.

Another pleasant walk takes you along Calle Bolívar, which turns into Avenida Miraflores, toward the neighborhood of Miraflores. The river can be crossed about 2km away from town on Avenida Los Guaytambos, which soon leads to the neighborhood of Ficoa and **La Quinta de Juan Montalvo** (admission $1; 9am-4pm Fri-Sun), where the 'Cervantes of America' built his villa close to two centuries ago. You can also take the bus marked 'Ficoa' from Parque Cevallos.

PARQUE JUAN MONTALVO

The northwest side of this handsome plaza is taken up by **Casa y Mausaleo de Montalvo** (☎ 282-4248; admission $0.50; 9am-noon & 2-6pm Mon-Sat), Montalvo's pied-à-terre and where he is

> **ECUAVOLLEY**
>
> A ride through the countryside is bound to involve a double take at the image of men playing volleyball. Actually, it's *Ecua*volley, played as fiercely and strategically as the classic game but with some distinctively local features. The net is hung about three meters high, ruling out knock-out spikes for relatively short-statured Ecuadorians, and three-player teams are allowed to briefly palm the ball, tricking their opponents with fake-outs and redirections. Local games are cutthroat and all bets are *on*.

CENTRAL HIGHLANDS

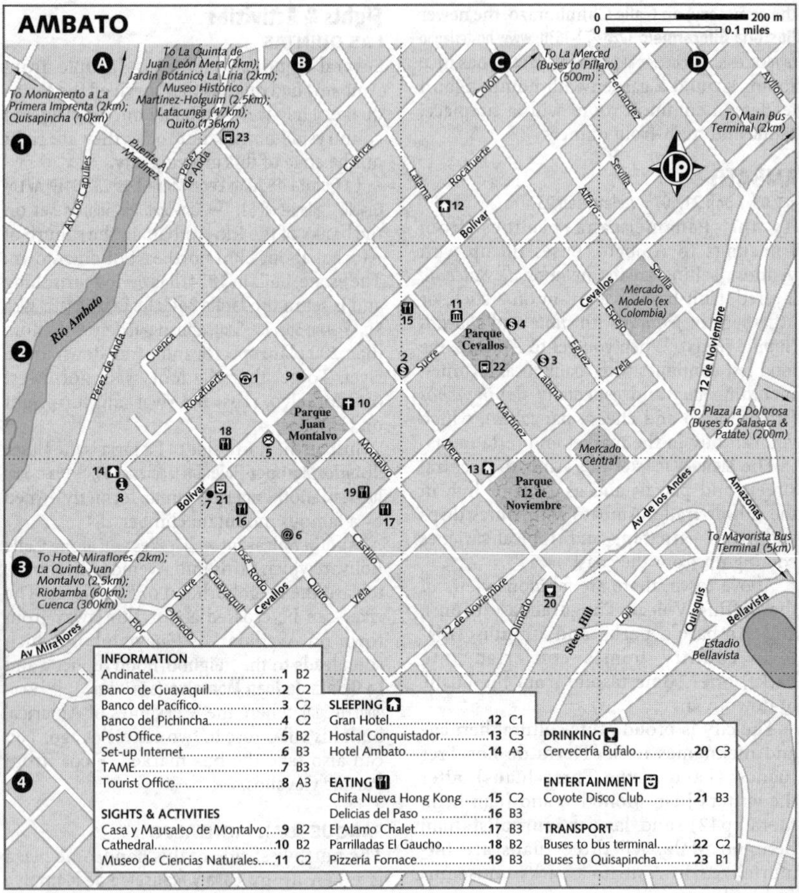

interred. On the northeast side of the plaza is the soaring, modern **cathedral** (see the boxed text, opposite), which recently got an interior facelift.

MONUMENTO A LA PRIMERA IMPRENTA

Ambato's best view of Volcán Tungurahua is at the **Monumento a La Primera Imprenta** on the northwest side of town. A taxi up to the top should cost no more than $2, and you can walk down to the bus stop to return downtown.

MUSEO DE CIENCIAS NATURALES

Although a bit dusty, this **natural history museum** (☎ 282-7395; Sucre & Lalama; admission $1; 8:30am-12:30pm & 2:30-5:30pm Mon-Fri, 9am-5pm Sat) in the Colegio Bolívar houses Ecuador's most thorough collection of stuffed birds, mammals and reptiles. The historical photograph collage and a gruesome display of farm freaks, such as two-headed calves and six-legged lambs, make great fun for the whole family.

Festivals & Events

Ambateños know that their province's natural beauty and fecundity go hand in hand with its earthquakes and eruptions. Starting soon after the devastating quake of 1949, they began to celebrate the good side of this combo during an annual **Fiesta de Frutas y Flores** (Festival of Fruit and Flowers), held during the last two weeks in February. Magnificent displays of, you guessed it, fruits and flowers

PRAISING NATURE

Ambato once had an old cathedral, but it was destroyed along with the rest of the city by an earthquake in 1947. Many people consider the replacement temple on Parque Juan Montalvo, with its minimalist vertical lines, boringly modern in comparison to Ecuador's antique, ornate churches, and it's never competed well with the glacier-topped peaks and active volcanoes in the background. The cathedral, however, has recently been attracting attention for what's inside: in 2007, the church got a makeover by a young *ambateño* landscape artist, David Moscoso, who steered clear of the usual religious motifs and instead expressed his devotion through daring representations of Ecuador's natural beauty.

Pointing up to the light-flooded cupola, which has more than 200 meters of painted surface, Moscoso describes why he depicted the Avenue of the Volcanoes, including a smoking Tungurahua, the cloud-enshrouded Llanganates and glaciered Chimborazo, instead of the usual flocks of cherubs.

Why did you only paint scenes of nature in the cathedral?

In more than 500 meters of murals in this cathedral I didn't paint a single human figure. No angels, no saints, not even Christ; only mountains, clouds and nature. I want to break down the old patterns that we see in the great cathedrals of the world and instead paint God through representations of the countryside and the volcanoes and through the vibrant use of colors and light. For me the greatest expression of faith is devotion to nature, God's creation. The old images of saints and angels are worn out and even opposed to the spirituality of the 21st century; the expression of God through nature is very appropriate for this city, for Ecuador and even the whole world.

Why is nature more appropriate than the traditional icons of the Catholic Church?

Ambato is subject to natural forces that have destroyed it in the past, and that could destroy it again at any moment. We *ambateños* and Ecuadorians are constantly aware of the cycles of nature in the eruptions of volcanoes that ebb and flow around us.

A Christ with white skin and blue eyes in the paintings of Europe makes sense because Europeans look like that, but we Ecuadorians are a cultural mix of Europeans, mestizos and *indígenas* [indigenous people], and we are aligned by our belief in the natural cycles. Images of nature speak to *all* of us, especially the indigenous.

You're a little like Michelangelo up there, aren't you? How did you do it?

The cupola is 60 meters up and required huge aluminum scaffolding. It was very expensive, so I had to work quickly, night and day, and at times I took medication to calm my muscles. It was very stressful at times.

How did the people react to this unorthodox form of religious art?

The bishop did not want the volcanoes in the church and he was actually terrified to show it to the people. We didn't know if the people who are extremely devout would reject it, but when it materialized before them, they reacted really positively. It responded to what was inside of them.

adorn bullfights, parades and the *Reina de Ambato* (Queen of Ambato) pageant.

Sleeping

Ambato has been investing heavily in its tourism infrastructure in recent years, but it still lacks decent hotels. Don't expect too much from your lodgings.

Hostal Conquistador (☎ 282-0391; Parque 12 de Noviembre; s/d $7/8) Among the *residenciales* (cheap hotels) around Parque 12 de Noviembre, this is a better one. It's clean, comfortable and central and, on the upper floors, less noisy.

Gran Hotel (☎ 282-4235; cnr Rocafuerte & Lalama; s/d incl breakfast $15/21) The Gran is definitely not so grand anymore, but the carpeted rooms have hot showers and TVs and the staff is helpful and pleasant.

Hotel Miraflores (☎ 284-3224; www.hmiraflores.com.ec; Av Miraflores 227; s/d incl breakfast $41/63) Set on expansive and immaculately landscaped grounds, this is one of several better hotels on Avenida Miraflores, located about 2km from downtown Ambato. Miraflores aspires to the status of a resort or a banquet center, but the rooms are large and quiet.

Hotel Ambato (☎ 242-1791/1792/1793; www.hotelambato.com; Guayaquil 01-08; s/d $43/61;) Built into a hillside over the Río Ambato, this 25-year-old downtown hotel has views of both the cathedral and the river. The rooms are spacious and well lit, and the whole place is quiet. High rollers can gamble at the casino and kiddos can splash around in the pool. The restaurant and café are just fine for everyone.

Eating

Mercado Central (12 de Noviembre; mains $1.50; 7am-7pm) The second floor of Ambato's indoor market has particularly good *llapingachos* (fried potato and cheese pancakes). Old ladies serve them with eggs, avocado slices and sausage (veggies can get it without the meat) for $1.50. The younger gals nearby blend superfresh juices made with bottled water ($1).

Delicias del Paso (☎ 242-6048; cnr Sucre & Quito; menu items $1-2; 10am-6pm) This cafeteria has all its tasty quiches and cakes in the display out front, and you can order them to go right from the street.

Chifa Nueva Hong Kong (☎ 282-3796; Bolívar 768; mains $2-4; noon-11pm) Hong Kong comes to Ambato with fried rice, *tallerines* (noodles) and *agridulce* (sweet and sour) dishes. The little egg rolls are yummy.

Pizzería Fornace (☎ 282-3244; Cevallos 17-28; pizzas $3-5; noon-10pm) With a wood-fired brick oven, thin crusts and fresh ingredients, this is easily the best pizza in town. Locals enjoy the cuts of meat here as well.

El Alamo Chalet (☎ 282-4704; Cevallos 17-19; mains $3-6; 8am-10pm) Easily identified by its chalet-style wooden facade, El Alamo serves good, diner-style food: meat and chicken dishes, *llapingachos*, a hearty *desayuno montubiano* (a Manabi-province breakfast of fish, eggs, beans and fried plantains) and more basic morning dishes.

Parrilladas El Gaucho (☎ 282-8969; cnr Bolívar & Quito; mains $7-10; noon-11pm Mon-Sat, to 4pm Sun) This Argentinean-style *parrillada* (grill) is popular with families because they bring a mountain of juicy, sizzling steaks, chicken or meat combos right to a tabletop grill.

Drinking & Entertainment

The **Coyote Disco Club** (Bolívar 20-57; 6pm-late), near Quito, is a huge, somewhat upscale bar and dance club geared toward Ambato's wealthier youth. The more egalitarian **Cervecería Bufalo** (Olmedo & Mera; noon-late) serves *cerveza* (beer) – but no buffalo. Dancing goes late.

Getting There & Away

BUS

Bus services to Quito ($2, two hours), Riobamba ($1.25, 1 to 1½ hours) and destinations beyond leave from Ambato's particularly down-and-out **main bus terminal** (☎ 282-1481; Av de las Américas at Av Colombia), located 2km from downtown. Head northeast on 12 de Noviembre to the traffic circle and then turn right on Avenida de las Américas.

Buses ($0.30, 25 minutes) to Quisapincha leave from the northwest end of Martínez (at the corner of Perez de Anda) in Ambato. A taxi will cost around $8.

Buses to Salasaca ($0.35, 25 minutes) and Patate ($1, one hour) leave every 20 minutes or so from Plaza La Dolorosa in the neighborhood known as Ferroviaria, a $1 cab ride from downtown. Any Baños-bound bus can drop you in these villages too, but the direct buses depart from a stop closer to downtown.

Buses leave for Baños ($1, one hour, hourly) from the **Mayorista Terminal**, about 5km south of the main bus terminal, near the roundabout at Amazonas and Julio Jaramillo. You can also catch passing buses, which are more frequent, at the roundabout itself.

BUSES FROM AMBATO

Destination	Cost (US$)	Duration (hr)
Baños	1	1
Cuenca	7	7
Esmeraldas	6	8
Guaranda	2	2
Guayaquil	6	6
Ibarra	5	5
Lago Agrio	9	11
Latacunga	1	¾
Loja	9-11	11
Machala	6	8
Manta	7	10
Otavalo	3.50	4½
Puyo	2.50	3
Quito	2.50	2½
Riobamba	1	1
Santo Domingo	4	4
Tena	5	6

Buses to Píllaro leave frequently from Colon and Unidad Nacional near Parque La Merced in Ambato ($0.40, 30 minutes). A taxi should run about $10.

Getting Around

The most important local bus service for travelers is the route between Ambato's main bus terminal and downtown. From the terminal, climb the exit ramp to Avenida de las Américas, which crosses the train tracks on a bridge. On this bridge is a bus stop, where a westbound (to your right) bus, usually signed 'Centro,' will take you to Parque Cevallos for $0.20.

Buses marked 'Terminal' leave from the Martínez side of Parque Cevallos. A bus that goes to Miraflores and Ficoa runs along the Sucre side. Buses for Atocha (for more quintas) leave from 12 de Noviembre and Espejo.

Taxis to the quintas from downtown cost $2.

AROUND AMBATO

☎ 03

From handicraft shopping to indigenous villages, from haciendas to rugged wilderness, the area around Ambato has it all. See opposite for transport options from Ambato to these destinations.

Quisapincha

pop 3860 / elevation 3120m

Quisapincha is a pretty adobe-filled town that somehow came to have dozens of stores selling leather jackets, handbags, wallets, shoes and soccer balls. The quality varies, but they have plenty of up-to-date styles (as well as some '70s holdouts). Most adult jackets run between $30 and $45 and the offerings for kids are extensive. If the sleeves are a bit long, ask for an alteration, generally free and done on the spot.

The ride up to Quisapincha (10km) from Ambato offers spectacular views of the city and Volcán Tungurahua on a clear day.

Parque Nacional Llanganates & Píllaro

Anyone who ventures far into this wilderness deserves bragging rights, for they have walked in the rubber boots of many intrepid explorers including orchid researcher Lou Jost, the 19th-century biologist Alfred Russell Wallace and the 'Stone-faced' General Rumiñahui himself, who was said to have buried the lost treasure of the Inca in its impenetrable wilderness.

Created in 1996, Parque Nacional Llanganates encompasses 219,719 hectares of *páramo,* cloud forest and tropical forest running across four provinces. It is home to mountain and Amazonian tapirs, pumas, jaguars, capybara and the spectacled bear, although its extremely high levels of biodiversity and endemism are protected more by its harsh weather conditions than by personnel or infrastructure. Unrelenting rain and fog, forests of thick *flechas* (arrows) grass with needle-sharp leaves, quaking bogs and impassable peaks reaching over 4000m have created near-complete isolation. Navigation is frequently blind and even the IGM topo maps show blank areas labeled only *nubes* (clouds), where satellites signals have never penetrated the area's thick mantel of weather. The best months, still soused and given to hypothermia, are December to February.

You can hire a guide and porters (about $20 per day, plus food for the guide) in the village of **Píllaro**, about 20km northeast of Ambato, which is the main entry point for the park. In theory you would pay $5 to enter, although there may be no one to collect your money. It could take a couple of days to arrange and outfit your trip. A few tour operators in Baños will arrange excursions (p175), but they may not penetrate as far into the park as you would like. Be specific about your wishes and insist that guides do no hunting (and preferably not bring a rifle).

Píllaro itself is an interesting village in a fruit-growing area that is known for its bulls, bullfights and bull runs. The beasts sprint through the streets on Quito's Independence Day (August 10) and during **Diablada Pillareña**, a celebration of independence from Spain during the first week of January. Both also have parades and dancing.

Salasaca

You'll know when you've reached Salasaca, about 14km south of Ambato, by the abundance of men walking around in long, black ponchos over crisp white shirts and trousers. Along with a broad-brimmed white hat, men wear the distinctive black Salasaca poncho. Women wear colorful shawls and long wool skirts with a woven belt called a *chumbi.*

The town and its environs are home to some 2000 indigenous folk, who are famous for their high-quality weavings. Salasaca is a poor but proud community where some older people only speak Quichua. Life is organized around the harvest and almost everybody uses some traditional medicine. Like the Saraguro people (p213), the Salasaca originally lived in Bolivia but were forcefully relocated north by the Inca in the late 15th century.

There is a **craft market** held every Sunday morning near the church on the Ambato–Baños road. Nearby are several craft stores that are open daily, and **Hostal Runa Huasi** (☎ 09-984-0125; www.hostalrunahuasi.com; Panamericana in Salasaca; r per person incl breakfast $12), a comfortable and friendly place run by the indigenous Pilla family. Next door is the weaving studio of Alonso Pilla, who sells his pieces and gives demonstrations on his backstrap loom. Señor Pilla can arrange tours of the area focusing on indigenous agriculture, medicine, textiles, music and more. Salasaca is small and all of these places are within close walking distance of wherever the bus drops you in town.

On the Sunday after Easter, a magnificent street dance takes place on the road (slowing traffic considerably) and on June 15 the Salasacas dress up in animal costumes for **Santo Vintio**. Both **Corpus Christi** (on a movable date in June) and the **feast of St Anthony** (end of November) are colorfully celebrated.

Patate & Around

Along the banks of the Río Patate and with great views of Volcán Tungurahua, Patate has became a popular destination for volcano watchers during recent eruptions (see p181). The village is known for its *chicha de uva* (a fermented grape beverage) and *arepas* (a squash-based spice cake wrapped and cooked in leaves), lovingly prepared in wood ovens around town. The best of them is said to be that of Luisa Cárdenas, or 'Mama Lucha,' on the main square. She's been at it for forty years. Once you're drunk and full of cake, some nice resorts in the area are good places to sleep it off. They also provide access to Baños (right) and Parque Nacional Llanganates (p171).

Jardín del Valle (☎ 287-0209/0508; Soria at Calderón; s/d $10/18) is the best option for accommodations in town – a simple but comfy little place with a dense green garden in back and friendly owners. It's a block off the main plaza.

From Patate, a back road called the Ruta Ecológica heads south to Baños. Ten km along this road the 300-year-old **Hacienda Leito** (☎ 285-9329; www.haciendaleito.com; r per person/ste $82/110; 🅿) beckons visitors with a history involving Jesuits, Spanish kings and seekers of lost treasure. A classic whitewashed hacienda, Leito has luxurious rooms with wooden rafters and big, comfy beds, a full-service spa and a spectacular view of Tungurahua.

About 2km further down the road, the **Hacienda Manteles** (☎ Quito 02-223-3484, 02-601-3290; www.haciendamanteles.com; s/d incl breakfast & dinner $111/156) is a beautiful upscale hotel engaged in certified ecotourism practices. Among other things, they support local communities in creating microbusinesses, have an organic garden and protect 200 hectares of cloud forest that you can explore. Rooms have broad views of the Río Patate valley and of Volcán Tungurahua in the distance. Horseback riding, bird-watching and zip-lining over the cloud forest are available.

BAÑOS

☎ 03 / pop 14,700 / elevation 1800m

Baños is perched on the slope of an impressive active volcano called Tungurahua ('throat of fire' in Quichua). Besides offering the thrilling backdrop of a crater that occasionally spits smoke and fire, Tungurahua bestows high waterfalls, steaming thermal baths, dense, jungly vegetation and deep river gorges that make a great playground for nature-lovers and adventure-seekers. Although it sometimes seems that hordes of Ecuadorian and foreign tourists come to town only to party (especially on weekends and holidays), Baños is a premier destination for hiking, rafting, horseback-riding, biking and climbing (volcano permitting). It's also where people come to relax, usually topping off a day in the outdoors with a muscle-soothing soak in the thermal baths and a meal from one of the town's restaurants.

Although Tungurahua giveth, it also taketh away. In late 1999, the volcano roared to life after years of silence, and *bañenos* (people from Baños) were forced to ring in the new millennium as evacuees far from the lava flows and ash fall. Only after Tungurahua's activity diminished in January (and a fierce fight with the Ecuadorian authorities) did residents trickle back to reestablish their agricultural and tourism businesses. Another large eruption and evacuation occurred in late 2006 and activity was recorded in early 2008. As of this writing, Tungurahua's crater has sealed significantly (with a massive plug of cooled and hardened lava), tourism is in full swing and there's much talk of declaring the volcano open for climbing.

A highway with sweeping views of the upper Amazon Basin plunges from Baños to the jungle town of Puyo. You can sail down this road on a rented mountain bike, passing the thundering Pailón del Diablo (Devil's Cauldron) waterfall, bromeliad-laden hiking trails and picnic spots along the way.

Orientation

Baños is tiny and the mountains towering over town make everything easy to reference. Almost everything is in walking distance from the bus terminal. Few buildings in Baños have street numbers.

Information

Ask your hotel staff about evacuation procedures in the event of an eruption.

Internet cafés come and go but are always plentiful.

Andinatel (☎ 274-0411; cnr Rocafuerte & Halflants) Telephone center.
Banco del Pacífico (cnr Halflants & Rocafuerte) Bank with ATM; changes traveler's checks.
Banco del Pichincha (cnr Ambato & Halflants) Bank with ATM; changes traveler's checks.
Direct Connect (Martínez; per hr $2; 🕑 9am-10pm) Internet access near Alfaro.
Hospital (☎ 274-0443/0301; Montalvo) Near Pastaza; pharmacies are along Ambato.
La Herradura (Martínez; per kg $0.70; 🕑 8:30am-12:30pm & 2:30-7pm) Same-day laundry service near Alfaro.
Ministerio del Ambiente Parque Nacional Llanganates (☎ 274-1662; bus terminal; irregular hr Mon-Fri) Administration office for Llanganates; has small, photocopied topo maps and lots of information.
Police station (☎ 274-0251; Oriente) Near Mera.
Post office (☎ 274-0901; Halflants) Near Ambato.
Tourist office (☎ 274-0483; mun_banos@andinanet.net; Halflants; 🕑 8am-12:30pm & 2-5:30pm Mon-Fri) Lots of info, free maps and emergency-evacuation information. Near Rocafuerte.

Sights & Activities

Most visitors here brave the outdoors on a horse or bicycle. Baños also offers an innovation in freefall insanity called *puenting* (think bungee jumping without the bounce). It crudely translates as 'bridging' but it's really swinging, in this case along a rope tethered to two bridges. Many tour operators can set you up.

Motorcycles, ATVs and go-carts (sometimes charmingly mislabeled 'goat-carts') rent at numerous shops around town, all for about $10 per hour. Be especially vigilant about using helmets and inspecting the equipment; there have been accidents in recent years.

SIGHTS

Within the town itself, the **Basílica de Nuestra Señora de Agua Santa** (Ambato at 12 de Noviembre; admission free; 🕑 7am-8pm) is dedicated to the Virgin of the Holy Water (the same one with a shrine over by the waterfall). This illustrious lady is credited with several local miracles. Inside the church, paintings depict her wonders with explanations in Spanish along the lines of: 'On January 30, 1904, Señor X fell off his horse as he was crossing the Río Pastaza bridge. As he fell 70m to the torrents below, he yelled "Holy Mother of the Holy Water" and was miraculously saved!' Other paintings show people being spared from exploding volcanoes, burning hotels and other misfortunes. The Virgin is particularly good at warding off transit accidents, so you may catch the site of a priest blessing a taxi or lorry with holy water.

ACTIVITIES

Baths

Bañenos really are water babies. You'll see them walking around town in flip-flops, wet and heading home from the baths that the town is named for. People go to splash around, to socialize and to take advantage of the water's curative properties, which are said to result from the healthful chlorates, sulfates and magnesium in the waters. The liquid heat feels great on aching muscles after a horse or bike ride too. Most of the baths are fed by thermal springs burbling from the base of Volcán Tungurahua. The water in the pools is constantly being recycled and only looks murky because of its mineral content.

Baños has four municipal baths. All but one are in town, and all have changing rooms and clothing storage. Towels are available for rent, but generally not until after 8am, and they can run out. Everyone is supposed to shower and put on a bathing suit before entering the pools. Technically, you're supposed to have a bathing cap too, but it's okay if you don't – just pull back your hair.

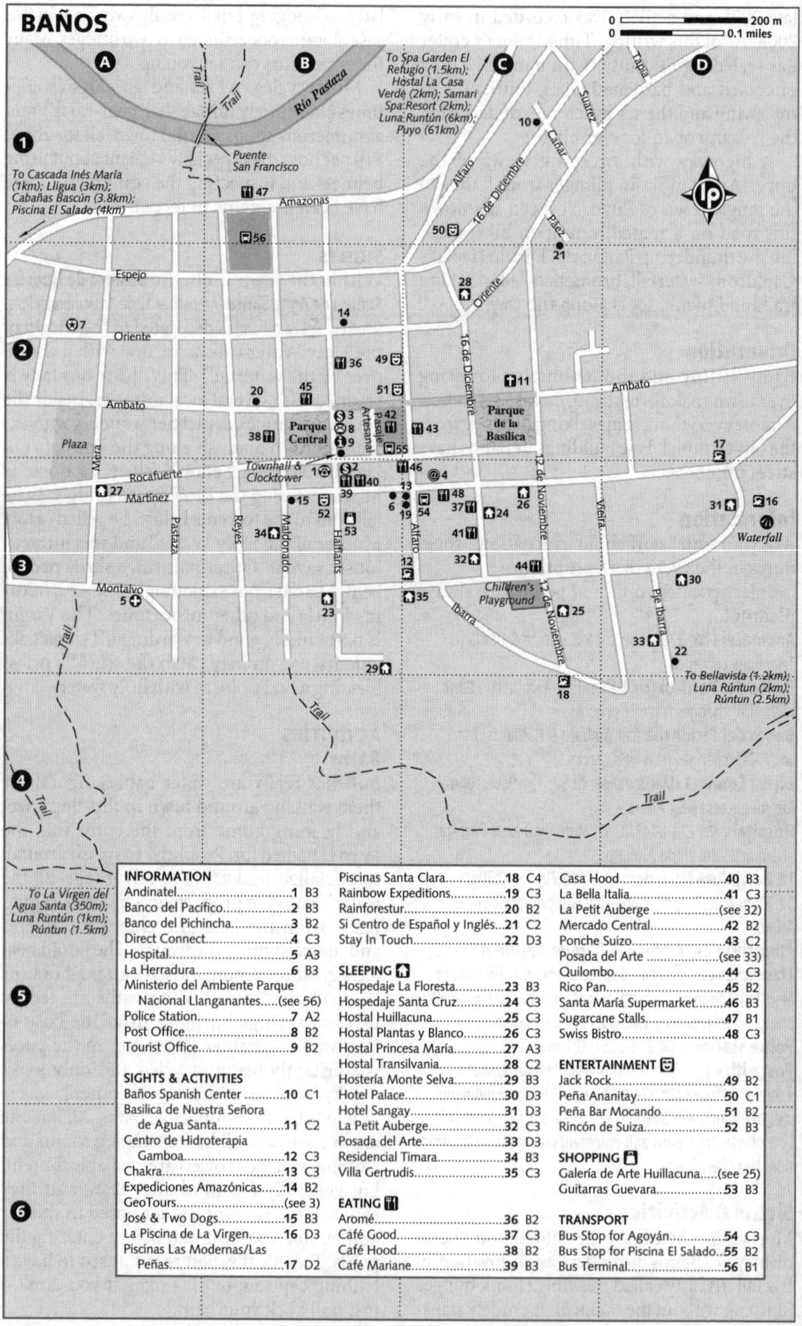

INFORMATION
Andinatel....1 B3
Banco del Pacífico....2 B3
Banco del Pichincha....3 B2
Direct Connect....4 C3
Hospital....5 A3
La Herradura....6 B3
Ministerio del Ambiente Parque Nacional Llanganantes....(see 56)
Police Station....7 A2
Post Office....8 B2
Tourist Office....9 B2

SIGHTS & ACTIVITIES
Baños Spanish Center....10 C1
Basilica de Nuestra Señora de Agua Santa....11 C2
Centro de Hidroterapia Gamboa....12 C3
Chakra....13 C3
Expediciones Amazónicas....14 B2
GeoTours....(see 3)
José & Two Dogs....15 B3
La Piscina de La Virgen....16 D3
Piscinas Las Modernas/Las Peñas....17 D2
Piscinas Santa Clara....18 C4
Rainbow Expeditions....19 C3
Rainforestur....20 B2
Si Centro de Español y Inglés....21 C2
Stay In Touch....22 D3

SLEEPING
Hospedaje La Floresta....23 B3
Hospedaje Santa Cruz....24 C3
Hostal Huillacuna....25 C3
Hostal Plantas y Blanco....26 C3
Hostal Princesa María....27 A3
Hostal Transilvania....28 C2
Hostería Monte Selva....29 B3
Hotel Palace....30 D3
Hotel Sangay....31 D3
La Petit Auberge....32 C3
Posada del Arte....33 D3
Residencial Timara....34 B3
Villa Gertrudis....35 C3

EATING
Aromé....36 B2
Café Good....37 C3
Café Hood....38 B2
Café Mariane....39 B3
Casa Hood....40 B3
La Bella Italia....41 C3
La Petit Auberge....(see 32)
Mercado Central....42 B2
Ponche Suizo....43 C2
Posada del Arte....(see 33)
Quilombo....44 C3
Rico Pan....45 B2
Santa María Supermarket....46 B3
Sugarcane Stalls....47 B1
Swiss Bistro....48 C3

ENTERTAINMENT
Jack Rock....49 B2
Peña Ananitay....50 C1
Peña Bar Mocando....51 B2
Rincón de Suiza....52 B3

SHOPPING
Galería de Arte Huillacuna....(see 25)
Guitarras Guevara....53 B3

TRANSPORT
Bus Stop for Agoyán....54 C3
Bus Stop for Piscina El Salado....55 B2
Bus Terminal....56 B1

The best-known baths in Baños are **Las Piscinas de La Virgen** (Montalvo; admission day/night $1/1.20; 4:30am-5pm & 6-10pm), the only hot pools in town. Built as a community project in 1928, they are named for the Virgin María, who is said to have come here to dip her own feet. One bath is cold, another warm and a third reaches an intense 42°C (118°F). If you go early in the morning, it'll just be you and a few old-timers. If you're curious, ask the basket woman to show you the *ojo del agua*, where the water, heated by the volcano, gushes from the earth at a scorching 50°C (122°F).

Piscinas Santa Clara (admission $1; 8am-5pm Sat & Sun) has two cooler pools (about 22°C or 72°F), which are higher in minerals than La Virgen.

With a waterslide, a swing set, water toys and cool pools, **Piscinas Las Modernas/Las Peñas** (Martínez; admission children/adults $0.50/1; 8am-5pm Fri-Sun) is packed with families on the weekends and holidays.

Up the hill and past the cemetery on Martínez, you'll end up on a track that crosses a stream (Quebrada de Naguasco) on a small wooden footbridge. The trail continues on the other side to a road, where you turn left to reach **Piscina El Salado** (admission $1; 5am-5pm). These are the only other hot pools, and because they're 2.5km out of town, they're usually less crowded. After simmering in the hot pool, masochists can jump into the ice-cold creek. Buses come out here ($0.20, 10 minutes), departing from the stop on Rocafuerte.

Private nonmineral baths are available around town as well. **Centro de Hidroterapia Gamboa** (☎ 274-2951; Montalvo & Alfaro; admission $3-12; 8am-9pm) has an indoor lap pool, *baños de cajón* (steam boxes), hot tub, mud masks and massages.

Massages & Spa Treatments

Baños offers an endless supply of spas with such treatments as the *baños de cajón*, medicinal mud baths and, yes, even intestinal drainage, although you can always just go for a relaxing massage if you're not game to have your colon cleansed. Most of the big hotels offer at least some of these services, and the **Spa Garden El Refugio** (☎ 274-0482; www.spaecuador.info; Camino Real; treatments $5-20; by appointment or walk-in) just outside of town has them all.

For excellent one-hour, full-body massages ($25) and herbal facials ($20), make an appointment or drop in to **Stay In Touch** (☎ 274-0973; Ibarra; by appointment or walk-in), owned by an Ecuadorian-American couple.

For one-hour Swedish, hot-stone and reflexology massages ($20), visit Carmen Sánchez at **Chakra** (☎ 274-2027; 09-355-6698; Alfaro & Martínez; 8am-7pm & by appointment).

Mountain Biking

Several companies rent mountain bikes starting at about $10 per day, but check that the bike, helmet and lock are adequately maintained or even ask to take a quick test ride before agreeing to rent. The most popular ride is the dramatic descent past a series of waterfalls on the road to Puyo (see p179), a jungle town 61km to the east. Various other mountain-biking options are available and the outfitters will be happy to tell you about them.

On the issue of safety, the Baños–Puyo road has several narrow, long and pitch-black tunnels. Bike riders should bypass the tunnels by veering down on the signed trails that swing around them.

Hiking

The tourist office provides a crude but useful map showing some of the trails around town.

The walk down to Río Pastaza is easy and popular. Just behind the **Sugarcane Stalls** by the bus station, a short trail leads to the **Puente San Francisco**, the bridge that crosses the river. You can continue on trails up the other side as far as you want.

Going south on Maldonado takes you to a path that climbs to **Bellavista**, where a white cross stands high over Baños. The path then continues to the settlement of **Runtún**, some two hours away, where the views are outstanding. You can then loop around and back down to Baños, ending up at the southern end of JL Mera. This takes you via the statue of **La Virgen del Agua Santa**, about half an hour from town. The whole walk takes four to five hours.

West of town, turn right by a religious shrine and walk down to Puente San Martín and visit the impressive falls of **Cascada Inés María**, a few hundred meters to the right of the bridge.

Jungle Trips

Many Baños tour operators lead trips to the jungle, but they vary in quality and experience. For more information, see p234.

Three- to seven-day jungle tours cost per person about $30 to $50 per day, depending on the destination (usually with a three- or four-person minimum). Always full of travelers, Baños is a good town in which to organize a group if you are not already with one.

Rainbow Expeditions (☎ 274-2957; rainbowexpeditions2005@hotmail.com; Alfaro at Martínez) is owned by Germán Shacay, a member of the Shuar indigenous community from the southern Oriente that offers culture-oriented trips into several areas of the Oriente including Shuar communities outside of Macas.

Some other recommended operators are **Rainforestur** (☎ 274-0743; www.rainforestur.com.ec; Ambato 800) and **Expediciones Amazónicas** (☎ 274-0506; www.amazonicas.banios.com; Oriente 11-68, near Halflants). Both lead culture and nature tours near Puyo and Lago Agrio for about $50 per day.

Climbing

The climbing conditions on Tungurahua (5016m), an active volcano, are naturally in flux. At the time of research, local authorities were carefully monitoring the situation and considering declaring the volcano open for climbing. For detailed information about other climbing and hiking peaks in Parque Nacional Sangay, see p180.

Expediciones Amazónicas (see above) rents well-maintained equipment and can arrange licensed guides; Rainforestur (see above) has rental equipment and licensed climbing guides and can tailor your itinerary to include acclimatization. Climbs, which generally involve an overnight stay in *refugios*, run between $120 to $150 per person, not including park and *refugio* fees.

Horseback riding

Horse rentals cost around $5 per hour or $35 per day. Many half- or full-day trips start with a long jeep ride out of town, and the actual riding time is short – inquire carefully to get what you want. **José & Two Dogs** (☎ 274-0746; josebalu_99@yahoo.com; cnr Maldonado & Martínez) is recommended by locals.

Rafting

Long in the business, **GeoTours** (☎ 274-1344; www.geotoursbanios.com; Ambato at Halflants; 🕑 daily) offers half-day trips on the Río Patate for $30. Trips last four hours (only two hours are spent on the river) and a snack is included. Also available is a full-day trip to Río Pastaza for $100 that takes 10 hours, with four hours on the river, lunch included and complete gear provided. GeoTours also offers a three-day kayaking course ($150).

Rainforestur (see left) offers excellent rafting trips.

Courses

One-on-one or small-group Spanish classes start around $4.50 and are offered by the following schools:

Baños Spanish Center (☎ 274-0632; www.spanishcenter.banios.com; Oriente 8-20) Near Cañar.

Sí Centro de Español y Inglés (☎ 274-0360; Paez) Near Oriente.

Festivals & Events

Baños became the seat of its canton on December 16, 1944, and an annual fiesta is celebrated around this date. There are the usual processions, fireworks, music and a great deal of street dancing and drinking. These festivities rev up again in October as the various barrios (neighborhoods) of Baños take turns paying homage to the local icon, Nuestra Señora de Agua Santa.

Sleeping

There are scores of competitively priced hotels in Baños. Rates are highest on weekends and during vacations, when they can all fill up.

BUDGET

Hospedaje Santa Cruz (☎ 274-0648; santacruzhostal@yahoo.com; 16 de Diciembre; dm $5.50, r per person incl breakfast $8) Another traveler's favorite brought to you by the owners of Plantas y Blanco, the Santa Cruz has tiled rooms and a garden full of plants and hammocks. It's nothing fancy, but the rooms are large and clean and the managers are friendly.

Hostal Plantas y Blanco (☎ 274-0044; Martínez & 12 de Noviembre; dm $5.50, r per person with bathroom $8.50; 💻) Attractively decorated, hyperclean and eternally popular, 'Plants and White' (you figure it out) scores big points for its rooftop terrace, outstanding breakfasts, on-site steam bath and overall value. Some rooms have weird layouts (such as walking through the shower to the toilet), but no one seems to mind.

Hostal Princesa María (☎ 274-1035; Juan León Mera & Rocafuerte; r per person $6) Readers have written to extol the virtues of this friendly, family-run hostal, which offers private baths, good security and a communal kitchen.

CENTRAL HIGHLANDS

Hostal Transilvania (☎ 274-2281; www.hostal-transilvania.com; 16 de Diciembre y Oriente; r per person incl breakfast $6) There's nothing Transylvanian about the simple, clean rooms with private bathrooms, but they come with free internet and there's a Middle Eastern restaurant on site.

Residencial Timara (☎ 274-0599; Maldonado; r per person with shared/private bathroom $6/10.50) This 40-year-old family business has recently added three stories of colorful new rooms with private bathrooms and cable TV. The older rooms with shared bathrooms are run down but well lit and acceptable. There are guest kitchen facilities too.

Hostal Huillacuna (☎ 274-2909; yojairatour@yahoo.com; 12 de Noviembre; s/d incl breakfast $13/15) If you love art, sleep in it. At Huillacuna, also an important local gallery, rooms are arranged around a large dining area filled with art, antiques and a cozy fireplace. It's an unusual but interesting concept and the warm and accommodating hosts offer a breakfast feast. Near Montalvo.

La Petit Auberge (☎ 274-0936; 16 de Diciembre; s/d $12/24, with fireplace $14/28) This French-owned, hacienda-style hotel has big rooms with *chimeneas* (fireplaces) and lofts. A huge games room makes it popular with families.

Villa Gertrudis (☎ 274-0441; www.villagertrudis.com; Montalvo 20-75; r per person incl breakfast $15; ☒) Low key and quiet, Gertrudis has a beautiful garden, '60s furniture, hardwood floors and a relaxing, vacationy feel. Inside a grand chalet-style home, it has been around for decades. Prices include use of the indoor pool across the street.

MIDRANGE

our pick **Posada del Arte** (☎ 274-0083; www.posadadelarte.com; Pje Ibarra; s/d incl breakfast $19-24/$32-42; ☐) They say that small is beautiful and that is certainly the case at Posada del Arte, an exquisite little guesthouse with colorful, comfortable rooms, wood floors, a rooftop terrace, gigantic breakfasts and art all around. The midrange rooms have views, as do the priciest rooms, which also have fireplaces. Wi-fi is free.

Hotel Sangay (☎ 274-0490; www.sangayspahotel.com; Montalvo; standard s/d $24/40, cabin $40/50, executive $56/70; ☐ ☒) The kind of place you'd stay if you're looking for typical high-end service, the Sangay, near Martínez, is another resort-style hotel right next to the Virgen and the waterfall. All rates include use of the pool, sauna, spa, Turkish bath and hydro massage (it's a Jacuzzi), and there are the usual spa treatments available for an additional charge.

Hotel Palace (☎ 274-0470; hotelpalace@hotmail.com; Montalvo 20-03; s/d $24/49; ☒) Down by the waterfall and conveniently close to La Virgen hot baths, Hotel Palace is a large resort hotel with faded glory like the paint on the walls. Still, with a garden, pool, sauna, spa, Turkish bath and a games room with darts and table tennis, it has a much to offer.

Hostal La Casa Verde (☎ 08-659-4189; www.lacasaverde.com.ec; Camino Real; dm/s $8/16, d $24-30; ☐) One of the surprisingly few environmentally sensitive hotels in Baños, the 'Green House,' about 2km outside of town along the Camino Real road, offers spacious rooms with balconies overlooking the Río Pastaza and a lush garden. The Kiwi owners strive for a welcoming, homey feel. Camping is $4.

Hospedaje La Floresta (☎ 274-1824; wwwlafloresta.banios.com; Montalvo & Haflants; s/d $22/35 ☐) This comfortable inn situated around a pretty interior garden is located in a quiet part of town that is still close to the baths and everything else. The staff here are friendly and the spacious, tile-floor rooms have big windows and comfortable beds. The wireless is free.

Hostería Monte Selva (☎ 274-0566, 274-0244; www.hosteriamonteselva.com; Halflants; s/d $29/49; ☒) Swanky, with wooden cabins and sauna facilities.

TOP END

Luna Runtún (☎ 274-0882/3; www.lunaruntun.com; superior/deluxe d $140; ☒ ☐ ☒) Perched at the top of a sheer cliff (2260m) looking high over Baños and up to the Tungurahua summit, Luna Runtún is all about location. Just laying eyes on the spa will relax you, and the restaurant serving traditional cuisine and food from their own garden is good. Ultimately, it's about the view, one of the most stunning offered by any central sierra hotel. Rates include the hot tub and sauna, but massages and treatments cost extra (also available to nonguests). It's 6km beyond Baños via the road to Puyo – get the bus or a taxi ($6) up to the hotel, and walk down to town via a well-maintained trail.

Samari Spa Resort (☎ 274-1855; www.samarispa.com; Vía a Puyo Km 1; s $122-254, d $187-254; ☐ ☒) A five-star resort built on the site of an 18th-century Jesuit monastery, Samari is by far the most luxurious hotel and spa in town and easily one of Ecuador's best. Whether it's the artisanal furniture, fluffy bedspreads, or the presentation of food grown right in its own garden, everything here has been thought out to minute detail. The spa is situated around a heavenly indoor pool, and can be accessed by nonguests all day for $20. Additional spa treatments are à la carte.

Eating

Baños has probably Ecuador's highest concentration of a-cut-above restaurants. With cuisine ranging from Italian to French to German to everyone's favorite roasted rodent, *cuy*, Baños is a worthy place to splurge.

Restaurants tend to close on slower days, principally Monday to Wednesday, and hours can vary during low season (although what constitutes low season in Baños depends on who you are talking to).

Baños is famous for its *melcocha*, a chewy taffy that's softened and blended by swinging it onto wooden pegs, usually mounted in the doorways of shops. Pieces of chewable *caña de azucar* (sugarcane) and *jugo de caña* (sugarcane juice) are sold at the **Sugarcane Stalls** across from the bus terminal.

Ponche Suizo (Alfaro; snacks $1-3; 🕑 8am-6pm) Between Ambato and Rocafuerte, this little spot serves cakes and coffee, but everyone comes for the 'Ponche Suizo', a trade-secret treat that's a cross between a shake and a mousse. It's really delicious and they also have the usual fruit and yogurt *batidos* (shakes).

Aromé (Haflants, near Ambato; coffee & treats $1-4; 🕑 9am-8:30pm Mon-Thu, to 10pm Fri-Sun) If you're jonesin' for chocolate or coffee, head to Aromé for both as well as the always flowin' fondue fountain.

Café Good (☎ 274-0592; 16 de Diciembre; mains $2-4, almuerzos $2; 🕑 8am-10pm) An imitator of the Hood joints, the Good also serves better-than-good veggie dishes with wholesome brown rice as well as some chicken and fish.

Rico Pan (☎ 274-0387; Ambato; mains $2-5; 🕑 7am-8pm Mon-Sat, to noon Sun) *Panaderías* (bread shops) in Baños tend to have good coffee and breakfasts. Rico Pan, near Maldonado, has one of the earliest served.

Casa Hood (☎ 274-2668; Martínez at Halfants; mains $3-4; 🕑 8am-10:15pm Wed-Mon) Named for owner Ray Hood, a long-standing gringo in residence, this excellent café has nourishing breakfasts, a $2 *almuerzo* and a menu of Thai, Mexican and Middle Eastern dishes. The Casa is a welcoming place to eat, exchange books, meet with friends, chill *solito* (alone), and even take yoga classes.

Café Hood (☎ 274-0537; Maldonado; mains $3-6; 🕑 10am-10pm) Of all the Hoods and Goods in Baños, this one, near Parque Central, *might* just be the best. Some of the dishes, such as the soft tacos or the chickpeas and spinach in curry sauce with yogurt and cucumbers, are simply excellent. The menu is mostly Tex-Mex with a splash of Thai, Greek and Indian.

Posada del Arte (☎ 274-0083; www.posadadelarte.com; Pje Ibarra; mains $3-7; 🕑 8am-10pm) Like the hotel it's part of, this restaurant is a welcoming and cozy place with a warming fireplace. It serves excellent international dishes, wonderful breakfasts (including Tungurahua pancakes – they don't explode!) and lots of great, small plates for snacking (try the fried yuca).

La Bella Italia (☎ 274-0121; 16 de Diciembre; mains $4-6; 🕑 7am-9pm) This elegant little Italian bistro serves pasta and pizzas in a quiet atmosphere.

La Petit Auberge (☎ 274-0936; mains $5-8; 16 de Diciembre; 🕑 noon-10pm) In the hotel by the same name, this restaurant has another wonderful French-inspired menu serving soups, meat dishes and pasta.

Swiss Bistro (☎ 274-2262; www.swiss-bistro.com; Martínez, near Alfaro; most mains $5-9; 🕑 daily) This small bistro's cow fetish is evident in its decor and delicious Swiss and European specialties, which include fondue, steaks, big, fresh salads and a Swiss potato dish called *roesti*. The service might be the best in Baños.

our pick **Café Mariane** (☎ 274-0911; Halflants at Rocafuerte; mains $5-12; 🕑 11am-11pm) Mariane's French-Mediterranean cuisine is a real standout in Baños. The cheese and meat fondues are a lot even for two people, and the pasta and meat dishes are quite elegant.

Quilombo (☎ 274-2880; cnr Montalvo & 12 de Noviembre; mains $8-12; 🕑 Wed-Sun) Quilombo (which means 'mess' or 'insanity' in Argentine slang) refers to the irreverent menu in the form of dice (just roll if you can't decide), hodge-podge decor and kooky Argentine owner who has imported Southern Cone-style *parrilla* (grilled meat) to Baños. Also in good Argentine style, the glasses of wine are properly large.

Santa María Supermarket (☎ 274-1641; Alfaro & Rocafuerte; 🕑 8:30am-8pm) This centrally located market is the place to stock up, while the **Mercado Central** (Alfaro & Rocafuerte; 🕑 7am-6pm) is a reliable place to find fresh fruits and veggies.

Drinking & Entertainment

Nightlife in Baños means dancing in local *peñas* (small venues that feature live folk music) or hanging out in one of many character-filled bars.

Peña Ananitay (16 de Diciembre; 9pm-3am) Near Espejo, this is the best place in town to catch live *folklórica* (Andean folk music). It can get packed, but that's part of the fun.

Peña Bar Mocambo (274-0923; Alfaro; 4pm-2am) Always popular thanks to its sidewalk bar with a funny Last-Supper-inspired mural, party atmosphere and upstairs billiards room. Near Ambato.

Jack Rock (Alfaro 5-41; 7pm-2am) Jack Rock boasts a rock-'n'-roll theme and the best pub atmosphere in town. It plays classic rock during the week and salsa, merengue and *reggaetón* on weekends.

Rincón de Suiza (Martinéz, near Haflants; 9am-midnight Tue-Sat, noon-midnight Sunday) The crowd at this Swiss-Ecuadorian hangout spills out on the sidewalk; billiards and drinks.

Shopping

At the **Pasaje Artesanal** (8am-8pm), between Ambato and Rocafuerte, you'll find endless quantities of locally made baubles and a regional craft called *tagua* carving – white, golf-ball-sized nuts that resemble ivory and are dyed and transformed into figurines and jewelry.

Galería de Arte Huillacuna (274 2909; yojairatour@yahoo.com; 12 de Noviembre, near Montalvo; 8:30am-9pm) exhibits and sells excellent Ecuadorian art. You're free to roam without buying.

Guitarras Guevara (274-0941; Halflants 2-84; daily) For more than 50 years, Jacinto Guevara has been hand-making guitars. Pick one up for anywhere from $75 to $300.

Getting There & Away

Buses from Ambato's **Mayorista bus terminal** leave about every half-hour for Baños ($0.75; 1 hour).

The Baños **bus terminal** (Amazonas) is within easy walking distance of most hotels. Transportes Baños offers frequent buses direct to Quito ($3.50, 3½ hours) that stop in Salasaca, Ambato and Latacunga as well. The first half of the Baños–Riobamba road (up to Penipe) remains closed – you will have to backtrack through Ambato. To the Oriente, buses depart regularly for Puyo ($2, 2 hours), Tena ($4, five hours) and Coca ($10, 10 hours). There are daily buses to Guayaquil ($7, seven hours).

Getting Around

Westbound buses leave from Rocafuerte, behind the Mercado Central. Marked 'El Salado,' they go to the Piscinas El Salado ($0.20, 10 minutes). Eastbound buses that go as far as the dam at Agoyán leave from Alfaro at Martínez.

FROM BAÑOS TO PUYO

03

Nicknamed 'La Ruta de las Cascadas' (Highway of the Waterfalls), the road from Baños to Puyo is one of the region's most dramatic routes. It hugs the Río Pastaza canyon as it drops steadily from Baños, at 1800m, to Puyo, at 950m and passes more than a dozen waterfalls on the way. The bus ride is great, but zipping down on a mountain bike is even better. The first third of the route is mostly downhill, but there are some definite climbs, so ready those legs (it's about 61km if you do the whole thing). For mountain-bike rentals, see p175.

Most people go only as far as the spectacular Pailón del Diablo waterfalls, about 18km from Baños, but if you're up for a much bigger ride, making it to Río Negro allows you to see the change in ecology as you head into the lower elevations.

Along the way, the road shoots through tunnels that seem to swallow you up like a black hole. Some are quite long and bikers or ATV riders should take the signed, dirt-trail detours that skirt around them. Watch your speed on curves and approaches to the tunnels and ride on the right side of the road. From Puyo (or anytime before), you can simply take a bus back to Baños, putting your bike on the roof (the bus driver's assistant will help you load it).

Make sure that you rent a helmet and a bike lock (and use both!). Insects on the trails can be unrelenting, so bring repellent and don't forget your raincoat.

Baños to Río Verde

Before the first tunnel, you'll pass the Agoyán hydroelectric project. After the tunnel, you'll catch a little spray from the first waterfall, and about 45 minutes' riding time from Baños you'll pass the spectacular **Manto de La Novia** waterfalls. For a closer look at the falls, take the engine-powered *tarabita* (cable car, $2), which transports you 500m across the river gorge at the hair-raising height of 100m.

From Manto de La Novia, it's a good 30- to 45-minute ride to the village of **Río Verde** (between the fourth and fifth tunnels), the access point for the 15-minute downhill hike to the thundering **Pailón del Diablo** (Devil's Cauldron). One view of the falls is from the suspension bridge (maximum capacity five people!) and the other is an up-close view from *behind* the falls (admission $1, at the Pailón del Diablo cafeteria).

our pick Just east of Río Verde, you'll find the wonderful **Hostal Pequeño Paraiso** (www.hostel-banos-pequenoparaiso.com; dm/r per person $17/20). It offers lodging and camping amid lush and beautiful jungle, as well as excellent opportunities for hiking, rock climbing and canyoning (a cool sport involving hiking, climbing, swimming and abseiling up river gorges and canyons). Prices include breakfast and dinner (including vegetarian options).

Another enchanting place to stay 500m east, further along the road, is called **Miramelindo** (☎ 288-4194; Km 18 on the Baños-Puyo rd; r per person $25), where prices include breakfast, a guide to Pailón del Diablo waterfall, sauna and Jacuzzi, *baños de cajón* (steam boxes) and wonderfully rustic rooms accented in wood and earthy colors. The orchid collection is outrageous.

Río Verde to Puyo

Shortly after leaving Río Verde, the road starts to climb. About a half-hour (riding time) uphill from Río Verde, you come to **Machay**, a nice place to stop for a picnic lunch and a dip in the river. A 2.5km trail leads into the cloud forest and past **eight waterfalls**, which range from wee tumblers to the beautiful Manantial del Dorado 2.5km in. You can lock your bike at the start of the trail.

After Machay, you have two good climbs, then it's downhill nearly all the way to Río Negro, 15km from Río Verde. As the road drops, the vegetation rapidly becomes more tropical and the walls of the Río Pastaza canyon are covered with bromeliads, giant tree ferns and orchids. Before you hit Río Negro, you'll pass through the village of **San Francisco**, which has a dirt plaza, a few simple eateries and places to buy water or beer.

After San Francisco, it's only another 10 to 15 minutes to **Río Negro**, a funky little town built up along the main road. There are restaurants (some of which are surprisingly slick) and plenty of places to buy refreshments. There's even a hotel.

After Río Negro, you start really feeling tropical. After 17km you pass **Mera**, which might have a police checkpoint (have your passport ready), and is slowly developing as a tourism spot. For folks who have some time and a love of animals, the **Merazonia Foundation** (☎ 279-0030; www.merazonia.org; r per volunteer per week $50), a refuge for injured rainforest animals just outside of Mera, offers volunteer opportunities with their projects rescuing and protecting birds, mammals and other creatures. They have facilities with composting toilets and hot showers.

Some 7km further, you pass **Shell**, an important air-transport hub into the jungle, where there might be another police checkpoint. They'll certainly be Cessnas and cargo jets banking over town. On the other side of the bridge, near the main square, **Alexander's** doubles as a small grocery store and serves good *almuerzos* ($1 to $2). Just east of the military base, **Aero Regional** (☎ in Puyo 03-279-5095) is an air-taxi company with charted flights to lodges and villages in the jungle.

At the end of the descent, 61km from Baños, you arrive at the humid jungle town of Puyo (p258).

PARQUE NACIONAL SANGAY

The 271,000-hectare Parque Nacional Sangay (admission $10) contains three of Ecuador's most magnificent volcanoes – the mightily active Sangay, the remittently active Tungurahua and the extinct El Altar – as well as flora, fauna and terrain of immense diversity. The Ecuadorian government established the park in 1979, and Unesco made it a World Heritage site in 1983.

From the *páramo* in the park's western heights, which climb to over 5000m around each of the three volcanoes, the terrain plunges down the eastern slopes of the Andes to elevations barely above 1000m. In between is terrain so steep, rugged and wet (over 4m of rain is recorded annually in some areas) that it remains a wilderness in the truest sense. The whole park is home to some 500 bird species and 3000 plant species and the thickly vegetated slopes east of the mountains are the haunts of very rarely seen mammals, such as spectacled bears, mountain tapirs, pumas, ocelots and porcupines.

Only two roads of importance enter the park. One goes from Riobamba to **Alao** (the main access point to Volcán Sangay) and peters out in the *páramos* to the east. Despite the protected status of the park, the newly completed Guamote–Macas road drives right through it, inviting the negative environmental impact of colonization and hunting.

Volcán Tungurahua

With a (pre-eruption) elevation of 5016m, Tungurahua is Ecuador's 10th-highest peak. It *was* a beautiful, cone-shaped volcano with a glacier plopped on top of its lush, green slopes, but since 1999 many eruptions have melted the snow and changed the shape of the cone and crater. Lava and lahar flows from the August 2006 eruption covered about 2km of the Ambato-Baños road (now repaired), and as recently as February 2008 there has been significant volcanic activity.

Until 1999, travelers liked to walk part of the way up the volcano, perhaps as far as the village of Pondoa and the (now destroyed) refuge at 3800m. People have made it up to the refuge during periods of calm in recent years, but climbing beyond Pondoa without a guide, preferably one specializing in Tungurahua, is ill advised. An entirely new topography up there has made all the old maps and pointers invalid. It only takes about three months of relative silence, however, from the carefully monitored Tungurahua to get an all-clear for climbing from local authorities, so ask in Baños about the current situation.

Recent eruptions created impressive pyroclastic 'rivers' that flowed down the east and west slopes. In late 2008, operators were considering developing tours in these areas, so ask about horseback riding and hiking excursions to Quebrada Ulba (west) and Quebrada Bascún (east) – see p173 for more information.

Volcán El Altar

At 5319m, this long-extinct volcano is the fifth-highest mountain in Ecuador and one of its most picturesque and fascinating peaks. Before the collapse of the western side of the crater in prehistoric times, the 'Altar' may have been one of the highest mountains in the world. The crater walls, which surround a gem-colored lake called Laguna Amarilla, actually form nine distinct peaks, most of which have religious-themed names like Obispo (Bishop, 5315m) and Monja Chica (Little Nun, 5080m). In 2000, part of a glacier fell into the lake, creating a massive wave of water that charged down the west slope and over the Collanes plane (3900m), leaving huge boulders strewn across the landscape.

To get to El Altar, take a bus from Riobamba to **Penipe**, a village halfway between Riobamba and Baños. A road between Ambato and Penipe via Baños exists, but recent Tungurahua eruptions have made the bridges between Baños and Penipe impassable; inquire locally about current conditions. From Penipe, take a bus or hire the occasional truck to the tiny village of **Candelaria** (3100m), 12km to the southeast. From Candelaria it's about 2km to **Hacienda Releche** (☎ 03-296-0848; per person $6), where you can sleep, and the nearby ranger station, where you pay the park fee ($10). The owners of Releche also own the thatched-roof **refugio** (per person $6) on the Collanes plane, and they rent horses ($8 each way plus $8 for a guide).

The hike to the Collanes plane, which is the best place to camp near the peak, is straightforward, but slick mud can make for a slow-going walk. Rangers and hacienda staff can indicate the beginning of the trail, and in dry weather a fit hiker could power from Candelaria to the Collanes plane in six to seven hours. Once up on the plane, you will encounter many bulls (keep your distance), and their poop spread all over the place (watch your step). Flooding occurs, but rarely.

The best times to go are December to March. The wettest months are April and May, and the foggiest are July and August.

Volcán Sangay

Constantly spewing out rocks, smoke and ash, 5230m-high Sangay is one of the world's most active volcanoes and highly dangerous ascent. For those who do try, some guides actually recommend carrying a metal shield as protection from rocks blown out of the crater (now *that'll* lighten your load). Hiking up to the base or perhaps just to **La Playa** (The Beach), where a refugio once stood, is possible, especially from December to February, when the area is driest.

The Instituto Geográfico Militar (IGM, p76) in Quito can provide topo maps. To get to Sangay, take a bus from Parque La Dolorosa in Riobamba to the village of **Alao** at 5:30am, 6:30am and hourly noon to 6pm ($1.50, 1½ hours). At the national-park entrance in Alao, you can pay the park fee and get information about a cooperative of local guides that works out of Alao and nearby **Guargualláa**.

Lagunas de Atillo & Ozogoche

With the opening of the Guamote–Macas road, the spectacular *páramo* lakes region of Lagunas de Atillo became easily accessible and the area is being slowly developed for horseback riding, hiking, trout fishing and even mountain biking. Still, Atillo gets very few visitors and it's an amazing place to see remote landscape and rural life.

About 79km from Riobamba, the road passes through **Atillo** (population 300), which is really two villages, Atillo Grande and Atilla Chico, spaced about 1km apart. From this area, which is surrounded by the Atillo lakes, you can hike six to eight hours over a nearby ridge to the **Lagunas de Ozogoche** and another three to four hours to the village of **Totoras**, where you can camp or ask around in the village for a *choza* (thatch-roofed hut, approximately $1) to sleep in. In Atillo Chico, a woman named Dora Paña at **Paradero Los Saskines** (☎ 03-260-6000; Vía Cebadas-Macas Km 38; r per person $5) offers basic lodging and meals, and close to Atillo Grande, the **Cabaña Atillo Grande** (Vía Cebadas-Macasal km 41; r per person $8) offers similar facilities. If you are camping, get your supplies in Riobamba and pick up a topo map at the Instituto Geográfico Militar (IGM; p76) in Quito.

From Atillo the road winds through the easternmost extremity of the national park, before ending in Macas in the southern Oriente (see p265 for details of tours and park access from Macas). Pro Bici in Riobamba (see p189) offers two- and three-day biking trips along the Guamote–Macas road passing through the lakes area.

Cooperativa Unidos buses to Atillo leave Riobamba at 5:30am, noon and 3:20pm (2:30pm on Sundays; $2, 2½ hours) from Velasco and Olmedo. All buses to Macas pass Atillo, leaving Riobamba's Terminal Oriental at 2:30am, 5:45am, 10am, 1pm, 4pm and 5pm.

GUARANDA

☎ 03 / pop 30, 987 / elevation 2650m

Half the fun of Guaranda is getting there. The 99km 'highway' from Ambato reaches altitude over 4000m and passes within 5km of the glacier on Volcán Chimborazo (6310m). From here, the mountain almost looks easy to climb. The road slices through windswept *páramo* grass and past little troops of *vicuña* (a wild relative of the llama), before suddenly plunging toward Guaranda.

The capital of Bolívar province, Guaranda is small and uneventful. It sits between and on seven steep hills that have prompted the moniker, 'the Rome of the Andes.' It certainly didn't get this nickname for its cultural offerings.

It's also the departure point for Salinas, described next.

Information

Andinatel (Rocafuerte) Telephone center near Pichincha; there are many others around town.
Banco del Pichincha (Azuay near 7 de Mayo) Bank with an ATM.
Clínica Bolívar (☎ 298-1278) One of several clinics and pharmacies near Plaza Roja, south of the hospital.
Hospital (Cisneros s/n)
Post office (Azuay) Near Pichincha.

Sights & Activities

The markets on Saturday and Wednesday take place at **Plaza 15 de Mayo** (Selva Alegre at 7 de Mayo), which has old adobe houses and a pleasantly quiet, forgotten colonial air. The market at Mercado 10 de Noviembre is held in a modern, concrete building.

Guaranda takes its name from a 16th-century indigenous chief named Guaranga, whose dignified stone monument, **El Indio Guaranga**, is situated about 3km west of town on the top of a hill ($2.50 by taxi).

Festivals & Events

Guaranda is famous for its February/March **Carnaval** celebrations. In the last few days before Lent, people stream in from all over for such festivities as water fights, dances and parades. Local musicians serenade people in their homes and receive a little 'Pájaro Azul' (Blue Bird), a liquor with local herbs, in return.

Sleeping

Hostal Marquez (☎ 298-1306; 10 de Agosto at Alfaro; s/d with shared bathroom $6/12, r with private bathroom $15) The staff isn't out to charm anyone here, but the rooms are bright and appointed with cable TV and firm beds.

Hostal de las Flores (☎ 298-0644; Pichincha 4-02; r per person with shared/private bathroom $8/10) This is Guaranda's most traveler-oriented hotel,

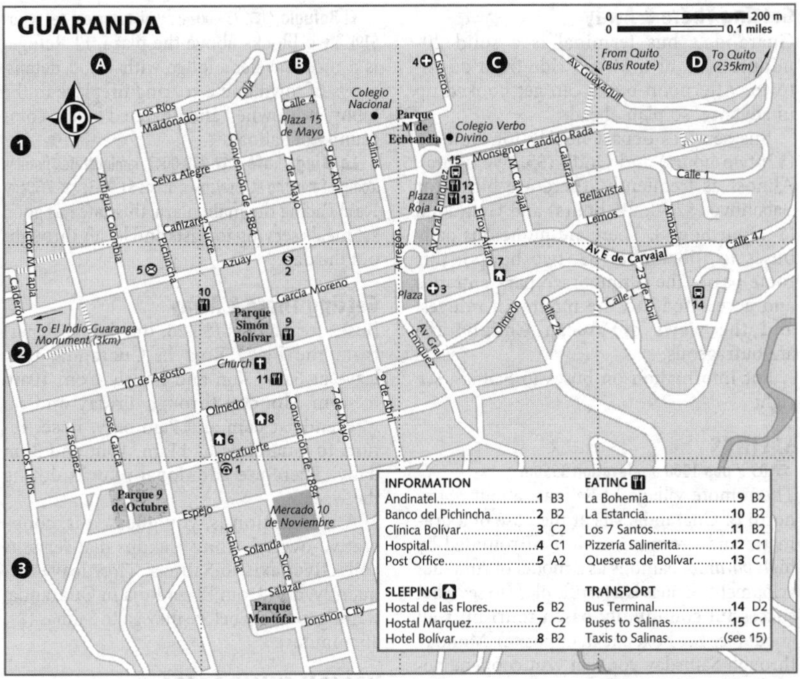

a pretty place in a nicely refurbished old building. The cheerful rooms open onto a small interior courtyard and have cable TV, firm beds and telephones.

Hotel Bolívar (☎ 298-0547; Sucre 7-04; s/d $8/16) Another good option for discerning travelers, the rooms here are welcoming and clean and there's a pleasant courtyard. The attached restaurant has good *almuerzos* ($2 to $3).

Eating

Los 7 Santos (☎ 298-0612; Convención de 1884; mains $1-3; ⏰ 10am-11pm Mon-Sat) Near 10 de Agosto, and thoroughly out of place in Guaranda, Los 7 Santos offer all that you would expect from an artsy café in Quito. The coffee's not quite up to snuff, but the cool atmosphere is a great place to pen your next novel – or just sit comfortably and read one. There's breakfast in the morning and small sandwiches and *bocaditos* (snacks) all day.

La Bohemia (☎ 298-4368; Convención de 1884 & 10 de Agosto; mains $2-4; ⏰ 8am-9pm Mon-Sat) Close to Parque Bolívar, La Bohemia serves *almuerzos* ($2) in a laid-back but attentive atmosphere. Chase your meal down with one of the giant *batidos*.

La Estancia (☎ 298-3157; García Moreno; mains $3-4.50; ⏰ noon-10pm Tue-Sat, to 4pm Mon) Restaurant by day, bar by night, La Estancia (near Sucre) is a cool little place with an old-fashioned sign, wooden tables and friendly staff. Most of the menu is steaks, chicken and pasta.

Pizzería Salinerita (☎ 298-5406; Av Gral Enriquez; pizzas $3-7; ⏰ noon-10pm Mon-Sat) From the folks who brought you the cheese, the pizza here has a good crust and sauce as well.

Queseras de Bolívar (☎ 298-2205; Av Gral Enriquez; ⏰ 8:30am-1pm & 2:30-6pm Mon-Sat, 8:30am-noon Sun) Stock up here on the province's famous cheeses ($6 to $7 for a whole wheel), chocolate and other treats.

Drinking & Entertainment

Two restaurants double as bars: Los 7 Santos has a laid-back, lodge kind of scene at night, while La Estancia transforms into a mellow bar after dinner. If you have to boogie, a *discoteca* or two pumps beats along 10 de Agosto just west of Eloy Alfaro.

Getting There & Away

Guaranda's bus terminal is a solid 20-minute walk or a $1 cab ride from downtown. Afternoon buses can get booked up in advance, so plan ahead.

Bus services depart hourly for Ambato ($2, two hours) and Quito ($5, five hours). Almost as frequently, there are buses for Babahoyo ($2.50, 2½ hours) and Guayaquil ($4, four hours). There are numerous daily buses to Riobamba ($2, two hours); this route passes the Chimborazo park entrance and access road to the mountain refuges, and the views of Volcán Chimborazo are outrageous.

For information on buses to Salinas, see right.

SALINAS

☎ 03 / pop 1000 / elevation 3550m

The remote village of Salinas, about 35km north of Guaranda, sits at the base of a dramatic and precipitous bluff surrounded by high *páramo*. Famous as a model of rural development, Salinas is a terrific place to see what successful community-based tourism is all about (see the boxed text, opposite). Monday through Saturday you can visit cooperative-run factories making cheese, chocolate, dried mushrooms, salami and *turón* (a taffylike, honey-based candy). Local guides lead walks and horseback rides to the factories, nearby salt, mushroom-picking areas or through the stunning countryside.

The **tourist office** (☎ 239-0022; www.salinerito.com; 9am-5pm) is located on the main plaza next to the post office, and can help you hire a guide and offer information on solo activities. If it's not open, you could head over to the El Refugio hotel for assistance. There are no banks or other tourist services in the village.

Tienda El Salinerito (Plaza Central; 9am-5pm) is Salina's local outlet for all the products made by the communities, including fuzzy wool sweaters and a cool comic book about the history of Salinas.

Sleeping & Eating

Hostal Samilagua (sadehm2@latinmail.com; r per person $6) Directly across from El Refugio, the privately run Samilagua is a simple place managed by a friendly local woman. Rooms are cement rather than wood, but they're colorfully painted and comfortable.

El Refugio (☎ 239-0024; r with bathroom per person $19) Two blocks above the plaza, El Refugio is a nice traveler's lodge with wood details, views of town and a roaring fireplace in the lobby. It is owned and operated by the community of Salinas.

La Minga Café (☎ 239-0042; lamingacafé@hotmail.com; El Salinerito at Guayamas; mains $1.50-3; 7:30am-10pm) Facing the main plaza, this café has good set meals serving tourists and locals throughout the day.

Getting There & Away

Buses for Salinas ($0.25, one hour) depart from the Plaza Roja in Guaranda; they leave at 6am, 7am and hourly from 10am to 4pm Monday through Friday and on weekends at 6am and 7am only. Buses return to Guaranda at 11am, 1pm and 3pm daily. There are additional returns during the week.

A new option is, you guessed it, cooperative-owned, white pickups that serve as collective taxis to Salinas. They leave frequently, also from Plaza Roja in Guaranda, waiting to fill up before they go to Salinas ($1, 45 minutes).

VOLCÁN CHIMBORAZO

Called 'Taita' (Father) by indigenous people in the area, Volcán Chimborazo (6310m) is the country's tallest mountain, a hulking giant topped by a massive glacier. Along with its smaller, craggier companion **Volcán Carihuairazo** (5020m) to the northeast, and the Río Mocha valley that connects them, Chimborazo makes up a remote, even desolate, area populated by only a few indigenous communities. The western side of Chimborazo is called the *arenal* (*arena* means 'sand') and is so arid that some people compare it to the *altiplano* of Bolivia.

Not only is the extinct Volcán Chimborazo the highest mountain in Ecuador but its peak (6310m), due to the earth's equatorial bulge, is also the furthest point from the center of the earth.

Chimborazo and Carihuairazo are both within the **Reserva de Producción Faunística Chimborazo** (admission $10). It is called a 'fauna-production reserve' because it is home to hundreds of vicuña (a wild relative of the llama). Once hunted to extinction, they were imported from Chile and Bolivia in the 1980s. Now prospering, it's easy to catch their elegant

FROM CHOZAS TO CHEESES

Not to be confused with the coastal town by the same name, Salinas de Guaranda sits high on the skirts of Volcán Chimborazo and gets its name from the surrounding deposits of salt. It is a proud indigenous and mestizo community with a self-sustaining economy, but it wasn't always that way.

When an Italian Salesian missionary named Antonio Polo rode into town one July day in 1971, Salinas was still a town of *chozas* (thatched-roof huts). For generations, *salineritos* (people of Salinas) had lived in dire poverty, unable to demand a fair price for their production of milk, vegetables and wool; half of all Salinas children died before the age of five.

Polo saw a better future for local families making and selling dairy-based products. He helped the *campesinos* (peasants) set up a credit cooperative, buy equipment and bring in technical expertise. A Swiss technician named José Dubach showed the cooperative how to build a *quesería* (cheese factory), which was soon producing high-quality cheeses with milk bought from local farmers. Emphasizing high standards of freshness and sanitation, the cooperative eventually opened more than twenty *queserías* around Salinas and branched out into other provinces. Their fresco, dambo, tilsit andino, mozzarella, gruyere and provolone are now sold in Queseras de Bolívar shops and supermarkets all over the country, under the name El Salinerito, generating profits that go straight back to communities.

They have also created new cooperatives that produce chocolate, dried mushrooms, wool clothing, salamis, candies and buttons, and they have even started a community tourism project that includes two hotels. Visitors can check out local salt mines and *queserías*, ride horseback to the surrounding farms and, of course, buy cheese.

Salineritos consider Señores Polo and Dubach true heroes, and their names and portraits are common around town. Their life's work is evident everyday in the high levels of health, education and pride enjoyed by the people of Salinas.

silhouettes in the mist on the bus ride between Guaranda and Riobamba, and you'll surely see them poking around if you explore the park.

Climbing Chimborazo or Carihuairazo is an adventure only for experienced mountaineers with snow- and ice-climbing gear (contact the guides listed under Riobamba or Quito). Reaching the refuge on Chimborazo or getting started with a multi-day hike requires hiring a car from Riobamba and assembling some gear and maps.

Activities

Care should be taken to properly acclimatize if you plan to do physical activities around Chimborazo and Carihuairazo. All of the accommodations listed under Sleeping are good sites to do this, although you should also consult a qualified guide if you are planning hard hiking or climbs on either peak. Temperatures can drop well below freezing at night. July to September, as well as December, are the driest (but coldest) times in this region.

HIKING

The walk from Urbina (p186) along the Río Mocha, reaching over the Abraspungo pass and emerging at the Ambato–Guaranda road, is particularly well trodden. Allow three days for this hike. Maps are available at the Instituto Geográfico Militar (IGM, p76) in Quito.

CLIMBING

Most climbers do multiple acclimatization ascents and spend the night at increasingly higher elevations before tackling Chimborazo, which is a notoriously laborious climb that also requires technical know-how. Most parties these days follow the **Normal Route**, which takes eight to 10 hours to the summit and two to four to return. The **Whymper Route** is currently unsafe.

There are no refuges on Carihuairazo, so guides usually set up a base camp on the south side of the mountain. The climb is relatively straightforward for experienced climbers, but ice-climbing gear is needed.

Sleeping

Two small lodges on the lower slopes of Chimborazo are interesting places to enjoy the countryside and learn a bit about local indigenous culture. The two high climbing refuges, on the other hand, are pretty much a place to eat some grub and catch a few winks before heading out on an all-night climb. All of these places are bone chilling from the late afternoon on, so bring appropriate clothing.

The cheapest place to stay in the area is **La Casa del Condor** (☎ 357-1379; r per person $5) in the small indigenous community of **Pulinguí San Pablo** (3900m) on the Riobamba–Guaranda road. This community of Puruhá people, who have lived on Chimborazo for centuries, owns the surrounding land and runs the ecotourism enterprise **Proyecto El Cóndor** (Condor Project; www.interconnection.org/condor). Families still live in the round *chozas* typical of the area, but La Casa del Condor is a stone building with rooms for a women's weaving cooperative and a *hostal* with hot showers and a communal kitchen. Locals provide basic guiding services, mountain bikes are available and there are fascinating interpretation trails in the area. Information can be obtained from Riobamba resident **Tom Walsh** (☎ 03-294-1481; twalsh@ch.pro.ec), who has been instrumental in helping the villagers set up the project.

Just outside of the reserve's boundary, southeast of Chimborazo, is **Urbina**, which at 3618m was the highest point on the Trans-Andean Railway. The former train station, built in 1905, now functions as **Posada La Estación** (☎ in Riobamba 294-2215; beds $7), a simple but comfortable *hostal* operated by Alta Montaña (see p189). Popular for acclimatization and scenic hikes, the posada has eight rooms, hot showers, a kitchen and meals. The only road access to Urbina is from the Panamericana. You'll need to arrange transport through Alta Montaña, or ask the bus driver to drop you at the turnoff and walk in 6km.

The lower **Refugio Hermanos Carrel** (beds $10) is at 4800m and the upper **Refugio Whymper** (beds $10), Ecuador's highest-altitude lodgings, is at 5000m and is named after Edward Whymper, the British climber who in 1880 made the first ascent of Chimborazo with the Swiss Carrel brothers as guides. Both accommodations have caretakers, equipped kitchens, storage facilities and limited food supplies.

Getting There & Away

Several buses go from Riobamba to Guaranda daily via a paved road. About 45 minutes from Riobamba, it passes Pulingui San Pablo, and about 7km further it passes the signed turnoff (4370m) for the Chimborazo refuges. From the turnoff, it is 8km by road to the parking lot at Refugio Hermanos Carrel and 1km farther to Refugio Whymper. If for some reason you are walking up this road, allow several hours to reach the *refugios*.

Most hotels in Riobamba can arrange a taxi service (about $35 round-trip) to Refugio Hermanos Carrel via this route.

To reach Posada La Estación *hostal*, take a bus along the Panamericana and ask the driver for the Urbina road, almost 30km north of Riobamba. Urbina lies about 1km up that road.

RIOBAMBA

☎ 03 / pop 181,960 / elevation 2750m

Riobamba takes its name from a combination of the Spanish word for 'river' and the Quichua word for 'valley.' This bilingual moniker describes the topography of the area as well as the rich mix of cultures that live here. Riobamba has a strong indigenous presence, which grows to wonderfully colorful proportions during the **Saturday market**, but the city's layout and architecture are imposing reminders of Spanish colonization.

The Puhurá Indians were the first people to live in the vicinity, followed by the Inca for a brief period. In 1534, the Spanish founded the city of Riobamba on the site of Cajabamba, 17km south on the Panamericana (see p192), but in 1797 a huge landslide destroyed the city and the people moved it to its present-day site. Spain's grip on Ecuador was officially broken in Riobamba with the signing of Ecuador's first constitution in 1830, which is why one of the main thoroughfares is called Primera Constituyente.

Riobamba lies at the heart of an extensive scenic road network and is the starting point for the spectacular train ride down the Nariz del Diablo (see p191). It gets so sleepy on Sundays, though, you might think the town had slipped into a coma.

Information

Andinatel (Tarqui at Veloz; 8am-10pm) Telephone center.

Banco de Guayaquil (Primera Constituyente) Bank with ATM.

Banco del Pichincha (cnr García Moreno & Primera Constituyente) Bank with ATM; other banks with ATMs are around town.

Clínica Metropolitana (☎ 294-1930; Junín 25-28) Locally recommended clinic.

CENTRAL HIGHLANDS

WHAT'S IN A GRAIN?

Ecuador is corn and potato country. Any look up toward the hills, with their patchwork of green and golden cultivation, shows that. But for thousands of years, quinoa (*Chenopodium quinoa*) was also king. A critical protein source, this morsel, the size of a pin head, sustained the Inca, who called it 'Mother Grain,' on their long marches, and to this day it is an important staple throughout the Andes

According to some agriculture experts, quinoa production has declined over the years because of cheap imported wheat. Others say that the long washing and drying process required to remove its bitter coating is simply too labor intensive for most poor farmers nowadays. In rural Ecuador, however, you'll still find the tiny grain in *sopa de quinua* (quinoa soup) and other recipes, thanks in part to its cultural importance and to its UN designation as a 'supercrop' for its high nutritional value. Some rural communities have even found a market overseas for their quinoa crops.

One such community is in, strangely enough, a community-based radio station called the Escuelas Radiofóica Populares del Ecuador (referred to locally as ERPE or *Radiofónica;* tune in at AM 710 or FM 91.7 or check out www.erpe.com.ec). ERPE started in 1962 as an education program that broadcast to *campesinos* (peasants) in surrounding provinces. In the 1980s they started an organic farm, something they already knew how to do well, to fund their activities and they soon realized that they could target the international market with their organic produce. ERPE taught more than 3500 farming families in four provinces how to grow organic quinoa, and in 1997 they received their first order from the United States. Since then, they have produced more than 700 tons of quinoa for export, increased local consumption of the supercrop and nearly doubled the salaries of many quinoa-farming families.

In 2002, Slow Food International awarded ERPE the prestigious Slow Food Prize, putting these farmers in the ranks of the world's finest organic food producers.

Hotel Los Shyris Internet (Rocafuerte & 10 de Agosto; per hr $0.49; 8am-10pm Mon-Sat) Internet access.

Hospital Policlínico (☎ 296-1705/5725/8232; Olmedo 11-01) Hospital, southeast of downtown.

Lavandería Donini (Villaroel; per kg $0.80; 9am-1pm & 3-6pm Mon-Sat) Same-day laundry service near Larrea.

Metropolitan Touring (☎ 296-9600/601; mtrioopr@andinanet.net; cnr Av León Borja & Francia) Local office of Ecuador's biggest travel agency.

Parque Nacional Sangay Office (☎ 295-3041; parquesangay@andinanet.net; Av 9 de Octubre; 8am-1pm & 2-5pm Mon-Fri) West of downtown, near Duchicela; get information and pay entry fees to Parque Nacional Sangay here.

Police station (☎ 296-1913/9300; Av León Borja)

Post office (cnr Espejo & 10 de Agosto)

Sights

MUSEUMS

Inside the beautifully restored, 16th-century convent of the Conceptas nuns, Riobamba's **Museo de Arte Religioso** (☎ 296-5212; Argentinos; admission $2; 9am-noon & 3-6pm Tue-Sat) houses one of the country's finest collections of 17th- and 18th-century religious art. Once upon a time, many upper-class girls were sent to this convent for confined education within its walls. The museum shows the nuns' bleak cells and even the scourges they used to 'punish' themselves. The museum's signature piece is a priceless, meter-tall monstrance inlaid with more than 1500 precious stones including emeralds, pearls, diamonds, rubies, amethysts and aquamarines. Made of solid gold with a solid silver base, it weighs over 360kg (making it incredibly difficult to steal).

PARKS

The handsome, tree-filled **Parque Maldonado** (Primera Constituyente at Espejo) is flanked by Riobamba's **cathedral** on the northeastern side. A few blocks southeast, **Parque La Libertad** (Primera Constituyente at Alvarado) is anchored, near Alvarado, by its neoclassical **basilica** (Veloz), famous for being the only round church in Ecuador. It's often closed, but try Sundays and evenings after 6pm. Just north of downtown, the **Parque 21 de Abril** (Orozco at Ángel León) has an observation platform with views of the surrounding mountains.

MARKETS

The Saturday market transforms Riobamba into a hive of commercial activity, when thousands of people from surrounding

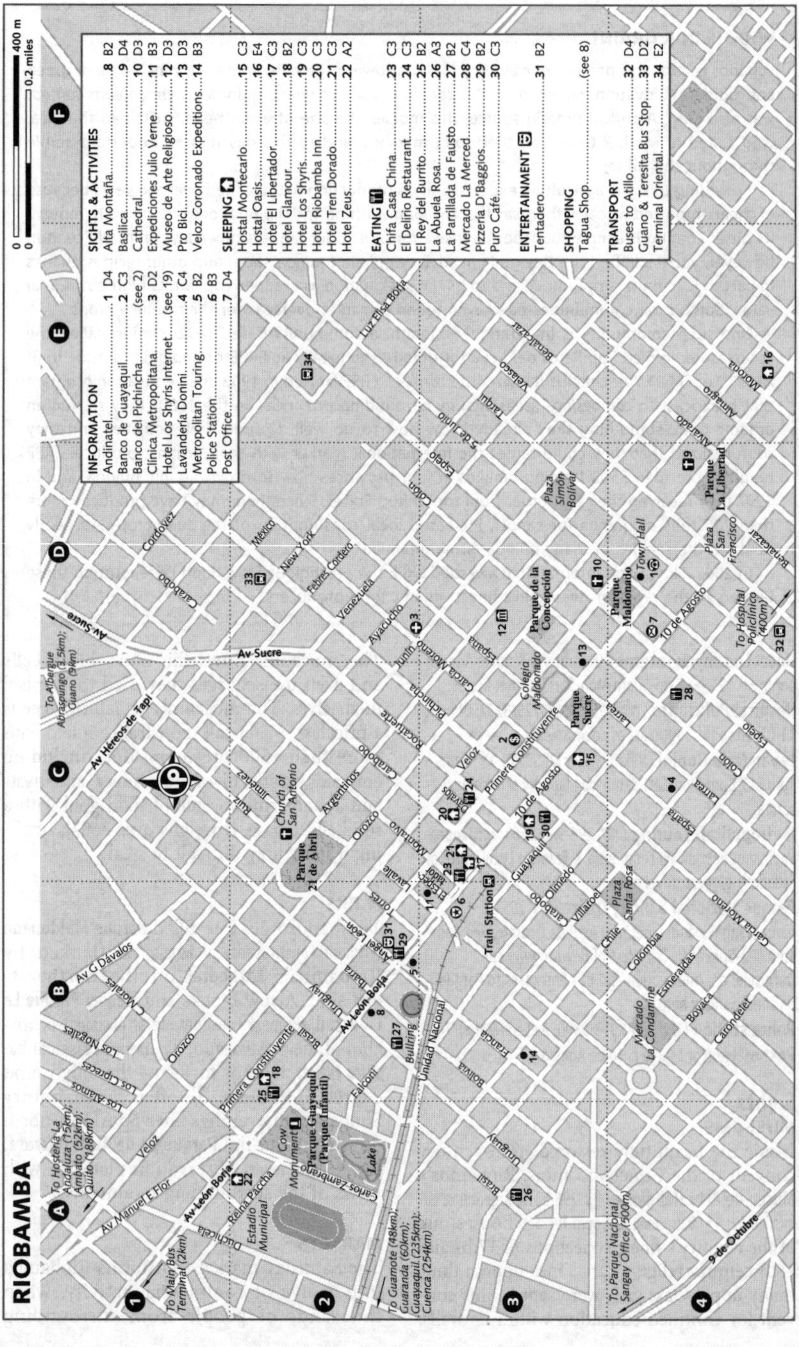
RIOBAMBA
0 400 m
0 0.2 miles
INFORMATION
Andinatel 1 D4
Banco de Guayaquil 2 C3
Banco del Pichincha (see 2)
Clínica Metropolitana 3 D2
Hotel Los Shyris Internet (see 19)
Lavandería Donini 4 C4
Metropolitan Touring 5 B2
Police Station 6 B3
Post Office 7 D4
SIGHTS & ACTIVITIES
Alta Montaña 8 B2
Basilica 9 D4
Cathedral 10 D3
Expediciones Julio Verne 11 B3
Museo de Arte Religioso 12 D3
Pro Bici 13 D3
Veloz Coronado Expeditions 14 B3
SLEEPING
Hostal Montecarlo 15 C3
Hostal Oasis 16 E4
Hotel El Libertador 17 C3
Hotel Glamour 18 B2
Hotel Los Shyris 19 C3
Hotel Riobamba Inn 20 C3
Hotel Tren Dorado 21 C3
Hotel Zeus 22 A2
EATING
Chifa Casa China 23 C3
El Delirio Restaurant 24 C3
El Rey del Burrito 25 B2
La Abuela Rosa 26 A3
La Parrillada de Fausto 27 B2
Mercado La Merced 28 C4
Pizzería D'Baggios 29 B2
Puro Café 30 C3
ENTERTAINMENT
Tentadero 31 B2
SHOPPING
Tagua Shop (see 8)
TRANSPORT
Buses to Atillo 32 D4
Guano & Teresita Bus Stop 33 D2
Terminal Oriental 34 E2

villages come to barter, buy and sell. They flood into town by truck, cart, donkey and foot, unloading impossibly giant loads and spreading out their wares along the streets northeast of Parque de la Concepción. Cows are often a common sight on the streets because Riobamba is the center of an important cattle-raising region.

The only place with handicrafts is **Parque de la Concepción** (Orozco & Colón). As you're walking around, keep your eyes peeled for locally made *shigras* (small string bags), *tagua*-nut carvings (see p179), and *totora* straw baskets and mats woven by the indigenous Colta from the reeds lining the shores of nearby Laguna de Colta.

Tours

Thanks to Riobamba's proximity to Chimborazo, the country's highest peak, the city is home to some of the country's best climbing operators and mountain guides. For more information on climbing Chimborazo, see p184. Two-day summit trips start around $160 per person for Chimborazo and include guides, gear, transportation and meals, but not park-entrance fees ($10).

One-day mountain-biking trips start at $35 per person. Downhill descents from the refuge on Chimborazo – an exhilarating way to take in the views – are very popular.

A pioneer in Ecuadorian mountaineering, and owner of **Veloz Coronado Expeditions** (☎ 296-0916; www.velozexpediciones.com; Chile 33-21 & Francia), Enrique Veloz is practically a historical personage in Ecuador. He and his sons are both certified with ASEGUIM (Asociación Ecuatoriana de Guias de Montaña; Ecuadorian Mountain Guides Association), and Veloz himself has climbed Chimborazo more than 500 times. They have high standards for safety, climb most of the peaks in the central sierra, and also offer mountain-climbing courses.

Expediciones Julio Verne (☎ 296-3436; www.julioverne-travel.com; Espectador 22-25; 9am-1pm & 3-6pm Mon-Fri, 9am-noon Sat) is a respected Ecuadorian-Dutch-owned, full-service operator offering affordable, two-day summit trips to Chimborazo and other peaks, as well as to the Oriente and Galápagos. The company arranges guided hikes, rents out climbing and hiking gear and offers clear information without pressuring customers. It also offers downhill mountain biking on Chimborazo (their routes are good for kids about ten years and up) and tons of interesting tours in the region.

Pro Bici (☎ 295-1759; Primera Constituyente & Larea) is one of the country's best mountain-bike operators, with many years of experience and excellent trip reports from clients. It offers mountain bike rentals (per day $15 to $25, depending on the bike), excellent maps, good safety practices and fascinating day tours. The friendly owners speak English, and the store is located on the second floor of a fabric factory.

Alta Montaña (☎ 294-2215; León Borja & Uruguay) is run by the well-known and amiable Rodrigo Donoso, an accomplished mountaineer. Apart from arranging guided climbs of the highest mountains in Ecuador, Alta Montaña manages three mountain refuges on Volcán Chimborazo and arranges acclimatization and training days before ascents.

Festivals & Events

Riobamba's annual fiesta celebrates the **Independence Battle of Tapi** of April 21, 1822. On and around April 21, there is a large agricultural fair with the usual highland events: street parades, dancing and plenty of traditional food and drink.

Sleeping

If you are in Riobamba to catch a train or go on a sunrise excursion, early breakfasts and proximity to the train station or your tour operator are primary considerations.

BUDGET & MIDRANGE

our pick **Hostal Oasis** (☎ 296-1210; Veloz 15-32; r per person $9-12; 💻) When it comes to friendliness, value and down-home cutesiness, it's hard to beat Oasis, a gem of a guesthouse behind the owners' home. Rooms (and two apartments) are grouped around a garden, complete with two squawking parrots. Transportation to and from train and bus stations is free and camping is available. Wi-fi is also on the house.

Hotel Tren Dorado (☎ 296-4890; Carabobo 22-35; r per person $10) Not surprisingly, the 'Golden Train' is close to the train station. It has spotless, comfortable, flowery rooms that would make Martha Stewart proud. A self-serve breakfast ($3 extra) is served at 5:30am on train days so you can fill up before the ride. The hot water seems infallible and the TVs are big.

Hotel Los Shyris (☎ 296-0323; Rocafuerte & 10 de Agosto; s/d incl breakfast $11.20/18) The large and modernish Shyris is great value for its central location and clean rooms with TV. Many of the rooms are sunny and recently renovated, and bathrooms are small but nice and clean. The lobby has Riobamba's cheapest internet ($0.49 per hour)

Hotel Glamour (☎ 294-4406; www.hotelglamour.com.ec; Primera Constituyente 37-85; r per person $12-25) This glass and glowing hotel probably was glamorous when it was first built, but nowadays it's dated and more funky than anything else. In an odd reversal from most hotels, the rooms here are nicer than the lobby – with carpets, good beds and cable TV – and the staff is lovely.

Hotel Riobamba Inn (☎ 296-1696, 294-0958; Carabobo 23-20; s/d incl breakfast $14/25) Holding on to the '70s like they never went out of style, the orange bedspreads, vinyl chairs and groovy Chimborazo mural offer the kitschiest comfort in Riobamba. Despite the blast from the past, the place is well kept and veers toward a business-traveler hotel.

Hostal Montecarlo (☎ 296-1577; montecarlo@andinanet.net; 10 de Agosto 25-41; s/d incl breakfast $15/19) The Montecarlo occupies an attractively restored, turn-of-the-20th-century house. The use of blue (blue couches, blue carpet, blue trim and blue plaid bedspreads) can be a bit overbearing, but it's a lovely place nonetheless. Breakfast is available in the café next door from 5am on train days.

Hotel El Libertador (☎ 294-7393; León Borja & Carabobo; s/d $15/23; 💻) This fancier hotel in a renovated building with wood floors sits conveniently across the street from the train station. There's a busy restaurant-grill downstairs that opens early and closes late, and wi-fi is available.

Hotel Zeus (☎ 296-8036/8037; www.hotelzeus.com.ec; León Borja 41-29; s/d $24/37, executive s/d $37/49) Between the bus terminal and downtown, Hotel Zeus is a seven-story hotel with a range of room styles and amenities as well as gym access. The pricier rooms are excellent (some have five-star views of Chimborazo).

AROUND RIOBAMBA

Like many countryside inns, these places can be full of families and groups on the weekends and deserted midweek.

Hostería La Andaluza (☎ 290-4223, 290-4248; s $54-68, d $63-88) About 15km north of Riobamba on the Panamericana, this renovated, colonial hacienda has panoramic views and beautiful grounds. Two restaurants, a small exercise room and sauna and a bar are among the amenities, but the best part is the isolated countryside setting. Nearly all the antique-furnished rooms have fireplaces, as well as cable TV and telephones. If you take a chance and just arrive, try to negotiate a lower price.

Albergue Abraspungo (☎ 294-0820; www.abraspungo.com.ec; s/d $68/92) Situated 3.5km northeast of town on the road to Guano, Abraspungo is a first-class hotel inbuilt around a whitewashed, tile-roofed hacienda. Filled with antiques and rustic details, Abraspungo offers spacious, themed rooms, a restaurant and bar, some spa services and horseback riding. It is also a certified ecotourism project with excellent local hiring practices.

Eating

On train days, early-bird breakfasts are available from 5am at Hotel Tren Dorado and Hostal Montecarlo; arrange the day before. Dining is scarce on Sundays, when Riobamba seems to stay in bed.

La Abuela Rosa (☎ 294-5888; Brasil & Esmeraldas; mains $0.80-1.50; 🕑 4pm-9:30pm Mon-Fri) Drop by Grandma Rosa's for *comida típica* (traditional Ecuadorian food) and tasty snacks including sandwiches, chocolate and cheese. Friendly, cozy and popular with locals.

our pick **Mercado La Merced** (Mercado M Borja; Guayaquil btwn Espejo & Colón; hornado $3; 🕑 7am-6pm) The ladies hawking *hornado* (whole roast pig) put on a pretty hard sell, yelling out for your attention and offering samples. If you can stand the pressure and you're up for dining in a (very sanitary) atmosphere of flayed Wilburs, then the market is fun and interesting. The pork is superfresh. Saturdays are busiest.

Chifa Casa China (Primera Constituyente; mains $2-4; 🕑 11am-11pm) Like most Chinese food in Ecuador, it's a little heavy on the grease, but the lovely Chinese family that runs this *chifa* (Chinese restaurant) serves large portions with plenty of fresh vegetables and seafood.

Puro Café (Pichincha 12-37; small plates $2-6; 🕑 9:30am-2pm & 3:30-9:30pm) Serving absolutely perfect coffees, cappuccinos and other caffeinated beverages, this narrow café tucked into a side street also has pressed sandwiches and cheese plates. It really is perfect if you're looking for a place to chill alone or chat with a friend.

CENTRAL HIGHLANDS

El Rey del Burrito (☎ 295-3230; Av León Borja 38-36; mains $3-5; 🕑 11am-11pm Mon-Sat, till 4pm Sun) 'The King of the Burrito' serves large burritos, tacos and enchiladas with super spicy salsa (*ole!*). There must be a vegetarian in the house, because they have wonderful options for herbivores. Service is friendly and the atmosphere is enlivened by some cool murals.

Pizzería D'Baggios (☎ 296-1832; León Borja & Angel León; pizzas $3-8; 🕑 noon-10pm Mon-Sat) Dozens of different kinds of medium-thick-crust pizzas are prepared before your eyes in Baggio's wood oven. They wouldn't make an Italian drool, but this corner pizzeria spins out a satisfying pie and the oven keeps the whole place nice and toasty.

La Parrillada de Fausto (☎ 296-7876; Uruguay 20-38; mains $4-6; 🕑 noon-3pm & 6-10:30pm Mon-Sat) This fun, Argentine-style grill serves great barbecued steaks, trout and chicken in a ranch-style setting. Don't miss the cool, cavelike bar in back.

El Delirio Restaurant (☎ 296-6441; Primera Constituyente 28-16; mains $6-9; 🕑 noon-10pm Tue-Sun) Named for a poem by the great liberator, Simón Bolívar, and located in his house that is a historical monument, the restaurant serves *comida típica* in a dimly lit, antique atmosphere. The hostess of many years is a bit on the eccentric side.

Entertainment

Nightlife, limited as it is, centers on the intersection of Avenida León Borja and Torres and northwest along León Borja toward Duchicela. Both areas have bars and discos.

Tentadero (Av Leon Borja; admission $3; 🕑 8pm-late Fri & Sat) near Ángel Leon is the town's hottest (both in terms of popularity and temperature) *discoteca*, spinning electronica and salsa well into the night.

Shopping

The **Tagua Shop** (Av León Borja 35-17; 🕑 9am-7pm Mon-Sat, 10am-5pm Sun) has Riobamba's best selection of *tagua* carvings. Vendors sell crafts at Parque de la Concepción throughout the week, although it's best on Saturday.

Getting There & Away

BUS

Riobamba has two bus terminals. The **main bus terminal** (☎ 296-2005; León Borja at Av de la Prensa), almost 2km northwest of downtown, has hourly buses for Quito ($4, four hours) and intermediate points, as well as buses for Guayaquil ($5, 4½ hours). Transportes Patria has a Machala bus at 9:45am ($6, six to seven hours) and there are several buses a day to Cuenca ($6, six hours). Buses for Alausí leave 20 times a day between 5am and 8pm with CTA ($1.50, two hours). Flota Bolívar has morning and afternoon buses to Guaranda ($2, two hours); some continue on to Babahoyo. Guaranda-bound buses pass the access road to Chimborazo and the mountain refuges.

For buses to the Oriente, you have to go to the **Terminal Oriental** (Espejo & Luz Elisa Borja), northeast of downtown. The direct road between Riobamba and Baños has been closed since 2006; although it is open as far as Penipe, you'll need to go to Ambato to transfer to Baños. Inquire locally about the road's current condition.

Buses to Atillo in Parque Nacional Sangay (p182) leave from the corner of Velazco and Olmedo.

TRAIN

The only service out of Riobamba is the famous ride south to Alausí and La Nariz del Diablo (see the boxed text 'The Devil's Nose,' p193); service to Riobamba from cities to the north may resume again sometime in 2009 (details may be available at www.efe.gov.ec). The train ($11) leaves Riobamba at 7am Wednesday, Friday and Sunday. It picks up more passengers in Alausí and goes only as far as Sibambe, immediately below La Nariz del Diablo, where there are no services. From Sibambe, the train ascends La Nariz del Diablo and returns to Alausí, where passengers can spend the night, continue on to Cuenca by bus or return to Riobamba

> **THE PANAMERI-WHAT?**
>
> Right around Cajabamba, the Panamericana splits: the easternmost branch is the Ecuadorian Panamericana, which becomes a regular road when it hits the border with Peru, and the westernmost branch is the international Panamericana, still referred to as such once it hits the Peruvian border. Throughout the rest of this chapter, references to the Panamericana should be understood as the Ecuadorian, not international, Panamericana.

by bus. Riding on the roof is permitted; cushions for that purpose are rented for $1 before departure.

Heavy rains and landslides sometimes damage the tracks and cause authorities to shut down the Riobamba–Alausí run. Your best bet is to call the **train station** (☎ 296-1909; Av León Borja at Unidad Nacional), which is also where you buy your tickets either the day before or the morning of the departure (starting at 6am).

Getting Around

North of the main bus terminal, behind the Church of Santa Faz (the one with a blue dome), is a local bus stop with buses to downtown, nearly 2km away. These buses run along Avenida León Borja, which turns into 10 de Agosto near the train station. To return to the bus terminal, take any bus marked 'Terminal' on Primera Constituyente; the fare is $0.25.

Three long blocks south of the main bus terminal (turn left out of the front entrance), off Unidad Nacional, is a smaller terminal with frequent local buses for Cajabamba, Laguna de Colta and the chapel of La Balbanera. Buses for Guamote also leave from there.

To visit the villages of Guano and Santa Teresita, take the local bus from the stop at Pichincha and New York.

GUANO & SANTA TERESITA

☎ 03

Besides serving as a playground for families from Riobamba on the weekends, the village of **Guano**, 8km north of Riobamba, is an important craft center that specializes in carpets and items made of leather and *totora*. Stores selling them are right around the main square (where the bus stops). Also near the main square is a **museum** (admission $1) holding the mummified remains of a Franciscan monk from the 16th century, and **ruins** of a convent dating to the 1660s. The **mirador** over town has excellent views (on a clear day) of El Altar.

There are no hotels; several restaurants serve *almuerzos*.

From the main plaza, you can continue by bus or walk to **Santa Teresita**, two kilometers away. At the end of the bus ride, turn right and head down the hill for about 20 minutes to **Parque Acuático Los Elenes** (admission $1; 🕓 8am-6pm), where swimming pools are fed by natural mineral springs. The water is quite cool (22°C or 72°F), but the views of Tungurahua and El Altar are marvelous.

Local buses to Guano and Santa Teresita leave Riobamba from the stop at Pichincha and New York.

SOUTH OF RIOBAMBA

☎ 03

About 17km south of Riobamba, the Panamericana speeds through the wee village of **Cajabamba**, the original site of Riobamba until an earthquake-induced landslide buried the city in 1797, killing thousands. You can still see a huge scar on the hillside as you arrive.

Further south and just off the Panamericana, you'll pass the unmistakable colonial-era chapel of **La Balbanera**. Although much of it crumbled in the 1797 earthquake, parts of the facade date from 1534.

About 4km south of Cajabamba, the waters of **Laguna de Colta** appear choked with a golden reed called *totora*. For anyone who has ever visited Lake Titicaca in Bolivia, this setting and the small *totora* rafts used to sail around Laguna Colta will look familiar. Ethnobiologists believe that *totora* seeds may have been brought here in prehistoric times, but whatever the case, the reeds form an important crop for the indigenous Colta who use them to make their famous baskets and *esteras*, (straw mats). Indigenous Colta women dye the fringes of their hair a startling golden color.

A trail with broad views of Chimborazo will take you around the lake in a couple of hours, and on the weekends small lakeside eateries serve the local specialty, *cariucho*, a kind of tuna stew.

You can easily visit any or all of these sites on a day excursion from Riobamba using local buses or by hiring a taxi. Buses from Riobamba heading south on the Panamericana will drop you at any of them. They're close enough to each other that you could walk between them too.

GUAMOTE

☎ 03 / pop 2788 / elevation 3050m

Guamote is famous for its unspoiled **Thursday market**, one of the largest in rural Ecuador. The town itself is also beautiful. Although a bit sleepy, it's a place where Quichua-speaking old-timers walk the streets in bare feet (as they have their whole lives) and everyone gathers

THE DEVIL'S NOSE

Train buffs will be excited to learn that an illustrious rail system known as the Ferrocarril Transandino (Trans-Andean Railway), built around the turn of the 20th century, once ran between Quito and Guayaquil. It was an economic lifeline between the coast and highlands and considered a technological marvel.

Sadly, however, the heyday of Ecuadorian rail transport has ended. Highway construction, along with constant avalanche damage from heavy rains, spelled its demise and by 2000 only a few short runs, mostly frequented by tourists, remained.

The best known and most exciting of these is the section from Riobamba to Sibambe, which includes the descent from Alausí (3350m) down La Nariz del Diablo (Devil's Nose), a 765-meter sheer cliff of solid rock. In 1902 track engineers devised a clever way up this monster by carving a zigzag route into the side of the mountain (many lives were lost in the process). The train tugs a bit north, switches track, tugs a bit south and again switches track, slowly making its way up and down the Devil's nose.

Somewhere along the Nariz, the old choo choo inevitably derails. Not to worry, though! The conductors ask everyone to get off and using advanced technology – big rocks and sticks – they steer the iron horse back on track.

Before reaching the Nariz del Diablo, the train winds through the Avenue of the Volcanoes, treating riders, most of whom sit on the roof, to views of Chimborazo, El Altar, Laguna Colta and the indigenous communities along their flanks and banks.

The Ferrocarril Transandino is in a bit of flux these days. Heavy rain can still cause temporary closures and rumors about the safety of the train, particularly riding on its roof, have persisted. In 2007, two women were killed in an accident while riding on top of an *autoferro,* which is actually a bus retrofitted to ride the rails.

These problems have not deterred the ongoing restoration of the Ferrocarril Transandino, which was prioritized as an important tourism development project by President Rafael Correa in 2007. A massive restoration of the whole network (including the long detour to Cuenca – more than 400km in all) and many of the 45 old train stations is underway. Despite controversy about the costs and even the environmental impact of harvesting wood for the sleepers (the wood planks on which the tracks rest, *not* sleeping cars), the revival of the Ferrocarril Transandino at the time of research was full steam ahead.

in the main square to greet the train, steaming and whistling, when it rolls in on Wednesdays, Fridays and Sundays. A charming maze of brightly painted adobe buildings, Guamote is a proud indigenous community in little (immediate) danger of losing its identity.

You can stay at **Inti Sisa** (☎ 291-6319; www.intisisa.org; JM Plaza at Garcia Moreno; r per person $12), part of a community tourist project run by a Belgian-Ecuadorian. It's a cozy, well-run place that also offers mountain biking and horseback-riding trips and can arrange local homestays and volunteer work. Call ahead if you can, especially for Wednesday-night stays.

Guamote is on the Riobamba–Cuenca bus route, which has several services per day. Unless your bus is actually going to Guamote (usually only on Thursdays), you will be dropped off on the Panamericana and will have to walk about 1km in.

At the time of research, it was not possible to board the train in Guamote, although there is nothing to stop you from getting off if you want to stick around.

ALAUSÍ

☎ 03 / pop 8111 / elevation 3323m

Set almost dizzyingly on the edge of the Río Chanchán gorge and presided over by a giant statue of St Peter, Alausí is the last place the train stops before its descent down the famous Nariz del Diablo. Many jump on the train here, rather than in Riobamba, although you're more likely to score a good seat in Riobamba and you would miss the beautiful ride down the Avenue of the Volcanoes. Alausí is wonderfully picturesque, especially near the train station and on the side, cobbled streets, where old adobe buildings with wooden balconies take you back in time. Alausí is really just a whistle stop these days, but it banks on train tourism and has renovated some of its old railroad infrastructure as well.

Alausí lies about 97km south of Riobamba and has a busy **Sunday market**. The train station is at the north end of 5 de Junio.

Sleeping & Eating

Most of Alausí's slim pickings are on Avenida 5 de Junio, the main street. Places fill up on Saturday nights with Sunday market-goers and weekend visitors.

Hotel Europa (☎ 293-0200; 5 de Junio 175 at Orozco; s with shared/private bathroom $5/8, d $8/14) With old wooden balconies and corridors, the renovated Europa is considered Alausí's best. The rooms don't quite live up to the promise, but they have hot water and cable TV. It's right across from the bus station. The *chifa* downstairs has good Cantonese-style dishes.

Hotel Panamericano (☎ 293-0156; 5 de Junio & 9 de Octubre; r per person with shared/private bathroom $6/10) The rooms without bathrooms don't have windows, but the others are clean and comfortable.

Hotel Gampala (☎ 293-0138; 5 de Junio 122; s/d $11/20) Believe it or not, this small, 35-year-old hotel has hosted several famous Ecuadorian statesmen and artists. The rooms are a bit cramped, but the beds are comfortable and there's reliable hot water. You can also hang out in a cute little sitting room or the downstairs café.

Three kilometers outside of town, there's an exception to Alausí's humdrum hotel offerings, **Hostería Pircapamba** (☎ 293-0181; www.pircapamba.com; r per person incl breakfast $20), which lies in a country setting with views of Alausí and the surrounding valleys. The spacious rooms and sitting area with fireplace are traditional whitewashed brick and wood. Horseback riding and excursions to area sites are available.

Aside from the traditional *comedores* (inexpensive eateries) along 5 de Junio, the railroad-inspired **Cafetería La Higuera** (☎ 293-1582; 🕑 8am-6pm) has breakfasts and *almuerzos* ($2.50).

Getting There & Away

The **bus station** is on Avenida 5 de Junio. Buses for Riobamba ($1.50, two hours) depart every hour or so. Buses for Cuenca ($4, four hours) and Quito ($5, five hours) depart several times daily. Many buses between Riobamba and Cuenca enter town – if not, it's a 1.5km walk (all downhill) into town from the Panamericana.

Old buses (or pickup trucks acting as buses) leave from 5 de Junio for nearby destinations. Some of the bus rides can be quite spectacular, especially the one to Achupallas, the departure point for the Inca Trail hike (see boxed text 'Camino del Inca,' p197), about 23km by road to the southeast.

TRAIN

Alausí used to be a major railroad junction, but services are now limited to the Nariz del Diablo and Riobamba run (see p191 for more details). The train leaves Alausí on Wednesday, Friday and Sunday at 9:30am and tickets go on sale at 8am. The fare is $11. The trip takes around two hours to go over the famous Nariz del Diablo (see boxed text 'The Devil's Nose,' p193). Roof riding is allowed, but it's often filled with folks who boarded in Riobamba.

Southern Highlands

Emerging out of the shadows of glaciers and active volcanoes in the north, the passage down the southern spine of the Ecuadorian Andes gives way to gently rolling mountains and valleys. No less impressive as scenery, these tamer peaks, along with rushing, trout-filled rivers and fields of patchwork cultivation, make splendid backdrops to scattered provincial capitals and isolated indigenous villages.

Southern *serranos* (people from the mountains) – from cultured city-slickers in Cuenca and Loja to the independent Saraguro and Cañari peoples – are a diverse group. They each have surviving craft and culinary traditions that have changed little in hundreds of years and unique holidays and festivals that fill the streets with celebration. Catholic processions and indigenous ceremonies – and sometimes fascinating combinations of both – mark the passage of the year as surely as the sowing and harvesting of the fields.

Even more diverse than the cultures of the south are its many varied landscapes. From humid lowland forest to chilly elfin woodland, the region is home to hundreds of bird species, thousands upon thousands of plant species, and scores of mammals. These habitats also provide unsurpassable hiking and horse- and bike-riding experiences that will leave you thinking there are a few unspoiled places left on this earth.

Although they may seem like it in places, the southern highlands are not Eden. A journey down here almost certainly involves exposure to both urban and rural poverty, whole mountainsides scarred by deforestation and mining, and terrible road conditions. These things are no less part of the region's immense and fascinating complexity than its wonderful riches.

HIGHLIGHTS

- Wander the cobblestone streets of colonial **Cuenca** (p199), a Unesco World Heritage Site.
- Keep your eyes peeled for orchids, birds, and rare mammals in the diverse habitats of **Parque Nacional Podocarpus** (p219).
- Perfect the art of relaxation in **Vilcabamba** (p223) with massages, horseback riding and strolls in the clean mountain air.
- Grab your boots for a hike in the eerie moors of **Parque Nacional Cajas** (p211)
- Ponder the engineering mysteries of the Incan ruins at **Ingapirca** (p196).

- AVERAGE TEMPERATURE IN CUENCA: 14°C (57°F)
- RAINIEST MONTHS IN CUENCA: APRIL & MAY

Climate

In Cuenca, and particularly south of Cuenca, altitudes diminish enough that the temperatures, especially around Loja and Vilcabamba, remain spring-like year-round. The rainy season, when it can be colder and wetter (but almost always with several hours of sunshine in the morning), is October to early May.

National Parks

The southern highlands' two national parks – **Parque Nacional Cajas** (p211) near Cuenca and **Parque Nacional Podocarpus** (p219) near Loja – are easily accessible and offer wonderful hiking opportunities. Podocarpus itself has a startling range of terrains within its own borders, so it's worth visiting both of its sectors (highlands and lowlands) for full effect. Part of **Parque Nacional Sangay** falls within this region, but its access points are further north (see p180).

Dangers & Annoyances

Theft of backpacks and other belongings on buses is common, especially on nighttime trips. If it can be avoided, do not carry valuables on day-hikes, especially in areas commonly visited by tourists. Fortunately, violent crime against travelers is rare.

Getting There & Around

Daily direct flights from both Quito and Guayaquil go to Cuenca as well as Loja. Loja is a convenient departure point for Peru, via Macará, Zumba (passing through Vilcabamba), or even Huaquillas to the west. Guayaquil, on the southern coast, is only about 3½ hours by bus from Cuenca.

INGAPIRCA

☎ 07 / elevation 3230m

For the unimpressionable, Ingapirca (Wall of the Inca) is about as much fun as staring at a pile of rocks. For the easily impressed, it might be akin to having lunch with Atahualpa (Inca ruler of Quito) himself. Somewhere in the middle is Ecuador's best-preserved archaeological site, dating from the brief period of Incan dominion over the indigenous Cañari during the 15th century. Although the remains of Ingapirca are limited, they provide a close-up view of the mysterious and uncanny precision of Incan stonemasonry.

And it is, indeed, close-up. Visitors are permitted to walk through, jump on, and snap shots all over the complex, including the Temple of the Sun, a large structure that was probably used for ceremonies and solar observation. Signs point to pits called *colcas* that were used to store food and to *acllahuasi*, which is where the ceremonial, and ultimately sacrificial, virgins lived. The trapezoidal niches are identical to those found in other ruins, such as Machu Picchu in Peru and San Agustín de Callo (p157) near Latacunga. The Inca fitted the stones together so perfectly that no mortar is needed to hold them in place. How the Inca accomplished this feat of transporting and carving the heavy rock still puzzles archaeologists.

The Spanish carted away much of Ingapirca's stone to build nearby cities. What's left of the **site** (admission $6; 8am-6pm) is still important to the indigenous Cañari, whose ancestors worshipped here long before the Inca (and then the Spanish) arrived. The Cañari people now control the administration of the ruins and the **museum** (admission included with Ingapirca) displaying Inca and Cañari artifacts.

Llamas graze the green grasses around the ruins, making for a postcard-worthy sight as visitors approach from the town of Ingapirca, about 1km away. For years, a local blind man has played his pipes at the entrance to the museum in exchange for a coin or two.

Sleeping & Eating

There are toilet facilities and a simple café near the site entrance. Camping is free.

Posada Ingapirca (☎ 221-5116, 282-7401 in Cuenca; Calle Larga 6-93 at Borrero; s/d $42/60) Just above the archaeological site, this converted hacienda offers the only lodgings in Ingapirca, and it's midrange, so tour groups use it a lot. Its cozy rooms would be considered lovely even without amazing views of the ruins.

Getting There & Away

Agencies in Cuenca organize day trips, starting at $37 per person (see p205 for details).

Transportes Cañar buses ($2.50, two hours) go direct from Cuenca, leaving at 9am and 1pm and returning at 1pm and 4pm Monday through Friday; on Saturdays and Sundays they leave at 9am and return at 1pm only.

Buses also leave every half-hour from Cuenca for El Tambo, 8km from Ingapirca. From El Tambo, buses leave about every half-hour to Ingapirca, or a taxi to the ruins will cost $5.

CAÑAR

☎ 07 / pop 16,470 / elevation 3104m

Cañar, a dusty town with gently leaning adobe buildings and wooden balconies, has been the Cañari people's most important crossroads since the 16th century. Sunday is *the* day, when hundreds of Cañari in their colorful woolens gather in town for the **market**.

The men wear *chumbis*, distinctive belts made by a local weaving method and decorated with Catholic and indigenous motifs. These are available in the market, but down at the jail the prisoners make and sell them too (some with distinctive 'prison' motifs). You will be allowed in to make purchases.

Hostal Canãr (☎ 223-5996; cnr 24 de Mayo & Nieto; r per person 4) has shared bathrooms with electricity-heated showers. **Hostal Ingapirca** (☎ 223-5201; Calle Sucre at 5 de Junio; r per person $5) has dark, compact and carpeted rooms for the budget set.

Cañar market stalls and simple restaurants serve *almuerzos* (set lunches, $1.50) and *meriendas* (set dinners, $1.50).

Buses frequently run to here from Cuenca's main bus terminal ($1.50, 1½ hours).

BIBLIÁN

☎ 07 / pop 6480 / elevation 2843m

As the Panamericana bends around the wee village of Biblián, about 26km south of Cañar, you'll notice one thing: the **Santuario de la Virgen del Rocío** (Sanctuary of the Virgin of the Dew), a castle-like church built into the hill over town. Hoof it up there (30 minutes from town) to see how the altar and neo-Gothic arches are carved right into the exposed rock face. There is a huge pilgrimage on September 8 and a lesser one on Good Friday. If you find yourself needing a bed, head 7km south to Azogues, where there are more options.

AZOGUES

☎ 07 / pop 41,300 / elevation 2500m

The capital of Cañar province has a highly visible hillside church, **Iglesia de la Virgen de las Nubes** (Church of the Virgin of the Clouds). This stone and stained-glass structure offers broad views of the countryside. At the lively **Saturday market** at Rivera and Sucre, woven panama hats are sold and sent to Cuenca for finishing.

Hostal Rivera (☎ 224-8113; cnr 24 de Mayo & 10 de Agosto; s/d $18/26) has straightforward carpeted rooms with mod cons. On the north end of town, **Hotel Paraíso** (☎ 224-4729; cnr Váscones & Veintimilla; s/d $21/32) is a glass-and-steel giant (by Azogues standards) with big, clean rooms and a business-hotel feel.

Several inexpensive restaurants around town serve *almuerzos* ($1.50) and *meriendas* ($1.50), and the restaurant at **Hotel Rivera** (cnr Váscones & Veintimilla; mains $4-7; 🕑 7am-10pm) has breakfast and a larger dinner menu.

CAMINO DEL INCA

Though it sees only a fraction of the traffic of the Inca trail to Machu Picchu, the three-day hike to Ingapirca is a popular hike. For approximately 40km, it follows the original Incan royal road (Ingañan) that linked Cuzco with Tomebamba (at present-day Cuenca) and Quito. In its heyday, this transportation and communication network rivaled that of the Roman Empire.

The starting point for the hike is the village of **Achupallas**, 23km southeast of Alausí (see p193). From there, it climbs, passing rivers and lakes and eventually the ruins of an Incan town. The next day takes you past the ruins of an Incan bridge and a large structure at **Paredones**, where some walls are still standing. At times you'll be able to easily make out the Ingañan itself. On the third day the hike lets out at the magnificent ruins at **Ingapirca** (see opposite).

You'll need a GPS and three 1:50,000 topographical maps – *Alausí, Juncal* and *Cañar* – available at the Instituto Geográfico Militar (IGM) in Quito (see p76). Also be prepared for extremely persistent begging from children; most travelers refuse to hand anything out in order to discourage begging for future walkers.

To get to Achupallas, take one of the daily midday buses from Alausí or, more reliably, hire a taxi-pickup for about $10 to $15 one-way. Alternatively, south-bound Panamericana buses from Alausí can drop you at **La Moya** (also known as **Guasuntos**), where you can wait for passing trucks headed to Achupallas, 12km up a slim mountain road. You can hire guides in Achupallas for about $30 per day, or **Tinamu Tours** (see p205) in Cuenca and **Expediciones Julio Verne** (see p189) in Riobamba both run the trip for about $250 per person. If you want to go on your own, check out a hiking guide, such as *Ecuador: Climbing and Hiking Guide* by Rob Rachowiecki and Mark Thurber.

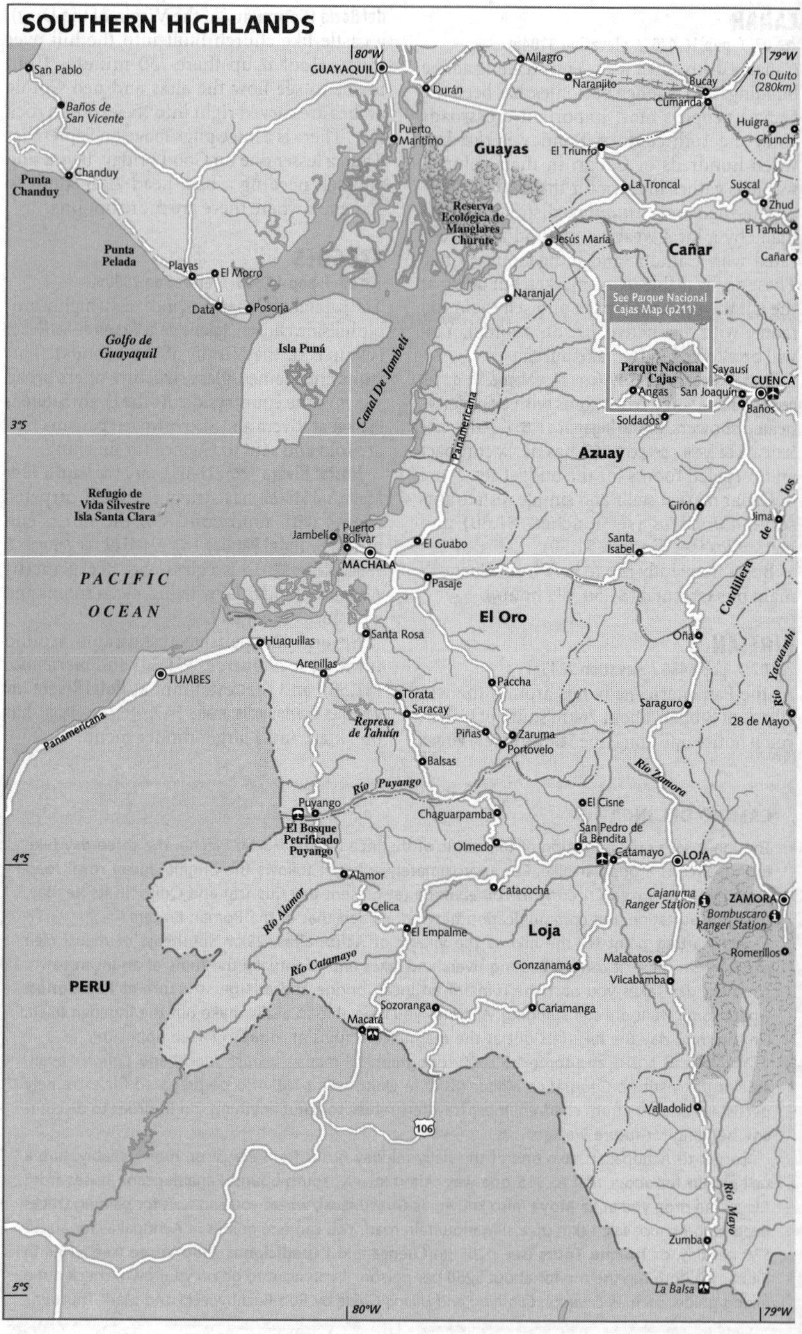
SOUTHERN HIGHLANDS
80°W
79°W
San Pablo
GUAYAQUIL
Milagro
Durán
Naranjito
Bucay
Cumanda
To Quito (280km)
Baños de San Vicente
Puerto Marítimo
Huigra
Chunchi
Guayas
El Triunfo
Punta Chanduy
Chanduy
La Troncal
Suscal
Zhud
Reserva Ecológica de Manglares Churute
El Tambo
Jesús María
Cañar
Punta Pelada
Playas
El Morro
Naranjal
See Parque Nacional Cajas Map (p211)
Data
Posorja
Golfo de Guayaquil
Isla Puná
Canal De Jambelí
Parque Nacional Cajas
Sayausí
CUENCA
Angas
San Joaquín
Baños
Soldados
3°S
Panamericana
Azuay
Refugio de Vida Silvestre Isla Santa Clara
Girón
Jima
Jambelí
Puerto Bolívar
El Guabo
Santa Isabel
MACHALA
Cordillera de los
PACIFIC OCEAN
Pasaje
El Oro
Santa Rosa
Oña
Huaquillas
Arenillas
TUMBES
Paccha
Torata
Saracay
Saraguro
Río Yacuambi
28 de Mayo
Represa de Tahuín
Piñas
Zaruma
Portovelo
Balsas
Río Zamora
Río Puyango
Puyango
El Cisne
Chaguarpamba
El Bosque Petrificado Puyango
San Pedro de la Bendita
Olmedo
4°S
Catamayo
LOJA
Alamor
Catacocha
Cajanuma Ranger Station
ZAMORA
Celica
Bombuscaro Ranger Station
Río Alamor
El Empalme
Loja
Romerillos
Río Catamayo
Gonzanamá
Malacatos
Vilcabamba
PERU
Sozoranga
Cariamanga
Macará
106
Valladolid
Río Mayo
Zumba
5°S
La Balsa

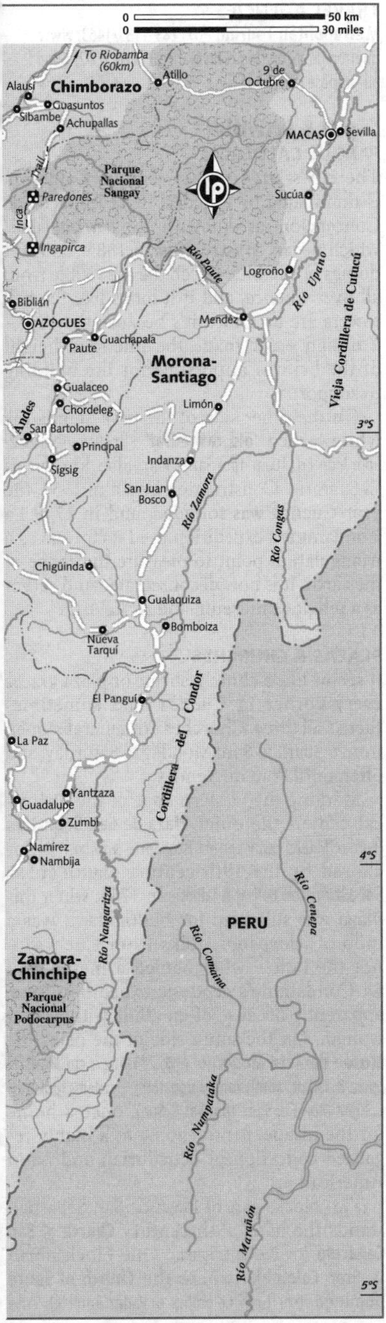

Buses to Cuenca ($1, 45 minutes) leave from the local bus terminal on Rivera, about three blocks south of the main market. There are daily departures to Quito ($8, eight hours) and Guayaquil ($6, four hours).

CUENCA

☎ 07 / pop 417,000 / elevation 2530m

After Quito, Cuenca is Ecuador's most important and beautiful colonial city. But don't tell that to the locals, who insist that their laid-back culture, cleaner streets, and more agreeable weather outclass the capital, hands down.

Dating from the 16th century, Cuenca's historic center, a Unesco World Heritage Site, is a place that time keeps forgetting, where nuns march along cobblestone streets, kids in Catholic-school uniforms skip past historic churches, and old ladies spy on promenading lovers from their geranium-filled balconies.

In addition to its trademark skyline of massive rotundas and soaring steeples, Cuenca is famous for its *barranco* (cliff) along Calle Larga, where the city's 18th- and 19th-century 'hanging houses' seem to hover over the rocky Río Tomebamba. The city is the center of many craft traditions, including ceramics, metalwork and the internationally famous panama hat. Also well known are intricate and vibrant weavings called *ikat* that are displayed in the clothing of Cuenca's *cholas cuencanas* (see the boxed text, p206).

At least three cultures have left their imprint on Cuenca. When the Spanish arrived in the 1540s, they encountered the ruins of a great, but short-lived Incan city called Tomebamba (Valley of the Sun). The Spanish eagerly dismantled what was left of it, incorporating the elegantly carved Incan stones into their own structures. Before the Inca, the indigenous Cañari people had lived in the area for perhaps three thousand years, and they too had a city here, call Quanpondelig (Plain as Big as the Sky). Except for a few limited but interesting sites, the physical remains of these pre-Columbian cultures have been erased.

Information

BOOKSTORES

Libri Mundi (☎ 284-3782; Miguel 8-14; 🕑 10am-8pm Mon-Fri, 10am-6pm Sat & Sun)

Carolina Bookstore (☎ 09-779-4057; cnr Miguel & Calle Larga; 🕑 10am-6pm Mon-Sat)

EMERGENCY
Police station (☎ 281-0068; Luís Cordero near Presidente Córdova)

INTERNET ACCESS
There are more internet cafés than you'll ever need, and new ones open regularly. Most charge $0.80 to $1 per hour and are open from 8am to 9pm daily.
Azuaynet (Padre Aguirre near Lamar)
Cybercom (cnr Presidente Córdova & Borrero)
Cybernet (Benigno Malo near Calle Larga)

INTERNET RESOURCES
www.cuenca.com.ec Cuenca's tourism website.
www.cuencanos.com Loads of Cuenca information, mostly in Spanish.

LAUNDRY
La Química (per kg $0.90; 8am-6:30pm Mon-Fri, 9am-1pm Sat) Borrero (Borrero near Cordero); Gran Colombia (cnr Gran Colombia & Montalvo)
Lavanda (☎ 283-5308; Honorato Vásquez 6-76; per kg $0.70; 8am-1pm & 3-6pm Mon-Fri, 8am-noon Sat)

MEDICAL SERVICES
The following medical clinics have some English-speaking staff. Consultations cost about $20.
Clínica Hospital Monte Sinai (☎ 288-5595; Miguel Cordero 6-111)
Clínica Santa Inés (☎ 281-7888; Daniel Córdova 2-113) Can help with referrals to local doctors.

SOUTHERN HIGHLANDS

MONEY
Banco de Guayaquil (Mariscal Sucre near Borrero) Bank with ATM.
Banco del Pacífico (cnr Gran Colombia & Tarqui) Bank with ATM.
Banco del Pichincha (cnr Solano & 12 de Abril) Bank with ATM; changes traveler's checks.

POST
Post office (cnr Gran Colombia & Borrero)

TELEPHONE
Etapa (Benigno Malo 726; 7am-10pm) Telephone call center.

TOURIST INFORMATION
Bus Terminal Information office (☎ 284-3888) In the bus terminal.
Tourist information (iTur; ☎ 282-1035; Mariscal Sucre at Luís Cordero; 8am-8pm Mon-Fri, 8:30am-1:30pm Sat) Friendly and helpful; English spoken.

TRAVEL AGENCIES
Metropolitan Touring (☎ 283-1185/1463; www.metropolitan-touring.com; Mariscal Sucre 6-62) Good all-purpose travel agency.

Sights & Activities
PARQUE CALDERÓN
The city's largest plaza, Parque Calderón, is dominated by Catedral de la Inmaculada Concepción, also known as the **'new cathedral,'** which began construction in 1885. Its giant domes of sky-blue Czech tile are visible from all over Cuenca, and if it looks like the bell towers are bit short, it's because they are – a design error made the intended height of the belfries impossible for the building to support.

On the other side of the park stands the whitewashed **'old cathedral'** (9am-1pm & 2-6pm Mon-Fri, 10am-1pm Sat & Sun), also known as El Sagrario. Construction began in 1557, the year Cuenca was founded, and in 1739 La Condamine's expedition used its towers as a triangulation point to measure the shape of the earth. It is now deconsecrated and serves as a religious museum and recital hall.

PLAZAS & CHURCHES
It seems like a church, shrine or plaza graces every corner in Cuenca, and sometimes there's all three. Churches are generally open from 6:30am to 5pm Monday to Saturday, and often until 8pm on Sunday.

Marking the western edge of the historical center, the quiet **Plaza de San Sebastián** (Parque Miguel León; cnr Mariscal Sucre & Talbot) is anchored by the 19th-century **Church of San Sebastián** (cnr Bolívar & Talbot). In 1739, when this plaza was still used for bullfights, it was a mob of *cuencanos* (folks from Cuenca) – not the bull – who mauled a member of La Condamine's geodesic expedition here, apparently because of an affair with a local woman. On the south side of the plaza the **Museo de Arte Moderno** (☎ 283-1027; cnr Mariscal Sucre & Talbot; admission by donation; 9am-1pm & 3-6:30pm Mon-Fri, 9am-1pm Sat & Sun), once a home for the insane, is now home to a highly regarded collection of Ecuadorian and Latin American art.

Two blocks east of Plaza de San Sebastián stands the bare, 19th-century **Church of San Cenáculo** (cnr Bolívar & Tarqui). One block north is **Gran Colombia**, where the **Church of Santo Domingo** (cnr Gran Colombia & Padre Aguirre) has

IT'S NOT A PANAMA, IT'S A MONTECRISTI!

For well over a century, Ecuador has endured the world mistakenly crediting another country with its most famous export – the panama hat. To any Ecuadorian worth his or her salt, the panama hat is a *sombrero de paja toquilla* (toquilla-straw hat), and to the connoisseur it's a Montecristi, named after the most famous hat-making town of all. It's certainly not a paaa…

The origin of this misnomer – surely one of the world's greatest – dates to the 1800s, when Spanish entrepreneurs, quick to recognize the unrivaled quality of *paja toquilla,* began exporting them via Panama. During the 19th century, workers on the Panama Canal used these light and extremely durable hats to protect themselves from the tropical sun and helped solidify the association with Panama.

Paja toquilla hats are made from the fibrous fronds of the *toquilla* palm *(Carludovica palmata),* which grows in the arid inland regions of the central Ecuadorian coast, particularly around Montecristi (p300) and Jipijapa (p301). A few Asian and several South American countries have tried to grow the palm to compete with the Ecuadorian hat trade, but none could duplicate the quality of the fronds grown here.

The work that goes into these hats is astonishing. First the palms are harvested for their shoots, which are ready just before they open into leaves. Bundles of shoots are then transported by donkey and truck to coastal villages where the fibers are prepared.

The preparation process begins with beating the shoots on the ground and then splitting them by hand to remove the long, thin, flat, cream-colored leaves. The leaves are tied into bundles and boiled in huge vats of water for about 20 minutes before being hung to dry for three days. Some are soaked in sulfur for bleaching. As the split leaves dry, they shrink and roll up into the round strands that are used for weaving.

Some of the finished straw stays on the coast, but most is purchased by buyers from Cuenca and surrounding areas, where the straw is woven into hats. Indeed, you'll see more panama hats in and around Cuenca than you'll see anywhere in Ecuador.

The weaving process itself is arduous, and the best weavers work only in the evening and early in the morning, before the heat causes their fingers to sweat. Some work only by moonlight. Weaves vary from a loose crochet (characteristic of the hats you see sold everywhere) to a tighter 'Brisa' weave, which is used for most quality panama hats.

Hats are then graded by the density of their weaves, which generally fall into four categories: standard, superior, *fino* (fine) and *superfino* (superfine). Most hats you see are standard or superior. If you hold a real *superfino* up to the light, you shouldn't see a single hole. The best of them will hold water and some are so finely woven and so pliable that they can supposedly be rolled up and pulled through a man's ring!

After the hats are woven, they still need to be trimmed, bleached (if they're to be white), blocked and banded. Then they're ready to sell. Although standard-grade hats start at around $15 in Ecuador, a *superfino* can cost anywhere between $100 and $500. While it may seem expensive, the same hat will easily fetch three times that amount on shelves in North America and Europe. And considering the work that goes into a *superfino,* it rightly should.

some fine carved wooden doors and colonial paintings inside. Although it looks older, the church was built in the early 20th century.

The stark, white **Church of El Carmen de la Asunción** (Padre Aguirre, near Mariscal Sucre), which was founded in 1682, contrasts beautifully with the colorful **flower market** (daily) held on the small Plazoleta del Carmen out front.

Just a few paces south along Padre Aguirre, the 19th-century **Church of San Francisco** features an important gold-leaf altar from the colonial period. It towers handsomely above the not-so-attractive (but still very interesting) **Plaza de San Francisco**, which is flanked by old arcaded buildings with wooden balconies as well as a permanent ramshackle street market.

On the east end of the historical center and occupying what was once known as the 'low neighborhood,' the **Church of San Blas**, on the Parque San Blas, is one of the city's largest and the only one built in the form of a Latin cross.

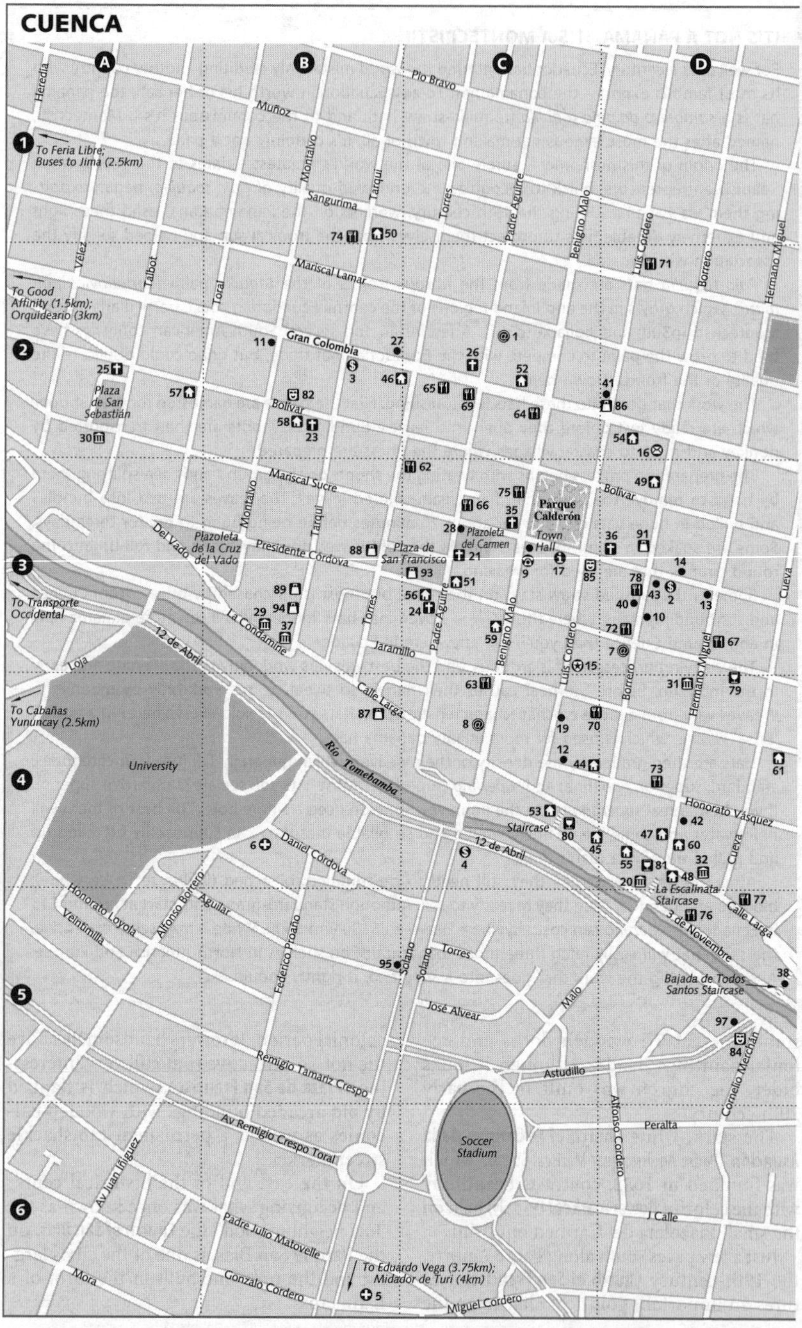
CUENCA
A
B
C
D
1
2
3
4
5
6
To Feria Libre; Buses to Jima (2.5km)
To Good Affinity (1.5km); Orquideario (3km)
To Transporte Occidental
To Cabañas Yununcay (2.5km)
To Eduardo Vega (3.75km); Midador de Turi (4km)
Pío Bravo
Muñoz
Sangurima
Mariscal Lamar
Gran Colombia
Bolívar
Mariscal Sucre
Presidente Córdova
Jaramillo
Calle Larga
La Condamine
Del Vado
12 de Abril
Loja
Río Tomebamba
Daniel Córdova
Honorato Loyola
Veintimilla
Aguilar
Alfonso Borrero
Federico Proaño
Solano
Torres
José Alvear
Malo
Remigio Tamariz Crespo
Av Remigio Crespo Toral
Av Juan Iñiguez
Padre Julio Matovelle
Gonzalo Cordero
Mora
Miguel Cordero
Astudillo
Peralta
J Calle
Alfonso Cordero
Cornelio Merchán
3 de Noviembre
Honorato Vásquez
Cueva
Heredia
Vélez
Talbot
Toral
Montalvo
Tarqui
Padre Aguirre
Benigno Malo
Luis Cordero
Borrero
Hermano Miguel
Plaza de San Sebastián
Plazoleta de la Cruz del Vado
Plaza de San Francisco
Plazoleta del Carmen
Parque Calderón
Town Hall
University
Soccer Stadium
Staircase
La Escalinata Staircase
Bajada de Todos Santos Staircase

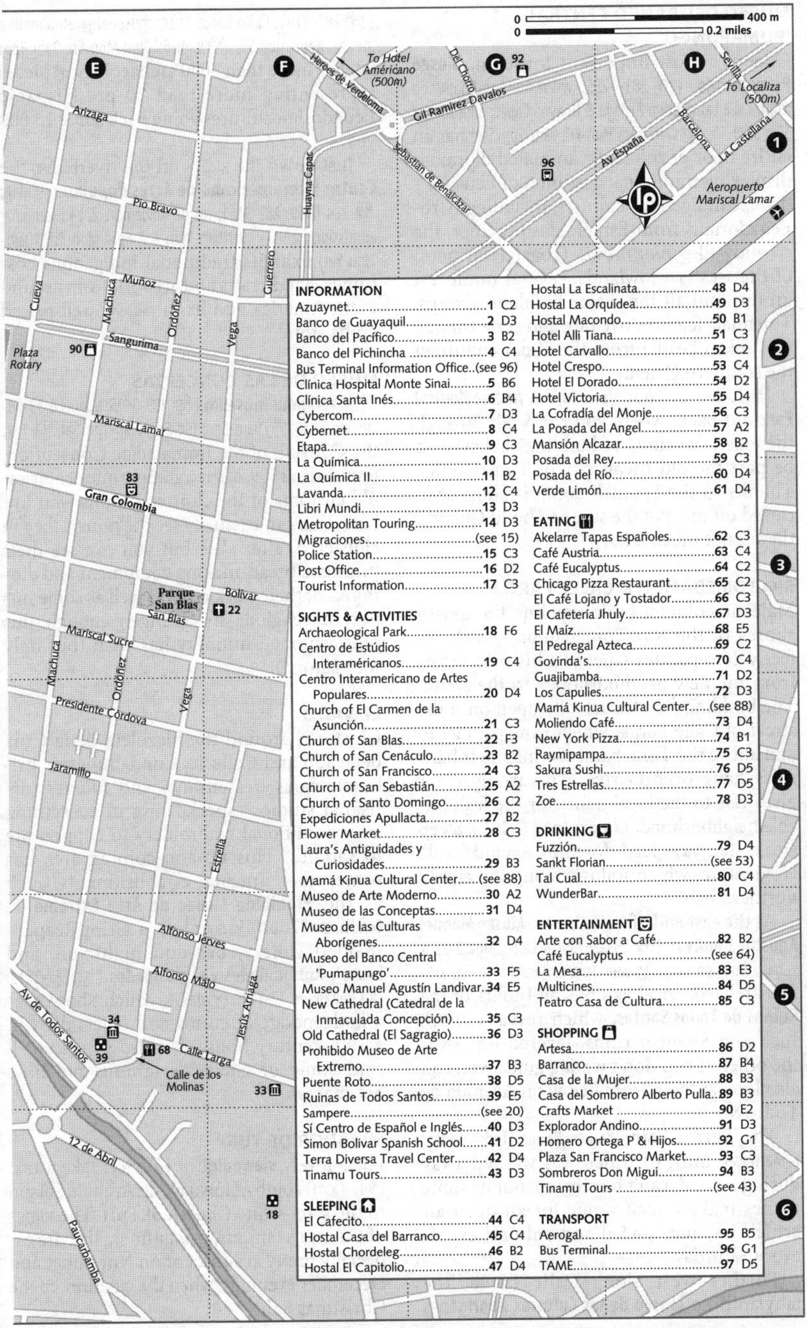

INFORMATION

Azuaynet 1 C2
Banco de Guayaquil 2 D3
Banco del Pacífico 3 B2
Banco del Pichincha 4 C4
Bus Terminal Information Office (see 96)
Clínica Hospital Monte Sinai 5 B6
Clínica Santa Inés 6 B4
Cybercom 7 D3
Cybernet 8 C4
Etapa 9 C3
La Química 10 D3
La Química II 11 B2
Lavanda 12 C4
Libri Mundi 13 D3
Metropolitan Touring 14 D3
Migraciones (see 15)
Police Station 15 C3
Post Office 16 D2
Tourist Information 17 C3

SIGHTS & ACTIVITIES

Archaeological Park 18 F6
Centro de Estúdios Interaméricanos 19 C4
Centro Interamericano de Artes Populares 20 D4
Church of El Carmen de la Asunción 21 C3
Church of San Blas 22 F3
Church of San Cenáculo 23 B2
Church of San Francisco 24 C3
Church of San Sebastián 25 A2
Church of Santo Domingo 26 C2
Expediciones Apullacta 27 B2
Flower Market 28 C3
Laura's Antiguidades y Curiosidades 29 B3
Mamá Kinua Cultural Center (see 88)
Museo de Arte Moderno 30 A2
Museo de las Conceptas 31 D4
Museo de las Culturas Aborígenes 32 D4
Museo del Banco Central 'Pumapungo' 33 F5
Museo Manuel Agustín Landivar 34 E5
New Cathedral (Catedral de la Inmaculada Concepción) 35 C3
Old Cathedral (El Sagragio) 36 D3
Prohibido Museo de Arte Extremo 37 B3
Puente Roto 38 D5
Ruinas de Todos Santos 39 E5
Sampere (see 20)
Sí Centro de Español e Inglés 40 D3
Simon Bolivar Spanish School 41 D2
Terra Diversa Travel Center 42 D4
Tinamu Tours 43 D3

SLEEPING

El Cafecito 44 C4
Hostal Casa del Barranco 45 C4
Hostal Chordeleg 46 B2
Hostal El Capitolio 47 D4
Hostal La Escalinata 48 D4
Hostal La Orquídea 49 D3
Hostal Macondo 50 B1
Hotel Alli Tiana 51 C3
Hotel Carvallo 52 C2
Hotel Crespo 53 C4
Hotel El Dorado 54 D2
Hotel Victoria 55 D4
La Cofradía del Monje 56 C3
La Posada del Angel 57 A2
Mansión Alcazar 58 B2
Posada del Rey 59 C3
Posada del Río 60 D4
Verde Limón 61 D4

EATING

Akelarre Tapas Españoles 62 C3
Café Austria 63 C4
Café Eucalyptus 64 C2
Chicago Pizza Restaurant 65 C2
El Café Lojano y Tostador 66 C3
El Cafetería Jhuly 67 D3
El Maíz 68 E5
El Pedregal Azteca 69 C2
Govinda's 70 C4
Guajibamba 71 D2
Los Capulies 72 D3
Mamá Kinua Cultural Center (see 88)
Moliendo Café 73 D4
New York Pizza 74 B1
Raymipampa 75 C3
Sakura Sushi 76 D5
Tres Estrellas 77 D5
Zoe 78 D3

DRINKING

Fuzzión 79 D4
Sankt Florian (see 53)
Tal Cual 80 C4
WunderBar 81 D4

ENTERTAINMENT

Arte con Sabor a Café 82 B2
Café Eucalyptus (see 64)
La Mesa 83 E3
Multicines 84 D5
Teatro Casa de Cultura 85 C3

SHOPPING

Artesa 86 D2
Barranco 87 B4
Casa de la Mujer 88 B3
Casa del Sombrero Alberto Pulla 89 B3
Crafts Market 90 E2
Explorador Andino 91 D3
Homero Ortega P & Hijos 92 G1
Plaza San Francisco Market 93 C3
Sombreros Don Migui 94 B3
Tinamu Tours (see 43)

TRANSPORT

Aerogal 95 B5
Bus Terminal 96 G1
TAME 97 D5

SOUTHERN HIGHLANDS

MUSEO DEL BANCO CENTRAL 'PUMAPUNGO'

Cuenca's most important museum, **Museo Pumapungo** (☎ 283-1255; www.museopumapungo.com; Calle Larga btwn Arriaga & Huayna Capac; adult/under 12yr $3/1.50; 9am-6pm Mon-Fri, 9am-1pm Sat) has an entire floor of colorfully animated dioramas displaying traditional costumes of Ecuador's diverse indigenous cultures, including Afro-Ecuadorians from Esmeraldas province, the cowboy-like *montubios* (coastal farmers) of the western lowlands, several rainforest groups and all the major highland groups. The finale features five rare and eerie *tzantza* (shrunken heads) from the Shuar culture of the southern Oriente.

Included in your visit is the **Archaeological Park** out back, where you can walk through the extensive ruins of buildings believed to be part the old Incan city of Tomebamba. Thanks to the Spanish conquistadors who carted off most of the stone to build Cuenca, there's not much left.

RÍO TOMEBAMBA & CALLE LARGA

Majestic colonial buildings line the grassy shores of the Río Tomebamba, which effectively separates Cuenca's historic sector from the new neighborhoods to the south. The building facades actually open onto the street of Calle Larga, which runs parallel to and above the Tomebamba, while their back sides 'hang' over the river. This arrangement gives rise to the local name for the fashionable neighborhood, El Barranco ('cliff'). Steep stone stairways lead down to Avenida 3 de Noviembre, which follows along the river's northern bank.

At the east end of Calle Larga, **Museo Manuel Agustín Landivar** (☎ 283-2639; cnr Calle Larga 2-23 & Vega; admission free; 9am-1pm & 3-6pm Mon-Fri) offers archaeological exhibits and tours of the **Ruinas de Todos Santos**, which reveal Cañari, Inca and Spanish ruins, layered one over the other. If you don't want a guide, you can also look at them from below on Avenida de Todos Santos.

The **Puente Roto** (Broken Bridge; Todos Santos & Machuca), most of which was washed away during a flood, can't be crossed, but its stone arches make a nice venue for an open-air **art fair** (10am-5pm Sat) and cultural events every Saturday.

Further west along Calle Larga, the labyrinthine **Museo de las Culturas Aborígenes** (☎ 283-9181; Calle Larga 5-24; museoarq@etapaonline.net.ec; admission $2; 9am-6:30pm Mon-Fri, 9am-1pm Sat) has more than 5000 archaeological pieces representing more than 20 pre-Hispanic Ecuadorian cultures going back some 15,000 years.

Just down the stairs on the riverbank, the **Centro Interamericano de Artes Populares** (Cidap; ☎ 284-0919, 282-9451; cnr de Noviembre & La Escalinata; admission free; 9:30am-1pm & 2-6pm Mon-Fri, 10am-1pm Sat) exhibits traditional indigenous costumes, handicrafts and artwork from around Latin America and has a classy, well-priced crafts store.

MUSEO DE LAS CONCEPTAS

This **religious museum** (☎ 283-0625; Miguel 6-33; admission $2.50; 9am-5pm Tue-Fri, 10am-1pm Sat;) in the Convent of the Immaculate Conception, founded in 1599, offers a glimpse into centuries-old customs of the cloistered nuns who live here. You can't actually see the nuns – they're cloistered, after all – but you can see their primitive bread-making equipment and dioramas of their stark cells, as well as some important religious art. Strangely enough, this old-fashioned nunnery has wi-fi (but only for visitors!).

EL VADO

Clustered around the Plazoleta de la Cruz del Vado and Calle La Condamine are galleries, cafés, restaurants and *talleres* (artisanal studios) specializing in everything from traditional embroidery to copperware to saddles. This up-and-coming area has some other unusual establishments, such as the **Prohibido Museo de Arte Extremo** (La Condamine 12-102; noon-late), a Grim Reaper–themed gallery, bar and nightclub, and **Laura's Antiguidades y Curiosidades** (☎ 282-3312; La Condamine 12-112; daily), which showcases a hodgepodge of curios and objets d'art in a 19th-century house. It's also where you'll find some of Cuenca's famous old-time hat makers.

MIRADOR DE TURI

For a lovely **viewpoint** of Cuenca, take a taxi ($4, 4km) south of town along Avenida Solano to the stark white Church of Turi. The views of Cuenca's famous, romantic skyline are especially pretty at sunset or on November and December evenings, when the city fires up the Christmas lights.

Courses

Most language schools charge $5 to $7 per hour for one-to-one classes.

Centro de Estúdios Interamériscanos (CEIDEI; ☎ 283-4353; www.cedei.org; Luis Cordero 5-66) A nonprofit school offering drop-in and/or long-term courses in Spanish, Quichua and Portuguese.

Sampere (☎ 282-3960; www.sampere.es; Hermano Miguel 3-43) A highly recommended and busy Spanish-owned school.

Sí Centro de Español e Inglés (☎ 282-0429; www.sicentrospanishschool.com; Borrero 7-67) Twenty-hr/one-week ($140) minimum.

Simon Bolivar Spanish School (☎ 283-9959; www.bolivar2.com; Luis Cordero 10-25) Offers homestays and excursions.

Tours

Local operators arrange no-hassle day trips to Ingapirca (p196), Parque Nacional Cajas (p211), nearby villages and markets, and other local attractions. Most operators charge $35 to $40 per person (excluding park entrance fees) and will pick you up at your hotel.

Expediciones Apullacta (☎ 283-7815/7681; www.apullacta.com; Gran Colombia 11-02) A big operation that organizes day tours to Ingapirca, Cajas and the Chordeleg area, among other sites.

Mamá Kinua Cultural Center (☎ 284-0610; Torres 7-45, Casa de la Mujer) A community tourism project offering tours and homestays in nearby indigenous communities ($48 per person per night; two persons minimum). You can participate in all kinds of activities, including folkloric music, cooking, farming, medicinal plant demonstrations, and cheese-making. All revenue goes to a community health network. No English is spoken.

Terra Diversa Travel Center (☎ 282-3782; www.terradiversa.com; Hermano Miguel 5-42) Specializes in biking and horseback-riding day trips (per person $48) as well as overnight horseback riding trips that stay at haciendas or camp along the Inca trail north of Ingapirca (see p196). Also Cajas and Amazon tours. Three-hour Cuenca city tours costs about $15. The center has maps and luggage storage.

Tinamu Tours (☎ 245-0143; www.tinamutours.com; Borrero 7-68) A recommended agency that rents camping gear, conducts tours all over the region, and offers parapenting (tandem hang-gliding) trips ($48).

Festivals & Events

Cuenca's **Independence Day** is November 3, which combines with November 1 and 2 (All Saints' Day and All Souls' Day) to form an important vacation period for the city and the whole country. April 12, the anniversary of Cuenca's founding in 1557, often comes on the heels of Easter celebrations. It's a time when school kids take loyalty pledges to the city, and the Reina de Cuenca (Queen of Cuenca) is selected. *Cuencanos* display their abundant civic pride with elaborate fireworks-laced floats from different neighborhoods.

Carnaval, as in other parts of Ecuador, is celebrated with boisterous water and talcum powder fights in which *no one* is spared.

In keeping with Cuenca's strong Catholic identity, the Pase del Niño **Christmas Eve procession** occupies participants with preparations throughout the whole year and culminates in one of Ecuador's most spectacular religious displays. **Corpus Christi** is usually on the ninth Thursday after Easter, and often coincides with the indigenous celebration called Inti Raymi on the June solstice. Carried out with the same fervor as other big Cuenca holidays, it spills over into a weekend full of processions and fireworks displays. Parque Calderón transforms into a big outdoor candy festival with vendors selling traditional sweets.

Sleeping

Cuenca has a great selection of hotels, many of which are located in old restored houses and mansions. They come in all price categories, but still run a tad higher than elsewhere. During vacation periods they fill up fast and go up in price.

BUDGET

Hostal La Escalinata (☎ 284-5758; Calle Larga 5-83; r per person with shared/private bathroom $5/6) The foam mattresses are a little Jell-O-ish, but the garret rooms have cool sloped ceilings, and the price is ridiculously low for the location.

Hostal El Capitolio (☎ 282-4446; Hermano Miguel 4-19; dm $6, r per person with private bathroom $8) This recommended place is right in the center and has shared and private digs, as well as use of the kitchen.

Posada del Río (☎ 282-3111; Hermano Miguel 4-18; dm $6, r per person with shared/private bathroom $8/10; 💻) Run by the sweet and earnest Torres sisters, this simple and tasteful inn near the river has a rooftop terrace with views (where you can barbecue) and a communal kitchen. Bright colors and woodwork adorn throughout, and the shared bathrooms are squeaky clean.

Verde Limón (☎ 283-1509, 282-0300; Jaramillo 4-89 near Mariano Cueva; dm $7, r per person with shared/private bathroom $7/12) 'Green Lime' refers to the neon walls that make this little hostel almost

CHOLAS CUENCANAS

In many parts of the Spanish-speaking world, *cholo* is a slur. In the United States, it refers to a gangster, and in the Andean nations to an indigenous person parading as a mestizo (of mixed indigenous and Spanish descent) or a white person. In Cuenca and in Azuay, however, the term identifies mestizo farmers and artisans who dress in a traditional, regional costume of dark-red ponchos for men and embroidered blouses and short colorful skirts for women.

The feminine half of this iconic group, the *cholas cuencanas,* are visible all over Cuenca, probably because they have retained their traditional dress more than their male counterparts. *Chola* skirts, called *polleras,* fall just below the knee and have a distinctive embroidered hem that can identify which community a woman comes from. Although fine *polleras* can cost hundreds of dollars, no part of the *chola* wardrobe is prized more than her *paño,* a beautiful fringed shawl made with a complicated pre-Columbian weaving technique called *ikat*. For the people of Cuenca, the *chola* hat, also made of straw and always stiffened with white paint and adorned with a black band, is as familiar as the panama. The whole look is topped off with two long braids and clunky metal earrings called *zarcillas*.

blindingly vibrant. The reception doubles as a bar, and some rooms resemble military barracks, but you can do your own laundry in the machines (per kg $0.50).

Cabañas Yanuncay (☎ 288-3716, 281-9681; Calle Canton Gualaceo 2-149; r per person $15) If you are looking for a place a bit outside of town, this quiet guesthouse on a working farm, 3km southwest of downtown, has two cabins and two rooms in the owner's house. The sauna and Jacuzzi are divine, the whole place is relaxing and quiet, and the organic dinners are nourishing ($7). You can also take advantage of the nice kitchen to whip up your own dishes. English and German spoken.

Hostal Macondo (☎ 284-0697, 283-0836; www.hostalmacondo.com; Tarqui 11-64; s/d incl breakfast with shared bathroom $13.50/20, with private bathroom $19/26) The colonial-style Hostal Macondo has palatial rooms in the front, older section, and small but cozy rooms situated around a big, sunny garden out back. Longer-staying guests will enjoy access to the well-equipped and spotless kitchen, and everyone likes the continental breakfasts with bottomless cups of coffee.

El Cafecito (☎ 283-2337; www.cafecito.net; Honorato Vásquez 7-36; dm $7, d with shared bathroom $15, s/d/t/q with private bathroom $25/25/30/36) This café-bar and *hostal* (small, reasonably priced hotel) is one of the two Canadian-owned El Cafecito's in Ecuador (see p107). It's a longtime favorite of the *mochilero* (backpacker) and local hipster scenes. The dorm rooms right off the café are spacious but close to nightly festivities (maybe too close for some), and the comfortable rooms looking onto the garden each have a touch of local art.

MIDRANGE

Hostal Casa del Barranco (☎ 283-9763; www.casadelbarranco.com; Calle Larga 841; s/d/ste incl breakfast $18/27/56) Some of the most inexpensive river views in town are in this friendly, family-run hostal's four back rooms. The remaining rooms are low on light, but the huge family suite is a great deal.

Hostal La Orquídea (☎ 282-4511, 283 5844; Borrero 9-31; s/d/apt $28/34/109) Only a block from bustling Parque Calderón, the 'Orchid' has immaculate rooms with hardwood floors, cable TV and mini-fridges. The apartment sleeps five.

Hotel Américano (☎ 283-7882; www.hotelamericano.net; cnr Francisco Tamaríz 1-14 & Héroes de Verdeloma; s/d/tr $24/36/48) Readers rave about this quiet, family-run hotel, a 10-minute walk from downtown. They especially like the free bus terminal and airport pickup, views of Cuenca's churches, bright rooms and the owners' down-home friendliness.

La Cofradía del Monje (☎ 283-1251; viniciocobojr@cofradiadelmonje.com; Presidente Córdova 10-33; s/d/ste incl breakfast $22/38/56) In a refurbished century-old home practically on top of the Church of San Francisco, the 'Brotherhood of Monks' B&B has high timbered ceilings and expansive views of the plaza and market below. With the thick wooden shutters closed, the rooms become as serene as a monastery, and kids will love the attic space in the two-floor family suite.

our pick **La Posada del Angel** (☎ 284-0695; www.hostalposadadelangel.com; Bolívar 14-11; s/d incl breakfast $37/52; 💻) This yellow-and-blue B&B in a – you guessed it! – colonial-era house has comfortable rooms with cable TV and big beds.

SOUTHERN HIGHLANDS

Those off the interior balconies have high ceilings, and several others reached by a narrow wooden staircase are tucked away in the quiet reaches. Breakfasts in the sunlit lobby are watched over by the eponymous angel.

Posada del Rey (☎ 283-2063; Gran Colombia 9-52; s/d/ste incl breakfast $30/55/75) In a restored colonial-style house, 10 rooms with hand-painted murals surround a central courtyard full of wood and iron. All the rooms have balconies and cable TV, and the family-size attic suite also has internet.

Hotel Victoria (☎ 282-7401; Calle Larga 6-93; s/d/tr incl breakfast $47/67/84; 💻) One of several grand 17th-century houses on the *barranco* over Río Tomebamba, the Victoria's 23 impeccable hacienda-style rooms are full of wooden touches. Two suites have giant terraces over the river, many rooms have views, and all have wi-fi.

Hotel Carvallo (☎ 283-2063; Gran Colombia 9-52; s/d incl breakfast $53/77, ste $122-146) A cut above the crop of renovated Cuenca houses, the Carvallo's 30 rooms along three stories of interior balconies have such details as down comforters and tin-pressed ceilings. Includes a big breakfast buffet.

Less exciting, but still nice in this price range are **Hostal Chordeleg** (☎ 282-2536; Gran Colombia 11-15; s/d incl breakfast $22/35) and **Hotel Alli Tiana** (☎ 282-1955; cnr Presidente Córdova & Padre Aguirre; s/d $16/26).

TOP END

Hotel Crespo (☎ 284-2571; www.hotelcrespo.com; Calle Larga 7-93; s/d $85/103; 💻) Overlooking Río Tomebamba, Crespo's lobby greets guests with a stunning ceramic mural by Eduardo Vega, one of Cuenca's most important artists (see 'Shopping,' p210). The rest of the hotel is less unusual, but the amenity-filled rooms, great views, and pleasant staff are all top-end.

Hotel El Dorado (☎ 283-1390; www.eldoradohotel.com.ec; Gran Colombia 7-87; s/d incl breakfast $110/122; 💻 🏊) This large hotel serves the business set with bright, minimalist decor, all the usual free gels and liquids, and a fitness center. Rates include a huge buffet breakfast.

Mansión Alcázar (☎ 282-3918; www.mansionalcazar.com; Bolívar 12-55; s/d 120/146; ⊠ 💻) With unsurpassed service and rooms decorated with unique themes, the 'Fortress' is one of Cuenca's best. A water fountain spills over with fresh flowers in the interior courtyard, and the sumptuous garden, library and international restaurant all convey the management's tireless attention to details.

Eating

Cuenca has an impressive number of restaurants aspiring to world-class international food, and plenty more that prepare traditional Ecuadorian food to a high standard. It's a great place to try both.

El Cafetería Jhuly (Hermano Miguel btwn Cordova & Sucre; treats $0.60-0.75; 🕑 8am-7pm Mon-Sat) The wait for a table at Jhuly's is worth it. All the great southern Ecuadorian treats (see the boxed text, p217) are prepared before your eyes at this Cuenca classic. It's deelish for breakfast.

El Café Lojano y Tostador (☎ 287-6724; Sucre 10-20; snacks $1; 🕑 8:30am-7:15pm Mon-Fri, to 6:30pm Sat) Sip southern Ecuador's famous coffee ($1), freshly roasted and ground before your eyes. You can also buy coffee by the pound ($2.60).

Mamá Kinua Cultural Center (Casa de la Mujer; ☎ 284-0610; Torres 7-45; mains $2-3; 🕑 8am-5:30pm Mon-Fri) This cooperative restaurant run by indigenous women has served tasty, traditional *almuerzos* ($2) for many years. It's wholesome, filling and helps out a great cause.

Chicago Pizza Restaurant (☎ 283-9864; Gran Colombia 10-43; mains $2-3; 🕑 9:30am-11pm Mon-Sat, 11am-10pm Sun) Thick-crust slices ($1.10) are the preference here, as well as pastas and sandwiches ($3.75 to $6).

New York Pizza (☎ 284-2792, 282-5674; Gran Colombia 10-43; mains $2-4; 🕑 9:30am-11pm Mon-Sat, 11am-10pm Sun) Pop in here for thin-crust pizza starting at $1.10 a slice.

Good Affinity (☎ 283-2469; cnr Gran Colombia 1-89 & Capulíes; mains $2-4; 🕑 8am-7pm Mon-Sat) This oddly named Taiwanese cafeteria is the king of soy, gluten and all things vegetarian. *Almuerzos* ($2) include a filling soup, entrée, and dessert. Outdoor seating is available.

Govinda's (Jaramillo 7-27; almuerzos $2, mains $2-4; 🕑 8:30am-3pm Mon-Sat) Pizzas, lentil burgers and a little good karma to wash it down.

Moliendo Café (☎ 282-8710; Honorato Vásquez 6-24; light meals $2-4; 🕑 9am-9pm Mon-Sat) From Ecuador's neighbors to the north, the hearty *arepas* (maize pancake) are a specialty here. Topped with anything from beans and cheese to slow-cooked pork, they go well with cold beer or a strong Juan Valdez. Whether you get a little or a lot, it's essentially old-fashioned comfort food, Colombian-style.

Akelarre Tapas Españoles (☎ 282-3636; General Torres 8-40; tapas & mains $2-8; 🕑 11am-10pm Mon-Fri, 11am-2pm & 6pm-10pm Sat & Sun) Akelarre serves petite plates of Spanish classics like 'Brave Potatoes' (spicy fried spuds) and Gallecian Squid nightly, and big plates of paella on Sundays.

our pick **Café Eucalyptus** (☎ 284-9157; www.caféeucalyptus.com; Gran Colombia 9-41; small plates $3-6; 🕑 5-11pm Mon-Tue, 5pm-midnight Wed-Thu, 5pm-1am Fri, 7pm-4am Sat) The irreverent Eucalyptus menu proudly declares that it doesn't serve 'customs officials, crazy bus drivers, or airline executives.' For the rest of us, dozens of Cuban, Vietnamese, Spanish and other reliably delicious international dishes are served at cozy tables near roaring fireplaces, and an extensive variety of wines and beers flow from the gorgeous bar. This wonderful restaurant should cure any gringo's hankering for home, and, thankfully, it still serves guidebook writers.

Los Capulies (☎ 284-5887; cnr Presidente Córdova & Borrero; mains $3.50-5.50; 🕑 9am-4pm & 6pm-late Mon-Sat) Los Capulies serves delicious, reasonably priced, traditional Ecuadorian meals and livens things up with entertainment on weekends. The cantina out back provides after-dinner fun.

Café Austria (☎ 284 -0899; Benigno Malo 5-95; mains $3-7; 🕑 9am-11pm) Every caffeinated drink known to humankind, dainty Austrian cakes, pressed sandwiches and goulash make for a great menu at this Austrian-owned café. English-language newspapers are always available.

Tres Estrellas (☎ 282-2340/6968; Calle Larga 1-174; most mains $4-5; 🕑 11:30am-3pm & 5:30pm-1am Tue-Sat) Long in the business, Tres Estrellas roasts up gourmet *cuy* (roast guinea pig, $17, serves two). If you're not up for that squeaky delicacy, there's outstanding grilled beef, chicken and pork on the menu too.

Guajibamba (☎ 283-1016, 09-845-8015; Luis Cordero 12-32; mains $4-6; 🕑 noon-3pm & 6-11pm Mon-Sat) This atmospheric restaurant has a small menu of traditional plates like *seco de chivo* (goat stew) and gourmet *fritada* (fried pork with hominy, avocado and other garnishes). It's also one of the best places to try *cuy;* if you're game, call an hour before you go for prep time ($17 for two).

El Maíz (☎ 284-0224; Calle Larga 1-279 y Calle de los Molinos; mains $4-7; 🕑 5-11pm Mon & Tue) Billing itself as purveyor of the 'new Ecuadorian cuisine,' El Maíz takes traditional ingredients like quinoa and *chochos* (marinated lupine beans) and turns them into modern and delicious fusion dishes. This restaurant feels more upmarket than its prices suggest.

Raymipampa (☎ 283-4159; Benigno Malo 8-59; mains $4-7; 🕑 8:30am-11:30pm Mon-Sat) This Cuenca institution is popular with locals and travelers and stays open late. The food hangs somewhere between Ecuadorian comfort food and diner fare.

El Pedregal Azteca (☎ 282-3652; Gran Colombia 10-29; mains $5-9; 🕑 noon-3pm & 6-10:30pm Mon-Sat, to 11:30pm Fri & Sat) El Pedregal serves delicious Mexican food, including lots of vegetarian options, in an atmosphere that's all ponchos, sombreros and *olé!* The portions can be a bit small, however, so fill up on the free homemade chips.

Sakura Sushi (☎ 282-7740; cnr Paseo 3 de Noviembre 2451 & Escalinata; rolls & mains $6-9; 🕑 noon-midnight) Cuenca's best sushi is fresh – the coast is only three hours away – and pretty authentic. The $3.50 lunch special includes soup, fish or chicken, teriyaki, rice, and a glass of wine.

Zoe (☎ 284-1005; cnr Borrero 7-61 & Sucre; mains $6-10; 🕑 5-11pm) This new, stylish restaurant, bar and gallery has laid modish decor over a colonial-style house. The food is also a hybrid, cooking up traditional meat and seafood dishes with some newer, imported techniques. For all this hipness, the service is pleasantly down to earth.

Drinking & Entertainment

BARS & NIGHTCLUBS

Cuenca has a lot of nightlife offerings, from intimate taverns to smart cafés featuring live music to Hollywood-style clubs catering to the hook-up scene. Discos are open Thursday through Saturday nights from 10pm, but things don't really get moving until around midnight. Bars are generally open nightly, often as early as 5pm.

There are numerous cozy and welcoming little bars along Honorato Vásquez, near El Cafecito. East of Hermano Miguel along Presidente Córdova, there are several wildly popular (and equally loud) bars with dance floors.

Sankt Florian (☎ 283-1274; www.sanktflorian.wordpress.com; Calle Larga 7-119) This classy café and bar in a historic Calle Larga house has billiards, live music, and a Happy Hour from 8pm to 10pm Wednesday to Saturday.

Fuzzión (Presidente Córdova near Cueva, drink minimum $2) Of the bars located along Presidente Córdova, this is the trendiest. It's nonstop dancing from about midnight to dawn Thursday to Saturday.

Tal Cual (☎ 285-0207; Calle Larga 7-57; ⌚ 5:30pm-midnight Tue-Thu, 5:30pm-late Fri & Sat) Tucked into a narrow stairway, this bar attracts a friendly local crowd, especially Thursdays through Saturdays when there's live music. Friday and Saturday it's salsa and merengue, and the chairs are cleared for dancing.

WunderBar (☎ 283-3359; Escalinata 3-43; ⌚ 11am-1am Mon-Fri, 3pm-1am Sat) This Austrian-owned place is *voon*derful if you want a classic bar with big wooden tables to sit around with friends. Food is served, and there's a Happy 'Hour' from 11am to 6pm.

Arte con Sabor a Café (☎ 282-9426; www.arteconsaboracafe.com; cnr Bolivar 12-60 & Montalvo; ⌚ 4pm-2am Mon-Sat) Cuban-owned and host to local, national and international acts of all kinds, this small café and bar has a $4 cover charge, small plates ($3 to $5) and great Cuba Libres, of course! Music starts at 10pm.

Café Eucalyptus (☎ 284-9157; www.caféeucalyptus.com; Gran Colombia 9-41; ⌚ 5-11pm Mon & Tue, 5pm-midnight Wed & Thu, 5pm-1am Fri, 7pm-4am Sat) A bar on each of the two floors serves drinks to lively salsa and Cuban rhythms most evenings, and for ladies, drinks are free (no kidding) on Wednesdays from 6pm to 10pm.

La Mesa (Gran Colombia 3-55) This is where the locals go when they want to salsa, and boy, can they salsa. It's fun to watch as much as dance. The tiny sign out front is easy to miss.

CINEMAS

Movies cost about $4 per person and are listed in Cuenca's newspaper *El Mercurio*. **Teatro Casa de Cultura** (Luís Cordero at Mariscal Sucre) screens recent movies. Get your stadium seats, buckets of popcorn and blockbuster Hollywood flicks in English (with Spanish subtitles) at **Multicines** (Milenium Plaza, Astudillo).

Shopping

Cuenca is the center of the *paja toquilla* (or 'panama') hat trade (see the boxed text, p201). Typical *cuencano* nested baskets, gold- and silver-filigreed jewelry from the nearby village of Chordeleg, and ceramics of varying quality are typical finds.

HATS

Cuenca produces panama and other kinds of straw hats, mostly for export, as well as the distinctive hats worn by local indigenous women known as *cholas cuencanas* (see the boxed text, p206). Nowadays Cuenca's traditional hatters on Tarqui focus on refurbishing the latter, and in their shops, you can see hundreds of them, tagged for their owners and waiting to be picked up. They usually have a few top-quality hats for sale, too. The larger shops have much bigger selections of panamas.

Casa del Sombrero Alberto Pulla (☎ 282-9399; Tarqui 6-91; ⌚ 6am-6pm) The hats of Cuenca's most famous hatter, the charming 81-year-old Alberto Pulla, have graced the noggins of presidents, celebrities and hundreds of local indigenous women. In the early days he worked with chemicals that damaged his throat and has since lost his voice, but he still welcomes visitors into his shop with a smile.

Sombreros Don Migui (Tarqui near Calle Larga) Another hatter that works more with the local market, this old place sells panamas from $15, including durable *dobles,* which are double woven.

Barranco (☎ 283-1569; Calle Larga 10-41; ⌚ 9am-6pm Mon-Fri, 9:30am-5pm Sat, 9:30am-1:30pm Sun) This old hat factory has an interesting museum where you can see how panamas were made over the years and witness them being made in the present. Upstairs there's a nice café and a cheesy exhibit where you can dress up as a *chola cuencana* – hat, skirt and all. Plenty of hats are for sale, and you can even custom order a panama (especially important if you have a big head).

Homero Ortega P & Hijos (☎ 280-9000; www.homeroortega.com; Gil Ramirez Davalos 386) More akin to a hat emporium, this is Ecuador's best-known hat seller. The company exports around the world and has a huge selection of high-quality men's and women's straw hats.

SANTA SOPA

During Semana Santa, the 'Holy Week' before Easter, signs go up all over Cuenca advertising *fanesca,* a codfish soup that accommodates the prohibition on red meat during the holiday. The base is made of pumpkin, and a dozen kinds of beans and grains representing the 12 apostles of Jesus are thrown in. Garnishes include hard-boiled eggs, fried plantains, and mini-empanadas. It's so rich and delicious you won't be hungry until the following Easter.

CRAFTS

Both the **crafts market** (cnr Sangurima & Machuca; 8am-5pm) near Plaza Rotary and the **Plaza de San Francisco Market** (cnr Padre Aguirre & Córdova; 8am-5pm) have an interesting combination of basketry, ceramics, ironwork, wooden utensils, plastic trinkets, gaudy religious paraphernalia and guinea pig roasters (great gift for mom, but tough to get home). The San Francisco market also has a large contingent of *otavaleños* (people from Otavalo) selling sweaters and weavings on its north side. On the west side of the plaza is the **Casa de la Mujer** (☎ 284-5854; Torres 7-33; 9am-6:30 Mon-Fri, 9am-5pm Sat, 9am-1pm Sun), which houses over 100 craft stalls selling handmade musical instruments, embroidered clothing, baskets, jewelry and more.

Just below the Mirador de Turi is the home, workshop and studio of **Eduardo Vega** (☎ 288-1407; www.eduardovega.com; Via a Turi 201; 9am-6pm Mon-Fri, 10am-1:30pm Sat), Ecuador's most important ceramic artist. His colorful terracotta and enamel murals grace walls all over Cuenca and the rest of Ecuador. Sculpture, vases and plates are for sale, and the affable artist is often hanging around and ready to chat.

Artesa (☎ 284-2647; www.artesa.com.ec; cnr Gran Colombia & Cordero; 8:30am-12:30pm & 2:30-5pm Mon-Sat) is a big Ecuadorian ceramics company that incorporates old Andean ceramic styles into high-quality, hand-painted pieces. If you just can't live without a dinner service, they will happily ship it home for you. Tours of the factory may be available, especially if you are with a group.

OUTDOOR EQUIPMENT

Explorador Andino (☎ 284-7320; Borrero 7-39; 9am-1pm & 2:30-7pm Mon-Fri, 9:30am-3pm Sat) Sells camping, fishing and mountaineering gear, and more.

Tinamu Tours (☎ 245-0143; www.tinamutours.com; Borrero 7-68 & Sucre) Rents most camping gear.

Getting There & Away

AIR

Cuenca's **Aeropuerto Mariscal Lamar** (☎ 286-2203; Av España) is located 2km from the heart of town and five minutes from the Terminal Terrestre bus station.

TAME (www.tame.com.ec); airport (☎ 286-2400); downtown (☎ 288-9097/9581; Astudillo 2-22; 8:30am-1pm & 2-6:30pm Mon-Fri, 9:30am-12:30pm Sat) flies daily to Quito ($79) and Guayaquil ($64). **Aerogal** (☎ 281-5250; www.aerogal.com.ec; Aguilar y Solano; 8:30am-1pm & 2-6:30pm Mon-Fri, 9:30am-12:30pm Sat) also flies daily to Quito ($66) and Guayaquil ($59).

BUS

Cuenca has two major bus stations. Some buses, including those to Parque Nacional Cajas (see p212), Jima (p213) and Girón (p213), leave from **Terminal Sur**, across from the Feria Libre, west of the center. To get there, take a cab ($2) or bus signed 'Feria Libre' from either Presidente Córdova or Mariscal Lamar.

The vast majority of buses (hundreds per day) leave from Cuenca's **Terminal Terrestre** (☎ 284-3888/2023; Av España), the main bus station about 1.5km from downtown.

Buses go daily from this station to Ingapirca (p196) and Gualaceo, Chordeleg and Sígsig (p212).

Two routes go to Guayaquil: the shorter via Parque Nacional Cajas and Molleturo ($8, four hours), and the longer via La Troncal and Cañar ($8, five hours). Buses leave hourly for Machala ($4.50, four hours); a few continue to Huaquillas ($8, seven hours).

Buses for Azogues ($0.60, 45 minutes) leave every 15 minutes, many continuing to Cañar ($1.50, 1½ hours).

Quito-bound buses go every hour ($10, 10 to 12 hours), and several buses depart daily to Riobamba ($6, six hours), Ambato ($7, seven hours) and Latacunga ($9, 8½ hours). All pass through Alausí ($4, four hours).

Buses leave every hour from 6am to 10pm to Loja ($7.50, five hours) via Saraguro ($5, three hours).

For the southern Oriente, daily buses go to Macas via Guarumales ($8.50, eight hours) or via Limón ($8.50, nine hours). Two daily buses (at 11am and 2pm) ride the rough and scenic road to Gualaquiza ($7, eight hours) via Sígsig.

CAR

The national chain **Localiza** (airport ☎ 280-3198/3193; España ☎ 286 3902, 286 0174; www.localiza.com; España 1485 near Granada) rents economy cars and 4WDs at the airport and another location 400m northeast of the airport.

Getting Around

In front of the bus terminal, buses depart regularly to downtown ($0.25). From downtown to the terminal, take any bus marked 'Terminal' from stops on Padre Aguirre near the flower market. Taxis cost about $2 between downtown and the airport or the bus terminal.

Local buses for Turi ($0.25), 4km south of the center, go along Avenida Solano.

AROUND CUENCA

☎ 07

Cuenca is an easy base for day trips to indigenous villages in the surrounding area. Some of those listed here are invested in community-based tourism, so you can support local people by hiring local guides and buying traditional crafts. Gualaceo, Chordeleg and Sígsig can all be done together in one day, while Principal, Cajas and the ruins at Ingapirca (p196) are really separate day trips of their own.

Parque Nacional Cajas

Only 30km west of Cuenca, **Parque Nacional Cajas** (admission $10) encompasses 2854 sq km of golden moor-like *páramo* dotted with hundreds of chilly lakes that shine like jewels against a bleak, rough countryside.

This extremely wet and foggy area feeds rivers that flow into Cuenca (and for that reason the park is run by the city's water authority) and is considered an important conservation area for birds, mammals and flora.

Especially important are small forests of *Polylepis* trees that are found in sheltered hollows and natural depressions. *Polylepis* grow at the highest altitudes of any trees in the world, and wandering into one of these dense dwarf forests is like entering a Brothers Grimm fairytale.

The park is called Cajas, according to some folks, because the lakes look (rather dubiously) like *cajas* ('boxes'). More likely, the name comes from *caxas,* the Quichua word for cold.

And cold it is…so cold that getting lost, which is easy, is a rather dangerous proposition. Night temperatures can drop below freezing, especially in the dry season. The driest months are August to January, but it can rain anytime.

INFORMATION

Three main recreational areas, all at scenic lakes, lie along the Cuenca–Molleturo road: **Laguna Llaviucu**, which is closest to Cuenca and

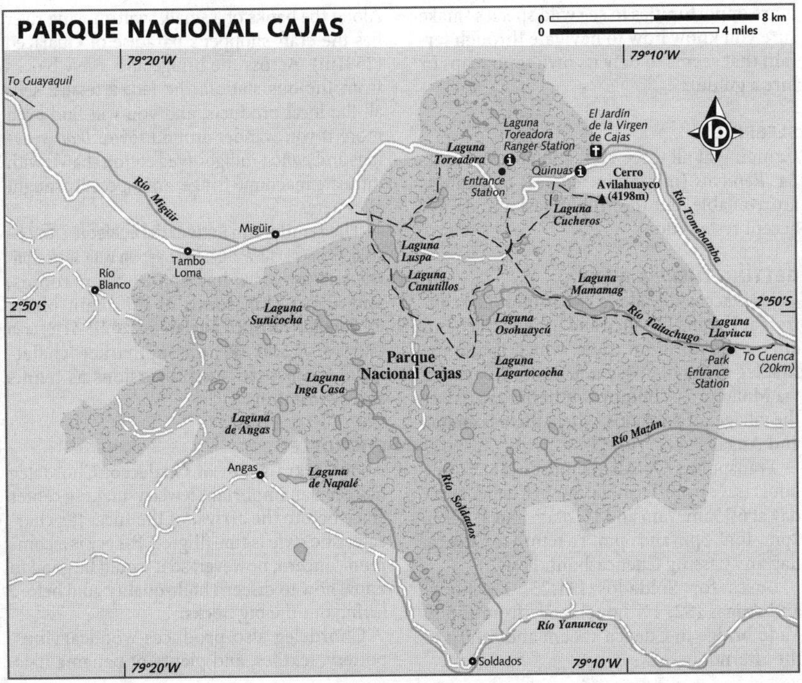

SOUTHERN HIGHLANDS

has a **control** where you can pay admission; **Laguna Cucheros**; and **Laguna Toreadora**, which has an information center. A second **control** appears at Quinuas, 3km before Cucheros. The controls provides free glossy topographical trail maps, which are also available at the tourist information office (p200) in Cuenca.

Outside the designated areas around Llaviacu, Cucheros and Toreadora, groups of eight or more are required to be accompanied by a guide, and *all* hikers outside these areas must register with the ranger stations (they must also carry a GPS or compass). Currently no overnight hiking trips may be conducted without an approved guide from Cuenca or the park itself. Most of the operators listed under 'Tours', p205, can arrange a guide.

ACTIVITIES

The park has some rock-climbing spots, but for real thrill seekers there's bird-watching, llama-viewing, and even fishing! All of the recreation areas offer these activities and signed **hikes** of up to a few hours. Several multiday **hikes** across the park pass through sublime deserted landscapes and present more opportunities to see wild species (make sure you know how to navigate through terrain that seems to defy its own topo maps or hire a guide).

SLEEPING

Camping at all three recreational areas costs $4. *Refugios* (mountain refuges) and cabins are available, but they fill up fast and do not accept reservations.

GETTING THERE & AWAY

Cajas is accessible along two routes. The controls at Laguna Llaviucu and Laguna Cucheros are on the northern route, which is also the first leg of the highway journey to Guayaquil via Molleturo. A bumpy southern road passes the villages of Soldados, where there is **control**, and Angas.

Transportes Occidental buses ($1.25, one hour) leave from Terminal Sur in Cuenca every day at 6:15am, 7am and 10:20am and at noon, 2pm, 4pm, 5pm and 6pm. To return to Cuenca, flag any passing Cuenca-bound bus.

Buses for Soldados ($1.25, 1¼ hour) and Angas ($2, 1¾ hour) leave from the El Vado bridge in Cuenca at 6am and return in the afternoon.

Apart from the bus, you can take a taxi (about $60 for the day) or go on a day trip with one of the tour agencies in Cuenca.

Gualaceo, Chordeleg & Sígsig

If you start out early, you could easily visit the Sunday markets at all three of these towns and be back in Cuenca for happy hour. Between them all you'll find many traditional handicrafts – woven baskets, fine filigree gold and silver jewelry, woodworking, pottery, guitars and *ikat* textiles, which are made using a pre-Columbian technique of weaving tie-dyed threads.

GETTING THERE & AWAY

From Cuenca's bus terminal, bus services leave every half-hour to Gualaceo ($0.80, one hour), Chordeleg ($1, one hour) and Sígsig ($1.25, 1½ hours). You can take a bus from Gualaceo the approximate 10km to Chordeleg. Buses pass Chordeleg's plaza for Sígsig ($0.50) every half-hour. Buses return from Sígsig to Cuenca about every hour for $1.

GUALACEO

Along the banks of a small, swift-moving river lies the craft shopper's paradise of Gualaceo (2591m). Across the bridge and a few blocks from the bus station, the **feria artesanal** sells all the local products, and you will find even more if you wander around town. *Ikat* weavings and *paños,* indigo-dyed cotton shawls with intricate macramé fringe, are especially sought after here.

The family-run **Residencial Gualaceo** (☎ 225-5006; Gran Colombia 3-02; r per person with shared/private bathroom $6/10) has spare, clean rooms, and about 1km south of the main plaza, the **Parador Turístico Gualaceo** (☎ 225-5110; Gran Colombia; s/d $30/; 🅿) has upmarket 'chalet-style' rooms and such diversions as tennis and swimming.

CHORDELEG

About 10km south of Gualaceo, Chordeleg has been an important jewelry-making center since before the arrival of the Inca. It's characteristic style is fine filigree. Fakery is a common concern, however, so it would be good to know how to discern high-quality gold before laying out the big bucks.

Chordeleg also produces woodcarvings, pottery, textiles, and plenty of panama hats.

SOUTHERN HIGHLANDS

On the central plaza, a small **museum** (admission free; 8am-5pm Tue-Sun) details the history and techniques of many of these handicrafts and sells some locally made work.

SÍGSIG

About 26km south of Gualaceo lies Sígsig (2684m), a charming vestige of a colonial-era indigenous town, best known for its panama hats. On the outskirts of the village, in the old hospital, a women's hat-making cooperative called the **Asociación de Toquilleras Maria Auxiliadora** (ATMA; 226-6014/6377; Vía Sígsig-Chigüinda, Río Santa Barbara; 8:30am-4:30pm Mon-Fri) sells hats far more cheaply than in Cuenca or Quito.

There are a couple of restaurants and *residenciales* (cheap hotels) near the main market plaza.

Principal

Just another half-hour beyond Sígsig, the small community of Principal (2791m) rests humbly in the shadow of **Volcán Fasayñan** (3907m), a huge pillar of rock where local legend says that the Cañari people originated.

To promote sustainability in the community, Principal has a small association of certified guides who can lead hikes ($10 per person) up Fasayñan, to the **Infiernillo** (little hell) waterfall, and the **Three Lakes**, which dot the *páramo* with crystal waters. All destinations are within three to five hours hiking, and *cabalgatas* (horseback-riding trips) to them are possible. Inquire about these activities and the local weaving cooperative that makes panama hats at **Hostal Anabel** (09-981-5821; r per person $6), which is a modern guesthouse with shared bathrooms and hot water; **Restaurante Huallo Kindi** has meals with vegetarian options.

Buses to Principal ($0.50, 30 minutes) leave every 40 minutes from 6:30am to 6:30pm, four blocks from the main square in Chordeleg.

Jima

Just above the Río Moya, where apple trees blossom for half the year, the happy agricultural village of Jima (spelled Gima on some maps; 2630m) enjoys a peaceful pace of life that goes about as fast the cows down the main street.

The townspeople run a sustainable tourism project, based principally on access to excellent hiking and to Tambillo cloud forest, a community-protected reserve. One component is the **Centro de Informes** (Information Center; 241-8270), where you can get trail information or hire local guides (about $10/20 for two people for a half/full day) for hikes ranging from shorter orchid-spotting jaunts to three-day tramps into the Oriente. Horseback riding can be arranged, and they can tell you how to reach a legendary 100-year-old adobe church nearby.

Also part of the project, **Hostal Chacapamba** (241-8035; r per person $4.50) offers simple but spotless lodgings in private rooms with comfortable beds.

Transportes Jima buses ($1, 1½ hours) leave from the Terminal Sur in Cuenca (see p210) daily at 6am, 8:30am and 11am (7am, 8am and 8:30am on Sundays).

Girón

Some 43km southwest of Cuenca along the road to Machala on the coast, the small town of Girón (2759m) comes into view. The walk to its famous 60-meter **Chorro de Girón** waterfall, lined with mosses and bromeliads, makes a beautiful day-hike. Actually three waterfalls are located in the area, but you'll need to hire a guide, which can be done at the first, to navigate to the second and third. Many operators in Cuenca visit the falls as a $35 day trip, although you can get there yourself on Transportes Girón buses ($1, one hour), which leave from Terminal Sur in Cuenca (see p210). In Girón hire a pickup truck ($5) to take you 5km to the entrance to the falls; to walk the 5km takes about two hours.

SARAGURO

07 / pop 4007 / elevation 2520m

Surrounded by golden-green hills that have been sown with hearty tubers and grains for perhaps thousands of years, Saraguro, 165km south of Cuenca, is the center of indigenous Saraguro culture. This prosperous and proud indigenous group originally lived near Lake Titicaca in Peru but ended up here in the 1470s due to the Inca empire's system of resettlement, or *mitimaes*.

During the last century, Saraguros have relocated (this time, of their own accord) to significantly lower altitudes to the southwest and often alongside Shuar communities in the Ecuadorian Amazon. In both the chilly mountains and humid lowlands, the Saraguro dress in traditional woolens. Women wear broad-brimmed white hats, long pleated skirts, ornate pins called *tupus* and elaborate beaded collars called *chakiras*. Men wear fedora-like hats, black ponchos and knee-length black shorts, and they may also don small white aprons and woven, double-pouch shoulder bags called *alfajoras*.

All the elements of Saraguro attire are important craft traditions maintained in nearby communities, which are fun to visit. The **Sunday market** draws Saraguros – dressed finely for the occasion – from the surrounding countryside.

An ATM and a call center are on the main square.

Sights & Activities

The villages around Saraguro, most within a half-hour walk or 10-minute bus ride ($0.20) are full of outdoor and cultural activities. **Baños del Inka**, just north on the Panamericana, has impressive waterfalls and large rock formations. The **Bosque Protegido Washapamba**, a protected forest just south of town, is great for hiking. In **Lagunas** Saraguro women make *tupus* and textiles, and the community of **Tuncarta** produces Saraguro hats.

Buses to any of these places leave from the main square in front of the cathedral. Information and trail maps are available at **iTur**, also on the main plaza.

Operadores de Turismo Saraurku (www.turismosaraguro.com) on the main plaza arranges tours to these sites and Saraguro communities in the Amazon for $40 to $60 per person per day. Horseback-riding and mountain-bike trips are available, and they can also set you up with a homestay in one of Saraguro's extensive community-based tourism projects.

Sleeping & Eating

Residencial Saraguro (☎ 220-0286; cnr Loja & Antonio Castro; r per person $5) This small establishment near the center of town is popular with travelers. Rooms and bathrooms are bare-bones, but the quiet garden and friendly owners add a touch of charm.

Hostal Samana Wasi (☎ 220-0315; www.turismosaraguro.com; cnr 10 de Marzo & Panamericana; r per person $10) Four blocks from the main plaza, this family-owned *hostal* has wood floors, cable, and a convenient internet café.

our pick **Hostal Achik Wasi** (☎ 220-0331; Calle Intiñan in Barrio La Luz; r per person $12) A 10-minute walk up and out of town (taxi $1), this large adobe and wood hostal has comfortable rooms with soft, wool blankets, tall ceilings, and great views. It's part of a well-run tourism project that benefits the community.

Mamá Cuchara (Parque Central; mains $1.50-2.50; 🕑 7am-10pm Sun-Fri) 'Mother Spoon,' as the name aptly means, serves up hearty, tasty meals right on the main plaza. Money goes to the indigenous women's association that runs it.

The **central market** west of the Plaza Mayor has stalls selling traditional Ecuadorian dishes for $1 to $2.

Getting There & Away

Any Loja-bound bus from Cuenca will drop you a block from the main plaza ($5, 3½ hours). Buses to Loja ($2, 1½ hours, 62km) leave hourly during the day. The bus office is a block from the main plaza.

LOJA

☎ 07 / pop 152,0018 / elevation 2100m

The provincial capital of Loja makes a convenient base for visiting Parque Nacional Podocarpus, Vilcabamba and the southern Oriente, but it is also a special place in its own right and one that many Ecuadorians admire for its dignified culture and romantic air. Despite being somewhat isolated in the far south of Ecuador, it boasts an important conservatory and a nationally renowned university that attracts many international students. It is a music-loving town with a proud history of local virtuosos, and one of the first municipalities in Ecuador to have a citywide recycling program, making it exceptionally clean and green. *Lojanos* (people from Loja) are also big foodies, well known throughout Ecuador for their succulent *cuy* (guinea pig), aromatic coffee and light café fare (see p217).

Information

EMERGENCY

Police Station (☎ 257-5606; Valdivieso btwn Imbabura & Quito)

INTERNET ACCESS

Cyberclub (cnr Sucre & Azuay; per hr $1; 🕑 7:30am-8pm)
Cyberpower (☎ 257-5212; cnr Riofrío & Sucre; per hr $1; 🕑 8am-8pm)

INTERNET RESOURCES

www.lojanos.com Loja's 'virtual community'
www.loja.gov.ec Municipal website

LAUNDRY

Lavandería Autoservicio (cnr de Mayo & Eguiguren; per kg $0.85; ⏰ 8am-7pm Mon-Sat, 8:30am-1pm Sun)

MEDICAL SERVICES

Clínica San Agustín (☎ 257-0314; cnr 18 de Noviembre & Azuay) Clinic with a good reputation.
Hospital (☎ 257-0540; cnr & San Juan de Diós)

MONEY

Banco de Guayaquil (Eguiguren near Valdivieso) Bank with ATM; changes traveler's checks. There are plenty of other banks around town.

POST

Post office (cnr Colón & Sucre)

TELEPHONE

Pacifictel (Eguiguren near Olmedo) Telephone call center.

TOURIST INFORMATION

Ministerio del Medio Ambiente (☎ 258-5421; Sucre 4-35) Responsible for administering Parque Nacional Podocarpus; provides information and simple maps.
Tourist office (iTur; ☎ 258-1251, 257-0407 ext 219/20; cnr Bolívar & Eguiguren; ⏰ 8:30am-1pm & 3-6:30pm Mon-Fri) Helpful, with some maps available.

Sights & Activities

Loja's historic center can be thoroughly covered in one full day. Living up to its ecologically friendly reputation, the parks are several and large and take more time to cover.

DOWNTOWN

The lively **Parque Central**, Loja's main square, is always busy with shoeshine boys, newspapers vendors and local devotees stepping into the **cathedral** for their daily devotions to the Virgen del Cisne (see the boxed text, p227). On the south side of the plaza, a republican-era building houses the **Museo del Banco Central** (10 de Agosto; admission $1; ⏰ 9am-1pm & 2-5pm Mon-Fri) and its small exhibit of local archaeology, ethnography and art.

One block east of Parque Central, the recently renovated **Museo del Monasterio de Monjas Concepcionistas** (10 de Agosto; admission $1; ⏰ 9am-1pm & 2-5pm Mon-Fri) has three public rooms housing religious treasures from the 16th to 18th centuries. The **Museo de la Música** (cnr Valdivieso & Rocafuerte; admission $1; ⏰ 9am-1pm & 2-5pm Mon-Fri), located in an old school one block south of the monastery, explores the lives of famous musicians that hailed from Loja. Many old instruments are on display.

Two blocks north of the Parque Central, **Plaza San Francisco** (cnr Bolívar & Colón) is crowned by a statue of the city's founder astride his horse. Two blocks south of Parque Central, on the Plaza Santo Domingo, the interior of the **Church of Santo Domingo** (cnr Bolívar & Rocafuerte) is adorned with religious paintings.

South along Bolivar, the **Plaza de la Independencia** (cnr Alonso de Mercadillo & Valdivieso) is hemmed in by the **Church of San Sebastián** and colonial-era buildings with pillared overhangs and shuttered wooden balconies. The narrow lane of **Lourdes**, the oldest colonial street in Loja, has some art galleries but otherwise hasn't changed much in the last half millennium.

AROUND TOWN

North of downtown, the **Puerta de la Ciudad** (Door to the City; ☎ 258-7122; admission free; ⏰ 10am-10pm Mon-Fri, 11am-10pm Sat & Sun) is a giant castle with an arched doorway spanning Sucre, a street entering downtown. Inside the castle are two floors of art galleries and several lookouts.

For a pleasant walk, head east from the center on Rocafuerte and cross Río Zamora. From there, climb the small hill to **El Pedestal**, where the base of the bronze statue of La Virgen offers a broad vista.

PARKS

Almost 5km south of the center, the 90-hectare reserve, **Parque Universitario La Argelia** (admission $1; ⏰ 9am-4pm), has excellent trails. Across the road from the park, the **Jardín Botánico Reynaldo Espinosa** (☎ 257-1841; admission $0.60; ⏰ 9am-4pm Mon-Fri, 1-6pm Sat & Sun) is a botanical garden with nearly 900 plant species.

North of town, **Parque Recreacional Jipiro** (Santiago de las Montañas at Salvador Bustamante) can induce the feeling you've been shrunk down and tossed into a miniature-golf course. Kids scramble all over little bridges, a giant chess board, a skate park, a Chinese pagoda, a pint-size Kremlin, small animal enclosures, and a paddleboat pond. Green buses ($0.25) go there from the southeast corner of Eguiguren and Peña.

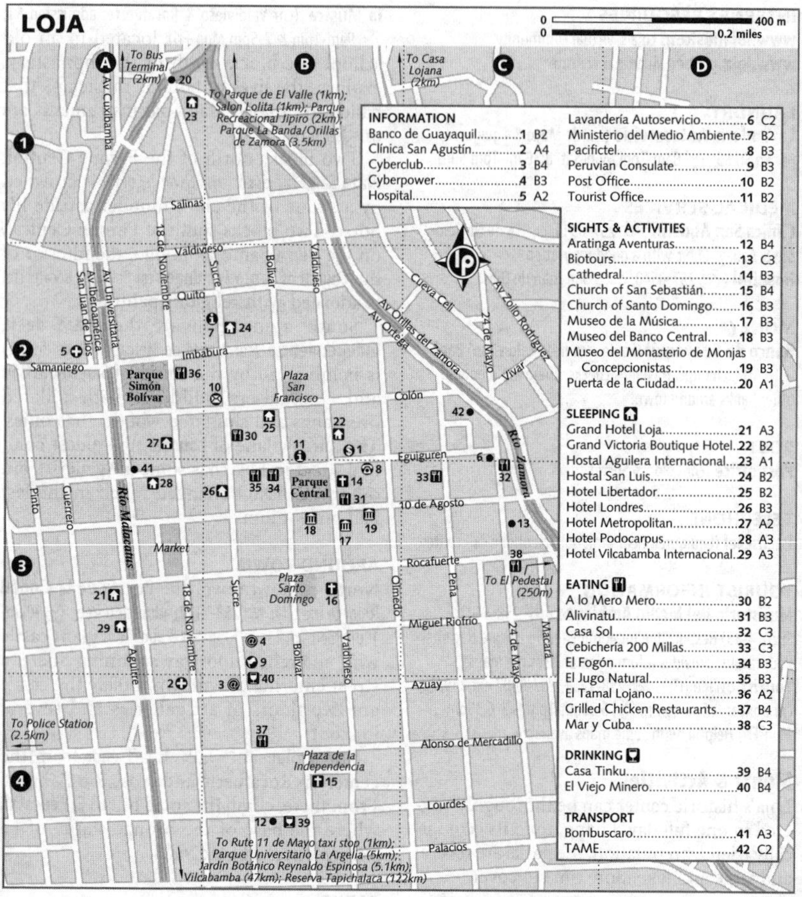

From Parque Jipiro it is about a half-hour walk to **Parque La Banda/Orillas de Zamora** (☎ 254-1202; 8 de Diciembre; admission $0.25; ⏲ 8:30am-5:30pm), where a small outdoor zoo shelters monkeys, ostriches and a pair of spectacled bears. The beautifully designed **Orquideario** (⏲ 8am-1pm & 2-6pm Mon-Fri, 8am-6pm Sat) maintains over 200 species of orchids from southern Ecuador.

Tours

Biotours (☎ 257-9387; biotours_ec@yahoo.es; 24 de Mayo 08-28) offers day trips to Parque Nacional Podocarpus from $35 per person plus park fee (minimum two, including lunch).

Aratinga Aventuras (☎ 258-2434; Lourdes 14-80; ⏲ closed for lunch) offers bird-watching day-tours in Podocarpus.

Festivals & Events

El Día de La Virgen del Cisne (see the boxed text, p227) is celebrated in Loja on September 8 with huge processions. The **Independence of Loja** celebrations on November 18 may go on for a week. *Lojanos* celebrate the feast of **San Sebastián** annually on December 8.

Sleeping

Loja's hotels are mostly superbudget or uninspiringly office-like and pricey.

BUDGET

Hotel Londres (☎ 256-1936; Sucre 07-51; r per person $5) With creaky wooden floors, big white walls and saggy beds, Hotel Londres is as basic as they come, but it's a tried-and-true travelers'

SOUTHERN DELIGHTS

For many Ecuadorians living overseas, nothing beckons home more than the smell of corn- and plantain-based *delicias* (delights or treats). They're common throughout the highlands, but everyone knows that they're better the closer you get to Loja. Many people wash them down with coffee or dress them with *ají* (a mild pepper-based sauce). Here's a primer:

Humita – A corn dumpling steamed in a corn husk. The *sal* (salty) versions come with cheese; the *dulce* (sweet) versions are often flavored with anise.

Quimbolito – A light corn-based cake steamed in achira leaves; usually topped with a raisin.

Tamales de Loja – Close to a *humita,* but usually stuffed with shredded chicken.

Empanada – A pocket of dough stuffed with sweet or savory fillings and fried to a golden, light crispiness. The *masa* (dough) in *empanadas de verde* is made with young plantain; *empanadas de maíz* are made of corn.

Tortilla de choclo – A grilled pancake made with rough corn flour.

Maduro con queso – A grilled, sweet plantain with cheese.

Bolón de verde – A molded ball of young mashed plantain, fried with sausage.

favorite, with spotless shared bathrooms and friendly young owners.

Hostal San Luis (☎ 257-0370; Sucre 4-62; r per person $8) Has 45 stark-white rooms with hot water. It's little more than a place to bed down for the night, but it's clean.

Hotel Metropolitan (☎ 257-0007/244; 18 de Noviembre 6-41; r per person $10) The Metropolitan is friendly and comfortable, with hardwood floors, decent beds and cable TV. It's dark, though, so try to score a window.

MIDRANGE

Hostal Aguilera Internacional (☎ 258-4660; Sucre 01-08 y Ortega; s/d $22/31) If you want to stay closer to the bus terminal, try this spot next to the Puerta de la Ciudad. Family-owned and family-friendly, the Aguilar also offers nice, well-lit rooms and big hot and dry sauna rooms.

Hotel Vilcabamba Internacional (☎ 258-1805; cnr Aguirre & Pasaje La FEUE; s/d incl breakfast $25/33; 💻) Rooms facing the street are big and have huge windows (and can be noisy). Interior rooms facing the corridors are small and quiet. All have cable and comfortable beds.

Hotel Podocarpus (☎ 258-1428, 257-9776; www.hotelpodocarpus.com.ec; Eguiguren 16-50; s/d $23/39; 💻) The Podocarpus has comfortable, cookie-cutter rooms with recently renovated bathrooms and nice, dark-wood furniture. The staff is eager to please.

Grand Hotel Loja (☎ 258-6600/6601; www.grandhotelloja.com; cnr Aguirre & Rocafuerte; s/d incl breakfast $37/49; 💻) Helpful and friendly, this large, modern hotel has comfortable rooms with 1970s-style golden bedspreads. It's also much quieter than most hotels.

Hotel Libertador (☎ 256-0779, 257-8278; www.hotellibertador.com.ec; Colón 14-30; s/d incl breakfast $61/71; 💻 🏊) This upmarket hotel throws in lots of extras, including wi-fi and a huge breakfast buffet. Some rooms have dining areas and big bathtubs. It frequently offers a weekend special on double rooms.

TOP END

Casa Lojana (☎ 258-5984; Paris 00-08 & Zoilo Rodréguez; www.casalojana.com.ec; s/d $73/98; 💻) In a beautiful converted home, Casa Lojana is run by the University of Loja's hotel and tourism school and is probably Loja's best lodgings. Everyone is raring to provide top-notch service, and everything from the creases in the sheets to the food gets an A.

our pick **Grand Victoria Boutique Hotel** (☎ 258-3500; www.grandvictoriabh.com; cnr Valdivieso & Eguiguren; s/d $110/134; 💻) Bringing the 'boutique hotel experience' to Loja, the Grand Victoria remembers all the little details, like bathrobes and rose petals, 800-thread-count cotton sheets, and aromatherapy in the pool area. The rooms are supremely comfortable, and service in the hotel and each of the three international restaurants is far above par.

Eating

Loja's biggest specialty, *cuy* (guinea pig), is commonly served on Sundays, although it's sometimes available during the week. Other local delights include *cecina* (salty fried pork served with yuca) and some of the country's best *humitas* (see the boxed text, above).

our pick El Tamal Lojano (☎ 258-2977; 18 de Noviembre 05-12; light items $0.70-1, almuerzos $2; ⏲ 9am-2pm & 4-8pm Mon-Sat) The *almuerzos* are good, but the real reason to come is for the delicious *quimbolitos, humitas, empanadas de verde* and *tamales lojanos*. Try them all!

Casa Sol (☎ 258-8597; 24 de Mayo 07-04; snacks $0.80-1.50; ⏲ 9am-11pm) The definition of a pleasant café, Casa Sol serves drinks and all the traditional snacks at balcony tables overlooking a little park and river. It's best in the evening, but if you go early, peek into the kitchen to see the whole family cooking up a storm.

Alivinatu (☎ 257-9945; 10 de Agosto btwn Validivieso & Olmedo; light meals $1-3; ⏲ 7am-6pm) Health-food nuts and vegetarians will find the juice bar and soy-meat sandwiches with greens a breath of fresh air. It also sells unusual teas and nutritious snacks to go.

El Jugo Natural (☎ 257-5256; Eguiguren 14-20; light meals $1-3; ⏲ 7am-8pm) Pure, all-natural juices, yogurt shakes, and fruit salads make up the menu at this small café. It's been in the juice business for 30 years.

A lo Mero Mero (Sucre 06-22; mains $3-4, almuerzos $2; ⏲ 9:30am-9pm Mon-Sat) The Mexican menu here has bulging burritos (great for vegetarians) and hearty enchiladas served in a friendly and colorful dining room. The guacamole is good, but the salsa is 100% Ecuadorian (not spicy).

Salon Lolita (☎ 257-5603; Salvador Bustamante Celi at Guayaquil, El Valle; mains $3-12; ⏲ 11am-10pm) North of downtown, this is *the* place for traditional food from Loja. The *cecina* is classic, and roasted *cuy* comes in $8, $10 or $12 sizes.

Cebichería 200 Millas (☎ 257 3563; Peña 07-41; mains $3.50-6; ⏲ 9am-3pm) Ceviche is really a late-morning dish, and that's when everyone shows up for superfresh seafood at this local favorite.

Mar y Cuba (☎ 258-5154; Rocafuerte 09-00 at 24 de Mayo; mains $4-5; ⏲ 10am-10pm Tue-Sat, 10am-4pm Sun) Despite its name, this local chain serves excellent Ecuadorian seafood and super-clean Peruvian ceviche, which unlike most ceviche, is actually raw (kind of like South American sushi).

El Fogón (☎ 258-4474; cnr Eguiguren & Bolivar; mains $4-9; ⏲ noon-8pm) Serves large portions of grilled meats in the Argentine tradition.

Succulent grilled-chicken joints line Alonso de Mercadillo, west of Bolívar, where you can pick up a quarter-chicken with soup and fries for about $2.

Drinking

Many cafés have unadvertised, low-key live music during the evenings, but otherwise Loja's nightlife is a pretty tame scene.

El Viejo Minero (Sucre 10-76) This rustic old watering hole is the perfect place for a relaxed beer and snacks in a friendly pub-like environment.

Casa Tinku (Lourdes btwn Bolivar & Sucre) Casa Tinku is a spirited little bar with a great vibe; there's usually live music on weekends.

Getting There & Away

AIR

Loja is served by La Toma airport, in Catamayo (see p227), some 30km to the west. TAME flies to/from Quito ($77) Monday to Saturday and Guayaquil ($79) Tuesday through Thursday. Tickets can be purchased in Loja at **TAME** (☎ 257-0248; Av Ortega near 24 de Mayo; ⏲ 8:30am-1pm & 2:30-6pm Mon-Fri, 9am-1pm Sat).

For transport, to the airport, ask your hotel or call **Aerotaxi** (☎ 257-1327, 258-4423), which charges $5 per person for the 40-minute shuttle service to the airport, or catch a bus to Catamayo ($1, 45 minutes) from the bus terminal.

BUS & TAXI

Almost all buses leave from the **bus terminal** (☎ 257-9592; Av Cuxibamba), about 2km north of downtown. There are daily departures to the following places:

Transportes Sur-Oriente has buses to Vilcabamba ($1, 1½ hours) once an hour, and Vilcabambaturis runs faster ($2, one hour) minibuses every 15 to 30 minutes from 6:15am to 9:15pm. Fastest of all are the *taxis colectivos* (shared taxis; $2, 45 minutes), which leave from Avenida Universitaria, about 10 blocks south of Mercadillo in Loja; ask a local taxi driver to take you to the Ruta 11 de Mayo taxi stop.

Huaquillas, on the main route to Peru, can be reached by a night bus in about seven hours, thus avoiding having to backtrack to Machala. Loja is also a departure point for buses to both southern border crossings into Peru: Macará (see p229) and Zumba (see p226).

You can go directly to Piura (Peru) from Loja without stopping in Macará. The service ($8, nine hours) is offered at 7am, 1pm, 10:30pm and 11pm with **Loja International** (☎ 257-9014/0505), and the bus stops at the border, waits for passengers to take care of

BUSES FROM LOJA

Destination	Cost (US$)	Duration (hr)
Ambato	$13	11
Catamayo	$1	¾
Cuenca	$7	5
Gualaquiza	$6	6
Guayaquil	$9	8-9
Macará	$6	6
Machala	$5	5
Piura (Peru)	$8	9
Quito	$15	14-15
Riobamba	$12	10
Zamora	$2.50	2
Zumba	$7.50	6

exits and entries, and then continues to Piura. It's advisable to buy your tickets at least a day before you travel.

There are no direct buses to Peru through Zumba; you will have to take a bus to Zumba, cross the border and transfer from there (see p226).

CAR

Localiza (☎ 258-1729; www.localiza.com; cnr Ayora & Nueva Loja; 🕑 8am-6pm Mon-Fri, 9am-1pm Sat & Sun) rents economy cars and 4WDs, which can be returned in other major cities. **Bombuscaro** (☎ 258-9293; cnr 10 de Agosto & Universitaria) is also recommended.

Getting Around

By law all taxi rides within the city of Loja cost $1, day or night, no matter how short or long the trip.

PARQUE NACIONAL PODOCARPUS

This **national park** (admission $10) fills in much of the triangle between Loja, Zamora and Vilcabamba as well as a huge swath to the southeast. Because altitude ranges so greatly within the park borders – from around 900m in the lowland sector to over 3600m in the highland sector – Podocarpus has some of the greatest plant and animal diversity in the world. Perhaps 40% of its estimated 3000 plant species are endemic (occur nowhere else in the world), and close to 600 bird species have been recorded. Rare mammals include foxes, deer, puma, mountain tapirs and bears.

Podocarpus' varied landscape is mesmerizing: high windy *páramo* that (especially when its foggy) looks vaguely like a coral-rich sea floor; jewel lakes that sit in glacier depressions formed long ago; fairy-tale elfin woodland buffeted by harsh weather; and lush, towering forests seething with the hum and whistle of insect and birdlife.

The park is named for the giant Podocarpus, Ecuador's only native conifer, but don't bank on seeing one, or any larger animals, for that matter. Loggers stole most of the Podocarpus years ago, and the mammals have been hunted down to small populations driven deep into the forest. On top of these threats, which continue despite the park's protected status, both legal and illegal mining and agriculture encroach on habitat throughout the park.

Birds, however, are abundant. In the highland sector, they include such exotic-sounding species as the lachrymose mountain-tanager, streaked tuftedcheek, superciliaried hemispingus and pearled treerunner; the lowland sector is home to coppery-chested jacamar, white-breasted parakeet and paradise tanager.

The park entry fee is valid for five days, so you can use the ticket to visit both areas of the park, and entrance is free on the first Monday of every month. Rainfall in both sectors is heavy and frequent, so be prepared for it. October through December are the driest months.

Highlands Sector

Access to the highland sector is through the **Cajanuma control**, which is located about 10km south of Loja. From the Cajanuma control, where you pay admission, a dirt road leads 8.5km uphill to the **refugio**, where seven basic **cabañas** (per person $5) with mattresses are available to the public, as well as a **camping area** (per person $3).

From the *refugio*, some short, self-guided trails wander through the cloud forest. More strenuous and wide-ranging is the 5km **Los Miradores loop trail**, a four-hour hike up through the cloud forest and into the *páramo*. Another trail that branches off the Miradores leads 14.5km to the highland lakes of **Lagunas del Compadre** and requires a minimum of three days round-trip for most hikers. There is no water between the trailhead and the lakes.

The Ministerio del Medio Ambiente (Ministry of Environment) in Loja (p215) can provide detailed information, and the control has simple maps.

PAUL J GREENFIELD, ARTIST & CONSERVATIONIST

Bird-watchers in Ecuador often carry a giant two-volume work called *The Birds of Ecuador*. This essential field guide has more than 3000 images of 1600 species painted by artist Paul J Greenfield, who is also a conservationist and leading bird guide. It took Greenfield, along with the American ornithologist Robert S Ridgely, more than 20 years to complete, and it represents more than 15% of the world's bird species.

Why is the bird-watching so good in Ecuador?
Coming here without bird-watching is like going to Paris without seeing the Eiffel Tower. The concentration of species here is spectacular. As you move up or down in the Andes, the temperature changes, something like two or three degrees per every 300 meters, which means a change in the vegetation, a change in the insects and a change in the birds. That's also cultural, you'll see changes in the people, the way they dress and in their homes. The bird element is just one way of focusing on something, and by focusing on one thing you're seeing a lot.

You work with the Jocotoco Foundation, named for a bird, the Jocotoco Antpitta (Grallaria ridgelyi), that your co-author discovered just as you were finishing the field guide. What does the foundation do?
Jocotoco's goal is to find and identify rare and endangered species that are not adequately protected in the national park protection scheme. They buy land where the species are found, and they are involved in tourism to sustain themselves. When Jocotoco began their land purchases, Ecuador was in dire straits in many ways, and many places that we identified needed to be purchased immediately. In Tapichalaca, where the Jocotoco Antpitta was found, you could hear the chainsaws nearby, and the mules were pulling the wood out of there (see p226). It was either buy this land or that's the end of the species; it's gone.

What are the biggest threats to birds and bird habitats in Ecuador?
The biggest threats have already happened, and that's the massive deforestation that went on through the 1970s to the 1990s. It's still going on to a certain extent. 'Progress' smacks head to head with this other need of a country to take care of its natural resources, in this case bird habitats, which of course can also bring a lot of money to a country.

How do birds translate into money for the country?
In the last five years there has been much more recognition by the Ministry of Tourism and Ecuadorians that Ecuador is a place for birds and nature. There are a lot of companies that lead bird-watching tours to Ecuador, and more and more independent bird-watchers are visiting too. Ecuador still doesn't have a reputation like Costa Rica, although it's far richer in diversity and it's getting more and more popular.

How does bird and nature tourism impact local communities?
When Jocotoco began to buy up land, the only thing that farmers thought that anybody would want was the pasture, but Jocotoco didn't want the pasture. They wanted the forest. It put value and concern into the natural vegetation, so people have started to look into reforestation. Now local people feel proud that foreigners are coming to see what they have, that they can participate in and benefit from it. That was not happening before. Now people are trying to figure out how to recover nature.

GETTING THERE & AWAY

A taxi all the way from Loja to the *refugio* will cost about $10. Set out early and you can hike for several hours before walking the 8.5km back to the Loja–Vilcabamba road. Then flag a passing bus back to Loja. The two-hour walk from the station to the main road (all downhill) is rather enjoyable itself. There are rarely cars on the park road, especially during the week, so don't expect to be able to hitchhike.

Lowlands Sector

The main access to the lowland sector is the **Bombuscaro control** (🕑 8am-5pm), 6km south of Zamora by a dirt road that follows the Río Bombuscaro. This river is a popular playground for locals and great for a dip. From the parking area at the end of the road it's a half-hour walk on a wide, uphill trail to the **control** where you pay the entry fee. Two basic **cabañas** (per person $5) without mattresses are available, and you can camp for $3.

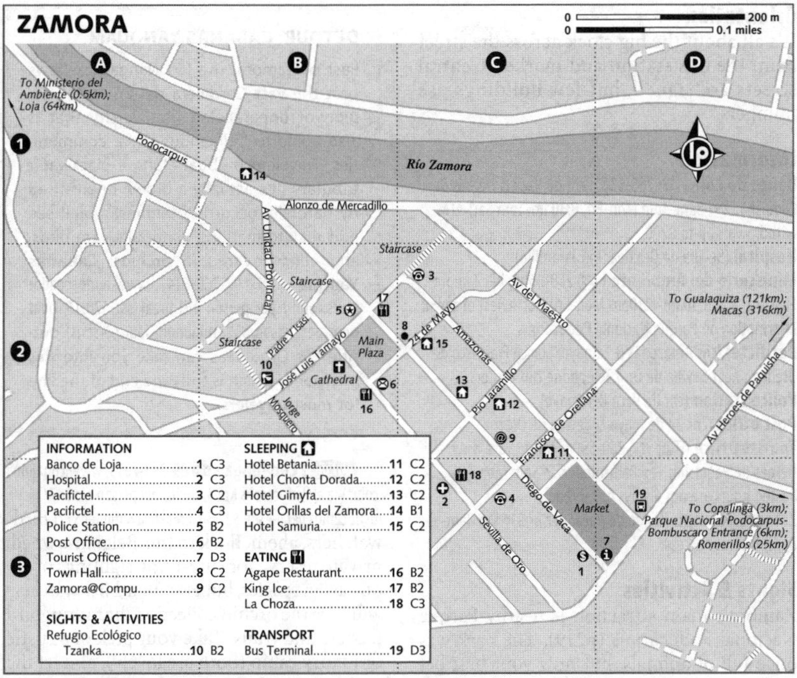

From the Bombuscaro control, there are several short, maintained (but sometimes muddy) trails that meander into the forest. The 6km **Los Huigerones** trail will lead you into some primary forest. Another trail leads to a deep (but very swift) swimming hole called the *área fotográfico* on the Río Bombuscaro.

Another infrequently used entrance is at the tiny village of **Romerillos**, about 25km south of Zamora by a different road.

The climate is hot and humid but beautiful, and the rainiest months are May through July. May and June are the best months for orchids.

GETTING THERE & AWAY

The easiest way to get to the Bombuscaro entrance is by taxi from Zamora; they hang out behind the bus terminal and charge $4 for the ride. You can have the driver return to pick you up at the end of the day (additional $4) or you can walk back in about an hour on the flat road. Buses to Romerillos ($1.50, two hours) leave at 6am and 2pm from Zamora's bus terminal.

ZAMORA

☎ 07 / pop 15,112 / elevation 970m

The hot, humid capital of Zamora-Chinchipe province is part Oriente and part Sierra. Perched between these regions in the Andean foothills, it attracts settlers from the high-altitude communities of Saraguro and Amazon Basin Shuar. The town bills itself as the 'City of Birds and Waterfalls,' and is important for its proximity to Parque Nacional Podocarpus and huge mining concessions.

A century ago, Zamora was a village of wooden houses at the end of the old Loja–Zamora road. But decades of colonization by miners and growth into a provincial hub have created a town of mostly unremarkable, concrete structures. Zamora has, however, experienced a bit of a revival, with renovations to bridges, a spruced-up bus station, and a brand new *malecón* (waterfront) along the Río Zamora. If you need to know what time it is, just look up: the big hill to the top has a massive clock. The minute hand is exactly 11 meters and 34 centimeters long. This may very well be the largest timepiece in Ecuador, and according to some, the biggest in the world.

Orientation

It's all about the big clock across the street from the bus station and market. Central streets are signed, but few buildings use numbers.

Information

Banco de Loja (☎ 260-5385; cnr de Vaca & Héroes de Paquisha; 8am-4pm Mon-Fri, 8:30am-1pm Sat) ATM withdrawals up to $200.

Hospital (Sevilla de Oro near Pio Jaramillo)

Ministerio del Ambiente (☎ 260-6606; Vía Zamora-Loja s/n; 8:30am-4:30pm Mon-Fri) Northwest of town; information on Parque Nacional Podocarpus.

Pacifictel (cnr Amazonas & Tamayo; branch Francisco de Orellana near Sevilla de Oro) Telephone call-centers.

Police station (cnr de Vaca & Tamayo)

Post office (cnr 24 de Mayo & Sevilla de Oro)

Tourist Office (iTur; ☎ 260-5996; cnr de Vaca & Av Heroes de Paquisha; 8am-noon & 2-5pm Mon-Fri) Posted hours are not always observed.

Zamora@Compu (Diego de Vaca; per hr $1; 8am-8pm) Internet access.

Sights & Activities

Zamora's main attraction is nearby Parque Nacional Podocarpus (p219). The park was once full of animals, but now your best bet for seeing them is at **Refugio Ecológico Tzanka** (☎ 260-5692; Jorge Mosquero at José Luis Tamayo; admission $2; 9am-5pm), a wildlife rescue center that has colorful parrots, coati (a great big, acrobatic rodent), monkeys, sloth and a boa constrictor.

Sleeping

Other than Copalinga, Zamora has a large stock of characterless but comfortable hotels.

Hotel Betania (☎ 260-7030; hotelbetaniaz@hotmail.com; Francisco de Orellana; s/d incl breakfast $12/17) The Betania is a comfortable and modern hotel with firm beds and an attached restaurant. It's one of the best in town.

Hotel Orillas del Zamora (☎ 260-5565; hotel_o_zamora@hotmail.net; Alonzo de Mercadillo; s/d incl breakfast $14/24) At the west end of the *malecón*, this hotel offers upper-floor rooms with clean, big bathrooms and great views of the river; some dingy rooms with low ceilings face the streets.

Hotel Samuria (☎ 260-7801; cnr 24 de May & Diego de Vaca; s/d incl breakfast $20/36) Zamora's newest is also its finest, featuring firm beds, hairdryers and relatively quiet rooms. There is a restaurant.

DETOUR: CABAÑAS YANQUAM

East of Zamora, the Río Nangaritza flows past the vast Cordillera del Cóndor, a region of unparalleled biodiversity that is also home to indigenous Shuar communities. Traveling by boat along a blackwater tributary (it's actually a brown hue caused by naturally occurring tannins), you'll see odd rock formations, waterfalls, rare birds, and cliffs covered in orchids. **Cabañas Yanquam** (☎ 07-260-6147; www.lindoecuadortours.com; r per person incl breakfast $20.16, boat rides per person $30, minimum four persons) outside Las Orquideas can take you into this lost world, which is truly the end of the line for most travelers.

our pick **Copalinga** (☎ 09-347-7013; www.copalinga.com; Via al Podocarpus Km 3; cabins per person s/d $47/36.50, rustic cabins per person $22.50; breakfast & dinner $12) Birdwatchers, ahem, flock to this Belgian-owned, private reserve for sure-thing sightings of exotic avian species, but even non-bird-watchers will love the orchid collection, hummingbird feeders and trails. Take your pick of a rustic or luxury cabin (both are lovely), and let the rushing river lull you to sleep. Hydropower runs the whole place, and meals are generous and tasty. Reservations are required. There's an additional charge of $15 on nonrustic cabins between December and March.

Also try the **Hotel Chonta Dorada** (☎ 260-6384/7055; hotelchontadorada@hotmail.com; Pío Jaramillo near Amazonas; r per person $9) and the modern, comfortable **Hotel Gimyfa** (☎ 260-6103; Diego de Vaca near Pio Jaramillo; r per person $9).

Eating

Unless you like *bagre* (catfish) and *ancas de rana* (frog's legs), eating in Zamora is a pretty humdrum affair. The nicer hotels serve better food, and the market has stalls selling soups and chicken plates.

King Ice (cnr Diego de Vaca & José Luis Tamayo; food $1.50-2.50; 8am-midnight) This ice-cream parlor serves burgers, hot dogs and frosty cold beers.

La Choza (☎ 260-5504; Sevilla de Oro; mains $2-3; 6:30am-8pm) Serving fried fish, fried frog's legs and *churrasco* (steak with eggs and rice), La Choza is a health foodie's nightmare, but it's good and the fish is local and fresh. Breakfast service starts at 6:30am.

Agape Restaurant (cnr Sevilla de Oro & 24 de Mayo; mains $3-5; 10am-9pm Mon-Sat) Near the cathedral, Agape has a friendly and slightly fancier atmosphere. It serves fish, meat and sometimes frog's legs.

Getting There & Away

The **bus terminal** (Av Heroes de Paquisha at Amazonas) is across the street from the big clock.

Buses leave almost hourly to Loja ($2.50, two hours) between 3am and 11pm. There are five daily buses heading north to Gualaquiza ($3.50, four hours) and a morning bus to Guayzimi ($2.25, three hours). For Cuenca (eight hours), Guayaquil (11 hours) or Quito (18 hours), head first to Loja and catch one of the frequent buses departing from there. See p221 for details about transport to Parque Nacional Podocarpus.

Buses to Las Orquideas (for Cabañas Yanquam; see opposite) leave from Zamora daily and pass through Guayzimi.

VILCABAMBA

07 / pop 4200 / elevation 1500m

Vilcabamba is synonymous with longevity all throughout Ecuador. It became famous for a high number of centenarian residents after *Reader's Digest* did stories on them many years ago. Although residents readily concede that few *vilcabambenses* (people from Vilcabamba) celebrate a 100th birthday anymore, most agree that their simple, stress-free lives and fresh, mountain air are conducive to long life.

The area's beautiful scenery, mild weather, and laid-back vibe attract waves of young backpackers and many American and European retirees, so many that Vilcabamba has experienced a sort of 'gringo boom.' The hills are dotted with big, new houses, and the gentrification has created some tension about the cost of land. The flip side is that jobs in tourism and construction are more plentiful than ever, and Vilcabamba is the rare, Ecuadorian pueblo where young people have little ambition to leave for the big city.

Vilcabamba offers perfect weather for hiking, horseback riding and access to remote sections of Parque Nacional Podocarpus, but it's also an excellent place to chill out. Legions of specialists are ready to facilitate your relaxation with inexpensive massages and facials.

Orientation & Information

Most of the town surrounds the plaza, and addresses are rarely used.

Craig's Book Exchange (1-5pm) Great book exchange 1.5km east of town on the road to Cabañas Río Yambala.
Hospital (267-3188; Av Eterna Juventud near Miguel Carpio)
Pacifictel (Sucre near Fernando de la Vega) One of several telephone centers in town.
Pepe Net (Fernando de la Vega near Sucre; per hr $1.15; 9am-9pm) Internet access.
Police station (264-0896; Agua de Hierro near Bolívar) By the post office.
Post office (Agua de Hierro near Bolívar)
Rosita's Laundry (Fernando de la Vega btw Toledo & La Paz; laundry per kg $0.80; 8-11am & 1-4:30pm) Same-day laundry service.
Tourist office (264-0090; cnr Bolívar & Diego Vaca de la Vega; 8am-1pm & 3-6pm)
Vilcanet (Huilco Pamba near Juan Montalvo; per hr $1; 9am-9pm) Outdoor internet café above Hotel Mandango (p224).

Sights & Activities

Most of the hotels have trail maps, and some even have their own trail systems. The most popular hike is up to Cerro Mandango (but there have been reports of robberies, so do not carry large amounts of money or valuables). Most naturalists and horse guides charge about $35 per day (not including park entrance fees).

Orlando Falco is an English-speaking naturalist guide who conducts walking tours to Podocarpus and other areas. Contact him at Primavera Handicrafts (p226) or at the Rumi-Wilco Ecolodge or Pole House (p225).

The folks at **Cabañas Río Yambala** (09-106-2762; www.vilcabamba.cwc.net) arrange two- and three-day hiking and horseback-riding trips into their private 350-hectare nature reserve on the edge of Podocarpus. Hiking trips cost $70/105 per person for two/three days, and riding trips around $40 per person per day. Prices drop for groups of three or more.

Caballos Gavilan (08-983051; gavilanhorse@yahoo.com; Sucre) is run by the highly recommended Gavin, a New Zealander who has lived here for years. He guides two- to three-day horse hikes with overnight stays in his refuge near the park. Gavin's excursions cost a bit more at $50 per day, but he's one of the town's best guides and his horses are treated superbly.

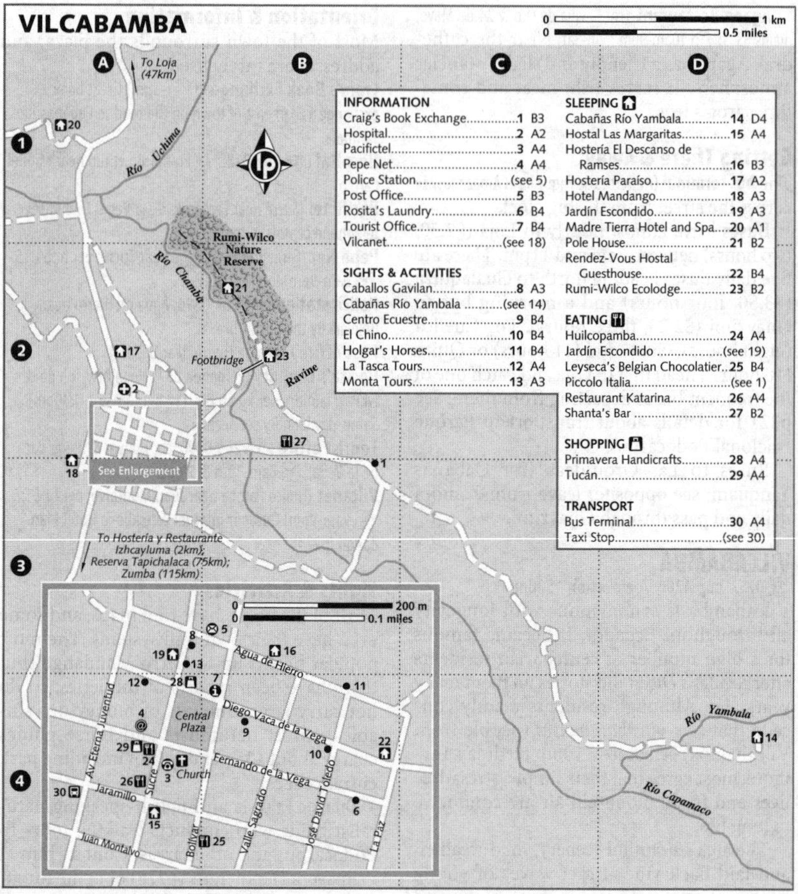

Centro Ecuestre (☎ 267-0151; Diego Vaca de la Vega) is a cooperative of local horse and mule owners offering tours lasting from two hours to three days. Most speak only Spanish.

Horseback-riding trips are also offered by the friendly René León at **La Tasca Tours** (☎ 09-152-3118, 09-184-1287; latascourts@yahoo.ec; Diego Vaca de la Vega), the French-owned **Monta Tours** (☎ 267-3186; solomaco@hotmail.com; Sucre), and the German-speaking Ecuadorian, Holgar, at **Holgar's Horses** (☎ 08-296-1238; Agua de Hierro & Toledo).

He is not really Chinese, but the proprietor of **El Chino** (☎ 264-0473; cnr Diego de la Vaca & Toledo) rents bikes for $1.50 per hour. He also offers biking day-tours starting at $15, as well as bike repair.

Sleeping

Vilcabamba has many inexpensive hotels, almost all with some version of a swimming pool. Those outside the village can be marvelously quiet and relaxing, while those in town are generally cheaper. Prices may fluctuate during high season and holidays.

CENTRAL

Hotel Mandango (☎ 264-0058; Huilco Pamba & Montalvo; r per person with shared/private bathroom $4/8) Behind the bus station, Mandango is a budget choice with electricity-heated hot showers and spartan rooms.

Hostal Las Margaritas (☎ 267-3130; www.vilcabamba.org/lasmargaritas.html; cnr Sucre & Jaramillo; r per person $10;) In a big, classy house with a garden

SOUTHERN HIGHLANDS

full of fruit trees, this family-run *hostal* has clean rooms with firm beds and cable TV.

Jardín Escondido (Hidden Garden; ☎ 264-0281; www.jardin-escondido.com; Sucre & Agua de Hierro; dm incl breakfast $9, r per person incl breakfast $12-17;) Built around a tranquil interior garden filled with songbirds, all rooms have tall ceilings and big bathrooms, and breakfast comes with homemade bread and good coffee.

Rendez-Vous Hostal Guesthouse (☎ 09-219-1180; rendezvousecuador@yahoo.com; Diego Vaca de Vega 06-43; s/d $14/22 low season, s/d $25/30 high season;) Call it adobe chic. Each of the meticulous rooms at French-owned Rendez-Vous has its own little terrace that looks out onto a calm interior garden. Breakfast, served on the terraces, comes with homemade bread. Wi-fi is $4 per day.

Hostería El Descanso de Ramses (☎ 264-0038/0039; www.vivavilcabamba.com/hosteriaeldescansoderamses; Aguas del Hierro & Bolívar; r per person low/high season $15/25;). This new, colonial-style *hostería* is popular with Ecuadorian families and groups. It has a big beautiful pool, meals on the veranda, and lots of games and diversions for kids.

OUTSIDE OF TOWN

Rumi-Wilco Ecolodge (www.rumiwilco.com; r per person $7) A 10-minute walk from the bus station, Rumi-Wilco and its separate Pole House (doubles/triples $24/30) are within the private Rumi-Wilco Nature Reserve, owned by knowledgeable, local naturalist guides Orlando and Alicia Falco. The adobe houses have attractive rooms with hand-tiled floors, shared bathrooms and communal kitchens (great for small groups). The Pole House, a traveler's favorite, is a rustic cabin on stilts with a hot shower, and hammocks looking over the river. To enter the reserve only is $2 per person (good for three visits).

Cabañas Río Yambala (☎ 09-106-2762; www.vilcabamba.cwc.net; cabins per person with 2 meals $10-14, without meals $5-9) Owned by a British/American couple who have lived locally for many years. The cabañas are a bit run down but still homey and comfortable. If you want to get away from it all, be close to great hiking and fall asleep to the sound of a rushing river, this is the place to be. A restaurant serves good dinners, including vegetarian food. You can walk there in about 45 minutes or hire a taxi for $4.

Hostería Paraíso (☎ 258-0266; r per person incl breakfast $9;) About 1km north of town, Hostería Paraíso has a great swimming pool, a flower-filled garden, a pyramid-shaped bioenergetic meditation room (really just a massage space) and rooms that don't quite measure up to everything else. Rates include use of the pool and spa facilities. It's not a bad deal midweek in low season, when you'll have the place to yourself.

our pick **Hostería y Restaurante Izhcayluma** (☎ 264-0095; www.izhcayluma.com; dm/s/d incl breakfast $9/19/28, cabins s/d $24/36;) Located 2km south of town, German-owned Izhcayluma packs excellent value into this casual but refined hilltop retreat. The outdoor dining area serves German and Ecuadorian cuisine and has sweeping panoramic views of the valley. A new 'holistic wellness room' offers massages and other treatments, and there is a bar and swimming pool. The cabins and rooms are quiet and spacious, and prices include use of a mountain bike to ride into town. Izhcayluma maintains up-to-date information about crossing into Peru as well.

Madre Tierra Hotel and Spa (☎ 264-0269; www.madretierra1.com; s/d incl breakfast $48/67;) On a hillside with waterfalls and gardens 2km north of town, Madre Tierra has a strong New Age vibe, replete with candles and healing ions. Rooms are meticulously decorated, and the newer suites have balconies and inset rock floors. Prices include organic breakfasts and dinners, served in a communal, outdoor dining area. Spa services are half-price for guests. The gleaming new Cosmos Conference Center has plenty of space for nightly movies, acting classes and 'eco-real-estate' seminars. Wi-fi is available for $4 per day.

Eating

In addition to some oldies but goodies, small cafés catering to tourists come and go around the main square. Hours can be irregular during low season, but there's always someone open for cold beers and snacks.

Layseca's Belgian Chocolatier (cnr Bolivar & Jaramillo; 10:30am-8pm Tue-Sun; snacks $0.50-1.50) Owned by a Belgian-Ecuadorian couple, this little café has delicious homemade chocolate, cookies, cakes, and bread and the town's best coffee and espresso. The bags of granola make great hiking snacks.

our pick **Shanta's Bar** (☎ 08-562-7802; 3/4km on road to Cabañas Río Yambala; mains $3-6; 1:30-9:30pm) Shanta's serves big plates of trout, pizza and frog's legs in an open-air, rustic setting with saddle seats at the bar and a bartender with a handlebar mustache.

Jardín Escondido (Sucre & Agua de Hierro; ☎ 264-0281, www.jardin-escondido.com; mains $3-7; ⌚ 8am-8pm) Not surprisingly, some of the best Mexican food in southern Ecuador comes from this little Mexican-owned café inside the hotel Jardín Escondido (see p225). Delicious dishes with *mole* (a chocolate-based spicy sauce), rich traditional soups and burritos are some of the specialties. You can get a big breakfast with homemade bread, too.

Hostería y Restaurante Izhcayluma (☎ 264-0095; www.izhcayluma.com; mains $4-7; ⌚ 8am-8pm) Bavarian specialties and classic Ecuadorian dishes are the fare here. Izhcayluma also offers excellent vegetarian substitutions for the meat dishes. It's worth the trip up the hill.

Piccolo Italia (☎ 09-939-3435; 1.5km on road to Cabañas Río Yambala; pizzas & mains $4-12; ⌚ 11am-4pm & 6-9pm Thu-Sun) This new pizzeria and bistro next to Craig's Book Exchange (p223) has an extensive menu that's more Venice than Vilcabamba. It serves all the traditional Italian pizzas and pastas, plus a couple of unusual ones.

Both **Huilcopamba** (cnr Sucre & Diego Vaca de la Vega; mains $2.50-4; ⌚ 8am-9pm) and **Restaurant Katerina** (Sucre at Jaramillo; mains $2.50-4; ⌚ irregular) are popular places serving Ecuadorian food.

Several restaurants along Eterna Juventud (the part of the Panamericana that goes through town) serve cheap Ecuadorian-style *almuerzos*.

DETOUR: TAPICHALACA RESERVE

The small **Tapichalaca Reserve** (admission $20), 75km south of Vilcabamba, protects one of Ecuador's most rare and endangered birds, the Jocotoco Antpitta (*Grallaria ridgelyi*), which has under 20 known breeding pairs. Some of the birds have been habituated to eating grubs put out by the caretaker, however, so a sighting is more or less guaranteed. The rest of the reserve is an oasis of cloud forest in a region of heavy deforestation, and the hummingbird feeders are abuzz all day. To get there in time for the Antpittas' breakfast, catch the 5am bus from Loja or spend the night at the reserve's beautiful **lodge** (☎ 02-227-2013; www.fjocotoco.org; r per person incl meals $100).

Shopping

Primavera Handicrafts (cnr Diego Vaca de la Vega & Sucre; ⌚ irregular) Primavera has nice, locally made products and postal services (including stamps), and is an office for Rumi-Wilco Ecolodge (p225).

Tucán (Fernando de la Vega near Sucre; ⌚ 10am-1pm & 2-6pm) Stock up on cheap souvenirs, postcards, jewelry and T-shirts.

Getting There & Around

Transportes Mixtos is a taxi-truck cooperative on the main plaza (you can't miss the green-and-white trucks). Most charge $1.50 to $4 for getting to nearby places.

Buses, minivans and taxis leave from the tiny **bus terminal** (Eterna Juventud & Jaramillo). *Taxis colectivos* ($2, 45 minutes) depart frequently to Loja after four people cram in, and there are buses ($1, 1½ hours) and Vilcabambaturis minibuses ($2, one hour) that leave on the hour.

Buses from Loja head south to Zumba ($6, five hours) and on to the Peruvian border (see below).

Vilcabambaturis (at the bus terminal) also sells tickets for the Loja–Piura (Peru) bus ride, which goes via Macará (see p228) It doesn't come through Vilcabamba, but it's good to purchase your ticket a day in advance if you're heading that way.

ZUMBA & THE PERUVIAN BORDER

☎ 07

Vilcabamba is the end of the road for most travelers. Those heading to Peru, especially those eager to see the ruins at Chachapoyas, may continue on to Zumba on the border.

Zumba was an important military outpost during the wars with Peru between the 1940s and 1990s. The war's over, but there's still an Ecuadorian military post here, and soldiers roam all over town, not doing much other than whistling at women. Basic *hostales* in Zumba have beds for about $5 per person, but there is little reason to stay. From Loja or Vilcabamba, it's an all-day journey to San Ignacio, Peru, the best place to spend the night.

Transportes Nambija ($7.50, six hours) buses leave from Loja for Zumba at noon and midnight, and **Sur Oriente** (☎ 256 1649) services go at 5am, 8am, 5:30pm and 9:30pm. All stop in Vilcabamba after leaving Loja.

SOUTHERN HIGHLANDS

LA VIRGEN DEL CISNE

Throughout Ecuador, but especially in Loja province, you'll see figurines, shrines, pendants and all manner of trinkets dedicated to the Virgen del Cisne (Virgin of the Swan). According to legend, the Virgin Mary protected a medieval knight who appeared before his lover in a boat shaped like a swan. The knight's chivalric acts and the Virgin's kindly auspices inspired Franciscan monks so much that they erected statues of the 'Virgen del Cisne' throughout Europe. The Franciscans later hauled one of these statues to Ecuador, where she was credited with miracles involving sickness and storms.

The Virgen you see today, installed by adoring campesinos (peasants) in 1594 in a little town also called El Cisne (70km west of Loja), wears gilded robes and a towering crown. This Virgen, the 'original,' lives in the town's El Santuario Gothic cathedral most of the year. Virgens del Cisne in other parts of Ecuador wear vestments inspired by local indigenous costumes, or even the Ecuadorian flag (especially when the national football team is playing a big game).

A huge festival is held in the Virgen's honor in El Cisne on August 15, after which thousands of pilgrims from Ecuador and northern Peru carry the statue on their shoulders to Loja, with many of the pilgrims walking the entire way. The Virgen finally arrives in Loja on August 20, where she is ceremoniously installed in the cathedral. On November 1, the process is repeated in reverse, and the Virgen rests in El Cisne until the following August. There is another major (if smaller) festival in El Cisne on May 30.

For most of the year, tours and buses make day trips to the village from Loja and Catamayo to see El Santuario and the statue. But on procession days, forget it! You walk like everybody else – the road is so full of pilgrims that vehicles can't get through. In recent years, cyclists have taken to riding this gorgeous route through the mountains alongside the pilgrims. No matter how you go, this display of devotion always amazes.

From Zumba, *rancheras* (open-sided trucks) leave at 8am, 10:30am, and 5:30pm for the border at **La Balsa** ($2, 1½-2½ hours) where you get your exit stamp (or entry stamp if coming from Peru). The condition of the road between Zumba and La Balsa can vary greatly, depending on recent weather. On the other side of the 'international bridge' in Peru there are *taxi colectivos* to **San Ignacio** ($3, 1½ hours), where you can spend the night.

From San Ignacio, there are regular mini-buses to **Jaén** ($3.50, three hours) beginning at 4am. Once you're in Jaén, take a *moto-taxi* (motorcycle taxi) to the *colectivo* stop and then get a *colectivo* to **Bagua Grande** (one hour). From Bagua Grande you then get a bus to **Chachapoyas** (three hours), the first town of any real size.

CATAMAYO & AROUND

☎ 07

Loja was founded twice. The first time was in 1546, on what is now **Catamayo** (population 21,982); the second time was on its present site, two years later. Despite its long history, Catamayo is a totally unremarkable town except for its airport, La Toma, which serves Loja 30km away.

About 15km west of Catamayo, a well-paved road passes through the village of **San Pedro de la Bendita**, which is the turnoff to the village of **El Cisne**, 22km to the north and home to the famous Virgin del Cisne (see the boxed text, above).

About 40km south of Catamayo, on the southernmost of two roads to Macará, **Gonzanamá** is noted for its weavers and for the production of *alforjas* (saddlebags); ask around if you want to buy. The route passes the villages of **Cariamanga** and **Sozoranga** before ending in Macará at the border. All three of these stops are little more than two- or three-horse towns and have only the simplest *residenciales*.

All of these places are served regularly from Loja's bus terminal.

CATACOCHA

☎ 07 / pop 5369 / elevation 1886m

The **Sunday market** is the most important event of the week in **Catacocha**, also known as Las Paltas. At dawn church bells call everyone to mass in the Plaza Independencia, and by 7am they are buying and selling homemade cheese, donkey saddles, farm-fresh eggs and mountains of veggies all over town. By dusk, the same plaza is a gathering spot for old-timers and bored teenagers.

Declared a National Cultural Heritage Site in 1994, Catacocha takes pride in its places of worship, sun-baked adobe houses and wooden balconies, but has yet to capitalize on the tourism potential of its vaunted status. As such, strolling its streets is the best way to appreciate the timeless cycle of highland life.

The **Templo de Lourdes** is worth a peek inside for its replicas of famous European religious paintings. You won't mistake this church for the Louvre, but the canvases by a local monk give the surroundings an earnestly faithful if not slightly kitschy feel.

The infamous **Peña de Shiricalupo** is a shrine-cum-mirador (lookout) known for its stomach-churning views of the Casanga Valley.

The **municipio** (town hall; ☎ 268-3157; 🕑 Mon-Fri) on the Plaza Independencia can provide tourist information. Internet and ATMs have recently arrived in Catacocha, which in addition to telephones can be found on the Plaza.

Hotel Tambococha (cnr 25 de Junio & Lauro Gerrero; s/d $8/12) has clean, well-lit rooms, many of which look over the Plaza Independencia. All have cable TV and electricity-heated showers. **Hotel Ejecutivo** (☎ 268-3092; cnr Calle Independencia & Domingo Meli; r per person $9) has identical amenities, as well as a *turco* (steam room) and roof access, but rooms with views over the market area can be noisy.

Dining options are spare, but you can get simple *menestras* (lentils and beans) with meat at **Casa Tradicional** off Plaza Independencia, or try the outdoor stalls serving *asodas* next to the big 'Indio' statue.

Buses from Loja ($2.50, two hours) stop here en route to Macará and Piura (Peru).

MACARÁ & THE PERUVIAN BORDER

☎ 07 / pop 14,727 / elevation 470m

The descent from Catacocha toward the Peruvian border offers sweeping views of mountains and deep valleys that give way to hilly dry tropical forest. Adobe ruins bake under the strong sun, and donkeys and cattle roam untethered along the road.

This arid forest's representative tree, the ceiba (kapok), with its green-tinted, swollen trunks and gnarly, usually leafless branches, stands out majestically – and sadly – on hillsides that have been logged and grazed. In these barren areas, the lonely giants have been spared the chainsaw because they are mostly hollow and of little utilitarian value.

To see this ecosystem in a healthier state, head to the **Jorupe Reserve** (admission $20) run by Fundación Jocotoco outside of Macará (see the boxed text, p220). Primarily a bird-watching reserve, Jorupe is home to the white-tailed jay, blue-crowned motmot, and Ecuadorian trogan. Hire a taxi ($3) to take you to the reserve about 5km down the road from Macará toward Sozorongo.

Most tourists heading south to the Peruvian border or north into Ecuador barely notice the sleepy border town of Macará. Surrounded by some fairly picturesque terraced rice cultivation, it's a bit infested with crickets that jump about the streets and hotel rooms. If you're entering the country through here, don't worry, it gets better as you head north.

Information

Banco de Loja (cnr Ventimilla & Calderón) has an ATM ($200 limit) but no currency exchange. For Peruvian *soles,* head to Parque Carlos Román and approach the conspicuous guy in mirrored sunglasses with a black briefcase. This busy market area is not the place to exchange a large quantity of cash; exchange only what you need until you reach the bank in Piura (Peru).

Internet at **Giullernet** (cnr Andrade & Ventimilla) and **SuperCompu** (cnr Sucre & Ventimilla) costs $1 per hour.

Sleeping & Eating

Accommodation is plentiful and cheap.

Hostal Santigyn (☎ 269-4539; cnr Bolívar & Rengel; s/d incl breakfast $7/14) Even with a painting of a joint-smoking Mona Lisa looming over the reception, this clean, smart hotel has well-lit rooms of various sizes. Some have air-conditioning, and all have private bathrooms with hot water and cable TV.

Hotel Karina (☎ 269-4764; 10 de Agosto at Antonia Ante; r per person incl breakfast with/without air-con $12/8) Situated on a bustling street corner, Karina's small rooms have private bathrooms, cable TV and include breakfast.

Hostal El Conquistador (☎ 269-4057; Bolívar at Abdón Calderón; r per person $10) All the rooms have air-conditioning, private bathrooms, and cable TV, but they're on the dark and small side.

Macará's dining options are slim and grim, but the friendly, service-oriented **El Buen Sabor Macareño** (☎ 269-4193; Manuel Rengel Bolivar) is an exception with its hit-the-spot *almuerzos* ($3), as is **D'Marco's** (Jaime Roldos near Amazonas; mains $5-6), which serves seafood.

Getting There & Away

Transportes Loja Internacional (Lázaro Vaca at Juvenal Jaramilla) buses leave six times a day to Loja ($6, six hours) and take the Catacocha route. **Union Cariamanga** (☎ 269-4047; www.unioncariamanga.com.ec; cnr Loja & Manuel E Rengel) has several buses a day to Loja ($6, six hours) via Cariamanga.

The crossing into Peru via Macará is much quieter than at Huaquillas and busier than at Zumba. Macará is 3km from the actual border crossing, or *puente internacional* (international bridge). Most people buy tickets direct to Piura (Peru) from Loja (see p218), but both companies listed above leave Macará for Piura (Peru) twice a day ($3, three hours). The bus stops at the border, waits for passengers to take care of exits and entries, and then continues to Piura.

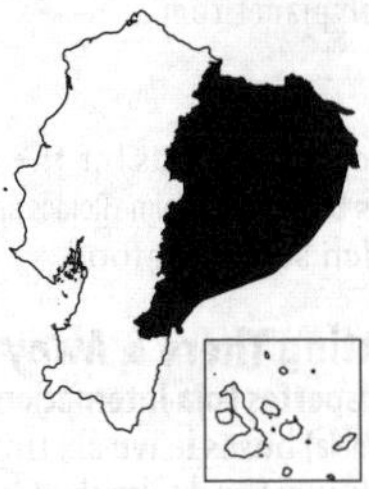

The Oriente

This vast landmass holds more drama than a rip-roaring flood or crackling lightning storm. Rivers churn from the snowcapped Andes into the dense, sweltering rainforest on course to the distant Atlantic Ocean. Along the way, ancient indigenous tribes call the riverbanks home.

Around many bends the modern world rubs up against the jungle and its inhabitants. Players include politicians, environmentalists, missionaries, indigenous peoples, and representatives of big industry, including oil companies, which pried open the Oriente in the 1960s. Here, everyone is angling for something, and the stakes couldn't be higher.

After all, this immense expanse holds an astounding amount of biodiversity. Beyond the cloud forests of the eastern Andean foothills, the rainforest is home to 50% of Ecuador's mammals, 5% of the earth's plant species and prolific birdlife. The most pristine parts of the Ecuadorian Amazon drip with life: orchids drop from mossy tree limbs, parrots fly in pairs, monkeys leap through the canopy and jaguars pad silently along paths. At night, the sounds of the jungle can be deafening.

Covering more than a third of Ecuador's land, the Oriente houses only a tiny percentage of the country's population, including the native Achuar, Cofán, Huaorani, Quichua, Secoya, Shuar, Siona and Zaparo tribes. Some cultures struggle to maintain traditional ways of life; many have retreated into the interior, and some have sworn off all contact with the outside world. But for others, adaptation has not made their cultures any less diverse or fascinating.

HIGHLIGHTS

- Spot pink dolphins in the blackwater paradise of **Reserva Producción Faunística Cuyabeno** (p240).
- Spend time with a **Huaorani tribe** (p241) with the help of a native guide.
- Tame some **white-water rapids** (p250) in a raft or kayak on the rivers outside of Tena.
- Soak in the pristine steaming waters at **Papallacta** (opposite).
- Descend into the dark underworld of **Cueva de los Tayos** (p266).
- Fish for piranhas in **Pañacocha** (p247).

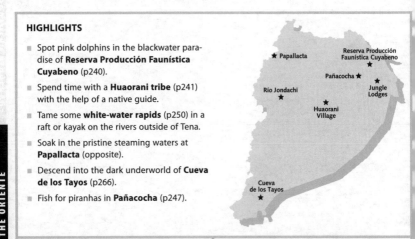

- AVERAGE TEMP IN NUEVO ROCAFUERTE: 10°C
- RAINIEST MONTH IN NUEVO ROCAFUERTE: JUL

Climate

The Oriente gets plenty of rain from April to July, its wettest months. Afternoon and evening rains are common year-round. August and December to March are the driest times. In some areas lagoons dry up entirely, tumbling waterfalls trickle and long-distance canoe rides become epic. Small rivers may become impassable due to low water levels.

You'll find a contrast between the sweltering flatlands (from Coca north toward Colombia and east to Peru) and cooler upland hills (around Tena, Misahuallí and Puyo). Damp jungle nights can feel downright chilly. Don't forget a sweater, although you can leave the woolen poncho in Otavalo.

National Parks

The remote **Parque Nacional Sumaco-Galeras** has 205,249 hectares of high peaks and dense tropical forest where jaguars and tapirs run wild. One of the few ways to access the park is on a white-water rafting trip on the stunning Río Hollín. South of the Río Napo is **Parque Nacional Yasuní**, a 9620-sq-km expanse of diverse wildlife (with 500 bird species), native populations, scientific stations and, astonishingly, oil exploration. Access is exclusively through tour operators. Further south, **Parque Nacional Sangay** straddles highlands and the Amazon Basin. Volcanoes Sangay, Tungurahua and El Altar sit within its 517,765 hectares. The peaks are best accessed via the highland side, but Macas is a good base for a strenuous hike to the upper lakes.

Dangers & Annoyances

Border crossings into Colombia from anywhere in the Oriente are not advised. Enter Peru from Nuevo Rocafuerte only.

Getting There & Away

Flights on national airlines go between Quito and Lago Agrio, Coca, Shell/Puyo and Macas. Otherwise, buses run from highland cities to major Oriente towns.

Getting Around

Many parts of the Oriente can only be reached by light aircraft, canoe and footpaths. Most canoes on the main rivers are motorized; some provide sunshade and seats with backs, which can make long journeys more pleasant. Light aircraft are more easily booked through a tour or lodge; they land on small airstrips in the jungle, a faster but more expensive way to reach remote regions. Bus travel in the south is less reliable due to bad roads and weather.

THE NORTHERN ORIENTE

Small drab cities are the gateways to the Amazon Basin, a place of unparalleled biodiversity. While it's tempting to dismiss the area as tainted by development and big oil, the rainforest thrives, home to more than 500 bird species, big cats, butterflies, freshwater dolphins, monkeys, fish, snakes and insects.

It's the most accessible part of the Ecuadorian jungle. Visitors travel down milky brown rivers to indigenous villages, parklands and lodges. While indigenous peoples are accustomed to outsiders jockeying for their land and resources, they still proudly share this unique region with the respectful visitor.

A paved road from Quito splits at Baeza; the north fork heads to Lago Agrio, the south fork goes to Tena. The other main road zips from highland Baños to Puyo in under two hours. In the rainiest months (June to August) roads can wash out and airports can close. Allow an extra day or two between important connections in Quito.

FROM QUITO TO LAGO AGRIO

☎ 06

Buses chug out of the Quito valley, fighting the effects of altitude, which on this ride reaches 4100m. That apex begins a dramatic descent through the Andes to gauzy lowland jungle. Two hours out of Quito you'll pass Ecuador's best thermal baths, Papallacta. A half-hour later the road forks at Baeza; Tena is to the right, Lago Agrio 170km to the left. Notice the large, snaking trans-Andean oil pipeline, a 500km-long eyesore that pumps hundreds of thousands of barrels each day to Esmeraldas province. It parallels the road all the way to Lago Agrio. Some 95km before Lago Agrio, the San Rafael Falls thunder and the 3562m Volcán Reventador, which erupted spectacularly in November 2002, sits shrouded in clouds.

Papallacta

elevation 3300m

Slip into this tiny village's steamy, therapeutic waters to soothe sore muscles or combat the high-altitude chill. At Termas de Papallacta,

THE ORIENTE

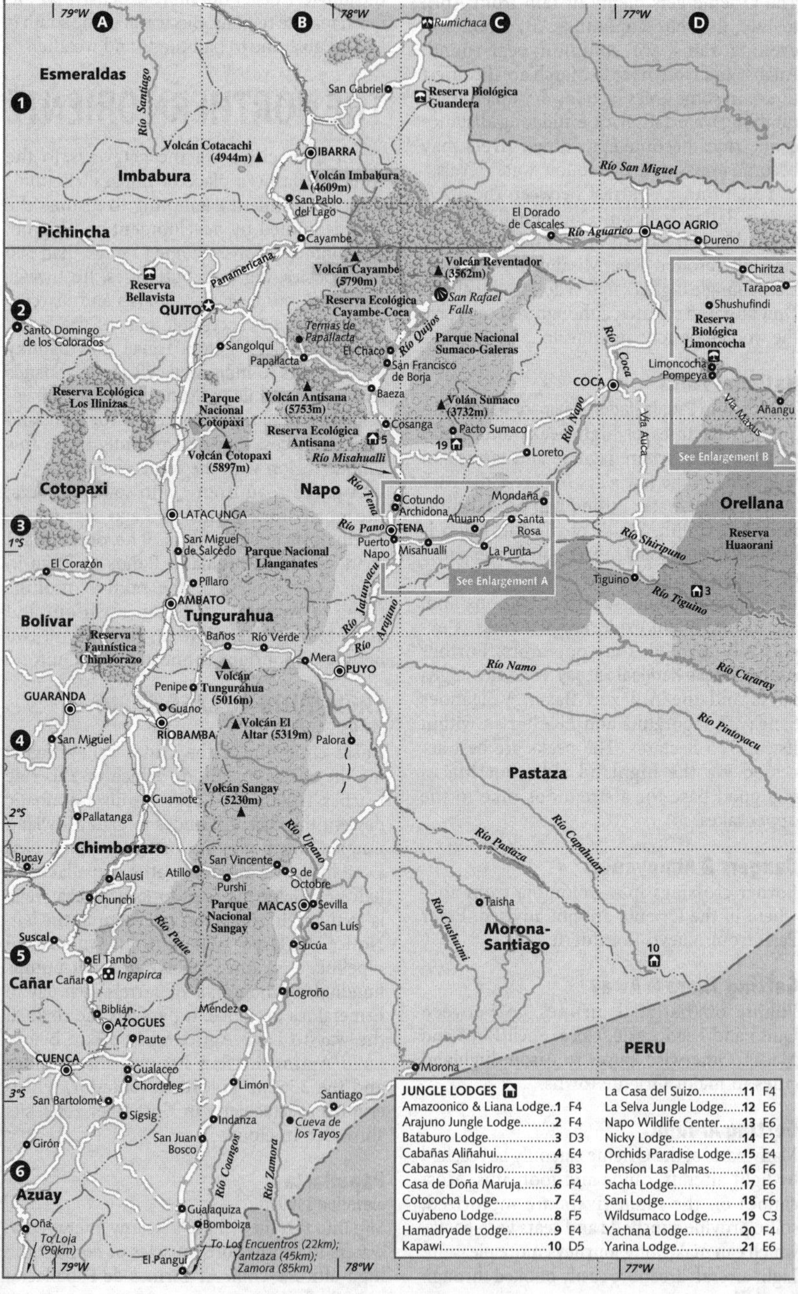
79°W
78°W
77°W
A
B
C
D
1
2
3
4
5
6
1°S
2°S
3°S
Rumichaca
Esmeraldas
Río Santiago
San Gabriel
Reserva Biológica Guandera
Volcán Cotacachi (4944m)
IBARRA
Imbabura
Volcán Imbabura (4609m)
Río San Miguel
San Pablo del Lago
El Dorado de Cascales
Río Aguarico
LAGO AGRIO
Dureno
Pichincha
Cayambe
Panamericana
Volcán Cayambe (5790m)
Volcán Reventador (3562m)
Chiritza
Tarapoa
Reserva Bellavista
QUITO
Reserva Ecológica Cayambe-Coca
San Rafael Falls
Shushufindi
Reserva Biológica Limoncocha
Santo Domingo de los Colorados
Termas de Papallacta
Río Quijos
Parque Nacional Sumaco-Galeras
Río Coca
Sangolquí
El Chaco
Papallacta
San Francisco de Borja
Limoncocha
Pompeya
COCA
Reserva Ecológica Los Ilinizas
Parque Nacional Cotopaxi
Volcán Antisana (5753m)
Baeza
Volán Sumaco (3732m)
Vía Maxus
Añangu
Reserva Ecológica Antisana
Cosanga
Pacto Sumaco
Río Napo
Vía Auca
Volcán Cotopaxi (5897m)
Río Misahualli
Loreto
See Enlargement B
Cotopaxi
Napo
Río Tena
Cotundo
Archidona
Mondaña
Orellana
LATACUNGA
Río Pano
TENA
Ahuano
Santa Rosa
Reserva Huaorani
Puerto Napo
Misahuallí
La Punta
Río Shiripuno
San Miguel de Salcedo
Parque Nacional Llanganates
El Corazón
Píllaro
See Enlargement A
Tiguino
Río Jatunyacu
Río Tiguino
AMBATO
Tungurahua
Río Arajuno
Bolívar
Reserva Faunística Chimborazo
Baños
Río Verde
Mera
Río Namo
PUYO
Río Curaray
Volcán Tungurahua (5016m)
Penipe
GUARANDA
Guano
RIOBAMBA
Volcán El Altar (5319m)
Palora
San Miguel
Río Pintoyacu
Pastaza
Volcán Sangay (5230m)
Guamote
Pallatanga
Río Upano
Río Capahuari
Río Pastaza
Chimborazo
Bucay
San Vincente
Alausí
Atillo
9 de Octobre
Purshi
Chunchi
Parque Nacional Sangay
MACAS
Sevilla
Taisha
Río Cushuimi
Río Paute
San Luís
Morona-Santiago
Suscal
Sucúa
El Tambo
Cañar
Ingapirca
Logroño
Biblián
Méndez
AZOGUES
Paute
PERU
CUENCA
Gualaceo
Morona
Chordeleg
Limón
San Bartolomé
Santiago
Sigsig
Indanza
Cueva de los Tayos
Girón
San Juan Bosco
Río Coangos
Río Zamora
Azuay
Gualaquiza
Bomboiza
Oña
To Loja (90km)
El Panguí
To Los Encuentros (22km); Yantzaza (45km); Zamora (85km)
JUNGLE LODGES
Amazoonico & Liana Lodge....1 F4
Arajuno Jungle Lodge....2 F4
Bataburo Lodge....3 D3
Cabañas Aliñahui....4 E4
Cabanas San Isidro....5 B3
Casa de Doña Maruja....6 F4
Cotococha Lodge....7 E4
Cuyabeno Lodge....8 F5
Hamadryade Lodge....9 E4
Kapawi....10 D5
La Casa del Suizo....11 F4
La Selva Jungle Lodge....12 E6
Napo Wildlife Center....13 E6
Nicky Lodge....14 E2
Orchids Paradise Lodge....15 E4
Pensíon Las Palmas....16 F6
Sacha Lodge....17 E6
Sani Lodge....18 F6
Wildsumaco Lodge....19 C3
Yachana Lodge....20 F4
Yarina Lodge....21 E6

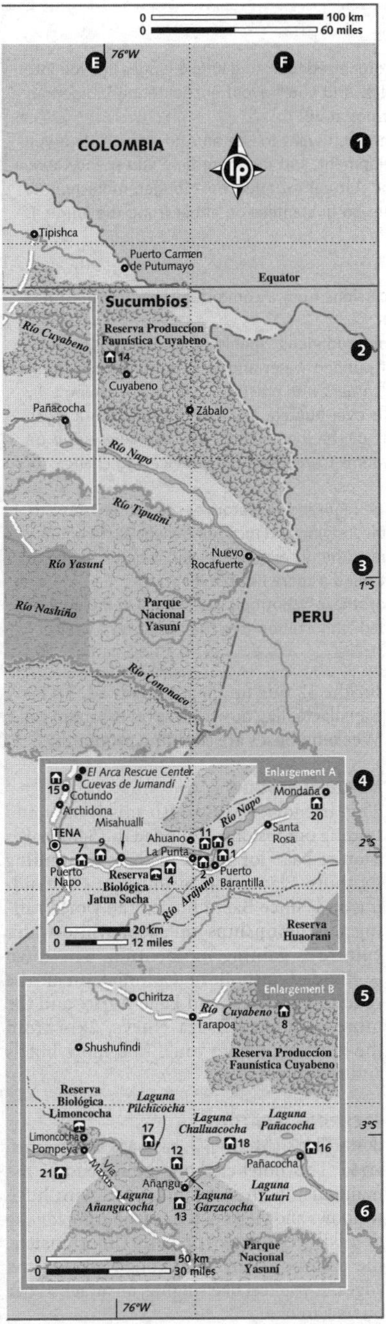

more than three-dozen sparkling pools offer the country's most luxurious thermal baths experience. The complex is about 3km outside the village of Papallacta and is a good day trip from Quito, 67km (two hours) away. Be prepared for on–off chilly rains or intense sun.

TERMAS DE PAPALLACTA

About 1.5km before the village, on the left as you approach from Quito, a marked dirt road leads 2km uphill to Termas de Papallacta. The setting is grand: on a clear day you can see the snowcapped **Volcán Antisana** (5753m), 15km south, beyond the lush hillsides. Unfortunately the hot springs are a poorly kept secret; opt for a weekday visit if possible. There are two sets of pools: the **Balneario** (admission $7; 9am-6pm) and the **Spa** (admission $18). The Balneario is paradisial, with more than 25 blue pools of varying temperatures surrounded by plush grass and red-orange blossoms. The nearby Río Loreto-Papallacta makes for an exhilarating plunge. Towels and lockers are available. There's little reason to spend the extra money on the Spa pools, although they are less crowded, smaller and filled with jets. An indoor sauna can loosen you up for a spa treatment, which can range from $10 to $45. Pool water is changed daily.

SLEEPING & EATING

Hostal Antisana (232-0626; r per person $17) This big, echoey *hostal* (small, reasonably priced hotel) sits in the shadow of Termas de Papallacta, just a few meters away. It's chilly, despite the friendly owner, so bring warm clothes if you spend the night. Pools out back look washed out compared with their counterparts up the road, but the on-site restaurant is a bargain.

Hostería La Pampa de Papallacta (232-0624; r per person incl breakfast $20-25) Flintstone-like adobe construction leaves few hard edges at this convenient (just off the Quito–Baeza road) hotel. Rooms are basic and without heat, which makes the on-site hot pools key. Two were under construction at the time of research.

Hotel Termas de Papallacta (Quito 02-250-4787, 02-256-8989; www.termaspapallacta.com; cnr Foch E7-38 & Reina Victoria, 4th fl; d $120-140, 6-person cabin $165-220;) A posh retreat of thatched adobe cabins with smart wood-paneled rooms. The outdoor hot springs hidden between the wings of the hotel are exclusively for hotel guests, while the other pool complexes welcome visitors

PREPARING FOR A JUNGLE TRIP

While it's possible to visit the jungle on your own, organized tours and jungle lodges get you into the wilderness quicker and without all the logistics. And you'll avoid encountering indigenous peoples who prefer to see tourists with guides or not at all.

First, figure out how much you can spend, what you want to see and how much time you have. The further you travel from roads and development, and the more time you spend there, the more wildlife you'll see. The same applies for cultural experiences – longer, more remote trips result in more-authentic encounters. There are no guarantees on either front; the jungle is neither an animal nor human zoo.

The Differences

Lodges and large hotel-style boats offer daily excursions from a comfortable base. Other tours may include camping or sleeping in communities.

Lower costs may translate to more basic accommodations, Spanish-speaking guides, non-naturalist guides, larger groups, boiled instead of purified water and visits to developed areas with less wildlife. In some cases, operators may cut corners with practices that are not ecologically sound, including hunting for food. The rainforest is over-hunted; a no-hunting policy is a must.

Different operators emphasize different aspects of the jungle, and each can advise you on the probability of seeing specific wildlife. Observation towers greatly enhance the chances of sighting birds and monkeys.

Visiting indigenous cultures can be done through high-end operators or community tourism. High-end programs will offer translators, comfortable lodging and may run beneficial community programs. Community tourism usually offers a more authentic experience, and is better suited to Spanish speakers with strong stomachs who don't mind a more flexible itinerary.

Some unscrupulous outfitters will offer *ayahuasca* or other psychotropics used ritually in indigenous cultures. These illegal substances should be regarded with caution (see the boxed text, p256).

(see p233). All accommodations have private bathrooms, heating, hot showers and tubs. Weekends must be reserved well in advance. Three restaurants (mains $5 to $12) – one each in the hotel, Balneario and Spa – have similar menus, but the hotel locale serves a wider range of international dishes including lamb chops, sea bass and filet mignon.

La Choza de Don Wilson (☎ 232-0627; mains $3-4) Almost everyone comes to this honky-tonk restaurant for an excellent fillet of trout and shots of *aguardiente* (sugarcane alcohol) to beat off the chills. You'll find it at the juncture with the road to Termas de Papallacta. Cement-floor rooms out back are plain but clean (per person $15), with views of the village below. An enclosed hot pool is a bonus. Situated 40km along the Quito–Baeza road.

GETTING THERE & AWAY

Any of the buses from Quito heading toward Baeza, Tena or Lago Agrio can drop you off in Papallacta, as can the occasional Papallacta bus. To visit the Termas de Papallacta complex, ask the driver to let you off on the road to the baths, 1.5km before the village. Then catch an awaiting *camioneta* (pickup or light truck) for the $2 ride up the bumpy road. To leave Papallacta, flag down a bus on the main road. Weekend buses are standing room only.

Baeza & Around

This friendly, old Spanish missionary and trading outpost, first founded in 1548, makes a quiet base for walks in the surrounding foothills. Plants and birdlife are outstanding and, since Baeza hosted the world rafting championships in 2005, white-water culture is gaining momentum. The town is divided into Baza Colonial, near the road to Papallacta and Lago Agrio, and the more populated Baeza Nueva, 2km from the junction, where you'll find more hotels and restaurants.

SLEEPING & EATING

Hostal Dido's (☎ 232-0357; Nueva Andalucía; r per person $6) This hotel anchors the far end of the main strip with spacious rooms with huge windows and views of the neighboring *tomate de arbol* (tree tomato) orchard. Unfortunately, the bathrooms are a bit rough around the edges. If you feel like singing, an attached bar offers karaoke.

Hiking alone is not advised (it is a jungle out there). Whatever choices you make, tread lightly and respect local communities.

Tour Bookings

In Quito, numerous operators' offices (see p96) allow for quick, comparative shopping. Agencies can usually get you into the jungle with a few days' notice. Once you've booked a tour, you usually have to travel to the town where the tour begins (usually Lago Agrio, Coca, Tena or Misahuallí). Thoroughly discuss costs, food, equipment, itinerary and group size before booking.

Booking a tour from Tena, Coca, Puyo or Macas is best if you want short, guided trips to nearby reserves or communities. The Cofán, Huaorani, Quichua, Shuar and other groups offer trips guided by their own community members.

Guides

A good guide will show you things you would have missed on your own, whereas an inadequate guide may spoil the trip. Guides should be able to produce a license on request and explain their specialties. Recommended guides are always preferable, and many lodges are known for their quality guiding services.

What to Bring

Jungle towns have only basic equipment, including bottled water, tarps (for rain) and rubber boots in an array of sizes. Many guided tours lend the essential boots and rain gear, but check beforehand. Mosquito nets are usually provided in places that need them. If you're serious about seeing wildlife, bring your own binoculars. Some guides will carry a pair, but will need them to make sightings. Besides your general travel supplies, bring a flashlight with extra batteries, sun block and repellant with DEET. Depending on the time of year and your destination, you may need malaria pills (see p405).

Hotel Samay (☎ 232-0170; Nueva Andalucía; r per person $6) Rooms in this friendly clapboard home come in all the colors of the rainbow. There's TV and hot water.

Hostal Bambu (☎ 232-0219/0615, Nueva Andalucía; r per person $8) Just a few doors down from its doppelganger in name only, a crumbling courtyard belies good basic rooms that have everything but direct sunlight.

Hostal Bambu's (☎ 232-0003; Nueva Andalucía; r per person $10) If you've ever wanted to sleep in a teenager's dream rec room, here's your chance. Rooms look out onto an indoor pool with diving board and inflatable toys, and there's a ping-pong table. The beds are unforgiving, but there's plenty of hot water.

El Viejo (☎ 232-0442; Nueva Andalucía; mains $5; 7am-9pm) A main gathering place, this warm restaurant with a clean, open kitchen serves trout in every possible way. Caters to tourists with an English/Spanish menu.

About 10km away on the road to Lago Agrio you reach the village of San Francisco de Borja and **Cabañas Tres Ríos** (☎ 09-792-0120; s/d $30/50), a group of lovely cabins east of the village and across Río Quijos. It can arrange Spanish classes, area tours, hikes, rafting and biking. A chef will cook meals on request. Catering mainly to kayakers (who may desperately need the on-site massages), the cabins are often full from November to March. Contact **Small World Adventures** (☎ USA 970-309-8913; www.smallworldadventures.com) for more information.

In a spectacular setting at 2000m, **Cabañas San Isidro** (☎ Quito 02-254-7403; www.cabanasanisidro.com; cnr Carrion N21-01 & Juan Mera, Quito; s/d incl 3 meals $80/130) is a former cattle ranch that's become a 3700-acre nature reserve. It offers first-class bird-watching, and co-owner Mitch Lsinger is one of the top bird-watchers in South America. Comfortable cabins have decks with forest views, and rooms have hot-water bathrooms. Nearby hiking trails weave through wonderful, subtropical cloud forest. Advance reservation is required. To get there, turn off the Baeza–Tena road just north of the village of Cosanga.

GETTING THERE & AWAY

Flag down one of the many buses going to and from Lago Agrio, Tena and Quito and hope there's room. Coming from Quito, take a Tena-bound bus from the main terminal.

El Chaco

Bigger than Baeza, but still sleepy, this one-stoplight town could experience a tourism boom as word gets out about its prime white water.

Get information about the area at **iTur** (☎ 234-9419; chacotourism@yahoo.com; 🕑 7:30am-5pm) on the main road by the intersection. Possibilities include hikes to local waterfalls, petroglyphs and an oil bird cave. **Waterdog Tours** (☎ 09-352-2152; www.waterdogtours.com) leads a variety of trips on the Río Quijos (site of the 2005 rafting championships), Río Salado and Río Due. **Huayra Causay** (☎ 02-224-8955; www.hcausay.org) offers local volunteer opportunities.

SLEEPING & EATING

Hosteria Katherine (☎ 232-9146; cnr Mari Chacon & Lago Agrio; s/d $8/12) A sunny, two-storied hotel holds spick-and-span rooms that enclose an empty cement courtyard. Rooms are somewhat generic but comfortable.

La Guarida del Coyote Hostería (☎ 232-9421; la guardia_del_coyote@hotmail.com; r per person $10; 🅿) Hidden on the hillside under the large cross, this hotel offers verdant views of the surrounding mountains. Paintings and murals decorate the walls of basic rooms and suites. The pool out back is uncomfortably green and murky. The large circular restaurant only serves large groups with prior arrangement.

With a glaring lack of restaurants in the town, the Colombian **Patacon Con Todo** (🕑 7am-5pm) on the main road is your only bet.

GETTING THERE & AWAY

Flag down a bus on the main road to Lago Agrio ($4, 3½ hours).

San Rafael Falls

Beyond El Chaco you'll pass thick patches of cloud forest harboring strange species of birds and plants. **San Rafael Falls** (admission $10) and a sash of Río Quijos can be glimpsed from the road. The entrance fee is steep, but visitors earn bragging rights to witnessing Ecuador's largest falls. To visit the falls, ask the bus driver to let you off just before the *puente* (bridge) crossing Río Reventador (not the community of the same name). You'll see a concrete-block hut on the right side of the road. From the hut, it's about 2.5km down a steep trail to the falls. Back on the main road, flag down a bus when you want to move on.

Volcán Reventador

After this volcano erupted in 2002, hiking to the summit was impossible. Intrepid explorers can reach the top (3562m), but because lava flows wiped out the already faint trail, it's easy to get lost; hire a local guide. **Victor Cansino** (☎ 09-471-6998; turismovolcanreventador@yahoo.com; per day $40, plus park entree fee $10) has experience leading vulcanologists up the mountain and knows about medicinal plants. Hike four to five hours to a camp site on the edge of the lava flow (Victor rents camping equipment), then depart early in the morning for a four-hour hike to the summit. Reventador is notoriously active and may not always be climbable. For updates consult the **Instituto Geofisico** (☎ 02-222-5655; www.igepn.edu.ec).

You can stay overnight at **Hostería Reventador** (☎ 09-312-9515; r per person $12; 🅿) a friendly, if run-down, concrete lodge by the San Rafael Falls, where you may also find Victor serving up fish and chips in the restaurant. The volcano is within the eastern boundaries of **Reserva Ecológica Cayambe-Coca**, which includes **Volcán Cayambe** (5790m; p121). There are no signs or entrance stations. The guard station is in the village of **El Chaco**, about 20km from Reventador on the road to Baeza.

LAGO AGRIO

☎ 06 / pop 55,917

This seedy, gray town pulses with the life of the oil industry, although as the provincial capital of Sucumbíos, a bit of normalcy underlies a chaotic market, dusty streets, thick traffic and gritty bars. The first oil workers nicknamed Lago Agrio 'bitter lake,' after Sour Lake, Texas, the former home of Texaco, which pioneered local drilling (see the boxed text, p239). The city's official name is Nueva Loja, although no one calls it that. Locals settle for 'Lago.'

Few tourists step foot here, and locals seem exasperated by the town's sad reputation. But certain realities exist, including a high amount of prostitution and crime related to the nearby Colombian border. Locals keep their heads down and mind their own business; visitors should do the same. Lago is the entry point to the spectacular and singular Cuyabeno reserve, which draws some overnight travelers on their way to the jungle.

Information

Lago Agrio has very few street signs and scant building numbers. *Casas de cambio* (currency-exchange bureaus) on Avenida

Quito near Avenida Colombia can change Colombian pesos.

Andinatel (cnr Orellana & 18 de Noviembre)

Banco de Guayaquil (cnr Av Quito & 12 de Febrero; 8am-4pm Mon-Fri, 9am-noon Sat) Changes traveler's checks; has an ATM.

Banco del Pichincha (12 de Febrero) Has an ATM.

Casa de Cultura (☎ 283-2505; cnr Manabí & Av Quito, 2nd fl; 2-9:30pm Mon-Fri) Offers movie viewings. Contact Manual Silva for local indigenous and environmental affairs.

Clínica González (☎ 283-0728/1691; cnr Av Quito & 12 de Febrero) The best medical attention.

Frente de Defensa de la Amazonía (☎ 283-1930; admin@fda.ecuanex.net.ec; Alfaro 352) Contact with Cofán indigenous guides; active in environmental issues.

Interactive (☎ 283-0529; Río Amazonas; per hr $3) Internet access inside the entrance to Hotel La Cascada.

Migraciones (Immigration Office; 18 de Noviembre)

Post office (Rocafuerte)

World System Internet (Av Quito 522 near Orellana; per hr $1; 9am-7pm Mon-Sat)

Dangers & Annoyances

The ongoing conflict in neighboring Colombia has made border towns such as Lago Agrio havens for Colombian guerrillas, antirebel paramilitaries and drug smugglers. It is not recommended to cross into Colombia here. In town, bars can be risky and side streets unsafe, so stick to the main drag, especially at night, or take a taxi to the restaurants further out. Tourists rarely have problems.

Intermittent armed robberies have taken place near the entry to the Cuyabeno reserve. But ranger presence has increased and lodges have coordinated to make the area safer.

Sights & Activities

Shop for Cofan handicrafts sold by tribal members (see p239) at the Sunday morning market.

Sleeping

There are decent hotels along Avenida Quito. Mosquitoes can be a problem, especially in the rainy months (June to August), making fans and mosquito nets essential. Unlike in most towns, hotels here charge extra for 'amenities' including hot water and fans. Be prepared for extensive mix-and-match price menus.

Hotel Selva Real (☎ 283-3867; cnr Avs Quito 261 & Colombia; r per person $15-20) Don't be put off by the driveway reception area. Rooms are neat and clean and have TVs. Bargain hunters won't mind the cold showers in the cheapest rooms.

Hotel D'Mario (☎ 283-0172; www.hoteldmario.com; Av Quito 1-171; r per person incl breakfast $15-45;) Tour groups favor this midstrip staple. While service is somewhat indifferent, there's free internet for guests, and the rooms, though cramped, make cozy efforts. All rooms have private bathroom and fans or air-con. The restaurant serves good sandwiches, but is known for its sloppy pizzas.

Hotel Gran Colombia (☎ 283-1032; Av Quito 265; s/d $22/26;) A multilevel megalith with a long layout much like the other hotels on the street. Rooms feel stuffy and overdressed, but all have air-conditioning. The restaurant is popular and most rooms have phones, mini-bars and cable TV.

Hotel La Cascada (☎ 283-2229; www.hcascada.com; Av Quito 291; s/d incl breakfast $25/43;) Off-street rooms are small yet snug, insulating guests from the gritty streets. Splash in the swimming pool alongside locals beating the heat. All rooms have cable TV and air-conditioning. Breakfast is served in the restaurant, which is also open for other meals. Located next door to an internet café.

Araza Hotel (☎ 283-1287/47; www.hotel-araza.com; cnr Av Quito 536 & Narvaez; s/d incl breakfast $35/46;) Caters to suited oil execs with a tropical courtyard, a professional staff and a bar with big-screen TV. Spotless, tasteful rooms have air-conditioning and wi-fi. If you have time, check out the gym and swimming pool.

Eating

Because oil workers end work on Sunday it's the busiest night for eating out or traveling. Most restaurants are closed Monday and Tuesday.

Gran Colombia Restaurant (Av Quito; mains $4-6; 7am-10pm) Oil workers refuel here at the end of the day with set meals doused in lip-burning *ají* (hot sauce). The regular menu offers tasty plates such as *chuleta* (pork chops) and ceviche.

Maytos (☎ 283-0641; Av Quito; mains $5; 2-11pm Mon-Sat) Serves *maitos* (fish grilled in palm leaves) Huaorani-style, but with a garlicky twist. Wrapped in banana leaves and steamed over hot coals, the flavors steam into the moist, flaky fish, served alongside *patacones* (plantain fritters) and rice. Perfect with a tall cold brew. Next to the Texaco station, just over 3km out of town.

Freedom (☎ 283-1180; cnr Av Quito & Circubalacíon; dinners $8; 6:30-11pm, closed Mon & Tue) This thatched-hut outdoor grill has tasty sides of homemade salsa, salad and yuca (cassava).

Other eateries, including chicken rotisserie stalls and fast-food vendors, line Avenida Quito.

Getting There & Away

AIR

Flying prevents the need for a long bus trip on a corkscrew mountain road. Reservations fill up fast with jungle-lodge guests and oil workers traveling home for the weekend; book early. If you can't get a ticket, go to the airport and get on a waiting list in the hope of cancellations, which are frequent as tour companies book more seats than they can use.

TAME (☎ 283-0113; Orellana near 9 de Octubre) flights leave Quito at 9am every day and return to Quito at 10am. In addition, on Friday flights leave Quito at 4:30pm and return from Lago Agrio at 5:30pm ($48, 30 minutes).

VIP (☎ 283-0333; www.vipec.com) has an office at the airport and runs one to three flights daily between Quito and Lago Agrio, with no flights on Saturday.

The airport is about 3km east of town (a 10-minute trip), and taxis (yellow or white pickup trucks) cost about $3.

BORDER CROSSINGS

The Colombian border is less than 20km north of town but it is best to avoid it. The area is notorious for smugglers and FARC (Revolutionary Armed Forces of Colombia) activity. The most frequently used route from Lago Agrio is to La Punta (about 1½ hours) on Río San Miguel. Taxi-trucks leave Lago Agrio from the corner of Eloy Alfaro and Avenida Colombia and go to La Punta during the day.

BUS

The drive from the jungle into the Andes (and vice versa) is dramatic and beautiful, and worth doing in daylight. Night buses have had occasional robberies.

The bus terminal, about 2km northwest of the center, has a wide selection of routes and options. Buses depart for Quito ($8, eight hours)

A CRUDE LEGACY

According to environmentalists, one of the greatest oil-related disasters of all time lies at the feet of the Texaco oil corporation (now Chevron), which, in partnership with state-owned Petroecuador, extracted some 5.3 billion liters of oil from the northern Oriente between 1964 and 1992.

In 2003, US attorneys filed a lawsuit in Lago Agrio (the case was moved from US courts after a decade of wrangling), on behalf of 30,000 Ecuadorians, against ChevronTexaco, claiming the company intentionally dumped 18 billion gallons of toxic oil wastewater into the rainforest, including 18 million gallons of crude – almost twice what was spilled by the *Exxon Valdez*. The plaintiffs say Texaco's practices helped decimate indigenous populations (especially the Cofán and Secoya), destroy ecosystems and create a toxic environment that's resulted in increased rates of cancer and aborted pregnancies. They're asking for $6 billion.

In 1992, state-owned Petroecuador took over a majority of Texaco's operations, and Chevron says the Ecuadorian company is responsible for any existing pollution. Chevron says Texaco cleaned up its share of spills through a $40 million remediation program prescribed by the Ecuadorian government. According to Texaco's website, existing health problems in the region 'are related to lack of water treatment infrastructure, the lack of sufficient sanitation infrastructure and inadequate access to medical care.'

In the spring of 2008, a court-appointed expert recommended Chevron pay between $8 billion and $16 billion to clean up the rainforest. But the official judgment is still out on the first-ever class-action environmental suit brought against a multinational oil corporation. A judgment is expected in 2009 in Lago Agrio. Chevron's lawyers have said if the company loses, they will appeal.

Supporters of the plaintiffs include the **Amazon Defense Coalition** (www.texacotoxico.org) in Lago Agrio, **Amazon Watch** (www.amazonwatch.org), **ChevronToxico** (www.chevrontoxico.com) and Texaco Rainforest (www.texacorainforest.org). **Texaco** (www.texaco.com) refutes the claims in detail – check out the website for further information.

almost every hour until 11:45pm. Cooperativo Loja and Cooperativo Esmeraldas have better *ejecutivo* (first-class) buses. Transportes Putumayo goes to Tulcán via a new route ($7, seven hours), the best option for crossing the border. Ruta Costa has seven departures daily for Guayaquil ($14, 14 hours). There are one or two overnight buses to Tena, Puyo, Ambato, Riobamba, Cuenca and Machala.

Buses to Coca aren't usually found in the bus terminal; catch a Petroleras Rancheras ($3, three hours) bus on the corner of Petrolera and Amazonas. They leave every 20 minutes until 6pm. Transportes Putumayo buses go through the jungle towns of Dureno and Tarapoa and have access to the Cuyabeno reserve.

ALONG RÍO AGUARICO

☎ 06

This region of the Cuyabeno reserve is home to the Cofán tribe. The Cofán numbered in the tens of thousands before early contact with whites decimated them (mainly by disease). It's estimated that 1200 Cofán people currently exist in Ecuador. Before the discovery of oil, most Cofáns' exposure to nonindigenous people was limited to the occasional missionary, and they still practice a traditional lifestyle. The Cofán are excellent wilderness guides with broad knowledge about the medicinal and practical uses of jungle plants.

The Cofán run well-organized **ecotourism trips** (www.cofan.org). Given the rapid environmental degradation of the area around Lago Agrio, multiday trips start at Chiritza but head to remote Zábalo.

Dureno

Within an hour from Lago Agrio, Dureno has some primary rainforest and a Cofán settlement, which makes for a good day trip. Although you won't see much wildlife, a local guide can show and explain jungle plants.

Trips to Dureno cost $65 per person per day and can be organized through Federacion Indigena de la Nacionalidad Cofán del Ecuador (FEINCE), the **Cofán Federation** (☎ 283-1200) or through the **Fundación Cofán** (☎ 283-2103) in Lago Agrio. Both offices are Spanish-speaking. Visiting the village without advance notice is discouraged.

Zábalo

This small Cofán community on Río Aguarico near the confluence with the smaller Río Zábalo is a seven-hour canoe ride from Lago

Agrio. Across the river from the village there is an interpretive center with a Cofán guide. Visiting the village without advance notice is discouraged and taking photographs is not allowed.

For information and to make reservations for a tour ($100 per day), contact **Randy Borman** (☎ in Quito 02-247-0946; randy@cofan.org), who is one of the few English-speaking guides in the area. The son of American missionaries who came to the Oriente in the 1950s, Randy was raised among the Cofán and formally educated in Quito. He later founded the settlement of Zábalo, where he still has a house with his Cofán wife and family. He is highly respected and one of the leaders of the Cofán Federation. Randy guides occasionally, but spends much of his time in Quito working to preserve the Cofán culture and the rainforest.

RESERVA PRODUCCIÓN FAUNÍSTICA CUYABENO

This beautiful **reserve** (admission $24) is a unique flooded rainforest covering 6034 sq km around Río Cuyabeno. Seasonally inundated with water, the flooded forest provides a home to diverse aquatic species and birdlife. Macrolobium and ceiba treetops thrust out from the underwater forest, creating a stunning visual effect. The blackwater rivers, rich in tannins from decomposing foliage, form a maze of waterways that feed the lagoons.

The boundaries of the reserve shift with the political winds, but the area is substantially larger than it was originally. The reserve was created in 1979 to protect rainforest, conserve wildlife and provide a sanctuary in which the indigenous inhabitants – the Siona, Secoya, Cofán, Quichua and Shuar – could lead customary ways of life. The numerous lakes and swamps are home to fascinating aquatic species, such as freshwater dolphins, manatees, caiman and anacondas. Monkeys abound, and tapirs, peccaries, agoutis and several cat species have been recorded. The birdlife is abundant.

Its protected status notwithstanding, Cuyabeno was opened to oil exploitation almost immediately after its creation. The oil towns Tarapoa and Cuyabeno and parts of the trans-Ecuadorian oil pipeline were built within the reserve's boundaries. Roads and colonists followed, and tens of thousands of hectares of the reserve became logged or degraded by oil spills and toxic waste. At least six oil spills were recorded between 1984 and 1989, and others occurred unrecorded. Many of the contaminants entered Río Cuyabeno itself.

Various international and local agencies set to work to try to protect the area, which although legally protected was, in reality, open to development. Conservation International funded projects to establish more guard stations in Cuyabeno, train local Siona and Secoya to work in wildlife management and support Cordavi, an Ecuadorian environmental-law group that challenged the legality of allowing oil exploitation in protected areas.

Finally, in late 1991 the government shifted the borders of the reserve further east and south and enlarged the area it covered. The new reserve is more remote and better protected. Vocal local indigenous groups – which are supported by Ecuadorian and international nongovernmental organizations (NGOs), tourists, travel agencies and conservation groups – are proving to be its best stewards.

Due to its remoteness, and to protect the communities within it, travelers should only visit the reserve on a guided tour.

Tours

Agencies in Quito offer Cuyabeno tours that are run by operators on location. Tour camps and lodges seem to open and close quickly here, but about 10 currently operate close to each other on the river; a few are close by on a lagoon. No location is significantly privileged; all have similar opportunities for spotting wildlife. Travel is mainly by canoe except between December and February, when low water levels limit canoe travel. Most visitors come during the wetter months of March to September. Annual rainfall is between 2000mm and 4000mm, depending on the location, and humidity is often 90% to 100%.

The best rates, especially for solo travelers, are obtained by squeezing into an existing trip. When booking, check to see if transportation to and from Lago Agrio is included, if the travel day is considered a tour day, if water is boiled or purified and whether you can expect naturalist or native guides. The entry fee to Cuyabeno reserve usually costs extra and is paid at the guard post in Tarapoa.

Cuyabeno Lodge (Map pp232-3; Laguna Grande; per person 3 nights $200-310, 4 nights $250-370) This recommended place is run by Neotropic Turis (Map p90; ☎ in Quito 02-252-1212, 09-980-3395; www.neotropicturis.com). Thatched huts spread out over a hillside offer a bit of privacy, and most have private bathroom and hot water. Solar power provides some electricity, but dinners are by candlelight. Rooms are rustic but comfortable, with firm beds and mosquito nets. Bilingual naturalist guides get top reviews from guests and the food and attention are excellent. Prices include transfers from Lago Agrio, a guide, drinking water, coffee and tea. Canoes and kayaks are available to paddle around the lake; many guests jump in for a swim.

Nicky Lodge (Map pp232-3) Run by Dracaena Amazon Rainforest Explorations (Map pp232–3; ☎ in Quito 02-254-6590; www.theamazondracaena.com; per person 3 nights $200), Nicky Lodge offers seven stilted cabins with private bathroom with running water. Daily expeditions include piranha fishing, wildlife viewing and a trip to a local community. A canopy tower enhances bird-watching opportunities. Eight- and six-day tours into more-remote parts of the rainforest involve camping. Prices do not include the park entrance fee or transport from Quito to Lago Agrio.

SOUTH FROM LAGO AGRIO

☎ 06

A smooth, winding strip of asphalt connects Lago Agrio and Coca, towns that before the 1970s were separated by wild jungle threaded with footpaths. These days, the heavily used road passes oil-worker camps, brothels and dilapidated towns. Buses that take the route stop frequently for locals. The bus crosses the Río Aguarico a few kilometers outside Lago and passes through small communities where children sell coconut milk and slices of fresh *sandia* (watermelon). Shortly before Coca, the bus goes through the small town of **La Joya de las Sachas**, then passes the belching wells of the Sacha oil works.

COCA

☎ 06 / pop 29,484

Coca exploded along with the oil boom, transforming a tiny river settlement with dirt roads into a hot and busy collection of concrete. The capital of the Orellana province since 1999 (and officially known as Puerto Francisco de Orellana), Coca sits on the Río Napo, once an all-important passageway that set the town's tone; these days grunting trucks and buses speak just as loudly. The bridge across the river begins the controversial Vía Auca, a road that plunges south into Huaorani territory.

The port attracts a mixture of oil execs and oil workers, soldiers, sailors, urbanized indigenous people and colonists. While the town lacks a single park, the new riverfront promenade draws crowds at weekends. There, squealing children feed monkeys showing off in the trees. If you're traveling to a jungle lodge on the lower Napo or to Peru, Coca is a lackluster but strangely compelling stop along the way.

Information

Andinatel office (cnr Alfaro & 6 de Diciembre)

Banco del Pinchincha (cnr Bolívar & 9 de Octubre) Has an ATM.

Clínica Sinai (cnr Napo & Moreno) This clinic is preferred to the hospital.

Pancho.net (Moreno; per hr $1; 🕑 7am-12pm) Internet service.

Post office (Napo near Montalvo)

Tourist information office (Transportes Fluviales Orellana Bldg, Chimborazo; 🕑 8:30am-1pm & 2-5:30pm Mon-Fri) Provides good info about the region.

Tours

Local tour companies have diminished in Coca. It's best to book from Quito, although a few independent guides operate in town.

Kem Pery Tours (Map p90; ☎ in Quito 02-250-5600; www.kempery.com; cnr Ramíres Dávalos 117 & Amazonas, Quito; lodge 3 nights with shared/private bathroom $310/330, 4 nights $350/370) Leads tours to Bataburo Lodge, on the edge of Huaorani territory, about nine hours from Coca by boat and bus. Canoes motor into the remote Ríos Tiguino and Cononaco and tours combine wildlife viewing with cultural visits. There is a $20 fee to enter Huaorani territory. Guides are both bilingual and native. The agency also runs longer trips in the same area that involve camping; see p244.

Otobo's Amazon Safari (www.rainforestcamping.com; per person 7-night tour incl airfare $1540) Operated by indigenous Huaorani Otobo and his family, this remote site on the Río Cononaco has platform tents and a thatched-roof lodge. Visitors hike in the Parque Nacional Yasuní with a native English-speaking guide, visit lagoons and a local village. The site can be reached by small plane from Shell/Puyo and motorized canoe, from Coca and the Vía Auca or by canoe only at a reduced price.

Tropic Ecological Adventures (Map pp88-9; ☎ in Quito 02-222-5907, in the US 703-879-1575; www.tropiceco.com; Av República E7-320, apt 1A, Quito) Provides tours to an ecologically sound lodge in Huaorani territory that is run by the Ecotourism Association of Quehueri'ono, which represents five communities on the upper Shiripuno River. The group also runs day trips, as well as one- and two-day tours into Secoya territory from Coca.

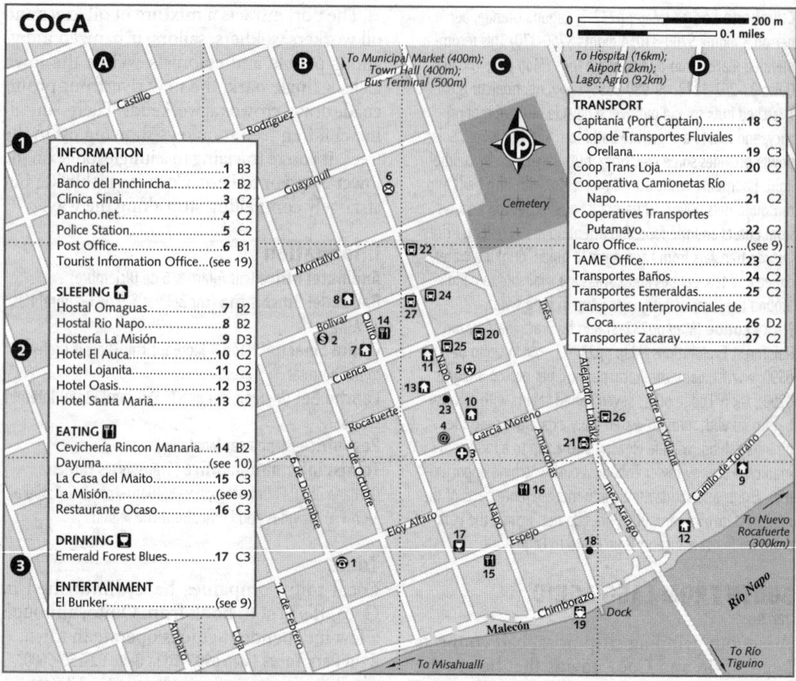

Jarol Fernando Vaca (☎ in Quito 02-227-1094; shiripuno2004@yahoo.com), a Quito-based naturalist and butterfly specialist, is a good independent guide. He can take visitors into the Shiripuno area and is authorized by the Huaorani to guide in their territory. **Sandro Ramos** (sandroidalio@hotmail.com) leads trips into Parque Nacional Yasuní, Huaorani territory and Iquitos, Peru. **Luis Duarte** (☎ 288-2285; cocaselva@hotmail.com) organizes customized tours, including river passage to Peru or stays with Huaorani families. Find him at La Casa del Maito, opposite.

Sleeping

Hotel Santa Maria (☎ 288-0097; Rocafuerte btwn Quito & Napo; r per person $8, with air-con s/d $15/20) Don't hit your head on the low ceiling in the stairwell on the way to cramped rooms with blistering paint.

Hotel Oasis (☎ 288-0206; yuturilodge@yahoo.com; Camilo de Torrano s/n; s/d with fan $9/12, with air-con s/d $12/25;) Despite basic, slightly battered rooms (the ones with air-conditioning hit refrigerator temps), you're away from the fray with a nice deck view of the river. The staff arranges trips to Yarina Lodge (see p245).

Hotel Lojanita (☎ 288-0032; hotelojanitacocaecuador@gmail.com; cnr Napo & Cuenca; s/d with fan $10/16, with air-con & hot water $15/24;) A remodel spruced up this hotel, which is convenient for catching buses. Most rooms have white walls and linens, and high ceilings, but some have held onto old decor; ask to see a few before choosing.

Hotel Rio Napo (☎ 288-0872; cnr Bolívar & Quito; s/d with fan incl breakfast $20/30, with air-con $25/40;) An orderly yet slightly generic spot, with good beds and neat rooms. All have private bathroom and cable TV.

Hostería La Misión (☎ 288-0260/0544; Camilo de Torrano s/n; s/d $23/34;) This longtime Coca staple has small, cool rooms overlooking the Río Napo. All rooms have cable TV, but hot water comes and goes. Multiple swimming pools are usually teeming with children. Sneaky monkeys live in the trees on-site, and the riverside restaurant and bar (see opposite) is the place to be on a warm evening.

Hotel El Auca (☎ 288-0127/0600; helauca@ecuanex.net.ec; Napo; s $25-47, d $40-50;) *Guatusas* (agoutis) overrun the grounds, but if you don't mind furry creatures (there are monkeys too) this hotel is the most upmarket place in town, catering to tour groups and oil workers alike. Choose from polished-wood cabins out back (with the critters), civilized rooms in a detached building, or rooms in the main hotel, which, at the highest price gets you more space and some street noise. The restaurant, Dayuma (below) is a good place to dial into the local scene; ask to dine in the luxuriant gardens.

Hostal Omaguas (☎ 288-0136; cnr Quito & Cuenca; s/d $27/48; ❄) Brightly tiled and gleaming clean, this welcoming spot has sparsely furnished rooms with cable TV and hot water. The restaurant is a cool, quiet haven from the sweltering streets.

Eating

Restaurante Ocaso (cnr Alfaro & Amazonas; mains $3-5; 🕒 6am-9pm) Locals recommend the saucy meat stews served alongside fluffy rice and hot *patacones*.

our pick **La Casa del Maito** (Espejo; mains $3.50; 🕒 7am-6pm) Stuff yourself between the noisy locals for the heavenly house specialty *maito*. Sometimes caiman caught upriver splashes onto the menu. The owner connects visitors with local guides (see opposite).

Cevichería Rincon Manaria (☎ 288-0957; Quito btwn Cuenca & Bolívar; mains $4-7; 🕒 9am-6pm) Plates piled with crispy *chifles* (banana slices) preview deep bowls of frothy ceviche served with little wedges of lime. Crowded tables and loud music create a beach-party vibe.

La Misión (Hotel La Misión, Camilo de Torrano; mains $7-12; 🕒 7am-10pm) Eat on the concrete patio overlooking the river or inside the bland restaurant. Dinner means delicious grilled white river fish, crispy salads and friendly service.

Dayuma (Hotel El Auca, Napo; mains $7-12; 🕒 6am-10pm) Large plates present standard combinations of surf and turf, meats in wine sauces and a few unimpressive pastas. Hit the attached *heladeria* (ice-cream shop) for dessert.

Drinking & Entertainment

Emerald Forest Blues (☎ 288-2280; Quito; 🕒 9am-late) An '80s soundtrack fills the background of this friendly little bar owned by Luís García, a popular local guide. Beer drinkers belly up to the bar well before lunchtime.

El Bunker (Hostería La Misión, Camilo de Torrano; 🕒 9pm-midnight Mon-Fri, to 2am Sat & Sun) The name suits this windowless, downstairs location that gets steamy on weekends with a mixture of *reggaetón* (a blend of Puerto Rican *bomba*, dancehall and hip-hop), Latin pop and hip-hop.

Getting There & Away

AIR

The airport terminal is almost 2km north of town on the left-hand side of the road to Lago Agrio. A 10-minute taxi ride there costs about $1.

TAME (☎ 288-0786/1078; cnr Napo & Rocafuerte; 🕒 7am-7pm Mon-Fri, 7am-1pm Sat, 9am-4pm Sun) flies from Coca to Quito Monday through Friday at 9:45am and 5pm, with a Saturday flight at 11am and a Sunday one at 3pm. Flights from Quito to Coca depart one hour earlier. The 30-minute flight costs $54.

Icaro (☎ 288-2767/68; www.icaro.com.ec; Hostería La Misión, Camilo de Torrano) flies from Quito four times per day Monday through Friday, three times on Saturday and twice on Sundays. Flights cost $56.

VIP (☎ 288-1742; www.vipec.com; airport office) runs one to three flights daily between Quito and back, with no flights on Sunday. Flights cost $55.

BOAT

Travelers arriving and departing by river must register their passport at the *capitanía* (port captain) by the landing dock. On tours, the guide usually takes care of this. Passenger canoe service to Misahuallí was suspended after the building of the Tena–Coca road. You could hire a private canoe (for 10 or more people) to Misahuallí for about $250, but they're hard to find. The upriver trip can take up to six hours, depending on water level (it takes four hours coming from the other direction).

Coop de Transportes Fluviales Orellana (☎ 288-0087; Chimborazo at docks; 🕒 8am-5pm Sun-Fri) offers an upriver passenger service in a covered 60-passenger canoe. Buy your ticket early. It departs Monday and Thursday at 7am for Nuevo Rocafuerte ($15, 10 hours) on the Peruvian border. It returns to Coca, departing Nuevo Rocafuerte at 5am on Sunday, Tuesday and Friday (12 to 14 hours). Although there's usually a stop for lunch, bring food and water for the long trip. For information on crossing to Peru by river, see p248. Canoes with an 18-passenger capacity can be rented for $60 per hour.

BUS

For most departures it isn't necessary to go to the bus terminal at the north end of town. Even so, ask where to board at the ticket purchase.

Transportes Baños (☎ 288-0182; cnr Napo & Bolívar) has several buses daily to Lago Agrio ($3, two hours), Tena and Quito ($10, eight to 10 hours). The trip to Quito by Vía Loreto is fastest. **Transportes Esmeraldas** (☎ 288-1077; cnr Napo & Cuenca) has two night buses to Quito. **Transportes Zacaray** (☎ 288-0286; cnr Napo & Bolívar) heads daily to Guayaquil ($16, 16 hours) and Ambato ($10, 10 hours). **Coop Trans Loja** (☎ 288-0272; cnr Cuenca & Amazonas) goes to Machala ($20, 22 hours) and Loja ($25, 27 hours). **Cooperatives Transportes Putamayo** (☎ 288-0173) goes to Quito, Guayaquil and Ambato.

At the bus terminal, 500m north of town, find several buses a day to Tena, evening departures to Santo Domingo, Quevedo, Babahoyo, Machala and Loja. Transportes Interprovinciales de Coca has buses that go south to Río Tiguino.

Rancheras (open-sided bus, or truck mounted with uncomfortably narrow bench seats – also known as *chivas*), leave from the terminal for various destinations between Coca and Lago Agrio, and to Río Tiputini to the south. Pickup trucks and taxis at **Cooperativa Camionetas Río Napo** (Alfaro) provide service in town and out.

VÍA AUCA

☎ 06

This road from Coca crosses Río Napo and continues south across Río Tiputini and Río Shiripuno, ending near the small community of **Tiguino** on Río Tiguino. Daily *rancheras* go as far as Tiguino. The area used to be Huaorani territory and virgin jungle, but when this oil-exploration road was built in the 1980s, the Huaorani were pushed eastward (some groups went westward). The area is being colonized, and cattle ranches and oil rigs are replacing the jungle in spite of conservationist efforts.

The rivers crossed by the road provide access to remote parts of both the Huaorani reserve and Yasuní, but you should enter with authorized guides. While some operators have long-standing relationships with the Huaorani, others do not, and the Huaorani insist on managing tourism on their own terms to protect their best interests.

Three to four hours downriver on Río Tiguino is the remote and simple **Bataburo Lodge** (Map pp232–3). Located in primary forest, the lodge has a canopy tower and rooms with shared and private bathrooms. Rates include meals, guiding and transportation from Coca. It's in a remote area, and upkeep of the trails is erratic. Safari Tours (p97) and Kem Pery Tours (p241) can book a trip.

LOWER RÍO NAPO

☎ 06

The Río Napo flows east from Coca on a steady course toward the Amazon River in Peru. Just after Coca, the river widens into a powerful waterway that can flood villages and islands. This long, lonesome stretch of the Napo houses some of Ecuador's best jungle lodges. Their watercrafts share the river with speedy oil-company boats and puttering dugout canoes loaded with tethered cows and sacks of rice. East of Pompeya and Limoncocha, the river flows just outside the northern border of Parque Nacional Yasuní and finally enters Peru at Nuevo Rocafuerte.

Pompeya & Limoncocha Area

Pompeya is a Catholic mission about two hours downriver from Coca on Río Napo near the **Reserva Biológica Limoncocha**. Road access and nearby oil drilling have created a depressing area devoid of wildlife. If you want to spend the night, ask about camping on the lake in the reserve. Pompeya's small **museum**, part of the Capuchin mission, houses a fine collection of indigenous artifacts from the Río Napo area as well as pre-Columbian ceramics. The area is easily accessed by buses from the oil town of **Shushufindi**, one hour from either Coca or Lago Agrio.

Manatee Riverboat

The **Manatee Amazon Explorer** (www.manateeamazonexplorer.com) offers a different way to see the jungle. Guests stay aboard a three-story, flat-bottomed riverboat and make day trips to Parque Nacional Yasuní, Limoncocha, Tiputini and other tributaries off the Río Napo. It's an interesting idea that results in access to a wider range of habitats thanks to efficient use of motor time (while guests are on excursions in motor canoes, the boat advances to its next destination). Cabins are basic but comfortable, and readers recommend the experience. Trips run for three, four or seven nights and can be booked through **Advantage Travel** (☎ in Quito 02-244-8985; www.advantagecuador.com; cnr El Telégrafo E10-63 & Juan de Alcántara, Quito; s/d 3 nights $895/1194, 4 nights $1194/1588).

Yarina Lodge

The small tributary Río Manduro meets the Napo an hour downstream from Coca. Navigate up this narrow green corridor to find **Yarina Lodge** (Map pp232-3; ☎ in Quito 02-250-4037/3225; www.yarinalodge.com; cnr Amazonas N24-236 & Colón; per person 2/3/4 nights $290/380/450), a hillside camp of 22 bamboo, thatched-roof cabañas. Yarina is geared toward budget travelers but provides good services. Meals, with vegetarian options, are well prepared in a communal lodge with hammocks, and cabins come equipped with mosquito nets, private bathroom, electricity 24 hours a day and hot water.

The lodge doesn't feel remote, but its pleasant surroundings offer river views, short trails, raised walkways and the opportunity to watch birds and paddle canoes. A collection of caged exotic animals in 'transition rehabilitation' leaves uneasy impressions. Rates include meals and tours with Spanish- and English-speaking local guides. Information can be obtained at Hotel Oasis (p242). Discounts are available for South American Explorers members (see p388).

Sacha Lodge

A spectacular setting, experienced guides and a convivial atmosphere have helped make **Sacha Lodge** (Map pp232-3; ☎ in Quito 02-256-6090, in Quito 02-250-9504, in the US 800-706-2215; www.sachalodge.com; cnr Zaldumbide 397 & Valladolid; s/d 3 nights $1035/1380, 4 nights $1305/1740) one of the more popular destinations on the Río Napo. Opened in 1992, the Swiss-run lodge is known for its punctuality and attentive service. The complex is built on the banks of Laguna El Pilche, a lake about 1km north of Río Napo. Getting there is an adventure in itself – a two-hour motorized canoe ride from Coca is followed by a walk through the forest on an elevated boardwalk, then a 15-minute paddle up a blackwater stream in a dugout canoe.

The central lodge is a circular two-story thatched hut with a restaurant, bar and small library. Its boardwalks tentacle out to 13 woodsy cabins, each with a modern bathroom, dry box for cameras, hot water and hammock deck for shady siestas. All rooms are screened and have electric lights and ceiling fans.

Meals are buffet-style with options for vegetarians and meat-eaters alike. Guests are divided into groups based on their interests, and eat meals together with their guides for the duration of their stay. Sacha is hopping with guests, which creates a summer-camp feel, and after-dinner drinks can be as lively as a Mariscal bar – that may be good or bad, depending on your taste.

In any case, small groups are the rule for excursions and serious bird-watchers get top treatment. Hikes and canoe trips typically consist of about five tourists, with a bilingual naturalist and local guide. The terrain includes flat and hilly rainforest, various lakes, coiling rivers and swamps. The 2000 hectares are visited by six kinds of monkey, toucans, poison dart frogs, peccaries, sloths, anacondas, caiman and black agoutis. You may see all or none, but keep your eyes peeled.

More cherished (and ganglier) than the Eiffel Tower, the lodge's showpiece, a massive metal canopy, stretches between three platforms at 60m off the ground. Bird-watchers from around the world covet the experience of standing on the creaking giant to watch the fog lift on an array of monkeys and birds. A separate 45m-high wooden observation deck atop a huge ceiba tree is another way to get high.

Choose from three- or four-night packages. The first runs Friday to Monday, the second from Monday to Friday. Airfare is an additional $120 round-trip from Quito to Coca, or you can travel by bus. Special interests, such as bird-watching, photography, plants or fishing, can be catered for with advance request.

Napo Wildlife Center

As the only lodge in the boundaries of Parque Nacional Yasuní, the **Napo Wildlife Center** (Map pp232-3; ☎ in Quito 02-600-5819, in the US 866-750-0830, in the UK 800-032-5771; www.napowildlifecenter.com; s/d 3 nights $1080/1440, 4 nights $1380/1840) offers a pristine setting with unparalleled access to wildlife. The ecotourism project is 100% owned by the Quichua community of Añangu, which makes up almost the entire lodge staff.

Guests hike in or paddle up a small tributary from the south banks of the Río Napo, which usually offers an easy glimpse of monkeys and birdlife. The cluster of thatched circular cabañas huddle on the far side of Laguna

Añangucocha like an emerald vision from a Gauguin painting. The communal hut is spacious and open, with a lovely wooden deck, small library and elevated viewing platform; it now boasts the first wireless internet on the Lower Napo. Meals here are artfully presented and occasionally you'll hear red howler monkeys calling nearby.

Trips are guided by local Añangans trained as Yasuní park rangers and bilingual naturalist guides. The focus and physicality of the outings are tailored to the interests of guests. Two parrot clay licks on the property are a major attraction for bird-watchers, who also come from surrounding lodges to see parrots, parakeets and macaws. Between late October and early April you are guaranteed to see between eight and 10 species of parrot – sometimes numbering in the thousands. A 36m steel tower, a short hike from the lodge, offers a spectacular canopy panorama and prolific birdlife. The rare zigzag heron has been spotted on the property.

The center has won numerous awards, not only for its connection to the local community, but for ecologically sound practices including an environmentally sustainable sewage system (there is persistent concern about how the rest of the lodges are disposing of their waste), composting latrines, solar panels and quality guiding.

Departures to the lodge are on Monday for four nights and Friday for three nights. Rates include lodging, meals, guided excursions and canoe transport from Coca. Round-trip airfare from Quito to Coca costs $125.

Sani Lodge

Founded and owned by the local Sani community, **Sani Lodge** (Map pp232-3; ☎ in Quito 02-255-8881; www.sanilodge.com; cnr Roca E4-49 & Amazonas; s/d 3 nights $750/1020, 5 nights $1100/1700) has set an impressive standard for jungle lodges. All profits from tourism go back into the lodge or Quichua community in the form of scholarships for study in Quito and abroad, a community store that eases the need for local hunting, emergency medical funds and other projects. Employees are members of the community, which creates a family feel. The setup will appeal to those who want a quieter, more intimate experience.

After traveling up a small tributary of the Río Napo, visitors encounter a group of thatched-hut buildings set on an enchanting blackwater oxbow lake. Ten circular cabins each sleep two to three people and have private cold-water bathroom, comfortable beds, mosquito screens and a small porch. There's some solar-generated electricity and no generators, which enhances the presence of wildlife; it's easy to spot impressive birds from the dining room over breakfast.

Monkeys, sloths and black caiman are regularly spotted, and the lodge's bird list records more than 570 species of birds in the area (the 30m-high tree tower will help you find them). Nocturnal mammals such as tapirs and capybaras live in the area, but are rarely seen. Even jaguar tracks have been spotted on the property, some 160 sq km of land. Guides here are excellent both for their knowledge of and respect for the jungle. Most enjoy showing visitors the Sani community to reinforce how the lodge has created an important, sustainable economy.

Tours are for three, four, five or seven nights, and include three meals a day, canoe transport to/from Coca (two to three hours upstream from the lodge), and daily excursions with both a native guide and an English-speaking naturalist guide. Readers consistently recommend this lodge.

La Selva Jungle Lodge

The North American–run **La Selva Jungle Lodge** (Map pp232-3; ☎ in Quito 02-254-5425, 255-0995; www.laselvajunglelodge.com; cnr Mariana de Jesús E7-211 & La Pradera; per person 3/4 nights $717/852) was one of the first in the area and still provides a high-quality tourism experience for no more than 40 people at a time.

Set on the shores of Laguna Garzacocha, a cluster of thatched-hut double cabins and one family cabin are connected by raised walkways. Each cabin has a private bathroom with hot water, ceiling fan, mosquito nets and generator-powered electricity. Details such as fresh flowers and candles help create a sense of luxury. Meals are delicious and presented in a spacious dining room overlooking the lake. An on-site masseuse offers massages in a dedicated room by prior arrangement.

With more than 500 bird species, bird-watching is a major attraction. About half of Ecuador's 44 species of parrots have been recorded near here, as well as a host of other exotic tropical birds. Some of the area's best guides work here, including biologists. Groups of no more than eight people explore the jungle by foot and dugout canoe. A 35m-high canopy platform, a 20-minute walk from the lodge, affords even better viewing. Look for the rare zigzag heron, a coveted sighting for bird-watchers from around the world. Monkeys and other mammals are frequently seen and there are tens of thousands of plant and insect species.

A small research facility offers project space for scientists and students by advance arrangement. Brilliantly colored butterflies flit about in a butterfly-breeding complex that's open to visitors.

The lodge is about 2½ hours downriver from Coca in a motorized canoe, plus a short walk through the jungle and a canoe ride across Garzacocha. Three-night stays begin on Wednesday or Friday, while four-night stays begin on Monday or Saturday. Prices include river travel from Coca, accommodations, meals and guide services. Even timid adventurers should consider the five-day 'Survival Package,' which involves camping with a native guide, foraging for food, then 'roughing it' in the remote, deluxe-style campsite with pillows and platforms, and a chef.

Pañacocha

This quiet, hidden blackwater lagoon is a short boat ride off the Río Napo. Pañacocha, which means 'Lake of Piranhas' in Quichua, is frequently visited by local lodges, but there's no infrastructure (although a new lodge is in the works on the banks of the lake). Reel in one of the sharp-toothed fish with your own trembling mitts then, if you're feeling brave, jump in for a swim (the fish won't attack unless you have a flesh wound). The biodiversity here is incredible – 251 plant species have been counted in a hectare, and pink freshwater dolphins are frequently spotted.

To get here, hire a local canoe where the Río Pañayacu meets the Río Napo, which can be reached by a Nuevo Rocafuerte canoe from Coca (see p243). Ask to be dropped at the small community on the shore of the Río Napo, where basic accommodations are available at **Pensíon Las Palmas** (riverfront; r per person $3), but you might be more comfortable camping. *Comedores* (cheap restaurants) are within view of the boat landing.

Pañacocha is four to five hours downstream from Coca (depending on your motor), or about halfway to Nuevo Rocafuerte.

Nuevo Rocafuerte

A distant dot on the map for many people, Nuevo Rocafuerte is certainly in no danger of losing its mystery. While backpackers may bubble with excitement at the idea of floating the Napo all the way to the Amazon River, only the most intrepid travelers should rise to the occasion. In this truly off-piste adventure, aspiring 'survivors' may have to endure cramped and wet travel, the possibility of seeing their next meal slaughtered, and immanent illness.

Nuevo Rocafuerte is on the Peruvian border, about eight to 10 hours from Coca along the Río Napo. This is a legal border crossing with Peru, albeit a highly independent one. Basic infrastructure such as regular boats and simple hotels are lacking. In the absence of cars, long tufts of grass sprout in the road and nighttime means outdoor barbecues with the TV hauled out to the sidewalk.

If you are continuing to Peru, try to time your arrival with one of the five boats from Iquitos. Inquire at the Coop de Transportes Fluviales Orellana (p243) in Coca, when you buy your ticket downstream, for cargo-boat phone numbers and possible arrivals. But nothing guarantees timing; there's a good chance you'll get stuck here, so be prepared. Bring adequate supplies of water-purification tablets, insect repellent and food. Also, consider getting Peruvian currency in Quito before arriving.

Due to a lack of any real lodging, some travelers have ended up staying on beds in the police station, a short walk from the port of entry. Consider getting a boat downstream to Pantoja, Peru, which has a hotel, restaurant and disco. Or arrange for a tour in Parque Nacional Yasuní or Cuyabeno reserve while you wait.

For local information, tours or to hire a boat, contact Juan Carlos 'Chuso' Cuenca (☎ 238-2182). His house is the second one after the marina. The town has an Andinatel phone office behind the marina.

GETTING THERE & AWAY

Passenger canoes to Coca depart at 5am on Sunday, Tuesday and Friday. The trip ($15) is 12 to 14 hours, with a lunch stop in Pañacocha. The canoe is covered but you should still bring rain gear, food and water. Low-water conditions may prolong the trip.

To/From Peru

Exit and entry formalities in Ecuador are handled in Nuevo Rocafuerte; in Peru, try your best to settle them in Pantoja, with Iquitos as backup. The official border crossing is at Pantoja, a short ride from Nuevo Rocafuerte. Boats from Nuevo Rocafuerte charge $40 per boat to Pantoja. Timing is the key: four or five cargo boats travel from Pantoja to Iquitos (a four- to six-day trip) when they have enough cargo to justify the trip. Call one **cargo-boat owner** (☎ 51-6-524-2082; one-way $35) to ask about arrival dates. A hammock and 19L of water, in addition to food, are recommended; food on the boats can be dodgy. Be warned that conditions can be rough: there may be only one bathroom, crowded conditions and lots of livestock on board. Boats vary in quality, but if you've been waiting a long time for one to arrive, you may not want to be picky.

About halfway to Iquitos (Peru), the village of Santa Clotilde has more transportation options including speedboats to Iquitos. Chartering a boat to Santa Clotilde from Nuevo Rocafuerte will set you back $200. Ask around at the marina for other options.

PARQUE NACIONAL YASUNÍ

Yasuní (admission $5, parrot clay lick $20) is Ecuador's largest mainland park, a massive 9620-sq-km section of wetlands, marshes, swamps, lakes, rivers and tropical rainforest. Its staggering biodiversity led Unesco to declare it an international biosphere reserve and it was established as a national park shortly after, in 1979. Because this pocket of life was untouched by the last ice age, a diverse pool of species has thrived here throughout the ages, including more than 500 bird species, some previously unknown elsewhere. Resident animals include some hard-to-see jungle wildlife, such as jaguars, harpy eagles, pumas and tapirs.

Yasuní stands today as one of the last true wildernesses in Ecuador. Its inaccessibility has preserved it in ways active protection cannot. Bordered by Río Napo to the north and Río Cururay to the southeast, the park encompasses most of the watersheds of Ríos Yasuní and Nashiño, as well as substantial parts of Río Tiputini. Its diverse habitats consist of 'terra firma' or forested hills, which are never inundated even by the highest floods; *varzea* or lowlands, which are periodically inundated by flooding rivers; and *igapó,* semipermanently inundated lowlands.

A small but not negligible number of Tagaeri, Taromenani and Oñamenane live within the park (see the boxed text, opposite). Park territory was altered in 1990 and 1992 to protect these traditional populations of hunters and gatherers who vehemently resist contact with the outside world. The nearby Reserva Huaorani contributes as an ecological buffer zone for the national park.

Oil discovery within the park has put a sinister spin on this conservation success story. In 1991, despite Yasuní's protected status, the Ecuadorian government gave the US-based company Conoco the right to begin oil exploration. Since then the concession has changed hands several times. Conoco was soon replaced by the Maxus Oil Consortium, whose legacy is the Maxus road, which slices through the park like a 150km coronary incision. While this 'ecological' road can be lifted up and removed (presumably when oil industry is no longer viable), the forest cut in its wake and the subsequent link to the interior for outsiders causes its own kind of degradation.

Oil pits and associated waste contaminate soil and drainage systems, while noise pollution and vegetation destruction cause an exodus of wildlife. There are claims that this degradation has been reasonably well contained, and that wildlife is abundant, but you can't go there to see it unless you're a researcher or oil worker.

Various international organizations – such as the **Nature Conservancy** (www.nature.org), **Conservation International** (www.conservation.org) and the **Natural Resources Defense Council** (www.nrdc.org) – in coalition with Ecuadorian groups such as **Fundación Natura** (www.fnatura.org), are working to avoid the destructive patterns that have occurred in other parts of the Amazon.

Recent logging within the Huaorani territory, by lumber companies that purchase trees (primarily cedar) from the Huaorani, is another way the park buffer zone is being denigrated.

Like most of Ecuador's preserved areas, Yasuní is woefully understaffed. At present, the only permanently staffed ranger station is at Nuevo Rocafuerte, with some seasonal stations on the southern park boundaries. Some guides in Coca lead trips into the park (see p96), as do many lodges in the area. You can stay within the park's boundaries at the Napo Wildlife Center (p245) and Bataburo Lodge (p244).

THE UNTOUCHABLES

The Tagaeri and Taromenani have a history of violent encounters with the outside world, which ultimately led to the withdrawal and self-imposed isolation of these subgroups of the Huaorani. In 1999 a presidential decree from the Ecuadorian government set up Intangible Zones to 'prevent more irreversible damage to indigenous communities and their environment.' They delineated 7000 sq km overlapping Parque Nacional Yasuní and Huaorani territory where these groups could live as they have for centuries without threat of contact with outsiders.

Mining, logging and oil exploration are forbidden in these areas, which also protects an estimated 500 species of birds, jaguars, pumas, manatees and other wildlife. But with evidence of illegal logging, and still more violent encounters between outsiders and the tribes, the government has promised to staff outposts to keep smugglers, poachers and loggers out. However, the tribes roam to hunt and collect food, making boundaries and outposts ineffective consolations from the modern world.

The annual rainfall is about 3500mm, depending on location. May to July are the wettest months; January to March are the driest.

PARQUE NACIONAL SUMACO-GALERAS

A smooth, paved road connects Coca to western cloud forest, preventing the need for expensive boat travel. This is commonly called the 'Loreto road,' taking its name from the town of **Loreto**. Just beyond the town, a dirt road heads south to meet the Río Napo, a good access point for the Yachana Lodge (see p258) and other Upper Río Napo spots. As the road presses west into the Andean foothills, the little-explored **Parque Nacional Sumaco-Galeras** offers stunning, remote wilderness.

The park consists of 2052 sq km of thick rainforest, hidden caves and cliffs. Its centerpiece is the 3732m Volcán Sumaco, which is plagued by wet weather. The volcano is dormant at this time, although vulcanologists believe it could become active. It lies about 27km north of the Loreto road.

Guides are essential for any summit attempts, which involve bushwhacking along poorly marked trails. The climb takes five to six days round-trip and includes overnight stays at one of the volcano's three new *refugios* (mountain refuges). Trails are muddy year-round, but drier between October and December.

Hire experienced guides for the climb in the village of **Pacto Sumaco**, 8km north of the Loreto road, for $20 to $30 per day. The **Sumaco Biosphere Reserve** (www.sumaco.org) can also help arrange guide services. Facilities are minimal, so bring all food and equipment.

Located 1km south of Pacto Sumaco, the new **Wildsumaco Lodge** (info@wildsumaco.com, www.wildsumaco.com; s/d incl 3 meals $155/270) at the **Wildsumaco Wildlife Sanctuary** makes a good base for climbing the volcano. Set on a hilltop with panoramic mountain views, a wooden house with a deck serves as a gathering spot for guests, most of whom come for the birds, a unique mixture of cloud forest, foothill and Amazonian species. Concrete rooms are simple but tasteful with wood floors, comfy beds, plenty of hot water and electricity. A web of trails starts at the lodge, providing access to the abundance of birds and wildlife. The price includes basic guide services; specialized bird guides can be requested in advance. The Swedish and American owners are conservation-minded and started the **Río Pucuno Foundation** (www.riopucunofoundation.org) to preserve forest in the area. The sanctuary accepts volunteers for $20 per day, which includes room and board.

Along the roadside outside of the park, you'll see stands selling oyster mushrooms harvested in the area. It's a good opportunity to stop and chat with locals, and the project funds sustainable agro-forestry.

PARQUE NACIONAL SUMACO-GALERAS TO TENA

☎ 06

The misty Andean foothills provide long, lush views of sprawling jungle and volcanic peaks. As the road descends into Tena, through cattle ranches and banana plantations, the temperature rises.

Further south, outside of the town of **Cotundo**, the **El Arca Rescue Center** (☎ 08-725-0640; admission $3.50; 🕑 8am-5pm) houses a myriad rehabilitated animals in well-kept cages. Walk with a guide on the winding pathway to see hawks, parrots, anacondas, turtles, caiman and monkeys. For $1 more, swim in the tiny blue pool by the river. Readers recommend El Arca over other animal-rescue centers in the area.

About 4km north of Archidona, you'll find **Cuevas de Jumandí** (☎ 08-445-2032; admission $1, with guide $5; ☉ 9am-5pm). This cave system, the best known in the area, has three main branches that remain partly unexplored. Forgo the sketchy waterslides that dump into a river-water pool, and tread slowly (with a flashlight) to see stalactites, stalagmites and odd formations. Rubber boots and old clothes will serve you well. For thorough exploration, you'll need a guide from Tena or on-site – ask guide companies in Tena for a customized day trip to include a trip to the caves.

Orchids Paradise Lodge (☎ 288-9232; www.orchidspara dise.com; r per person incl 3 meals $52; ☒), a gem just off the main road, has an amoeba-shaped pool, a spacious thatched-hut restaurant-bar, and cabins with screened windows and hot water. The lodge operates a monkey-rescue program – see the results swinging in the trees – and can arrange for day trips and multiday packages.

The faded pastel facades and manicured palm plaza make the yawning village of **Archidona** an agreeable stop. A mission founded in 1560 (the same year as Tena, 10km to the south), the town has maintained its smallness and tranquility. Sundays are choice for milling around, seeing the rural folk (including indigenous Quijos) coming to the market and checking out the zebra-striped concrete-block church near the plaza. A few small inexpensive hotels and restaurants line the square.

TENA
☎ 06 / pop 27,753 / elevation 518m

Tena is a cheerful, welcoming vortex, the kind of place visitors forget to leave. The pleasant, balmy climate encourages adventures to nearby waterfalls, petroglyphs, jungle and indigenous communities. But the rivers, including the Río Tena and Río Pano, which meet here, get the most attention. Whitewater fanatics from around the globe come to paddle and play on the high concentration of surrounding rivers. Town awaits with cold beer, good food and soft beds.

The capital of Napo province, Tena was founded in 1560 and plagued by early indigenous uprisings. Jumandy, chief of the Quijos, led a fierce but unsuccessful revolt against the Spaniards in 1578. The anniversary of the

foundation is celebrated on November 15 with live music and community events.

Every January, the town hosts the **Festival Río Napo** (www.kayakecuador.com), with rafting and other events designed to raise awareness about the Napo watershed.

Information
Andinatel (Olmedo)

Banco del Austro (15 de Noviembre) Changes traveler's checks in the mornings only. Has an ATM.

Clínica Amazonas (☎ 288-6495; Santa Rosa; ☉ 24hr)

Cucupanet (per hr $1.20; ☉ 8am-9:30pm) Internet on the main plaza.

Hospital (☎ 288-6305) South of town on the road to Puerto Napo.

Police station (☎ 288-6101; cnr Suares & Muyuna)

Post office (cnr Olmedo & Moreno) Northwest of the footbridge.

Tourism office (☎ 288-8046; Agusto Rueda; ☉ 7am-5pm Mon-Fri) Provides useful information on local attractions.

Sights & Activities
On a clear day, visitors to Tena are sometimes puzzled by the sight of Volcán Sumaco (p249) looming from the jungle 50km away.

Stroll over a small bridge to **Parque Amazónico** (btwn Ríos Pano & Tena; admission $2; ☉ 8am-5pm), a 27-hectare island with a self-guided trail passing labeled local plants and animal enclosures. Picnic areas, a swimming beach and a bathroom are available.

Market days are Friday and Saturday.

RIVER RAFTING
Tena offers Ecuador's best white-water rafting. Trips range from gentle scenic floats to exhilarating rapids and first descents in gorgeous landscapes. Serious outfitters will have everything you would expect – decent life jackets, professional guides, first aid supplies and throw bags. Many use safety kayakers who paddle alongside the boat in case of capsizings. It's worth signing up with one of these. Kayakers can hire guides or arrange for transport and put-ins through the places mentioned here.

The most popular river is the Jatunyacu, which means 'big water' in Quichua, where rafters tackle a fun 25km stretch of Class III+ white water, suitable for all levels. For more excitement, the Río Misahuallí has wild Class IV+ rapids and includes a portage around a waterfall.

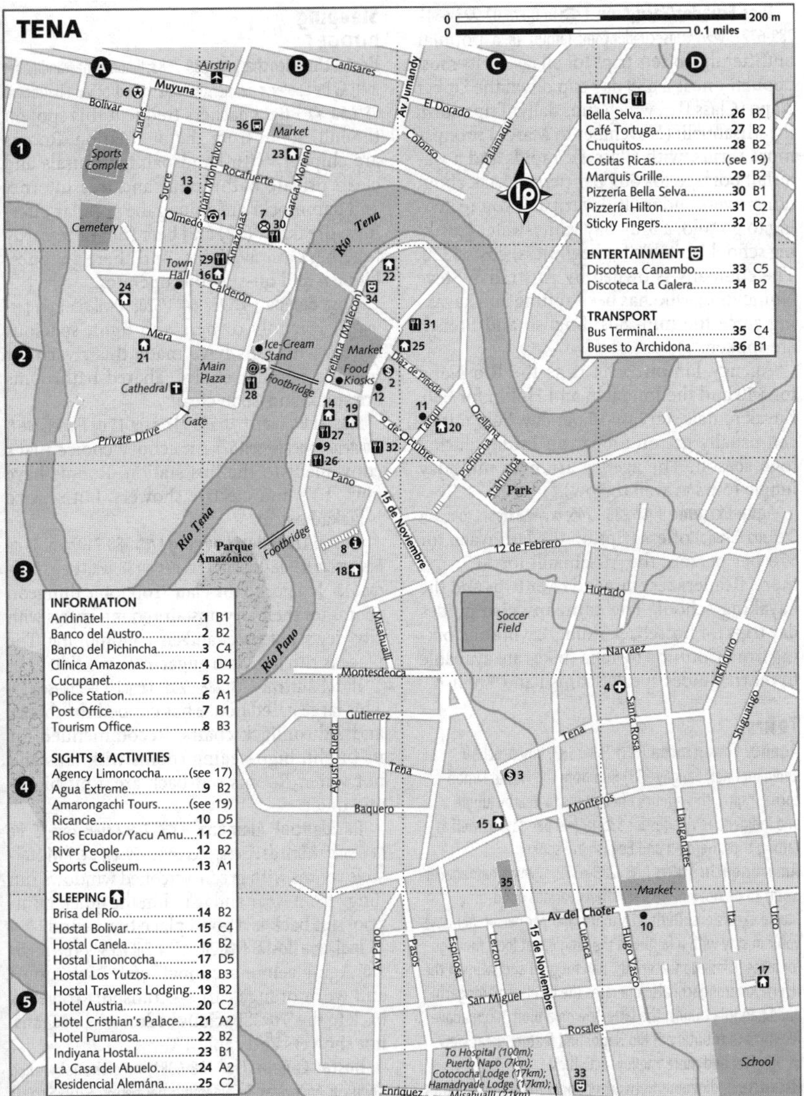

River People (☎ 288-8384/7887; www.riverpeople raftingecuador.com; cnr 15 de Noviembre & 9 de Octubre), run by English guide Gary Dent, his sons and one of his daughters, is a top-notch outfitter that consistently gets rave reviews. Day trips to the Jatunyacu are $50. Trips also run the Quijos (Class IV) for $70 per day, the spectacular Jondachi and the very remote Hollin (in Sumaco-Galera), Class III/IV. If you're feeling extra adventurous, try the Upper Hollin (Class V) between September and January, a $100, two-day trip. Guides have a minimum of eight years' experience and speak English. Jungle camping, kayaking instruction and tailor-made trips are possible. Check out the Dent family's café, Sticky Fingers (p254).

Ríos Ecuador/Yacu Amu (☎ in Quito 02-223-6844, 288-6727; www.riosecuador.com; Tarqui) is a popular outfitter that offers trips for all tastes. Its most popular one is a $59 day trip down the Upper Napo (Class III), which runs daily. Trips down the Misahuallí (November to March) promise more thrills, with Class-IV rapids and a waterfall portage for $69 per person. Ask about other rivers and multiday trips. If you're itching to go solo, a four-day white-water kayaking school (suitable for beginners) costs $330. The company is owned by Australian Steve Nomchong, who has been rafting and kayaking since the mid-'80s. English and French are spoken.

Agency Limoncocha runs the Río Napo for $40 and the Jondachi and Hollin for $50. Kayak rentals start at $15 per day. Solo rafters can usually get on a boat on Friday during high season. The agency arranges multiday jungle tours as well (below).

Agua Extreme (☎ 288-8746; www.axtours.com; cnr Orellana & Pano) offers trips on the Jatunyacu for $70 per person, the Misahuallí for $75, and more. Readers recommend river trips and the kayaking school. The company also guides day trips for horseback riding, caving and biking from Cotundo to Tena (bikes are available to rent). Guides speak Spanish and English.

Tours

Agency Limoncocha (☎ 288-7583; limoncocha@andinanet.net; Sangay 533) Run from the Hostal Limoncocha (right), this agency offers tours to nearby jungle and indigenous villages for $35 to $40 per day, as well as rafting trips. German and English are spoken.

Amarongachi Tours (☎ 288-6372; www.amarongachi.com; 15 de Noviembre 438) Offers various good-time jungle excursions. During its tours ($45 per person per day) you can stay with a family in the jungle, eat local food, go for hikes, climb up waterfalls, pan for gold and swim in the rivers. Amarongachi also operates the lovely Amarongachi and Shangrila cabins; the latter are on a bluff 100m above Río Anzu (a tributary of Río Napo) and feature great views of the river and more-mellow activities.

Ricancie (Indigenous Network of Upper Napo Communities for Cultural Coexistence & Ecotourism; ☎ in Quito 02-290-1493, 288-8479; www.ricancie.nativeweb.org; cnr Av El Chofer & Vasco; 🕑 8am-6pm) Ten Quichua communities have joined to improve life for their 200 families through ecotourism. They offer adventure tours, bird- and animal-watching, demonstrations of healing plants, handicrafts and cooking for $45 per day. Guides speak Quichua and Spanish, but little English. The staff can arrange stays in local villages and know the local caves and petroglyphs. Recommended.

Sleeping

BUDGET

Hostal Limoncocha (☎ 288-7583; limoncocha@andinanet.net; Av De Chofer; r per person with shared/private bathroom $5/7.50; 💻) Backpackers frequent this spot on the hill, 300m from the bus station. Rooms are chipper, with hand-painted murals and clean private bathrooms, and free internet and hammocks are among the popular offerings. Breakfast ($2) and beer (not necessarily together) are available, and there's a guest kitchen and on-site tour operator.

Brisa del Río (☎ 288-6444/6208; Orellana; r per person $7) Friendly owners and light, spacious rooms with fans have made this riverfront *hostal* a popular choice. Shared bathrooms are spick-and-span clean.

Hostal Bolivar (☎ 288-7176; cnr 15 de Noviembre & Monteros; r per person $7) An echoey choice that's convenient to the bus station. Rooms have fans, TVs and electric showers, but service is lackadaisical.

Hostal Travellers Lodging (☎ 288-7102; cnr 15 de Noviembre & 9 de Octubre; r per person $8, with views & air-con $18; ❄) Forgo the claustrophobic dungeon rooms for their airy upstairs counterparts with city views, hot water and air-conditioning. The place is run by Amarongachi Tours (left).

Hotel Austria (☎ 288-7205; Tarqui; r per person $9) This large gated house has clipped shrubbery and Adirondack chairs. Recommended for its bright, high-ceiling rooms with fans and hot water. Rooms out back are a bit bigger and quiet.

Residencial Alemána (☎ 288-6409; cnr 15 de Noviembre & Díaz de Piñeda; r per person $9-11; 🏊) Motel-style rooms with green-screened windows run dingy from wear and tear, but the quiet, mini-pool out back is a good place to unwind.

Indiyana Hostal (☎ 288-6334; Bolívar 349; r per person $10) Aging velour sectional sofas, dark rooms and worn orange carpets transport travelers back to the '70s. Spacious bedrooms have fans, hot showers and cable TV.

Hostal Canela (☎ 288-6081; canelahostal@yahoo.com; cnr Amazonas & Calderón; r per person $10) Small floor fans whisper in these warm, spacious rooms with plaid bedspreads. Large windows overlook two busy streets and all rooms have private bathroom and TVs.

MIDRANGE

Las Heliconias (☎ 288-7995, www.complejoheliconias.com; r per person $15; 🏊) This popular pool complex ($2 admission for nonguests) by the

WHAT'S IN A NAME?

In the Oriente, 'Kichwa' and 'Quichua' are used interchangeably to describe both an indigenous group and an Inca language that's spoken by people from other ethnic groups as well. The words are pronounced in the same way, but the spelling differences are highly symbolic.

'Quichua' was first penned by Spanish missionaries who wrote what they heard, replacing 'k' and 'w,' nonexistent letters in the Spanish alphabet, with 'qu' and 'u.' Since the conquest, Spanish has been the country's official language, which meant few people asked whether the traditional system of recording Kichwa sounds in written form made sense. But now a growing number of Kichwa speakers, writers and readers are standing up for their linguistic rights by choosing 'Kichwa' over 'Quichua,' which represents autonomy from Spanish oppressors.

And as if that's not complicated enough, Peruvians and Bolivians speak 'Quechua,' another version of the dialect. For this guidebook, we've chosen to use the more common 'Quichua' for the Ecuadorian indigenous peoples and the language.

river recently added new two-story buildings for overnight guests. The rooms are still shiny and new, and are well away from pool noise. Suites have two bathrooms and a kitchen.

our pick **La Casa del Abuelo** (☎ 288-6318; runanambi@yahoo.com; Mera 628; s/d $15/20) This ample refurbished colonial-style home with large, medieval wooden doors and comfortable, light rooms is tucked away on a quiet street. Rooms have hot water and ceiling fans, and the friendly owners can make tour arrangements. Ask the owners about their rural guesthouse on the river, 5km away.

Hotel Pumarosa (☎ 288-6320; Orellana; s/d $15/25;) Inviting lilac rooms have high wooden ceilings, large armoires and modern white-tile bathrooms. There is reliable hot water, cable TV, a telephone in every room, lush gardens and billiards in the open-air lobby. The disco and roller rink next door means noisy weekends.

Hotel Cristhian's Palace (☎ 288-6047; Mera; r per person incl breakfast $22;) This large, impersonal hotel is less than palatial, and, somehow, fresh yellow rooms, a pool and gym equipment add to a corporate feel. Breakfast is usually a buffet, and bells from the neighboring cathedral might serve as a wake-up call.

Hostal Los Yutzos (☎ 288-6717; www.geocities.com/losyutzos; Agusto Rueda 190; s/d incl breakfast & wi-fi $22/36, with air-con $31/42, ste $27-43;) The rooms at this riverside gem are spacious and tasteful. There's a tiled balcony with wooden loungers, overlooking the gurgling river and the city's northern bank. The garden is thick with green and hammocks. Internet access, cable TV, hot water and breakfast are additional perks.

OUTSIDE OF TOWN

Cotococha Lodge (Map pp232-3; ☎ in Quito 02-223-4336, in the US; 888-790-5264 www.cotococha.com; per person 2/3 nights $155/260) Located 17km from Tena along the south shores of the Río Napo, a quiet collection of thatched-roof bungalows are connected by winding river-rock pathways in a lush setting. Oil lanterns create a romantic glow and cabins have nice linens, hot water and private decks overlooking the river. Guests relax in wicker chairs around a fire pit after dinner. English-speaking guides lead walks and trips to waterfalls; tubing, rafting and visits to local communities can be arranged.

Hamadryade Lodge (Map pp232-3; ☎ 08-590-9992, in the US 800-327-3573; www.hamadryade-lodge.com; s/d per person incl breakfast & dinner $205/250) Perched on a jungle hillside, this ambitious French-owned lodge departs from 'standard jungle' with sleek, contemporary decor. Chic, private bungalows have balconies with gorgeous views, and an ozone-treated pool is perfectly perched over the rolling landscape. With a maximum of 11 guests, no space ever feels cramped, especially the lounge with leather chairs, a curvaceous bar and striking mural. The lodge's bumpy dirt road may require 4WD; ask for transportation options. Located 17km east of Tena on the north side of Río Napo.

Eating

our pick **Café Tortuga** (☎ 09-529-5419; cafetortuga@yahoo.com; Orellana; snacks $2; 7:30am-11am Mon, to 9pm Tue-Sat, 7:30-11am & 4-9pm Sun) A Swiss-run riverfront spot where tourists plan their next move. Start the day with pancakes and fruit, crepes or espresso. Post-river trip, try a house specialty: beer floated with vanilla ice cream and fresh pineapple.

Sticky Fingers (15 de Noviembre; breakfasts $3-5; 7:30am-10pm) A cozy new location serves wonderful cakes, salads and snacks. The Spanish chef/baker recently added a popular happy hour from 8pm to 9pm.

Cositas Ricas (15 de Noviembre; mains $3-7; 7:30am-9:30pm) Inside the Hostal Travellers Lodging complex (p252), this favorite serves vegetarian and Ecuadorian plates, salads and fresh juices.

Pizzería Bella Selva (288-8293; cnr Olmedo & Moreno; mains $3-7, pizzas $3-15; 5-10pm) This thatched-hut pizzeria serves heavily loaded cheese slicks and large piles of pasta. Overlooks the bridge.

Chuquitos (288-7630; main plaza; mains $4-7; 7:30am-9:30pm Mon-Fri) An old favorite over the wide ribbon of the Río Tena creates the perfect spot for a meal or a drink downstairs in the bar. Watch out for tour groups if you're not in the mood for lingering.

Pizzería Hilton (287-0750; 15 de Noviembre 195; pizzas $4-15; 5-11pm) Gets rave reviews for its reliable pizza menu, which looks much like the other pizzerias in town. Also serves up good rigatoni and lasagna.

Marquis Grille (288-6513; Amazonas 251; mains $6-20; noon-3pm & 6-11pm Mon-Sat) With white tablecloths, classical music and attentive service, this is the most formal restaurant for miles. Browse the Chilean wine list then choose from steamed tilapia, rich pastas and lobster. The ocelot skin, which offended many patrons, has been replaced by murals depicting regional mythology. If you're lucky, the resident sloth will be 'active.'

Entertainment

The dance floors pulse on the weekends, so slip into the mix. Discos open from 8pm to 2am, or until 3am from Thursday to Saturday. Descend into the mirrored **Discoteca Canambo** (cnr Enriquez & 15 de Noviembre; admission $2). Next to Hotel Pumarosa (p253), **Discoteca La Galera** (Orellana; admission $2) has a fun, slightly more grown-up atmosphere, even though there's an attached roller-rink.

Getting There & Away

The **bus terminal** (15 de Noviembre) is at the southern end of town. Numerous daily departures go to Quito ($5, five hours) via Baeza and to Coca ($7, six hours). Multiple daily departures go to Puyo ($2.50, three hours), Ambato ($5, six hours) and Baños ($4, five hours). Jumandy has a night bus to Lago Agrio ($7, eight hours). Café Tortuga (see p253) keeps a list of current bus times.

Getting Around

Local buses to Archidona ($0.25, 15 minutes) leave about every half-hour during the day from the west side of the market. Other local buses leave from 15 de Noviembre, outside the terminal, to Ahuano ($1.20, one hour), Misahuallí ($0.70, 45 minutes) and Santa Rosa/San Pedro ($3, three hours).

MISAHUALLÍ

06

Once a bustling connection for jungle tours, Misahuallí (Mee-sah-wah-*yee*) is a sleepy jungle town that pines for the past. Positioned between two major rivers – at the literal end of the road – the town has popular sandy beaches and a famous cadre of monkeys adept at swiping sunglasses and cameras from visitors.

Before the Tena–Coca road existed, the town was an important port for tour agencies and jungle lodges. These days, Misahuallí is an afterthought. Tourists who arrive without an air of purpose may feel like juicy bait among the warring tour operators (some of whom deserve more business for their top-quality jungle trips). But it's worth enduring their advances if only for a mellow day away from Tena.

The surrounding area has been colonized for decades, which means wildlife has diminished. What you can see, if you keep your eyes open – or better still, with a local guide – is a variety of jungle birds, tropical flowers, army ants, dazzling butterflies and other insects.

Information

There is no bank or post office. Internet has just appeared in a few hotels, which means more is on the way. Carry your passport on buses, boats and tours in the region, and have a stash of small bills for boat travel.

Sights & Activities

Pack a picnic and hit the dirt roads by foot, bicycle or bus.

A nearby **waterfall** is a sweet spot for a swim. You can easily reach it on your own. Take a Misahuallí–Puerto Napo bus and ask the driver to drop you at Río Latas, about 15 or 20 minutes from Misahuallí. All the drivers know *el camino a las cascadas* (the trail to the falls). Follow the river upstream to the falls, which takes an hour, passing several swimming holes en route. Be prepared to wade.

Dazzling giant *morphos* flutter about the **butterfly farm** (Centro de Reproducción de Mariposas; admission $2.50; 8:30am-noon & 2pm-5pm), a block off the plaza. It's run by Pepe and Margarita of Ecoselva (see below) and offers a close look at the developing stages of rainforest butterflies.

Tours

With most tours arranged in Quito, independent travelers will have a hard time finding a group on-site. The perk is a slightly cheaper rate. You'll find an accommodating guide (and price) far more quickly if you already have four or more people together when you arrive in Misahuallí.

Most guides who approach you in the main plaza are inexperienced and unlicensed. It's best to hire a guide recommended here or by other travelers. Tour prices should include the guide, food, water, accommodations and rubber boots.

Douglas Clarke's Expeditions (☎ 289-0002; douglasclarkeexpediciones@yahoo.com) Readers recommend this longtime operator with one- to 10-day tours for $35 to $45 per day. Most overnight trips involve camping. Some English is spoken.

Ecoselva (☎ 289-0019; ecoselva@yahoo.es) Pepe Tapia González takes visitors on fun one- to 10-day tours with overnight stays at his rustic lodge or jungle camps. He speaks English, has a biology background and is knowledgeable about plants and insects. Tours cost about $45 per person per day. Located on the Plaza.

Luis Zapata (☎ 289-0071; zorrozz_2000@yahoo.com) An independent, recommended guide who speaks English.

Misahullí Tours (☎ 288-7616) Carlos Lastra runs one- to four-day tours on the Upper Río Napo for $35 per day. He's experienced and well respected. Located on the plaza.

Sleeping & Eating

You'll find plenty of cheap lodging, especially on the main square, where a handful of restaurants serve typical foods.

Hostal Marena Internacional (☎ 289-0002; Av Principal s/n; r per person $6) The upper levels of this cotton-candy-colored multistory place have a delicious breeze. Half a block from the plaza, neat tiled rooms have hot-water bathrooms; some have TV and refrigerators. It's owned by Douglas Clarke's Expeditions (above).

Hostal Shaw (☎ 289-0019; r per person $6) Run by Ecoselva (left), this *hostal* on the plaza has simple rooms with fans and private bathroom with hot water. You'll find espresso and a good book exchange at the downstairs café, as well as morning pancakes and vegetarian dishes. Browse the native crafts for sale.

El Paisano (☎ 289-0027; Rivadeneyra s/n; s/d $8/16) A backpacker haunt with cement rooms, tiny bathrooms, hot water, fans and mosquito nets. The staff is friendly and provides laundry service and vegetarian dishes at the open-air restaurant. It's just off the plaza.

El Albergue Español (☎ 08-469-1271; www.albergueespanol.com; r per person incl breakfast & dinner $16) Basic, clean hotel-style rooms with private bathroom are just off the plaza. There's a popular pizzeria downstairs, and the staff organizes tours, including trips to Pañacohca and Iquitos.

our pick **France Amazonia** (☎ 289-0009; www.france-amazonia.com; Av Principal s/n; r per person incl breakfast $18;) Located just outside of town on the lip of the river, shady thatched huts surround a sparkling pool and sandy fire pit. Beds are ultranarrow but rooms are pleasant. Meals may be ordered in advance from the friendly French owners. The garden offers plenty of nooks for enjoying the pleasant climate and sound of the river, which can be accessed via a small trail.

Hostería Misahuallí (☎ in Quito 02-252-0043, 289-0063; www.misahuallijungle.com; r per person incl 3 meals $75;) A fussy, manicured version of a jungle camp, this *hostería* (small hotel) sits across the Río Misahuallí on the north side of Río Napo, a short canoe ride away from any town riffraff. New hotel-style rooms are sophisticated and cool, while some stilted cabins feel like ovens. Guests enjoy a swimming pool, volleyball courts and upmarket restaurant and bar.

Getting There & Away

Buses leave from the plaza approximately every hour during daytime; the last bus is at 6pm. The main destination is Tena ($1, one hour).

The Tena–Coca (Loreto) road and others along the Río Napo have dried up the need for passenger canoes. You can arrange trips with boat drivers on the beach for about $40 per hour, but nearby agencies offer better deals. If you're staying at a lodge on the Río Napo, transport is usually arranged by the lodge.

WHAT KIND OF TRIP IS THIS? *Oswaldo Muñoz*

Think twice if your jungle tour offers *ayahuasca,* a psychotropic plant used ritually in Amazon cultures, as part of the authentic experience. Only a professional shaman (not necessarily 'dressed-up' for the occasion) has the trained ability to carry out 'readings' for patients as part of his diagnostic arts. And it is only on rare occasions and with due preparation on the part of the patient that the intake of this psychotropic plant should be considered.

There are many factors that should be taken into account prior to taking *ayahuasca,* such as dietary preparation, professional supervision and menstrual cycles, making true professional supervision and guidance essential. Dangerous side effects from *ayahuasca,* either due to medication you might be taking at the time or negligent preparation of the plant, could ruin your trip.

There are a number of books available on the subject. An operator should be capable of providing you with these for a deep-rooted, preliminary understanding of what a genuine *ayahuasca* ritual entails, a good way to screen a tour operator.

UPPER RÍO NAPO

☎ 06

The Río Napo rushes northeast from Misahuallí toward Coca, gaining breadth as it passes nature reserves, small jungle communities, oilrigs and lodges. Unfortunately, road construction has altered wildlife habits for good, and visitors will see fewer animals and birds here now than in the past.

Reserva Biológica Jatun Sacha & Cabañas Aliñahui

In Quichua, **Jatun Sacha** (admission $7) means 'Big Forest,' an appropriate name for the spectacular diversity here: 850 butterfly species, 535 bird species and thrilling quantities of fungi. This 2500-hectare biological station and rainforest reserve is located on the south side of Río Napo, 23km east of Puerto Napo. It is run by **Fundación Jatun Sacha** (☎ in Quito 02-331-7163; www.jatunsacha.org; cnr Eugenio de Santillán N34-248 & Maurián, Urbanización Rumipamba), an Ecuadorian nonprofit organization formed to promote rainforest research, conservation and education.

With neighboring areas being rapidly cleared for logging and agriculture, the biodiversity of Jatun Sacha seems precious. Besides counting and tracking local species, the foundation develops reforestation initiatives and agro-forestry alternatives with local farming communities and indigenous groups. Volunteers ($240 for a two-week stay) can apply for a variety of projects, such as bringing internet to rural schools.

Biostation workers and other guests stay in **Cabañas Aliñahui** (Map pp232-3; ☎ in Quito 02-227-4510; www.ecuadoramazonlodge.com; r per person incl 3 meals $50) high up on a bluff with views of the twisting river basin. Situated amid a 2-hectare tropical garden, hammocks hang under eight stilted, rustic cabins with detached, shared bathrooms that have solar-heated water. The restaurant serves healthy Ecuadorian and international meals. Go bird-watching or meander through the surrounding forest, then check out the plant conservation center and botanical garden. There are discounts for groups and students.

To get to Jatun Sacha or Cabañas Aliñahui from Tena, take an Ahuano or Santa Rosa bus and ask the driver to drop you at either entrance. Aliñahui is about 3km east of the Jatun Sacha research station, or 27km east of Tena on the road to Santa Rosa.

Ahuano

Uniformed schoolchildren skip through the puddles and dogs sleep in the road in this tiny village, a half-hour downriver from Misahuallí. Besides poking around the folksy mission church, there's not much to do. Buses arrive from Tena at La Punta with a short canoe ride across the river. Ahuano is the end of the road. Boating to Coca from here is expensive and difficult to arrange; return to Tena and go by bus.

The friendly **Casa de Doña Maruja** (☎ 09-130-4668; r per person $5, with 3 meals $10) offers bare-bones rooms with split-plank floors beside the swift river. Bathrooms are shared and meals are on the patio with the family. A canoe can be rented for excursions.

Most visitors come to stay at **La Casa del Suizo** (Map pp232-3; ☎ in Quito 02-256-6090, 250-9504; www.lacasadelsuizo.com; cnr Zaldumbide 397 & Valladolid; s/d per person incl meals $105/178; 🏊), a walled fortress from the outside. The Swiss-owned lodge proffers a pampered glimpse of the jungle. A maze of covered boardwalks links thatched hotel-style rooms that have high-ceilings, pale adobe walls, electricity, fans, hot showers, and balconies with a hammock overlooking the river.

Run much like its sister operation Sacha Lodge (see p245), La Casa del Suizo assigns guests to tables for buffet-style meals. The turquoise pool kisses the lip of the overhang; you can cavort in its crystalline waters with an eye to the murky Napo just below. While the scenery is stunning, the area feels less remote and pristine than it once did. Included in the daily rate are meals and excursions with Spanish-speaking guides that include river trips, jungle hikes, community and mission visits, access to an on-site butterfly house, and wildlife walks.

Guests pay $60 per boatload for canoe transport from Misahuallí. For independent travelers, bus services from Tena run eight times a day to La Punta, about 28km east of Puerto Napo on the south side of Río Misahuallí. Although the bus doesn't actually go to Ahuano, it's called the Ahuano bus since most passengers transfer in dugout canoes across the river to Ahuano. Boats are frequent and cost $15 per boat to Casa del Suizo.

AmaZOOnico & Liana Lodge

You're guaranteed to see all manner of critters at **AmaZOOnico** (Map pp232-3; ☎ 09-414-3395; www.amazoonico.org; admission $2.50), a well-known animal rehabilitation center. The center is located on the grounds of Selva Viva, a 1500-hectare reserve of primary forest on Río Arajuno, a narrow tributary of the Napo about 3km east of Ahuano. A Swiss/Quichua couple founded the center in 1995 to care for confiscated or displaced rainforest animals, from toucans and capybaras to monkeys and boa constrictors.

While cages may not be the ideal setting for your first glimpse of jungle wildlife, the circumstances belie an ugly reality. These animals have been displaced because their habitats were destroyed or illegal traffickers sold them for quick cash. The center has its critics, who see it more as a zoo than a steppingstone to the wild, but an unfortunate number of animals arrive here too domesticated to be re-released. Some healthy animals are released back into the rainforest. Many animals have been maimed and suffer from mental and emotional trauma; the costs of caring for them are astronomical.

Bilingual volunteers, who know the animals intimately, lead all tours. The center is always looking for volunteers ($100 per month living expenses), especially veterinarians, for a two-month-minimum stay.

At the nearby **Liana Lodge** (Map pp232-3; ☎ 09-980-0463; per person 2/3/5 nights $87/141/219), six cabins are scattered throughout a forested hillside. Each has crafty touches such as bamboo beds and hand-carved clothes hangers built with leftover wood from road building. Cabins have two double rooms, a hot shower and no electricity. The carefree riverside atmosphere revolves around bonfires, walks through the woods and a round bar overlooking the river. Packages include meals, tours (including lessons on making chica and building a balsa raft) and canoe transport from Puerto Barantilla. Ask about **Runi Huasi**, a nearby indigenous-run lodge that's managed by the Liana owners. Quichua, English, Spanish, German and French are spoken here.

To reach the lodge, AmaZOOnico or Runi Huasi, take a Tena bus to Santa Rosa and get off at Puerto Barantilla. Walk down the dirt road to the river, a spot frequented by transport canoes.

Arajuno Jungle Lodge

If small and out of the way is your speed, check out former Peace Corps volunteer Thomas Larson's **Arajuno Jungle Lodge** (Map pp232-3; ☎ 08-268-2267; www.arajuno.com; r per person 2/3 nights $215/250), slung in a bend of the Río Arajuno. A handful of hillside cabins are snug and screened and have solar-powered hot water. The thatched main lodge has a sprawling wooden deck and dining area perched over the river. Guests can roam the 80 hectares of forest, hike, canoe and visit the nearby AmaZOOnico (left). The lodge works with local communities to develop new food sources and spread information about health and nutrition. Volunteers are accepted for stays of three to six months. The chef cooks up locally inspired gourmet food such as smoked *cachama maitos* (fish grilled in palm leaves) and *tortilla de yuca* (manioc bread). Grown-up kids will love the rope swing launching into the river. Services are bilingual.

Yachana Lodge

Set on a scenic bend in the Río Napo, **Yachana Lodge** (Map pp232-3; ☎ in Quito 02-252-3777, in the US 888-922-4262; www.yachana.com; cnr Vicente Solano E12-61 & Av Oriental; r per person incl all meals $175, bunkhouse per person incl all meals $100; 💻) offers guests a chance to experience 'geotourism' – tourism that sustains an environment, culture and residents – at its finest.

Located halfway between Misahuallí and Coca, a campus of stilted wooden buildings, groomed grounds and colorful gardens is upriver from the tiny community of Mondaña. The lodge has 18 rooms, which includes three cabins with a double and a triple room. Rooms have modern bathrooms with hot and potable tap water (the septic system can even accommodate toilet paper, a rarity in Ecuador), a balcony with hammock and solar-powered electricity. The kitchen serves delicious, mostly vegetarian meals in an open, covered dining area overlooking the river. In addition, there's a conference center, library and internet access.

Guests visit the adjacent community, where fees from the lodge help fund a high school for rural, mestizo (mixed indigenous and Spanish descent) and indigenous kids (see the boxed text, opposite), and a medical center. Other daytime activities include hiking, bird-watching, participating in a traditional healing ceremony, swimming and touring nearby protected forest in a *chiva*. Shuar and Quichua indigenous guides speak English and provide treasure troves of information about the forest. A new culinary program funded by the National Geographic Society lets visitors harvest and cook local, native foods.

Costs include all meals and guide services, with optional additional airfare from Quito to Coca. From Coca, it's a 2½-hour motorized canoe ride upriver to the lodge. The lodge operates as one arm of the Yachana Foundation, a project that's won numerous accolades, including a 2008 award for geotourism from National Geographic and Ashoka Changemakers.

PUYO

☎ 03 / pop 35,000

A lazy river slinks through this concrete outpost, the informal dividing point between the northern and southern Oriente. Part mellow jungle town and part commercial, government hub, Puyo gets some of its vitality as the capital of the Pastaza province. The streets are filled with missionaries, vendors pushing street carts piled with purple-and-orange crabs and speckled eggs, and indigenous people from far-flung corners of the Amazon. Dense green jungle flourishes around the town's edges and jagged snowcapped mountains rise in the distance. It's a good starting point for reaching indigenous villages.

Fiestas de Fundación de Puyo, the weeklong celebration of Puyo's founding, take place in early May.

Information

Amazonía Touring (☎ 288-3064; Atahualpa; 🕑 9am-8pm Mon-Sat, 9am-noon Sun) The only place to change traveler's checks; charges a 3% commission.
Andinatel (Orellana)
Banco del Austro (Atahualpa) Has an ATM.
Banco Internacional (Villamil) ATM only takes four-digit pins.
Banco Pinchicha (10 de Agosto) Has an ATM.
Cámara de Turismo (☎ 288-3681; Marín, Centro Commercial Zuñiga; 🕑 8:30am-12:30pm & 3-6pm Mon-Fri) Provides regional maps and info about nearby destinations.
Lavandaria La Mocita (☎ 288-5346; cnr Marín & Bolívar; 🕑 7am-7pm Mon-Fri, to 5pm Sat & Sun) Cheap and efficient laundry service.
Post office (27 de Febrero) Northwest of the market.
Red Cross (☎ 288-5214)
Voz Andes Mission Hospital (☎ 279-5172; Shell) American-owned and staffed. The best medical services in the area.

Sights & Activities

Early risers may see the jagged white teeth of **Volcán El Altar** (5319m), the fifth-highest mountain in Ecuador, about 50km southeast. On clear days look southwest to see **Volcán Sangay** (5230m).

Walk past the kids plunging from the bridge into Río Puyo (think twice about joining them, because of polluted water) to **Parque Omaere** (☎ 288-7656; 08-525-0864; www.fundacionomaere.org; admission $3, minimum per group $5; 🕑 9am-5pm), less than 1km north of the city center. The ethnobotanical park offers guided tours (free with admission) of rainforest plants and indigenous dwellings, by mostly indigenous guides. The park is run by Shuar plant expert Teresa Shiki and her husband, Chris Canaday, an American biologist, author of *Common Birds of Amazonian Ecuador* and

HIGHER LEARNING

In July 2008, 47 students from remote Quichua, Shuar and Secoia villages graduated from high school in the village of Mondaña, on the banks of the Río Napo. They took turns wearing the few caps and gowns during the ceremony. It was a proud moment for their parents, many of whom received little formal education. That's because in the remote Amazon Basin only 15% of kids finish secondary schooling, a dismal figure that contributes to the area's ongoing struggles with poverty and environmental degradation. Part of the problem stems from irrelevant classroom lessons.

But at the Yachana Technical High School, the curriculum focuses on the applicable, with hands-on courses in ecotourism, sustainable development, agronomy, animal husbandry and micro-enterprises. Students learn how to create hydroelectric power, plant yuca (cassava), graft citrus trees, raise algae for animal feed, serve meals to tourists, keep books and install water filters. They even practice at the adjacent Yachana Lodge (opposite). Students stay in dorms at the school for three weeks on and one week off, and can return to their families to help with farming and other essential tasks.

'The future of the rainforest is inextricably linked to the well-being of the people who call it home,' says Juan Kunchikuy, a native Shuar who works as a guide at the lodge, which helps fund the school through the fees paid by visitors.

All projects fall under the umbrella of the **Yachana Foundation** (☎ in the US 888-922-4262, 02-223-7133/7278; www.yachana.org.ec), which works to improve education, develop community-based medical care, create sustainable agriculture and conserve rainforest. Director Douglas McMeekin landed in the Amazon as a bankrupt American businessman who found work with the oil companies. But he saw a need for education among the Amazon natives and started the foundation in 1991 to do just that. The organization accepts volunteers.

a font of knowledge about everything from jungle plants to ecological dry toilets (see the boxed text, p261). Teresa helped found and plant the park and prepares natural medicine. Stomach troubles? Ask for a cure for parasites made from local fruits, seeds and sap.

Get there by following Loja north of town for about 500m until you reach the bridge over the river, then follow the sign. The park receives volunteers (one-month minimum), who speak Spanish and pay their own expenses.

A pleasant **trail** (called the *paseo turístico*) continues past Omaere for 1.7km along the river to the Puyo–Tena road, where you can flag down a bus back to town every 20 minutes, or return along the trail.

Visitors rave about the **Jardín Botáncio las Orquídeas** (☎ 288-4855; admission $5; 🕓 8am-6pm), located 15 minutes south from Puyo on the road to Macas. Enthusiastic owner Omar Taeyu guides visitors through hills of lush foliage and fishponds to see gorgeous plants and countless rare orchids. Call ahead.

At **Paseo de los Monos** (☎ 09-474-0070; admission $1.50; 🕓 8am-5pm) you can see a variety of rescued animals, including six kinds of monkeys, turtles and birds. Some animals are caged, while others run free. For an extra $2, guides lead four-hour walks into the surrounding jungle to see more of the center's animals.

The new **Museo Etnográfico Huaorani** (☎ 288-6148; Severo Vargas s/n; admission $3; 🕓 10am-5pm) has a small exhibit and guided tour. Perhaps more engaging than the artifacts themselves is the Huaorani's take of their culture and problems. Upstairs is Onhae, the political body of the Huaorani, which can help arrange visits to communities.

The **Museo Etnoarqueológico** (☎ 288-5605; cnr Atahualpa & 9 de Octubre; admission $1; 🕓 noon-6pm Mon-Fri) has ceramics, artifacts and an excellent map showing distribution of native populations.

Mountain bikers can do a beautiful 65km downhill **ride** from the central highlands town of Baños to Puyo, via the Podunk hamlet of **Shell**. Throw the bike on the roof of a bus in Puyo for the round-trip.

Tours

Fundecopia (☎ 09-029-4808; www.fundecopia) Runs trips to the Arutam Rainforest Reserve and Shuar homestays with some volunteer opportunities. Tourists pay $20 per day, and volunteers pay $75 per week, which includes meals and lodging. Comes recommended.

Madre Selva Tours (☎ 289-0449; www.madreselvaecuador.com; cnr Marìn & 9 de Octubre) Operates one- to four-day tours to visit local communities, raft, hike and more. Day trips start at $15 per person.

Papangu-Atacapi Tours (☎ 288-7684; papanguturismo@yahoo.es; cnr 27 de Febrero & Sucre; 8am-12:30pm & 2-6pm Mon-Sat) An indigenous-run agency with a focus on community tourism. Trips go to Sarayaku and Mango Wasi (Quichua communities) and Cueva de los Tuyos (Shuar). Sarayacu (www.sarayaku.com/tourism) requires a rural charter flight ($125 round-trip per person) and the cost is $63 per day for a two-night trip. Other trips start at $40 per day. Guides are indigenous and speak Spanish and Quichua, and some of the fees go to participating communities. Highly recommended by readers.

Sleeping

An explosion in offerings in all price ranges makes Puyo's grubby dives a thing of the past.

BUDGET

Hotel Libertad (☎ 288-3282; cnr Orellana & Manzano; r per person $6) This tranquil spot offers cramped but spotless rooms.

Hotel Los Cofanes (☎ 288-5560; loscofanes@yahoo.com; cnr 27 de Febrero & Marín; r per person $10) Right in the heart of the action. This modern hotel's hushed corridors lead to tiled rooms that seem ripe for a remodel, but the attention is good and rooms include phone, fan and cable TV.

MIDRANGE

Hostal del Rio (☎ 288-6090; cnr Loja & Cañar; r per person incl breakfast $10) Cool and quiet rooms surround an oversized indoor dining space. The private bathrooms may induce claustrophobia.

Hostal Mexico (☎ 288-5668; cnr 9 de Octubre & 24 de Mayo; r per person incl breakfast $11) Parquet floors and dark interior rooms are forgettable minus some strange, carpeted walls. Only some rooms have private bathroom. Breakfast happens across the street.

Las Palmas (☎ 288-4832; cnr 20 de Julio & 4 de Enero; r per person incl breakfast $13;) This big yellow colonial place features attractive gardens and chattering parrots. The rooms here are neat and bright. There's on-site internet access and a café serving wine and coffee. Take advantage of the hammocks and the outdoor fire pit.

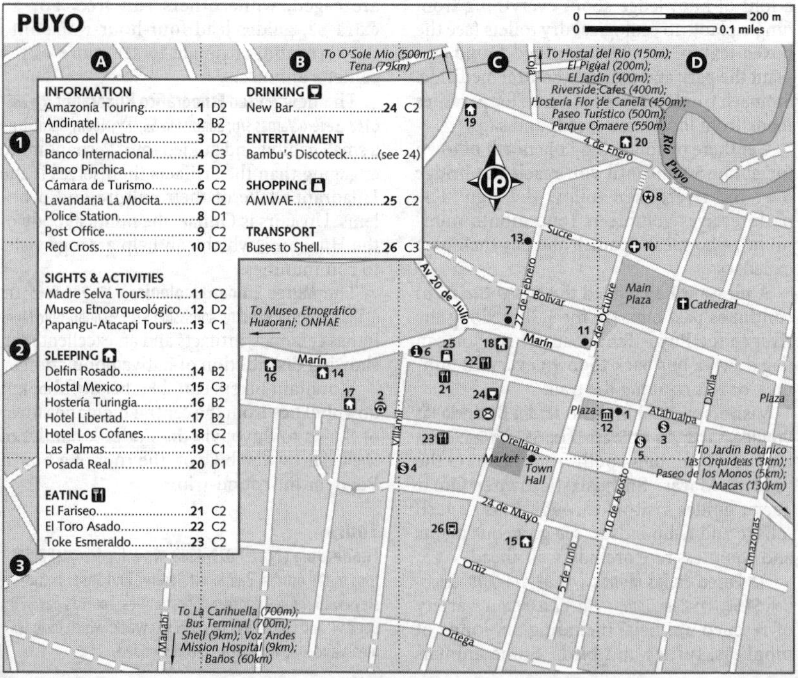

WASTE NOT

Chris Canaday, an American biologist who's been living in Ecuador for 17 years, started thinking about sanitation when he noticed the sewage from his house outside Tena flowing directly into a stream where kids played and fished.

So he built and installed an 'ecological dry toilet' (www.ecosanres.org, inodoroseco.blogspot.com), which converts human waste into safe, organic compost in six months in tropical climes. After a few months of odor-free, self-contained waste processing, he realized that the toilets could change the world.

'It's irrational to think we can defecate in precious drinking water and trust that someone will effectively clean it,' Canaday says. 'Flush toilets are explained as the only civilized option, but in the end they're not all that civilized.'

The toilets separate urine and feces without using water or chemicals (or petroleum, Canaday points out). After use, one dumps a cup of dry material, such as ash or sawdust, down the hole, to keep flies off the feces and to dry them out. Even in the humid Amazon Basin, the toilets don't smell because they're constructed above ground, away from water. Not only do they prevent disease, the toilets create compost, valuable nutrients for crops.

Since 2000, Canaday has helped install more than 100 dry toilets, mostly in the Ecuadorian Amazon. 'This approach can be applied throughout the world, even in big cities,' he says. 'Swedish experts are helping the Chinese build a whole city where no one defecates in water, even in multistory apartment buildings.'

See examples of Canaday's work at Parque Omaere (p258) and the Napo Wildlife Center (p245).

Delfin Rosado (☎ 288-8757; www.delfinrosadohotelspa.com; Marín & Atahualpa; r per person incl breakfast $15; 🅿) New paint, dark wood furniture and a spiral staircase creates a modern, clean option, but it's a bit loud. A Quito-based pizza chain is downstairs. The tiny pool out back is basic but private.

Hostería Turingia (☎ 288-5180; turingia@andinanet.net; Marín 294; s/d $22/36; 💻 🅿) This walled, Tyrolean outpost offers painted brick rooms with firm double beds and a full-service restaurant. There's patio seating under the bougainvillea, a tiny, green plunge pool and for a bit of kept wildness, a caged snake. Accommodations have fans, TV, telephone and hot water.

El Jardín (☎ 288-7770; www.eljardin.pastaza.net; r per person incl breakfast $25) A welcoming spot just across the footbridge. A rustic wooden building wraps around a charming garden infused with wi-fi. Comfortable rooms with firm beds and thick comforters have balconies and plenty of hot water. Breakfast is fruit and yogurt served in the excellent attached restaurant (see above). Ask the friendly owners about the orchid collection.

Posada Real (☎ 288-5887; www.posadareal.pastaza.net; 4 de Enero at 9 de Octubre stairs; r per person incl breakfast $25) A beautiful, mustard-yellow house with a formal, European atmosphere. Beds have plush spreads and thick pillows and rooms are elegant and tasteful. A guard poodle keeps watch.

Hostería Flor de Canela (☎ 288-5265; hosteriaflordecanela@hotmail.com; Paseo Turístico, Barrio Obrero; s/d $35/54; 🅿) Part wooded getaway, part Disneyland, this complex of elaborate jungle-style buildings sits near the Río Puyo next to Parque Omaere. Dated stone and wood cabañas are dark and dank, which may seem authentic to some.

El Pigual (☎ 288-7972; www.elpigualecuador.com; end of Tuguragua; s/d incl breakfast & dinner $32/57; 🅿) The expansive grounds of this former farm are manicured and green with a pool, volleyball court, quiet cement-and-wooden cabins and a good restaurant. Visit the pool as a nonguest ($3), but time your visit to avoid kiddie swim lessons. Popular with large groups.

Eating

Try the riverside cafés for a typical dish of *ceviche boquetero,* literally 'dumptruck ceviche,' a combination of toasted corn kernels and banana chips with a can of tuna elegantly dumped on top.

Toke Esmeraldo (Orellana s/n; mains $1.50; 🕑 7am-7pm) A cheery street-shack where you can pull up a stool for some fresh, fast seafood including ceviche and fried tilapia. Sip on a range of fresh juices.

El Fariseo (☎ 288-3795; cnr Atahualpa & Villamil; mains $2-5; 🕑 7am-9pm Mon-Fri, 8am-9pm Sat) Sit streetside for a frothy cappuccino and slice of cake. *Platos fuertes* (heavier dishes) include burritos and burgers. Largest cocktail list in town.

El Toro Asado (☎ 08-494-8156; cnr Atahualpa & 27 de Febrero; mains $4; 🕑 7am-11pm) In addition to more-common meats and fish, this elegant grill house serves *guanta*, an Amazonian…er, rodent, five different ways. The owner swears it tastes like pork, but we'll leave it to you to find out.

our pick **El Jardín** (☎ 288-6101; Paseo Turístico, Barrio Obrero; mains $5-11; 🕑 noon-10pm Tue-Sat, noon-5pm Sun) The best grub in the Oriente may be at this ambient house by the river. The award-winning chef-owner Sofia prepares fragrant *pollo ishpingo* (*ishpingo* is a type of cinnamon native to the Oriente), whose decadent, delicate flavors awake the palate. Try the *lomo plancho* (grilled steak) for a tender, perfectly cooked slab among artfully arranged vegetables.

La Carihuella (☎ 288-3919; Zambrano; mains $5-13; 🕑 noon-4pm & 6-9pm Mon-Sat, noon-5pm Sun) Missionaries converge in large groups here, but even nonbelievers are welcome for meaty meals cooked over an open grill. Hungry? The two-person barbecue plate ($12.50) has two kinds of sausage, chicken, pork chop, sirloin, tripe and kidney. Close to the bus station.

O'Sole Mio (☎ 288-4768; cnr Pichincha & Guaranda; pizzas $6; 🕑 6-10pm Wed-Sun) A new, modern Italian restaurant, with outdoor patio overlooking twinkling town lights, that serves uncommonly authentic pizzas. Lightly charred crusts are topped with tasty ingredients such as spinach, salami and ricotta. Pastas also make the grade. Ask the owners about upstairs suites.

Drinking & Entertainment

Twilight's frenetic buzz concludes around 9:30pm, when most good citizens and internet addicts head for home. If you're in the mood, try **New Bar** (27 de Febrero; 🕑 6pm-2am Mon-Sat), whose dim ambience encourages karaoke. See if the attached **Bambu's Discoteck** (🕑 Thu-Sat) lives up to its claim as 'the best' during endless sessions of pumping Latin rock.

Shopping

AMWAE (Asociacion De Mujeres Waorani De La Amazonia Ecuatoriana; ☎ 288-8908; amwae@latinmail.com; cnr Atahualpa & Villamil; 🕑 7:30am-1pm & 2pm-7:30pm Mon-Sat, 7:30am-2pm Sun) Sells artisan crafts made by Waorani women, including jewelry, spears, hammocks, blowguns and palm string bags. Artisans receive a portion of every sale.

Getting There & Away

Charter flights from the provincial airstrip in Shell cost about $350 per hour, but chances are if you're headed into the deep green yonder, it will be on a tour. **Aero Regional** (☎ 279-5095/768) flies anywhere with a landing strip, and can take groups to Kapawi lodge (p265) for $700 per plane.

The bus terminal is about 1km southwest of town. There are buses via Baños ($1.75, 1½ hours) to Ambato ($2.50, 2½ hours). Buses to Quito ($5, 5½ hours) leave about every hour and go via Baños or Baeza. Buses to Tena ($2.50, 2½ hours) leave hourly. San Francisco has one bus nightly to Guayaquil ($9, eight hours). Buses to Macas ($5, four hours) leave six times daily. There is a 5:45am departure to Coca ($10, nine hours). Seven buses a day go to Riobamba ($3.50, 3½ hours).

Centinela del Oriente, located at the bus terminal, runs ancient buses to various small villages in the surrounding jungle.

Getting Around

A taxi ride from downtown to the bus terminal costs $1, as should all rides within the city. Small local buses go to Shell ($0.25) every 30 minutes or so from south of the market along Calle 27 de Febrero.

THE SOUTHERN ORIENTE

The southern Oriente may be the envy of its northern sister: the wilder, more pristine territory is defined by unknowns. Just look at a map. Rivers snake through vast jungle dotted with tiny indigenous settlements. Roads? Who needs 'em? Inaccessibility remains, for the most part, because of a lack of industry, although mining and oil exploits may change all that in the future. Most visitors come to see indigenous tribes, an adventurous pursuit that usually involves few creature comforts – the tourism industry has yet to bloom.

The region's main road skirts the eastern edge of jungle, running south from Puyo through Macas, tiny villages and eventually,

Zamora. Beautiful highland roads swoop down from Cuenca and Loja to join with the central highway. With broken buses, unpaved roads and rainy-season landslides, travelers need patience and fortitude. June through August is the rainiest time.

MACAS

☎ 07 / pop 17,000

Most denizens of the southern Oriente eventually pass through Macas, the provincial capital of Morona-Santiago, a century-old trading post. At the bus station, men from nearby Shuar and Achuar territories wear traditional beads over logo T-shirts. Glass-and-concrete hotels rise with a surprising frequency, an odd modern facade in a town with unkempt corners. Visitors discover a welcoming place accustomed to shuffling people and goods into the remote, surrounding regions.

Information

Banco del Austro (cnr Comin & Soasti) ATM and cash advances on Visa.

Banco del Pinchincha (cnr 10 de Agosto & Soasti) Has an ATM.

Cámara de Turismo (☎ 270-1606; Comin; 🕒 8am-noon Mon-Sat) Useful information kiosk.

Centro de Interpretación (cnr Juan de la Cruz & 29 de Mayo) Small exhibit and information about Parque Nacional Sangay.

El Rincon de Vago Cyber Cafe (cnr 29 de Mayo & Amazonas; per hr $1; 🕒 8am-10pm)

Orientravel (☎ 270-0371; ortravel@mo.pro.ec; cnr 10 de Agosto & Soasti) Books national and international airline tickets and organizes local tours.

Pacifictel (24 de Mayo; 🕒 8am-10pm)

Post office (9 de Octubre)

Sights & Activities

In **Our Lady of Macas cathedral**, a Technicolor Virgin looms over the manicured plaza. Inside, a tranquil, column-free space draws attention to the tiled altar depicting a peaceful Macas in front of a bellowing volcano. Miracles are attributed to the painting of the Virgin of Macas (c 1592) on the altar.

The **casa de la cultura** (admission free; 🕒 8am-noon & 1:30-5pm Mon-Fri) has an extensive 1st-floor library with information about cultural events and the Shuar people.

The perfect snow-covered cone of **Volcán Sangay** (5230m), some 40km to the northwest, can be glimpsed on a clear day. It's Ecuador's seventh-highest mountain and one of the world's most active volcanoes; early missionaries construed it as hell.

A few blocks northeast of the center is a small **children's park** (cnr Don Bosco & Zabala).

During the last week of May, the **Chonta Festival** is the most important Shuar celebration of the year. A Shuar guide can help you garner an invitation to this grand event, where participants dance for four consecutive hours to help ferment the *chicha* (a fermented corn or yuca drink; see the boxed text, p266).

Tours

Macas is the place to book trips into the southern Oriente, but services are not as comprehensive here as those in the north. Be aware that the Shuar do not want unguided visitors in their villages; certain villages refuse visitors entirely. Given the negative impact of outsiders in the past, this stance is understandable.

Insondu Mundo Shuar (☎ 270-2533; www.mundoshuar.com; Soasti & Bolívar) Organizes two- to five-day trips into Shuar territory with some English-speaking guides.

Planeta Tours (☎ 270-1328; Comin at Soasti; 🕒 8am-9pm) Offers cultural tours in Shuar territory, waterfall hikes, fishing, white-water rafting on the Río Upano, and canoeing. Some English is spoken. Multiday trips cost $40 to $75 per day.

Yacu Amu Rafting (☎ in Quito 02-290-4054; www.yacuamu.com) Runs five-day trips through Río Upano's wild Namangosa Gorge, whose magnificent scenery comes from high waterfalls. The Class III/IV white water is suitable for kayakers. See p97.

Independent guides include Shuar guide **Nanki Wampankit Juank** (nanki_82@hotmail.com) and the experienced **Rafael Telcán** (☎ 09-101-1075).

Sleeping

Hostal Acupulco (☎ 270-0713; cnr Amazonas & 10 de Agosto; r per person with shared/private bathroom $6/8) A twisting maze of peachy walls creates a dingy impression. Shared bathrooms are shinier than private ones.

Hotel La Orquidea (☎ 270-0970; cnr 9 de Octubre & Sucre; r per person $8) Hard single beds and prim pink rooms add to the monastic ambience of this large, old-fashioned *pensión* (an inexpensive boarding house). Run by a friendly family, it's well situated away from the noise.

Hotel Milenium (☎ 270-0805; cnr Amazonas & Tarqui; r per person $8) An open shared balcony is lined with plants and overlooks the busy street. Rooms have humid bathrooms, and TVs.

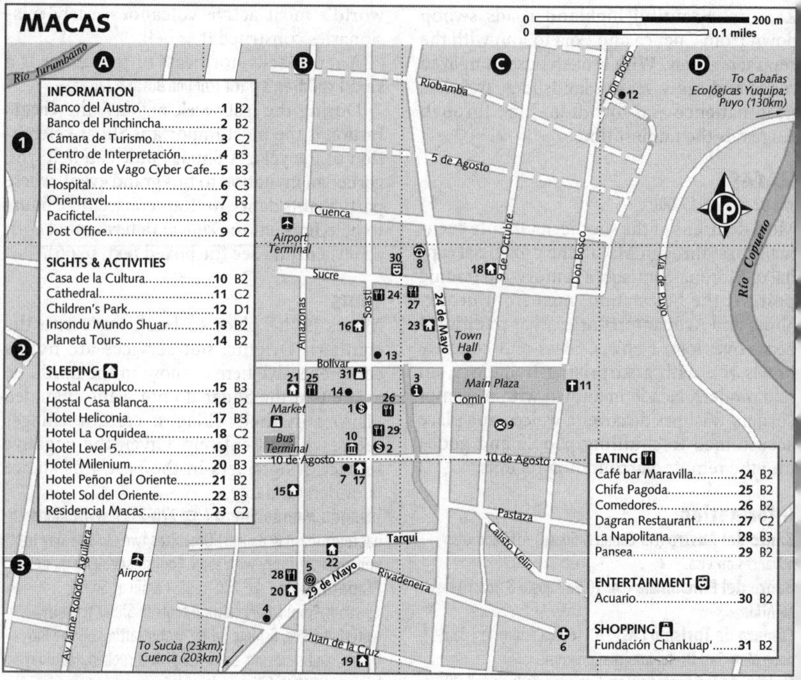

Hotel Peñon del Oriente (☎ 270-0124; cnr Amazonas & Comín; r per person $8) Make sure you have a sense of humor for the Barbie bedspreads and bible sayings, but with rooms this worn, consider venturing further from the bus station.

Residencial Macas (☎ 270-0254; 24 de Mayo; s/d per person with shared bathroom $5/10, with private bathroom $10/15) Clean slat-board rooms could be considered roughing it. Located across from the school.

Hotel Level 5 (☎ 270-1240; cnr Juan de la Cruz & Soasti; r per person $10) The most recent glass-walled addition to town still smells new. Rooms are a bit smaller than those at its counterparts, but it's comfortable, clean and has good views and a friendly staff.

Hostal Casa Blanca (☎ 270-0195; cnr Soasti & Sucre; r per person incl breakfast $12, garden r $15) A modern white multistory place whose most coveted rooms line the garden out back. Interior rooms are dim and airless, but clean. Has a restaurant and a pool in progress.

Hotel Heliconia (☎ 270-1956; cnr Soasti & 10 de Agosto; s/d $15/25) This high-rise, decked out with parquet floors and glass-walled panoramic views, has lost its sparkle. Rooms have cable TV, phones and finer furnishings, but don't count on clean bathrooms or consistent hot water.

Cabañas Ecológicas Yuquipa (☎ 270-0071; r per person incl meals $35) Rudimentary huts (no electricity or hot water) offer a rural experience near Río Yuquipa, a small tributary of Río Upano. Your Shuar guide will take you to primary jungle and San Vicente, a Shuar outpost. Ask for info in the Pansesa bakery (below).

Eating

Pansea (☎ 270-0071; 🕑 6am-1pm & 3-9pm) The place for a warm, flaky pastry. Operates Cabañas Ecológicas Yuquipa (above).

Dagran Restaurant (☎ 09-835-7923; mains $2-6; 🕑 6:30am-9pm) A large, bright cafeteria with wooden tables ready for the masses. Try the barbecued ribs, but don't expect to be transported to Texas.

La Napolitana (☎ 270-0486; cnr Amazonas & Tarqui; mains $2-9; 🕑 8am-11pm) Patrons eat cheesy pizzas and bowls of pasta swimming in sauce, under a tented patio.

Café bar Maravilla (☎ 270-0158; Soasti near Sucre; mains $4-6; ⏲ 4pm-1am Mon-Sat) This blue casita is all ambience, from the twinkling porch lights to the stuffed red-leather armchairs. It is a great place to chill, with *tablas* (cutting-boards) of meat and cheese and yuca fries. The drink menu gets creative, with herbal aphrodisiacs and *hueso de chuchuguazo* (a root mixed with rum).

Chifa Pagoda (☎ 270-0280; cnr Amazonas & Comín; mains $4-6; ⏲ 11am-10:30pm) The decor is part–wedding cake and part-diner at the best *chifa* in town, which serves tasty wonton soup, sweet-and-sour shrimp and fried noodles.

The *comedores* on Comín near Soasti sell tasty *ayampacos*, a jungle specialty of meat, chicken or fish grilled in *bijao* leaves.

Entertainment

Break up your mellow weekend with a trip to Café bar Maravilla (above) for live Andean music or head to **Acuario** (☎ 270-1601; Sucre; ⏲ 9pm-3am Thu-Sat, 3-7pm Sun), a dark smoky disco that heats up even during the Sunday 'matinee.'

Shopping

Fundación Chankuap' (☎ 270-1176; www.chankuap.org; cnr Bolívar & Soasti; ⏲ 9am-noon & 2-6pm Mon-Fri, 8am-1pm Sun) This foundation aids the Shuar and Achuar by selling crafts, herbal remedies and beauty products.

Getting There & Away

AIR

Monday through Friday **TAME** (☎/fax 270-1162/1978; airport) flies from Quito to Macas ($71) at 11:15am and returns at 12:15pm. On the flight to Quito, the left side of the plane offers the best mountain views, including Sangay and Cotopaxi on clear days.

Small aircraft can be chartered to interior villages, but it's expensive. Contact a local tour agency or guide instead.

BUS

Coop de Trans Banos (Cooperativo de Transportes Banos) heads to Quito at 2am ($8, eight hours). A few companies head to Riobamba ($5, five hours) on the new, controversial road through Parque Nacional Sangay, while Coop Trans Riobamba continues on to Guayaquil four times daily ($10, 10 hours). Buses to Cuenca ($8.50, eight hours) go through Limón or Guarumales, which knocks an hour off the ride. Head to Yaupi, near the Peruvian border, on Orient Rut ($6.50, seven hours). Buses to Sucúa ($1, 45 minutes) leave every 30 minutes from 6am to 7pm.

Buses to Puyo ($4, four hours) leave 10 times a day; some continue to Tena. Locals are proud of the new bridge spanning the Río Pastaza along the way.

Transportes Macas runs small buses and pickup trucks to various remote destinations, including 9 de Octubre (for Parque Nacional Sangay) and Morona.

PARQUE NACIONAL SANGAY

For more on this **national park** (admission $10), see p180. Most access to the park is from the north and west; access from the south and east is difficult. If starting from Macas, make your goal the alpine lakes, including the scenic Lagunas de Tinguichaca or the popular Sardina Yaca lagoons, which are teeming with wildlife. The volcano itself is inaccessible from here.

Buses from Macas go to 9 de Octubre and San Vicente, a good starting point for most hikes. The small settlement of Purshi is the official entrance. It's best to enter with a guide as trails are faint and require acute navigation and machete skills. Trips here are not for the uninitiated outdoors person.

At one point, the park was put on the List of World Heritage in Danger largely due to construction of a road between Macas and Guamote. The road, which was finally finished in 2006, offers greater access to the park but also caused irreversible damage.

KAPAWI ECOLODGE & RESERVE

Located in the heart of Achuar wilderness, in one of the most remote parts of the Ecuadorian Amazon, **Kapawi** (Map pp232-3; www.kapawi.com) offers a pristine, ecologically and culturally sound experience. Many outfits claim similar practices, but few execute like this. The lodge has received many accolades for its approach.

Ecuadorian tour operator Canodros opened the lodge in 1996, but rented the land from the Achuar and trained locals in guiding and tourism. Management has slowly been transferred to the Achuar over the years, and in 2008 the tribe became the lodge's sole owners and operators.

CHICHA, THE BREAKFAST OF CHAMPIONS

Before you could get a Coke and a smile in the Amazon Basin, there was *chicha* – not the boiled highland version, but a highly portable nutritional drink. Stored as a paste wrapped in leaves, *chicha* materializes when you add water.

The recipe is simple – *chicha* is yuca or chonta palm masticated by women (yes, just women). For millennia, *chicha* has been a prime source of nutrition and vitamins for remote communities. It's an important staple in the jungle, where people eat very little and drink up to 6L a day. When fresh, *chicha* tastes mild and yogurtlike, but as time passes, it becomes more alcoholic as bacteria from the saliva turn carbohydrates into simple sugars. The older the *chicha,* the more potent it is. The flavor depends on who made the stuff; each woman's bacteria creates a distinctive taste.

Really terrible *chicha* is considered a portent that something bad will happen. Will something bad happen to you, the visitor, if you try it? Contrary to what you might think, problems result not from the saliva, but unfiltered river water that may have been mixed with the paste. As it's considered very bad form to refuse *chicha,* in one way or another, you'll be taking your chances.

Ask for *chicha* at any jungle lodge or at restaurants frequented by locals, especially in Coca and Puyo.

Visitors arrive by air only – the nearest town is a 10-day walk away. The lodge is made up of 19 thatched cabins built on stilts over a lagoon, each with private bathroom and a balcony. Low-impact technology such as solar power, trash management, recycling, sound water treatment and biodegradable soaps are used in daily operations.

Instead of just photographing the Achuar, guests are invited to their homes and offered manioc beer, which begins a unique cultural exchange. Small groups are accompanied by an Achuar guide and a bilingual naturalist, who work in tandem to explain the intricacies of the rainforest, both from an ecological and a cultural perspective.

The lodge is just off Río Pastaza, on an oxbow lake on Río Capahuari, and is reached by canoe from the nearby landing strip. Make reservations at the main **office** (☎ in Quito 02-600-9003; cnr Mariscal Foch E7-38 & Reina Victoria; s 3/4/7 nights $975/1250/1790, d 3/4/7 nights $1390/1790/2790). Transportation from Quito costs $238 roundtrip. Packages include meals and guided tours.

THE JUNGLE FROM MACAS

Maps show tracks or trails leading from Macas into the interior, most of which lead to Shuar indigenous villages and missions deep in the Oriente. Going to these areas on your own is not recommended, as tourists may be unwelcome. Most communities that welcome guests insist they come with a guide.

Frequent buses from Macas go to the mission (church and school) of **Sevilla** (Don Bosco) on the other side of Río Upano. This is a good place to buy Shuar crafts from local artisans. From here a broad track leads south to the village of **San Luís**, a good day trip from Macas that offers a glimpse of indigenous life.

Trails leading to remote jungle communities are an unmarked tangle, just one more reason to hire a guide. A charter *expreso* (light aircraft) can take you to some of the better-known villages, including **Taisha**, 70km east of Macas. Salesian mission aircraft fly there, but locals are given preference and flights are often full. It's difficult to hire your own aircraft, but isn't unheard of. Expect delays when there's inclement weather.

To satisfy your craving for **caving**, or to see the rare oil bird, a nocturnal, fruit-eating bird that's prized by the Shar for its medicinal oils, grab a guide and head to **Cueva de los Tayos** between Méndez and Morona. A five-hour trail leads to the extensive Coangos cave system, where you could easily spend a week exploring the caverns spiked with stalactites and stalagmites. One route requires technical equipment, as the journey starts with a 70m-straight-descent underground, while another follows a slippery underground trail to an underground river. Even for routes that don't require technical equipment, you'll need gloves, rubber boots and a flashlight (or two).

A river trip down Río Santiago toward Peru (not an authorized crossing), which often includes some good white water, will get you way off the beaten path. Arrange this kind of trip with an experienced guide in Macas (see p263).

SUCÚA

☎ 07 / pop 9525

This tiny town is the transition from Macas' bustle to serene jungle. Old men slowly pedal bicycles as a vendor grills meats under the town's singular stoplight, across from a small plaza with ficus trees and chirping cicadas. From the plaza, it's a short walk down the main street to **Federacíon Shuar** (☎ 274-0108; Domingo Comín 17-38), which is of little interest to casual visitors, but useful to people working with the Shuar. Market day is Sunday.

Hotel Romanza (☎ 274-0943; r per person incl breakfast $11) is a bright spot with minty-green bedspreads and wood furniture. A block off the main plaza, **Tisho's Pizzeria** (☎ 274-1131; cnr Pástor Bernal & Sangurima; mains $3-5; 11am-11pm) offers American dishes inspired by the owner's years in the States, including Philly cheese-steak sandwiches and a 'Texas' pizza.

Frequent buses or pickups leave for Macas ($1, one hour) from dawn until dusk at the corner of the main plaza. Others head south to Gualaquiza.

FROM MÉNDEZ TO LIMÓN

☎ 07

The road south passes banana plantations and papaya groves surrounded by shaggy tropical forest. Buses pause in small towns with overgrown squares populated by stray dogs and chickens. **Méndez**, an hour-and-a-half south of Sucúa, at the bend in the Río Paute, is a quaint but sleepy town, with bright colonial buildings and a tiny cemetery pressed into the hillside.

It's the crossroads for travel west to Cuenca (five hours), east toward the Peruvian border via Santiago (a rough and bumpy road), north to Macas (three hours) and south to Gualaquiza.

A few *hostales* circle the square, but **Los Ceibos** (☎ 276-0133; Cuenca near Comín; r per person $6) is your best bet: a spick-and-span hotel with peach and terra-cotta tiles and frilly bedspreads. Eat at the popular **Restaurant Sucus** (Cuenca near Comín; meals $3-5) a few doors down for good *carne apanada* (breaded beef steak) and rice.

South from Méndez, the road can be a muddy mess, but the scenery is in perfect order. On either side of the Río Upano, lush conical hills rise shrouded in mist or glowing in sunshine as cows graze on soft grasses.

About two hours south of Méndez, **Limón**, also known as General Leonidas Plaza Gutiérrez, is a small, unprepossessing jungle town. Walk uphill to the town's center on the other side of the river for a few simple hotels, basic restaurants, internet and a Pacifictel. **Hotel Joya Limonense** (☎ 270-1047; r per person $7) offers spacious rooms with hardwood floors and private bathrooms. **Restaurant D'Gust** (☎ 277-0440; 28 de Mayo; meals $2-5; noon-10pm) is a popular local gathering spot with daily dishes such as tender, saucy chicken legs and *papas fritas* (french fries). Buses to Cuenca pass through here. Locals know bus times for travel west, south and north.

An hour south of Limón the road passes through the missions of San Juan Bosco and Indanza (also known as Plan de Milagro), then continues through the countryside to Gualaquiza, four hours from Limón.

GUALAQUIZA

☎ 07 / pop 9564 / elevation 950m

Spread against a gently sloping hillside surrounded by beautiful jungle, this town wants for nothing but more of the same. Even an influx of internet cafés hasn't made the rest of the world seem relevant. Families meander through the town square at the base of a hillside church with a fan of turquoise-painted steps. In the market by the bus station, women tend to piles of citrus, yuca and chamomile. Lodging is limited, but adventures are plenty in the surrounding tropics.

Information isn't easy to rustle up in Gualaquiza but the locals are friendly and patient. A **tourist booth** (☎ 278-0109; García Moreno near Pesantez; 9am-5pm Mon-Fri) has information about nearby Inca sites and attractions. There's supposedly excellent **caving** 15km west of town near the village of Nueva Tarquí (spare flashlights and batteries are essential), as well as **waterfalls** and sandy river **beaches**. Visit **Ciclos** (☎ 278-0579; Orellana 4-35 near the market; 8am-6pm), a bike shop run by Angel and Erwin Barros, for advice on outings. An excellent **ride** swoops through the hills to La Florida (2½ hours by bike). It's best to have your own bike, but they may be willing to rent.

Your best bet is **Hotel Internacional** (☎ 278-0637; cnr Cuenca & Moreno; r per person incl breakfast $11), a modern multistory place with narrow rooms and varnished plywood floors. A half-block off the plaza, **Residencial Guadalupe** (☎ 278-0113; cnr

Pezántez & Moreno; r per person with shared/private bathroom $5/7) is a friendly old bunkhouse with faded rooms. Head to **Canela y Cafe** (☎ 278-0201; Pezántez; mains $2-4; ⏰ 9am-11pm) for hot ham sandwiches and big salads. For some tasty *comida rapida* (fast food), visit **Los Pinchos** (☎ 09-767-8022; ⏰ noon-midnight), diagonal from the square.

The bus terminal is downhill from the center. Ten buses a day go to Loja ($6, six hours) via Zamora ($4, four hours). There are two routes to Cuenca – the Sigsig route ($7, six hours) saves two hours. Buses north go to Limón ($4, four hours), Sucúa and Macas ($7.50, nine hours). *Rancheras* outside the terminal go to villages in the pretty hillsides, which make for interesting outings.

FROM GUALAQUIZA TO ZAMORA

☎ 07

Several kilometers south of Gualaquiza, a turnoff to the right leads to **Bomboiza**, where a **Salesian mission** educates Shuar and colonist children. Visitors are encouraged to stop by to learn about Shuar craft making.

Soon after, the road crosses the provincial line into Zamora-Chinchipe province and then rises before passing through the village of **El Panguí**. Ask locals here for directions to *la cascada,* a beautiful **waterfall** two hours east on foot. South of El Panguí the road descends from tableland hills into a gaping, lush valley.

The road continues through the village of **Los Encuentros** and, about 3½ hours from Gualaquiza, reaches **Yantzaza**, the only sizable village before Zamora, 1½ hours further south. In Yantzaza there are restaurants and some basic hotels (likely to be full of gold miners) near the main plaza. Even if you don't stay, try a soft-serve ice cream cone drizzled with chocolate syrup from a street vendor on the square.

Río Zamora zigzags the emerald valley floor parallel to the road. These rich-soil floodplains are populated with colonists from Loja, and native Shuar. Indigenous hamlets and *fincas* (farms) grow tropical produce such as coffee, sugarcane and citrus fruit.

Just before Zamora you'll hit **Nambija**, which translates to 'the place no one can find.' A 1980s gold rush created a Wild West atmosphere of prostitution and crime against the backdrop of frenzied mining action. A tragic landslide in the late 1980s killed many. Rather than stay in a basic hotel here, it's preferable to move on.

About five hours from Gualaquiza, you finally reach the southern belle of **Zamora**, an excellent base for exploring **Parque Nacional Podocarpus**. Although Zamora is geographically part of the Oriente, it's best accessed from the highland city of Loja (two hours west by bus). For more information see p221.

North Coast & Lowlands

Charming beach towns, little-explored mangrove forests, indigenous settlements and delectable Afro-Ecuadorian cuisine are just a few reasons to venture to the coastal provinces stretching from Manabí southwest of Quito all the way to the Colombian border.

While the north coast and lowlands usually take low priority on most Ecuador itineraries, there's much for the independent traveler to discover – particularly those looking to get well off the beaten path.

The jungle beckons in Esmeraldas province. Visitors can catch a motorized canoe up a palm-lined river to the magnificent reserve of Playa de Oro, home to a superb array of wildlife including big cats. Catching a boat on another river leads to the heart of the indigenous Chachi community, settled amid species-rich rainforest.

Those looking for a beach getaway have many options, from brash and brazen Atacames, where the music never stops, to laid-back Same, with its wide stretch of empty sands that invite long sunset walks. For uncrowded waves without the fuss, Mompiche, further south, is the place to go. Surf lovers and those looking for a sleepy spot to unwind opt for Canoa and its ramshackle assortment of beachfront guesthouses, bars and restaurants.

The northern coast and lowlands hold many surprises – from the ecologically forward city of Bahía de Caráquez to the world's tallest mangroves near San Lorenzo. There's the handicraft village of Montecristi (home to beautifully made 'panama' hats), the rich archaeological site of Chirije, great nightlife in Manta, and a number of forest reserves that draw far fewer visitors than the rainforests of the Oriente.

HIGHLIGHTS

- Take in the laid-back beach and nightlife scene at hard-to-leave **Canoa** (p290).
- Hike beneath the jungle canopy at the lush **Playa de Oro Reserva de Tigrillos** (p279).
- Take an ecocity tour of **Bahía de Caráquez** (p292) followed by a trip to the **Chirije archaeological site** (p292).
- Frolic in the waves in the idyllic beachside setting of **Same** (p287).
- Marvel at the verdant scenery of the wildlife-rich **Reserva Biológica Bilsa** (p274).

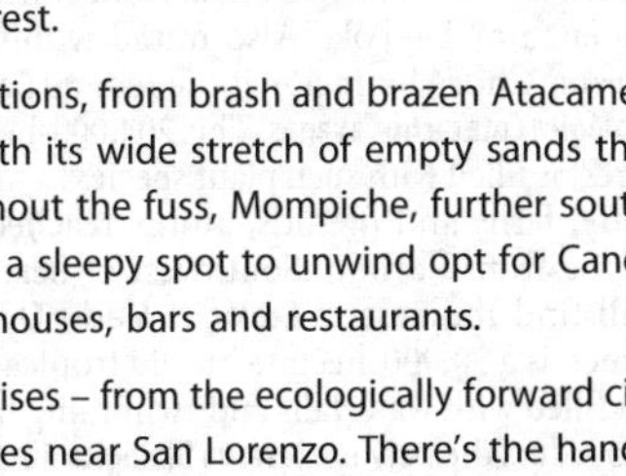

- AVERAGE TEMP IN ESMERALDAS: 26°C (79°F)
- RAINIEST MONTH IN ESMERALDAS: MAR

Climate

The northern coast has two seasons: rainy and dry. The rainy season, which lasts from December to May, is marked by sporadic downpours but also by the hot, bright sun. The dry season, from June to November, is often overcast, gray and cool. Ecuadorians jam the beaches during the rainy season, for July and August school vacations and from January to Easter, when the water is warmest. The coast is relatively abandoned from September to November.

Malaria can be a problem in the northern region, mostly during the rainy season. It's less prevalent south of Esmeraldas province.

National Parks

Mangroves, estuaries and beaches comprise the **Reserva Ecológica de Manglares Cayapas Mataje**, which is best accessed by boat from either San Lorenzo or La Tola. Also found within the diverse Chocó bioregion is the remote **Reserva Ecológica Cotacachi-Cayapas**. This 204,000-hectare forest is filled with such plant species as mahogany, ferns and orchids, and is reached via canoe from Borbón. Southwest of here you will find the **Reserva Ecológica Mache Chindul**, which is a 70,000-hectare humid tropical forest filled with waterfalls and swimming holes. It borders the private **Reserva Biológica Bilsa** and also the areas of Atacames and Muisne.

Dangers & Annoyances

Solo female travelers get stares, dares and offers from some local males, who are far less reserved than their highland counterparts. Take care when exploring towns along the north coast; certain areas are best avoided after dark.

Getting There & Around

A direct bus from Quito can zip you to the coast in just a day. If you're coming from another area you can get a connection in Santo Domingo, the transportation hub between the Andes and the coast. From Quito two roads reach Santo Domingo de los Colorados. The new road takes three hours, and the old road via Mindo takes about five hours, but also distracts with some fabulous diversions (for information on this route, see p149).

San Lorenzo can be reached by paved road from Ibarra (in the northern highlands) in only four hours. From Latacunga in the central highlands, a spectacular five-hour bus ride will take you to Quevedo in the western lowlands, from where it's about four hours to Portoviejo.

Boat service still exists along certain parts of the coast, notably between La Tola, Limones and San Pedro. Boats also provide the only way of reaching certain jungle communities like San Miguel and the Playa de Oro Reserva de Tigrillos.

WESTERN LOWLANDS

Fertile farmland and rolling hills stretch off toward the coast, with a swath of rivers traversing the region on their journey from Andean heights to the ocean. Between mountain and sea, big plantations now crisscross the land, bearing the fruits that help power the agricultural economy: cacao, African palm oil and bananas spread across the green horizon, where primeval forest once grew. In between lie grimy and fast-growing cities.

Botanists estimate that about half the plant species that once grew on the western Andean slopes and lowlands were found nowhere else. The last forested pockets of this unique ecosystem, vastly distinct from the Amazonian rainforest, merit a good look before they disappear from the globe.

Highlights here include the fantastic birdwatching of Tinalandia in wet premontane forest, several forest reserves packed with distinctive flora and fauna, and the indigenous community of Los Tsáchilas, who welcome visitors to their small village.

QUITO TO SANTO DOMINGO DE LOS COLORADOS

☎ 02

Dramatic scenery is a big part of the journey, with steep pitches plunging toward the misty void as lush hills appear around sharp curves. It is best to travel this stretch in the morning, when skies are more likely to be clear. The route is treacherous, with white crosses dotting the road.

For visitors headed to the coast, the road from Quito through Santo Domingo is the most direct route. From there you can head south through Quevedo and Babahoyo, in the lowland province of Los Ríos, and on to Guayaquil, on the south coast; or you can go northwest toward Esmeraldas, on the north coast.

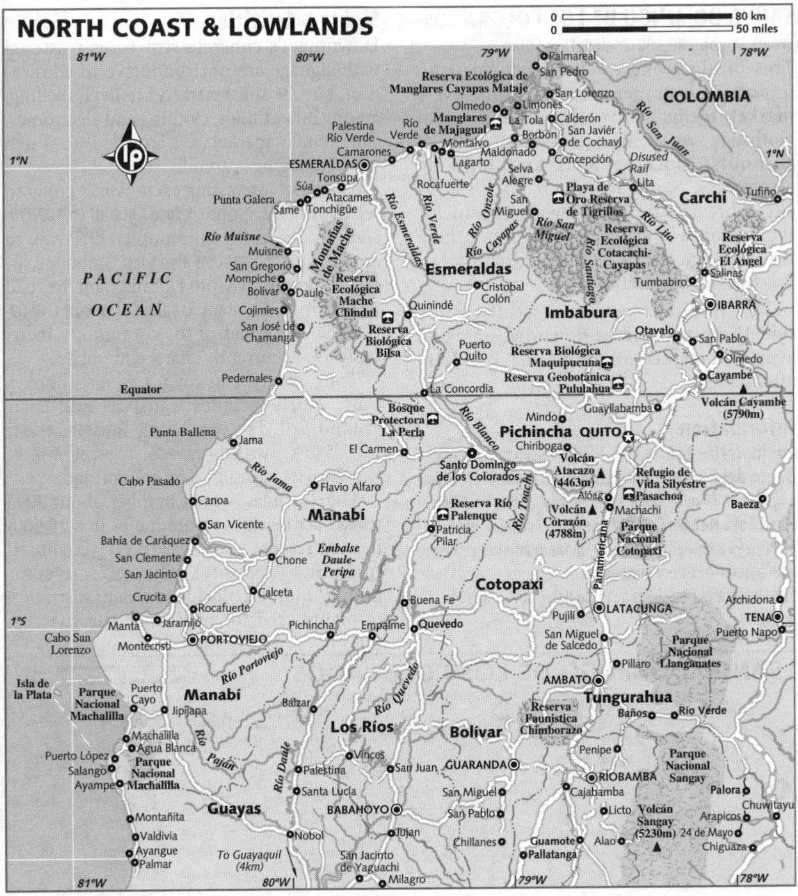

Outside of Quito the road climbs into the high *páramo* (Andean grasslands), with views of the extinct **Volcanes Atacazo** (4463m) and **Corazón** (4788m) to the north and south, respectively. The tortuous descent leads into the Río Toachi valley, where the air thickens and tropical plants begin sprouting up. The trans-Ecuadorian oil pipeline parallels the road for the last third of the distance. If your bus is continuing beyond Santo Domingo it may bypass the city altogether.

About 16km outside of Santo Domingo, **Tinalandia** (off Map p272; ☎ Quito 02-244-9028; www.tinalandia.com; s/d $65/85) was built for golfing but receives much greater acclaim for its top-notch bird-watching. This rustic resort sits at 600m in a wet premontane forest. Guests stay in weathered bungalows with private bathrooms and hot showers. The driest months (May and June) are particularly popular with bird-watchers, who can come for day visits (day pass $10). Delicious meals with fresh veggies from the hydroponics farm cost extra. Reservations may be necessary – make them on your own or through major travel agencies in Ecuador. Staff can arrange transport from Quito with advance reservations.

Tinalandia is about 86km after the turn-off from the Panamericana in Alóag. Ask your driver to drop you off at Tinalandia, or watch out for the small stone sign on the right-hand side of the road as you drive from Quito. The hotel is 500m away on the left.

SANTO DOMINGO DE LOS COLORADOS

☎ 02 / pop 200,500 / elevation 500m

This bustling and sweltering town is an important commercial center. Its lively market teems willy-nilly with piles of clothing, greasy machine parts, sacks of coconuts, clucking hens and blinking electronics. Santo Domingo (as it's usually abbreviated) offers few attractions for the visitor. The chief reason to stop here is to arrange a visit to the fascinating Los Tsáchilas community.

This tropical town has a scruffy, seedy side. Visitors should be somewhat wary and avoid the market area and Calle 3 de Julio after dark.

Information

Andinatel (Av Quito near Río Toachi) Telephone call centre.

Banco del Pichincha (Iturralde, Main Plaza) There's also a branch on Avenida Quinindé. Both branches have ATMs.

Hard Soft Net (Av Quito 127 near Los Tsáchilas; per hr $0.80; ⏰ 8am-8pm) A friendly, modern internet center with a quiet 2nd-floor location.

Post office (Av Tsáchilas near Río Baba) Just north of downtown.

Sights & Activities

Downtown's concrete structures plastered with signage are not conducive to admiration, but the **street markets** are lively, selling, among other things, clothing and electronics. The Sunday market gets crowded, so watch your belongings carefully.

The most interesting excursion is going to see the **Tsáchila**. Contact **José Aguabil** (☎ 09-770-8703), leader of the community El Poste, to arrange a visit. You can also visit Chihuilpe, located 17km from Santo Domingo on the road to Quevedo. Contact **Tsapini Calasacón** (☎ 09-750-3320), the leader of the community there. Visitors are currently charged about $5.

Tour agencies in town can also book a tour, which includes transport and costs around $20. Try contacting **Turismo Zaracay** (☎ 275-0546; www.turismozaracay, in Spanish; Av 29 de Mayo 200 & Cocaniguas) in Santo Domingo.

The Tsáchilas, which number about 3000 spread across eight communities in a 10,500-hectare reserve, are eager to revive cultural traditions (opposite). They offer a community tour that includes a demonstration of plants used for medicinal purposes, an

LOS TSÁCHILAS

In a yard of thatched huts surrounded by sugarcane, a river that no longer has fish, and tattered forest remnants that no longer bear wild game, stands grandfather Oeido Aguabil. Dressed in traditional Tsáchila finery, he sweeps a look at his surroundings and family and wonders aloud, 'Do you think this is worth it?'

The family, part of the small community of 70 families in El Poste, 12km outside of Santo Domingo, belongs to a group interested in reviving customs and dress and sharing its culture with the public in hopes of keeping what's left of it intact. The many alterations to their environment and the often abrasive contact with the outside world makes the challenge justifiably daunting.

The Tsáchilas, dubbed the Colorados by colonists, have well-known *curanderos* (medicine men) and the women craft beautiful wovens in shocks of rainbow colors on the backstrap loom. The group's signature dress is easy to recognize: they paint their faces with black stripes and men dye their bowl-shaped haircuts red. Aguabil says that the natural dye from the achiote plant was long ago used as a protection from yellow fever. Ritual painting, such as the black stripes, is also considered a form of shield or protection.

Nowadays it is much more probable to see Westernized Tsáchila. With bus drivers protesting that the hair dye stains the backs of their seats, curio shops selling their postcard images, and gawkers in the city calling them 'painted tigers', it's no wonder that the Tsáchilas have closeted their customs. Nevertheless, there have been some important victories for the Tsáchilas in recent years, most notably the creation of their own province in 2007, granting the group a much more prominent role in the nation's political system.

The most important Tsáchila celebration was shelved for 30 years and began again only in 1998. Kasama, the New Year, is a time for the Tsáchila to reaffirm their roots. Coinciding with the Catholic Holy Saturday (the day before Easter Sunday), it unites all of the villages to wish prosperity for one another. Cane sugar *chicha* (a fermented drink) is served and the festive atmosphere ignites with music, dance and theater. With the return of this celebration springs the small hope that other important features of the landscape – such as the *guatusa* (agouti, a type of rodent) and the armadillo, will eventually return as well.

While most communities are reticent to welcome visitors (much less have their photograph taken), travelers are welcome in Chihuilpe and El Poste, both south of Santo Domingo on the road to Quevedo. Apart from going to the tourist center in Chihuilpe, you can also visit one of the *curanderos,* who sell curative herbs or offer treatments. El Poste welcomes visitors to the above-mentioned annual Kasama festival.

explanation of customs and traditions, and even dancing. They produce lovely hand-woven goods in their signature wild rainbow colors, as well as jewelry. They speak only Tsa'fiki and Spanish. Learn more about them on Spanish-language sites www.ciudadcolorada.com/tsachilas and www.tsachilas.com.

Festivals & Events

Santo Domingo celebrates its **cantonization day** on July 3, when the town packs with visitors attending the fairs and agricultural festivals. Rooms are scarcer during this week.

Sleeping

There's a string of adequate hotels along Avenida 29 de Mayo. Cheaper guesthouses lie near the market area, which is not very safe at night.

Hotel El Colorado (☎ 275-4299; Av 29 de Mayo 110; s/d $8/16) This bare-bones place is cheap but fairly clean, with thin curtains and trashy artwork. Rooms have phones but no hot water.

Hotel Diana Real (☎ 275-1380; cnr Av 29 de Mayo & Loja; s/d $14/21) The friendly Diana Real offers quiet rooms decorated in earth tones with stone paved floors. Some are quite large.

Hotel Del Pacífico (☎ 275-2806; Av 29 de Mayo 510; s/d $19/33) This good midrange place has simple, clean and spacious rooms with tile floors and glazed windows. Back rooms are quieter.

Gran Hotel Santo Domingo (☎ 276-7950; www.granhotelsd.com; cnr Río Toachi & Galapagos; s/d/ste $50/72/87;) This elegant hotel is a surprise find in Santo Domingo. Rooms are handsomely set with nice woodwork and comfy fittings. Suites have balconies with hammocks overlooking the pool. The on-site restaurant is reputable.

Eating

Chifa Tay Happy (☎ 275-0121; Tulcán 117; mains $2-4; ⏰ noon-10pm) Chinese food right on the plaza. The steamed veggies and lo mein are on the salty side.

Restaurante Timoneiro (Av Quito 115; mains $2-5; ⏰ 7am-4pm) Sunken and softly lit, this traditional restaurant has hearty fare, full dinners and chicken soup with all the bones.

La Tonga (☎ 276-7950; cnr Río Toachi & Galapagos; mains $4-5; ⏰ 7am-10:30pm) A crisp and formal setting with a varied menu of well-prepared international dishes, vegetarian options and criollo (of Spanish influence) specialties. Located in the Gran Hotel Santo Domingo.

Drinking & Entertainment

Lined on the far end of Avenida Quito are a number of small atmospheric joints geared mostly to the younger crowd. For salsa dancing, hail a taxi to **Salsoteca the Jungle** (⏰ 9pm-2am Thu-Sat), east on Avenida Quito.

Getting There & Away

Santo Domingo is an important transportation hub, with connections all over Ecuador. The bus terminal, almost 2km north of downtown, has frequent buses to many major towns, as well as internet access, an ATM and left luggage ($0.60 per item). Quito ($3, three hours) and Guayaquil ($5, five hours) are the most frequent destinations, with several buses going every hour. Those headed to Guayaquil pass Quevedo. To get to Mindo ($4, 3½ hours) try **Transportes Kennedy** (☎ 275-8740).

Coast-bound buses include **Transportes Occidentales** (☎ 275-8741), with daily departures to Machala ($5 to $6, seven hours), and Reina del Camino, which goes to Puerto Lopez ($7, eight hours). Every hour buses depart to the north-coast town of Esmeraldas ($4, 3½ hours), stopping at La Concordia and Quinindé. After going through Esmeraldas, some may continue to Atacames or Muisne. Buses also go to Bahía de Caráquez ($6, six hours) and Manta ($6, six hours).

Highland-bound buses go to Ambato ($4, four hours), Baños ($5, five hours), Riobamba ($5, five hours) and Loja ($13, 12 hours). Several companies have a daily trip to Lago Agrio ($10, 12 hours) and Coca ($12, 14 hours).

The local bus plaza at the west end of Avenida 3 de Julio serves nearby villages.

Getting Around

Look for the city bus marked 'Centro.' It loops past the bus terminal, through downtown and out along Avenida Quito. The return bus, signed 'Terminal Terrestre,' heads west along Avenida 29 de Mayo, picking up passengers for the terminal.

NORTH OF SANTO DOMINGO DE LOS COLORADOS

☎ 02

The road rumbles northwest of Santo Domingo to Esmeraldas, almost 200km away. Amid African oil palm and banana groves you'll find **Bosque Protectora La Perla** (☎ 272-5344; admission $5), a 250-hectare reserve ideal for bird-watching and guided walks. You can even stake a tent on the grounds. Obtain exact directions when making a reservation.

Shortly after the village of **La Concordia** (about 50km northwest of Santo Domingo) a paved road leads eastward toward Mindo via Puerto Quito and Pedro Vicente Maldonado (see p149), eventually spitting out at Mitad del Mundo.

On the way to Esmeraldas, the small town of **Quinindé** (also known as Rosa Zárate; the area code is ☎ 06), 86km from Santo Domingo, has a couple of basic hotels.

Rugged adventurers should head to **Reserva Biológica Bilsa**, 30km west of Quinindé. Crashing waterfalls and spectacular wildlife adorn this biological station. This 30-sq-km reserve in the Montañas de Mache is administered by **Fundación Jatun Sacha** (☎ 243-2240; www.jatunsacha.org). Biodiversity is exceptionally high in these last vestiges of premontane tropical wet forest. Visitors may see howler monkeys and endangered birds such as bird-watchers' coveted long-wattled umbrella bird. Jaguar and puma are also afoot. This trip is not for the feeble or frail: rainy season access (January to June) requires hiking or mule-riding a mud-splattered 25km trail. Contact Jatun Sacha for reservations and volunteer or research information (rooms per person with three meals $40; discounts for groups and students).

SOUTH OF SANTO DOMINGO DE LOS COLORADOS

The road from Santo Domingo descends 100m to Quevedo through banana plantations and African palm and papaya groves. Villages off the main road are part of the shrinking territory of the indigenous Tsáchila (known also as the Colorados; see p273), whose *curanderos* (medicine men) have great acclaim.

About 46km south of Santo Domingo, you'll see a sign for the **Reserva Río Palenque**, a 110-hectare reserve run by Fundación Wong. It has one of the few remaining stands of western lowlands forest in the area. There are facilities for researchers, 3km of trails and excellent bird-watching. Past counts noted 1200 plants and 360 bird species, but with infringing development some species have become scarce. The proposal of a government-sponsored dam on Río Palenque threatens to flood part of this important biodiversity pocket.

An overnight stop here is a relaxing countryside alternative. Visitors can sleep in the **field station** (☎ Guayaquil 04-220-8670, ext 1470, 09-751-9465; fundacion@grupowong.com; per person dm/r $12.50/30), where rooms are quite comfortable and meals are $3. Advance reservations are necessary. Any bus between Santo Domingo and Quevedo can drop you off or pick you up at the entrance road to the field station.

QUEVEDO

☎ 05 / pop 120,380

Hot and sticky, Quevedo is a busy hub of motorbikes, street vendors and Chinese immigrants. For most people, the main attraction is the route to the coast via the gorgeous drive linking Latacunga to Quevedo.

If you need a place to stay try **Hotel Casablanca** (☎ 275-4144; Décima 416 near Av 7 de Octubre; s/d with fan $12/16, with air-con $20/24), whose echoey tiled rooms beg a homey touch. On the south end of town the high-end **Hotel Olímpico** (☎ 275-0455; Calle 19na 107 & Av Jaime Roldós; s/d $42/52; 🏊) falls short of high expectations but it's coveted by lap swimmers. Meals here are $7 to $10.

Quevedo claims to have the best Chinese food in the country. At **Café Fenix** (☎ 276-1460; Av 12 de Octubre; mains $3-6; 🕒 9:30am-9pm) you'll note the blending of cultures in dishes such as *mondongo* (tripe stew) curry.

The new bus terminal is located off Avenida Walter Andrades on the edge of town. The following companies are all found within the terminal.

Transportes Macuchi has regular direct buses to Quito ($5, four hours). Transportes Sucre has buses to Santo Domingo (one hour), from where there are frequent buses to Quito. Transportes Sucre and TIA go frequently to Guayaquil ($3, 2½ hours) both via Daule or Babahoyo. Transportes Cotopaxi has hourly departures from 3am to 5pm to Latacunga ($5, 5½ hours), as well as buses at 8am and 1pm to Portoviejo ($5, four hours).

THE NORTH COAST

The north coast is a lush green swath of tropical rainforests and tangled mangroves, with a sprinkling of inviting beaches, dodgy backwater villages and laid-back surf towns. This is home to the country's largest Afro-Ecuadorian population, which gives the area its marimba music and lively fests as well as outstanding seafood dishes.

Good sense and a taste for adventure are essential tools for travelers to this region, some of whom may be turned off by its rawness and lack of upkeep.

SAN LORENZO

☎ 06 / pop 15,000

Encircled by verdant jungle, at the edge of a dank, still river, San Lorenzo is a decrepit, lively hodgepodge of blaring heat, tropical beats and crumbling storefronts. Hollow marimba notes and salsa flavor this mostly African-Ecuadorian outpost, which goes all out in August with an annual music festival.

With road access only completed in the mid-1990s, the area still has the air of a forgotten outpost. It is extremely poor, tourism is barely developed and getting around isn't easy. Its treasure is its people, the most spirited you'll encounter, and the real reason to come all this way. With little in common with the Ecuador that most visitors know, San Lorenzo makes an intimidating but nonetheless fascinating destination.

Orientation

Coming in to San Lorenzo you'll pass the old train station and follow Calle Imbabura, the main street, for several blocks. The better hotels are to the left. The road narrows and ends at the small plaza of Parque Central near the Río San Antonio. The main pier is to the left, a few blocks beyond the park.

The town itself is extremely poor with cracked, flooded streets and falling-down buildings all around. Locals are the first to warn visitors to stay safe in San Lorenzo, not to wander off the main road and plaza area, and not to stay out long after dark.

North Coast Delicacies

Traveling along the North Coast, keep an eye out for some of the scrumptious local dishes. Fresh seafood, plantains and coconut milk are combined to great success. Many Ecuadorians rate *cocina esmeraldeña* (dishes from Esmeraldas) as the country's best. Here are a few reasons why:

- *Encocado* – fresh mixed seafood or fish cooked with coconut milk and spices, often served with rice. Simply outstanding.
- *Pusandao* – a hearty dish of fish or pork prepared with coconut milk, plantain and yuca.
- *Cazuela* – A mixed seafood (or fish) stew made with peanut sauce and plantains, served in a clay pot.
- Ceviche – the classic seafood dish of shrimp, squid, mussels or raw fish, cooked in lemon juice and served with banana chips (and preferably a cold beer). Prepared with panache in Esmeraldas.
- *Tapao* – an elegant dish of fish and plantains, seasoned with coconut and *chillangua* (a type of wild cilantro) and steamed beneath banana leaves.
- *Mazato* – A dish made of boiled ripe banana mashed with coconut milk, cheese and egg, then baked in a *bijao* leaf.
- *Bolas de platano* – A soup with shrimp, coconut milk and a cheese-and-plantain mixture shaped into balls.
- *Cocada* – a round sweet made of brown sugar, coconut, milk and peanuts.
- *Frutipan* – Made by indigenous Chachis, *frutipan* is made of bread-tree fruit that is mixed with sweet spices, butter and cheese, then baked.
- *Cazabe* – A type of sweet made from cooked corn, coconut juice, cinnamon, clove and other spices.

Information

The **police station** (☎ 278-0672) faces the Parque Central, and the **capitanía** (port captain) is at the main pier. If you're traveling into or out of Colombia (which is not recommended; see the Getting There & Away section on opposite), take care of passport formalities at one of these places.

San Lorenzo's Catholic hospital, a short taxi ride from downtown, is reputedly the best in the area north of Esmeraldas.

Andinatel (Calle Imbabura) Telephone call centre; opposite Gran Hotel San Carlos.

Ministerio del Ambiente (☎ 278-0184; main plaza; 🕑 usually 9am-12:30pm & 2-7pm Mon-Fri) On the far side of the park; offers information on Reserva Ecológica de Manglares Cayapas Mataje.

Sleeping

Pickings are slim, but consider mosquito nets and fans as essentials, especially in rainy season. The following places all have mosquito nets.

Hotel Carondolet (☎ 278-1119; Parque Central; r per person with shared/private bathroom $6/8) The small rooms at Carondolet are adequate with wide plank floors, and some rooms offer views over the tin roofs toward the river.

Gran Hotel San Carlos (☎ 278-0284; cnr Imbabura & José Garcés; s/d with shared bathroom $6/12, s/d with private bathroom $10/16) A recent makeover has left San Carlos with clean, bright rooms with large windows. Kitschy, rainbow-hued decor prevails in the common areas.

Hotel Pampa de Oro (☎ 278-0214; Tácito Ortíz; s/d $7/14) This is the pick of the hotels, with very clean rooms with wood floors. Some are quite bright and open onto a shared balcony. Colorful murals on the stairs and friendly service sweeten the deal. Located on a side-street off Imbabura.

Hotel Continental (☎ 278-0125; Imbabura; r per person with fan/air-con $8/12; ❄) This aging place has fading fishing murals and creaky floorboards. The rooms are sizable and fairly clean, with tile floors, TVs and warm showers.

Eating

El Chocó (☎ 278-0338; Imbabura near Tácito Ortiz; mains $2-5; 🕑 6am-10pm) On the main street, this clean and well-liked spot serves all the local seafood favorites including ceviche and *encocado de camarones* (shrimp and coconut stew).

Ballet Azul (Imbabura; mains $3-6; 8:30am-10pm Mon-Sat) Shrimp is the specialty at this popular open-sided place. *Ceviche de camarón* (shrimp ceviche) and *camarones al ajillo* (garlic shrimp) mate perfectly with a bottle of beer.

Getting There & Away

BOAT

Ecuador Pacífico (☎ 278-0161; andrescarvache@yahoo.es) services depart to Limones ($3, 1½ hours) at 7:30am, 10:30am and 1pm, and continue to La Tola ($5, 45 minutes). At La Tola, you can connect with a bus to Esmeraldas. Trips to nearby beaches leave at 7:30am and 2pm ($3). Tour guide Andres Carvache arranges these and other trips. He can be found on the pier in a stilted storefront to the right of the pier.

To cross the Colombian border there are departures at 7:30am, 2pm and 3pm ($3), which also requires bus connections to Tumaco in Colombia. Given nearby guerilla activity that occasionally sends refugees spilling over, it is not recommended to cross the border here.

Touring the mangroves isn't really possible via public transportation. To arrange a trip contract **Cooperativa San Lorenzo del Pailón** (☎ 278-0039), an authorized service offering private tours in boats for $20 to $30 per hour. You can also arrange tours through Sr Carvache for $60 and $80 for a two- to three-hour trip.

BUS

La Costeñita and Transportes del Pacífico alternate departures for Borbón ($1.20, one hour) and Esmeraldas ($5, five hours). They leave the Parque Central hourly from 5am to 4pm. The road is mostly paved except for a few monstrous potholes and jackhammer-rough patches.

Aerotaxi buses leave at 1pm and 3pm to Ibarra ($4, four hours) from the corner of Imbabura and Tácito Ortíz. Both buses continue on to Quito ($5, five to six hours).

TRAIN

The scenic highland-to-coast train from Ibarra was washed out in 1998's El Niño storms. Locals yen for its return, but as of yet there are no projects in the works to rebuild.

RESERVA ECOLÓGICA DE MANGLARES CAYAPAS MATAJE

Millions of migratory birds pass through this coastal reserve in June to July, creating a cacophonous and memorable spectacle. This 51,300-hectare reserve supports five species of mangrove, and includes the tallest mangrove forest in the world, Manglares de Majagual, near the villages of La Tola and Olmedo. The town of San Lorenzo lies in the middle of the reserve and makes a good base. Most of the reserve is at sea level and none of it is above 35m. A highlight of the reserve is the pristine 11km island beach of **San Pedro** near the Colombian border, but visitors should inquire about safety before venturing into this area.

There are basic, community-run cabañas nearby at the settlement of **Palmareal**. If you stay, bring a mosquito net and water (or purification tablets). The reserve is accessible almost solely by boat.

LIMONES TO LA TOLA

☎ 06

The island lumber town of **Limones** scratches out a living at the deltas of Ríos Santiago and Cayapas. You'll find wilting wooden homes perched above the water, a humble plaza flanking the foot of the pier, and all the bananas you can peel. Most of the timber logged in the area is floated downriver to Limones' sawmill. Rough-and-tumble, the place has few amenities, but it's interesting nonetheless. Sometimes indigenous Chachis (formerly known as the Cayapas) come to trade. There's a basic guesthouse in town.

See left for details about boat travel.

La Tola is another tiny fishing village near the mangroves, but it's usually bypassed now that road travel is the norm. The main attraction is the Tolita archaeological site on the nearby island of **Manta de Oro**, but since the gold ornaments found here are now in museums there is not much left to see.

Hoof it for 20 minutes from La Tola's pier to Olmedo, a spit of land in the estuary, engulfed in mangroves, shrimp farms and the sea. This mostly Afro-Ecuadorian fishing village offers boat and fishing tours. You can stay at **Cabañas de los Manglares de Olmedo** (☎ San Lorenzo 278-0357, La Tola 278-6133, Olmedo 278-6126; r per person $6), a welcoming but basic community-run *hostal* (small hotel) right on the estuary – at high tide the water laps the deck. The shared bathrooms have

MANGROVES UNDER THREAT

Ecuador's coastal mangroves are an important habitat. In addition to helping to control the erosion of the coast, they provide homes, protection and nutrients for numerous species of bird, fish, mollusk and crustacean. Unfortunately, mangroves have been in no-man's land, and it has been difficult to say who owns these coastal tropical forests that are semipermanently inundated. Squatters took over areas of mangroves as their own, but this was not a problem in itself because their livelihood was based on low-impact fishing and gathering crabs and shellfish. The mangroves also supported cottage industries such as fishing, shrimping and crabbing, as well as some sport fishing. Thousands of families along the coast were gainfully employed in these industries while coexisting with the mangroves.

This all changed in the 1980s with the arrival of shrimp farms, which produced shrimp in artificial conditions in numbers many times greater than could be caught by traditional shrimping methods. To build the farms, it was necessary to cut down the mangroves. The prospective owner of a shrimp farm purchased the land from the government, cut down the mangroves and began the shrimp-farming process. The net profits of the shrimp farms were very high, and the idea soon caught on and spread rapidly along the coast, resulting in the removal of 80% to 90% of Ecuador's mangroves during the 1980s and early 1990s. Although there are now laws controlling this destruction, these are difficult to enforce in the remote coastal areas.

The shrimp farms have had many negative short- and long-term effects. Previously, many families could find a sustainable livelihood in the mangroves, whereas shrimp farms employ only a handful of seasonal workers. Where before there were mangroves protecting a large diversity of species, now there's just commercial shrimp. Coastal erosion and pollution from the wastes of the shrimp farms have become serious problems.

In 1999, the shrimp industry suffered dramatically when diseases such as *mancha blanca* (whitespot) wiped out entire shrimp farms in a matter of days. Many farms now lie abandoned. Meanwhile, desperate efforts are being made in Muisne, Bahía de Caráquez and a few other coastal towns to start replanting mangroves.

cold showers, and meals are $5. At low tide roll up your pant legs and grab a pail to go clamming on the wide silty beach.

The nearby **Manglares de Majagual** boasts the tallest mangrove forest in the world (64m). Visit the forest on your own or hire a guide in Olmedo or La Tola.

BORBÓN TO SAN MIGUEL

☎ 06

Borbón is a muddy and ramshackle lumber port, its main strip lined with *comedores* (cheap restaurants) where men play dominoes and drink beer at any given hour. The attraction here is to make boat connections upriver to the remote settlements of Afro-Ecuadorians and indigenous Chachi. Boats up Río Cayapas continue up Río San Miguel to the Reserva Ecológica Cotacachi-Cayapas. Boats also depart sporadically for Río Santiago.

Owing to assorted drifters passing through town, Borbón isn't a safe place to linger, and if you're planning a trip up the Río San Miguel it's best to make arrangements in advance. **Javier Valencia** (☎ 09-139-1649; pandafinu@hotmail.com) in Esmeraldas and **José Chapiro** (☎ 09-781-1122), based in Borbón, are two guides who can assist with boat transport and other arrangements up the Río Cayapas.

Borbón's daily passenger boat to San Miguel is a fascinating trip into the little-explored interior, described by one visitor as 'the other heart of darkness.'

The boat to San Miguel leaves daily at 10am and stops at a number of communities and missions. Passengers here range from nuns to indigenous Chachi embarking or disembarking in the various ports, which are usually no more than a few planks at the water's edge.

The first mission is the Catholic **Santa María** where there is a clean dormitory for six guests, a basic *pensión* (boarding house) and camping. The next mission, Protestant **Zapallo Grande**, also offers basic accommodations. There are a number of other villages, such as Pichiyacu, Playa Grande, Atahualpa and Telembi, where Afro-Ecuadorians or indigenous Chachi live, some with crafts for sale.

San Miguel

San Miguel is a modest and friendly Afro-Ecuadorian community of stilted thatched huts set in the forest. Chachi homes are scattered nearby along the shores of the river. The village is the main base from which to visit the lowland sections of the Reserva Ecológica Cotacachi-Cayapas.

Accommodation is available in a simple guesthouse, run communally by the women's association. Prices are around $5 per person, and you can arrange for home-cooked meals for an extra $7 per day.

The **ranger station** (per person $5) perched on a small hill with spectacular views of the rainforest and river, has basic accommodations. Ask the *guardaparque* (park ranger) for permission to stay here. The station has a cold-water shower, a toilet and kitchen facilities. A shop in the village sells basic provisions or travelers can ask around, as sympathetic locals are eager to cook up simple meals of soup, rice and plantains for about $5.

The driver of the daily passenger canoe from Borbón spends the night about 15 minutes downriver from San Miguel. He will not return to San Miguel unless passengers have made previous arrangements, so advise ahead. The canoe leaves San Miguel around 4am.

Getting There & Away

La Costeñita and Transportes del Pacífico run buses to Esmeraldas ($3, four hours) or San Lorenzo ($1.30, one hour) about every hour from 7am to 6pm. Most of the roads are paved, although some sections have murderous potholes.

A daily passenger boat leaves at 11am for San Miguel ($8, five hours). This boat can drop you at any location on Río Cayapas or at San Miguel. Various boats run irregularly to other destinations – ask around at the docks. *Fletes* (private boats) can usually be hired if you have the money, but these are not cheap: expect to pay at least $100 per day per group.

PLAYA DE ORO

The other river leading inland from Borbón is Río Santiago. The furthest community up the river is the settlement of **Playa de Oro** (p280), near Reserva Ecológica Cotacachi-Cayapas. Playa de Oro means 'Beach of Gold.'

Half an hour upstream from Playa de Oro is the **Playa de Oro Reserva de Tigrillos**, a 10,000-hectare reserve owned and operated by the community of Playa de Oro. The reserve, which borders Cotacachi-Cayapas, protects native jungle cats, which are more plentiful here than elsewhere, but nonetheless elusive. The best way to experience it is by staying at the community-operated riverside **jungle lodge** (www.touchthejungle.org; r per person per day $50). Prices include three meals, laundry service and local guides. Make sure when you arrive that you insist on staying in the rainforest lodge, not in the village. (Both accommodations cost the same, but offer a significantly different experience; your hosts may try to steer you toward the village digs.)

Playa de Oro's charm is its authenticity. Locals do what they and their ancestors have always done, whether that be roaming the forest, riding the river current, panning for gold, making drums or encouraging their children in traditional dances. When visitors find that interesting, locals are quietly proud.

The village of Playa de Oro is about five hours upstream from Borbón, but there are no regular boats. You have to take the 7:30am bus from Borbón to Selva Alegre ($3, two hours). From Selva Alegre, if you made a reservation, a boat from Playa de Oro will motor you up to the village or the reserve (each way per boatload $50). If you didn't make a reservation, your best bet is to time your visit with the once-a-week market boat that currently goes out on Saturdays (leaving around noon and costing $10 per person). The river trip from Selva Alegre takes two hours (2½ hours if you're going to the reserve). Another option of getting there is hiring Playa de Oro's point of contact, **Ramiro Buitron** (☎ 09-960-6918), who can drive travelers to the boat launch site from Otavalo, a four-hour trip. Reservations must be made at least two weeks in advance with **Tracy Jordan** (tracy@touchthejungle.org), who speaks English.

RESERVA ECOLÓGICA COTACACHI-CAYAPAS

This 204,420-hectare **reserve** (admission $7) is by far the largest protected area of Ecuador's western Andean habitats. Altitude ranges from about 200m above sea level around San Miguel to 4939m at the summit of Cotacachi. Habitats change quickly from lowland, tropical, wet forest to premontane and montane cloud forest to *páramo*, with many intermediate habitat types. This rapid

JOURNEY INTO THE JUNGLE

Playa de Oro's end-of-the-earth location is the defining point of its existence. The huffing of margays can be heard at night outside a cabin window. The village is populated with the Afro-Ecuadorian descendants of slaves brought here to pan for gold 500 years ago. Located hours inland from the coast in a remote, roadless wilderness, Playa de Oro's near-inaccessibility has kept it a natural paradise.

To ensure that it would stay that way, the community designated 10,000 of its hectares as Playa de Oro Tigrillos Reserve, a wildlife area protecting all species of indigenous wildcats: jaguars, cougars, ocelots, margays, oncillas and jaguarundi. They decided against registering the reserve with the national government, given its history of favoring big industry over sustainable development, and locals decided to manage it as a community.

In Playa de Oro, every villager over the age of 14 has a vote on important issues. The far-sighted among them have long argued that ecotourism is the sensible, nondestructive way to go. But their insistence on maintaining control of their own ecotourism, and not allowing it to fall into the hands of large tour agencies who take a big cut, forces them to rely on independent travelers and small groups.

Much of the area around the reserve has changed dramatically in the last 15 years owing to gold-mining activity. Small villages have disappeared and in their place lie heaps of gravel piled up by machinery sluicing for gold; the river water has become contaminated by cyanide and arsenic used in the mining process. So far the villagers have resisted overtures from gold-mining and lumber companies to receive goods and services (a generator, a new road, jobs to log their own forest) in exchange for their land. The question remains whether the income that trickles in will sustain the reserve for the years to come.

For more information on Playa de Oro, see p279.

change of habitat produces the so-called 'edge effect' that gives rise to an incredible diversity of flora and fauna.

These hills are the haunts of such rarely seen mammals as giant anteaters, Baird's tapirs, jaguars and, in the upper reaches of the reserve, spectacled bears. The chances of seeing these animals are remote, however. You may see monkeys, squirrels, sloths, nine-banded armadillos, bats and a huge variety of bird species.

To visit the reserve you can approach from the highlands (see p133), or San Miguel (p278). Hiking between the two regions may well be impossible; the steep and thickly vegetated western Andean slopes are almost impenetrable. This is good news for the species existing there – they will probably be left alone for a little while longer.

The lower reaches of the reserve and rivers are the home of the indigenous Chachi. About 5000 remain, mostly fishermen and subsistence farmers, living in open-sided, thatched river houses built on stilts. The Chachi are famous for their basketwork; try buying their crafts directly from the river folk, although many speak only Chachi. Over the last few decades, the Chachi have been swept by an epidemic of river blindness carried by black flies, which are particularly prevalent in April and May. Some 80% have the disease to some extent. To protect yourself while traveling use insect repellent and take malaria pills.

When to Go

River levels are high during rainy season (December to May), making for swifter travel. At this time mosquitoes, black flies and other insects are at their highest concentrations; definitely cover up at dawn and dusk when they come out in full force.

Even during the rainy months, mornings are often clear. Up to 5000mm of rain has been reported in some of the more inland areas, although San Miguel is somewhat drier. The drier months of September to the start of December are usually less buggy, and there is a better chance of seeing wildlife, although river navigation may be limited.

Getting There & Around

Entrance into the reserve is payable at the ranger station in San Miguel (p279). The rangers can serve as guides, and charge about $10 per day, plus food. Two guides are needed for trips – one for each end of the dugout canoe (these canoes are paddled and poled; engines are scarce out here). Alternatively, you can visit on a guided tour with one of the lodges. The lodge in Playa de Oro (p279) is also an access point for the reserve.

It is about two or three hours by canoe from San Miguel to the park boundaries. Another one or two hours brings the visitor to a gorgeous little waterfall in the jungle. A guide is essential as the few trails are poorly marked. There are places to camp if you have tents and the necessary gear.

THE ROAD TO ESMERALDAS

☎ 06

The bus journey to Esmeraldas from San Lorenzo via Borbón is dusty in the dry season, muddy in the wet season and bumpy year-round. It starts along the Ibarra road and turns inland through the forest. Beyond Borbón, there are a number of villages, most with a basic *residencial* (cheap hotel) if you get stuck. One of these villages is **Lagarto**, where Río Lagarto is crossed.

Soon after crossing Río Lagarto, the routes from Borbón and La Tola unite. The road then continues to the coastal village of **Rocafuerte**, which has very basic *residenciales* and simple restaurants selling tasty fresh seafood to weekenders from the city out for a stroll in the countryside.

A few kilometers further, the road passes through the two coastal villages of Río Verde: **Palestina de Río Verde**, just beyond the river, and then **Río Verde**, a few kilometers further. Río Verde was the setting of Moritz Thomsen's fine memoir *Living Poor* (1969). At the river crossing, look for a large frigate-bird colony visible in the trees along the banks. Palestina de Río Verde has a few simple hotels.

Almost 20km beyond Río Verde is the village of **Camarones**, which, as its name implies, sells fresh shrimp concoctions in its simple beachfront restaurants (open weekends and vacations). Ask around about cabins for rent if you want to stay by the beach; Cabañas Fragatas is one such place.

A few kilometers beyond Camarones, the road passes the Esmeraldas airport on the east side of Río Esmeraldas. The city is on the west side, but there is no bridge until San Mateo, about 10km upriver. It is a half-hour drive from the airport to Esmeraldas.

ESMERALDAS

☎ 06 / pop 98,000

The Spanish conquistadors made their first Ecuadorian landfall on this broad, sandy bank flanked by a sparkling river and surrounded by low green hills. Esmeraldas has been an influential port town throughout history, though its modern incarnation is not pretty. Many of its cement structures are either half-finished or half-fallen, the frenzied streets harbor drugs and petty crime, and the forests have surrendered to scrub brush.

These days fishing and shipping take a backseat to the oil refinery processing the contents of the trans-Ecuadorian oil pipeline, which adds its share of noise and pollution. This, combined with the fact that Esmeraldas is considered one of Ecuador's most dangerous major cities, makes it an improbable destination.

Still, visitors should know that *esmeraldeños* (residents of Esmeraldas) are seriously preoccupied about their reputation and some will go out of their way to prove how amenable they are. If you can negotiate the mean streets, you'll find a fun and gregarious culture under hard times. Most tourists just spend the night (if they have to) and continue southwest to the popular beach destinations of Atacames, Súa and Mompiche.

Information

Andinatel (cnr Malecón Maldonado & Montalvo)

Banco del Pichincha (cnr Olmedo & Mejía; cnr Bolívar & Calle 9 de Octubre) Has an ATM.

Hospital (☎ 271-0012; Libertad) Between Esmeraldas and Las Palmas, at the north end of town.

Immigration office (☎ 271-0156, 272-4624) At the Policía Civil Nacional, 3km out of town (take a taxi). Have your passport stamped here for entry or exit via the rarely used – and not recommended – coastal route to Colombia.

Planeta Cybercafé (cnr Olmedo & Cañizares; per hr $1; 🕑 9am-9pm) Internet access.

Police station (cnr Bolívar & Cañizares) Two blocks south of the plaza.

Tourist office (☎ 272-7340; Bolívar; 🕑 9am-noon, 2-6pm) Located between 9 de Octubre & Piedrahita. For info on San Miguel, you're better off visiting the shop Mandagua in the Centro Artesenal (p282).

Dangers & Annoyances

Esmeraldas is striving to beat its notorious rap. In the meantime, avoid arriving after dark or take a taxi if you do. Busy Olmedo is

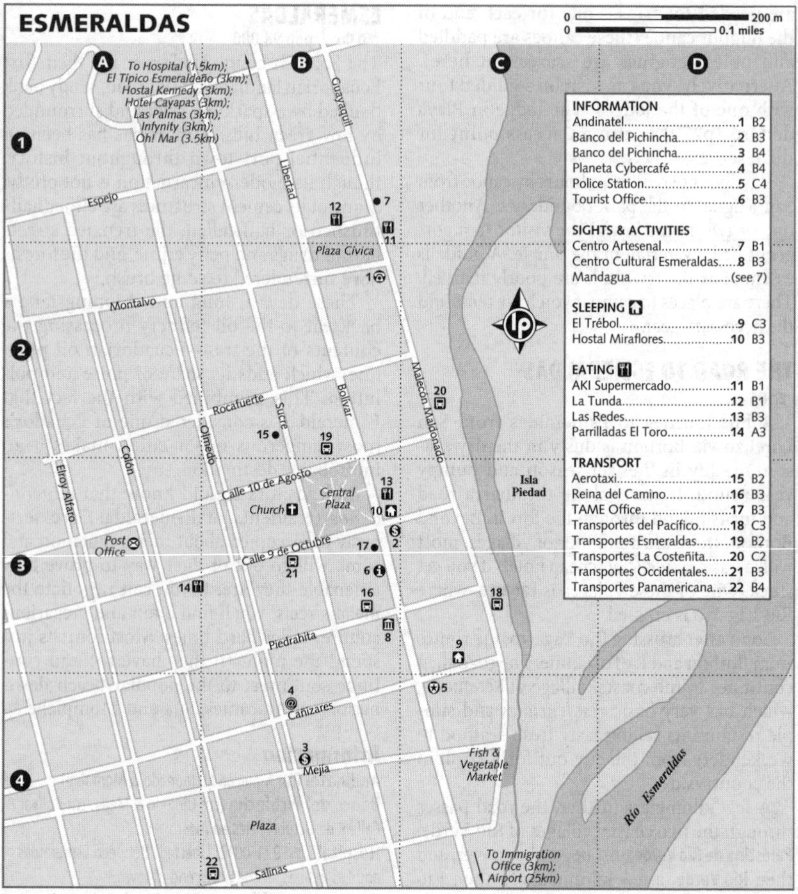

the safest street to walk at night. Be careful at any time of day in the market areas (especially along Malecón Maldonado) and away from the main streets. Single women get hit on and hooted at more often than elsewhere; it's best to ignore them. Incidences of malaria increase during the wet months.

Sights & Activities

The **Centro Cultural Esmeraldas** (☎ 272-2078; Bolívar 427; admission $1; ⏲ Tue-Fri 9am-5pm, Sat & Sun 10am-4pm) houses a museum, a library and a bookstore. Material ranges from recent local history to fine ceramics and gold work from the ancient Tolita culture. Some exhibit signs and documentary videos are in English, and the staff is very obliging.

The **Centro Artesenal** (cnr Malecón Maldonado & Plaza Cívica) is a new handicrafts center. Browse for tapestries, baskets, tagua carvings and other Chachi pieces. The first shop, **Mandagua**, is also a good place to get info about visiting off-the-beaten-track locations in the province. Ask for **Javier Valenciana** (☎ 09-139-1649; pandafinu@hotmail.com).

Sleeping

Hotels are plentiful, but the cheapest ones tend toward intolerable. During the wet months you should have a fan or a mosquito net in your room. The resort-suburb of Las Palmas, 3km north of downtown, offers better accommodations. Most of the hotels and restaurants are on Avenida Kennedy, which is the main street parallel to the beach.

Hostal Miraflores (☎ 272-3077; Bolívar 6-04, 2nd fl; r per person $5) The best bet for backpackers. Granny is your decorator at this old wooden *hostal* on the plaza, adorned with bubblegum colors and plastic bouquets. Pocket-sized rooms have high ceilings and mosquito nets, and the shared bathrooms are clean.

El Trébol (☎ 272-8031; Cañizares 1-18; s/d $12/24; ❄) Immaculate fern-lined modern hotel offering oversized rooms with a crisp finish and cable TV, but no hot water.

Hostal Kennedy (☎ 272-1141; Av Kennedy 7-03; s/d $25/30; ❄) Snug and spacious rooms in an attractive house with a gated patio out front. Hostal Kennedy is family-run. Cable TV included.

Hotel Cayapas (☎ 272-1318; Av Kennedy 401; s/d $33/45; ❄) Decorated with festive paintings by local artists, rooms are comfortable and bright, with cushiony mattresses, phone, TV and hot water. There's also an open-sided restaurant in front with good seafood dishes.

Eating

The food in the many cheap sidewalk cafés and *comedores* is often good – try along Olmedo between Mejía and Piedrahita.

Las Redes (☎ 272-3151; Bolívar; mains $2.50) On the east side of the central plaza, this teeny café crammed with wooden benches serves *almuerzos* (set lunches). Bring your local inquiries to the owner, who enjoys chatting with travelers.

La Tunda (☎ 272-2137; Plaza Cívica; mains $2-6; 🕒 10am-10pm Mon-Sat) One of several new cafés overlooking the Plaza Cívica, La Tunda has a large menu of ceviche, lasagna, pastas and hamburgers, as well as breakfast plates. There's outdoor seating on the square.

El Típico Esmeraldeño (☎ 272-6830; cnr Puerto Rico & Av del Caribe, Las Palmas; mains $3-4; 🕒 7.30am-3pm) This charming little spot in Las Palmas is a local favorite for its home cooking. Enjoy daily lunch specials (fish soup, plus chicken, beef or pork dishes) on the breezy fenced-in patio.

Parrilladas El Toro (Calle 9 de Octubre 4-23; mains $6-10; 🕒 5pm-midnight) Beyond the mafioso decor you'll find a decent steakhouse specializing in beef and chops. The thatched courtyard seating is preferable.

Oh! Mar (☎ 272-0688; Malecón de las Palmas; mains $6-12; 🕒 9am-6pm) Out in Las Palmas, this casual open-sided beachfront restaurant serves delicious seafood dishes like *encocado de langosta* (lobster in coconut milk) and *ensumacao* (soup with coconut and peanuts).

AKI Supermercado (cnr Malecón Maldonado & Montalvo) is a good supermarket for stocking up on provisions.

Entertainment

Esmeraldas is the pulsing heart of African-influenced marimba music. The best way to find out what's happening is to ask the locals, but impromptu gatherings are the norm – especially on weekends.

A LEGENDARY SHIPWRECK

Travelers in the Esmeraldas province may hear about the legendary slave ship that was wrecked offshore – giving rise to the black population living now along the north coast. Although some Ecuadorians dismiss it as pure myth, the shipwreck is indeed based on fact. In 1553, a vessel belonging to the wealthy Spanish merchant Sebastian Alonso de Illescas was en route from Panama to Callao, Peru, with 23 African slaves (17 men and six women) from the coast of Guinea.

After a month at sea, the ship anchored off the Esmeraldas coastline. The crew of Spaniards disembarked with slaves to hunt game and refill the ship's drinking water. As they were returning to the ship, a thunderstorm erupted over the sea and wrecked the ship against the reefs.

The slaves seized their chance and revolted, killing their captors and fleeing into the forest. The group established themselves in their new world, mingling with other *ladinos* (Hispanicized black people) and intermixing with indigenous peoples – sometimes battling them over limited resources and land. By 1599, black people had established themselves with solid authority as 'la República de Zambos' (the Zambo Republic). (Zambo was a word used to describe the offspring of Africans and the indigenous.) Their group numbered perhaps 100,000 and it remained largely autonomous throughout the colonial era.

The story of the ship's early survivors, incidentally, was confirmed by Spanish chronicler Miguel Cabello Balboa, who obtained the information in 1577 from one of the shipwrecked former slaves.

The discos in Las Palmas are considered the best; the concrete and thatch-roofed **Infynity** (Av del Caribe), with a tropical flavor, is one of them. Note: an unescorted woman may encounter serious hassles.

Getting There & Away

AIR

The **TAME office** (☎ 272-6863; Bolívar near Calle 9 de Octubre; 8am-12:45pm & 3-5:30pm Mon-Fri) is just off the central plaza. TAME has daily flights to Quito ($54 one-way, 30 minutes), and less-frequent service to Guayaquil ($98 one-way) and Cali, Colombia ($115 one-way). You can also purchase a plane ticket at the **airport office** (☎ 272-9040) if the flight isn't full; be early and make sure you get a seat assignment.

BUS

There is no central bus terminal. **Transportes Esmeraldas** (Calle 10 de Agosto at Plaza Central), near the central plaza, has nine daily buses to Quito ($7, six hours), plus departures to Guayaquil ($9, nine hours), Manta ($8, 10 hours), Portoviejo ($8, nine hours) and Santo Domingo ($3, 3½ hours). **Aerotaxi** (Sucre, btwn Rocafuerte & Calle 10 de Agosto) and **Transportes Occidentales** (Calle 9 de Octubre) both go to Quito ($6, five hours) and Guayaquil ($7, nine hours). **Transportes Panamericana** (Colón & Salinas) has the most luxurious buses to Quito, but the fare is a few dollars more, and the trip takes seven to eight hours.

Transportes La Costeñita (Malecón Maldonado) and **Transportes del Pacífico** (Malecón Maldonado) have buses for Atacames and Súa (both $1, one hour), which leave frequently from 6:30am to 8pm. There are also several buses a day to Muisne ($2.20, two hours), plus services to Borbón ($3.50, four hours) and on to San Lorenzo ($4.50, five hours).

Reina del Camino (Piedrahita) is a reliable bus company going to Manta ($8, seven hours) and Bahía de Caráquez ($8, 8 hours), once daily.

Note that buses from Esmeraldas to Borbón pass the airport. Passengers arriving by air and continuing by bus to towns on the way to Borbón don't need to backtrack to Esmeraldas.

Getting Around

The airport is 25km from town, across the Río Esmeraldas. Passengers and taxi drivers gather in front of the TAME office in town a couple of hours before the flight, and four or five passengers cram a taxi for $3 per person (15 minutes). Incoming passengers get together to do the same thing at the airport. A taxi charges about $25 to go directly from the airport to Atacames, thus avoiding Esmeraldas completely.

A taxi to the beach costs $1, or otherwise take a Selectivo bus signed 'Las Palmas No 1' northbound along Bolívar.

Taxis charge a $1 minimum, which doubles after 11pm.

To avoid the area of the bus terminals you can catch buses to Atacames on Calle Olmedo after Calle Quito.

ATACAMES

☎ 06 / pop 10,200

The raucous beach town of Atacames inspires pure excitement or dread depending on how you like your beach vacations. For some *serranos* (highlanders), Atacames equals nonstop party, with a wide packed beach, bustling guesthouses and a jumble of thatch-roofed bars blaring salsa and *reggaetón* at all hours of the day. Plenty of international travelers join the festive atmosphere, which reaches its peak in the high season (July to mid-September, Christmas through New Year, Carnaval and Easter).

Meanwhile, those seeking a quieter getaway bypass the town altogether, heading instead to Súa (p286), Same (p287) or Mompiche (p289) further south, all of which offer open, empty expanses of sun and sea.

Orientation

The main road from Esmeraldas goes through the center of town and continues south past Súa and Same. Ask the bus driver to leave you at *taxis ecológicos,* the tricycle rickshaw stand. The beach is on a peninsula on the opposite bank of the Río Atacames. Take Prado west a couple of blocks to the small footbridge over the river to the beach and hotel area. Hotels and restaurants line the east–west Malecón.

The beach itself is a pretty strip extending 4km to its southern terminus at 'suicide rock.' Buses do not reach the beach area. To skip the walk, hail a tricycle 'ecotaxi' to take you (via the other bridge) to your hotel for $1. The actual center of town is inland from the highway but there is little reason to go there other than to go to the bank.

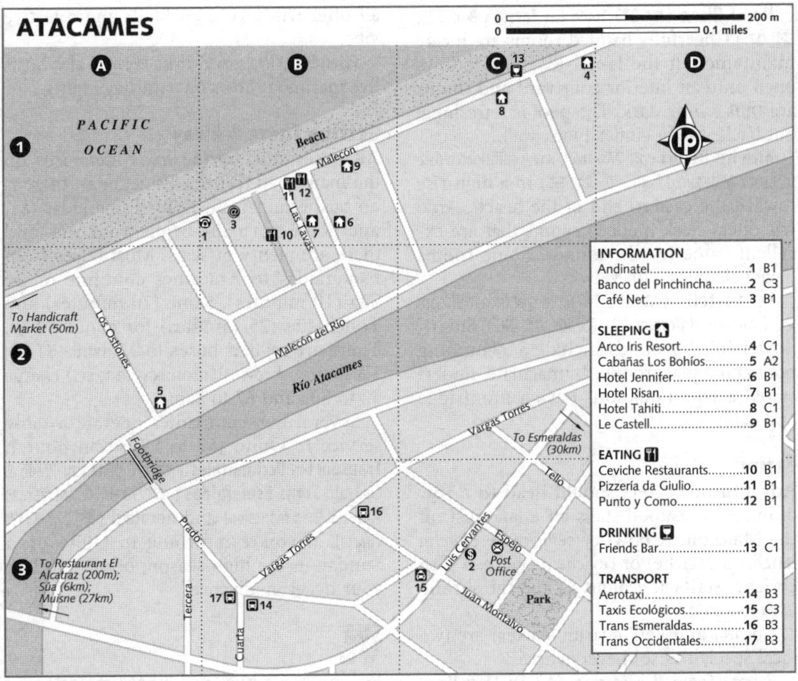

Information

Andinatel (Malecón)

Banco del Pichincha (Luis Cervantes s/n; 🕑 8am-2pm Mon-Fri) Has an ATM.

Café Net (Malecón; per hr $1.50; 🕑 8am-11pm) A popular internet café facing the beach.

Sights & Activities

Fishermen on the beach can take you on a boat tour around the area, passing by Isla de Pajaros just off shore. Plan on about $20 per person for a 75-minute tour, and $40 per person for a fishing trip. Ask around or contact **Fidian Franco** (☎ 09-055-6409) to arrange an excursion.

There's a tiny **handicraft market** (Malecón; 🕑 9am-8pm Sat & Sun) on weekends at the west end of the Malecón.

Dangers & Annoyances

The beach has a strong undertow and lifeguards work only midweek to weekends. People drown here every year, so stay within your limits.

The beach is considered unsafe at night, when assaults and rapes have been reported. Stay near the well-lit areas in front of the hotels, and avoid the isolated stretch between Atacames and Súa, as knifepoint robberies have been reported. Needless to say, the beach is not a place to bring your valuables.

Sleeping

Atacames is packed with hotels, but it can get awfully crowded on holiday weekends. Reserve in advance if arriving at peak season.

Hotel Jennifer (☎ 273-1055; near Malecón; s/d without hot water $8/15, s/d with hot water $10/20) This simple, straightforward place has clean, spartan rooms that get a decent amount of light (windows in every room). Kind staff.

Cabañas Los Bohíos (☎ 272-7478; Calle Principal; s/d $10/20) Near the dark, fetid Río Atacames, Los Bohíos offers clean, inexpensive rooms with tile floors and wood and bamboo details. Cabins are slightly smaller and made entirely of bamboo. It's surrounded by a concrete parking area with a few flowers and palms.

Hotel Tahiti (☎ 273-1078; Malecón; s & d $20-40; 🏊) The nicely landscaped pool is the centerpiece of this whitewashed five-story hotel near the beach. Rooms are clean and fan-cooled, and many have balconies with partial sea views.

Hotel Risan (☎ 273-1609; Las Tavas; s & d $25;) Cheerfully painted rooms are nicely maintained at the Hotel Risan. Windows open onto an interior courtyard and rooms are thus a little dark. The pool is refreshing, but backed by a cinder-block wall.

Arco Iris Resort (☎ 273-1654; www.edificioarcoirisresort.com; Malecón; d from $30;) In a high-rise toward the eastern end of the beach, Arco Iris offers sleek modern rooms that are excellent value for the money. Some rooms have balconies with views.

Le Castell (☎ 273-1476; www.lecastell.com.ec; Malecón; s/d/cabins $22/35/56;) Smart, flower-filled grounds include a swimming pool and a playground. Immaculate, understated accommodations have a minifridge and cable TV.

Eating

Adventurous eaters should head to a row of open-air seafood stalls on a lane just off the Malecón. A bowl of *ceviche de concha* (shellfish ceviche) or *ceviche de pescado* (fish ceviche) starts at around $4 and the shrimp is precooked.

Cocada and *batido* (fruit shakes) are two local specialties sold everywhere.

Punto y Como (Malecón; mains $3-7; 11am-10pm) Punto y Como is a small cozy seafood restaurant that packs in the crowds. Its recipe for success? Big family plates that are piled high with fresh seafood, plus daily lunch specials.

Pizzería da Giulio (☎ 273-1603; Malecón; mains $6-9; 5:30pm-midnight Tue-Fri, 10:30am-midnight Sat & Sun) Run by a Sicilian, this handsome restaurant serves up excellent thin-crust pizzas with fresh ingredients and old-world flavors (including real prosciutto). There's upstairs balcony seating, as well as grappa, sambuca and other spirits rarely seen around these parts.

Restaurant El Alcatraz (☎ 273-1453; road to Súa; mains $7-10) Though it's not on the beach, El Alcatraz serves great Esmeraldan seafood, and it's well worth the trip. A full plate of *mariscos* (seafood) features various clams and shellfish simmered in spices.

Drinking & Entertainment

Music-blaring thatch-roofed bars line the Malecón. Virtually indistinguishable from one another (except each cranks up a different song list), these beach-facing places all offer fruity rum cocktails and a festive vibe.

Friends Bar (Malecón; noon-midnight) also hosts live marimba shows on Saturday nights.

Getting There & Away

All buses stop by the *taxis ecológicos* on the main road to/from Esmeraldas; there is no bus terminal. Buses for Esmeraldas ($1, one hour) normally begin from Súa, and there are plenty of seats. Most buses from Esmeraldas to Atacames continue on to Súa (10 minutes), Same (20 minutes) and Tonchigüe (25 minutes) for about $0.30. There are regular buses to Muisne ($1.50, 1½ hours). *Ecovias* (motorcycle taxis) charge $2 to Súa and $7 to Same.

Several bus companies operate a daily service to Quito ($7 to $8, seven hours): **Transportes Occidentales** (☎ 276-0547; cnr Prado & Cuarta), **Trans Esmeraldas** (☎ 273-1550; cnr Vargas Torres & Juan Montalvo) and **Aerotaxi** (☎ 273-1312; Cuarta). If you're returning to Quito on a Sunday in the high season, be sure to buy your ticket in advance.

SÚA

☎ 06

Fishing boats bob in the bay, encircled by frigate birds, pelicans and other seabirds. This village boasts tranquil waters ideal for a dip and a slow-churning pace, although early morning finds the bay busy with trawlers. Súa is family-oriented, quieter and less popular than Atacames, with more reasonable weekend prices. Humpback whales can be seen off the coast from June to September.

Sol de Súa (☎ 273-1021; www.folklorehotelsua.com, in Spanish; Malecón; cabin per person $5) On the southern end of the Malecón, Sol de Súa consists of nine basic cabins scattered around a sandy yard. Each has wood ceilings, concrete walls, a cold-water bathroom and a little porch. There's a small bar for guests, and the owners can arrange boating tours.

Hostal Las Buganvillas (☎ 273-1008; Malecón; r per person $8;) Buganvillas has clean-swept rooms with tile floors and cold-water showers. Some rooms are sunnier than others, so have a look before committing.

Hotel Chagra Ramos (☎ 273-1006; Malecón; r per person $8) Nestled against the beach, this friendly, wind-battered classic is the most popular guesthouse in town. Rooms are clean if a little weathered, with antiquated bathrooms but nice views. There's no hot water. There's a good-value restaurant here, too.

For a bamboo beachfront eatery, try **Kikes** (Malecón; mains $4-5; 9am-6pm). It serves up mouth-watering *encocada de camarón* (shrimp and coconut stew).

Bus services to and from Esmeraldas run about every 45 minutes. It takes 10 minutes to get to Atacames ($0.30) and about an hour to get to Esmeraldas ($1). If you want to go further along the coast to Muisne, you have to wait out of town along the main road for a bus headed south from Esmeraldas.

SAME & TONCHIGÜE

06

Same (pronounced sah-may) boasts the prettiest beach in the area, a striking 3km-long stretch of palm-fringed coast only lightly touched by development. The village itself, which lies 7km southwest of Súa, is quite small, with only a sprinkling of guesthouses and restaurants. Expect to pay more here.

Tonchigüe is a tiny fishing village about 3km west of Same, along the same stretch of beach. Go early in the morning to see the fishermen unloading their catch.

Sleeping & Eating

La Terraza (247-0320; Same; r per person $12-15) Spanish-owned La Terraza offers a wide range of rooms in a white-washed beachfront guesthouse. The best rooms are spacious with sea views and small balconies strung with hammocks. It's a simple but pleasant setting, and there's an open-sided restaurant overlooking the waves.

Playa Escondida (273-3122, 09-973-3368; www.playaescondida.com.ec; campsites per person $5, r per person low-season $10-15; high season d $20-35) The lovely but rustic Playa Escondida offers accommodation in rustic cabins with composting toilets. There's a restaurant serving seafood, meat and vegetarian dishes, and the host offers tours and other activities. It's located 3km west of Tonchigüe and 10km down the road to Punta Galeras. It's an out-of-the-way and precious stretch, backed by rumpled woods, and run by a Canadian named Judy.

Casa de Amigos (247-0102; www.casadeamigosecuador.com; Same; r per person $25-30) A lovely addition to the Same beachfront, Casa de Amigos is an Adobe-style guesthouse with a friendly, welcoming vibe. Rooms are nicely designed with terra-cotta tile floors, wood trim and comfortable beds, and the artwork throughout adds color to the place. The meals at the restaurant are an even bigger attraction, with delicious Caribbean- and Mexican-influenced dishes. English, German and Spanish are spoken.

Isla del Sol (273-3470; www.cabanasisladelsol.com; Same; low-season r per person $18, high-season s & d $56) Pleasant beachfront cabins here are a good deal for the money. The best rooms have wood floors with beamed ceilings and small verandas, and all have hot water and cable TV. There's also a basketball court and a swimming pool.

Hotel Club Casablanca (273-3159; Same; s/d incl breakfast from $35/61) This sprawling resort on the north end of Same has a wide range of rooms, each with its own deck or balcony. The property includes a golf course, two tennis courts, a large pool and a laid-back beachfront bar and restaurant. An airport shuttle from Esmeraldas is offered.

El Acantilado (273-3466; www.hosteriaelacantilado.com; s/d/tr/cabañas low season $25/50/60/80, s/d/cabañas high season $75/80/110) Perched on a cliff above the crashing waves, El Acantilado offers unobstructed sea views from its rooms and common areas (including the pool). Rustic suites and cabañas have blue tiles, wood furnishings and hot water. Cabins fit up to eight occupants. Each room has a garden hammock, and there's a glassed-in restaurant with views. Run by a hospitable young family who speak English. Located 1km south of Same.

Seaflower (247-0369; Same; mains $9-12; noon-4pm & 6-9pm) Boasting one of the best chefs along the North Coast, Seaflower serves delicious plates of grilled seafood. The house's countryside ambience is warm and eclectic, with bright candlelit tables both indoors and out. It's around the corner from La Terraza.

There are a handful of simple *comedores* right on the beach in Same offering plates of *encocado* (shrimp or fish cooked in a rich, spiced coconut sauce) or *pescado* (fish) for around $5.

Buses heading east to Esmeraldas and south to Muisne pick up and drop off passengers at both Same and Tonchigüe. *Rancheras* (open-sided buses) head to Tonchigüe from Esmeraldas.

MUISNE & AROUND

☎ 05

Muisne is a tumbledown, working-class island surrounded by river and sea, off the end of the road from Esmeraldas. Its little ramshackle port bustles with a minor banana-shipping industry. Relatively remote, Muisne attracts far fewer visitors than the more popular beaches, but it makes an interesting foray off the beaten track. The long and lonely palm-lined beach at its back is its best feature.

The few remaining mangroves in the area are protected and worth a visit (see the boxed text, p278).

Orientation

Buses from Esmeraldas get as far as the cement launch of El Relleno. From here take a motorized canoe across the mottled blue Río Muisne to the island ($0.20). Muisne's main road leads directly away from the pier, crossing the center to the beach. It's 2km end to end. Ecotaxis vie for passengers at the pier. It's worth the $1 for the wild ride at top rickshaw speed through muddy potholes and over sharp, rolling rubble. The beautiful beach is fronted by worn wooden boarding houses.

Information

There's no bank in Musine and the post office, near the telephone office, is open sporadically. An Andinatel office is just off the main plaza.

Dangers & Annoyances

Some beach cabins have had thefts, so check the security of the room you choose before you head out. Single travelers, women especially, should stick to the area of hotels and restaurants on the beach.

Tours

Community and mangrove tours are organized by **Fundecol** (☎ 248-0519; www.fundecol.org), the Foundation for Ecological Defense. Costs range from $25 to $50 per person per day (depending on the tour and the group size) and include boat trips up Río Muisne to see the remaining mangroves and the impact of commercial shrimping (see the boxed text, p278).

Only 2km from Muisne is the **Congal Biostation**, a 250-hectare marine reserve working with mangrove conservation and organic aquaculture. Volunteers are needed, but visitors are welcome as well. There are great opportunities for snorkeling and scuba diving, plus comfortable private cabins with seafood on the menu. Contact **Fundación Jatun Sacha** (☎ 02-243-2240; www.jatunsacha.org; r per person with 3 meals $40, discounts for groups & students).

Sleeping & Eating

There are only budget options in Muisne. Avoid the bleak hotels across the river and head to the island where you'll find beachfront cabañas. During the rainy months mosquitoes can be bad, so get a room with a net.

Calade Spondylus (☎ 248-0279; r/cabin per person $6/8) This basic place facing the beach has simple but clean rooms and wooden cabins. The best rooms have private bathrooms and open onto a shared balcony with ocean views. There's a sandy palm-filled yard surrounding the place. Cold water only.

Hostal Las Olas (☎ 248-0782; s/d $10/15) Facing the sea, Las Olas is a large well-maintained guesthouse with nice woodwork throughout. Try to score room 11 up top, with a big sitting area adjoining the room. There's a popular open-sided restaurant on the ground floor.

Playa Paraíso (☎ 248-0192; r per person $14) Under new management, this beachfront guesthouse was receiving a makeover at the time of research. The friendly owner aims to bring something slightly more upscale to Muisne, with handsome rooms and cabins with private hot-water bathrooms.

A few cheap restaurants line the beach, including the town favorite **Las Palmeiras**. Enjoy inexpensive shrimp or fish plates with a sea view.

Getting There & Away

Several companies have buses departing from El Relleno across the river about every 30 minutes to Esmeraldas ($2, 2½ hours) passing Same, Súa and Atacames en route. There are five buses a day to Santo Domingo de los Colorados ($5, five hours), where connections to Quito or Guayaquil are made. **Transportes Occidentales** (Calle Principal at El Relleno) has a nightly bus to/from Quito ($8, 8½ hours). Buses or pickups (depending on road conditions) go south to Daule about every hour, from where boats go on to Cojimíes. It's easier, however, to take an Esmeraldas bus for 30 minutes ($0.50) to El Salto (a road junction with a basic *comedore*) and wait there for southbound traffic heading to Daule. To get further south, get a bus to El Salto and then a bus to Pedernales ($3, three hours), from where there are buses heading in all directions. Between El Salto and Pedernales, you often have to change buses in San José de Chamanga (you'll know you're in Chamanga by the floating piles of garbage and stilted houses). Ask your driver.

MOMPICHE

☎ 05

Besides a fabulous stretch of palm-fringed sands, Mompiche has little else. That's the beauty. Its claim to fame is its world-class wave – a left point-break that you'll find during big swells. Fanatics can click onto the latest **surf reports** (www.surf-forecast.com/ breaks/Mompiche).

You can get your forty winks at **Gabeal** (☎ 09-969-6543; east beach; r per person low/high season $10/15, camping $3), a set of basic bamboo cabins with cold-water bathrooms. The amenable owner can arrange horseback riding and surf lessons. You'll find it two blocks to the right of the bus stop.

Run by a friendly group of Colombian surfers, **DMCA Surf Hostel** (r per person $6-8; camping $3 per person) offers a range of sleeping options in a rustic hostel on the narrow road along the beach. Some rooms have private cold-water showers. There's a rooftop terrace with hammocks, and you can order food by advance notice.

Iruña (☎ 09-754-725; r per person $10), with its pale Easter-egg cabins, offers isolated tranquility. Talk to Marco to arrange a visit; you'll need to arrive by boat or truck at low tide.

Rancheras go to and from Esmeraldas every day ($3.50, 3½ hours), passing Atacames on the way.

COJIMÍES

☎ 05

The small friendly fishing village of **Cojimíes** lies on an attractive headland, which is slowly being eroded by the ocean. The village has to keep moving inland, which means that the cemetery is gaining beachfront vistas. There is a Pacifictel office here, and a few basic accommodations scattered around town.

El Sueño de Teo (☎ 08-297-3198; s/d from $7/15) This family-run place offers pleasant bamboo-and-wood cabañas, each with a thatched roof, a mosquito net and a private bathroom. Teo, the friendly owner, can arrange boat trips to Isla del Amor. It's located on the way out to the beach (along the road to Pedernales); El Sueño is about 200m walk from the crashing waves.

Restaurant Aurita (☎ 239-1236; Malecón; mains $6-10; 🕑 6am-7pm) Overlooking the fishing boats bobbing on the water, this simple waterside restaurant serves delectable Manabí seafood. It's famous for the huge shrimp native to the area, but also prepares tasty ceviche, *concha* (shellfish) and *encocado de pescado*. The vibe is casual: dine at plastic picnic tables and dig your heels into the sand.

Hotel Coco Solo (☎ Pedernales 09-921-5078, 05-268 1156; cabins per person $8) is a coconut grove hideaway 14km south of Cojimíes. Some visitors have commented that it is becoming run down, but it still offers seaside cabins and horses to gallop the deserted beaches. The restaurant offers just a limited menu, and there's a pool table for entertainment. The hotel is notoriously difficult to reach by phone; visitors can also reserve through Guacamayo Tours (p293).

The Costa del Norte bus office on the main street can give transportation information. Trucks run along the beach at low tide, racing the tide at breakneck speeds, to Pedernales (from $3, 40 minutes). Buses take the 'road' ($1.50, 1½ hours); the last one leaves at around 3pm. To head north, you have to take a boat across to Daule, from where there are buses to the junction of El Salto. From there you can change direction to Muisne or Esmeraldas (buses to Esmeraldas pass through other coastal towns).

PEDERNALES

☎ 05

Chevys with tinted windows thump down the strip, where street-side grills soak up the action. The beach here attracts *serranos* but there are better options around. This unattractive yet important hub and shrimping center 40km south of Cojimíes may be a necessary juncture for connections south to Canoa or north to Esmeraldas.

Hotel Arenas (☎ 268-1170; Av Plaza Acosta & Robles; r per person with fan/air-con $8/10; ❄) is the best value, with spacious, airy rooms and cable TV. It's located a few blocks from the beach. The modernish **Hotel América** (☎ 268-1174; García Moreno; r per person $8; ❄) is well-kept but the walls are paper thin.

Buses leave the terminal for destinations south along the coast including Canoa ($4, three to 3½ hours) and San Vicente ($3, four hours). Regular buses go to Santo Domingo ($4, three hours), Quito ($6, six hours) and Guayaquil ($9, seven hours). The road via Chamanga to El Salto leaves you near Muisne to make connections there or further north. Full-speed trucks take the beach north to Cojimíes ($1.45) during low tide.

CANOA

☎ 05 / pop 6100

A sleepy village with a heart of gold, Canoa has a lovely stretch of beach framed by picturesque cliffs to the north and a disappearing horizon to the south. Despite its growing popularity with sunseekers and surfers, Canoa remains a low-key place, where kids frolic on the sandy lanes at dusk and fishermen head out to sea in the early hours before dawn. In the evenings the beachfront bars and guesthouses come to life as expats swap travel tales over rum-filled cocktails.

International surf competitions come in high season (December to February), when waves reach over 2m and accommodations become downright scarce. Obviously, the swimming is better after surf season. At low tide you can reach caves at the north end of the beach, which house hundreds of roosting bats. Canoa is also a good place to make arrangement to visit the lush Río Muchacho Organic Farm.

Orientation & Information

Buses between Pedernales and San Vicente come through Canoa about every thirty minutes. The bus lets passengers off on the Calle Principal (main street) in town. From here it's just a few short blocks to the beach, where many of the accommodation options are located.

There are no banks (you'll have to go to San Vicente for ATMs), but there are several public phone centers on the main street, and (slow) internet access at **Net Café** (per hr $1.25; 8:30am-9pm), just off the main street.

Note that because of unreliable phone service in town, most local businesses use mobile phones.

Sights & Activities

Surfboard rental is available at many guesthouses as well as a few local outfits like **Coquitos Bar** (bike or surfboard per hr/day $3/10; 8am-4pm), which rents surfboards as well as bikes. It's located around the corner from Hotel Bambu. Ask around about horseback riding, kayaking and rafting trips.

For paragliding adventures, contact Kentucky exile **Greg Gilliam** (☎ 08-519-8507; www.flycanoa.com). You can also ask after him at Surf Shack (opposite). He currently charges around $30 per tandem flight and offers lessons as well.

On Saturday mornings, Río Muchacho (opposite) sponsors an organic market on the main street.

Sleeping

Linda Onda (☎ 261-6339, 08-023-5719; www.lindaonda.com; dm $5, s/d with private bathroom from $10/15) This newly opened guesthouse offers clean rooms in a peaceful setting two blocks from the beach. The bar has a festive vibe, and you can get the lowdown on the surf from the friendly Aussie owners.

Coco Loco (☎ 09-544-7260; hotalcocoloco@yahoo.com; dm $5, s/d with shared bathroom $10/14, s/d/tr with private bathroom $16/18/28) The current backpacker favorite in town, Coco Loco has clean rooms with decent mattresses and bamboo details, and a sand- and palm-filled yard in front. People tend to stick around longer than planned: there's a laid-back happy hour, barbecue nights (Thursday to Sunday), and lots of activities on offer.

Hotel Bambu (☎ 08-926-5225; www.hotelbambuecuador.com; s/d with shared bathroom $7/10, d with private bathroom/balcony $18/20) A beachfront surfer resort able to sustain your urges for fruit shakes, hammock naps, big meals and bigger waves. Firm beds fill these smallish thatched rooms, kept cool with a bamboo-plaster construction. Shared bathrooms are spotless and all have hot water. You can rent surfboards, body boards and a beach sailer, or hang out in the communal lounge with games.

Hostal Shelmar (☎ 08-450-5391; Calle Principal; r per person $7) This locally owned place may not have much of a traveler vibe, but it does offer friendly service and nicely furnished rooms with wood floors, fans, mosquito nets and piping hot showers. Sandwiched in the middle of the main strip, it's a few blocks from the beach.

Hotel País Libre (☎ 261-6536; r per person with shared/private bathroom $7/12;) Owned by an Ecuadorian surf pro, País Libre is a colorful multistory wood-frame building with hewn-log banisters and bamboo-crafted rooms.

It has its own disco and swimming pool, and hammocks on the upper decks. The rooms come equipped with fans as well as hot water.

La Posada de Daniel (☎ 09-750-8825; r per person $8, camping $3; 🖳 🏊) One of Canoa's first guesthouses, La Posada de Daniel offers a range of wooden cabins, some of which are rather beat-up. Still, the hammocks on the porches are nice (with views over town to sea), and the campsites have tents and thick air mattresses good to go. There's also a small pool and a casual thatch-roofed bar. It's located a few blocks inland.

La Vista (☎ 08-647-0222; Malecón; s/d $16/24; 🖳) La Vista is a slightly more upscale four-story guesthouse. Its spacious, nicely designed rooms have beamed ceilings and glass (rather than bamboo) windows.

Eating & Drinking

Café Flor (☎ 08-560-8255; mains $3-6; 🕑 9am-3pm & 6-9.30pm Mon-Sat) This sweet, family-run café serves a range of delicious, carefully prepared dishes, including pizzas, burritos, hamburgers and veggie burgers, American-style breakfasts and more. Enquire here about inexpensive surfing or Spanish lessons. You can also rent a simple but tidy room. It sits two blocks from the beach near the ballfields.

Surf Shack (Malecón; mains $3-6; 🕑 8am-11pm Wed-Mon) Another popular beachfront bar-restaurant, Surf Shack serves up pizzas, burgers, filling breakfasts and plenty of rum cocktails to a fun-seeking foreign crowd. There's also plenty of gear for hire here: kayaks, rafts, motorbikes, surfboards and more. This is the place to find high-flier Greg Gilliam, who offers paragliding tours (from $30 per person).

Shamrock (☎ 09-781-2752; Malecón; mains $3-6; 🕑 10am-midnight Tue-Sun) Run by a friendly Irish expat, the Shamrock is a low-key place for a pint and tasty chili, shepherd's pie, burgers and other pub grub.

Amalur (☎ 08-294-1187; mains $3-7; 🕑 noon-9pm) Owned by a talented Spanish couple ('Amalur' means 'Mother Earth' in Basque), this trim, minimalist restaurant is a great place to dine. A chalkboard lists the day's delicacies: fresh calamari in ink, gazpacho, grilled pork with red peppers, nicely seasoned eggplant in salsa and a marvelously tender sea bass are a few recent favorites. Find Amalur a few blocks inland overlooking the ball field.

El Oasis (Calle Principal; mains $4-10; 🕑 8am until last customer) One block from the beach, El Oasis is a simple thatch-roofed restaurant that serves excellent seafood. The welcoming chef, who hails from Esmeraldas, cooks up tasty Manabí recipes including ceviche, *encocado* and nicely spiced grilled fish and shrimp.

AROUND CANOA

The **Río Muchacho Organic Farm** (☎ 09-147-9849; www.riomuchacho.com) is a tropical organic farm where guests and locals get their hands dirty engaging in and learning about sustainable farming practices.

The farm is proactive in the community and built a primary school that teaches children about reforestation and waste management as well as their ABCs.

Lying along the river of the same name, Río Muchacho Organic Farm is reached by a rough 8km track branching inland from the road north of Canoa. Transportation to the farm is normally on horseback, which is how the local *montubios* (coastal farmers) get around.

After touring the farm, inspecting the crops and learning about permaculture and organic farming, visitors are free to choose from a variety of activities. They can help with farm chores, fish for river shrimp or make ornaments from tagua nuts. Those who want unadulterated nature can take guided hikes, go horseback riding or bird-watching.

Cabins are Thoreau-approved rustic, with shared showers and composting toilets. The coveted spot is a treehouse bunk. Guest groups are kept small, and reservations are a must. Current rates are $30 for one night, and cheaper the longer you stay.

Volunteers are welcome to stay longer and work in the school or on the farm, and are charged $130 for one week (or $350 a month) for food and lodging. Spanish courses are offered, and the farm offers a month-long apprenticeship in organic agriculture (billed as a course).

For more information contact the **Río Muchacho office** (☎ 09-147-9849), just off the main street in Canoa. You can also arrange tours through Guacamayo Tours in Bahía de Caráquez (see p293).

SAN VICENTE

☎ 05

Most travelers stop in busy San Vicente either to get cash from an ATM before returning to Canoa or to catch a boat across the bay to Bahía. If you have time to look around, check out the brisk market and the colorful murals and stained glass in the church on the beach. Buses to various destinations can be found here.

If you get stranded here, there are several decent lodging options on the main street, including **Hotel Vacaciones** (☎ 267-4116; r per person with fan/air-con $8/10;). Rooms with tile floors are set around a pool and back courtyard. It's located on the Malecón, a short stroll from the boat dock. There's a decent restaurant on hand.

Buses leave hourly from near the market (by the passenger-ferry dock) to Pedernales ($3, three hours). Reina del Camino has several buses a day to Chone ($1.50, 1½ hours), Santo Domingo and Guayaquil (both $7, six hours), as well as morning and evening buses to Quito ($8, eight hours). Buses head regularly to Canoa ($0.35, 30 minutes).

Passenger ferries cross Río Chone several times an hour between 6am and 10pm ($0.35). It takes 10 minutes to reach Bahía de Caráquez. A car ferry leaves about every half-hour – foot passengers can cross at no charge.

BAHÍA DE CARÁQUEZ

☎ 05 / pop 20,000

Chalk-colored high-rises and red-tile roofs fill this tiny peninsula, whose manicured yards and swept sidewalks give a tidy impression. In the first half of the 20th century the city was Ecuador's principal port, but eroding sandbanks let the honor drift to Guayaquil and Manta, and Bahía (as the locals call it) was left to its housekeeping.

Despite a string of natural disasters (including the landslides induced by the 1998 El Niño and a bad earthquake that same year), Bahía has done a remarkable job of picking itself up and starting anew – at times reinventing itself. In recent years it has become a vanguard of Ecuador's fledgling green movement. In 1999, Bahía declared itself an 'ecocity,' creating a community culture of recycling and sustainable living that has attracted worldwide attention.

Bahíans get an ecocity pamphlet full of environmental tips. The market recycles, and organic farms are within a stone's throw of town. Reforestation projects target hillsides damaged after 1998's El Niño and mangroves desiccated by shrimp farming. Various other agroecological and recycling ventures are promoted by a handful of visionary locals.

Information

Banco de Guayaquil (☎ 269-2205; cnr Bolívar & Riofrío) Cashes traveler's checks and has an ATM.

Genesis Net (Malecón Santos 1302; per hr $1; 9am-9:30pm Mon-Sat, 10am-8pm Sun) Internet and cheap international calls.

Post office (Aguilera 108)

Sights & Activities

A good introduction to the area's indigenous history is the **Museo Bahía de Caráquez** (☎ 269-0817; cnr Malecón Santos & Peña; admission $1; 9am-4:30pm Tue-Sat, 11am-2:30pm Sun). The modern museum, which opened in 2004, has hundreds of pieces of pre-Columbian pottery, as well as local crafts for sale. A guided tour in Spanish is included with admission.

The **Mirador La Cruz** (lookout) at the south end of town gives good views of the area, and can be reached on foot or by a short taxi ride.

Chirije archaeological site, 15km south of Bahía and 3km north of San Clemente, is riddled with artifacts, including ceramics, burials, cooking areas, garbage dumps and jewelry, dating mainly from the Bahía culture (500 BC to AD 500). The site is owned by Bahía Dolphin Tours (p294), and to visit you must arrange a guided trip through the agency. The sheer number of remains leads archaeologists to think this was once an important port. Only small sections of the site have been professionally excavated, and some pieces are exhibited in the tiny on-site museum, but visitors will find shards of pottery all over the place.

Chirije is cut off by high tides, so visits have to be planned with this in mind (Bahía Dolphin Tours will have this info). Visitors can spend the night and take advantage of trails into the coastal tropical dry forest. Four large solar cabins sleep up to eight (a squeeze) and have a porch, a private bathroom and a kitchen. Rates are $70 per cabin, and meals are available on request. A day tour of Chirije, including lunch, costs $35 per person.

Tours

The following agencies are useful local resources. In addition to describing tours and attractions, they can provide information on

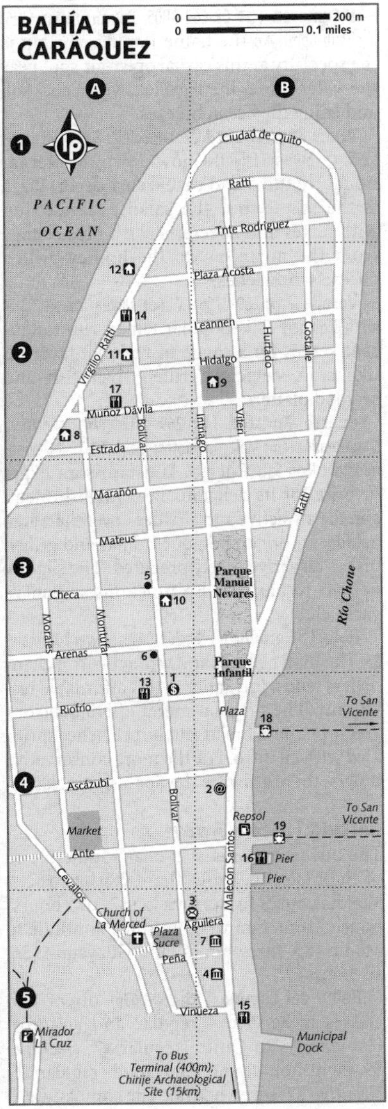

INFORMATION
Banco de Guayaquil....1 A4
Genesis Net....2 B4
Post Office....3 A5

SIGHTS & ACTIVITIES
Bahía Dolphin Tours....(see 8)
Casa de Cultura....4 B5
Ceibos Tours....5 A3
Guacamayo Tours....6 A3
Museo Bahía de Caráquez....7 B5

SLEEPING
CasaGrande Oceanfront Guesthouse....8 A2
Centro Vocational Life....9 B2
Hotel Italia....10 A3
Hotel La Herradura....11 A2
Hotel La Piedra....12 A2

EATING
Arena Bar....13 A4
D'Camaron....14 A2
La Herradura....(see 11)
Puerto Amistad....15 B5
Riverside Restaurants....16 B4
Vereda....17 A2

TRANSPORT
Car-Ferry Dock....18 B4
Passenger-Ferry Dock....19 B4

volunteering in local schools and other excellent opportunities for community work.

Guacamayo Tours (☎ 269-1412; www.guacamayotours.com; cnr Bolívar & Arenas; 🕑 8:30am-7pm Mon-Fri, 9am-4pm Sat, 10am-2pm Sun) is owned by an Ecuadorian/New Zealand couple. The company arranges tours to Río Muchacho Organic Farm (p291) and offers fascinating ecocity tours, where travelers can learn about the grassroots community projects (organic shrimp farming, environmental education in schools, mangrove replanting and more) that have made Bahía a model for sustainable development. Three-hour tours take in a reforestation project, followed by a visit to the waterfront via *ecotaxi* (bicycle taxi) and a stop at Ecopapel, a paper-recycling center where discarded paper is combined with fruit and vegetable fibers to make lovely handcrafted paper products. Guacamayo also organizes a number of activities-based tours. Río Muchacho goods and products from the recycling workshop are on sale here.

Canoe tours through mangrove forests with abundant birdlife are paddled by a local fisherman. Trips to local islands with seabird colonies (including one of the coast's largest frigate-bird colonies) also educate about the problems facing the mangrove habitat, and visit a private zoo. Whale-watching runs from late September to early October.

Ceibos Tours (☎ 269-0801; www.ceibostours.com; Bolívar 200; 🕑 9am-5pm Mon-Fri, 11am-3pm Sat) offers whale-watching tours (July to September), as well as day trips to Isla Corazon ($33 per person). Bike hire is available ($1 per hour, $5 per day).

Bahía Dolphin Tours (☎ 269-0257; www.chirije.com; CasaGrande Guesthouse, Virgílio Ratti 606) owns the Chirije archaeological site, and offers day visits or overnight tours to the site. The staff can arrange packages with overnight stays at Chirije and in Bahía, combined with visits to panama-hat workshops, an organic shrimp farm, frigate-bird islands and other local points of interest. Guides speak English, French and German.

Sleeping

Some of the cheap places have water-supply problems.

Hotel Italia (☎ 269-1137; cnr Bolívar & Checa; r per person $10) An old-fashioned four-story hotel with comfortable high-ceiling rooms, fans, hot water and cable TV. Make sure your room has been cleaned adequately. Downstairs is a decent restaurant.

Centro Vocational Life (☎ 269-0496; Octavio Vitteri & Muñoz Dávila; r per person $10;) Ideal for families, six small cabins sit on this gated grassy lot with a playground. Sturdy and functional with a very Brady Bunch aesthetic. Each cabin has cable TV and a kitchenette, and some have hot water. There's a separate games room.

Hotel La Herradura (☎ 269-0446; Bolívar 202; s/d from $20/30;) An old Spanish home with antiques and artwork brimming from its nooks. The cheaper rooms are smaller with funky old chenille spreads; you'll find better options upstairs, where the ambience is more airy and contemporary. Look for the upper-level balconies and the two rooms with ocean views.

Hotel La Piedra (☎ 269-0780; apartec@uio.satnet.net; Virgilio Ratti; s/d $44/54;) This big full-service hotel offers large, spotless rooms with spectacular ocean views. The palm-shaded pool ringed with lounge chairs is lovely, and just steps from the crashing waves.

CasaGrande Oceanfront Guesthouse (☎ 269-0257; www.chirije.com; Virgílio Ratti 606; d incl breakfast $60-80;) Facing the ocean, the lovely CasaGrande offers six handsomely furnished rooms with polished wood floors and modern bathrooms. The best rooms have balconies strung with hammocks and views of the sea. There's a comfy lounge and a refreshing pool. Wi-fi access.

Eating

You'll find a slew of weathered restaurants on the river pier, with perfect sunset ambience. They're popular for seafood, especially ceviche, and open from morning until midnight.

D'Camaron (☎ 08-662-3805; Bolívar; mains $2-5; 9am-6pm) As the name implies, shrimp is the specialty at this casual open-air spot near the water. Order them grilled, with a cocktail, and enjoy the ocean breezes.

Arena Bar (☎ 269-2024; cnr Bolívar & Riofrio; mains $2-5; 5pm-midnight) Chow down to international rhythms and casual surf decor. Pizza is the staple, but the salads, spruced up with olives and cheese, make a nice change from the norm, as do the homey grilled cheese sandwiches.

Vereda (☎ 269-2755; Muñoz Dávila; mains $3-5; lunch & dinner) This popular family-run restaurant serves up a range of regional favorites like crab, ceviche, grilled river fish and seafood platters.

Puerto Amistad (☎ 269-3112; www.puertoamistadecuador.com; Malecón Santos; mains $4-7; noon-midnight Mon-Sat) Puerto Amistad is an expat favorite for its delicious fare, English menu and the attractive and airy deck over the water. Salads, savory crepes, quesadillas and grilled dishes all arrive nicely prepared. The slightly upscale restaurant also functions as Bahía's yacht club.

Hotel La Herradura (☎ 269-0446; Bolívar 202; mains $5) The high ceilings and wrought-iron chandeliers lend a formality to this affordable restaurant. The original menu offers delicious green-plantain bread and tart ceviches sprinkled with cilantro. For the more conservative diners, there's always the Spanish omelet.

Getting There & Away

The bus terminal is at the far southern end of the Malecón. From there **Coactur** (☎ 267-4466) has buses to Portoviejo ($2, two hours) hourly from 4am to 8pm; some continue to Manta ($3, three hours) and Guayaquil ($6, six hours).

Reina del Camino (☎ 269-0636) offers two classes of service – regular and *ejecutivo* (1st class) – to Quito (regular $7, *ejecutivo* $9, eight hours) and Guayaquil (regular $6, *ejecutivo* $7, seven hours). The company also serves Santo Domingo ($4.50, four hours). Buses to local towns such as Chone are often *rancheras*, and they leave from various places in town.

To Canoa and points north, cross the river to San Vicente – see p292 for boat information. The passenger and car-ferry docks are on the eastern side of town, off Malecón Santos.

PORTOVIEJO

☎ 05 / pop 175,000

If charm were a deck of cards, Portoviejo would be holding a pair of deuces. Workers, business people, everyone in this city rushes around its bleak, stuffy streets. Despite an industrious appearance, the town is uninspiring to visitors. Founded in 1535, Portoviejo is the capital of Manabí province and vital for coffee, cattle and fishing. Much of its commercial success is based on the agricultural-processing industry. If it doesn't float your boat, it has scores of bus connections and is a reasonable overnight stop from Quito to the coast.

Information

Banco de Guayaquil (Parque Central, cnr Bolívar & Ricaurte)

Banco del Pacífico (cnr Calle 10 de Agosto & Chile)

Clínica Metropolitana (☎ 263-4207; cnr Calle 9 de Octubre & Rocafuerte)

Sights

Despite the town's colonial history, there's little to see. Wander down to the pleasant **Parque Eloy Alfaro**, for a look at its modern **cathedral**. One block east of the cathedral is a **statue of Francisco Pacheco**, the founder of Portoviejo.

The **street market** (Chile), between Duarte and Gual, makes for an interesting stroll; it's impassable to cars during the day. If you want to browse around a mall, **Paseo Portoviejo** by the Parque Central has some shops.

Sleeping

Hotel Conquistador (☎ 263-1678; Calle 18 de Octubre near Gual; s/d with fan $10/16, with air-con $15/20) This budget place has worn floorboards, cold water and sagging beds, but at least the staff is friendly. Rooms with fans lack windows.

Hotel New York (☎ 263-2395; cnr Olmedo & F de Moreira; s/d $18/20, d with window $22; ❄) A step up from the Conquistador, Hotel New York is a friendly spot with a decent location by the plaza. The rooms are plain and fairly clean, with tile floors. Exterior rooms are bright and open onto a shared balcony. There's hot water and cable TV.

Hotel Ejecutivo (☎ 263-0840; Calle 18 de Octubre near Calle 10 de Agosto; s/d $45/65) Polished and elegant rooms are tasteful and snug. Considered the best hotel in town, with an attitude to match.

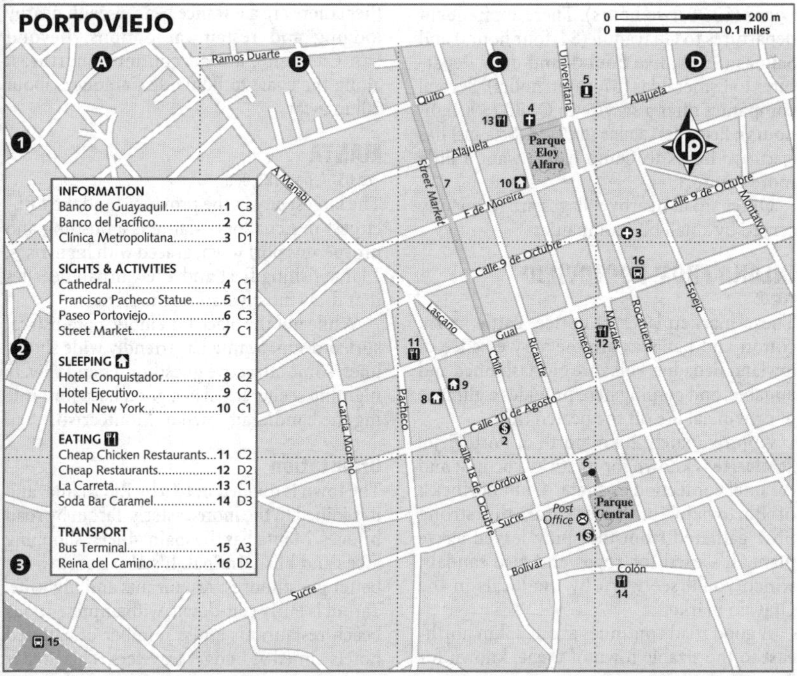

The fully equipped, carpeted rooms are often booked. The hotel provides car rental and has a good, but not cheap, restaurant.

Eating

Soda Bar Caramel (Colón; 8am-10pm) A popular place for young and old with old-fashioned wood booths, a checkered floor and a satisfying assortment of cold drinks, sandwiches and other snack fare.

La Carreta (265-2108; Olmedo; mains $2-5; 7am-10pm Mon-Fri, to 3pm Sat) Tie-clad waiters serve up tasty Ecuadorian fare in this slick and starched eatery by the cathedral.

Chicken roasters and other cheap eateries can be found on Gual between Calle 18 de Octubre and Pacheco, as well as on the block of Morales south of Gual.

Getting There & Away

Most travelers arrive at the bus terminal 1km southwest of downtown. Take a taxi ($1) to/from the terminal for security reasons.

Buses depart every half-hour or so to Manta ($0.85, 40 minutes) and every 45 minutes to Jipijapa ($1.40, 40 minutes). Carlos Aray buses to Jipijapa continue on to Puerto López ($2.20, two hours). There are frequent departures to Guayaquil ($4, four hours) and Salinas ($5.50, five hours), and daily departures to Esmeraldas ($7, seven hours). Several companies offer a service to Quito ($9, eight hours); **Reina del Camino** (cnr Gual & Rocafuerte) has *ejecutivo* buses to Quito if you want a little more comfort.

Other small nearby villages are frequently served by small bus companies.

INLAND FROM PORTOVIEJO

05

These marketplaces of coffee, cattle, corn, cotton and bananas are the very essence of lowland Ecuador. Folks are old-fashioned and amiable, and coming here provides a glimpse of provincial life off the beaten track.

Approximately 20km north of Portoviejo, **Rocafuerte** is known for its sticky coconut and caramel confections. **Calceta**, 43km northeast of Portoviejo, produces sisal, the strong fiber gathered from the spiny-leaved agave plant. It's used for ropes and also sandals, which you'll see worn by the locals in the Otavalo market.

A good road continues about 25km northeast to the sizable town of **Chone**, known for cowboy machos who supposedly keep the local beauties under wraps. Keep this in mind when seeking a dance partner.

From Chone, a paved road continues northeast, linking the coastal lowlands with Santo Domingo. This road climbs to over 600m above sea level as it crosses the coastal mountains, then drops over the eastern side to the canton capitals and market towns of **Flavio Alfaro** and **El Carmen** before reaching Santo Domingo. From El Carmen buses loop back to the coast via Pedernales.

CRUCITA AREA

05

North of Manta you'll find small villages popular with national tourists. The fishing town of **Crucita** has superlative winds for paragliding and kite-surfing. If you're interested in taking the leap, call Raúl or Luis Tobar at the friendly and family-oriented **Hostal Los Voladores** (234 0200; hvoladores@hotmail.com; r per person with shared/private bathroom $6/8;). **Hostería Zucasa** (234 0133; r per person with cold/hot water $14/17;) offers comfortable cabins around a shady pool area.

Sandwiched between **San Jacinto** (13km beyond Crucita) and **San Clemente** (3km further) there are a few nice beaches with nearby lodging and restaurant options. Beyond San Clemente, a road continues northeast along the coast to Bahía de Caráquez, about 20km away.

MANTA

05 / pop 185,000

The largest city in the province (and the fifth-largest in Ecuador), Manta is a bustling and prosperous port town, graced with high-rises, a large fishing fleet and a few urban beaches that draw mostly national tourists.

While not the place for empty, paradisiacal surf and sun, Manta has friendly wide shorelines, some attractive guesthouses and a lively nightlife scene. It's also a good base for visiting the handicraft town of Montecristi.

Orientation

The town is divided in two by Río Manta, and it is joined to the more easterly Tarqui by road bridges. Manta has the main offices, shopping areas and bus terminal. It's also home to the better guesthouses, restaurants and nightlife. Tarqui is fairly run-down, with unpretentious beach restaurants and a number of battered hotels aimed at budget travelers. This area is more prone to theft and security problems, particularly at night. The main residential areas are to the southwest of the Manta business district, while the cleanest beaches are to the northwest of Manta. Addresses are rarely used.

Information

Banco del Pacífico (☎ 262-3212; cnr Av 2 & Calle 13; 8:30am-5pm Mon-Fri) Has an ATM.
Banco del Pacífico ATM (cnr Av 107 & Calle 103) In Tarqui.
Cámara de Turismo (☎ 262-0478; cnr Malecón de Manta & Circunvalación, Tramo 1; 9am-6pm) Tourist information near Playa Murcielago.
Clínica Manta (☎ 292-1566) Has doctors of various specialties.
Cool Web Cybercafé (Av 3 near Calle 11; per hr $1; 8:30am-7pm Mon-Fri, to 4pm Sat) Slow internet.
Municipal tourist office (☎ 262-2944; Av 3 10-34; 8am-12:30pm & 2:30-5pm Mon-Fri) Friendly and helpful.
Mutualista del Pichincha ATM (cnr Calle 9 & Av 4) Best place to get cash near the bus station.
Police station (☎ 292-0900; Av 4 de Noviembre) Tourist embarkation-card extensions can be done in the immigration office. This street is a continuation of Malecón de Manta.
Post office (Calle 8) At the town hall.

Sights & Activities

The **Museo del Banco Central** (☎ 262-4099; Malecón, near Calle 20; admission $1; 9am-4:30pm Tue-Sat, 11am-2:30pm Sun) reopened in its new location in 2009, and showcases valuable artifacts from pre-Columbian Manta culture, as well as quirky fishing memorabilia.

You know you're in Tarqui when you stumble upon the enormous **Manabí fisherman statue** (Calle 101). Beyond it is **Tarqui beach**, whose east end is a hive of activity early in the mornings. Vendors' carts tail the morning crowd, selling row upon row of shark, tuna, swordfish, dorado and others (whose size decrease with each passing year). Nearby is Manta's **boatyard**, where giant wooden fishing boats are built by hand on the edge of the sand. The whole scene merits an early wake-up call. The **fishing-boat harbor**, between Manta and Tarqui, is busy and picturesque at high tide and dead in the mud at low tide.

In Manta, **Playa Murciélago** is a less-protected beach and has bigger waves (although they're not very big, there's a powerful undertow). It's a couple of kilometers northwest of downtown and is the town's most popular beach, backed by snack bars and restaurants and umbrella rental spots. Shopping can be done at the new **Supermaxi**, located diagonally across from Hotel Oro Verde. Further northwest, **Playa Barbasquillo** is a more tranquil resort area.

Sleeping

Prices rise during vacation weekends and during the high seasons (December to March, and June to August). While most of the better restaurants and bars are in Manta proper, the cheaper hotels are in Tarqui. If you stay here definitely take a taxi if you're out after dark.

TARQUI

Hotel Panorama Inn (☎ 261-1552; Calle 103 near Av 105; r per person $7, annex s/d $20/25;) The budget version of this hotel is worn out but welcoming. Large tiled rooms have teeny balconies, and some have views of the water. The staff is attentive. Its newer incarnation across the road has air-conditioning and a courtyard pool.

Hostal Miami (☎ 261-1743; Calles 102 & 107; s/d with fan $10/15, s/d with air-con $14/24;) This friendly place offers simple but pleasant rooms, some with ocean views. The old-fashioned porch lined with plants is a nice detail.

MANTA

Leo Hotel (☎ 262-3159; Av 24 de Mayo; s/d $15/25;) Across from the bus station, Leo offers small, clean rooms, some of which lack windows. Convenient if you're just passing through.

Hotel Macadamia's (☎ 261-0036; cnr Calle 13 & Av 8; s/d $18/25;) This tidy guesthouse has clean, bright accommodations (all six rooms have windows) with tile floors and sturdy furnishings.

Antares Hostal (☎ 262-6493; www.hostal-antares.com; cnr Calle 29 & Flavio Reyes; s/d $25/50;) In a peaceful residential neighborhood above Playa Murciélago, Antares offers trim and cheerfully painted rooms with wood details. Guests can take advantage of the pool, Jacuzzi and spa services.

Manakin (☎ 262-0413; cnr Calle 20 & Av 12; s/d/tr incl breakfast $35/45/60;) Near the heart of all the nightlife, Manakin is a converted one-story house with a pleasant laid-back vibe. Narrow, well-ordered rooms are nicely furnished, and the house offers fine places to unwind – including the front patio.

MANTA

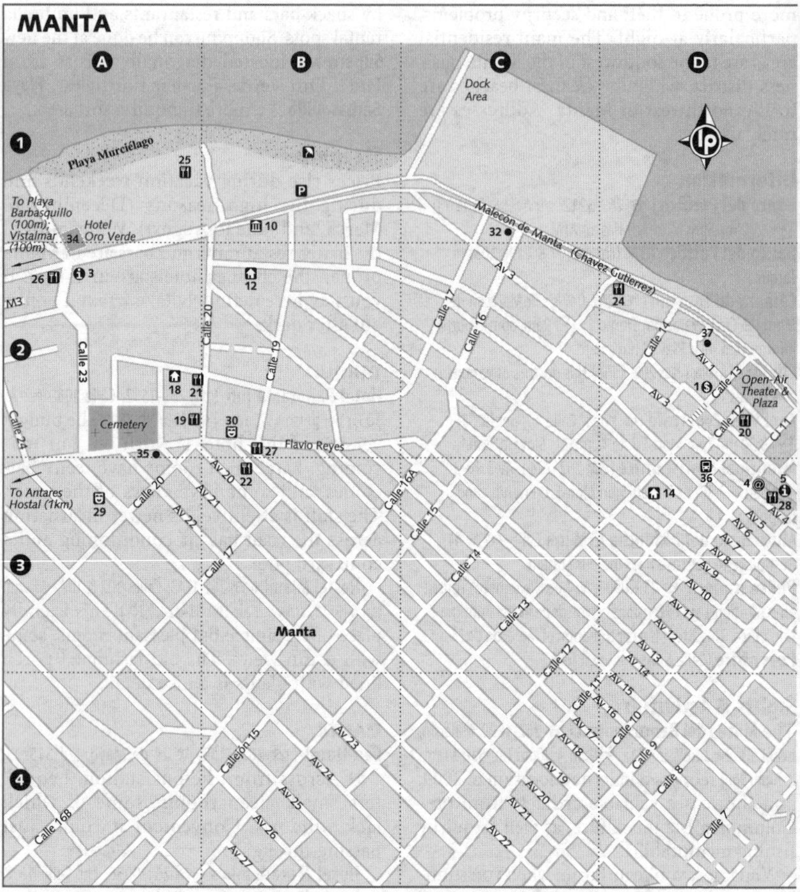

Hotel Lun Fun (☎ 262-2966; lunfunhotel@yahoo.com, Calle 2; s/d $39/55; ✗ ▯) Slick, Asian-influenced decor sets the mood for this upscale hotel. Plush, modern rooms have hot water, air-con, a minifridge, a TV and a telephone. The attached Chinese restaurant is excellent (right). The location isn't very convenient.

Vistalmar (☎ 262-1671; www.hosteriavistaalmar .com; cnr Calle M1 & Av 24; s/d/cabaña incl breakfast $50/60/80; ✗ ▣) A beautiful place for the money, Vistalmar is set on a hill over Playa Murciélago. Two handsomely designed rooms with wood floors and peaked thatched roofs open onto a small deck with excellent views. The three cabins have two bedrooms each, full kitchens and ample space. The inviting pool is perched on the edge of the cliff.

Hotel Balandra (☎ 262-0316; www.hotelbalandramanta .com; cnr Av 7 & Calle 20; s/d/cabin $70/80/150; ✗ ▯ ▣) This small hillside hotel offers pleasantly furnished rooms and swish two-bedroom cabins, some with balconies looking out to sea. Outside you'll find sculpted shrubbery, a small gym and sauna, a pool and a playground.

Eating

Seafood *comedores* line the east end of the beach on Malecón de Tarqui. Playa Murciélago has cafés front and center to enjoy beach action.

Trovador Café (☎ 262-9376; cnr Av 3 & Calle 11; coffee $0.50-1.50; ☺ 8am-8pm Mon-Sat) On a pleasant pedestrian lane near the center, this place offers frothy cappuccinos, sandwiches and inexpensive lunch plates. Outdoor seating.

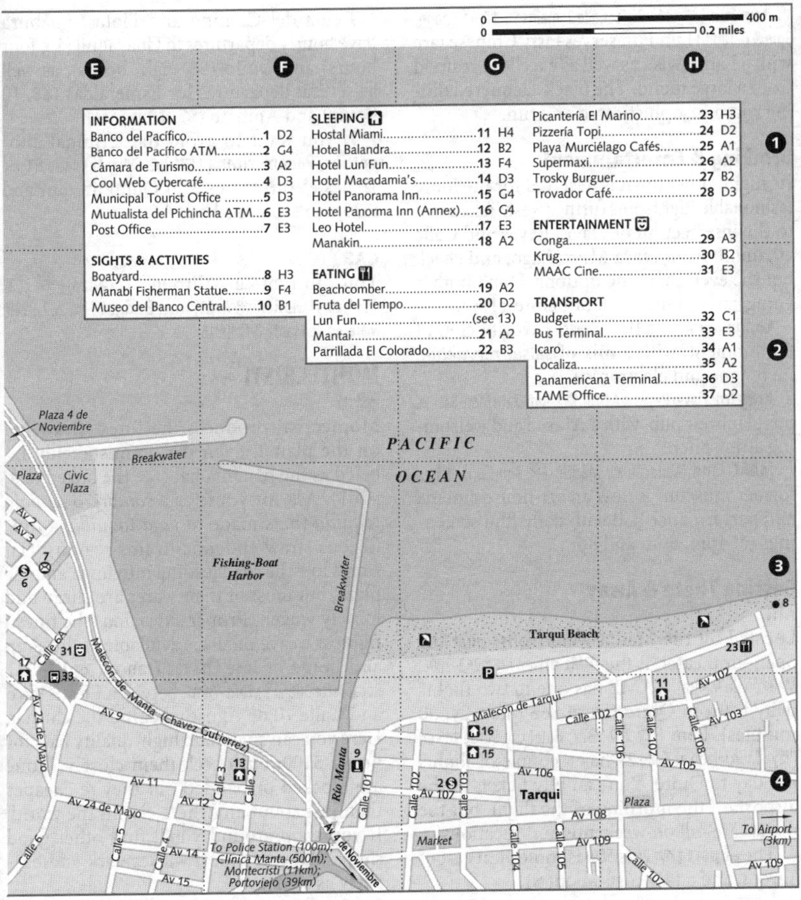

Fruta del Tiempo (☎ 262-5920; cnr Av 1 & Calle 12; mains $1-3; 🕐 7:30am-11pm) Slip into a bamboo chair near the plaza for juices, breakfasts, filling lunches and ice-cream sundaes.

Trosky Burguer (cnr Av 18 & Flavio Reyes; mains $2-5; 🕐 6pm-3am Tue-Sun) This popular surfer-run snack spot serves juicy burgers grilled to order amid rock and reef sounds. Friendly English-speaking owner.

Beachcomber (☎ 262-5463; cnr Calle 20 & Flavio Reyes; mains $2-7; 🕐 6pm-midnight) Near the heart of the nightlife, the popular Beachcomber is a favorite for its grilled meats. Dine in the lush backyard garden or on the open-sided front porch.

Picantería El Marino (☎ 261-0071; cnr Malecón de Tarqui & Calle 110; mains $3-7; 🕐 8am-5pm) This casual but nicely set café serves delectable seafood plates. It's a popular place with a subdued marine theme and reliable plates of ceviche, grilled fish and several types of shrimp dish.

Mantai (cnr Calle 20 & Av 12A; mains $3-7; 🕐 7pm-2am Mon-Sat) The big drawcard of Mantai is its pretty outdoor setting, featuring paper lanterns, fairy lights and potted plants. This restaurant also offers good-looking wait staff, electronic music and enjoyable bistro meals.

Parrillada El Colorado (cnr Av 19 & Flavio Reyes; mains $3.50; 🕐 5pm-midnight) Another popular but very casual spot, with patrons sitting at sidewalk tables next to a sizzling grill.

Pizzería Topi (☎ 262-1180; Malecón de Manta; mains $5-9; 🕐 noon-11pm) A popular spot with a huge menu of pizza, pasta and fish specials.

Lun Fun (☎ 262-2966; Calle 2; mains $6-12; ⌚ noon-3pm & 6-10pm) Lun Fun serves tasty Chinese fare with a Latin twist, as well as excellent seafood from a large menu. The black-lacquered dining room is sophisticated and fun.

Drinking & Entertainment

At night, downtown is deserted for the more fashionable nightspots further west. Take a taxi to the intersection of Flavio Reyes and Calle 20, uphill from Playa Murciélago, and check out the ever-changing options. Don't bother going early in the week or before 11pm.

Conga (cnr Av 23 & Flavio Reyes) Favorite club of the moment, with a mix of salsa, *reggaetón*, merengue and electronica.

Krug (cnr Flavio Reyes & Av 18; ⌚ 5pm-3am Mon-Sat) A popular brew pub, with a relaxed and welcoming atmosphere.

MAAC Cine (Malecón de Manta; ⌚ Thu-Sun) This former museum is now an art-house cinema and performance hall with daily film screenings (at 4pm, 6pm and 8pm).

Getting There & Away

AIR

Located on the Manta waterfront, past the open-air theater, is the **TAME office** (☎ 262-2006; Malecón de Manta). TAME has one to two flights daily to/from Quito (from $65 one-way, 30 minutes). **Icaro** (☎ 262-7327; Hotel Oro Verde tower, Playa Murciélago at Calle 23) has a couple of flights per day to Quito. You can buy tickets at the airport on the morning of the flight, but the planes are full on weekends and vacations.

The **airport** (☎ 262-1580) is some 3km east of Tarqui, and a taxi costs about $1.

BUS

Most buses depart from the central bus terminal in front of the fishing-boat harbor in Manta. Buses to nearby Manabí towns and villages such as Montecristi ($0.30, 15 minutes) also leave from the terminal.

Trans Crucita goes hourly to Crucita ($1.50, two hours). Reales Tamarindo has frequent departures to Portoviejo ($0.85, one hour), Jipijapa ($0.85, one hour) and Quevedo ($6, six hours). Transportes Manglaralto goes to Montañita ($5.50, 3½ hours), La Libertad ($6.50, five hours), Puerto López ($3, 2½ hours) and Manglaralto ($6, 4½ hours). Coactur goes to Pedernales ($5, seven hours), Canoa ($4, 3½ to four hours) and Guayaquil ($5, four hours).

Reina del Camino and Flota Imbabura have hourly departures to Guayaquil ($5, four hours) and Quito ($8, eight hours), as well as several departures for Esmeraldas ($8, 10 hours) and Ambato ($7, 10 hours).

If you want to avoid the terminal altogether, **Panamericana** (☎ 262-5898; Av Cuatro & Calle 12) has *ejecutivo* buses to Quito at 9pm and 9:30pm ($10, nine hours).

CAR

You can rent cars through **Localiza** (☎ 262-2434; cnr Flavio Reyes & Av 21) and **Budget** (☎ 262-9919; Malecón de Manta & Calle 16).

MONTECRISTI

☎ 05

Montecristi produces the finest straw hat on the planet, even if it is mistakenly labeled as the panama hat (see the boxed text, p201). Ask for yours as a *sombrero de paja toquilla* (hats made of *paja toquilla*, a fine, fibrous straw endemic to this region). Hat stores line the road leading into town and the plaza, but most of their wares are cheap and loosely woven. Proper *superfino* (the finest, tightest weave of all) is available at the shop and home of **José Chávez Franco** (☎ 231-0343; Rocafuerte 386; ⌚ 7am-7pm), between Eloy Alfaro and Calle 10 de Agosto, behind the church. Here you can snatch up high-quality hats for under $100, but check them closely. None are blocked or banded but they're cheaper than just about anywhere else in the world. If you shop around you'll find other good shops that carry local wickerwork and basketry as well.

Montecristi was founded around 1628, when Manteños fled inland to avoid the frequent plundering by pirates. The town's many unrestored colonial houses give the village a rather tumbledown and ghostly atmosphere. The main plaza has a beautiful church dating back to the early part of the last century. It contains a statue of the Virgin (to which miracles have been attributed) and is worth a visit. In the plaza is a statue of Eloy Alfaro, who was born in Montecristi and was president of Ecuador at the beginning of the 20th century. His tomb is in the town hall by the plaza.

For a peek at some of the indigenous artifacts found in the region, visit the privately maintained **Museo Arqueológico** (Calle 9 de Julio 436; admission by donation; ⌚ 9am-6pm Mon-Sat). Highlights of the small exhibition space include a primitive percussion instrument, giant funereal urns and elaborate carvings in stone.

Montecristi can be reached during the day by frequent buses ($0.40, 30 minutes) from the bus terminal in Manta.

JIPIJAPA

☎ 05

This hill city is surrounded by burned fields, set among the gnarled, spooky ceibas. Pronounced 'Hipihapa,' it is an important agricultural center, especially busy on Sundays when market stands hawk fish and vegetables. You can buy *paja toquilla* hats here. Signs outside many stores read 'Compro Café' (Coffee Bought Here) but you'd be hard pressed to find a decent cup because it's bought, not sold.

The bus terminal on the outskirts facilitates fast onward travel. A few basic hotels are available.

From the terminal, buses to Portoviejo, Manta and Puerto López leave frequently; fares are about $1. Buses to Guayaquil and Quito ($9, 10 hours) leave several times a day. Vendors board the buses with baskets of sticky *pan almodón,* delicious gooey buns baked with yuca root. It's worth buying a hot handful for the journey.

South Coast

Some would sum up the south coast in two words: sun and surf. But this region can't be so easily pigeonholed. Stretching all the way from Puerto López in the north to the Peruvian border in the south, it does indeed feature a long, sandy coastline. This draws a motley crew of international travelers, who head mostly to mellow hangouts such as Montañita and around the Parque Nacional Machalilla.

Combining industrial sprawl and the beachside resort of Salinas, the Santa Elena Peninsula is usually bypassed by foreign travelers on their way between Guayaquil and the Ruta del Sol. *Guayaquileños* pack the hotels and condominiums from mid-December through April, and sport fishermen and international yachties stop here too. During the low season, some of the coastal resorts feel like ghost towns – missing only a piece of scrub brush blowing in the wind.

But the south coast also includes Guayaquil: Ecuador's largest city, its commercial and business capital and, more importantly for travelers, an emerging destination. The rejuvenated waterfront, a far cry from the old *malecón* (waterfront) of concrete and shady characters, is more like Disneyworld these days: filled with children and families and couples succumbing to the universal romance of a bench, a river and piped-in salsa music.

South of Guayaquil is mostly banana country, with miles and miles of the green fruit – or *oro verde* (green gold), as it's referred to down here. The regional capital is Machala: while not especially appealing in its own right, there's a range of accommodations, it makes a good base for exploring nearby mountain towns, and it's a convenient stopover for those heading to Peru.

HIGHLIGHTS

- Get up close and personal with nesting boobies and other birdlife on **Isla de la Plata** (p305)
- Go off-road into the mountains anywhere along the **Ruta del Sol** (p303)
- Slow down and do some serious chilling at surf mecca **Montañita** (p311)
- Take a Sunday stroll along the **Malecón 2000** (p321), Guayaquil's amusement-park-like riverfront promenade
- Breathe in the cool air and spectacular views around **Zaruma** (p338)

- AVERAGE TEMP IN GUAYAQUIL: 26°C (79°F)
- RAINIEST MONTH IN GUAYAQUIL: MAR

Climate

The south coast is generally drier than the north coast, and the rainy season lasts only from January through April. During this time the coast is oppressively hot and humid, but it's also sunny, unlike the dry season from May through December, which is often overcast and pleasantly cool. During the dry season, visitors are often disappointed to find it's just a little too cool out for sunbathing. Ecuadorians visit the coast during the rainy season and in July and August.

Getting There & Away

Guayaquil is serviced by many direct international flights as well as frequent connections to Quito. All flights to the Galápagos Islands leave from here as well. By road from Quito, most travelers head first to Manta (about nine hours from the capital) or Puerto López (nearly 11 hours from the capital) and work slowly down the coast from there (although there are also plenty of direct buses to Guayaquil). Guayaquil is about five spectacular hours from Guaranda (in the central highlands) and less than four hours from Cuenca via the road through Parque Nacional Cajas.

Getting Around

You can get to most destinations around the south coast direct from Guayaquil. For spots along the Ruta del Sol, it's usually one easy bus transfer in Santa Elena or La Libertad. Direct minivan services also link Guayaquil with several of these towns. For smaller towns south of Guayaquil, Machala is the secondary transport hub. Roads almost everywhere are paved, however the highway between Guayaquil and Huaquillas at the Peruvian border is a narrow, two-lane patchwork of potholes, bumps and continual construction. Throw in heavily laden trucks, speeding buses, pickups that should have been decommissioned decades ago and a general lack of concern for road-safety rules and you have a nerve-shattering and potentially dangerous mix.

RUTA DEL SOL

The PR-approved title of the coastline stretching from the Parque Nacional Machalilla south to the Santa Elena Peninsula is somewhat misleading, in part because a thick foggy mist blankets the landscape during the *garúa* *(drizzly)* months. More importantly, the area's geography comprises more than just immaculate stretches of sand. It runs the gamut from an uninspiring and lifeless mix of dry scrub and cactus to lush mountain-covered cloud forests and offshore islands teeming with unique flora and fauna.

PARQUE NACIONAL MACHALILLA

☎ 05

Ecuador's only coastal national park is an Arcadian memento mori – a reminder of what much of the Central and South American Pacific coast once looked like. Now, having almost entirely disappeared, it's one of the most threatened tropical forests in the world. The park, created in 1979, preserves a small part of the country's rapidly vanishing coastal habitats, protecting about 50km of beach (less than 2% of Ecuador's coastline), some 40,000 hectares of tropical dry forest and cloud forest, and about 20,000 hectares of ocean (including offshore islands, of which Isla de la Plata is the most important).

The tropical dry forest found in much of the inland sectors of the park forms a strange and wonderful landscape of characteristically bottle-shaped trees with small crowns and heavy spines (a protection against herbivores). In the upper reaches of the park, humid cloud forest is encountered. Some of the most common species include the leguminous algarobo, which has green bark and is able to photosynthesize even when it loses its leaves. The fruits of the ceiba (kapok) tree yield a fiber that floats and doesn't get waterlogged. Before the advent of modern synthetics it was used in life jackets. Fig, laurel and palo santo trees are also commonly seen. Tall, spindly candelabra cacti are abundant on the hillsides, as is prickly pear.

Within this strange-looking forest is a variety of bird and animal life. Well over 200 species of bird have been recorded, including a range of coastal parrots, parrotlets and parakeets, as well seabirds such as frigate birds, pelicans and boobies – some of which nest on the offshore islands. Other animals include deer, squirrels, howler monkeys, anteaters and a variety of lizards, snakes and iguanas.

Most of the park's archaeological sites date from the Manta period, which began around

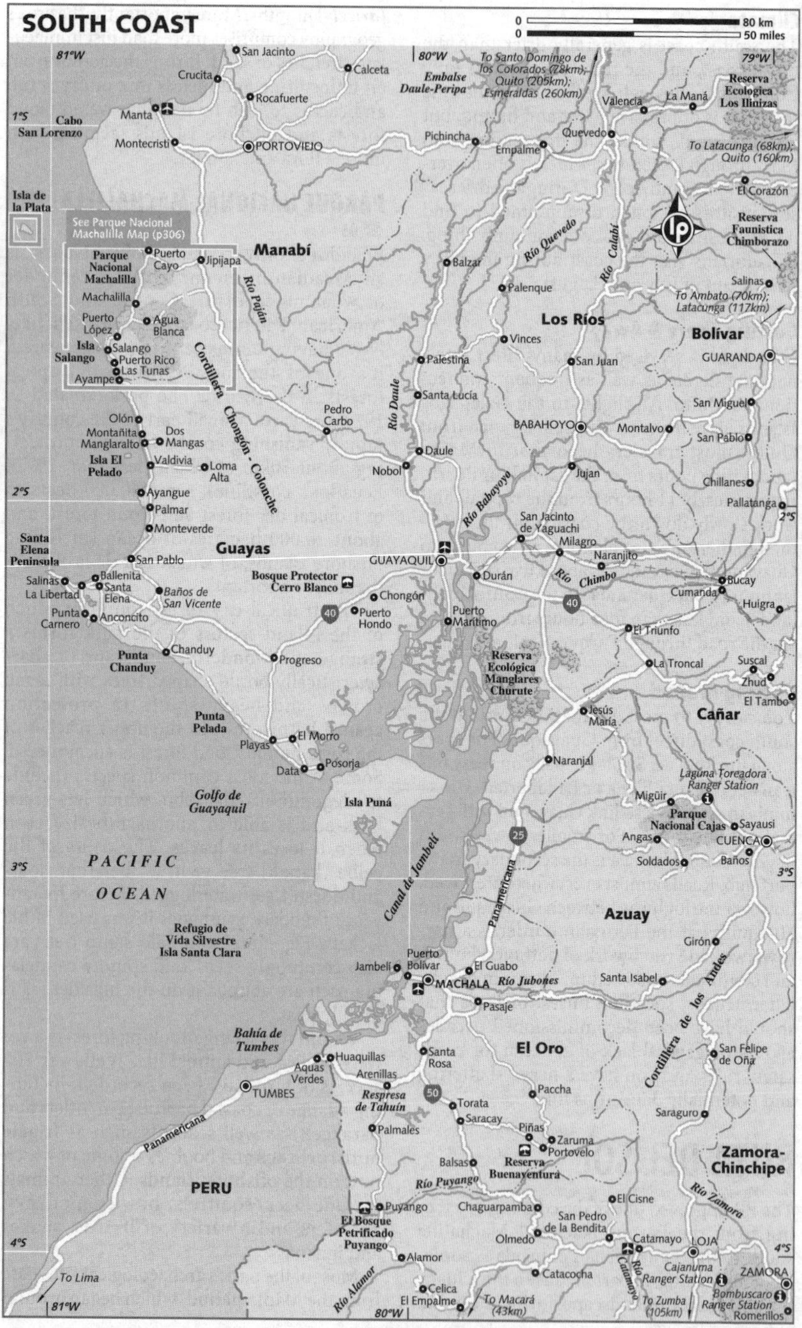
SOUTH COAST
0 80 km
0 50 miles
81°W
80°W
79°W
1°S
2°S
3°S
4°S
To Santo Domingo de los Colorados (78km); Quito (205km); Esmeraldas (260km)
To Latacunga (68km); Quito (160km)
To Ambato (70km); Latacunga (117km)
To Lima
To Macará (43km)
To Zumba (105km)
San Jacinto
Calceta
Crucita
Rocafuerte
Embalse Daule-Peripa
Manta
Cabo San Lorenzo
Montecristi
PORTOVIEJO
Pichincha
Empalme
Quevedo
Valencia
La Maná
Reserva Ecologica Los Ilinizas
El Corazón
Reserva Faunistica Chimborazo
Salinas
Isla de la Plata
See Parque Nacional Machalilla Map (p306)
Parque Nacional Machalilla
Puerto Cayo
Jipijapa
Machalilla
Puerto López
Agua Blanca
Isla Salango
Salango
Puerto Rico
Las Tunas
Ayampe
Manabí
Río Paján
Cordillera Chongón - Colonche
Balzar
Río Quevedo
Río Calabí
Palenque
Los Ríos
Vinces
Bolívar
GUARANDA
Palestina
San Juan
Santa Lucía
Río Daule
Pedro Carbo
BABAHOYO
Montalvo
San Miguel
San Pablo
Olón
Montañita
Manglaralto
Dos Mangas
Isla El Pelado
Valdivia
Loma Alta
Daule
Nobol
Jujan
Chillanes
Pallatanga
Ayangue
Palmar
Monteverde
Río Babahoyo
San Jacinto de Yaguachi
Milagro
Naranjito
Santa Elena Peninsula
San Pablo
Guayas
GUAYAQUIL
Durán
Río Chimbo
Bucay
Cumandá
Huigra
Salinas
La Libertad
Ballenita
Santa Elena
Baños de San Vicente
Bosque Protector Cerro Blanco
Chongón
Puerto Hondo
Puerto Marítimo
El Triunfo
Punta Carnero
Anconcito
40
Punta Chanduy
Chanduy
Progreso
Reserva Ecológica Manglares Churute
La Troncal
Suscal
Zhud
El Tambo
Jesús María
Cañar
Punta Pelada
Playas
El Morro
Data
Posorja
Naranjal
Golfo de Guayaquil
Isla Puná
Laguna Toreadora Ranger Station
Migüir
Parque Nacional Cajas
Sayausí
Angas
CUENCA
Soldados
Baños
25
PACIFIC OCEAN
Canal de Jambelí
Panamericana
Azuay
Refugio de Vida Silvestre Isla Santa Clara
Girón
Jambelí
Puerto Bolívar
MACHALA
El Guabo
Río Jubones
Santa Isabel
Pasaje
Cordillera de los Andes
Bahía de Tumbes
Huaquillas
Aguas Verdes
Santa Rosa
El Oro
San Felipe de Oña
Arenillas
TUMBES
Represa de Tahuín
50
Paccha
Torata
Saracay
Saraguro
Palmales
Piñas
Zaruma
Portovelo
Balsas
Reserva Buenaventura
Zamora-Chinchipe
Río Puyango
PERU
Puyango
El Bosque Petrificado Puyango
Chaguarpamba
El Cisne
Río Zamora
San Pedro de la Bendita
Olmedo
Catamayo
LOJA
Alamor
Catacocha
Río Catamayo
Cajanuma Ranger Station
ZAMORA
Celica
El Empalme
Río Alamor
Bombuscaro Ranger Station
Romerillos

AD 500 and lasted until the conquest. There are also remains of the much older Machalilla and Chorrera cultures, dating from about 800 BC to 500 BC, and the Salango culture (from 3000 BC). While important, none of the sites are particularly striking for the casual visitor.

The northern border of the park is marked by the somewhat desolate fishing village of Puerto Cayo. From the highway above town, it looks substantial enough, strung along the length of the shoreline. Upon closer inspection, especially at midday, it seems like a ghost town. If stopping for a break, head to **Restaurant Caprichos** (mains $3), a basic open-air eatery for heaping rice dishes, ceviches and grilled seafood. It's located between the beach and town square.

From December to May, it is sunny and uncomfortably hot, with frequent short rainstorms. From June to November, it is cooler and often overcast.

Information

The **park headquarters** (☎ 260-4170; 🕒 8am-noon & 2-5pm Mon-Fri) and a regional tourism office share a building in Puerto López. The park entrance fee of $20 covers any or all sectors of the park (including the islands) and is valid for five days. If you plan to visit only Isla de la Plata, the fee is $15; the mainland-only fee is $12. The fee is charged in all sectors of the park, so carry your ticket.

Sights & Activities

ISLA DE LA PLATA

Isla de la Plata (Silver Island) is a reasonably accurate facsimile of an island in the Galápagos. Only an hour or so by boat from Puerto López, this is not to be missed if you're traveling in the area. After passing through various private hands, including a businessman from Guayaquil who built a hotel (now the park office and the only facilities on the island) and an airstrip, the island was later incorporated into the national park. A good thing too, for the survival of the birdlife – fishermen used to club clumsy albatross until they dropped their day's catch.

The origin of the island's name is variously explained as an allusion to claims that Sir Francis Drake buried treasure here, or to the color of the guano-covered cliffs in the moonlight. Home to nesting colonies of **seabirds**, the island is a revelation for anyone who hasn't been to the Galápagos. A large number of blue-footed boobies reside here; frigate birds, red-footed boobies and pelicans are frequently recorded, as are a variety of gulls, terns and petrels. Albatross can be seen from April to October, dolphins pass by, and there's year-round snorkeling in the coral reefs around the island.

Only the muscular ballet of mating **humpback whales**, which abound in these waters between mid-June and early October (especially July and August), can compete with the island's natural wonders. Whale-watching is a booming business here, and despite the strict guidelines and legally enforced rules and etiquette, scientists are concerned with tourism's impact on the mating habits of these gentle beasts.

It's a steep climb from the boat landing to two loop hikes, one to the east and one to the west: the 3.5km **Sendero Punta Machete** and the 5km **Sendero Punta Escaleras**. Either way, the trail is rough and exposed, so good footwear and plenty of water are essential.

The only way to enjoy this 'poor person's Galápagos' is by taking a guided boat tour from Puerto López (see p307).

LOS FRAILES BEACH

Marked by dramatic headlands on either side, this truly breathtaking stretch of beach is worth the price of admission. Look for the turnoff about 10km north of Puerto López, just before the town of Machalilla. After purchasing or showing your ticket at the ranger station, it's another 3km along a dirt road to the beach (swimmers take caution, there are strong undertows). There's also a 4km nature trail that runs through the dry forest to two secluded beaches and lookouts – keep your eye out for blue-footed boobies.

AGUA BLANCA

A visit to this small indigenous community and its surrounding territory is a chance to escape tar-and-concrete modern Ecuador. Though the village of Agua Blanca itself is nothing more than a scattering of simple wood-and-bamboo dwellings, it's noteworthy for what's missing: no noise, no pollution, just fresh air and strong breezes. You'll find the turnoff, where you pay a $5 charge (which also covers museum admission and a guide) about 5.5km north of Puerto López on the right side of the road. From here it's another 6km down a dusty, bumpy road to the village. The **archaeological museum** (🕒 8am-6pm) is well worth

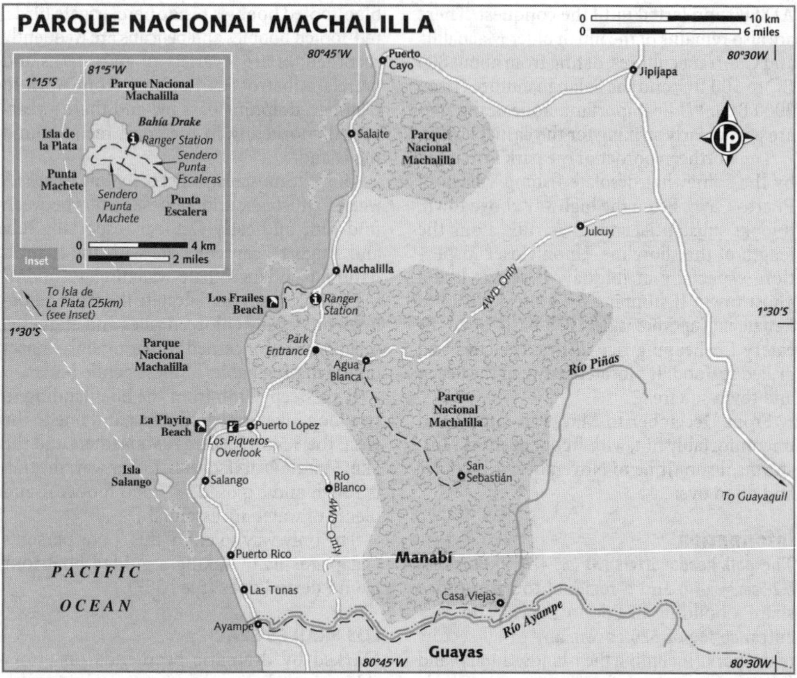

a visit; Spanish-speaking guides explain the significance of the artifacts, including well-preserved ceramics and funeral urns. The tour continues a short walk away at the **Manta site**, believed to have been an important political capital of the Manta people. Only the bases of the buildings can be seen, but there are thought to be approximately 400 buildings, some waiting for more complete excavation.

Then it's a fairly delightful hour-plus walk, across a bone-dry riverbed and through an equally arid tropical forest. You can stop along the way to soak in the **sulfur pool**, where the combination of hot water and therapeutic mud are the equal of any spa treatment. Close to the end of the walk there's a raised platform with outstanding views and plenty of interesting **bird** and **plant life** for knowledgeable guides to point out. Because of the merciless sun it's easy to succumb to heat exhaustion walking in the area, so bring a hat, sunscreen and water.

SAN SEBASTIÁN & JULCUY

This excellent four-hour hike or horseback ride lies to the southeast of Agua Blanca. The trail ascends a transition zone to humid remnant cloud forest at San Sebastián, about 600m above sea level. Horses ($10 to $15 per person) can be hired if you don't want to hike the 20km round-trip, and guides ($20) are mandatory. Contract one in Puerto López, Agua Blanca or San Sebastián. It's best to stay overnight, but camping or staying with local people are the only accommodations.

Another option is to continue through Agua Blanca up the Río Julcuy valley to the northeast. From Agua Blanca, it is a six- to seven-hour hike through the park, coming out at the village of Julcuy, just beyond the park boundary. From Julcuy, it's about another three hours to the main Jipijapa–Guayaquil road. Four-wheel drives may be able to pass this road in good weather, but it is mainly a horse trail. Some tour agencies in Puerto López and guides in Agua Blanca (the latter don't provide bicycles) can arrange full-day mountain-biking trips ($17 per person) from Jipijapa to Julcuy to Agua Blanca; only the aerobically fit should consider this option.

Another option to reaching the high forest in and around San Sebastián is to go via **El Pital** (☎ 269-042) community ecotourism project, 9km east of Puerto López. There's a small 'community lodge', a brick and thatch-roofed hut with four double rooms, and meals are available.

Sleeping

Camping is allowed in much of the park, and is most often done as part of an overnight tour booked through an agency in Puerto López. There's also a designated **campsite** (per person $5), nothing more than a fenced-off patch of land with bathroom facilities in the forest a few kilometers from Agua Blanca, a short walk from the sulfur pool. For camping and possible homestay opportunities in San Sebastián and Agua Blanca, inquire at the museum in the village; tents and sleeping bags are provided. Check with park authorities about the availability of water, particularly during the dry season (May to December).

Getting There & Away

At least every hour, buses run up and down the coast between Puerto López and Jipijapa (hippy-happa). You should have no difficulty in getting a bus to drop you off at the park entrance or finding one to pick you up when you're ready to leave. However, while there is the occasional truck from the main road to Agua Blanca, it can be a long, hot wait; walking the 5km is an option for the aerobically fit (bring water). The most sensible plan is to hire a taxi in Puerto López ($10 round-trip, includes a stop at Los Frailes).

Boat trips to Isla de la Plata are arranged through tour agencies in Puerto López (see right) or anywhere you are staying along the Ruta del Sol coast.

PUERTO LÓPEZ

☎ 05 / pop 14,000

There's little to distinguish this ramshackle town apart from a handful of hotels and tour agencies catering to foreigners. What it lacks in physical charm, it more than makes up for in its proximity to the wonders of the Parque Nacional Machalilla. During whale-watching season especially, tourists wander the long beach, the *malecón* and the dusty streets, transforming this otherwise quiet fishing village into a bustling and amiable base camp. In the wee morning hours – before tour groups escape for the day and the handful of sunbathers take up positions on the sand – fishermen gut their catch on the beach, and the air teems with frigate birds and vultures diving for scraps.

Information

A small medical clinic is north of town. The **tourism office** (Malecón Julio Izurieta; ⏰ 9am-2pm Mon-Fri) is on the *malecón,* next to the post office. **Banco del Pichincha** (cnr Machalilla & Córdova) changes traveler's checks and has an ATM – however, it has a very unreliable reputation so it's best to bring enough cash along. **Muyuyo Internet** (Córdova; ⏰ 8am-11pm) and **Cyber Junior** (Malecón Julio Izurieta; ⏰ 9am-9pm) both charge $1.25 per hour and also operate as call centers. Several drop-off machine-wash laundries catering to foreign travelers are along the *malecón,* including one next to Cyber Junior, and **Lavandería Burbujas** (Malecón Julio Izurieta; per load $3), just south of the intersection with Sucre.

Tours

Numerous agencies offer tours to Isla de la Plata and/or the mainland part of the park. Hiking, horseback-riding, mountain-biking and fishing trips are also offered. Some companies have English-, German- and French-speaking guides.

From June through September, whale-watching tours combined with visits to Isla de la Plata are popular ($35 to $40 plus the park-entry fee, which is $15 to $20; whale-watching only $25). During both July and August, good whale sightings are pretty much guaranteed, and in June and September sightings may be brief, distant or just of single animals. On Isla de la Plata groups have lunch, a guided hike and a brief opportunity to snorkel. The trip to the island takes well over an hour and can be rough, so take motion-sickness medication if necessary, and bring a rain jacket for the wind and spray.

Licensed companies all have boats with two outboard engines and are equipped with life jackets, radios and basic toilet facilities. Most are found along Córdova and Malecón Julio Izurieta; boats will sometimes have guests booked from different agencies. Bargain hunting for cheaper whale-watching trips on the street is discouraged since these fishing boats tend to be slower, smaller and lack bathrooms, life jackets, radios and other officially mandated equipment. If the park fee is not mentioned you will not be visiting the island.

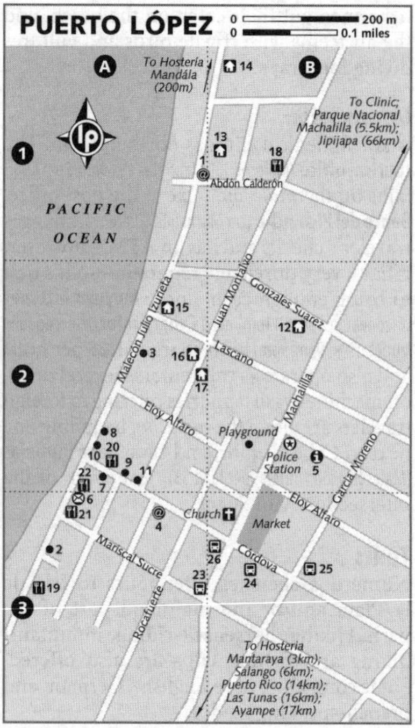

INFORMATION

Banco del Pichincha .... (see 26)
Cyber Junior **1** A1
Lavanderia Burbujas **2** A3
Machalilla Tours **3** A2
Muyuyo Internet **4** A3
Parque Nacional Machalilla Headquarters & Museum **5** B2
Post Office **6** A3
Tourism Office .... (see 6)

SIGHTS & ACTIVITIES

Bosque Marino .... (see 6)
Ecuador Amazing **7** A2
Exploramar Diving **8** A2
Mantaraya Tours **9** A2
Mares Dive Center **10** A2
Naturis **11** A2

SLEEPING

Hostal Maxima **12** B2
Hostería Itapoá **13** B1
Hosteria Playa Sur **14** B1
Hotel Pacífico **15** A2
Machalilla Hostal **16** A2
Sol Inn **17** A2

EATING

Bellitalia **18** B1
Café Ballena/The Whale Café **19** A3
Mayflower .... (see 22)
Patacón Pisa'o **20** A2
Picantería Rey Hojas **21** A3
Restaurant Carmita **22** A2
Restaurant Spondylus .... (see 8)

TRANSPORT

Cooperativa Transportes Jipijapa **23** A3
Manglaralto Buses .... (see 26)
Reina del Camino **24** B3
Taxis .... (see 26)
Trans Turismo Manta **25** B3
Transportes Carlos A Aray & Other Buses **26** B3

Outside of the whale-watching season, similar tours to the island (same price as above) are offered to see birds and sea lions, and you may well see dolphins too. Most of the operators will also arrange a variety of other local trips, such as fishing (June to January), visits to local beaches, and camping and/or horseback riding in the Agua Blanca and San Sebastián areas. It is usually cheaper to make your own way to Agua Blanca. The $5 entry to the area includes a museum guide and visit.

Bosque Marino (☎ 230-0004; Malecón Julio Izurieta; www.bosquemarino.com) Half-day fishing trips $300 for up to six persons.

Ecuador Amazing (☎ 230-0239; www.ecuadoramazing.com; Córdova)

Exploramar Diving (☎ 230-0123; www.exploradiving.com; Malecón Julio Izurieta)

Machalilla Tours (☎ 230-0234; machalillatours@yahoo.com; Malecón Julio Izurieta)

Mantaraya Tours (☎ 230-0233; Córdova at Juan Montalvo)

Mares Dive Center (☎ 230-0137, 09-990-0300; Malecón Julio Izurieta) Costs $95 for two dives.

Naturis (☎ 230-0218; General Córdova at Juan Montalvo)

Sleeping

Because most of the accommodation is located within a few blocks of the *malecón* it's easy to explore your options before booking. Reserve ahead during the busy whale-watching season, and during the coastal high season (January to April). Some hotels advertise hot water when in fact it's not available – it's best to verify if that's important to you.

BUDGET

Sol Inn (☎ 230-0248; hostal_solinn@hotmail.com; Juan Montalvo near Eloy Alfaro; r per person with shared/private bathroom $5/7) What the compact wood-and-bamboo rooms lack in size, they make up for in funky character at this mellow backpacker retreat. There's just enough space for front-porch hammocks, but there's more elbow room in the outdoor kitchen and living area. English and French are spoken.

Hostal Maxima (☎ 09-953-4282; www.hotelmaxima.org; Gonzáles Suarez near Machalilla; r per person with shared/private bathroom incl breakfast $6/10) This no-frills hotel looks a bit like a work site, but the concrete rooms are spacious and clean, and the owner is eager to please. The grassy courtyard has a lounge area with a TV and a DVD player for any guest craving entertainment.

Machalilla Hostal (☎ 230-0155; Juan Montalvo; r per person $7) Compared with the Sol Inn on the other side of the street, this hotel is strictly utilitarian. It does have a small central courtyard with a hammock and a plastic table or two, however the most flattering thing to remark about the concrete rooms is that the TVs are large.

Hosteria Playa Sur (☎ 864-4255; playasurpuertolopez@hotmail.com; Malecón Julio Izurieta; r per person $8) If you're not claustrophobic, these stand-alone cabañas at the northern end of the beach are worth considering. There is barely enough room to slide past the bed but each of these tidy wooden structures does have its own private bathroom with hot water, and there's little noise to disturb your sleep.

Hostería Itapoá (☎ 255-1569, 09-314-5894; itapoa_25@hotmail.com; Malecón Julio Izurieta; cabañas incl breakfast per person $9.50) A handful of thatch-roofed cabins tucked back in a lush courtyard, Itapoá is a friendly, family-run operation. Rooms are tidy and efficient, and breakfast is served in the raised wooden platform café out front along the *malecón*. A Jacuzzi and Turkish bath are available when functioning.

MIDRANGE

Hotel Pacífico (☎ 230-0133, 09-382-7061; www.hotelpacificoecuador.com; cnr Lascano & Malecón Julio Izurieta; s/d with fan $15/20, with air-con $30/40; ❄ 🏊) Maybe the largest, most modern hotel on the *malecón*, the Pacífico offers ordinary but uninspiring rooms; ask for one of the sea-facing ones with a balcony to feel like you're at the beach (although street noise can then be an issue). Its raison d'etre, however, is a pool set in a lovely and lush backyard garden.

our pick **Hostería Mandála** (☎ 230-0181, 09-951-3940; www.hosteriamandala.info; s/d/q cabin $24/39/73) Catering beautifully to the modern obsession with ecoconscious comfort, the Mandála is easily the nicest place to stay in town. Boasting a beachfront location north of the *malecón*, its entrance is marked by a few towering sculptures of whale tails decorated with peace signs. The room decor is decidedly more subdued: wood, bamboo and colorful textiles combine to make a charming, cozy hideaway. The cabins are scattered throughout a thick and lush flower garden. Out the front, you'll find a large, attractive lodge with a bar and a restaurant serving delectable breakfasts as well as Italian and seafood entrees.

Hosteria Mantaraya (☎ 244-8985; www.mantarayalodge.com; r from $80; 🏊) A Mediterranean villa transported to a hillside with views of Puerto López below, the Mantaraya is a surprising splash of pastel colors. Popular with groups or those with their own vehicles, it's one of the nicer places in which to base yourself in the area – the only downside is noise from downshifting trucks on the passing roadway. Vaulted archways and Spanish-style stucco are signatures of the property, and the light-filled rooms are charming – ask for a second-story one with balcony and views. A nice restaurant, a trellis-covered outdoor sitting area and a pool offer alternative lounging areas for a day off. It's a few kilometers north of Salango.

Eating

A handful of seafood restaurants line the *malecón* south of the intersection with Córdova. Carmita, Picantería Rey Hojas, Spondylus and Mayflower serve up comparable fresh fare (fish $3, lobster $10).

Café Ballena/The Whale Café (Malecón Julio Izurieta; mains $2-6; 🕑 noon-9pm, closed mid-Nov–Dec) For good veggies, pasta and pizzas, walk toward the southern end of the *malecón* to this American-owned café.

Patacon Pisa'o (Córdova; mains $3) Looking for a little variety in your *almuerzo* (set lunch)? Nothing more than a few small outdoor tables, it serves delicious Colombian specialties such as crepes, *arepas* (maize pancakes) and its namesake dish: large, thin, crisply fried plantains with your choice of meat topping. Good for breakfast, brewed coffee and an afternoon hang out.

Bellitalia (Juan Montalvo s/n; 🕑 from 6pm) Yummy Italian food that's served in romantic candlelight.

Getting There & Away

There have been reports of several armed robberies on long-distances buses in the area; if you want to be extra cautious, try to avoid nighttime journeys.

TO QUITO

Reina de Camino (☎ 230-0207; Córdova) has the fastest, most secure service to Quito, with 1st-class buses at 8am and 8pm ($12, 10 hours). Passengers can get off at Santo Domingo de los Colorados, but new passengers cannot board there. It doesn't stop for dinner either. Show up 20 minutes early for security checks.

Transportes Carlos Aray (☎ 230-0243; cnr Córdova & Machalilla) also has direct buses to Quito ($10, 11 hours) at 5am, 9am and 7pm. Alternatively, you can catch the bus to Portoviejo or Manta to make connections.

TO SOUTH COAST & GUAYAQUIL

Manglaralto (cnr Córdova & Machalilla) buses leave frequently for Montañita ($2.50, 1½ hours) and La Libertad ($4, three hours). Several other companies between Jipijapa and La Libertad stop at the corner of Córdova and Machalilla at least every hour during daylight hours; you can get off at any point you want along the coast.

The rickety, dilapidated-looking buses of Cooperativa Transportes Jipijapa have eight departures daily to Guayaquil ($4, 4½ hours) via Jipijapa. Another option is the crowded Jipijapa-bound Trans Turismo Manta service. Buses leave from the corner of Córdova behind the market; from here you can transfer to services for Guayaquil or other northbound destinations.

Getting Around

The whole town is walkable, but if you're feeling sluggish look for coati tricycles on the *malecón* or near the buses. The Asociación de Camioneros has cars and pickups in front of the church. The 24-hour service goes to Agua Blanca for $10 round-trip and to Los Frailes and Agua Blanca for $15.

SOUTH OF PUERTO LÓPEZ

Only 6km south of Puerto López is the sleepy little fishing town of **Salango**. You can hire fishing boats ($10 per person) to buzz the 2km out to **Isla Salango**, a haven for birdlife including blue-footed boobies, pelicans and frigate birds. In the town itself take a peek in the small archaeological **Museo Salango** (admission $1.50; 9am-6pm Mon-Fri). Most of the explanations are in Spanish; a gift shop offers crafts by local artisans. There are two good seafood restaurants in town: **El Delfín Mágico** (mains $4-6) and **El Pelicano** (☎ 09-185-1812; mains $4-6), within a block of one another near the central church. The latter can organize fishing, diving, snorkeling and camping trips to Isla Salango; ask for Ivo Gutiérrez.

The turnoff for the beachfront refuge **Hostería Piqueros Patas Azules** (☎ 04-278-0279; www.hosteriapiqueros.com; s/d from $29/42) is a few kilometers south of Salango. Another 2km or so past a large gatehouse, you come to a somewhat messy complex of a restaurant, a mini archaeological museum and garishly colored rooms perched on a small hill. The rooms themselves are simple and no better than many budget ones in town, however the broad, private stretch of sand right out your front door is more than adequate compensation.

The village of **Puerto Rico**, about 8km south of Salango, is on the traveler's roadmap solely because of the **Hostería Alandaluz** (☎ Guayaquil 04-278-0686, 02-406-670; www.alandaluzhosteria.com; camping $5, s $16-45, d $29-75, tr $40-96;), a sprawling, low-key ecoconscious resort that features composting, recycling and its own organic garden. A variety of accommodation types is scattered on both sides of the highway. The seaside ones, found at the end of paths snaking through the forest, are recommended, especially the charming wood cabins – besides an open-air shower and toilet, there's a separate semicircle-shaped living space–office attached to the bedroom. Swimmers should proceed with caution as there are strong currents. The restaurant, housed in a large open-air wooden pavilion and more creative than most, does superb seafood cooked with unique, locally grown fruits and veggies. All Parque Nacional Machalilla tours can be arranged here, as well as walking and cycling trips to **Cantalapiedra**, a property deep in the lush mountains of the Cordillera Chongón-Colonche east of Ayampe; there's also a zip-line and an organic farm.

Continuing south, you come to the beachside village of **Las Tunas**, which is immediately recognizable for the **Hosteria La Barquita** (☎ 04-278-0051, 09-369-8818; www.labarquita-ec.com; r per person from $24), whose whimsically designed restaurant-bar resembles a large wooden boat complete with portholes and thatch-roofed sails. The surrounding cabins, charming and cozy, are set amid a beautifully landscaped garden right on the beachfront. Puerto López tours, as well as horseback riding and trips to the Ayampe river, are available. Only a few meters away is **Hosteria La Perla** (☎ 04-278-0701, 09-210 2200; s/d incl breakfast $25/40), a haphazardly decorated, weathered beach house with several clean wood-floored cabañas.

At **Ayampe**, where the Río Ayampe empties into the ocean (the strong undertow here makes swimming difficult), the luxuriant green hills close in on the beach. Tucked back into one of these, surrounded by dense woods, is **Finca Punta Ayampe** (☎ 09-488-8615, 09-189-0982; www.fincapuntaayampe.com; r $14 per person), which feels like an end-of-the-road hideout. The high-ceilinged bamboo bedrooms are filled with light. Surfing, scubadiving, kayaking and bird-watching tours can be arranged here. Nearby, perched on a denuded hillside, is the less rustic **Hostería Almare** (☎ 04-278-0611/12; r per person low/high season $10/15, mains $5-7), which has an attractive cedar deck and central patio, and simple all-wood rooms. **Cabañas La Tortuga** (☎ 04-278-0613, 09-383-4825; www.latortuga.com.ec; s/d/tr $15/24/30), the only beachfront accommodation in Ayampe, has a collection of well-maintained thatch-roofed cabins. Kayaks and bikes can be rented here, and there's a restaurant, a bar and satellite TV. Its camping annex, **Tortuga Tent Camp** (per person $6), a row of fairly developed blue-canvas shelters, is just below Hostería Almare.

OLÓN

A few kilometers north of Montañita, before the province of Guayas ends and Manabí begins, is the coastal village of **Olón**. It has a long though not especially attractive beach, however the inland landscape is a dramatic departure from the dry scrubland further south. This lush cloud forest is part of the **Cordillera Chongon-Colonche**, climbing over a low coastal mountain range. Only 1% is officially protected by a statute in the Ecuadorian constitution and in practice by the local community. It's one of the few places in the world with a cloud forest and a beach in such close proximity; jaguars, howler monkeys and the endangered Great Green Macaw all reside here.

Taking advantage of this truly unique setting, with paths deep into the forest, are two hilltop resorts. Between Olón and Ayampe, in the highlands above the village of San José, is the magical **Samaí Retreat** (☎ 04-278-0167; www .sacred-journey.com; Km700; s/d $27/45; ☒ ☐). Owner Tania Tuttle and her husband, practitioners of alternative healing, meditation and yoga, have

created an idyllic oasis, combining a sophisticated aesthetic sensibility with rustic charm. A handful of cabañas are scattered throughout the property; room 2 has fantastic floor-to-ceiling windows with views all the way to the coast. There's a Jacuzzi, a pool and tasty vegetarian food. Wi-fi is available throughout.

Closer to Olón itself is the more generic **El Retiro Finca Hosteria** (☎ 09-910-4109; www.elretiro .com.ec; s/d $50/75; ☒ ☐), frequented by families, groups and those seeking standard hotel-style lodgings. There are nice views throughout the complex, whether from the rooms, the pool or the restaurant, however the scale and character of the development subtract somewhat from the beauty. A very short zip-line is available.

MONTAÑITA
☎ 04 / pop 1000

An all-pervasive laid-back ethos as much as good year-round surf draws a steady stream of cosmopolitan backpackers – as many South Americans as gringos – to the beachfront village of Montañita. The cheap digs and Rasta vibe mean some travelers put down temporary roots by taking up hair braiding and jewelry making or staffing their guesthouse's front desk. No *localismo* here, it's an easygoing surfing community willing to share its waves. Montañita is ideal for the kind of person who balks at the typical restaurant dress code: bare feet and no shirt are practically de rigueur.

The beach break is rideable most of the year (though it's best from December to May) but beginners should keep in mind that waves can get big, and riptides are common. Real surfers ride the wave at the north end of the beach at *la punta* (the point), a right that can reach 2m to 3m on good swells. An international surf competition is usually held around Carnaval. Most *hostales* (small and reasonably priced hotels) can arrange surfboard rentals ($10 full day) and lessons ($15 for two hours). Wet suits and bodyboards are also available.

Information
Banco de Guayaquil and Banco Bolivariano have ATMs in town. There's a handful of internet cafés charging $1.50 per hour, including **Montañita Express** (☾ 8am-midnight) and **Mis Cabinas Internet** (☾ 8am-midnight). Most hotels provide laundry services, and there are several stand-alone *lavanderías* (laundries) in town.

Sleeping

Noise is an issue and earplugs are recommended at many of the hotels in town during the high season. The partying is more subdued at other times of the year, but if you're interested in peace and quiet it makes sense to check out the places just outside of town.

Unless specified, the prices quoted here are for the high season (mid-December through April). Almost all hotels cut their rates significantly for the rest of the year, and discounts are available for extended stays.

Calle Principal is the main drag down to the beach. Most hotels in town are on the streets leading away from Calle Principal. Most have mosquito nets and sea breezes for ventilation; some places only have cold water.

IN TOWN

Tiki Limbo Backpackers Hostel (☎ 254-0607; www.tikilimbo.com; r per person from $5) Especially good for groups of three or four, Tiki Limbo outdoes its cheapie competitors in terms of style: the pastel-colored rooms have four-poster beds made of bamboo. The 2nd floor lounge area is a good place to crash or journal or play guitar. There's a good seafood and vegetarian restaurant attached.

Casa Blanca (☎ 218-2501; r per person $8) One of the anchors of the busiest intersection in town. Unlike some of the budget crypts, Casa Blanca is a good deal. The small bamboo rooms here come with private bathrooms with hot water and balconies with hammocks. Queen-size beds (which can be hard to find elsewhere) are available.

Hotel Hurvínek (☎ 08-454-5354; Calle 10 de Agosto; r per person $10) Escape from the dark and claustrophobic budget flophouses just on the other side of Calle Principal to this bright and sunny guesthouse. The spacious rooms are beautifully crafted, from the polished wood floors to the charmingly tiled bathrooms. To find the Hurvínek, make your first left after turning into town from the highway; it's located halfway down on the right.

Hostal Las Palmeras (☎ 08-541-9938; dlgpalmeras@yahoo.com; r per person $15) Compared to many of the buildings in town, this sensible option away from the party strip looks permanent and well-constructed (which it is, of course). Owned and operated by an Ecuadorian-American from New York City, the three-story Las Palmeras offers clean and basic modern rooms – many with bunk beds good for groups – if at something of a loss of atmosphere. Coming from the highway, make the second and final left; the hotel is located halfway down this beachfront road on the right.

Charo Hostal (☎ 206-0044; www.charoshostal.com; r per person $15; ⊠ ⊠) Lacking the laid-back rustic vibe of other hotels in town, Charo tends to attract a somewhat older clientele. While the majority of the rooms are unfortunately evocative of a city hotel – wall-mounted TV, concrete, antiseptic furnishings – Charo can be recommended for its beachfront location and courtyard pool and Jacuzzi.

Other recommended crash pads are **Montezuma** (☎ 09-718-2965; r $6) and **Surfing Inn Hostal** (☎ 09-490-4860; www.surfinginn@yahoo.com). The longstanding Pakoloro was under renovation at the time of research.

OUT OF TOWN

All of these places, with the exception of Kamala Hostería, are on or near the beach only a short walk north of town.

Kamala Hostería (☎ 242-3754; dm per person $5, cabañas $20-40; ⊠ ⊠) South of Montañita, closer to the town of Manglaralto, is this beachside hodgepodge of cabañas owned, staffed and frequented by backpackers. When not booked by big groups or during monthly full-moon parties, it's a low-key alternative that offers loads of empty beachfront. Accommodations are fairly ragged and meals are generally only offered when enough guests make it worthwhile. Kayak rental ($5 per hour), horseback riding ($15 per hour) and other trips are available.

Hostal Kundalini (☎ 09-954-1745; www.hostalkundalini.com; cabañas per person $10) Just on the other side of the small creek that marks the northern border of town, the Kundalini nevertheless feels very far away from the party. Certainly a good thing if you're looking for some low-key quiet – and it's immediately in front of one of the surf breaks. It's nothing more than a thatch-roofed building set out on a lawn with beachfront access. Four small rooms have bamboo walls and furniture, and private hammocks.

Paradise South (☎ 09-787-8925; r $12-30; ⊠) Another good option to lay low, this place just north of the river on the way to the point has a large, well-kept central lawn surrounded by several low-slung buildings. The thatch-roofed stone cottages sporting adobe walls and ceramic tiled floors are worth the extra bucks; more-ordinary rooms meant for groups feature several bunk beds.

Casa del Sol (☎ 264-8287; amada@casasol.com; r per person incl breakfast $20) Directly across from Hanga-Roa, the three-story, palm-roofed Casa del Sol has something of a Swiss ski chalet in its genes. No bamboo here – the rooms done in stone, stucco and red-tile floors are extremely cozy and stay cool even without a fan. There's a bar and restaurant out front.

Hanga-Roa Cabanas (☎ 235-2955; www.montanita.com/hangaroa; r per person $20) One of the few places directly on the beach, Hanga-Roa unfortunately doesn't fully exploit its position. A pleasant concrete patio, great for sunset drinks, hangs over the sand, however the four rooms themselves are in a low-slung building extending out to the road. They're good-sized and colorful, with bamboo walls and modern bathrooms. The wood-and-bamboo house next door with a 2nd-floor balcony is available for rent.

Eating

Almost every street-side space has been converted into an informal restaurant. Spanish and English menus cater to foreigners' taste buds, serving everything from pizzas to empanadas and bubbling *cazuelas* (seafood stews). Those serving Ecuadorians are more likely to offer economical *almuerzos* ($2.50) and *meriendas* (set dinners). Many double as game rooms during the day and bars at night.

A prime people-watching spot is **Karukera** (mains $4), a small, stylish café serving pastas, sandwiches, crepes, ice cream ($2), cake and coffee. **Funky Monkey** (mains $4), a mellow and mod popular restaurant and bar, is just across the street. For a few Israeli-inspired dishes, large breakfasts and grilled meats and seafood, try **Café Hola Ola** (mains $4). Enormous seafood and chicken empanadas, as well as omelets and ceviches are on the menu at **Tiburón Restaurant** (Calle Principal; mains $4.50). Toward the end of Calle Principal is one of the nicest restaurants, the 2nd-floor **Machu Picchu** (mains $3-7), which has an eclectic menu and excellent juice shakes and cocktails. Down a side street towards the beach is **Marea** (mains $6), the place for brick-oven pizza.

Drinking & Entertainment

Several wooden cabañas operating as bars are set up on the north end of the town beach, right in front of a small pond. The side street that ends at this part of the beach is lined with carts doling out inexpensive mixed drinks ($2), beers and shakes until late every night. Also on this street is the Caño Grill, an open-air bar with live music and DJs most weekend nights.

Otherwise, drinks can be had at many of the restaurants.

Getting There & Away

CLP buses pass by Montañita on their way south to Guayaquil ($5.50, 3½ hours; Tuesday through Thursday at 5:15am, 1:15pm and 5pm; Friday through Monday at 4:15am, 5:15am, 10:15am, 1:15pm, 3pm and 5pm). These are more comfortable than other buses that stop on their way to Santa Elena ($1.50, two hours), La Libertad or north to Puerto López ($1.50, one hour). These depart every 15 minutes or so.

Roca Tour (☎ 221-1611; ramonrocatour@hotmail.com) has minivans that travel to and from Guayaquil ($10).

SANTA ELENA PENINSULA TO GUAYAQUIL

The area around La Libertad and Santa Elena toward the end of the peninsula is a dusty urban zone. East of Santa Elena Peninsula, the landscape seems fit for a cowboy. It becomes increasingly dry and scrubby, and the ceiba trees give way to 5m-high candelabra cacti. To the south along the coast, the resorts draw *guayaquileños* but few foreigners, since the beachfronts – primarily Salinas and to a lesser extent Playas – are backed by concrete and buildings, and outside of the water itself the towns hold little appeal.

LA LIBERTAD & SANTA ELENA

☎ 04

The road forks at Santa Elena, where you can head west to La Libertad, the largest town on the peninsula and a noisy, unattractive place with a mainly rubble beach. Santa Elena has an oil refinery, a radio station and the archaeological museum **Los Amantes de Sumpa** (☎ 09-783-2081; admission $1; 9am-1:30pm & 2:30-5pm Mon-Tue & Thu-Fri). Located a couple of blocks from the main road on the west side of town, the

DETOUR FROM THE SUN

Most often visited as a side trip from Montañita a few kilometers away, the inland village of **Dos Mangas** is a starting point for walks or horseback rides further into the Cordillera Chongon-Colonche – coastal hills reaching an elevation of 834m and covered by tropical humid forest. Tagua carvings and *paja toquilla* (toquilla straw) crafts can be purchased in the village.

Travelers have the chance to visit remote coastal villages and stay overnight with local families for a nominal fee that also includes meals, guides and mules. The villages are usually an easy day's walk or horse ride from Manglaralto and each other. Overnight tours can be arranged for bird-watching and visiting remote waterfalls and other natural attractions.

Guides and horses can be hired at the Centro de Información Sendero Las Cascadas, a small kiosk in the village. The friendly guides speak Spanish only, and will take you on a four- to five-hour hike through the forest to an elevation of 60m and to the 80m **waterfalls** (these dry up in the dry season). They charge $10 for up to three people and an extra $3 per person for horses, and lunch can be arranged in local homes. The park entrance fee is $1.

Trucks to Dos Mangas ($0.25, 15 minutes) leave the highway from Manglaralto every hour or so. Taxis from Montañita are more convenient and only $1.

A 40-minute, 17km bus ride from the coastal village of Valdivia will bring you to **Loma Alta** (☎ in the USA 212-279-7813; www.pansite.org; entrance $10), a community-protected, 2428-hectare cloud forest (for overnight visits, call several days in advance for planning and coordination). The ride passes through the villages of Sinchal and Barcelona before a final 10km stretch over a rough road leading to the forest. This watershed ecopreserve has howler monkeys and more than 200 species of bird, and is ideal for hiking or taking horses or mules the four to six hours to its simple cabins and camp sites. With a guide, you can also hike from Loma Alta to the village of El Suspiro.

museum displays several 8000-year-old skeletons, including two embracing as *amantes* (lovers) in the position they were found.

On the outskirts of Ballenita, just north of Santa Elena, is the charmingly idiosyncratic **Hostería Farallón Dillon** (☎ 295-3611; www.farallondillon.com; s/d $35/60;), a more interesting and even convenient alternative to the conventional hotels in Salinas if you're passing through. A whitewashed complex perched on a cliff with views to the horizon, from here it's possible to see migrating whales from June to September. Appropriately enough for a hotel with its own extensive maritime museum, the ruling aesthetic is eclectic nautical – from the trippy restaurant to the all-wood rooms, seafaring is the name of the game. At the very least it's worth stopping here for a meal or a drink.

Getting There & Away

La Libertad is the center of bus services on the peninsula, but if you're not headed to Salinas it's easier to simply be let off in Santa Elena, bypassing La Libertad, and make the transfer to another bus heading either north along the Ruta del Sol or east to Guayaquil.

Frequent buses to Salinas run all day from Calle 8 and Avenida 2 in La Libertad. A taxi between the two costs about $2. To get to Santa Elena from La Libertad, flag down one of the minibuses that run frequently along 9 de Octubre.

TO GUAYAQUIL

To get to Guayaquil ($3, 2½ hours, every 15 minutes), you can take buses with either **Cooperativa Libertad Peninsular** (CLP; cnr 9 de Octubre & Guerro Barreiro) or **Cooperativa Intercantonal Costa Azul** (CICA; 9 de Octubre & Diagonal 2), opposite the Residencial Turis Palm in La Libertad. The CLP bus terminal in Salinas is at Calle 7, behind the water park at the western end of the *malecón;* if you pick up the bus here keep in mind that it will make a long stop in La Libertad for more passengers. Buses coming from Guayaquil carry on to Salinas, entering town along the *malecón* and continuing to the naval base, where they turn around and head back along Enríquez to La Libertad ($0.25, 20 minutes). You can ask the driver to let you off anywhere along the way.

A more convenient option is **Turismo Ruta del Sol** (☎ 277-0358), which runs minivans between Salinas and Guayaquil ($10) every hour between 6am and 8pm. Its office is attached to the Hotel Calypso I on the *malecón* in Salinas.

Also in La Libertad, Transportes San Agustín has buses to Chanduy to the east of the peninsula.

TO THE NORTH

To continue further north to destinations along the Ruta del Sol such as Montañita ($1.50, two hours) and Puerto López ($4, three hours), catch a CITUP, Cooperativa Manglaralto or CITM bus in La Libertad at a terminal near the market. Note that buses may be booked out in advance during weekends in the high season. These buses also service other coastal villages to the north, including Ballenita, Valdivia, Ayangue and Palmar.

Trans Esmeraldas has three buses daily from La Libertad for Quito ($8, 10 to 12 hours, 7:30pm, 8:30pm and 9:30pm); the 8:30pm trip is nonstop and costs $9.

SALINAS

☎ 04 / pop 31,000

From afar Salinas looks like Miami beach, a row of tall white condominiums fronting a pale sandy expanse filled with sun worshippers, and yachts docked nearby. Up close it's not so glamorous, especially since only a block behind the beach the streets look more down-and-out than like a playground for wealthy Ecuadorians. Nevertheless, Salinas is the biggest resort town on the south coast, and is the most westerly town on the Ecuadorian mainland.

Salinas is overpriced and crowded during the high season (mid-December through April), when international yachts dock at the yacht club on the west end of the waterfront. The water is warmest for swimming from January to March. In July and August, Salinas is overcast and dreary and, although the sunbathing is lousy during this time, whale- and bird-watching is fairly good. During Carnaval (in February), the place is completely full.

Orientation

Upon entering Salinas, before reaching the beach, you pass through blocks and blocks of blighted semi-industrial landscape. The resort itself stretches for several kilometers along the beachfront, the more visited and popular part where most of the hotels are located is fronted by a *malecón* with restaurants and bars. On one side it ends at the large Barcelo Colón hotel; on the other is the town plaza and church. West of here is an equally nice sandy stretch, though the apartment buildings are directly on the beach. At the far western end, there's a water park (open in high season) right behind the *malecón*. Most locals go by landmarks rather than street names.

Information

Banco de Guayaquil, Banco Bolivariano and Banco Pinchincha all have ATMs and are located along the *malecón*.

Camara de Turismo (☎ 09-623-6725; www.municipiodesalinas.gov.ec; Enríquez Gallo, btwn Calles 30 & 36; 🕑 8am-5pm Mon-Fri, to 2pm Sat) Only open during high season.

Capitaña del Puerto (☎ 277-2720; Malecón) Where to go if arriving by private boat or looking to sign on with one as a crew member; next to the Hotel Calypso.

Cybermar (Calle Fidon Tohala Reyes; per hr $1; 🕑 9.30am-10pm) The only internet just off the *malecón*.

Lavenderia de Todtito (Calle Ruminahui) Around the corner from Hostal Francisco II; per pound $0.45.

Sights & Activities

Beginning about 13km offshore from Salinas, the continental shelf drops from 400m to over 3000m (about 40km offshore), so a short, one-hour sail can take you into really deep water for excellent **sportfishing**. Swordfish, sailfish, tuna, dorado and black marlin call these waters home. **Pesca Tours** (☎ 277-2391, in Guayaquil 244 3365; www.pescatours.com.ec; Malecón), run by Ben Hasse of the Oystercatcher Bar and pioneer of whale-watching in the area, charters boats for about $350 a day (6am to 4:30pm). Boats take up to six anglers and include a captain, two crew members and all fishing gear, but you have to provide your own lunch and drinks. The best season (for marlin, dorado and wahoo) is September to December. **Avista Travel** (☎ 277-0331), on the *malecón*, books similar tours.

Bird-watchers need to seek out the **Oystercatcher Bar** (☎ 277-8329; bhaase@ecua.net.ec; Enríque Gallo), between Calle 47 and Calle 50. The owner, Ben Haase, knows more about coastal birds than anyone in the area and is permitted to lead tours (group of eight $30) to the private Ecuasal lakes by the Salinas salt factory, where 120 species of bird have been recorded. The bar, which has a small whale museum and a 10m humpback-whale skeleton out the back, is an equally good place to set up **whale-watching** trips (June through October only).

Along the *malecón* near Guayas is the **Museo Naval y Arqueológico Salinas Siglo XXI** (admission $2; 10am-6pm), with well-organized exhibits displaying seagoing artifacts and figurines and ceramics from the Valdivía period.

Sleeping

Accommodations aren't geared towards foreign travelers looking for a laid-back beach getaway. Prices quoted here are for the high season – they often drop 20% to 30% from May to mid-December and are higher during Easter week, Christmas, New Year and Carnaval.

Hotel Marvento (277-0975; Guayas & Enríquez Gallo; www.hotelmarvento.com; r per person incl breakfast $20;) If sea views aren't a priority, the recently built Marvento, only a block from the *malecón*, is excellent value. Everything from the polished marbled floors to the rustic wooden furniture is in mint condition. The rooftop has a small pool, there's a good restaurant attached, and wi-fi is available throughout.

El Carruaje (277-4282; Malecón 517; r from $25;) Sea views aside, the rooms at this *malecón* hotel could use a makeover. Some are weirdly designed and have oversized bathrooms, others mix and match furniture styles. There is a café and a rooftop bar attached.

Hotel Francisco I (277-4106; Enríquez Gallo & Rumiñahui; s/d $25/35;) Another good option also a block off the *malecón*, Francisco's large rooms are aging but clean, although some air-cons supply as much noise as cold air. Rooms are tucked back in a concrete building off the street, and a small pool occupies the courtyard. The entrance faces the Mi Comiserato supermarket.

Hotel Francisco II (277-3751; Malecón 723; s/d $25/35;) On the *malecón* between Calle 17 and 19. Slightly more modern rooms than its sister hotel; seafront rooms are worth the extra cost (from $35).

Barceló Colón Miramar (277-1610; www.barcelo.com; Malecón; s/d from $125/160;) The largest and most luxurious hotel in town. It boasts international-standard facilities: a pool, a Jacuzzi, a gym, a spa and tennis courts, plus three restaurants, including a generic Japanese place, and several bars and lounges. Discount all-inclusive deals available in low season.

Eating & Drinking

Most of the restaurants are located either on the *malecón* or a block or two away. Many, however, may be closed or have limited hours during the low season. There's a half-dozen or so similar seafood places with tables spilling onto the street on the *malecón* toward the western end. Cevichelandia, the nickname for a highly recommended series of cheap seafood stalls at the corner of Calle 17 and Enríquez, are mainly open for lunch. The bars and discos on the *malecón* come alive during high-season weekends; it's almost comatose during the low season.

The best pizza on the *malecón* is **La Bella Italia** (277-1361; mains $4), which has a wood-burning oven; seafood is served here as well. Between the Banco del Pichincha and Calypso Hotel is the trellis-covered **Cafeteria del Sol** (mains $5; 7am-midnight), with everything from burritos ($4) to seafood paella ($13). One of the nicer places to eat, also with a similarly wide-ranging menu, is the **Amazon Restaurant** (277-3671; Malecón & 24 de Mayo; mains $5) next to the Banco de Guayaquil; it also has a nice rooftop bar.

Getting There & Away

See p314 for transport information.

PLAYAS

04 / pop 27,000

It's something of a relief to come upon Playas (called General Villamil on some maps), even when it reveals itself to be crumbling and dusty like the absolutely parched and desiccated landscape you pass through upon approach. But weekending *guayaquileños* don't come here looking for urban sophistication; they come for the long, broad and relatively proximate expanse of beach. There's some good **surfing** in the area – the best place for information is **Playas Club Surf** (cnr Paquisha & Avenida 7), based at Restaurant Jalisco de Doña Elvita (opposite).

Playas is still an active fishing village: a handful of the old balsa rafts used a generation ago, nothing more than three logs tied together with a sail attached (similar to those used before the Spanish conquest) can be seen unloading their catch at the west end of the beach. Several impressive-looking condominiums tower above; however up close, like many of the buildings in town, they appear to be mere empty shells.

The town is busy from December to April but quiet at other times. On an overcast midweek day in the low season it can feel downright gloomy.

Information

Banco de Guayaquil and Banco Bolivariano are on the central plaza, and have ATMs; the former has a larger branch at Avenida Guayaquil at Paquisha. **Cyber Claudia.com** (9am-8:30pm) and **Cyber Playas** (9am-1am), internet cafés and call centers, are both only a few blocks from the plaza.

Sleeping

En route to Data, southeast of the center, are several quiet places near the beach that tend to fill up and overcharge on high-season weekends. They're usually empty midweek when they can feel forlorn.

Hostería Los Patios (☎ 276-1115; hosterialospatios@gmail.com; r per person $15) This friendly complex just off the beach does come with a small pool and lounge area in the back, however the basic, mostly concrete rooms don't measure up. There's a restaurant as well.

Hotel Las Redes (☎ 276-0222; Roldos Aguilera; r with fan/air-con from $20/25) The rooms at this low-slung, horseshoe-shaped complex could use an update – some of the walls are adorned with posters of '80s supermodels and movie stars. A bunch of hammocks hang in the concrete central courtyard.

Hotel Nevada (☎ 276-0759; www.hotelnevadaplayas.com; Paquisha; s/d $20/30) Only two blocks from the beach, the Nevada has comfortable rooms with chintzy decor and bath towels the size and thickness of a dishrag. Spacious family rooms, good for up to six, are in the new building attached. The little rooftop pool, no larger than a compact car, is sometimes filled with water; at least there is a hammock and good views of the city.

Hotel Arena Caliente (☎ 276-1580; www.hotel-arenacaliente.com; Paquisha; s/d $25/35) Across the street from the Nevada, the Arena Caliente is a small step up in quality. The tiled rooms are larger, as are the TVs, and the linens are certainly better, but the real added value is the nice courtyard swimming pool and lounge area. The ground-floor restaurant is good for breakfast and the standard *almuerzo*.

Hotel Ana (☎ 276-1770; www.hotelanaplayas.com; r $28) One of the last hotels you come to on the way to Data, this is probably also the most pleasant. Look for the faux-red-brick building along the beachfront. There's a small plunge pool in the front, good enough for not much more than a toe in the water.

Eating & Drinking

It's *comedore* (cheap restauran around the intersection of Roldos Agu and Paquisha (next to and across the street from Hotel Arena Caliente and Hotel Nevada). They have piles of oysters and crabs on display and do a variety of ceviches, grilled fish and meat and rice dishes; a few serve thick and sizzling shrimp, calamari or fish *cazuelas*. For a slightly more upscale version, at least as far as seating and decor go, try **Las Velas** (Paquisha; mains $6), just down the street.

There is a handful of *comedores* along the beach, where staff compete for your patronage by waving menus and shouting seafood specials upon your approach.

Empanadas de Playas (Roldos Aguilera) and **Empanadas Chilenos** (Roldos Aguilera) are no-frills restaurants with plastic tables, serving cheap chicken and meat empanadas (each $0.70). On Avenida Aguilera just before Chilenos are two informal *parrilladas* (steak houses) serving inexpensive chicken and meat dishes.

Restaurant Jalisco de Doña Elvita (cnr Paquisha & Av 7; mains $3; 8am-5pm), a local institution, has been serving cheap *almuerzos* and seafood plates for some 40 years.

In high season, *discotecas* (nightclubs) are open nightly, but only on weekends during low season. Most are fairly ad-hoc affairs near the central plaza. Three similar dives are Norman Café, Vanessa Bar and El Pescador.

Getting There & Away

Transportes Villamil (☎ 276-0190; Mendez Gilbert) and **Transportes Posorja** (☎ 214-0284) have buses to Guayaquil ($2.50, two hours, 97km); Villamil is a much better choice coming from Guayaquil since it goes direct rather than passing through Posorja. Buses leave every 15 minutes with either company from 4am until 8pm. **Transportes 9 de Marzo** (Guayaquil at Paquisha) has frequent buses to Posorja ($0.50, 30 minutes) during the day.

To get to Santa Elena and then further north along the Ruta del Sol, go to Progreso ($0.50, 25 minutes) on any Guayaquil-bound bus and change there. However, the buses that you may catch in Progreso for Santa Elena are often full upon leaving Guayaquil during the holidays.

On Sunday afternoons in the high season (December to April), everybody is returning to Guayaquil. The road becomes a one-way bus-fest and few (if any) vehicles can travel south into Playas.

…O BLANCO

…il, this is one of … forests left in the …s, pumas, monkeys, …ng its wildlife. More …ncluding the rare Great …serve's symbol), which is cons… endangered – call the 6078-hectare C…co home. There are stands of dry forest wi… uge ceiba trees and more than 100 other tree species, as well as views of coastal mangrove forests in the distance. Several trails take you into this area of rolling coastal hills.

This is a private **reserve** (adult/child $4/3; ⌚ 9am-4pm Sat & Sun, weekdays by reservation) owned by construction conglomerate Holcim Ecuador SA and administered by **Fundación Pro-Bosque** (☎ 04-287-4946; www.bosquecerroblanco.com). There's an organic farm, an education center with exhibits on the local ecology and birdlife in Spanish, and a wildlife **rescue center** where endangered species are cared for, including a large aviary for several Guayaquil macaws. Spanish-speaking guides for one of the nature-trail hikes (two to four hours) are available for $9 to $12 per group (up to eight).

From January to May there's plenty of water and the plants are green, but there are lots of mosquitoes so bring repellent. From June to December (the dry season) the trees flower and it's easier to see wildlife since the animals concentrate in the remaining wet areas. Early morning and late afternoon are, as always, the best times to see wildlife. The visitors center sells a bird list and booklets, and dispenses information and trail maps.

Just west of Cerro Blanco, on the south side of the Guayaquil–Salinas highway near the small community of Puerto Hondo, are the **Puerto Hondo Mangroves**. Charged with the protection of this threatened environment is the **Club Ecológico Puerto Hondo** (⌚ 9am-4pm Sat & Sun, weekdays by reservation), which arranges pleasant canoe rides ($7) through the area; dozens of bird species can be seen. Contact Fundación Pro-Bosque for more information.

Sleeping

Cerro Blanco has a visitors center and **camping ground** (3-person tent rental $8), with the charge for camping included in the reserve admission price. The ground features barbecues, bathrooms and running water (even showers), while one cabin, called the ecolodge – basically a large thatch-roofed hut with two basic rooms and a shower and bathroom – is also available, as is spotty, solar-powered electricity. Back-country camping may be permitted. For any of these options, advance reservations are always recommended. Contact Fundación Pro-Bosque, which has a reservation form on its website, or otherwise through the director, **Eric Horstman** (☎ 04-287-4946; vonhorst@ecua.net.ec), who speaks English.

Getting There & Away

To get to Cerro Blanco and Puerto Hondo, take a Cooperativa de Transportes Chongón bus from the corner of 10 de Agosto and García Moreno in downtown Guayaquil, or hop on any Playas- or Salinas-bound bus from the central bus terminal in the northern suburbs. Ask to be dropped off at the park entrance at Km16. Get off before the cement factory; you'll see a sign. A taxi will cost about $7 to $10.

From the reserve entrance, it is about a 10-minute walk to the visitors center and camping area.

GUAYAQUIL

☎ 04 / pop 2.16 million

A far cry from its unsavory reputation of yesteryear, Guayaquil is not only the beating commercial heart of the country but a vibrant sprawling city growing ever more confident. A half-dozen or more high rises give it a big-city profile and several hillsides are engulfed by shantytowns, but it's the *malecón* along the Río Guayas, the city's riverfront town square–cum-eatery-cum-playground, which defines the city's identity. The picturesque barrio of Las Peñas, which perches over the river, anchors the city both geographically and historically, while the principal downtown thoroughfare Avenida 9 de Octubre funnels office workers, residents and shoppers into one hybrid stream. Amid revitalized squares, parks and massive urban renewal projects, the city has a growing theater, film and arts scene and lively bars, fuelled in part by several large universities.

Note that all flights to the Galápagos Islands either stop at or originate in Guayaquil, so the city is the next best place after Quito to set up a trip.

HISTORY

Popular legend has it that Guayaquil's name comes from Guayas, the great Puna chief who fought bravely against the Incas and later the Spanish, and his wife, Quill, whom he is said to have killed rather than allow her to be captured by the conquistadors, before drowning himself. Several historians claim the city's name actually comes from the words *hua* (land), *illa* (beautiful prairie) and Quilca, one of Río Guyas' tributaries, where the Quilca tribe lived until being wiped out in the 17th century. Thus Guayaquil is literally 'the land like a beautiful prairie on the land of the Quilcas.'

A settlement was first established in the area around 1534, which moved to its permanent home of the Santa Ana Hill in 1547. The city was an important port and ship-building center for the Spanish, but it was plagued by pirate attacks and several devastating fires, including one in 1896 – known as the Great Fire – in which huge parts of the city were simply burnt to the ground. Guayaquil achieved its independence from the Spaniards on October 9, 1820, and was an independent province until Simón Bolívar annexed it as part of Gran Colombia in 1822. When Bolívar's experiment failed in 1830, Guayaquil became part of the newly formed republic of Ecuador.

ORIENTATION

Most travelers stay in the center of town, which is organized in a gridlike fashion on the west bank of Río Guayas. Most of the streets are known interchangeably by a number or proper name – the latter often changes depending on how far north or south one goes. The main east–west street is Avenida 9 de Octubre, which runs from the Estero Salado (a brackish estuary bordering the west side of the center) to La Rotonda (the famous statue of liberators Simón Bolívar and José de San Martín) on the Río Guayas. La Rotonda marks the halfway point of the Malecón 2000, which stretches along the bank of the Río Guayas from the Mercado Sur (near the diagonal Blvd Olmedo) at its southern tip to Las Peñas and the hill of Cerro Santa Ana to the north.

The airport is about 5.5km north of the center and the bus terminal is about 2km north of the airport entrance. The suburb of Urdesa, which is frequently visited for its restaurants and nightlife, is about 4km northwest of downtown and 1.5km west of the airport. The city sprawls in other directions including across the river, but most of these areas are residential or industrial and of little interest to the traveler.

INFORMATION

Bookstores

The best selection of books, both in Spanish and English, are in the Mr Books shops in the Mall del Sol (Map p324) and San Marino mall (Map p324) in the northern suburbs. The few downtown, such as the **International Bookshop** (Map pp322-3; Luque near Pichincha), have extremely limited selections in both Spanish and English.

Cultural Centers

Alliance Française (Map pp322-3; ☎ 253-2009; cnr Hurtado 436 & Mascote) French cultural center located near the American embassy holds exhibitions, concerts and various courses and lectures.

Casa de Cultura (Map pp322-3; ☎ 230-0500; cnr Av 9 de Octubre & Moncayo; 🕑 10am-6pm Tue-Fri, 9am-3pm Sat) Holds art exhibitions, lectures and poetry readings. Also a bookstore, a small café and a cinema (see p331) that shows foreign and art-house films.

Centro Ecuatoriano Norteamericano (Map pp322-3; ☎ 232-6505; Roca btwn Rocafuerte & Cordova) Aka the Ecuador–United States Cultural Center; periodically hosts concerts, exhibitions and other performances.

Emergency

Cruz Roja (Red Cross; ☎ 131)

Police (☎ 101)

Internet Access

Many of the top-end hotels and a few of the midrange ones offer wi-fi in their lobbies and sometimes in the rooms, or at the very least have their own terminals for internet access. The stand-alone internet cafés scattered throughout downtown all charge about $1 per hour.

Laundry

Most laundries in Guayaquil specialize in dry cleaning rather than washing, drying and folding – **Secomatico** (Map pp322-3; cnr Colón & Boyaca) is one. Most are closed weekends. Midrange and top-end hotels offer laundry at often exorbitant prices. The best bet for reasonable rates is to inquire at one of the respectable budget hotels. **Lavandería Pato** (Sauces 1, Isidrio; 🕑 9am-7pm Mon-Fri, to 4pm Sat) has standard machine wash and dry ($2.50 per load).

Media
El Universo and *El Telégrafo* are Guayaquil's two main local papers and have all the cultural goings-on about town.

Medical Services
A number of 24-hour pharmacies can be found on Avenida 9 de Octubre.

Clínica Kennedy (Map p324; ☎ 238-9666; Av del Periodista) One of the better hospitals in Guayaquil, by the Policentro shopping center in the Nueva Kennedy suburb. Avenida del Periodista is also known as San Jorge.

Dr Serrano Sáenz (Map pp322-3; ☎ 256-1785; Boyacá 821 & Junín) Takes drop-ins and speaks English.

Money
All of Ecuador's major banks are represented in Guayaquil, including several branches of each scattered around the downtown area. All change traveler's checks and have ATMs. There are stand-alone ATMs all over downtown, especially around Plaza de la Merced.

Post
Post office (Map pp322-3; 🕑 8am-7pm Mon-Fri, to noon Sat) Part of a huge building bounded by Ballén and Carbo.

Telephone
Most of the internet cafés also double as call centers. Pacifictel and other phone companies also have offices all over the city.

Tourist Information
Centro de Informacíon (Map pp322-3; Malecón Simón Bolívar; 🕑 10:30am-1pm & 2-7pm Mon-Sat) This train car on the *malecón* offers 15 minutes' free internet access, plus good city maps and info on cultural events and happenings.

Dirección Municipal de Turismo (Map pp322-3; ☎ 252-4100, ext 3477/9; www.visitguayaquil.com; cnr Malecón Simón Bolívar & 10 de Agosto) If you can't get what you need from the train car, try this office in the town hall.

Subsecretario de Turismo Litoral (Map pp322-3; ☎ 256-8764; infotour@telconet.net; Paula de Icaza 203, 6th fl; 🕑 9am-5pm Mon-Fri) Provides general tourist information about Guayas and Manabí Provinces.

Travel Agencies
Although Guayaquil is the last stop for the Galápagos, prices are no lower here than they are in Quito, and Quito definitely has more travel agencies catering to foreigners. However, you do save about $45 on the flight to the islands (and over an hour's flying time). More details are given in the Galápagos Islands chapter (p342).

Canodros (☎ 228-5771; www.canodros.com; Urbanización Santa Leonor, Manzana 5, Solar 10, Vía Terminal Terrestre; 🕑 9am-6pm) Operator for *Galápagos Explorer II*, one of the more expensive cruise ships in the islands; prides itself on its ecotourism credentials.

Centro Viajero (Map pp322-3; ☎ 230-1283, 09-397-1917; centrovi@telconet.net; Baquerizo Moreno 1119 at Av 9 de Octubre, Office 805, 8th fl; 🕑 9am-7:30pm) A travel agency that provides honest and personal service in organizing Galápagos packages. Spanish, English and French spoken. Ask for the manager Douglas Chang.

Dreamkapture Travel (☎ 224-2909; www.dreamkapture.com; Alborada 12a etapa, Av Benjamín Carrión at Francisco de Orellana) Good deals on Galápagos cruises and also arranges surfing trips. French, Spanish and English are spoken.

Ecuadorian Tours (Map pp322-3; ☎ 228-7111; Boyacá) Books high-end tours; Amex representative.

Galasam Tours (Map pp322-3; ☎ 230-4488; www.galapagos-islands.com; 9 de Octubre 424, Office 9A; 🕑 9am-6:30pm Mon-Fri, 10am-1pm Sat) Known for economical Galápagos cruises, however go in with your eyes open.

Metropolitan Touring (Map p324; ☎ 233-0300; www.metropolitantouring.com; Hilton Colón Hotel, Francisco de Orellana) Can arrange luxury trips to the Galápagos and also books tours throughout the country.

DANGERS & ANNOYANCES
Although Guayaquil is statistically and anecdotally no more dangerous than Quito, its reputation is still unfairly tarred, often by foreigners who spend no more than a night in town. Of course the city has its fair share of poverty and urban woes, but nothing to justify paranoia. Post-ATM-withdrawal robberies are a continuing problem, however the main tourist areas of Avenida 9 de Octubre, the Malecón 2000, Las Peñas and the restaurant strip in Urdesa are perfectly safe – not simply because there is a visible police presence but also because these are lively, vibrant areas clogged with couples and families going about their daily routines. The area directly north and south of the Parque del Centenario can feel dodgy at night, but simply use common sense and take the normal precautions when visiting any large city.

SIGHTS & ACTIVITIES
While the majority of visitors breeze in and out on their way to the Galápagos, the city has a fair share of sights, most within walking distance of one another. If your time is limited

be sure to walk the Malecón 2000 (also called Malecón Simón Bolívar or simply *el malecón*) and visit the northern neighborhood of Las Peñas – an especially pleasant destination at night, when cool breezes blow off the Río Guayas and the bright lights of the city sparkle below. Sunday is a good day to foot it because traffic is limited.

Malecón 2000

The riverfront promenade is where Guayaquil comes to shop, eat, stroll and just plain congregate. **Malecón 2000** (Map pp322-3; 7am-midnight), one of the most extensive urban-renewal projects in South America, is made up of ponds, playgrounds, sculptures, gardens and river views. From its southernmost point at the Mercado Sur to Cerro Santa Ana and Las Peñas in the north, the *malecón* stretches 2.5km along the bank of the wide Río Guayas. It's a gated, policed public space with restaurants, a museum, a performance space, an IMAX movie theater and a shopping mall.

At the southern end of the *malecón* stands the handsome steel **Mercado Sur** (Map pp322–3), sometimes called the Crystal Palace. When this Belgian-designed covered market was built in 1907, it was the biggest marketplace in Guayaquil. It has now been restored, with giant glass walls, and is periodically filled with art and commercial exhibitions.

Just north of the Mercado Sur is the **Olmedo monument** (Map pp322–3) honoring José Joaquín de Olmedo (1780–1847), who was an Ecuadorian poet and the president of the first Ecuadorian territory independent of Spanish rule. Just to the north, outside the *malecón's* blue fence, is the sprawling street market known as La Bahía (p332), where you can pick up everything from underwear to DVDs of the Latin Grammy awards.

Where 10 de Agosto hits the *malecón* you'll see the famous Moorish-style **clock tower** (Map pp322-3; 9am-6pm Mon-Fri), which originally dates from 1770 but has been replaced several times. The 23m-high tower is open to visitors to climb the narrow spiral staircase inside.

Across the street is the **Palacio Municipal** (Map pp322–3), an ornate, gray building that is separated from the simple and solid **Palacio de Gobierno** by a small but pleasant pedestrian mall. Both buildings date from the 1920s. The Palacio de Gobierno replaced the original wooden structure, which was destroyed in the great fire of 1917.

A few blocks away in the Plaza de Administración building is the **Museo Nahim Isaias** (Map pp322-3; ☎ 232-4182; www.museonahimisaias.com; cnr Pichincha & Ballén; adult/child $1.50/0.50; 10am-6pm Tue-Sat, 11am-3pm Sun & holidays), which exhibits an excellent collection of sculptures, paintings and artifacts of the colonial period.

Continuing north along the *malecón*, you will soon come to the famous statue of **La Rotonda** (Map pp322–3), one of Guayaquil's more impressive monuments, particularly when illuminated at night. Flanked by small fountains, it depicts the historic but enigmatic meeting between Bolívar and San Martín that took place here in 1822.

To the east is **Avenida 9 de Octubre** (Map pp322–3), downtown Guayaquil's main commercial street, stretching off toward Parque del Centenario. Several blocks north of La Rotonda is a large and well-manicured **tropical garden** (Map pp322–3) with footpaths, small ponds, benches and, most importantly, shade.

At the far northern end of the *malecón* there are good views of the colonial district of Las Peñas and Cerro Santa Ana and, far beyond, the impressive Guayaquil–Durán bridge – the biggest in the country. Marking the end of riverfront is the modern **Museo Antropológico y de Arte Contemporáneo** (MAAC; Map pp322-3; ☎ 230-9383; www.museomaac.com; cnr Malecón Simón Bolívar & Loja; admission Tue-Sat $1.50, Sun free; 10am-5:30pm Tue-Sat, 11am-3:30pm Sun), a museum of anthropology, archaeology and (most importantly for the average visitor) a superb and well-curated collection of contemporary Ecuadorian art. MAAC also has a modern 400-seat **theater** (☎ 230-9400; www.maaccine.com; admission $2) for plays, concerts and films. Behind the museum is an open-air stage, where musical and theatrical performances are occasionally given. Beside the museum is a modern food court, and immediately to the south is a large IMAX cinema ($4).

Las Peñas & Cerro Santa Ana

These two historic neighborhoods (Map pp322–3) have been refurbished into an idealized version of a quaint South American hillside village, all brightly painted homes and cobblestone alleyways. If you peek inside an open door or window, however, you realize it's a bit of a Potemkin village that's not entirely sanitized, as residents still live their everyday lives as they would elsewhere in the city.

GUAYAQUIL – CITY CENTER

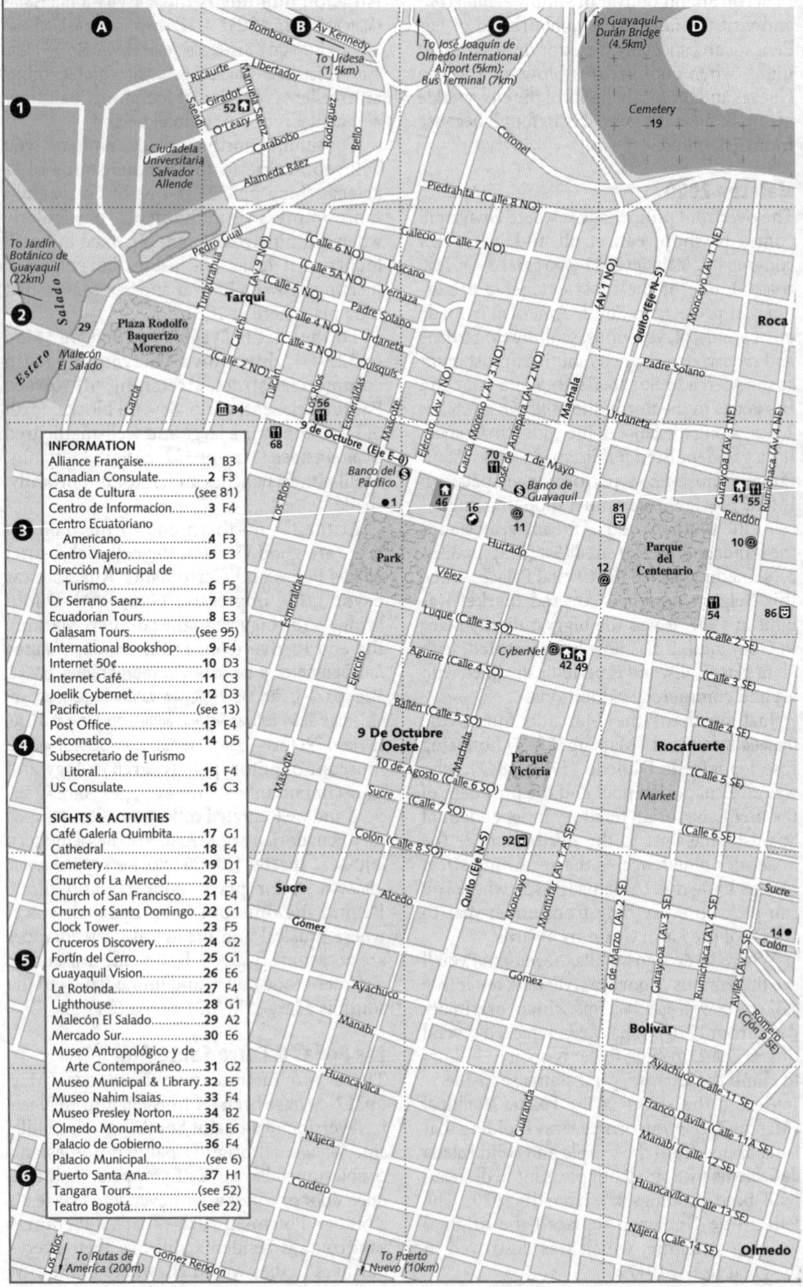

INFORMATION

Alliance Française........1 B3
Canadian Consulate........2 F3
Casa de Cultura........(see 81)
Centro de Informacíon........3 F4
Centro Ecuatoriano Americano........4 F3
Centro Viajero........5 E3
Dirección Municipal de Turismo........6 F5
Dr Serrano Saenz........7 E3
Ecuadorian Tours........8 E3
Galasam Tours........(see 95)
International Bookshop........9 F4
Internet 50¢........10 D3
Internet Café........11 C3
Joelik Cybernet........12 D3
Pacifictel........(see 13)
Post Office........13 E4
Secomatico........14 D5
Subsecretario de Turismo Litoral........15 F4
US Consulate........16 C3

SIGHTS & ACTIVITIES

Café Galería Quimbita........17 G1
Cathedral........18 E4
Cemetery........19 D1
Church of La Merced........20 F3
Church of San Francisco........21 E4
Church of Santo Domingo........22 G1
Clock Tower........23 F5
Cruceros Discovery........24 G2
Fortín del Cerro........25 G1
Guayaquil Vision........26 E6
La Rotonda........27 F4
Lighthouse........28 G1
Malecón El Salado........29 A2
Mercado Sur........30 E6
Museo Antropológico y de Arte Contemporáneo........31 G2
Museo Municipal & Library........32 E5
Museo Nahim Isaias........33 F4
Museo Presley Norton........34 B2
Olmedo Monument........35 E6
Palacio de Gobierno........36 F4
Palacio Municipal........(see 6)
Puerto Santa Ana........37 H1
Tangara Tours........(see 52)
Teatro Bogotá........(see 22)

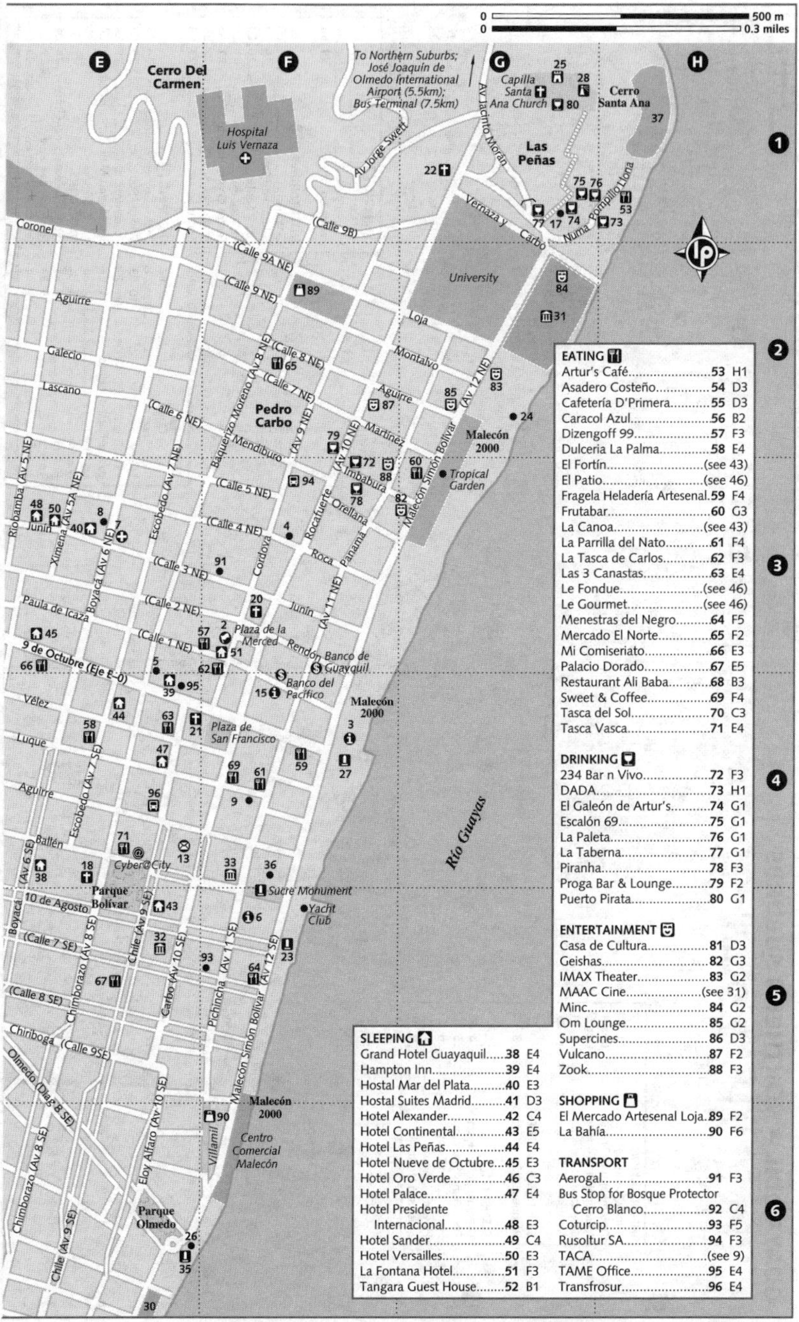

EATING

- Artur's Café........53 H1
- Asadero Costeño........54 D3
- Cafetería D'Primera........55 D3
- Caracol Azul........56 B2
- Dizengoff 99........57 F3
- Dulceria La Palma........58 E4
- El Fortín........(see 43)
- El Patio........(see 46)
- Fragela Heladería Artesenal........59 F4
- Frutabar........60 G3
- La Canoa........(see 43)
- La Parrilla del Nato........61 F4
- La Tasca de Carlos........62 F3
- Las 3 Canastas........63 E4
- Le Fondue........(see 46)
- Le Gourmet........(see 46)
- Menestras del Negro........64 F5
- Mercado El Norte........65 F2
- Mi Comiseriato........66 E3
- Palacio Dorado........67 E5
- Restaurant Ali Baba........68 B3
- Sweet & Coffee........69 F4
- Tasca del Sol........70 C3
- Tasca Vasca........71 E4

DRINKING

- 234 Bar n Vivo........72 F3
- DADA........73 H1
- El Galeón de Artur's........74 G1
- Escalón 69........75 G1
- La Paleta........76 G1
- La Taberna........77 G1
- Piranha........78 F3
- Proga Bar & Lounge........79 F2
- Puerto Pirata........80 G1

ENTERTAINMENT

- Casa de Cultura........81 D3
- Geishas........82 G3
- IMAX Theater........83 G2
- MAAC Cine........(see 31)
- Minc........84 G2
- Om Lounge........85 G2
- Supercines........86 D3
- Vulcano........87 F2
- Zook........88 F3

SLEEPING

- Grand Hotel Guayaquil........38 E4
- Hampton Inn........39 E4
- Hostal Mar del Plata........40 E3
- Hostal Suites Madrid........41 D3
- Hotel Alexander........42 C4
- Hotel Continental........43 E5
- Hotel Las Peñas........44 E4
- Hotel Nueve de Octubre........45 E3
- Hotel Oro Verde........46 C3
- Hotel Palace........47 E4
- Hotel Presidente Internacional........48 E3
- Hotel Sander........49 C4
- Hotel Versailles........50 E3
- La Fontana Hotel........51 F3
- Tangara Guest House........52 B1

SHOPPING

- El Mercado Artesenal Loja........89 F2
- La Bahía........90 F6

TRANSPORT

- Aerogal........91 F3
- Bus Stop for Bosque Protector Cerro Blanco........92 C4
- Coturcip........93 F5
- Rusoltur SA........94 F3
- TACA........(see 9)
- TAME Office........95 E4
- Transfrosur........96 E4

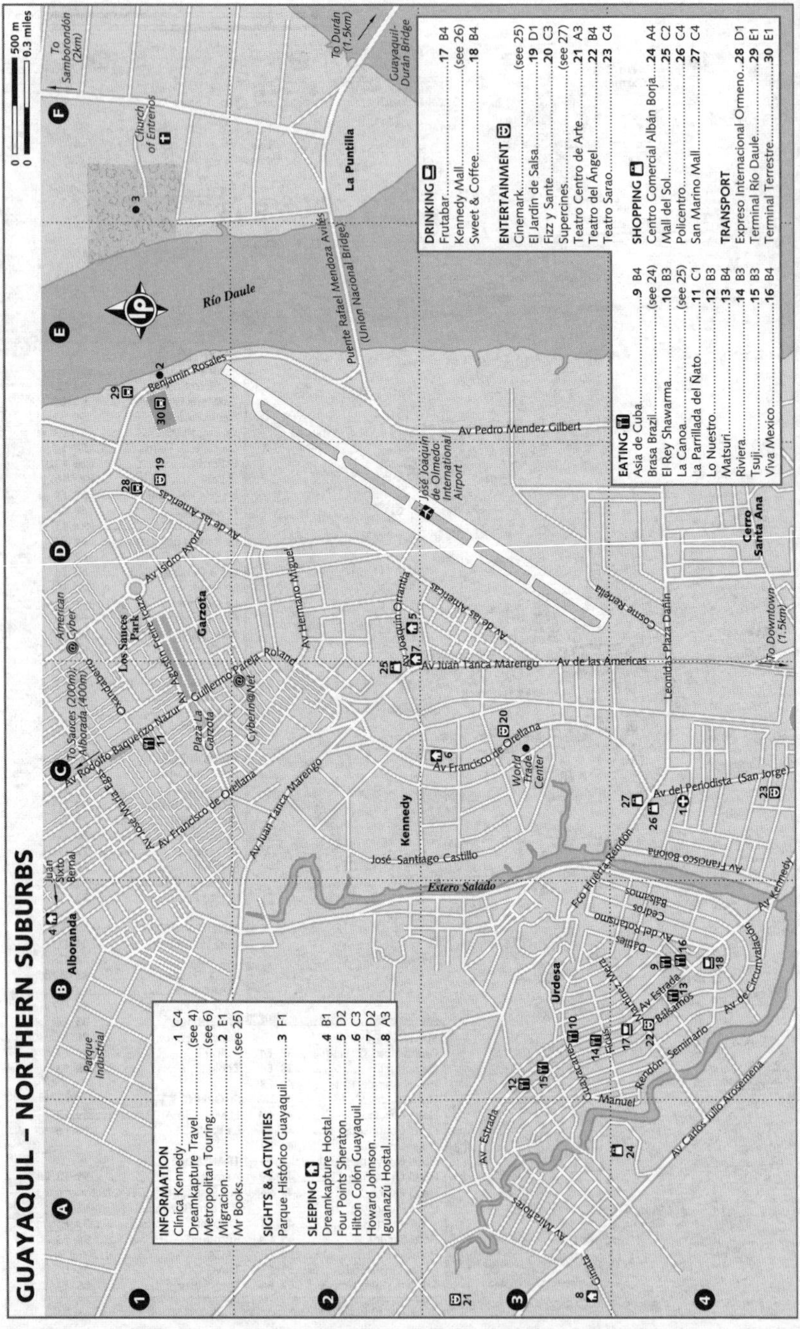
GUAYAQUIL – NORTHERN SUBURBS
INFORMATION
Clínica Kennedy 1 C4
Dreamkapture Travel (see 4)
Metropolitan Touring (see 6)
Migracion 2 E1
Mr Books (see 25)
SIGHTS & ACTIVITIES
Parque Histórico Guayaquil 3 F1
SLEEPING
Dreamkapture Hostal 4 B1
Four Points Sheraton 5 D2
Hilton Colón Guayaquil 6 C3
Howard Johnson 7 D2
Iguanazú Hostal 8 A3
EATING
Asia de Cuba 9 B4
Brasa Brazil (see 24)
El Rey Shawarma 10 B3
La Canoa (see 25)
La Parrillada del Ñato 11 C1
Lo Nuestro 12 B3
Matsuri 13 B4
Riviera 14 B3
Tsuji 15 B3
Viva Mexico 16 B4
DRINKING
Frutabar 17 B4
Kennedy Mall (see 26)
Sweet & Coffee 18 B4
ENTERTAINMENT
Cinemark (see 25)
El Jardín de Salsa 19 D1
Fizz y Sante 20 C3
Supercines (see 27)
Teatro Centro de Arte 21 A3
Teatro del Ángel 22 B4
Teatro Sarao 23 C4
SHOPPING
Centro Comercial Albán Borja 24 A4
Mall del Sol 25 C2
Policentro 26 C4
San Marino Mall 27 C4
TRANSPORT
Expreso Internacional Ormeno 28 D1
Terminal Río Daule 29 E1
Terminal Terrestre 30 E1
Río Daule
Puente Rafael Mendoza Avilés (Union Nacional Bridge)
La Puntilla
Church of Entrenos
To Samborondón (2km)
To Durán (1.5km)
Guayaquil-Durán Bridge
José Joaquín de Olmedo International Airport
Av Pedro Mendez Gilbert
Benjamin Rosales
Av de las Americas
Los Sauces Park
Garzota
Alboranda
Parque Industrial
Kennedy
Urdesa
Estero Salado
World Trade Center
Cerro Santa Ana
To Downtown (1.5km)
To Sauces (200m); Alborada (400m)
American Cyber
Cyberin@Net
Plaza La Garzota
Av Francisco de Orellana
Av Juan Tanca Marengo
Av del Periodista (San Jorge)
Av Francisco Boloña
Av Kennedy
Av de Circunvalación
Av Carlos Julio Arosemena
Av Miraflores
Av Estrada
Víctor Emilio Estrada
Juan Sixto Bernal
0 500 m
0 0.3 miles

Everyone strolling the *malecón* ends up here, especially at night, when the views from the top are spectacular. Small, informal, family-run restaurants and neighborhood bars line the steps and it's completely safe, patrolled by friendly security officers making sure foot traffic up the steep stairway flows unimpeded.

The historic street of **Numa Pompilio Llona**, named after the well-known *guayaquileño* poet (1832–1907), begins at the northern end of the *malecón,* to the right of the stairs that head up the hill called Cerro Santa Ana. This narrow, winding street has several unobtrusive plaques set into the walls of some of its houses, indicating the simple residences of past presidents. The colonial wooden architecture has been allowed to age elegantly, albeit with a gloss of paint. Several artists live in the area, and there are a few good galleries, including the eponymous **Café Galería Quimbita** (Map pp322-3; ☎ 231-0785; Escalón 27, Cerro Santa Ana; 🕑 5pm-1am Wed & Sun, 5pm-3am Thu-Sat), which doubles as a happening bar (cocktails $5), restaurant (mains $7) and showpiece for the large canvasses of this highly regarded artist; live folk and Latin rock music are played on weekends.

Numa Pompilio Llona dead-ends at steps that lead down into Guayaquil's latest redevelopment project, **Puerto Santa Ana** (Map pp322–3), a high-end condominium and office complex with a few ice-cream and fast-food kiosks. Much of the area was unfinished and unoccupied at the time of research but the paved walkway along the river makes for a nice stroll.

Retrace your footsteps back along Numa Pompilio Llona and instead of continuing south along the *malecón,* hang a sharp right and head up the 444 steps of **Cerro Santa Ana** (Map pp322–3). The stairs lead past dozens of refurbished, brightly painted homes, cafés, bars and souvenir shops, and up to the hilltop **Fortín del Cerro** (Fort of the Hill; Map pp322–3). Cannons, which were once used to protect Guayaquil from pirates, aim over the parapet toward the river and are still fired today during celebrations. You can climb the **lighthouse** (Map pp322-3; admission free; 🕑 10am-10pm) for spectacular 360-degree views of the city and its rivers.

Back at the bottom of the hill, walk inland from the stairway to reach the open-air theater **Teatro Bogotá** (Map pp322–3). Behind the theater is the oldest church in Guayaquil, the **Church of Santo Domingo** (Map pp322–3). Founded in 1548 and restored in 1938, it's worth a look.

Downtown Area

There are several ordinary colonial-era buildings in the streets immediately south of Las Peñas, but soon all the architecture turns mostly modern and dull. The **Church of La Merced** (Map pp322-3; Rendón at Rocafuerte) dates from 1938 and has a richly decorated golden altar; the original wooden church built in 1787, like most of Guayaquil's colonial buildings, was destroyed by fire.

The **Church of San Francisco** (Map pp322-3; Av 9 de Octubre near Chile), originally built in the early 18th century, was burnt down in the devastating fire of 1896 that destroyed huge swathes of the city, then reconstructed in 1902 and beautifully restored in the late 1990s. The plaza in front contains Guayaquil's first public monument, a statue of Vicente Rocafuerte, Ecuador's first native president, who held office between 1835 and 1839. (Ecuador's first president, Juan Flores, was a Venezuelan.)

The main thoroughfare, **Avenida 9 de Octubre** (Map pp322–3), is the commercial heart of downtown. It's lined with cheap second-hand clothing stores, high-end electronics shops, department stores and fast-food restaurants.

Parque Bolívar Area

Guayaquil may be the only city in the world that has land iguanas, some over a meter in length, living downtown. These prehistoric-looking animals, a different species from those found in the Galápagos, are a startling sight in one of Guayaquil's most famous plazas, **Parque Bolívar** (Map pp322–3), which is also known as Parque Seminario. Around its small ornamental gardens are many of Guayaquil's top-end hotels.

On the west side of Parque Bolívar is the **cathedral** (Map pp322–3). Its original wooden building dates from 1547, but like much of Guayaquil, it was destroyed by fire. The present structure, completed in 1948 and renovated in 1978, is simple and modern, despite an extremely ornate front entrance.

A block south of Parque Bolívar, you find the **Museo Municipal** (Map pp322-3; ☎ 252-4100; Sucre; admission free; 🕑 8:30am-4:30pm Tue-Fri, 10am-2pm Sat & Sun) and the municipal **library**. The archaeology room on the ground floor has mainly Inca and pre-Inca ceramics, and several figurines from the oldest culture in Ecuador, the Valdivia (c 3200 BC). Also on the ground floor is a colonial room with mainly religious paintings and a few period household items. Upstairs, there is a jumble of modern art and ethnography rooms with regional costumes, handicrafts and several shrunken heads.

Parque del Centenario

This plaza, found along Avenida 9 de Octubre (Map pp322–3), is the largest in Guayaquil and marks the midway point between the Río Guayas and the Estero Salado. It's four square city blocks of manicured gardens, benches and monuments, the most important of which is the central **Liberty column** surrounded by the founding fathers of the country.

Parque Histórico Guayaquil

Historic Williamsburg meets the zoo at this large **park** (Map p324; ☎ 283-2958; www.parquehistoricoguayaquil.com; Av Esmeraldas; adult/child Wed-Sat $3/1.50, Sun $4.50/3; 9am-4:30pm Wed-Sun) across the Guayaquil–Durán bridge, on the east side of Río Daule. The park is divided into three 'zones': the Endangered Wildlife Zone, which has 45 species of bird, animal and reptile in a seminatural habitat; the Urban Architecture Zone, which has a restaurant and showcases the development of early-20th-century architecture in Guayaquil; and the Traditions Zone, which focuses on local traditions, with an emphasis on rural customs, crafts and agriculture.

A taxi from the city costs between $3 and $4, or take the red-and-white Duran 4/30 bus. It's easier to catch the bus back to the city from in front of the large mall on the main road about a 200m walk from the park.

Malecón El Salado

Like its more famous sister development on the Río Guayas to the east, the Malecón El Salado is an attempt to reclaim the city's waterfront for the everyday use of its residents. There are several eateries and cafés in a streamlined modern mall-like building along the estuary. Previously known as the Guayaquil Park, the large square just south of the *malecón,* now called the **Plaza Rodolfo Baquerizo Moreno**, is dominated by a large modernist structure. Expositions and events are held here periodically. A series of less refined gardens, playgrounds and public walkways, collectively called Parque Lineal, is on the other side of the waterway just to the north.

A few blocks south of here is the **Museo Presley Norton** (☎ 229-3423; 9 de Octubre; admission free; ☎ 9am-5pm Mon-Sat), an impressive collection of archaeological artifacts, including pottery and figurines made by the original settlers of Ecuador, housed in a beautifully restored ornate mansion. It occasionally hosts film screenings and live music.

City Cemetery

Incorporated into the city landscape a short ride from the center is this **cemetery** (Map pp322-3; Coronel & Moncayo) containing hundreds of aboveground tombs stacked atop one another so that it resembles a mini apartment complex rather than a final resting place. A walkway leads to several monuments and huge mausoleums, including the impressive grave of President Vicente Rocafuerte.

Jardín Botánico de Guayaquil

About a half-hour drive north of town near Cerro Colorado, this **botanical garden** (☎ 241-7004; jbotanic@interactive.net.ec; Francisco de Orellana; adult $3, child & student $1.50; 8am-4pm) has more than 80 orchid varieties and nearly 700 plant species. Paths and trails lead you past the plant exhibits and tropical birds flutter overhead. There is a gift shop, a café, a butterfly garden and an auditorium. Insect repellent is recommended in the rainy months. With a few days' advance notice, a guided tour can be arranged.

The most efficient way of getting there is to take a taxi and ask for Urbanización de Los Orquídeas.

TOURS

Cruceros Discovery (Map pp322-3; ☎ 230-4824; www.crucerosdiscovery.com; Malecón Simón Bolívar) River cruises from Tuesday to Sunday every two hours. Music, dancing and some information.

Ecua-Andino (☎ 232-6375; www.ecua-andino.com) A panama-hat exporter and an organizer of local tours, especially to see how toquilla (fine, fibrous straw) is split, boiled, bleached and dried in preparation for weaving. Ask for Alejandro Lecaro; Spanish, English and German are spoken.

Guayaquil Vision (Map pp322-3; ☎ 288-5800; www.guayaquilvision.com; adult/child $6/3) Double-decker bus tours of the downtown and surrounding suburbs (1½ hours). Five tours a day starting from the Plaza Olmedo on the *malecón*; the first is at 10:40am. There are four other hop-on and hop-off points.

Nancy Hilgert de Benavides (nancyperegrinus@yahoo.com) Expert bird-watching guide. Works with professional and academic tour groups as well as individuals.

Sans Souci Tours (☎ 288-7492; www.sanssouci.com.ec) Offers half-day tours of banana and cocoa plantations, as well half- and full-day city tours.

Tangara Tours (formerly Chasquitur; ☎ 228-2828; www.tangara-ecuador.com; Ciudadela Bolivariana, Manuela Sáenz & O'Leary, Block F, Casa 1) Run out of the guesthouse of the same name (single $37, double $49). Good for local day tours and ecotourism, including trips to the Reserva Ecológica Manglares Churute (p334).

FESTIVALS & EVENTS

Carnaval Movable feast held on the days immediately preceding Ash Wednesday and Lent, which, in addition to the traditional throwing of water, is 'celebrated' by dousing passersby with all manner of unpleasant liquids.

Simón Bolívar's Birthday & Founding of Guayaquil Falling on July 24 and 25 respectively. The city goes wild with parades, art shows, beauty pageants, fireworks and plenty of drinking and dancing. Hotels are booked well in advance, and banking and other services are usually disrupted.

Independence Day & Día de la Raza These two combine to create another long holiday full of cultural events, parades and bigger-than-usual crowds on the *malecón*. Independence Day is October 9 (1820) and Día de la Raza is October 12.

New Year's Eve Celebrated with bonfires and life-sized puppets called *viejos* (the old ones), which are made by stuffing old clothes – they represent the old year. The *viejos* are displayed on the main streets of the city, especially the *malecón,* and then burned at midnight in bonfires.

SLEEPING

Some people choose to stay in the northern suburbs, but it's really no more convenient to the airport or bus terminal than staying downtown and you'll be forced to take taxis wherever you go. It's also no safer than downtown, so if you do choose to stay here, decide on the merits of the accommodations alone.

Each hotel is officially required to post its approved prices near the entrance. You may be charged up to 22% tax on the listed price – this is especially the case when booking online – but most of the cheaper hotels don't bother. The better hotels often have a two-tiered pricing system for foreigners and residents.

During holiday periods, finding a room can be problematic, especially in the better hotels, and prices are usually higher than the listed price. Outside the holiday season, some of the budget and midrange places are willing to negotiate.

The heat and humidity in Guayaquil are especially oppressive from January to April, and air-conditioning is highly desirable.

Downtown

BUDGET

Cheap hotels aren't built with budget-minded foreigners in mind, and there are no backpacker havens like those found elsewhere in the country. Most of the budget options are found within several blocks of the Parque del Centenario and street noise can be an annoyance.

Hotel Sander (Map pp322-3; ☎ 232-0030; www.sanderguayaquil.com; Luque 1101; r with fan/air-con $9/12; P ❄ 🖳) While the lobby has been upgraded to make room for several comfy couches and computers for guests' use, the bunkerlike rooms are holdovers from another era. Don't let the website photos or brochures fool you – most of the rooms are bare bones and lack natural light; some have hot water. It is, however, a clean and secure cheapie option.

Hostal Mar del Plata (Map pp322-3; ☎ 230-7610; Junín 718 & Boyacá; s/d with fan $12/20, with air-con $18/23; ❄) Rooms here are similar in quality to Hostal Suites Madrid except the TVs here are noticeably old and some of the toilets are seat-free. It's clean and secure and still a good choice.

Hotel Nueve de Octubre (Map pp322-3 ☎ 256-4222; Av 9 de Octubre 736; r with air-con $13; P ❄) Hospitality is on the backburner at this behemoth occupying prime real estate in the heart of the downtown shopping strip. The perpetually busy ground-floor front desk is a model of efficiency, and the Soviet-era-style hallways and basic rooms are paragons of cleanliness to make up for their lack of character. No hot water or internet despite the advertising.

Hostal Suites Madrid (Map pp322-3; ☎ 230-7804; Quísquis 305; r with fan/air-con $15/20; P ❄) One of the few budget hotels run for foreign travelers, Madrid offers a superclean and secure refuge only a block north of the Parque del Centenario. Unlike some hotels in this category, hot water is guaranteed; unfortunately the lack of shower curtains and toilet seats make the bathroom a bit of a Slip 'N Slide. But the high ceilings, bright and cheerful color scheme and helpful manager are more than compensation.

MIDRANGE

Hotel Versailles (Map pp322-3; ☎ 230-8773; infohotelversailles@yahoo.es; Quísquis & Ximena; r with air-con $25; ❄ 🖳) While it inevitably falls short of its namesake, the Versailles is a remarkably good deal only a few blocks from Avenida 9 de Octubre. The large marble-floored rooms are spotless and they even sport high-end flat-screen TVs and shower fixtures.

Hotel Alexander (Map pp322-3; ☎ 253-2651; hotelalexander@hotmail.com; Luque 1107; s/d $32/36; P ✻ ▣) Located roughly equidistant from both riverside *malecóns*, the Alexander is accustomed to travelers as much as local businesspeople. Unfortunately, dark carpeting, poor lighting and few windows mean it can feel a little like sleeping in a crypt. Couples pay a little more for a room with a matrimonial bed. Intentionally or not, wi-fi access is free pretty much throughout the hotel, and the lobby has computers available for use as well. A restaurant is attached.

Hotel Presidente Internacional (Map pp322-3; ☎ 230-6779; www.presidenteinternacional.com; Quísquis near Riobamba, s/d $35/50; ✻ ▣) A traditionally outfitted doorman is a bit of an anomaly in this rather worn-down part of the city but it's a comforting gesture. The nine-story Presidente is a real value considering the polished wood floors, quality bathrooms and low-key artwork – there's even a small gym for the fitness obsessed.

Hotel Las Peñas (Map pp322-3; ☎ 2323355; www.hlpgye.com; s/d $40/50; ✻ ▣) Although it's already a few years old, good-value Las Peñas looks and feels like it's just rolled off the assembly line. The bright green hallways lead to large tile-floored rooms with cable TV and minifridges. Have breakfast at the attached California café.

Another good centrally located option is **La Fontana Hotel** (Map pp322-3; ☎ 230-3967; hlafontana@ecutel.net; Paula de Icaza 404 & Córdova; s/d $70/80; ✻ ▣).

TOP END

Grand Hotel Guayaquil (Map pp322-3; ☎ 232-9690; www.grandhotelguayaquil.com; Boyacá & 10 de Agosto; r from $85; P ✻ ▣ ◙) Only a block from Parque Bolívar and a short walk from the *malecón* and Avenida 9 de Octubre, this large complex does live up to its name, at least in terms of size. One entire side of the sunny inner courtyard is backstopped by the cathedral next door. This magnificence aside, the carpeted rooms, while spacious, aren't as modern or well maintained as the lobby. Buffet breakfast is included, as are 30 minutes' free internet a day, plus wi-fi is available throughout. There's a pool, a rooftop gym and saunas, as well as two restaurants and a bar.

Hampton Inn (Map pp322-3; ☎ 256-6700; www.hampton.com.ec; Av 9 de Octubre 432 & Baquerizo Moreno; r $85-350; ✻ ▣) This centrally located high-rise is your standard comfortable chain hotel.

Hotel Palace (Map pp322-3 ☎ 232-1080; www.hotelpalaceguayaquil.com; Chile 214; r incl breakfast $100; P ✻ ▣) Only steps from Avenida 9 de Octubre and a few blocks from Malecón 2000, the professionally run Palace is the best-located high-end hotel. The small but tastefully done rooms are efficiently designed to take advantage of every square inch (and there aren't that many to go around), packing in boutique-style touches with high-end TVs and internet cable hookups (wi-fi is free in the lobby). A small screen in the lobby displaying the status of all outbound flights is a nice touch, and a good restaurant is attached.

Hotel Continental (Map pp322-3; ☎ 232-9270; www.hotelcontinental.com.ec; Chile 510; r $100-175; P ✻ ▣) One of the oldest of the city's luxury hotels, the fortresslike Hotel Continental has comfortable though not especially large rooms. It's right across from Parque Bolívar and has several good restaurants (see p330).

Hotel Oro Verde (Map pp322-3; ☎ 232-7999; www.oroverdehotels.com; Av 9 de Octubre & García Moreno; r $152-317; P ✻ ▣ ◙) About four blocks west of Parque del Centenario. It still maintains its status as the classiest of the bunch, less for superior-quality rooms as much for its high-end facilities, casino and several excellent restaurants.

Northern Suburbs

BUDGET & MIDRANGE

our pick **Iguanazú Hostal** (☎ 220-1143, 09-986-7968; www.iguanazuhostel.com; Cuiadadela La Cogra, Km3.5, Villa 2, Cuidadela La Cogra; dm $12, r per person $40; ✻ ▣ ◙) An oasis of tranquility perched on a hill a few blocks from a busy roadway, the Iguanazú is an ideal base to explore the city. The only downside is that it's hard to find on your own – it's just north of Miraflores off Carlos Julio Arosemena. The owner, a former backpacker herself, and her friendly bulldog will make you feel at home. Besides charming wood-floored rooms, there's a terrace with hammocks and wonderful views of the city below, a lush and well-tended lawn, a pool and a living room–restaurant area. Breakfast is included in all rates, and wi-fi is available throughout the property.

Dreamkapture Hostal (Map p324; ☎ 224-2909; www.dreamkapture.com; Alborada 12a etapa, Manzana 2, Villa 21, Juan Sixto Bernal; s/d with shared bathroom $17/22, with private bathroom $18/28; ✻ ▣ ◙) A small, friendly Canadian-Ecuadorian-owned *hostal* on a side street in the suburb of Alborada, with a garden courtyard and a tiny pool for cooling off. There are several rooms including one good for groups of four or five, and tasty breakfast is included. One of the owners operates a travel agency (p320). Even with the address the *hostal* is hard to find – look for the fantasy paintings on the compound walls.

Another good option in the area is **Tangara Guest House** (Map pp322-3 ☎ 228-2828; www.tangara-ecuador.com; Ciudadela Bolivariana, Manuela Sáenz & O'Leary, Block F, Casa 1; s/d $37/49;).

TOP END

Hilton Colón Guayaquil (Map p324; ☎ 268-9000; www.hiltoncolon.com; Francisco de Orellana; r from $185;) This massive complex, including several restaurants, shops, a pool, a gym and a casino, is the most luxurious choice. Pony up for a suite and you get a balcony with spectacular views.

Next to one another and the Mall de Sol are the fairly indistinguishable **Four Points Sheraton** (Map p324; ☎ 269-1888; www.fourpoints.com; Av Joaquin Orrantia G; r from $140;) and **Howard Johnson** (Map p324; ☎ 239-7374; www.hojo.com; Av Juan Tanca Marengo; r from $150;); both are standard international business-class hotels.

EATING

Guayaquileños love their *encebollado*, a tasty soup made with seafood, yuca and onion and garnished with popcorn and *chifles* (crispy fried bananas). The best *encebollados* are sold in cheap mom-and-pop restaurants. They usually sell out by lunchtime. *Cangrejo* (crab) is another local favorite. Some of the better restaurants are in hotels downtown or in the northwestern suburb of Urdesa.

Downtown

There are bunches of little inexpensive eateries catering to working folk, though there are few standout restaurants. Informal *parrillas* are everywhere, with a particular cluster around the Parque del Centenario, and there are several concentrations of bright, clean fast-food restaurants serving seafood and Ecuadorian rice, beans and meat dishes along the Malecón 2000 and the Malecón Estero Salado. American chains can be found on Avenida 9 de Octubre.

For fresh fruits, vegetables and meat, try the outdoor Mercado El Norte, a block south of El Mercado Artesenal Loja between Aguirre and Martínez.

The cavernous grocery **Mi Comisariato** (Av 9 de Octubre btwn Avilés & Boyacá) is the most convenient downtown place for self-catering.

RESTAURANTS

Asadero Costeño (Map pp322-3; Garaycoa 929; almuerzos $1.50) Rotisserie chicken is a dime-a-dozen in Guayaquil, but this place on the east side of Parque del Centenario stands out for its size and efficient ordering system – pay at the caged cashier before sitting. Next door is the curiously named Parrallidas Beefs & Salads.

Menestras del Negro (Map pp322-3; Malecón & Sucre; mains $2) If you want to avoid the KFCs and Pizza Huts, this homegrown chain is a good fast-food alternative. Grilled meat, fish and chicken dishes are on the menu along with heaping servings of beans, an Ecuadorian staple and the restaurant's namesake.

Restaurant Ali Baba (Map pp322-3; Av 9 de Octubre; mains $2) One of the only Middle Eastern options downtown, Ali Baba serves staples such as hummus, falafel, juicy *shawarmas* and filling empanadas ($0.80). Service may not come with a smile but it's still a good place for a quick eat or a lazy drink at one of the street-side tables.

Dizengoff 99 (Map pp322-3; Paula de Icaza & Cordova; mains $3) The La Fontana Hotel's otherwise ordinary restaurant looks like a stage set for La Bohème. Whatever the owner's Parisian fantasies, the menu is decidedly uninspiring – basic *almuerzos* and grilled meats with rice.

La Parrilla del Nato (Map pp322-3; Luque & Pichincha; mains $5) A staple for lunching office workers, this two-story Guayaquil institution (there's another branch in Urdesa) is always crowded and bustling, even in such a large space. Specializing in personalized grills – meat or seafood – fired up at your table, almost everything is available on the menu, from pastas ($7), pizzas ($3) and sandwiches to good ole standard *almuerzos* ($4).

Artur's Café (Map pp322-3; ☎ 231-2230; Numa Pompilio Llona 127, Las Peñas; mains $6; noon-3am Mon-Thu, 6pm-4am Fri & Sat) A longstanding hideaway perched over the Río Guayas in Las Peñas, Artur's does average food (Ecuadorian and international standards such as pasta). Despite the chintzy decor and dark lighting, it's still a pleasant spot. There's live music on many weekends.

Caracol Azul (Map pp322-3; ☎ 228-0461; Av 9 de Octubre 1918 & Los Ríos; mains $10-20; noon-3:30pm & 7pm-midnight Mon-Sat) A fine dining institution, this gourmet French-Peruvian restaurant has been serving scrumptious seafood and

SOUTH COAST

steak for more than 30 years. *Langostinos encocoadas* (shrimp in coconut-milk sauce) is especially good. The relatively elegant dining room is more welcoming than stuffy.

Several Spanish-style restaurants – all unduly focused on getting things accurate aesthetically, from the waiters' uniforms to the wall hangings, at the expense of culinary attention – serve passable paellas, tortillas and other traditional dishes. **La Tasca de Carlos** (Map pp322-3; ☎ 230-3661; Cordova 1002 & Paula de Icaza; mains $8-14) is maybe the best of the bunch. **Tasca del Sol** (Map pp322-3; ☎ 228-2902; José de Antepara 802; mains $8-14) and **Tasca Vaca** (Map pp322-3; ☎ 253-4599; Ballén 422 & Chimborazo; mains $8-14; ⏰ noon-11pm Mon-Sat) are other options.

There are a handful of indistinguishable *chifas* (Chinese restaurants) on the blocks south of Parque Bolívar including **Palacio Dorado** (Map pp322-3; Chile 712 & Sucre; mains $3), serving low-cost and filling dishes.

CAFÉS

Perhaps the most atmospheric place downtown is the old-school **Dulceria La Palma** (Map pp322-3; Escobedo btwn Vélez & Luque). For specialty hot and cold coffee drinks, cakes and free wi-fi, head to the Starbucks imitator **Sweet & Coffee** (Map pp322-3; Carbo & Luque); a much larger branch on Estrada in the northern suburb of Urdesa is very popular. Several hotels are within a few blocks of **Cafeteria D'Primera** (Map pp322-3; cnr Rumichaca & Quísquis), a bright spot on a relatively blighted street, making it perfect for a morning (instant) coffee or fresh-squeezed juice ($1.25); empanadas ($0.40) and tortillas ($0.60) can cure the hunger pangs.

The two best places for fruit shakes and fruit juices are the surfer-themed **Frutabar** (Map pp322-3; Malecón; drinks from $2.50; ⏰ 8am-midnight) and **Las 3 Canastas** (Map pp322-3; cnr Velez & Chile; drinks from $2), a busy daytime spot with street-side tables. The former, which also has sandwiches ($4.50), snacks and light meals, has a branch on Avenida Estrada in Urdesa.

Heladerías (ice-cream shops) are easy to find downtown. **Fragela Heladería Artesenal** (Map pp322-3; Av 9 de Octubre btwn Malecón 2000 & Pichincha; ice-cream cone $1.75) does excellent sundaes ($3.75).

HOTEL RESTAURANTS

All of the top-end and a few of the midrange hotels have at least one restaurant. Most are dressed to impress but the value and quality of the food are only mediocre. One of the more recommended places for a taste of Ecuadorian-style diner food is **La Canoa** (Map pp322-3; ☎ 232-9270; Chile 510; mains $3-7; ⏰ 24hr) in the Hotel Continental. Instead of hamburgers, the quick dish of choice is ceviche or fried rice with crab. Also in the hotel is the chichi and pricey **El Fortín** (mains $17).

The best bet for a splurge is **Le Gourmet** (Map pp322-3; ⏰ 232-7999; Av 9 de Octubre & García Moreno; mains $20; ⏰ 7pm-1am), a top-flight French restaurant in the Hotel Oro Verde. El Patio, serving Ecuadorian standards at upscale prices, and Swiss restaurant Le Fondue are also here.

Northern Suburbs

Avenida Estrada, the main drag in the suburb of Urdesa 4km northwest of downtown, is lined with fast-food joints and restaurants – some slick and upscale. Other good eateries are scattered throughout the suburbs of Alborada, La Garzota and Los Sauces. There are large food courts and other restaurants in the Mall del Sol and San Marino mall.

our pick **Lo Nuestro** (☎ 238-6398; Estrada 903; mains $6-15) Housed in a century-old mansion complete with wooden shutters and period furniture, Lo Nuestro is one of the most atmospheric places in Guayaquil to eat seafood dishes typical of the region. Musicians play on Friday and Saturday evenings, when reservations are recommended. At lunchtime the place fills up with local bigwigs.

Riviera (☎ 288-3790; Estrada 707 & Ficus; mains $11) Every night looks like Christmas Eve at this festively lighted Italian. Serving conventional Italian fare, it offers an extensive wine selection.

For more ethnic variety try **Asia de Cuba** (☎ 600-9999; Dátiles 205; mains $12), **Brasa Brazil** (☎ 220-6043; Centro Comercial Albán Borja, Carlos Julio Arosemena; mains $13) or **Viva Mexico** (☎ 238-9752; Dátiles; mains $7). The latter is uber-Mexican with mariachi bands, burritos and excellent tortillas.

There are around a half-dozen Japanese restaurants alone along Estrada, including unpretentious **Matsuri** (☎ 260-0641; Estrada 511; mains $10-15), which is open Sunday when much of the area is shut down, and the upscale and stylish **Tsuji** (☎ 288-1183; Estrada 816; mains $15).

One of the better spots for cheap eats is the intersection of Estrada and Guayacanes, where more than five Middle Eastern *shawarma* and kebab joints are congregated. All of them, including **El Rey Shawarma** (mains $3) are open-air informal spots.

DRINKING & ENTERTAINMENT

The *farra* (nightlife) in Guayaquil is spread around town. Though particular places tend to come and go, there are specific areas to check out: the former red-light district, still called the Zona Rosa, behind Malecón 2000 between Aguirre and Orellana has more than a dozen bars and clubs, from trendy to seedy; Las Peñas, the hillside to the north of downtown, has more modest hangouts; the northern suburb of Urdesa and the Samborondón area, across Río Daule near the Parque Histórico, are where the beautiful and chic mix; while the places in Alborada and Kennedy Norte are less class conscious. The city's luxury hotels all have casinos and sedate bars.

Guayaquileños bleed yellow and black, the colors of their beloved soccer team, **Barceloña Sporting Club** (BSC; www.bsc.ec). On game days much of the city looks like it's gone into hiding, since those not at the 90,000-seat Estadio Monumental Banco del Pichincha in the northern suburb of El Paráso are glued to their TVs at home or in bars.

Local newspapers *El Telégrafo* and *El Universo* have entertainment listings.

Bars

It's easy to barhop in the Zona Rosa; **Proga Bar & Lounge** (Map pp322-3; Rocafuerte), **234 Bar n Vivo** (Map pp322-3; cnr Imbabura & Rocafuerte) and **Piranha** (Map pp322-3; Imbabura) are a few within steps of one another. Found along the cobblestone streets of Las Peñas is **DADA** (Map pp322-3; ☎ 230-2828; Numa Pompilio Llona 177; ⌚ Tue-Sat 6pm-3am), at once hip and stylish and warm and welcoming. Just down the street is **La Paleta** (Map pp322-3; ☎ 231-2329; Numa Pompilio Llona; ⌚ 8pm-3am Tue-Sat), which is all cavelike nooks, comfy benches and dark wood. Both serve beers and high-end cocktails such as $8 martinis.

Just to the left at the bottom of the steps in Las Peñas is **La Taberna** (Map pp322-3; Cerro Santa Ana), a grunge drinking bar with Latin rock and pop in the background. Also at the bottom is **El Galeón de Artur's** (Map pp322-3; ☎ 230-3574; Cerro Santa Ana; ⌚ 6pm-1:30am), a casual place for a drink if you don't mind the loud music. **Escalón 69** (Map pp322-3; ☎ 230-9828; Cerro Santa Ana; ⌚ noon-2am Tue-Sun) is a few flights up and has DJs and live music on weekends. The **Café Galería Quimbita** (Map pp322-3; ☎ 231-0785; Escalón 27, Cerro Santa Ana; ⌚ 5pm-1am Wed & Sun, 5pm-3am Thu-Sat) is one of the more popular late-night spots in the neighborhood.

If you need a drink after climbing to the hill's summit, stop in at **Puerto Pirata** (Escalón 384; ⌚ noon-midnight); you can't miss this faux pirate ship below the lighthouse. It has drinks and food (mains $5), and live music on weekends.

Barhopping is easy at **Kennedy Mall** (Map p324; Francisco de Orellana), a concentration of bars and discos in Kennedy Norte. Most have a cover charge, but also an open bar, meaning you drink for free after paying admission.

Nightclubs

Some of the Zona Rosa clubs to check out are **Geishas** (formerly Macarena Lounge; Map pp322-3; Malecón Simón Bolívar 602 & Imbabura; ⌚ 7pm-4am Mon-Fri), **Zook** (Map pp322-3; Panamá) and **Om Lounge** (Map pp322-3 cnr Malecón & Aguirre). A few blocks away, between the MAAC and Las Peñas, is **Minc** (Map pp322-3; ☎ 277-2511; Malecón at Vernaza y Carbo; cover $10; ⌚ 6.30pm-late Wed-Sat).

Urdesa has a few happening clubs despite the wealthy neighborhood's preference for low-key quiet. Names, locations and hotspots change with frequency. **Fizz y Sante** (Francisco de Orellana 796 & Cornejo), opposite the World Trade Center office building in Kennedy Norte, is particularly popular. **El Jardín de Salsa** (Map p324 ☎ 239-6083; Av de las Américas), near the airport, has one of the largest dance floors in Ecuador.

One of the few downtown gay and lesbian clubs is **Vulcano** (Map pp322-3; Rocafuerte 419 & Aguirre), which has drag shows Friday and Saturday nights and otherwise moves to techno rhythms.

Cinemas

El Telégrafo and *El Universo* publish show times for all cinemas in the city. English-language movies with Spanish subtitles are usually shown, although downtown there are a few B-rated movie houses screening porno flicks and schlock. For Hollywood fare downtown, check out the six-screen **Supercines** (Map pp322-3; ☎ 252-2054; Av 9 de Octubre 823 & Avilés; $2) or the **IMAX theater** (Map pp322-3; ☎ 256-3078; cnr Malecón Simón Bolívar & Loja; $4) on the *malecón*, connected to the MAAC. The latter also has the **MAAC Cine** (Map pp322-3; ☎ 230-9400; cnr Malecón Simón Bolívar & Loja; $2), a nice art-house cinema. The **Casa de Cultura** (Map pp322-3; cnr Av 9 de Octubre & Moncayo) periodically shows foreign films and art flicks.

Filmgoers in the northern suburbs head to the multiscreen **Cinemark** (Map p324; ☎ 269-2014; www.cinemark.com.ec; Av Juan Tanca Marengo) in the Mall del Sol or the **Supercines** (Map p324; ☎ 208-3268; www.supercines.com; Av Francisco Orellana) in the San Marino Mall.

Theater

Besides the performance space at the MAAC, several other venues to check out for contemporary theater and live music include **Teatro Sarao** (Map p324; ☎ 229-5118; Oeste 313 & Av del Periodista, Kennedy), **Teatro del Ángel** (Map p324; ☎ 238-0585; Bálsamos 620 & Las Monjas, Urdesa) and **Teatro Centro de Arte** (☎ 235-0718; sfdc@gye.com; Av del Bombero, Km4.5).

SHOPPING

El Mercado Artesanal Loja (Map pp322-3; Baquerizo Moreno; 9am-7pm Mon-Sat, 10am-5pm Sun) A large artisans' market taking up an entire block downtown. It has a huge variety of crafts from all over Ecuador, including Otavalo-style sweaters, panama hats, carved chessboards, mass-produced paintings, Barcelona (the hometown soccer team) apparel and just about every knickknack imaginable. Absolutely safe to wander, and bargaining is expected.

La Bahía (Map pp322-3; Carbo & Villamil) A sprawling street market between Olmedo and Colón is a crowded maze of vendors selling everything from knock-off name-brand watches to brassieres and bootleg CDs.

If you prefer a more sedate shopping atmosphere, try one of the indoor shopping malls along the *malecón* or the department stores along Avenida 9 de Octubre. One of the largest malls in all of South America, similar to any you find in the US, is **Mall del Sol** (Map p324; Av Juan Tanca Marengo), near the airport. **San Marino** (Map p324; Av Francisco Orellana) in the Kennedy suburb is a large, equally high-end mall. Also in Urdesa is **Centro Comercial Albán Borja** (Av Carlos Julio Arosemena).

GETTING THERE & AWAY

Air

Guayaquil's sleek and modern **José Joaquín de Olmedo International Airport** (airport code GYE; off Map pp322-3; ☎ 216-9209) is one of Ecuador's two major international airports and is about as busy as Quito's. It's located on the east side of Avenida de las Américas, about 5km north of downtown. Anyone flying to the Galápagos Islands either leaves from here or stops here on their way from Quito; those flying from Quito rarely have to change planes.

The terminal, completed in 2006, has every amenity including a *casa de cambio* (currency-exchange bureau), several ATMs, car-rental agencies, international telephone facilities, restaurants and coffee shops, and free wi-fi access is available throughout. A desk with accommodation and transport information is immediately outside the arrivals hall.

About 1km south of the main airport is the Terminal de Avionetas (Small Aircraft Terminal).

DOMESTIC

There are many internal flights to all parts of the country, but times, days and fares change constantly, so check the following information. The most frequent flights are to Quito with TAME, which charges about $59 one-way. For the best views, sit on the right side when flying to Quito.

TAME also flies to Cuenca ($65) and Loja ($80) daily, as well as Lago Agrio ($65, via Quito). There are usually flights to Tulcán ($65) and Esmeraldas ($57) as well.

TAME and AeroGal fly to Baltra and San Cristóbal in the Galápagos. There are two morning flights every day, costing $365 per round-trip ($320 in the low season – mid-January to mid-June and September to November). Ecuadorian residents pay $256 all year.

Icaro flies to Quito ($57) four times a day Monday to Friday and twice daily on weekends and to Cuenca ($45) twice daily (except weekends).

All the aforementioned flights leave from the main national terminal. Several small airlines have flights leaving from the Terminal de Avionetas. These airlines use small aircraft to service various coastal towns, such as Portoviejo and Esmeraldas. Flights are subject to demand. Baggage is limited to a 10kg bag and passenger weight is limited to 100kg.

The following is a list of domestic airline offices in Guayaquil.

AeroGal (☎ 231-0346; www.aerogal.com.ec; Junín 440)
Icaro (☎ 229-4265; www.icaro.com.ec; main airport)
TAME Gran Pasaje (Map pp322-3; ☎ 256-0778, ext 211; www.tame.com.ec; Av 9 de Octubre 424); main airport (☎ 216-9163).

INTERNATIONAL

A $27 departure tax for international flights must be paid before passing through security.

AeroGal, the Ecuadorean airline listed above, also has daily direct flights between Guayaquil and Miami. The following is a list of some international airlines serving Guayaquil.

Avianca (☎ 216-9130; www.avianca.com)
Copa (☎ 230-3211; www.copaair.com)
KLM (☎ 216-9070; www.klm.com)
Lan (☎ 269-2850; www.lan.com) Direct flights to New York City.
TACA (☎ 288-9789; www.taca.com; Luque btwn Carbo & Pichincha)

Bus & Van

The cavernous Terminal Terrestre (Bus Terminal; Map p324), just north of the airport, received a makeover in 2007. It's now as much a high-end mall (shops, restaurants, internet cafés etc) as it is a transportation facility. There are more than 100 bus companies with small offices lined up along one side of the bottom floor of the building. The kiosks are grouped by region, and most of the destinations and departure times are clearly marked. Buses depart from the 2nd floor. Fortunately, there are several comfortable seating areas if you have lots of time to kill. Check out the 'Servicios' section of the daily edition of *El Universo*, Guayaquil's city paper, or the website www.terminalguayauil.com for a listing of departures.

DOMESTIC

For the Santa Elena Peninsula, you can take Transportes Villamil or Transportes Posorja, which have buses every 10 minutes to Playas ($2.50, two hours); Costa Azul, Co-op Libertad Peninsular and CICA have buses to Salinas ($3, 2½ hours) every 15 minutes. **Rusoltur SA** (☎ 256-1675; rusoltur@hotmail.com; Córdova 601 & Mendiburo) has minivans that shuttle between downtown Guayaquil and Salinas ($10) every hour between 6:30am and 8:30pm.

To get to Bosque Protector Cerro Blanco (p318), take a bus marked 'Chongón' from the stop at Moncayo and Sucre. All the drivers know where to stop for the entrance to the reserve.

The best services to Quito are with the companies **Transportes Ecuador** (☎ 214-0592), **Flota Imbabura** (☎ 214-0649) and **Panamericana** (☎ 214-0638). They all cost around $9 and do the trip in eight hours.

From downtown, **Coturcip** (Map pp322-3; ☎ 251-8895; Sucre 202 & Pichincha) has comfortable air-conditioned vans to Machala ($8), and **Transfrosur** (Map pp322-3; ☎ 232-6387; www.transfrosur.com; Chile 416) has a similar service to Huaquillas ($12).

BUSES FROM GUAYAQUIL

Destination	Cost ($)	Duration (hr)
Ambato	6	6
Atacames	10	9
Baños	7	7
Cuenca	7	3½-4½
Esmeraldas	7	7
Huaquillas	5.50	4
Latacunga	6.50	7½
Loja	6	9
Machala	4	3½
Manta	4.50	3½
Montañita	6	3½
Muisne	9	9
Playas	2.50	2
Portoviejo	4.50	4
Puyo	9	7
Quito	9	7-10
Riobamba	5	5
Santo Domingo	5	5
Tulcán	13	13
Zaruma	6.50	6

Most bus companies sell tickets in advance, which will guarantee you a seat. Otherwise, just show up at the terminal and you'll often find a bus to your destination leaving soon. Friday nights and holidays can get booked up. The boxed table (above) should give you an idea of fares and travel times.

INTERNATIONAL

Ecuadorian bus companies such as CIFA, Transportes Rutas Orenses and Ecuatoriana Pullman go to Machala and Huaquillas on the Peruvian border. Transportes Loja has one bus in the evening to the border at Macará.

The easiest way to Peru, however, is with one of the international lines. **Rutas de America** (off Map pp322-3; ☎ 223-8673; www.rutasdeamerica.com.ec; Los Rios 3012 at Letamendi), whose office and terminal is south of downtown, has direct buses to Lima ($50, 24 hours) every Wednesday at 11am and Sunday at 7am and 11am.

More highly recommended is **Expreso Internacional Ormeno** (Map p324; ☎ 214-0362; Centro de Negocios El Terminal, Bahia Norte, Office 34, Bloque C), which has Sunday departures for Lima ($65) at 11:30am, stopping in Tumbes ($20, eight hours). Its office and terminal is on Avenida de las Americas, just north of the main bus terminal. These services are very convenient because you do not have to get off the bus to take care of border formalities.

GETTING AROUND

Walking is the easiest and most convenient way of getting around downtown. Yellow taxis, a quick and relatively inexpensive way of covering long distances, are everywhere. Buses, both the older blue-and-white *selectivos* and the new Metrovia system are convenient for travel between downtown and the suburbs.

To/From the Airport

The **airport** (Av de las Américas) is about 5km north of downtown. A taxi in either direction should cost no more than $4. The majority of taxis at the airport are yellow and labeled **Cooperativa de Transportes Aeropuerto Guayaquil** (☎ 216-9141; www.taxiecuadorairport.com); these will take you into the city or for that matter anywhere else in the country, from Ambato ($150) to Quito ($250). Rates are posted online and in the backseats.

Cross the street in front of the airport to take a bus downtown. From the center, the best bus to take to the airport is bus 2 Especial, which only costs $0.25 and takes under an hour. It runs along the *malecón* but is sometimes full, so you should leave yourself plenty of time.

To/From the Bus Terminal

The bus terminal is about 2km away from the airport. You can walk the distance if you want, although it means crossing a busy highway and is not recommended if you're carrying heavy bags. Turn right out of the airport and head for the obvious huge terminal. A taxi between the two is $1.

Buses from the center to the bus terminal leave from Parque Victoria, near Calle 10 de Agosto and Moncayo.

Several buses leave from the terminal for downtown including bus 71. A taxi to or from downtown is about $3.

Also see the Metrovia (below).

Bus

City buses are cheap (about $0.25) but the routes are complicated and are not much use for getting around downtown. With waiting and traffic, you're better off walking.

The **Metrovia** ($0.25), a new rapid transit system, has articulated double-sized buses (the kind with an accordion middle) running along designated lanes from downtown to northern suburbs. Terminal Río Daule, opposite the Terminal Terrestre, is the end of one of the lines. These newer and faster buses are recommended.

Car

There are several car-rental agencies at the airport including **Budget** (☎ 228-8510; www.budget-ec.com), **Hertz** (☎ 216-9035; www.hertz.com.ec) and **Localiza** (☎ 390-4523; www.localiza.com.ec). All of these also have offices in the city, though these tend to keep more limited hours. Pay attention to the kilometers included in your rate and ask about the condition of the roads where you'll be driving; a 4WD vehicle is often worth the extra cost. Driving in the city is not for the faint of heart – rules, regulations, safety, everything is out the window. See p398 for more details.

Taxi

Agree on the fare before you get into the cab, otherwise you may be overcharged. Another strategy, however, is simply to hand the driver what you suspect is the lower end of the proper price and if he accepts it without comment, great. If he asks for more, you know you have probably low-balled him. You should be able to get between any two points downtown for about $1.50 and to the airport, the bus terminal or Urdesa for between $3 to $4.

If you can't find a taxi on the street try **Cooperativa de Taxis Paraíso** (☎ 220-1877).

SOUTH OF GUAYAQUIL

Though primarily seen by travelers simply as a place to pass through on their way south to Peru, this agriculturally important part of the country boasts several nature reserves and a charming mountain town.

RESERVA ECOLÓGICA MANGLARES CHURUTE

☎ 04

This 50,000-hectare **national reserve** (admission $10) protects an area of mangroves southeast of Guayaquil. Much of the coast used to be mangrove forest – an important and unique habitat (see p56). This is one of Ecuador's few remaining mangrove coastlands; the rest have been destroyed by the shrimp industry. Inland is some tropical dry forest on hills reaching 700m above sea level.

Studies of the area within the reserve indicate that the changing habitat from coastal mangroves to hilly forest supports a wide biodiversity with a high proportion of endemic species. Dolphins have frequently been reported along the coast, and many other animal and bird species are seen by wildlife-watchers, who are the main visitors.

The reserve entrance is on the left side of the main Guayaquil–Machala highway, about 50km south of Guayaquil. Here you'll find an **information center** (☎ 09-276-3653, 229-3131), where you pay the entrance fee. Park rangers can arrange boats for you to visit the mangroves (about $60 for the whole day for four or five people). There are also several kilometers of hiking trails. The best season for boats is January to May, when water levels are high (but there are more insects then).

Bordering the reserve is an area protected by Fundación Andrade. Nancy Hilgert (p326) is the contact and she can guide you. Tangara Tours (p327) also does tours to Manglares Churute.

A few basic **cabañas** ($5) near the information center, little more than concrete shelters, are available. **Camping** ($3) can be arranged if coordinated in advance with the reserve office.

Any bus between Guayaquil and Naranjal or Machala can drop you off at the information center. When you are ready to leave, flag a bus down – there is a sign on the road and drivers know it.

MACHALA

☎ 07 / pop 228,000

Surrounded by banana plantations – the *oro verde* (green gold), which is the province's moniker – Machala is the commercial and administrative capital of El Oro province. The city is a convenient stop south from Guayaquil on the way to the Peruvian border, or as a place to base yourself for journeys further into the mountains directly to the east. Puerto Bolívar (p337), only 7km away, is the local international port and seafood central.

Information

The **tourism office** (9 de Mayo & 9 de Octubre), on the ground floor of the municipal building at the southeast corner of the central plaza has city and area maps. A handful of major banks with ATMs are located around the central plaza. More than half a dozen internet cafés doubling as call centers are on 9 de Octubre between Guayas and Las Palmeras.

Festivals & Events

Machala celebrates the **Feria Mundial del Banano** during the third week in September, when an international contest is held to elect La Reina del Banano (The Banana Queen).

Sleeping

Machala has a number of good-value hotels and it makes sense to spend the night here rather than in Huaquillas if heading to or from Peru.

Hotel Bolívar Internacional (☎ 293-0727; falvarado@hotmail.com; cnr Bolívar & Colón; s/d $18/26; ❄ 💻) This squeaky clean and friendly hotel is only a short walk from the busy center. Some of the tiled rooms are actually too large with too many beds, better for slumber parties.

Hostal Saloah (☎ 293-4344; Colón 1818; s/d incl breakfast $18/29; ❄ 💻) On a bustling block only steps from several bus companies, the well-kept rooms at the Saloah are surprisingly quiet all things considered – tiny windows help. Each of the four floors has a larger, brighter street-facing suite worth the few extra dollars. There's also a computer with internet access on every floor, and a rooftop patio where breakfast is served with panoramic views of the city.

Grand Hotel Americano (☎ 296-6400; www.hotelesmachala.com; Tarqui & 9 de Octubre; r from $25; ❄ 💻) The best choice in terms of overall value, the Grand Hotel Americano has clean, modern rooms, professional staff and a central location. The one downside here is the potentially annoying street noise. All rooms have air-conditioning and cable TV, and breakfast in the attached restaurant is included.

Rizzo Hotel (☎ 293-3651; Guayas 2123; s/d incl breakfast $30/45; ❄ 💻 🏊) The architecture of the Rizzo screams '70s and the furniture probably hasn't been replaced since then, but there is a pool and a patio area. Rooms at the Rizzo are clean and have cable TV, though they are a little dark. Wi-fi is available in the attached café.

SOUTH COAST

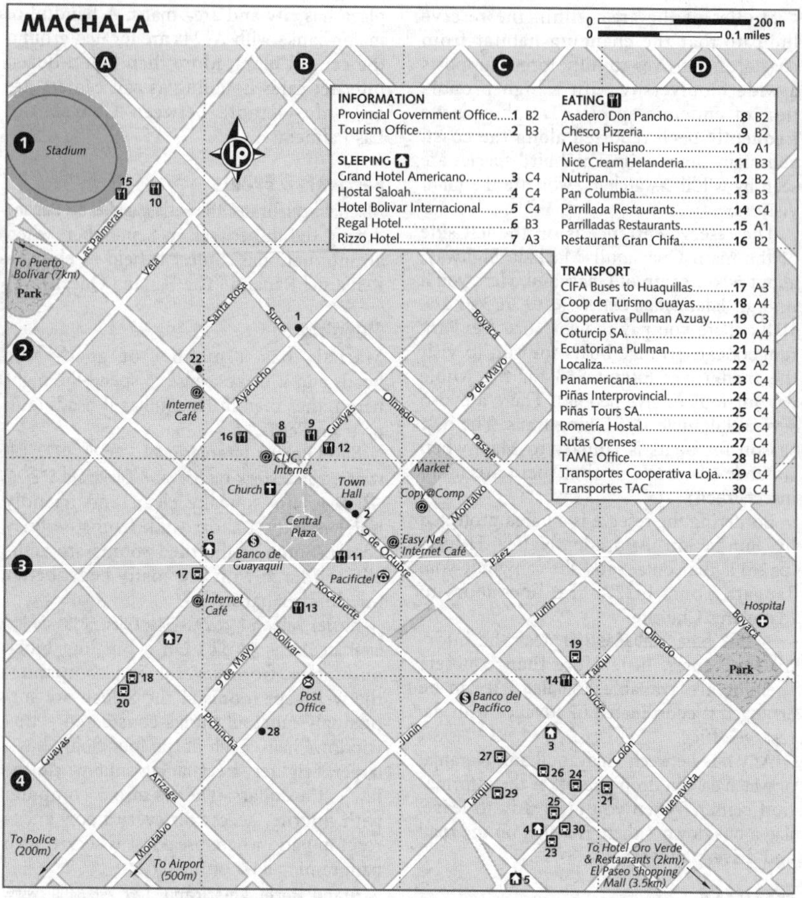

Regal Hotel (☎ 796-0000; www.regalhotel.com.ec; Bolívar near Guayas; s/d $57/70;) A big step up in terms of price though not a huge one in terms of comfort, the Regal nevertheless is the classiest hotel in downtown Machala. There are hints of Spanish villa in the floor tiles and the wall murals. Look for the tall glass-fronted building only a block from the main plaza. A small restaurant is attached, and wi-fi is available throughout.

Eating

There's a concentration of *parrillada* restaurants serving inexpensive grilled chicken and steaks on Sucre near Tarqui and on Las Palmeras in front of the stadium – an especially good choice on Sunday and holidays, when much of the city shuts down. Most of the hotels reviewed here have restaurants. Consider heading over to Puerto Bolívar (opposite) for a fresh seafood lunch.

Nice Cream Helandería (9 de Mayo; burgers $3) Cool off with shakes ($1.75), sundaes and cold coffee drinks at this popular place on the southern side of the central plaza. Pizza and burgers are of the reheated, video-arcade variety.

Asadero Don Pancho (9 de Octubre; almuerzos $3) Always bustling at lunchtime, the deep and narrow dining room is filled with diners enjoying cheap *almuerzos* and juicy rotisserie chicken.

Chesco Pizzeria (☎ 293-6418; Guayas 1050, near 9 de Octubre; mains $4) Chesco serves up piping-hot, deep-dish pizzas plus pasta and hamburgers in a modern dining room.

Meson Hispano (☎ 293-6769; Las Palmeras & Sucre; mains $5-12; 11am-midnight Mon-Thu, to 1am Fri & Sat) Qualifying as swank for Machala, this restaurant has uniformed waiters, tablecloths and a large sophisticated menu – Caesar salad ($5) to chateaubriand ($9).

Restaurant Gran Chifa (9 de Octubre; mains $2-5; 11am-10pm) is one of the many family-style Chinese restaurants scattered throughout town. There's a bar, a deli and an upmarket restaurant in the **Hotel Oro Verde** (☎ 293-3140; www.oroverdehotels.com; Circunvalación Norte & Calle Vehicular V7), Machala's only luxury hotel, a few kilometers to the southeast. El Paseo, a modern shopping mall 3.5km south of town, has an enormous department store with a grocery section, a food court and a cinema.

For midday snacks, nothing beats a piping-hot sweet roll or pastry served at one of the many bakeries; try **Nutripan** (Guayas btwn 9 de Octubre & Sucre) or **Pan Columbia** (9 de Mayo btwn Rocafuerte & Bolívar).

Getting There & Away

AIR

Weekday morning flights to Quito ($98), are available with **TAME** (☎ 293-0139; www.tame.com.ec; Montalvo near Pichincha). The airport is 1km from downtown and a taxi ride there will cost about $1. If you're on foot, walk southwest along Montalvo.

BUS

Machala has no central bus terminal. There are **CIFA** (☎ 293-1164; Guayas & Bolívar) buses that go to the Peruvian border at Huaquillas ($1.50, 1½ hours) every 20 minutes during daylight from the corner of Bolívar and Guayas. These buses go via the towns of Santa Rosa and Arenillas. CIFA buses also go to Guayaquil ($4, three hours). **Rutas Orenses** (☎ 293-7661; Rocafuerte near Tarqui) and **Ecuatoriana Pullman** (☎ 293-1164; 9 de Octubre near Colón) have slightly more comfortable air-conditioned buses and frequent services to Guayaquil and Huaquillas as well.

Piñas Interprovincial (☎ 229-3689; Colón & Rocafuerte) and **Transportes TAC** (Colón) both leave regularly from early morning to around 7pm for Piñas ($2, two hours) and Zaruma ($3, three hours).

Panamericana (☎ 293-0141; Colón near Rocafuerte) has regular daily buses to Quito ($7, 11 hours). It also has buses to Santo Domingo ($6, eight hours) and an evening bus to Tulcán.

Cooperative Pullman Azuay (☎ 293-0539; Sucre at Tarqui) has many buses daily to Cuenca ($4, four hours). A few direct buses take three hours.

Transportes Cooperativa Loja (☎ 293-2030; Tarqui near Bolívar) goes to Loja ($4.50, five hours).

MINIVAN

A handful of minivan companies line Guayas between Pichincha and Serrano, including **Coturcip SA** (☎ 296-0849, Guayaquil 225-1889) and **Coop de Turismo Guayas** (☎ 293-4382). These have several departures daily to Guayaquil ($10).

Romería Hostal (☎ 292-1739; Rocafuerte) has vans to Zaruma ($4) and **Piñas Tours SA** (☎ 296-6894; Colón & Rocafuerte) has vans to Piñas ($3) several times a day.

SOUTH COAST

Getting Around

Crowded bus 1 goes northwest from the central plaza along 9 de Octubre to Puerto Bolívar ($0.20, 15 minutes). It returns along Pichincha and goes southeast to the statue of El Bananero, almost 2km from the center. A taxi to Puerto Bolívar costs no more than $2.

Localiza (☎ 293-5455; 9 de Octubre near Santa Rosa) rents out cars. Hotel Oro Verde (opposite) also arranges car rental.

PUERTO BOLÍVAR & JAMBELÍ

☎ 07

An otherwise banal stretch of concrete, the port of Puerto Bolívar, only 7km from Machala, is of interest to seafood connoisseurs and those who want to glimpse the final stop for the southern coast's bananas and shrimp before they're shipped overseas. The port itself is really nothing more than a concrete *malecón* with around 20 informal *cevicherías* (ceviche restaurants) and a slightly dodgy feel at night. The **Waikiki Restaurant** (☎ 292-9810; mains $5) is a more upscale and modern version of these, and a secure destination if you visit after dark.

Motorized dugouts can be hired for cruising the mangroves, for **bird-watching** or to visit the nearby island beach at **Jambelí** (mosquito-ridden during the wet months). While it's understandably popular for Machala residents seeking a quick escape from the city, it's not an especially attractive destination in and of itself. Jambelí can be busy on weekends and completely overcrowded during Carnaval and Semana Santa. There's some good snorkeling around the nearby mangrove island of **Isla de Amor**, part of a community ecoproject to preserve the marine environment.

Maria Sol (☎ 293-7461; r per person $5) and **Toa Toa** (☎ 267-6067; r per person $7) both have small basic bamboo cabañas on the beach. A number of beach-side shacks serve seafood on weekends, but many are closed midweek.

Take bus 1 or bus 13 from Machala's central plaza, or take a taxi (about $2). To Jambelí you can either charter a boat from Puerto Bolívar or take one of the passenger shuttle boats (round-trip $2.40, 25 minutes, every two hours from 7:30am to 6pm). The boats drop you off on a canal on the mainland side of the island and you have to walk the few hundred meters to the beach.

ZARUMA

☎ 07 / elevation 1150m

After winding your way up and over lushly covered mountains with gushing streams pouring through the foliage, the final climb up to Zaruma feels like the end of a pilgrimage. And for those traveling along the washboard-flat coastal roadway, the narrow, hilly streets of this old gold-mining town in the mountains southeast of Machala are a revelation.

Architecturally more modern and less charming, **Piñas** is probably best visited as a side trip while based in Zaruma. In 1980 a new bird species, the El Oro parakeet, was discovered near here. The best place to see the bird is Fundación Jocotoco's **Reserva Buenaventura** (entry $15), a 1500-hectare cloud-forest reserve about 9km from Piñas.

Information

While the mines are mostly exhausted, you can arrange a visit to one nearby at the friendly and helpful **tourism office** (☎ 297-3101; turismo zaruma07@yahoo.com; 8am-noon & 2-6pm Mon-Fri, 9am-4pm Sat, 8:30am-12:30pm Sun), just off the Plaza de Independencia. In town there's a Banco de Guayaquil and a Banco de Machala, both with ATMs, several internet cafés with call centers, and a wash-and-dry laundry.

Sleeping & Eating

Because of the cool nighttime air temperatures, air-conditioning is unnecessary. The one place to truly take advantage of the scenery is the **Roland Hotel** (☎ 297-2800; s/d $18/25;), the first place you come to on the main road from Piñas up to town. The main building has small modern rooms with hot-water bathrooms and TVs – be sure to ask for one with windows opening onto the valley below. There are slightly more expensive, small, pastel-colored chalets surrounding the pool in the concrete courtyard. The only downside is the short uphill slog to eat, since the hotel's restaurant only gets going for groups.

The next-best options are up the hill, closer to the central plaza. Only a block or so above the bus stop is the **Hotel Blacio** (☎ 297-2045; www.hotelblacio.com; Calle Sexmo 015 & Sucre; r per person $10), a small, friendly place with hot water and well-cared-for rooms. Watch your head climbing the stairs of the family-run **Hotel Cerro de Oro** (☎ 297-2505; s/d $7/15); if you don't mind the climb, the top-floor room gets lots of light.

Just below Plaza Independencia are two casual eateries, Rincon Zarumen and Café Zarumeño, both of which serve basic chicken and rice dishes ($2.50) as well as *tigrillos*, an area specialty made of green bananas, eggs and cheese. **Tangobar Restaurant** (mains $3), on the plaza itself, has charming wood floors and good and cheap *almuerzos*. Both Café con Aroma Zarumeña and 200 Miles (mains $2) are located further down the main road from the plaza; the former is a good place for breakfast and coffee, and the latter has a small dining room with good views of the valley below.

Getting There & Away

Piñas (☎ 297-6167) has departures every hour on the half-hour, and TAC has four daily departures for Piñas (1$, one hour) and Machala ($3, three hours).

Romería (☎ 297-2173) runs minivans with direct connections to Machala ($4, hourly from early morning to 6:30pm), Guayaquil (3am, 7am and 1pm) and Cuenca (1pm and 5pm).

In your own vehicle it's no more than a two-hour drive to Machala.

EL BOSQUE PETRIFICADO PUYANGO

☎ 07

This is the largest petrified forest (2659 hectares) in Ecuador and probably the whole continent. Fossilized araucaria tree trunks – many of them millions of years old – up to 11m long and 1.6m in diameter have been found. The reserve is also home to more than 130 bird species.

Puyango is in a valley at about 360m above sea level, some 55km inland from the coast. The valley is separated from the ocean by the Cordillera Larga, which reaches over 900m above sea level. Despite the separation, the area experiences a coastal weather pattern, with warm temperatures and most of the annual 1000mm of rainfall occurring from January to May.

The entrance fee is $5 and camping is allowed for a small fee; ask at the information center. A lookout point and trails have been constructed.

In the small nearby village of **Puyango** there is no hotel as such, although the villagers will find you a bed or floor space. Locals know the reserve and some will act as guides. The nearest village with basic *hostales* is **Alamor**, just south of Puyango.

For more information, call the **Provincial Government Office** (Map p336; ☎ 293-5871; Ayacucho btwn Pasaje & Sucre).

Transportes Cooperativa Loja buses from Machala and Loja will drop you in Puyango. Alternatively, take a CIFA bus to the town of Arenillas, where you can catch an infrequent local bus for the further 55km to Puyango. You may be stopped for a passport check since the park is close to the border.

TO/FROM THE PERUVIAN BORDER

It's about 80km from Machala to the border town of Huaquillas, the route taken by most overland travelers to Peru. The highway passes through banana and palm plantations, as well as the dusty market towns of **Santa Rosa** and **Arenillas**. The border itself is at **Río Zarumilla** (🕑 24hr), a mostly dry riverbed which is crossed by an international bridge linking Huaquillas to **Aguas Verdes** in Peru. Many travelers report that crossing at night is easier in some respects – it allows you to avoid the touts and overzealous immigration officials (as opposed to the sleepy immigration officials who, in the middle of the night, simply want you on your way).

The **Ecuadorian Immigrations Office** (🕑 24hr) is inconveniently located about 4km north of the bridge; all entrance and exit formalities are carried out here. The Peruvian immigration office is about 2km south of the border.

If you are leaving Peru and entering Ecuador, first obtain an exit stamp in your passport from the Peruvian authorities. After walking across the international bridge you'll find yourself on the main road, which is crowded with market stalls and stretches out through Huaquillas. Take a taxi (about $1.50) or a Machala-bound bus to the Ecuadorian immigration office; you'll probably then have to return to Huaquillas to catch onward northbound transport. Be aware that readers report hassles and scams with taxis from Tumbes to Huaquillas – choose your driver carefully. The safest and most convenient bet are the daily CIFA buses direct from Tumbes to Guayaquil.

If leaving Ecuador, stop at the Ecuadorian *migraciones* office, 4km before the border. If you're traveling by bus from Machala, the driver does not wait for you. You must save your ticket and board the next Machala–Huaquillas bus (they pass every 20 minutes or so) or continue on to the border by taxi.

It's extremely unlikely you'll be asked to show the exit stamp in your passport to any Ecuadorian and Peruvian (Aguas Verdes) bridge guards, and you can cross back and forth as you please. You won't be bothered until full entrance formalities are carried out in the Peruvian immigration building about 2km from the border. Taxis are available for about $0.50 per person.

From the immigration building in Peru, *colectivos* (shared taxis; about $1.50 per person) go to Tumbes – beware of overcharging. Tumbes has plenty of hotels, as well as transportation to take you further into Peru. See Lonely Planet's *Peru* for more information.

Huaquillas

☎ 07 / pop 45,000

Both sides of the frontier are hectic and crowded, and hold little appeal except as necessary way stations to more pleasant destinations. The Río Zarumilla, which is the border, is a dry riverbed for much of the year. There is a busy street market by the border where Peruvians come to shop on day passes.

There are several **internet cafés** located around the intersection of La Republica and Santa Rosa near the town square.

INFORMATION

It's best to avoid the informal moneychangers on either side of the border. On the Ecuadorian side they're the guys with the briefcases sitting on plastic chairs. Problems with fake currency aren't uncommon. In order to get your business, moneychangers will tell patent lies like 'banks are closed' or 'the machines don't work'. Banks in Huaquillas or Aguas Verdes don't normally do exchange transactions, but it's worth trying. There are a number of ATMs on the Ecuadorian side including a branch of **Banco de Machala** (Av de la Republica & Santa Rosa).

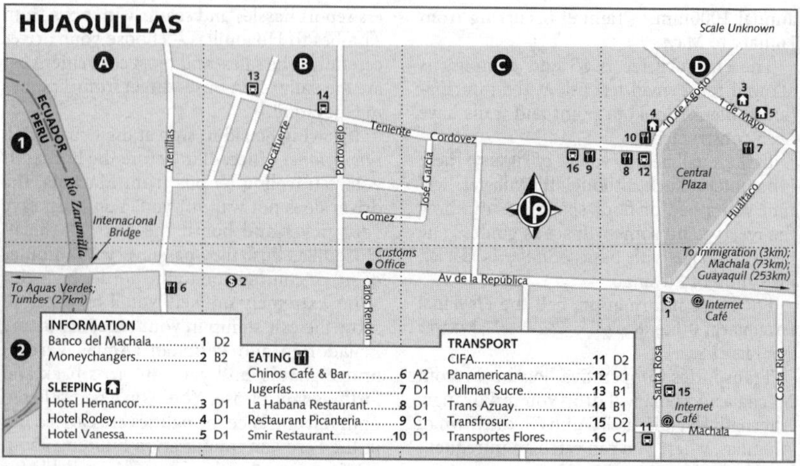

If you're leaving Peru, it's best to get rid of as much Peruvian currency as possible before you arrive in Ecuador, and preferably before arriving at the border. If you're leaving Ecuador, your US currency is easily exchanged in Peru, but again it's best to wait to do the bulk of your transactions further south.

SLEEPING & EATING

Most travelers leaving Ecuador sleep in Machala and go straight through to Tumbes (or vice versa); both places have plenty of hotels. If you're stuck for the night, however, there are a few adequate options. The **Hotel Rodey** (☎ 299-5581; Teniente Cordovez & 10 de Agosto; s/d from $5/10) has the smallest and least well-maintained rooms. A step up in quality is the friendly **Hotel Vanessa** (☎ 299-6263; 1 de Mayo & Hualtaco; s/d $14/18; ❄), which can usually at least guarantee hot water – some of the rooms in the back even get sunlight. The grand dame of town is the **Hotel Hernancor** (☎ 299-5467; grandhotelhernancor_@hotmail.com; 1 de Mayo; s/d $16/20; ❄); with its facade of reflecting glass and prominently displayed flags, it could pass for the Chinese embassy. The high-socialist theme extends inside with wide hallways, high ceilings and large but impersonal rooms. Staff at the front desk can answer transportation questions.

If you need a breather after enduring the border hassles and before tackling onward transport, **Chino's Café & Bar** (Av de la Republica), immediately after you cross the bridge into Ecuador, is a good spot. Grab a beer or a juice and an outdoor table to watch the comings and goings.

Smir Restaurant (cnr 10 de Agosto & Teniente Cordovez; mains $4) serves ceviches, tortillas and other fare in an air-conditioned modern dining room. **La Habana Restaurant** (Teniente Cordovez) and **Restaurant Picanteria** (Teniente Cordovez) are both across the street; the former does good *parrilladas,* and the latter has cheap *almuerzos.* There are several *juguerías* (juice shacks) selling delicious mango, papaya and other flavors just behind the municipal government building.

GETTING THERE & AWAY

Huaquillas does not have a main bus terminal; the various companies are scattered within half-a-dozen blocks of one another and the border. **CIFA** (Santa Rosa & Machala) has five daily departures for Guayaquil ($5, four hours, 9:15am, 11:15am, 1pm, 3:15pm and 5pm) and three for Machala ($1.80, 1½ hours, 8am, 10am and noon). Of course you can also board any Guayaquil-bound bus and get off in Machala. **Transfrosur** (Santa Rosa) runs frequent minivans to Guayaquil ($12, four hours).

Panamericana (Teniente Cordovez & 10 de Agosto) has seven buses a day heading to Quito ($10, 13 hours), some via Santo Domingo and others via Ambato ($8, 11 hours). The earliest is at 9:45am and the last at 9pm. If you're in a rush to make it to Colombia, there's a daily 4:30pm trip to Tulcan ($15, 19 hours) near the Colombian border. **Pullman Sucre** and **Trans Azuay**, both on Teniente Cordovez, have frequent buses heading to Cuenca ($5, five hours).

Crossing into Peru, taxi drivers at the border will tell you there are no buses or *colectivos* running to Tumbes when in fact there are. **Transportes Flores** (Teniente Cordovez 116) has five daily departures from the Peruvian side of the border south to Lima ($18, 20 hours) and points in between. The 3:30pm and 6:30pm trips are more-comfortable double-decker buses with reclining seats, bathrooms, TVs and dinner ($25).

Note that from Guayaquil the international bus companies Rutas de America and Expreso Internacional Ormeno (see p333) offer direct services to Tumbes and Lima in Peru, allowing you to avoid changing buses at Huaquillas or the border.

See p339 for information about crossing the border into Peru.

The Galápagos Islands

Much like the revolutionary scientific idea with which they've become synonymous, the Galápagos Islands may inspire you to think differently about the world. Nowhere else can you engage in a staring contest with wild animals and lose. You can't help thinking you've stumbled upon an alternate universe, some strange utopian colony organized by sea lions – the golden retrievers of the Galápagos – and arranged on principles of mutual cooperation. Don't come expecting to see bizarre wildlife – there are no half-penguin, half-turtle 'pen-urtles,' no large mammals with shark fins. What's truly special is this: the creatures that call the islands home act as if humans are nothing more than slightly annoying paparazzi.

This is not the Bahamas – though some of the cruise boats will remind you of a Caribbean luxury resort – and these aren't Pacific paradises; in fact, most of the islands are devoid of vegetation and look more like the moon than Hawaii. There are more humans living here than is commonly assumed – more than 30,000 and growing – and for such isolated specks of land (over 1000km from mainland Ecuador), there's a surprising level of development, most of it is geared toward sustaining a thriving tourism industry.

The islands have taken on a mythological status, and their relationship with Charles Darwin, the most famous visitor, who undoubtedly violated several park rules in riding and eating the Galápagos turtles, has become distorted and romanticized. Yet you don't have to be an evolutionary biologist or an ornithologist to appreciate one of the few places left on the planet where the footprint of the human presence is kept to a minimum.

HIGHLIGHTS

- Just off Isla Floreana, relax and let the current zip you past rays, turtles and sharks while snorkeling around **Devil's Crown** (p374).
- On northern Isla Isabela, huff it up to the trail above **Darwin Lake** (p371) for inspired views.
- On Isla Española, witness the pageantry of wildlife on the dramatic cliffs at **Punta Suárez** (p375)
- In the highlands of Santa Cruz, see who blinks first in a staring contest with the massive beasts in the **El Chato Tortoise Reserve** (p355)
- Pick your outdoor adventure – surf, snorkel, kayak, bike or dive – within minutes of the sleepy town of **Puerto Baquerizo Moreno** (p365) on Isla San Cristóbal.

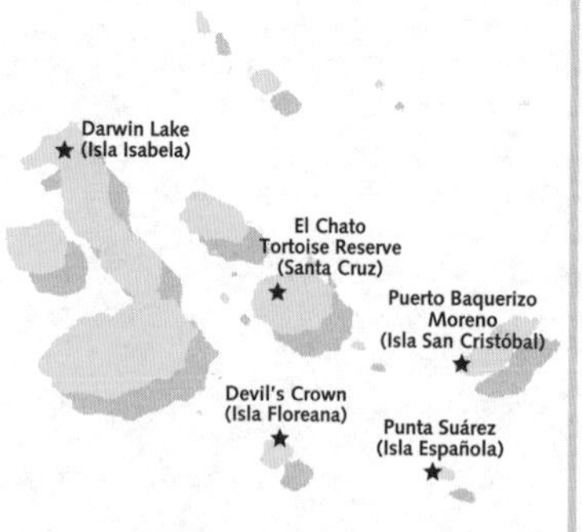

- AVERAGE TEMP IN PUERTO BAQUERIZO MORENO: 23°C (73°F)
- RAINIEST MONTH IN PUERTO BAQUERIZO MORENO: FEB

Orientation

There are around 12 main islands and 12 minor islands. Five of the islands are inhabited. About half the residents live in Puerto Ayora, on Isla Santa Cruz in the middle of the archipelago, which is also the most important island from the traveler's point of view. North of Santa Cruz, separated by a narrow strait, is Isla Baltra, home to one of the islands' major airports. A public bus and a ferry connect the Isla Baltra airport with Puerto Ayora (see p362).

Puerto Baquerizo Moreno on Isla San Cristóbal, the easternmost island, has become more important with regards to tourism. Its airport receives an almost equal number of flights from the mainland and while more tours start from Isla Santa Cruz, Puerto Baquerizo Moreno is another option.

The other inhabited islands are Isla Isabela, with the small port of Puerto Villamil, and Isla Santa María (Floreana), with Puerto Velasco Ibarra – both have places to stay and eat. Regular public ferries or private boats provide interisland transportation (see p353).

The remaining islands are not inhabited by people but are visited on tours. See p14 for information on planning your trip and for recommended books about the islands. See p65 for a brief introduction to the wildlife of the islands.

History

The Galápagos Archipelago was discovered by accident in 1535, when Tomás de Berlanga, the first Bishop of Panama, drifted off course while sailing from Panama to Peru. The bishop reported his discovery to King Charles V of Spain and included in his report a description of the giant Galápagos tortoises, from which the islands received their name, and an amusing note about the islands' birds that any visitor today can appreciate: '…so silly that they didn't know how to flee and many were caught by hand.'

It is possible that the indigenous inhabitants of South America were aware of the islands' existence before 1535, but there are no definite records of this and the islands don't appear on a world map until 1570 when they are identified as the 'island of the tortoises.' In 1953, Norwegian explorer Thor Heyerdahl discovered what he thought to be pre-Columbian pottery shards on the islands, but the evidence seems inconclusive. The first rough charts of the archipelago were made by buccaneers in the late 17th century, and scientific exploration began in the late 18th century.

For more than three centuries after their discovery, the Galápagos were used as a base by a succession of buccaneers, sealers and whalers. The islands provided sheltered anchorage, firewood, water and an abundance of fresh food in the form of the giant Galápagos tortoises, which were caught by the thousands and stacked, alive, in the ships' holds. More than 100,000 are estimated to have been taken between 1811 and 1844. The tortoises could survive for a year or more and thus provided fresh meat for the sailors long after they had left the islands. The fur seal population was also decimated, thousands killed for their valuable pelts.

The first resident of the islands was Patrick Watkins, an Irishman who was marooned on Isla Santa María in 1807 and spent two years living there, growing vegetables and trading his produce for rum from passing boats. The story goes that he managed to remain drunk for most of his stay, then stole a ship's boat and set out for Guayaquil accompanied by five slaves. No one knows what happened to the slaves – only Watkins reached the mainland.

Ecuador officially claimed the Galápagos Archipelago in 1832 and General Villamil was named the first governor – basically in charge of a single colony on Floreana of ex-rebel soldiers. For roughly one century thereafter, the islands were inhabited by only a few settlers and were used as penal colonies, the last of which, on Isla Isabela, was closed in 1959.

The Galápagos' most famous visitor was Charles Darwin, who arrived in 1835 aboard the British naval vessel the *Beagle*. Darwin stayed for five weeks, 19 days of which were spent on four of the larger islands, making notes and collecting specimens that provided important evidence for his theory of evolution, which he would later formulate and publish, but not until decades later. He spent the most time on Isla San Salvador observing and, for that matter, eating tortoises. The truth is that Darwin devoted as much of his attention to geology and botany as he did to the animals and marine life of the Galápagos.

Some islands were declared wildlife sanctuaries in 1934, and 97% of the archipelago officially became a national park in 1959. Organized tourism began in the late 1960s and in 1986 the government formed the Marine Resources Reserve.

Geography

The Galápagos are an isolated group of volcanic islands that lie in the Pacific Ocean on the equator about 90 degrees west of Greenwich. The nearest mainland is Ecuador, some 1000km to the east, and Costa Rica, almost 1100km to the northeast. The land mass of the archipelago covers 7882 sq km, of which well over half consists of Isla Isabela, the largest island within the archipelago and the 12th-largest in the South Pacific. There are 13 major islands (ranging in area from 14 sq km to 4588 sq km), six small islands (1 sq km to 5 sq km) and scores of islets, of which only some are named. The islands are spread over roughly 50,000 sq km of ocean. The highest point in the Galápagos is Volcán Wolf (1646m), on Isla Isabela.

Most of the islands have two – sometimes three – names. The earliest charts gave the islands both Spanish and English names (many of these refer to pirates or English noblemen assigned by Ambrose Cowley who drew up the first navigational charts of the islands), and the Ecuadorian government assigned official names in 1892. An island can thus have a Spanish name, an English name and an official name. The official names are used here in most cases.

Geology

The oldest of the islands visible today were formed roughly four to five million years ago by underwater volcanoes erupting and rising above the ocean's surface (the islands were never connected to the mainland). The Galápagos region is volcanically very active – more than 50 eruptions have been recorded since their discovery in 1535. The most recent eruption occurred in May, 2008 when Cerro Azul on Isabela spewed small amounts of lava and ash; overall, Fernandina is probably the most active. Thus, the formation of the islands is an ongoing process; the archipelago is relatively young compared with the age of the earth (which is about 1000 times older).

Geologists generally agree that two relatively new geological theories explain the islands' formation. The theory of plate tectonics holds that the earth's crust consists of several rigid plates that, over geological time, move relative to one another over the surface of the earth. The Galápagos lie on the northern edge of the Nazca Plate, close to its junction with the Cocos Plate. These two plates are spreading apart at a rate of about 1km every 14,000 years, pretty fast by plate-tectonic standards.

The hotspot theory states that deep within the earth (below the moving tectonic plates) are certain superheated areas that remain stationary. At frequent intervals (measured in geological time), the heat from these hotspots increases enough to melt the earth's crust and produce a volcanic eruption of sufficient magnitude to cause molten lava to rise above the ocean floor and, eventually, above the ocean's surface.

The Galápagos are moving slowly to the southeast over a stationary hotspot, so it makes sense that the southeastern islands were formed first and the northwestern islands formed most recently. The most ancient rocks yet discovered on the islands are about 3.25 million years old and come from Isla Española in the southeast. In comparison, the oldest rocks on the islands of Isla Fernandina and Isla Isabela are less than 750,000 years old. The northwestern islands are still in the process of formation and contain active volcanoes, particularly Isabela and Fernandina. In addition to the gradual southeastern drift of the Nazca Plate, the northern drift of the Cocos Plate complicates the matter, so that the islands do not get uniformly older from northwest to southeast.

Most of the Galápagos are surrounded by very deep ocean. Less than 20km off the coasts of the western islands, the ocean is over 3000m deep. When visitors cruise around the islands, they can see only about the top third of the volcanoes – the rest is underwater. Some of the oldest volcanoes in the area are, in fact, completely underwater. The Carnegie Ridge, a submerged mountain range stretching to the east of the Galápagos, has the remnants of previous volcanic islands, some of which were as much as nine million years old. These have been completely eroded away; they now lie 2000m beneath the ocean surface and stretch about half the distance between the Galápagos and the mainland.

Most of the volcanic rock forming the Galápagos Islands is basalt. Molten basalt has the property of being more fluid than other types of volcanic rock, so when an eruption occurs, basalt tends to erupt in the form of lava flows rather than in the form of explosions. Hence the Galápagos Islands have gently rounded shield volcanoes rather than the cone-shaped variety most people associate with the formations.

Ecology & Environment

Every plant and animal species arrived in the Galápagos from somewhere else after journeys of several hundred to thousands of kilometers on fortuitous wind, air and sea currents, mostly from South America and the Caribbean. Of course some flora and fauna arrived later more unnaturally, brought by settlers and others visiting the islands. There are no large terrestrial mammals. For more on the fascinating wildlife of the Galápagos, see the Galápagos Wildlife chapter (p65).

Concern about the islands' environment is not new. Even as early as the beginning of the 1900s, several scientific organizations were already alarmed. In 1934, the Ecuadorian government set aside some of the islands as wildlife sanctuaries, but it was not until 1959, the centenary of the publication of *The Origin of the Species,* that the Galápagos were officially declared a national park. Approximately 97% of the total land mass is included – the rest is taken up by urban areas and farms that existed prior to the park's creation. The construction of the Charles Darwin Research Station on Isla Santa Cruz began soon after, and the station began operating in 1964 as an international nongovernmental organization (NGO) dedicated to conservation. The Galápagos National Park Service (GNPS) began operating in 1968 and is the key institution of the Ecuadorian government responsible for the park. Both entities work together to manage the islands. In 1986, the Ecuadorian government granted more protection to the islands by creating the 133,00 sq km Galápagos Marine Resources Reserve. A law that was passed in 1998 enables the park and reserve to protect and conserve the islands and surrounding ocean; it also encourages educational and scientific research while allowing sustainable development of the islands as an Ecuadorian province.

TOURISM

Until the mid-1960s, few tourists visited the islands, other than tycoons and princes on their private yachts or the extremely intrepid willing to bed down with livestock on a cargo ship. After the research station opened and charter flights began operating, organized tourism was inaugurated with a trickle of a little over 1000 visitors a year. This figure soon increased dramatically. By 1971, there were six small boats and one large cruise ship operating in the islands. In less than two decades, the number of visitors had increased tenfold; in the early 1990s, an estimated 60,000 visited annually. Current figures indicate that around 180,000 tourists visited the islands in 2008, including Ecuadorian residents as well as foreign visitors. There are around 85 boats (with sleeping accommodations) carrying four to 96 passengers; the majority carry fewer than 20. The resident population of the islands is growing at about 10% annually to provide labor for the booming tourism industry.

While this is good for the economy of Ecuador, inevitable problems have resulted. Fortunately, the Ecuadorian government has seen the sense of preventing the building of luxurious high-rise hotels and introducing as many cruise ships as demand calls for. All too aware of the growing threat, the Ecuadorian government and environmental organizations are left with no other choice than to try to reverse, or at the very least halt, the direction of development for the benefit of the flora, fauna and people of the Galápagos.

INVASIVE SPECIES

The introduction of domestic animals on every one of the main islands, except Fernandina, is one of the major challenges the archipelago faces. Feral goats and pigs and introduced rats decimated (or caused the extinction of) native species in just a few years – the goats themselves are thought to be responsible for the extinction of four to five species. It took more than 127 years to eliminate the feral pig population on the island of Santiago.

Cattle, cats, dogs, donkeys, frogs and rats are other threats to the survival of endemic flora and fauna; an introduced wasp species is feared to be the cause of a declining number of caterpillar larvae, an important food for finches. More than 800 plant species have been introduced to the islands.

OVERFISHING

A major problem in all the world's seas, overfishing is a continuing source of tension in the islands. There have been periodic protests, and several quite serious incidents, organized by fishermen (there are over 1000 authorized) unhappy with the restrictions on various fisheries, primarily sea cucumbers and lobster, two of the more lucrative catches.

GALÁPAGOS ISLANDS

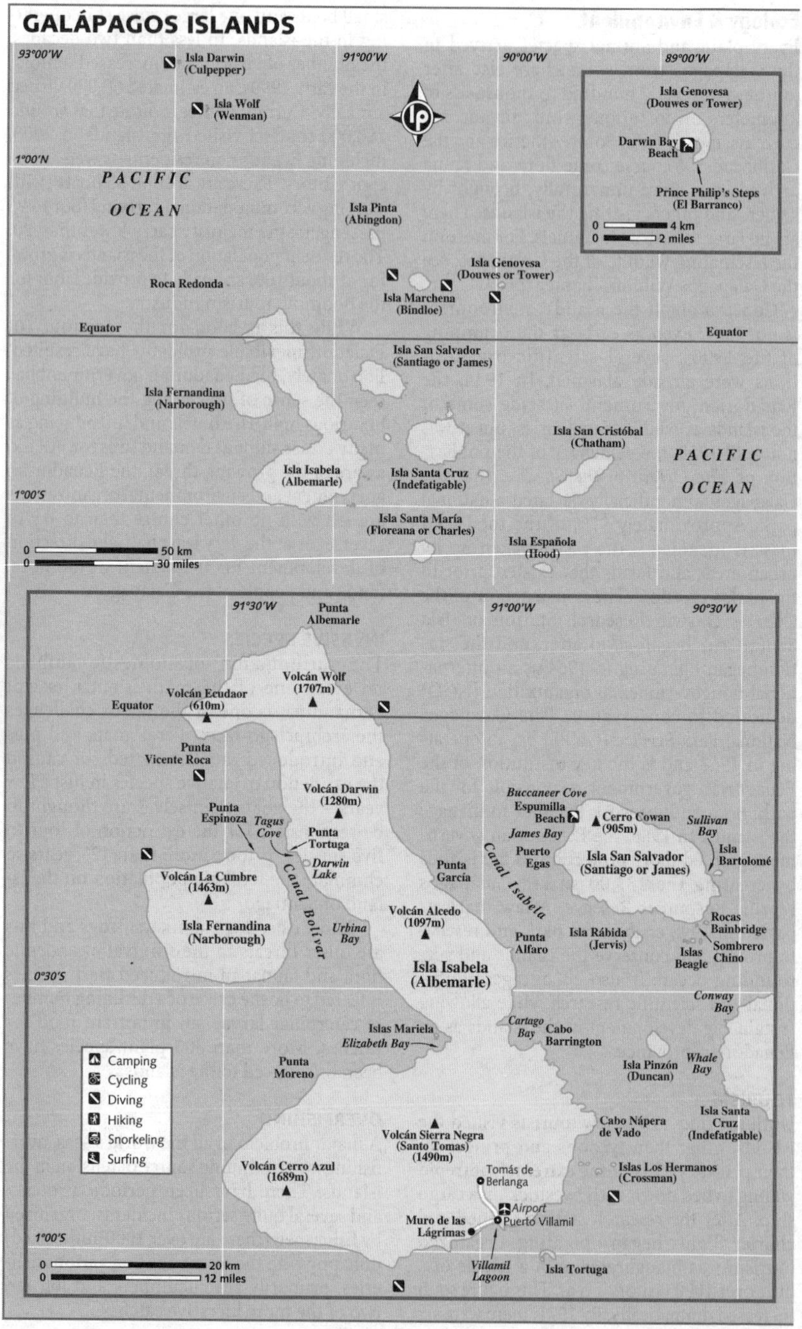
93°00'W
91°00'W
90°00'W
89°00'W
1°00'N
1°00'S
Isla Darwin (Culpepper)
Isla Wolf (Wenman)
PACIFIC OCEAN
Isla Pinta (Abingdon)
Roca Redonda
Isla Marchena (Bindloe)
Isla Genovesa (Douwes or Tower)
Equator
Isla San Salvador (Santiago or James)
Isla Fernandina (Narborough)
Isla San Cristóbal (Chatham)
Isla Isabela (Albemarle)
Isla Santa Cruz (Indefatigable)
Isla Santa María (Floreana or Charles)
Isla Española (Hood)
0 50 km
0 30 miles
Isla Genovesa (Douwes or Tower)
Darwin Bay Beach
Prince Philip's Steps (El Barranco)
0 4 km
0 2 miles
91°30'W
91°00'W
90°30'W
0°30'S
1°00'S
Punta Albemarle
Volcán Wolf (1707m)
Volcán Ecudaor (610m)
Equator
Punta Vicente Roca
Volcán Darwin (1280m)
Punta Espinoza
Tagus Cove
Punta Tortuga
Darwin Lake
Canal Bolívar
Volcán La Cumbre (1463m)
Isla Fernandina (Narborough)
Urbina Bay
Punta García
Volcán Alcedo (1097m)
Isla Isabela (Albemarle)
Canal Isabela
Buccaneer Cove
Espumilla Beach
James Bay
Cerro Cowan (905m)
Sullivan Bay
Puerto Egas
Isla San Salvador (Santiago or James)
Isla Bartolomé
Punta Alfaro
Isla Rábida (Jervis)
Rocas Bainbridge
Islas Beagle
Sombrero Chino
Conway Bay
Cartago Bay
Cabo Barrington
Islas Mariela
Elizabeth Bay
Punta Moreno
Isla Pinzón (Duncan)
Whale Bay
Cabo Nápera de Vado
Isla Santa Cruz (Indefatigable)
Volcán Sierra Negra (Santo Tomas) (1490m)
Volcán Cerro Azul (1689m)
Tomás de Berlanga
Islas Los Hermanos (Crossman)
Airport
Puerto Villamil
Muro de las Lágrimas
Villamil Lagoon
Isla Tortuga
Camping
Cycling
Diving
Hiking
Snorkeling
Surfing
0 20 km
0 12 miles

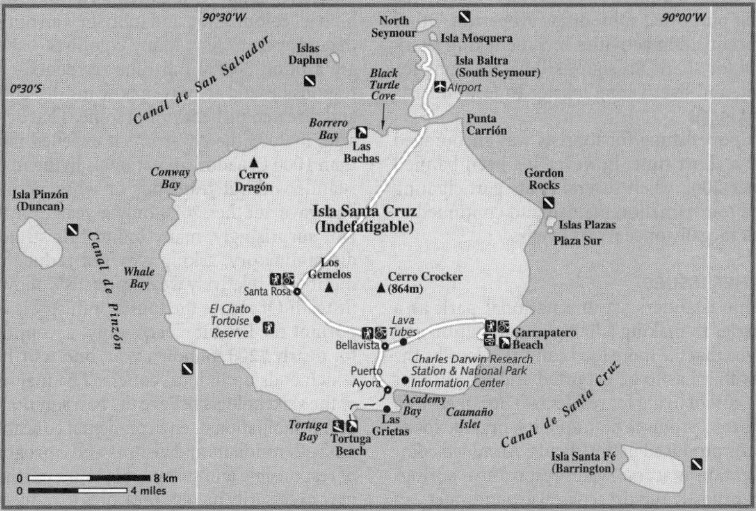
90°30'W
90°00'W
0°30'S
North Seymour
Isla Mosquera
Islas Daphne
Canal de San Salvador
Isla Baltra (South Seymour)
Airport
Black Turtle Cove
Borrero Bay
Las Bachas
Punta Carrión
Conway Bay
Cerro Dragón
Gordon Rocks
Isla Pinzón (Duncan)
Isla Santa Cruz (Indefatigable)
Islas Plazas
Plaza Sur
Canal de Pinzón
Whale Bay
Los Gemelos
Cerro Crocker (864m)
Santa Rosa
El Chato Tortoise Reserve
Lava Tubes
Bellavista
Garrapatero Beach
Charles Darwin Research Station & National Park Information Center
Puerto Ayora
Academy Bay
Las Grietas
Caamaño Islet
Canal de Santa Cruz
Tortuga Bay
Tortuga Beach
Isla Santa Fé (Barrington)
0 8 km
0 4 miles

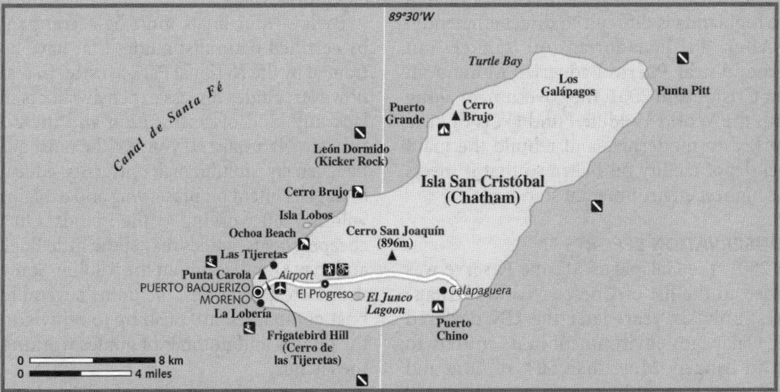
89°30'W
Turtle Bay
Los Galápagos
Punta Pitt
Canal de Santa Fé
Puerto Grande
Cerro Brujo
León Dormido (Kicker Rock)
Isla San Cristóbal (Chatham)
Cerro Brujo
Isla Lobos
Ochoa Beach
Cerro San Joaquín (896m)
Las Tijeretas
Punta Carola
Airport
PUERTO BAQUERIZO MORENO
El Progreso
El Junco Lagoon
Galapaguera
La Lobería
Puerto Chino
Frigatebird Hill (Cerro de las Tijeretas)
0 8 km
0 4 miles

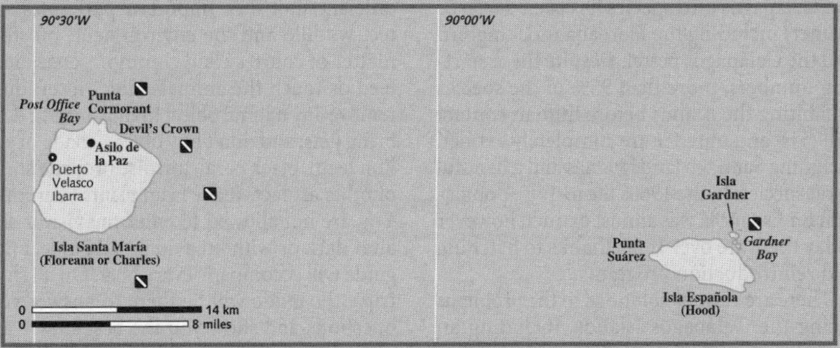
90°30'W
90°00'W
Post Office Bay
Punta Cormorant
Devil's Crown
Asilo de la Paz
Puerto Velasco Ibarra
Isla Santa María (Floreana or Charles)
Isla Gardner
Punta Suárez
Gardner Bay
Isla Española (Hood)
0 14 km
0 8 miles

Although sea-cucumber fishing became illegal back in 1994, hundreds of thousands are exported illegally every year, chiefly for their purported aphrodisiac properties. Other illegal fishing activities include taking shark fins for shark-fin soup, killing sea lions for bait, and overfishing lobster to feed tourists and locals.

Sport fishing for tourists was encouraged for a short time, however it's been banned since 2005 when several boats participating in a tournament remained and continued to fish illegally once it was over.

OTHER ISSUES

Some islanders see the national park as a barrier to making a living in agriculture and argue that the more food cultivated locally, the less that has to be exported and the cheaper the cost of living for residents. Thus, there's an effort to promote high-quality, organic foodstuffs produced in the islands. An added complication is scarce water resources – springs have mostly run dry, coastal groundwater can be polluted and the little there is to be found in the highlands is difficult to direct efficiently.

After an Ecuadorian oil tanker ran aground near Puerto Baquerizo Moreno on San Cristóbal in 2001, the government along with the World Wildlife Fund (WWF) have worked to modernize and rebuild the main fuel depot facility on Baltra so that it meets the highest environmental standards.

CONSERVATION EFFORTS

In 2001, the Galápagos Marine Reserve was added to the list of Unesco World Heritage sites; only six years later the UN declared the Galápagos environment in its entirety to be 'in danger'. More than 50% of flora and fauna species are threatened or endangered (no Galápagos bird species has been declared extinct) including the Floreana mockingbird and the Galápagos petrel. Despite these startling numbers, more than 95% of the species inhabiting the islands before human contact still exist and only 1% are completely extinct, including Santiago land iguanas and a handful of rat species. In the 1960s the tortoise population on Española was almost extinct, however today there are over 1000, thanks to hatching and reintroduction programs.

There are various solutions to the problems facing the Galápagos Islands, including an emphasis on sustainable tourism over extracting limited resources, both underwater and underground, that could alter the environment irreparably. One extreme view is to prohibit all colonization and tourism – an option that appeals to few. Many colonists – there are around 30,000 full-time residents – act responsibly and actively oppose the disruptive and threatening behavior of some. That being said, in 2008 the government expelled more than 1000 Ecuadorean nationals living in the islands without residency or work permits and gave another 2000 only a year to leave. Not surprisingly, many found this strategy discriminatory, asking why not reduce the number of relatively wealthy tourists allowed instead? Of course the tourist industry is important for Ecuador's economy, accounting for nearly $200 million a year, one-fourth of which ends up in local coffers. The majority of the stakeholders believe the best solution to be a combination of environmental education for both residents and visitors and a program of responsible and sustainable tourism which may necessarily involve measures to reduce or cap tourist visits.

By law, tour boats must be accompanied by certified naturalist guides that have been trained by the National Park Service. In reality however, guides on less expensive boats may lack any kind of certification and there are very few Naturalist III Guides (the most qualified, usually multilingual, university-educated biologists intent on preserving and explaining wildlife) left working in the islands. On the cheapest boats, guides may speak little English and may know less about the wildlife. Some of the interested parties, including several tour boat companies, are pushing to reinvigorate the quality and number of guides working in the islands.

Visitors to the islands are restricted to the official visitor sites. Important park rules protect wildlife and the environment, mostly a matter of courtesy and common sense: don't feed or touch the animals; don't litter; don't remove any natural object (living or not); don't bring pets; and don't buy objects made of sea-lion teeth, black coral, tortoise or turtle shells, or other artifacts made from plants or animals. You are not allowed to enter the visitor sites after dark or without a qualified guide, and a guide will accompany every boat. On all shore trips, the guide will be there to answer your questions and show you the best sites – and also to ensure that you follow park rules.

WHEN TO VISIT

There really isn't a bad time to visit, however there are several factors to keep in mind in determining when to go. The islands have two distinct seasons: the warm/wet season from January to May, with strong but short periods of rain but generally sunny and warm (average air temperature is 25°C); and the cool/dry season often known as the *garúa* for the misty precipitation which impacts the highlands, lasting from June to December, when water temperatures as a result of the dominant Humboldt Current can become decidedly chilly (18° to 20°C) and air temperatures average 22°C.

High season in the Galápagos is roughly the same as the warm/wet season and also coincides with vacation periods in the USA such as Christmas and Easter. This means more boats and more groups. The low season, generally the same as the cool/dry season, means fewer visitors which is a plus, but while the air temperature is extremely pleasant, the water is colder (wet suits are definitely needed) and the seas can be rough during the overnight passages between islands. Seasickness is not uncommon and some people have difficulty sleeping.

Keep in mind that the Galápagos is one hour behind mainland Ecuador time.

Tours

There are basically three kinds of tours in the Galápagos: the most common and most recommended because of its relatively low environmental impact are boat-based trips with nights spent aboard; there are also day trips returning to the same hotel each night and hotel-based trips staying on different islands. Once you decide on what kind of tour you want, you can either fly to the islands and find a tour there, or make reservations in advance on the mainland or through a travel agency in your home country. There is public transportation only between Isla Santa Cruz, Isla San Cristóbal and Isla Isabela, and the crossings can sometimes be rough.

BOAT TOURS

Most visitors tour the Galápagos on boat tours, sleeping aboard the boat. Tours can last from three days to three weeks, although tours lasting from four to eight days are the most common. It's difficult to do the Galápagos justice on a tour lasting less than a week, but five days is just acceptable. If you want to visit the outlying islands of Isabela and Fernandina, a cruise of eight days or more is recommended. On the first day of a tour, you arrive from the mainland by air before lunchtime, so this is really only half a day in the Galápagos, and on the last day, you have to be at the airport in the morning. Thus, a five-day tour gives only three full days in the islands. Shorter tours are advertised, but with the travel time at either end, they aren't recommended.

You can find boats to go to almost any island, although it takes more time to reach the outlying ones. Cramming as many ports of call as possible into your cruise means you probably won't have time to do justice to any. Boats have fixed itineraries, so think ahead if you want a tour that visits a specific island. Make sure the tour doesn't include more than one night or half a day in either Puerto Ayora or Puerto Baquerizo Moreno since you can always tack on a few days (or weeks for that matter) at the beginning or end on your own.

Tour boats range from small yachts to large cruise ships. By far the most common type is the motorsailer (a medium-sized motor boat), which carries eight to 20 passengers. Conditions on the cheapest boats can be cramped and primitive. Ask about washing facilities – they can vary from deck hoses on the cheapest boats to communal showers on the better boats and private showers on more expensive boats. Also inquire about water – on the cheaper boats, you may need to bring your own large containers of water. Bottled drinks are carried but cost extra – make sure that enough beer and soda is loaded aboard. There's nothing to stop you from bringing your own supply.

If you're going to spend such a large chunk of change to get to the islands, then seeing the Galápagos is probably important to you, so it might be worthwhile to consider spending an extra few hundred dollars to go on a more comfortable, reliable boat and getting a decent guide (although more expensive boats have their problems too). For about $1500 to $2400 for eight days, you can take a more comfortable tourist-class tour – the usual extra costs (airfare, fees and tips) apply. Many companies in Quito offer tours at about this price.

It is customary to tip the crew and guide at the end of a trip. On exceptionally good and higher-end boats, a tip amount is usually suggested and you aren't responsible for dividing the amount up among the crew members as you might on the cheaper boats where the guide generally gets the most, then the cook and captain, and then the other crew members.

Arranged Locally

Most people arrive in the islands with a prearranged tour, although it's usually cheaper to arrange a tour in Puerto Ayora or Baquerizo Moreno. As a general rule, only the cheaper boats are available for booking once in the Galápagos; the better boats are almost always booked. Don't fly to the Galápagos hoping to get on a really good boat for less money. Arranging a tour from the Galápagos is not uncommon, but neither is it as straightforward as it sounds. It can take several days – sometimes a week or more – and is therefore not a good option for people with a limited amount of time.

The best place to organize a tour is from Puerto Ayora; it's also possible to arrange it in Baquerizo Moreno. If you are alone or with a friend, you'll need to find more people, as even the smallest boats take no fewer than four passengers. There are usually people looking for boats, and agencies can help in putting travelers and boats together.

Finding boats both in August and around Christmas and Easter is especially difficult. The less busy months have fewer travelers on the islands, but boats are often being repaired or overhauled at this time, particularly in October. Despite the caveats, travelers who arrive in Puerto Ayora looking for a boat can almost always find one within a week (often in just a few days) if they work at it. This method isn't always cost effective since by the time you pay for hotels and meals in Puerto Ayora or Baquerizo Moreno, you may not save anything.

The most important thing to find is a good captain and an enthusiastic naturalist guide. You should be able to meet both and inspect the boat before booking. Agreeing on a quality itinerary is also paramount.

Prearranged

Most visitors arrange tours before arriving at the islands. You can do this in your home country (expensive but efficient), or you can arrange something in Quito, Guayaquil, Cuenca etc (cheaper, but you sometimes have to wait several days or weeks during the high season and you don't want Galápagos trip planning to take time away from enjoying the rest of Ecuador). One other word of caution if planning a Galápagos trip while in Ecuador – internet and telephone charges add up quickly and the default security protocols of some banks and credit-card companies make it difficult to pay for such relatively large amounts without hassle. See p354, p96 and p320 for more information on agencies that book Galápagos tours.

Dangers & Annoyances

There are some common pitfalls and hassles to Galápagos boat tours. It's difficult to make blanket statements concerning specific boats or companies, however it does seem safe to say that the cheaper the trip the more likely you are to experience problems. That's not to say costly boats are glitch free, only that because the crew and company expect you to have higher expectations, they are more attentive and quick to respond to any complaints.

Some of the recurring complaints involve last-minute changes of boat (which the contractual small print allows), poor crew, lack of bottled drinks, changes in the itinerary, mechanical breakdowns, insufficient and poor-quality snorkeling gear, hidden charges ($5 per day for wet suits is common), bad smells, bug infestations and overbooking. Passengers share cabins and are sometimes not guaranteed that their cabin mates will be of the same gender. Always ask to see a photograph or layout of the boat including those of the cabins before booking.

It's frustrating but not uncommon to discover shipmates have paid substantially less than you for the same services, especially if you've booked abroad and they've arranged things locally and at the last minute – there's little recourse, so it's best to move on and enjoy the trip.

When things go wrong, a refund is difficult to obtain. If you have a problem, report it to the *capitanía* (port captain) in Puerto Ayora and contact the agency where you booked the boat. You should also report problems (in person or by email) to the **Cámara de Turismo** (tourist information office; www.galapagostour.org) in Puerto Ayora, which keeps a database of complaints

THE GALÁPAGOS ISLANDS

to share with agencies and tourists. Reports are taken seriously, and repeat offenders get their comeuppance.

There have also been reports of crew members of tourist boats and, more commonly, small fishing boats illegally fishing and killing wildlife. Complaints of this kind should be reported to the Natural Reserve office, a green building just to the left of the information booth at the entrance to the Charles Darwin Research Station in Puerto Ayora.

Though not usually publicly disclosed, there have been a handful of shark attacks over the years. Odds are slim to nil that this will happen, but it's worth mentioning it here in the interests of full disclosure.

With all the boats cruising the islands, it's easy to forget that these are remote, inhospitable and dangerous places to be marooned. Seventeen people have disappeared since 1990 – most were found alive, though a few have died after straying from the designated paths.

LIVE-ABOARD DIVING TOURS

Not surprisingly for a place with an underwater habitat resembling a well-stocked aquarium, scuba diving in the Galápagos is world class. The conditions aren't suitable for beginners because of strong currents, sometimes murky visibility and cold temperatures. When the water is warm there's not much of a current so it's also a little murky (January to March); there is better visibility but colder water temperatures from July to October. Besides an array of tropical fish, there are plenty of whale sharks, hammerheads, manta rays and even sea horses to be seen.

Standard overnight boat tours, called naturalist trips in the tour-agency vernacular, are no longer allowed to offer scuba diving as an option. Four or so boats – Ecoventurer's M/Y *Sky Dancer* and *Deep Blue*, and the Aggressor's *Albatross* and *Jesus de Gran Poder* (☎ 800-348-2628; www.aggressor.com) – are currently the only options. *Sky Dancer* is the most recommended, followed by the Aggressor boats. Because there are so few options, these boats are usually booked months in advance. The majority of divers take day trips from either Puerto Ayora or Puerto Baquerizo Moreno – see those sections for more information.

The average cost of one week on a live-aboard is from $3500 to $4500 and includes up to four or five dives a day plus stops at some visitor sites on land. Most live-aboard boats go to Wolf and Darwin, northwest of the major islands, where there's a large number of different species of sharks. The best month to dive with whale sharks is July but they're around from May to October.

DAY TOURS

Day trips are out of either Puerto Ayora or Baquerizo Moreno. Several hours are spent sailing to and from the day's visitor site(s), so only a few central islands are feasible destinations. Some trips may involve visiting sites on other parts of Isla Santa Cruz or Isla San Cristóbal.

One of the downsides of this kind of tour is that there is no chance of visiting the islands early or late in the day. The cheapest boats may be slow and overcrowded; their visits may be too brief; the guides may be poorly informed; and the crew may be lacking an adequate conservationist attitude. Nevertheless, day trips are useful for severe seasickness sufferers and if your time and budget is extremely limited.

Operators in Puerto Ayora and Baquerizo Moreno typically charge from $40 to $120 per person per day, depending on the destination on offer and the quality of the boat and guides.

HOTEL-BASED TOURS

These tours go from island to island, and you sleep in hotels on three or four different islands: Santa Cruz, San Cristóbal, Santa María, Isabela. Tours typically last a week and cost $800 to over $1000 per person, plus airfare and park fee. Several of the travel agencies in Puerto Ayora and Puerto Baquerizo Moreno book these, as does **Surtrek** (☎ 02-223-1534; www.galapagosyachts.com; Av Amazonas 897), based in Quito (p97) and the **Red Mangrove Inn** (see p359) in Puerto Ayora. Also check with other agencies in Quito or Puerto Ayora, and possibly Baquerizo Moreno.

GALÁPAGOS ON A SHOESTRING

Regardless of the corners you cut, a trip to the Galápagos takes a significant chunk of change. Travelers touring the continent usually take a pass since a week in the islands may cost as much as a month or two backpacking elsewhere. There are, however, some strategies to reducing costs, though these may reduce the pleasure involved in a trip.

Talk to the ship owners directly to avoid having to pay commission to an agency. Ecuadorian agencies are generally at least 30% cheaper than agencies booking trips in the USA and Europe. You may find that you can get a substantial discount by checking various agencies and seeing if they have any spaces to fill on departures leaving in the next day or two. Particularly out of the high season, agencies may well let you travel cheaply at the last minute rather than leave berths unfilled. It's probably always worth a little back-and-forth negotiation, indicating that you have been offered another less expensive deal or simply that your budget will only allow you to spend such and such amount of money.

Individuals and couples have a better chance of grabbing a last-minute discounted spot than do large groups. All cabins are not the same size; book the smaller ones to save money. For boats in the lower price range, owners, captains, guides and cooks all change frequently; in addition, many boats make changes and improvements from year to year. Generally speaking, a boat is only as good as its crew. You can deal with a crew member or boat representative during your search, but don't hand over any money until you have an agreed itinerary in writing to avoid disagreements with other passengers and the crew during the cruise.

Alcoholic drinks are usually not covered in any boat tour's rates. One way to keep costs down is to stock up on wine, beer, etc from supermarkets in Puerto Ayora or Puerto Baquerizo Moreno.

Getting There & Away

AIR

Flights from the mainland arrive at two airports: Isla Baltra just north of Santa Cruz and Isla San Cristóbal. There are almost an equal number of flights to Baltra and San Cristóbal.

The two major airlines flying to the Galápagos Islands are TAME and Aerogal (p361); LanChile plans to begin servicing the route in the near future. TAME and Aerogal both operate two morning flights daily from Quito via Guayaquil to both the Isla Baltra airport, just over an hour away from Puerto Ayora by public transportation and the San Cristóbal airport. All return flights are in the early afternoons of the same days.

Flights from Guayaquil cost round-trip \$362/318 (high season/low season) and take 1½ hours. From Quito, flights cost \$412/356 round-trip and take 3¼ hours, due to the layover in Guayaquil (you do not have to get off the plane). It's also possible to fly from Quito and return to Guayaquil or vice versa; it's often more convenient to fly into Baltra and out of San Cristóbal or vice versa. If you're booked on a boat through an agency, they will likely make the arrangements for you, however if you are booking the flight independently, it's difficult to do this online. There is a limit of 20kg of checked luggage (per person) on the flight to the Galápagos. A transit control fee of \$10 must be paid at the Instituto Nacional Galápagos (INGALA) office next to the ticket counter in either Quito or Guayaquil airport; the charge is already included in the price of many pre-arranged boat tours.

Ecuadorian nationals can fly from Guayaquil for half the price foreigners pay, and Galápagos residents pay half that again. Some foreign residents of Ecuador or workers in the islands are also eligible, so if you have a residence visa you should make inquiries.

There is a Hercules military plane that flies to the islands every other Monday, but it's generally reserved for Galápagos residents and Ecuadorians, although it occasionally has room for foreign passengers, primarily volunteers or students performing research. Make inquiries at Avenida de la Prensa 3570, a few hundred meters from the Quito airport (ask for Departamento de Operaciones, Fuerza Aerea del Ecuador). Flights go from Quito via Guayaquil and stop at both San Cristóbal and Baltra. Foreigners pay about \$300 round-trip for either destination.

Flights to the Galápagos are sometimes booked solid well in advance, but often there are many no-shows. Travel agencies book blocks of seats for their all-inclusive Galápagos Islands tours, releasing the seats on the day of the flight when there is no longer any hope of selling their tour.

Getting Around

Most people get around the islands by organized boat tour, but it's very easy to visit some of the islands independently. Santa Cruz, San Cristóbal, Isabela and Santa María (Floreana) all have accommodations and are reachable by affordable interisland boat rides or more expensive flights. Keep in mind, however, that you'll only scratch the surface of the archipelago's natural wonders traveling independently.

AIR

The small airline **EMETEBE** (Puerto Ayora ☎ 05-252-6177, San Cristóbal ☎ 05-252-0615, Puerto Villamil ☎ 05-252-9255, Guayaquil ☎ 04-229 2492; www.emetebe.com.ec) flies a five-passenger aircraft between the islands. It offers daily flights between Baltra and Puerto Villamil (Isla Isabela), between Baltra and San Cristóbal, and between San Cristóbal and Puerto Villamil. Fares for foreigners are about $130 one-way, and there is a 9kg baggage limit per person (although this is flexible if the plane isn't full).

BOAT

Private speedboats known as *lanchas* or *fibras* (short for fiberglass boats) offer daily passenger ferry services between Santa Cruz and San Cristóbal and Isabela (there are no direct trips between San Cristóbal and Isabela). Fares are $30 on any passage and are purchased either on the day before or the day of departure. Ask around in Puerto Ayora, Puerto Baquerizo Moreno and Puerto Villamil; see the Getting There & Away sections of these towns for more information.

ISLA SANTA CRUZ (INDEFATIGABLE)

The island of Santa Cruz has the largest and most developed town in the Galápagos; almost every visitor to the islands spends at least some time here even if it's simply commuting from the airport on nearby Isla Baltra to a cruise ship in the harbor of Puerto Ayora. However, to anyone who stays for longer, the island of Santa Cruz is more than just a way station or place to feel connected to the modern, man-made world; it's a destination in itself, full of visitor sites, easily accessible beaches, remote highlands in the interior and a base for adventurous activities far from the tourism trail.

Visitor Sites

CHARLES DARWIN RESEARCH STATION

About a 20-minute walk by road northeast of Puerto Ayora, the **Charles Darwin Research Station** (www.darwinfoundation.org; 6am-6pm) can also be reached by dry landing from Academy Bay. More than 200 scientists and volunteers are involved with research and conservation efforts, the most well known of which involves a captive breeding program for giant tortoises. It contains a national-park information center; an informative museum where a video in English or Spanish is presented several times a day; a baby-tortoise house with incubators (when they weigh about 1.5kg or are about four years old, the tortoises are repatriated to their home islands) and a walk-in adult tortoise enclosure, where you can meet the Galápagos giants face to face. Several of the 11 remaining subspecies of tortoise can be seen here. **Lonesome George**, the only surviving member of the Isla Pinta subspecies, has been living here since 1972. Thirty-five years after park rangers first tried to mate George with tortoises of closely related subspecies, two of his longtime female companions finally became pregnant in July, 2008. To the dismay of all, the eggs that were laid proved to be unviable, leaving researchers to return to Isabel to continue their search for closer matched mates.

Other attractions include a small enclosure containing several land iguanas and explanations in Spanish and English concerning efforts to restore their populations on islands where they've been pushed to the brink of extinction. Several paths lead through arid-zone vegetation, such as salt bush, mangroves and prickly pear and other cacti. A variety of land birds, including Darwin's finches, can be seen. Outside of the islands, the research station is supported by contributions to the **Galápagos Conservancy** (formerly the Charles Darwin Foundation; www.galapagos.org).

Just after the entrance to the site is a sign for **Playa Estación**, a small patch of sand fronted by large rocks and a nice little swimming area good for children.

TURTLE BAY

In terms of sheer white-sand beauty, this beach at the end of a 2.5km paved trail southwest from Puerto Ayora, is the rival of any in South America. But in addition to swimming (a spit of land provides protection from the strong and dangerous currents on the exposed side), surfing or just sunbathing you can see sharks, marine iguanas, pelicans and the occasional flamingo. There's no drinking water or other facilities. It's about a half-hour walk from the start of the path – often used by local runners – where you must sign in between 6am and 6pm. At the foot of the hill before the start of the path is the **Marine Reserve Exhibition Hall** (8am-noon & 2-5:30pm Mon-Sat), a good place to learn about conservation efforts and issues in the waters around the archipelago.

SHOPPING FOR A SMOOTH SAIL

There are five boats (*Explorer II, Expedition, Galápagos Legend, Santa Cruz* and *Polaris*) that carry up to 98 passengers and four boats (*Isabela II, Eclipse, La Pinta* and *Islander*) that carry up to 48 passengers; all are considered luxury or first-class ships. The majority of the close to 75 boats or yachts carry up to 20 people or less. There are several catamarans as well.

The $100 park fee, airfare and bottled drinks are not included in fare quotes. Boats are divided roughly into the following categories (prices are per day except for live-aboards):

- Luxury ships: $400 and up
- First-class yachts: $300 to $400
- Tourist-class yachts: $200 to $300
- Economic-class yachts: less than $199
- Dedicated Dive Live-Aboards: per week $3500 to $5000

To avoid disappointment, the following questions should always be asked before booking:

- 'Does this boat do overlapping tours?' If you want to do an eight-day tour, it's best to book a boat that only does eight-day tours. A large number of boats operate by continually shuffling passengers on overlapping four-, five- and eight-day tours. In addition to a lack of continuity in terms of group cohesion, this means you'll likely spend more time in port picking up and dropping off passengers and are less likely to travel to outer islands and less-visited tourist sites.
- 'Is the guide a freelancer?' The quality of the guide is one of the most important factors in your enjoyment of the trip. Guides affiliated with one company or boat are more likely to feel responsible for their passengers' satisfaction and to not take a laissez faire approach to complaints.
- 'How many towns do we stop at?' Always look at the itinerary in detail. Refer to the map and text of this chapter in order to understand the wildlife and activities common at each site. At least two half-days will be dedicated to either Puerto Ayora and/or Baquerizo Moreno at the beginning and end of your trip – many of the activities involved with these stops can be done independently. A stop in and around Puerto Villamil on Isabela is not uncommon, but for trips of five days or fewer this will probably seem like too much civilization.
- 'Is snorkeling equipment in my size guaranteed?' Masks, snorkels and fins are generally supplied, however some boats may lack enough fins in certain sizes for all passengers. This is even more of a problem with wet suits, which usually cost an additional $5 per day.

HIGHLANDS

Several sites of interest in the highlands of Santa Cruz can be reached from the trans-island road and are part of the itineraries of many cruises. Access to some sites is through colonized areas, so respect private property. From the village of Bellavista, 7km north of Puerto Ayora by road, one can turn either west on the main road continuing to Isla Baltra or east on a road leading about 2km to the **lava tubes** (admission $3). These underground tunnels are more than a kilometer in length and were formed by the solidifying of the outside skin of a molten-lava flow. When the lava flow ceased, the molten lava inside the flow kept going, emptying out of the solidified skin and thus leaving tunnels. Because they are on private property, the tunnels can be visited without an official guide. The owners of the land provide information, guides and flashlights ($1). Tours to the lava tubes are offered in Puerto Ayora.

North of Bellavista is the national park land known as the highlands. A path from Bellavista leads toward **Cerro Crocker** (864m) and other hills and extinct volcanoes. This is a good chance to see the vegetation of the Scalesia, Miconia and fern-sedge zones (see p57) and to look for birds such as the vermilion flycatcher, the elusive Galápagos rail and the paint-billed crake. It is around 5km from Bellavista to the crescent-shaped hill of Media Luna, and 3km further to the base of Cerro Crocker. This is national park, so a guide is required.

Part of the highlands that can be visited from the road are the twin craters called **Los Gemelos**. These are actually sinkholes, not

- 'What's the refund policy?' Read the fine print and clarify how much money you can get back in case of a mechanical breakdown or other unforeseen circumstance that results in the cancellation or alteration of your trip.
- 'How would you rate the food?' This can be difficult to determine since chefs come and go and some agencies may be less than forthright in assessing their own product. Nevertheless, it's worth pressing if this is an important issue for you.
- 'One bed or two?' Couples be warned: all the boats have a limited number of cabins with matrimonial beds. Unless you reserve early, you may be stuck with two narrow single beds.

For practical reasons, it's obviously impossible to provide reviews for all or most of the boats servicing the islands. It's also quite common for boats and companies to receive favorable reviews from some people and unfavorable reviews from others. Expectations and standards differ and sometimes things go wrong on one trip but smoothly on another. The chemistry between you and your fellow passengers is another important factor; the smaller the boat the more important it is that you get along.

These caveats aside, there are a few boats and companies that are worth checking out:

Columbus Travel (Quito ☎ 02-254-7587; www.columbusecuador.com) Full service agency with excellent customer service; can book range of boats depending on budget and dates of travel.

Ecoventura (Quito ☎ 02-290-7396, Guayaquil ☎ 04-283-9390; www.ecoventura.com) One of the pioneers in conservation and sustainable tourism. Its four boats, including the diving live-aboard M/Y *Sky Dancer* and the M/Y *Eric*, which is partly powered by wind turbines and solar panels, are highly recommended.

Ecuador Travel (www.ecuador-travel.net/Galapagos.htm) Dependable and honest broker for a wide range of boats, from luxury to economic.

Explorer's Corner (☎ 877-677-9623; www.explorerscorner.com; Berkeley, CA) Passengers cruise long distances on a catamaran and explore the nooks and crannies of the islands by kayak (seven nights $4500) – the only tour of its kind in the Galápagos.

Galacruises Expeditions (Quito ☎ 02-290-3391; www.galacruises.com) Books tourist-class yachts *Sea Man Catamaran*, *Guantanamera*, *Yolita II* and *Floreana*.

Happy Gringo Travel (Quito ☎ 02-255-0532; www.happygringo.com) Despite its unfortunate name, this agency, on balance, can be recommended for those looking for last-minute deals on first-class and lower boats.

Metropolitan Touring (Quito ☎ 02-298-8200; www.metropolitan-touring.com) Affiliated with the Finch Bay Hotel in Puerto Ayora (p360); books several first-class and luxury yachts.

Sangay Touring (Quito ☎ 02-255-0180; www.sangay.com) An experienced outfit that books over 60 boats.

volcanic craters, and they are surrounded by Scalesia forest. Vermilion flycatchers are often seen here, as well as short-eared owls on occasion. Los Gemelos are reached by taking the road to the village of Santa Rosa, about 12km west of Bellavista, and continuing about 2km beyond Santa Rosa on the trans-island road. Although the craters lie only 25m and 125m on either side of the road, they are hidden by vegetation, so ask your driver to stop at the short trailhead.

EL CHATO TORTOISE RESERVE & RANCHO PERMISO

Near Santa Rosa, is El Chato Tortoise Reserve ($3), where you can observe giant tortoises in the wild. When these virtually catatonic prehistoric-looking beasts extend their accordion-like necks to feed, it's an impressive site. The reserve is also a good place to look for short-eared owls, Darwin's finches, yellow warblers, Galápagos rails and paint-billed crakes (these last two are difficult to see in the long grass).

A trail, downhill and often muddy, from Santa Rosa leads through private property to parkland about 3km away. Horses can be hired in Santa Rosa – ask at the store/bar on the main road for directions to the outfitter's house. The trail forks at the park boundary, with the right fork going up to the small hill of **Cerro Chato** (3km further) and the left fork going to **La Caseta** (2km). The trails can be hard to follow, and you should carry water. The reserve is part of the national park and a guide is required.

Next to the reserve is **Rancho Permiso** (admission $4), a private ranch owned by the Devine family. This place often has dozens of giant tortoises, and you can wander around at will

FEES & TAXES

As of January 2009, the Galápagos national park fee is around $200. It must be paid in cash at one of the airports after you arrive, or in advance through a pre-booked tour, and you will not be allowed to leave the airport until you pay. Make sure you have your passport available when you pay your fees and hang onto your ticket until you leave.

and take photos for a fee. The entrance is beyond Santa Rosa, off the main road – ask locals for directions. Remember to close any gates that you go through. There is a café selling cold drinks and hot tea, which is welcome if the highland mist has soaked you.

OTHER SITES

There are several attractive spots in and around Puerto Ayora. The small **white-sand beach** in front of the Finch Bay Hotel (p360) is a good place to while away a few hours. The water here is pristine and sharks have been known to pass through the cove. For nice swimming and snorkeling head to **Las Grietas**, a water-filled crevice in the rocks. Talented and fearless locals climb the nearly vertical walls to plunge gracefully and sometimes clumsily into the water below. Take a water taxi (per person 6am-7pm $0.60) to the dock for the Angermeyer Point restaurant (p361), then walk past the Finch Bay Hotel, then past an interesting salt mine and finally scramble up and around a lava-rock-strewn path to the water. Good shoes are recommended for the walk which takes about 30 minutes. Just behind the Casa de Lago and Hotel Fiesta is the **Laguna Las Ninfas**, an emerald-green watering hole popular with cannon-balling children.

A beautiful 40-minute taxi ride from Puerto Ayora (per person $5) through the highlands brings you to **Garrapatero beach**, which has tidal pools good for exploring, a lagoon with flamingos and nice snorkeling on calm days.

The remaining Santa Cruz visitor sites are reached by boat and with guides. On the west coast are **Whale Bay** and **Conway Bay**, and on the north coast are **Black Turtle Cove** (Caleta Tortuga Negra) and **Las Bachas**; between these two areas is **Cerro Dragón**. Conway Bay has a 1.5km trail passing a lagoon with flamingos; north of here is Cerro Dragón, which has two small lagoons that may have flamingos and a 1.75km trail that leads through a forest of palo santo (holy wood) trees and opuntia cacti to a small hill with good views. There are some large repatriated land iguanas here.

There is no landing site in Black Turtle Cove, which is normally visited by *panga* (small boats). The cove has many little inlets and is surrounded by mangroves, where you can see lava herons and pelicans. The main attraction is in the water: marine turtles are sometimes seen mating, schools of golden mustard rays are often present and white-tipped sharks may be seen basking in the shallows. The nearby Las Bachas beach, although popular for sunbathing and swimming, is often deserted.

Puerto Ayora

☎ 05 / pop 18,000

This town, the largest in terms of population and size in the Galápagos, is a surprise to most visitors, who don't expect to find anything but plants and animals on the islands. Puerto Ayora looks and feels like a fairly prosperous mainland Ecuadorian coastal town, that is if it weren't for the sea lions and pelicans hanging around the waterfront. Most of the hotels, restaurants and tourist facilities line Avenida Charles Darwin, and the airport is on Isla Baltra, around an hour away to the north.

INFORMATION

Internet Access

Some of the midrange and top-end hotels offer internet access and have wi-fi available in the lobby – rooms, less often. Internet cafés have sprouted up throughout town – most charge around $2.50 per hour and have headsets for Skype. Some, including **Galápagos Online** (Av Charles Darwin; per hr $3; 8am-10pm) and **Sistem@s.com** (Av Bolívar Naveda) also offer wi-fi access for those with their own computers for the same fee.

Laundry

Convenient mom-and-pop shops have popped up all over to meet the dirty traveler's needs. **Laundry Lava Flash** (Av Bolívar Naveda; per kg $1; 8am-1pm & 2-7pm) allows you to drop it off or do it yourself. **Lavandería La Peregrina** (Av Indefatigable) is attached to the guesthouse of the same name.

Medical Services

Protesub (☎ 09-283-995; 18 de Febrero; 🕑 8am-12:30pm & 3-5pm) Has a state-of-the-art recompression chamber for divers with the bends and offers 24-hour emergency medical service. Several languages are spoken.

Money

Banco del Pacífico (Av Charles Darwin; 🕑 8am-3:30pm Mon-Fri, 9:30am-12:30pm Sat) Has an ATM and changes traveler's checks. Another ATM for this bank and for Banco Bolivariano can be found steps from the water-taxi pier in front of Proinsular Supermarket.

Post

There's a post office near the harbor.

Telephone

There are Pacifictel and *multicabinas* (telephone cabins) shops on Avenida Charles Darwin and Avenida Padre Julio Herrera. Most internet cafés are also calling centers.

Tourist Information

Cámara de Turismo (tourist information office; ☎ 252-7135; www.galapagostour.org; Av Charles Darwin; 🕑 7:30am-5pm Mon-Fri) Has hotel information, maps and schedules for local boat transportation; some staff speak English. Report any complaints here about boats, tours, guides or crew.

i-Tur (Water-taxi pier) A small kiosk with flyers, maps and basic hotel and travel-agency info.

ACTIVITIES

Diving

Because live-aboards are expensive and space is limited, most divers experience the underwater wonders of the Galápagos on day trips booked from here. Suitable for intermediate to advanced divers, currents can be strong and most are drift dives.

Gordon Rocks, Caamaño Islet, La Lobería, Punta Estrada and Punta Carrión off the Puerto Ayora bay are popular dives sites as is North Seymour Island, a short boat trip from Baltra. Devil's Crown, Enderby or Champion off the northern tip of Santa María are good for barracudas, rays and sharks. One of the recommended sites for those with a few dives under their belt is Academy Bay off the Puerto Ayora harbor; because of strong currents, Gordon Rocks is considered one of the most challenging sites.

Rates vary from about $80 to $120 for two dives per day ($150 for three), depending on the destination; most also offer PADI certification courses to newcomers. The following is a list of several recommended dive shops:

Galápagos Sub-Aqua (☎ 230-5514; www.galapagos-sub-aqua.com; Av Charles Darwin) The longest-running full-service dive center in the Galápagos. Guides are friendly and most speak English.

Galayachts (☎ 252-6542; www.galayachts.com; Av Charles Darwin) A full service agency supplying and supporting private yachts, also runs a high quality dive operation.

Nauti Diving (☎ 252-7004; www.nautidiving.com; Av Charles Darwin) Across from the turtle statue, runs hotel-based diving tours as well as day trips.

Scuba Iguana (☎ 252-6497, 09-300-8749; www.scubaiguana.com; Hotel Galápagos; Av Charles Darwin) Run by two of the most experienced divers in the Galápagos. Offers full-certification courses, and trips can be booked online.

Surfing

Surfers tend to be an adventurous bunch and obstacles like inaccessibility and sea lions aren't usually enough to deter them. There are several good surf breaks near Puerto Ayora itself including La Ratonera and Bazán near the Charles Darwin Research Station beach. If hauling your board a few kilometers is no problem, Tortuga Bay has several good breaks.

An hour or so by boat takes you to Punta Blanca and further north to Cerro Gallina, Las Palmas Chica and Las Palmas Grande, considered to be three of the best breaks in the Galápagos. There are also several breaks off the west side of Isla Baltra. Stop by **Santa Cruz Surf Club** (Av Charles Darwin) for more information.

TOURS

Albatross Tours (☎ 252-6948; albatrosstours@gpsinter.net; Av Charles Darwin) Santa Cruz day tours, equipment rental and diving.

Iguana Travel (Av Charles Darwin) Rents bicycles (per day $15), arranges day tours and books last-minute overnight yachts on the lower end of the pay scale.

Joybe Tours (☎ 252-4385; Av Charles Darwin) Last-minute overnight boat deals and day tours.

Lonesome George Travel Agency (☎ 252-6245; lonesomegrg@yahoo.com; (cnr Av Opuntia & Av Padre Julio Herrera) Rents snorkeling equipment (per day $8), kayaks (per half-day $30), bicycles (per hour $2), surfboards (per half-day $20) and wet suits (per day $8).

Metropolitan Touring (☎ 252-6297; www.metropolitan-touring.com) Located at the Finch Bay Hotel, it books the M/V *Santa Cruz* and luxury *Isabel II* and *La Pinta* yachts and any land or water-based tours in and around Santa Cruz.

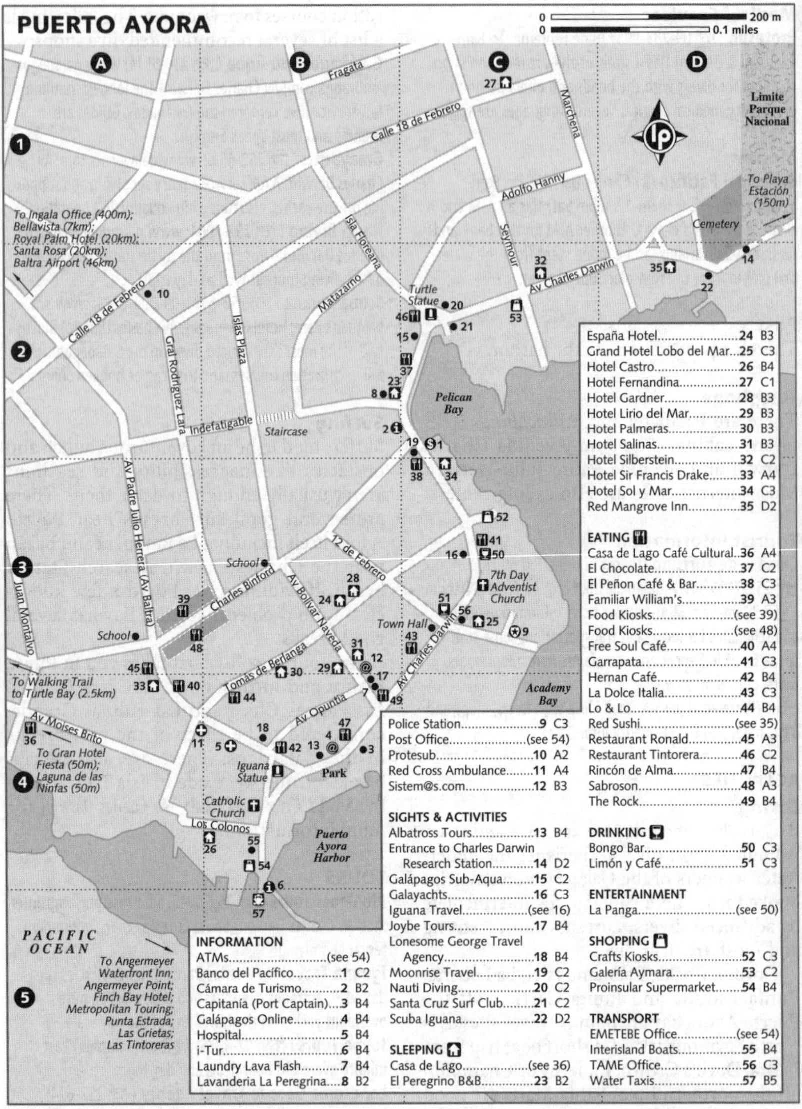

Moonrise Travel (☎ 252-6348; www.galapagosmoonrise.com; Av Charles Darwin) Run by a family of Galápagos experts and guides, who can arrange camping at their private highlands ranch, plus boat- and hotel-based tours and diving trips.

Red Mangrove Inn (see opposite) Offers day tours, diving and hotel-based tours of the islands, and camping; rents sea kayaks, surfboards, mountain bikes and snorkel equipment.

SLEEPING

You get much less bang for your buck compared to the mainland. Most of the hotels are within a few blocks of Avenida Charles Darwin, and prices tend to rise during the heaviest tourism seasons (December to January and June to August), but are somewhat negotiable the remainder of the year.

Family-run B&Bs pop up all the time; look for flyers posted by the harbor. Street numbers aren't used.

For a budget recommendation, try **Hotel Lirio del Mar** (☎ 252-6212; Av Bolívar Naveda; r per person $15). There's nothing but the basics here, with unadorned concrete rooms and cold-water bathrooms. Fans are hard to come by, but many of the second-floor rooms catch breezes.

Midrange

Hotel Salinas (☎ 252-6072; Av Bolívar Naveda; s/d from $18/36;) Across the street from Hotel Lirio del Mar, the Salinas can be hit or miss. Get one of the small, dark ground-floor rooms and you'll be disappointed. However, the second-floor rooms with high ceilings and sun exposure aren't bad value – all have hot water and cable TV. A small, central courtyard has a few plastic tables and chairs.

El Peregrino B&B (☎ 252-7515; Av Charles Darwin; s/d incl breakfast $20/40) This small place, with only four simple rooms, is popular because of its central location and warm, family-like atmosphere. Breakfast is included.

Hotel Sir Francis Drake (☎ 252-6221; Av Padre Julio Herrera; s/d $20/40) From the outside it doesn't look like much, sandwiched between shops and with nothing more than a dark hallway marking its entrance. However, this friendly hotel, only a short walk up from the pier, is one of the best value in town. Ask for one of the ground-floor rooms all the way in the back – these have large windows which let in lots of natural light. All of them are well maintained and are brighter than most of the competition, with the only downside being no common space.

Hotel Castro (☎ 252-6173; Av Padre Julio Herrera; s/d $40/60) Located down a quiet street winding away from the harbor, the Castro looks like a Mexican villa. However, none of the warmth and charm of the exterior extends inside: although the rooms are clean and well maintained, they have little character and some of those tucked away in back are quite dark.

Gran Hotel Fiesta (☎ 252-6348; s/d incl breakfast $45/60;) The quiet Fiesta is almost directly in front of the Laguna Las Ninfas, perfect for a quick dip. Rooms in this orange-and-yellow concrete building are well kept and have hot water. There's a pool table and modern restaurant on the grounds.

Hotel Fernandina (☎ 252-6499; www.hotelfernandina.com.ec; cnr 18 de Febrero & Los Piqueros; s/d $50/80;) Only a short walk from Avenida Charles Darwin, this friendly, family-run hotel nevertheless feels pleasantly secluded. Rooms are surrounded by a nicely landscaped garden, and there's a pool and Jacuzzi on the premises.

Next to one another are two hotels of similar value, with ordinary rooms: **España Hotel** (☎ 252-6108; www.elhotelespana.com; Islas Plazas; r incl breakfast with fan/air-con $20/30;) and **Hotel Gardner** (☎ 252-6979; www.hotelgardnergalapagos.com; Islas Plazas; s/d $25/30;). The España has one ground-floor room with four beds ($10 per person) for the budget minded; the Gardner has a covered rooftop patio with lounge chairs and hammocks. **Hotel Palmeras** (☎ 252-6139; s/d $50/70;), a large, institutional-looking complex, is worth considering for its second-floor outdoor pool area.

Top End

Casa de Lago (☎ 271-4647; www.galapagoscultural.com; Moisés Brito & Juan Montalvo; r $100;) Nothing like others in the same price range, Casa de Lago is best for families looking to recreate a little sense of home in the islands. Choose from one of two large suites with full-service kitchens: everything is made from recycled materials and filled with attractive tiles and textiles. A short walk from the harbor and the Laguna Las Ninfas, it's owned and operated by a friendly couple who are culturally and environmentally conscious, and who regularly host photographic exhibitions and music and theater performances in the charming, wooden main building.

Red Mangrove Inn (☎ 252-7011; www.redmangrove.com; Av Charles Darwin; s/d from $115/145;) This charmingly decorated inn at the northern end of Avenida Charles Darwin has the most character of any top-end hotel in Puerto Ayora. Each of the rooms are bright and sunny with white adobe walls and colorful, tiled bathrooms. The common areas are outfitted with hammocks and a Jacuzzi, and all manner of day and overnight trips can be arranged.

Hotel Sol y Mar (☎ 252-6281; www.hotelsolymar.com.ec; Av Charles Darwin; s/d from $155/175;) The recently renovated Sol y Mar bears little resemblance to its previous incarnation, save the sought-after waterfront location with pelicans and sea lions as neighbors. The A to Z makeover transformed the rooms into no-nonsense, efficient and comfortable refuges, each with a small private balcony. The seaside Jacuzzi, pool, bar and restaurant are the highlights, and there is wi-fi available throughout.

Finch Bay Hotel (☎ 252-6297; www.finchbayhotel.com; r from $275;) This hotel across the bay from Puerto Ayora is in a class by itself, in part because it's the only one with the beach right out its front door. The rooms themselves, a mix of tasteful wood and modern appliances, aren't especially large or luxurious but the grounds, which include a pool, Jacuzzi and barbecue area, justify the splurge. Metropolitan Touring (see p79) is based in the hotel, and can arrange any outdoor activity imaginable in the Galápagos.

Noteworthy for its waterfront location and indoor pools, the rooms at the **Grand Hotel Lobo de Mar** (☎ 252-6188; www.lobodemar.com.ec; 12 de Febrero; s/d incl breakfast from $75/100;) are less than grand. A big step up in quality is the **Hotel Silberstein** (☎ 252-6277; www.hotelsilberstein.com; Av Charles Darwin; s/d $98/142;), a Mexican-style villa with rooms surrounding an attractive inner courtyard with a pool and garden.

Across the harbor, accessible by water taxi, is the **Angermeyer Waterfront Inn** (☎ 09-472-4955; angermeyerwaterfrontinn@fmail.com; r $150;), a sun-splashed complex with simple rooms and outstanding views from the garden patio. If Puerto Ayora is too 'bright lights, big city' for you, try the **Royal Palm Hotel** (☎ 252-7408; www.royalpalmgalapagos.com; r from $375;), a beautifully designed luxury hotel in the highlands around Santa Rosa.

EATING

Often it's only higher prices that distinguish the restaurants that cater to locals from those that cater to tourists, although all the latter are congregated along Avenida Charles Darwin from the harbor to the Charles Darwin Research Station. Many of the hotels have restaurants.

Budget

There's a handful of popular kiosks selling inexpensive and hearty meals – mainly meat and fish dishes – along Charles Binford, just east of Avenida Padre Julio Herrera. The best time to go is a weekend night, when there's a festive atmosphere with tables set out on the street and couples and families chowing down at their favorites.

Free Soul Café (Av Padre Julio Herrera) Nothing more than a few shaded tables set outside in a rocky patio, this place is good for a quick empanada fix ($0.80) or coffee, juices and shakes.

Casa de Lago Café Cultural (www.galapagoscultural.com; Moisés Brito & Juan Montalvo; mains $5) With indoor, outdoor and balcony tables, there's no better place to while away a few hours with a book and coffee. This boho café serves excellent homemade fruit drinks, homemade ice cream and empanadas. It schedules periodic readings, photo exhibits and live music.

Familiar William's (Charles Binford; mains $5-7; 6-10pm Tue-Sun) stands out for its delicious *encocados* (fish, shrimp or lobster in a savory coconut sauce). Across the street, **Sabroson** (mains $7) is always busy, serving a wider variety of meat, seafood and rice dishes. The fried shrimp platter ($7) is enough for two.

El Chocolate (Av Charles Darwin; mains $3-6; 7:30am-10pm Mon-Sat) A popular *malecón* (waterfront) eatery, El Chocolate has outdoor patio tables and serves seafood, sandwiches and burgers besides good, fresh ground coffee and chocolate cake.

Midrange

Restaurant Ronald (Av Padre Julio Herrera; mains $6) Formerly a hole-in-the-wall, strictly *almuerzo* (set-lunch) place, Ronald's has gone slightly upscale, at least in terms of décor. It's still a mom-and-pop-run place but with nice tablecloths and a charming wood floor, and it has standard pasta, chicken and meat dishes and several hearty soups ($3) on the menu.

Garrapata (Av Charles Darwin; mains $4-9; 7-10pm Mon-Sat) More sophisticated than other tourist haunts, this popular outdoor restaurant serves substantial meat, seafood and chicken dishes with Italian and Ecuadorian flavors. Good wine, nice shore breezes and a pebble floor make it an attractive place for the night.

Restaurant Tintorera (Av Charles Darwin; mains $5-15) This spot at the northern end of town has an outdoor patio and turns atmospheric at night. There's a wide selection of fare, from burgers ($4.50) and lasagna ($4.50) to Cajun blackened fish ($9) and lobster ($15). Homemade ice cream and a good selection of cakes are available for desert. It's open for breakfast as well.

Hernan Café (Av Padre Julio Herrera; mains $6-12) The Hernan is a standout, not because of its near-standard menu of pasta, pizza, fish and meat dishes, but because of its location occupying prime real estate at the busiest intersection in town. There's even a bit of a nighttime buzz when groups pack the outdoor dining room till late.

Rock (☎ 252-7505; Av Charles Darwin & Plazas; mains $7) Something of a TGI Friday's with an Ecuadorian twist, this restaurant/bar is popular with students, volunteers and tour groups out for the night. The menu is more varied than most, and the linguini with coconut sauce and lobster ($12) is especially recommended.

La Dolce Italia (☎ 09-455-4668; Av Charles Darwin; mains $9; 11am-3pm & 6-10pm) With its warm, nautically inspired decor and gregarious Sicilian owner, this upscale Italian bistro is popular with groups on break from boat buffets. A number of excellent pizzas and pastas are served and if you just can't be bothered to go ashore, it does deliver to boats.

Other options include **Rincón de Alma** (Av Charles Darwin; mains $6-9; 7am-9pm), a casual street-side restaurant that serves ceviche and other seafood dishes, including lobster omelet ($16). **Lo & Lo** (Islas Plazas; mains $8), a little open-air place, does *balones* and empanadas, while **El Peñon Café & Bar** (Av Charles Darwin; mains $5) is a good hangout for a drink, a snack such as tortillas ($2), or something more substantial.

Top End

Angermeyer Point (☎ 252-7007; mains from $11; 5-10pm) Rustic and romantic, a candlelit dinner at this picturesque spot perched over the water is highly recommended (grab a water taxi at the pier). With better-than-average seafood and a few international dishes, as well as sushi on Friday nights and tapas in the early evenings, it's often booked by large groups, so reservations are a good idea.

Red Sushi (Red Mangrove Inn, Av Charles Darwin, mains from $10) Thanks to this upscale hotel restaurant, sushi lovers don't have to go hungry. It has a rustically elegant dining room and a large menu with Japanese specials, from sashimi to teppanyaki.

DRINKING & ENTERTAINMENT

Most of the restaurants are also good places for a relaxing drink, especially the Rock (see above), which doubles as a happening bar.

What nightlife there is to speak of centers mainly on the **Bongo Bar** (Av Charles Darwin; 6pm-2am), a trendy spot replete with flat-screen TVs showing videos (often of the islands themselves), loud music, a pool table and a lubricated mix of locals, guides and tourists. The downstairs disco, **La Panga** (Av Charles Darwin; 8:30pm-2am), is where to go to grind the night away ($10 cover on weekends).

A more mellow and younger crowd head to the **Limón y Café** (Av Charles Darwin), a modest outdoor bar with a gravel floor and pool tables.

SHOPPING

Every imaginable item has been covered with a Galápagos logo and is on sale in Puerto Ayora. The profits from gifts and clothes sold at the Charles Darwin Research Station go to support the institution, and the national park boutique is the only place to get things emblazoned with its logo.

Galería Aymara (☎ 252-6835; cnr Av Charles Darwin & Seymour) is a high-end artists' boutique selling uniquely designed handicrafts, jewelry and ceramics. Avoid buying objects made from black coral, turtle and tortoise shell – these threatened species are protected and it is illegal to use these animal products for the manufacture of novelties.

Food, beer, wine, toiletries, sun block and other necessities are available at the **Proinsular Supermarket** (Av Charles Darwin) near the water-taxi pier.

GETTING THERE & AWAY

Air

For more information on flights to and from Santa Cruz, see p352. Reconfirming your flight departures at either the **Aerogal** (☎ 252-6798; www.aerogal.com.ec; Av San Cristobál & Lara) or **TAME** (☎ 252-6527; www.tame.com.ec; Av Charles Darwin; 8am-noon & 2-5pm Mon-Fri, 9am-noon Sat) offices is essential. Flights are often full, and there is sometimes difficulty in changing your reservation or buying a ticket.

EMETEBE (☎ 252-6177; Proinsular Supermarket, 2nd fl, Av Charles Darwin) has small aircraft that fly between Baltra and San Cristóbal and Isabela. You must reserve your ticket at least a few days in advance, and departure times vary. See p353 for more information.

Boat

Private speedboats head daily to Isabela and San Cristóbal at 2pm. They reach the islands in less than three hours and charge about $30. There are no toilets on these little boats and the ride can be rough and frightening to some. Advance reservations aren't required, however, during high season especially, it's recommended to purchase tickets a day in advance. Every tour and travel agency sells these, or ask to be directed to the small kiosk near the water-taxi pier for whatever company is operating at the time.

The *capitanía* has information about (infrequent) boats to the mainland and details of every boat sailing from Puerto Ayora.

GETTING AROUND

Hotels, travel agencies, tour agencies and some cafés rent bicycles (per hour $2). To reach boats docked in the harbor or one of the several hotels or sites southwest of town, take a water taxi (per person 6am to 7pm $0.60, 7pm-6am $1).

To/From Airport

The airport is on Isla Baltra, a small island practically touching the far northern edge of Isla Santa Cruz. If you are booked on a prearranged tour, you will be met by a boat representative upon arrival and ushered onto a bus for the 10-minute drive to the channel (separating Baltra from Santa Cruz) and the boat dock.

If you are traveling independently, take the public bus signed 'Muelle' to the dock (a free 10-minute ride) for the ferry to Isla Santa Cruz. A 10-minute ferry ride ($0.80) will take you across to Santa Cruz, where you will be met by a CITTEG bus to take you to Puerto Ayora, about 45 minutes away ($1.80). This drive (on a paved road) provides a good look at the interior and the highlands of Santa Cruz. You should be in Puerto Ayora around an hour after leaving the airport; if going to the airport to make a flight, it's a good idea to allow yourself an hour and a half.

You can buy your ticket on the bus or at one of the ticket booths near the airport exit. The ride is always crowded.

Buses from Puerto Ayora to Baltra (via the ferry) leave every morning at 7am, 7:30am, 9:15am and 9:30am. Tickets are sold at the CITTEG bus station around 2km north of the harbor at the corner of Padre Julio Herrera and Charles Binford; a taxi to here will cost $1. Taxis to and from town to the Santa Cruz side of the channel are $15 (35 minutes).

Buses & Taxis

Taxis from anywhere in town to the CITTEG bus station cost $1. Buses from Puerto Ayora to Santa Rosa (about $1) leave from the bus station four or five times a day Monday to Saturday and less often on Sunday.

The most convenient way of seeing the interior, and ensuring that you don't get stuck, is to hire a bus or truck for the day with a group of other travelers.

All taxis are pickups, which means you can toss your bike in the back if you want to return to Puerto Ayora by pedal power. To Bellavista by taxi is around $2 and to Santa Rosa is around $7 – both one-way.

AROUND ISLA SANTA CRUZ

The one sizable island in the central part of the archipelago that has no visitor sites is **Isla Pinzón** (Duncan). It is a cliff-bound island, which makes landing difficult, and a permit is required to visit it (permits are usually reserved for scientists and researchers).

Isla Baltra

Most visitors' first experience of the Galápagos is from the archipelago's main airport at Isla Baltra. Baltra is a small island (27 sq km) off the north coast of Santa Cruz. The majority of tours begin here or in the town of Puerto Ayora, about one hour away (by a bus-boat-bus combination) on Isla Santa Cruz. There are no visitor sites or accommodations. Formerly a US military base during WWII, today the Ecuadorian armed forces call Baltra home. Those on a prearranged tour are often met at the airport and taken to their boats – a host of pelicans and noddies will greet you as you arrive at the harbor. Public transportation for here is described under Puerto Ayora (see left).

Islas Seymour & Mosquera

Separated from Isla Baltra by a channel, Isla Seymour is a 1.9-sq-km uplifted island with a dry landing. There is a rocky, circular trail (about 2.5km) leading through some of the largest and most active seabird-breeding colonies in the islands. Magnificent frigate birds and blue-footed boobies are the main attractions. Whatever time of year, there is always some kind of courtship, mating, nesting or chick rearing to observe. You can get close to the nests, as there is always at least one pair of silly boobies that chooses the middle of the trail as the best place to build their nest. Swallow-tailed gulls also nest here, and other birds are often seen as well. Sea lions and land and marine iguanas are common, while occasional fur seals, lava lizards and Galápagos snakes are seen too. It's well worth visiting for the wildlife.

Isla Mosquera is a tiny sandy island (about 120m by 600m) that lies in the channel between Islas Baltra and Seymour. There's no trail, but visitors land on the sandy beach to see or swim with the sea lion colony.

Islas Plazas

These two small islands, just off the east coast of Santa Cruz, can be visited on a day trip from Puerto Ayora. They were formed by uplift due to faulting. Boats anchor between them, and visitors can land on **South Plaza** (the larger of the islands), which is only about 13 hectares in area. A dry landing on a jetty brings you to an opuntia cactus forest, where there are many land iguanas. A 1km trail circuit leads visitors through sea-lion colonies and along a cliff-top walk where swallow-tailed gulls and other species nest. The 25m-high cliffs offer a superb vantage point to watch various seabirds such as red-billed tropicbirds, frigate birds, pelicans and Audubon's shearwaters. Snorkeling with the sea lions is a possibility.

Islas Daphne

These two islands of obviously volcanic origin are roughly 10km west of Seymour. **Daphne Minor** is very eroded, while **Daphne Major** retains most of its typically volcanic shape (called a tuff cone). A short but steep trail leads to the 120m-high summit of this tiny island.

There are two small craters at the top of the cone, and they contain hundreds of blue-footed booby nests. Nazca boobies nest on the crater rims, and a few red-billed tropicbirds nest in rocky crevices in the steep sides of the islands.

The island is difficult to visit because of the acrobatic landing – visitors have to jump from a moving *panga* on to a vertical cliff and scramble their way up the rocks. The steep slopes are fragile and susceptible to erosion, which has led the national park authorities to limit visits to the island. You must arrange special permission in advance, and groups must be no larger than 12 people.

Isla Santa Fé (Barrington)

This 24-sq-km island, about 20km southeast of Santa Cruz, is a popular destination for day trips. There is a good anchorage in an attractive bay on the northeast coast, and a wet landing gives the visitor a choice of two trails. A 300m trail takes you to one of the tallest stands of opuntia cactus on the islands, some over 10m high. A somewhat more strenuous 1.5km rough trail goes into the highlands, where the Santa Fé land iguana (found nowhere else in the world) may be seen if you are lucky. Other attractions include a sea-lion colony, excellent snorkeling, marine iguanas and, of course, birds.

ISLA SAN CRISTÓBAL (CHATHAM)

Some local boosters say that San Cristóbal is the capital of paradise, which it technically is since the port town of Baquerizo Moreno on the southwest point is the political seat of the Galápagos. It's the only island with fresh water and an airport in town, and it has several easily accessible visitor sites, all of which means that its tourism profile is second only to Santa Cruz. San Cristóbal is the fifth-largest island in the archipelago and has the second-largest population. The Chatham mockingbird, common throughout the island, is found nowhere else.

Though first settled in 1880, it was the establishment of a sugar factory by Manuel J Cobos in 1891 that signaled the start of any significant human presence on the island. Cobos recruited jailed mainlanders to work in his factory at El Progreso, imported train cars and minted his own money called the cobo. The experimental utopian project lasted for 25 years until the workers revolted and killed him in 1904; his son took over but was not very successful. The site is now a small village, where you can see the factory ruins and the site where Cobos is buried.

Visitor Sites

EL JUNCO LAGOON

A good paved road leads from the capital to the village of **El Progreso**, about 8km to the east and at the base of the 896m-high Cerro San Joaquín, the highest point on San Cristóbal (buses go here several times a day from Puerto Baquerizo Moreno or you can hire a taxi to take you for about $20 round-trip). For an ordinary meal in a less than ordinary setting, head to **La Casa del Ceibo** (☎ 252-0248; mains $4), a small shed built halfway up an enormous ceiba tree.

Rent a jeep or walk east along a dirt road about 10km further to El Junco Lagoon – a freshwater lake at about 700m above sea

THE MAN BEHIND THE MYTH

The life and work of Charles Darwin is so closely connected in the general public's mind with the Galápagos Islands that most people assume he spent a significant amount of time here and that the inspiration for ideas he sketches out in the *Origin of Species* came to him in a 'Eureka!' moment while touring the islands. Neither assumption is in fact true.

Darwin spent only five weeks in the Galápagos, at first primarily interested in geology rather than biology, and his later observations of pigeons and the methods of dog breeders in England were both much more influential to Darwin than the finches that have become the poster children for the short-hand of evolutionary theory.

Darwin lived in London for five years after he returned from the Galápagos, and then retreated to an estate in the countryside. From then on he hardly traveled and was confined to a sedentary lifestyle, in part because of chronic health concerns.

From an early age, he was inspired more by free-thinking religious figures than secular atheists and was never motivated to disprove the role of a divine figure. After he spent 22 years trying to prove his theory, he renounced Christianity in his middle age and described himself as an agnostic.

Originally sent to Cambridge to be a clergyman, Darwin instead became inspired by the botany lessons of his mentor JS Henslow. He collected beetles as a hobby and formed a club organized around the eating of animals unknown to the European kitchen. It was only after his uncle Josiah Wedgwood intervened that Darwin's father allowed him to go on a voyage at the age of 22. Darwin slept in a hammock on the *Beagle,* rode on top of Galápagos turtles, and in what is surely a violation of park rules today, dined on their meat.

From 1831 to 1836, the *Beagle* was tasked to survey the South American coastline and chart harbors for the British navy, stopping in Brazil, the Falklands, Argentina and Chile before the Galápagos. Darwin returned with more than 1500 specimens, though for many of those from the Galápagos, he neglected to label where each was found.

By the time the boat reached Bahía, Brazil, in 1836, Darwin was ready to return, writing in his journal, 'I loathe, I abhor the sea and all ships which sail on it.' In 1859, the *Origin of the Species* sold out on its first day in print. Only 1% of the book refers to the Galápagos.

level. It's one of the few permanent freshwater bodies in the Galápagos. Here you can see frigate birds shower in the freshwater to remove the salt from their feathers, white-cheeked pintails and common gallinules, and observe the typical highland Miconia vegetation and endemic tree ferns. The weather is often misty or rainy.

The road to El Junco continues across the island to the isolated beach of **Puerto Chino**, one of two places where camping is a possibility with permission from the Galápagos National Park office in Puerto Baquerizo Moreno (opposite).

PUERTO GRANDE

Smaller than its name suggests, Puerto Grande is a well-protected little cove on San Cristóbal's northwestern coast. There is a good, sandy beach suitable for swimming and various seabirds can be seen. Reachable by kayak, camping is allowed with prior permission.

ISLA LOBOS

An hour northeast of Puerto Baquerizo Moreno by boat is the tiny, rocky Isla Lobos, the main sea-lion and blue-footed booby colonies for visitors to San Cristóbal, with a 300m-long trail where lava lizards are often seen. Both the boat crossing and the trail tend to be rough, and there are better wildlife colonies elsewhere.

LEÓN DORMIDO (KICKER ROCK)

About a half-hour boat ride northeast of Puerto Baquerizo Moreno, this little rocky island is so named because of its resemblance to a sleeping lion, although it's more commonly referred to as Kicker Rock. The island is a sheer-walled tuff cone that has been eroded in half; smaller boats can sail between the two rocks. Because there's no place to land, this site is usually only seen from a passing boat or from the top of Cerro de las Tijeretas outside of Puerto Baquerizo Moreno, often to dramatic effect when the sun is setting.

LOS GALÁPAGOS

At the northern end of San Cristóbal is Los Galápagos, where you can often see giant Galápagos tortoises in the wild, although it does takes some effort to reach the highland area where they live.

One way to reach Los Galápagos is to land in a bay at the north end of the island and then hike up – it takes about two hours to get to the tortoise area following the trail. Some visitors report seeing many tortoises, while others see none.

It's also possible to get to Los Galápagos by taking the road from Puerto Baquerizo Moreno through El Progreso and on to El Junco Lagoon from where you can hike in.

OTHER SITES

The northeasternmost point of the island is **Punta Pitt**, where volcanic tuff formations are of interest to geologists (and attractive in their own right), but the unique feature of the site is that it's the only one where you can see all of the Galápagos booby species nesting. The walk is a little strenuous but rewarding.

Maybe one of the nicest beaches in the Galápagos is **Cerro Brujo**, a huge, white, expanse found at the northeast end of the island. The sand here feels like sifted powdered sugar. A colony of sea lions and blue-footed boobies call Cerro Brujo home, and behind the beach is a lagoon where you'll find great egrets and great blue herons. There's also good snorkeling in the turquoise waters.

Nearby is **Turtle Bay**, where you can see flamingos, turtles and other wildlife; both Turtle Bay and Cerro Brujo can be visited as part of a trip to Punta Pitt and Los Galápagos.

On the northwest side is **Ochoa Beach**, a horseshoe-shaped cove with a white sandy beach and shallow water good for snorkeling. Sea lions, frigate birds, pelicans and blue-footed boobies can all be found frolicking here, however it's only accessible by boat and usually with a guide. Kayaks are a possibility.

Part of the national park on the southeastern part of San Cristóbal is **Galapaguera**, a corral of giant tortoises living in seminatural conditions. A taxi can take you there and back for around $30.

Puerto Baquerizo Moreno

☎ 05 / pop 10,000

In an attempt to come out from under the shadow of Puerto Ayora, its larger and more high profile sister city in the Galápagos, Puerto Baquerizo Moreno is experiencing something of a mini boom. Not that it's in danger of losing its sleepy, time-stands-still fishing-village feel, but there are more hotels, restaurants and gift shops going up than in years past. More flights are arriving daily and some boat companies begin their island tours from here. The surfing is world-class, and you can explore many places on the island from here on your own. Locals affectionately call it 'Cristóbal'.

INFORMATION

Internet Access

There are several internet cafes including **Georgina's** (Teodoro Wolf; 🕑 8am-9pm; per hr $1.50). Internet access is also available at the **Mockingbird Café** (p368), a popular hangout with good coffee and snacks.

Laundry

There's an efficient machine-wash and dry **laundry** (Av Alsacio Northia; per kg $1; 🕑 8am-1pm & 2-8pm Mon-Sat, 8am-1pm Sun) next to the church, and **Lavandería Sebastion** (12 de Febrero; 🕑 8am-8pm Mon-Sat, 9am-noon & 3-7pm Sun; per kg $1) a few blocks away.

Money

Banco del Pacifico (Av Charles Darwin; 🕑 8am-3:30pm Mon-Fri, 10am-noon Sat) Has an ATM and changes traveler's checks.

Telephone

Dolphin (Av 12 de Febrero) has a long row of *multicabinas* (telephone cabins), as well as internet service. A few other *multicabinas* are scattered around town.

Tourist Information

Cámara de Turismo (☎ 252-1124; www.caturcrist.com; Igancio Hernández, 3rd fl), Has Galápagos-wide information, although less useful for travelers.

Municipal Tourism Office (☎ 252-0119; www.sancristobalgalapagos.com; Av Charles Darwin & 12 de Febrero; 🕑 8am-12:30pm & 2-5pm Mon-Fri) Maps, accommodation and transportation information.

Parque Nacional Galápagos (☎ 252-0138; www.galapagospark.org) A block north of Cabañas Don Jorge, on the way to the Interpretation Center.

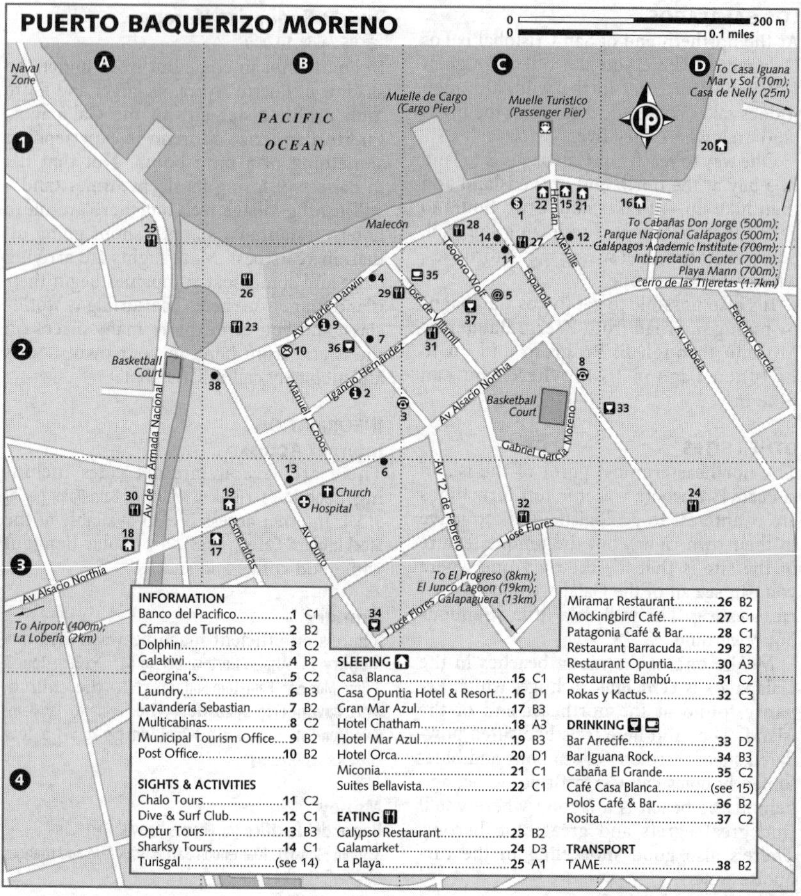

SIGHTS & ACTIVITIES

The newly restored *malecón* is Baquerizo Moreno's de facto town plaza. Built of high-quality, all-natural materials, it has benches, a small plaza for nighttime concerts and water slides where local kids play. You can see Leon Dormido from the second-floor viewing deck over the passenger pier.

The modern and easy to digest **Interpretation Center** (☎ 252-0358, ext 102; admission free; 🕒 8am-6pm) on the north side of the bay explains the history and significance of the Galápagos better than anywhere else in the islands. Exhibits deal with the biology, ecology, geology and human history of the islands, and it definitely deserves a visit even if you've already been inundated with facts from boat guides.

From the center, there are various well-marked trails (wear shoes, not sandals) that wind around the scrub-covered **Cerro de las Tijeretas** (Frigate Bird Hill). One trail leads over the hill to the small Las Tijeretas bay, which has excellent **snorkeling**; there's no beach here – just step in from the rocks.

Directly in front of the Interpretation Center is **Playa Mann**, a small beach popular with locals and tourists alike, especially during the lovely sunsets and on the weekends. The large, salmon-colored building across the street houses the **Galápagos Academic Institute** (☎ Quito 02-297-1845; www.usfq.edu.ec/gaias), which hosts semester-abroad international students and special marine-ecology and volunteer programs.

From the end of the dirt road that passes in front of the Interpretation Center, there's a short trail to the narrow beach of **Playa Cabo de Horno**, nicknamed 'Playa del Amor' (Beach of Love) because the sheltering mangrove trees are favorite make-out spots (the sea lions here show little interest in the goings on). Surfing off nearby **Punta Carola** is excellent, and other high-quality breaks near town are **El Cañon** and **Tongo Reef**, both of which are best accessed by the military zone. Stop by the **Dive & Surf Club** (☎ 252-1345) or one of the tour companies in town for information.

Just after the school, and before the airport, a road leads several kilometers (about a 30-minute walk) to **La Lobería**, a rocky beach with a lazy sea-lion colony, and that's also good for surfing year-round. There are lots of land iguanas along the trail leading past the beach. Bring water and protection from the sun. Taxis charge about $2 to take you out here and you can walk back (or pay an extra $4 for the driver to wait).

There are several good spots for **diving** nearby. Eagle rays, sea turtles, sea lions, hammerheads and white-tip sharks can be found at Kicker Rock. Schools of jacks, eagle rays, stingrays and seahorses are seen around Stephanie's Rock. Roca Ballena is a cave at about 23m to 24m down with corals, parrotfish, and rays; strong currents mean it's for experienced divers only. There are also several wreck dives including the *Caragua*, a 100m-long cargo ship near the site of the *Jessica* oil spill. Several companies in town offer diving – see below.

Tours

Chalo Tours (☎ 252-0953; chalotours@hotmail.com; Espanola) Offers day and overnight scuba trips, day trips on San Cristóbal and more expensive day trips to nearby islands; also rents snorkel, kayaking and biking equipment.

Dive & Surf Club (☎ 09-409-6450; www.divesurfclub.com; cnr Hernán Melville & Ignacio Hernández) Offers surf lessons and diving, and can arrange camping and horseback tours.

Galakiwi (☎ 252-1562; www.southernexposuretours.co.nz; Av Charles Darwin) Run by a New Zealand-Galápagean couple, offering land tours and snorkeling around San Cristóbal (per person $30); full-day tours to Española Island ($85); overnight boat tours; snorkeling gear for rent; and daily dive tours (two dives $100).

Optur Tours (☎ 252-1150; jmoralespolit@hotmail.com; Northia & 12 de Febrero) Books EMETEBE flights and boats to Santa Cruz and Isabela, and can arrange other charter boat services.

Sharksy Tours (☎ 09-954-0596; www.sharksky.com; Española) Customized daily (including mountain biking and snorkeling) and overnight tours, and scuba diving and probably the best resource for surfing information and board rentals.

Turisgal (☎; Española) Daily land and snorkel tours, and kayak and bike rentals ($25 per day).

SLEEPING

Budget

Cabañas Don Jorge (☎ 252-0208; Av Alsacio Northia; r per person $8-15) Looking very much like a survivalist camp or wilderness ranger station, this is a hodgepodge of rustic cabañas. Everything is aging including the kitchens, although they are fully stocked and good for self-catering. Look for Don Jorge on your right on the way to Playa Mann.

Hotel Mar Azul (☎ 252-0139; hotelmarazul_ex@hotmail.com; Av Alsacio Northia; s $12-20, d $20-25; ❄ 💻) A surprisingly good choice, considering the Mar Azul looks like a 1970s-era school building. Your best bet is one of the rooms that opens onto a small, sunny courtyard with a hammock. All rooms are comfortable and modern with hot water and cable TV, although you should avoid the handful of rooms that open directly onto the street because noise can be an issue. Wi-fi access is available in theory but the service is spotty.

Hotel Chatham (☎ 252-0137; Av Alsacio Northia; s/d $15/25; ❄) The anti-Don Jorge, the Chatham is strictly for the lover of concrete. The bare-bones rooms have no character, but at least there is a patio with hammocks and it's only a short walk from the airport.

Midrange & Top End

Gran Hotel Mar Azul (☎ 252-0901; granhotelmarazul@hotmail.com; Av Alsacio Northia; r from $22; ❄ 💻) The larger, more modern-looking building across the street from the Hotel Mar Azul, this is a less intimate option since the rooms, though equally comfortable and modern, open onto hallways.

Casa de Nelly (☎ 252-0112; jnagama@easynet.ec; Av Alsacio Northia; r with fan/air-con $30/40; ❄) This B&B, a three-story family home, can be found just outside of town on the way to Playa Mann. Some of the rooms, all fairly unadorned affairs, have private bathrooms; some don't. The owner, Nelly Saltos de Agama, can prepare breakfast for you if she's around.

our pick **Casa Blanca** (☎ 252-0392; jacquivaz@yahoo.com; Av Charles Darwin; s/d $40/60;) There's no better place to base yourself in town: not only does this whitewashed adobe have charmingly decorated rooms and tile floors, but it sits on the *malecón* directly across from the passenger pier, meaning rooms with sea-facing balconies have great views. Reception is on the third floor, where there's also a little breakfast nook.

Miconia (☎ 252-0608; www.miconia.com; Av Charles Darwin; s/d incl breakfast $55/75;) Just a few steps from the passenger wharf on the waterfront, this hotel is ever expanding. The seven attractive suites in the original low-slung building have separate living-room areas with wicker furniture and earthy pastel colors, and there's a tiny pool and Jacuzzi back here as well. Less spacious but equally finished are four floors of rooms next door. There's a full-service gym and excellent restaurant and café overlooking the harbor, plus an internet café as well.

Suites Bellavista (☎ 252-0352; Av Charles Darwin; r $60;) On the *malecón* across the street from Casa Blanca, this is another good option. The second and third floor of this utilitarian building have a handful of nice, warm rooms with gleaming wood floors, mini-fridges, cable TV and modern bathrooms. Look for the office in the street-level store.

Casa Opuntia Hotel & Resort (☎ 252-0632; teclagenoa@yahoo.com; s/d $60/80;) This white villa next to the Miconia, formerly known as the Teclas Surf Resort, isn't good value unless you can negotiate a lower price – which is possible, especially during low season. The sunny, whitewashed rooms are blandly decorated, however some have screen doors opening onto balconies. There's a pool and Jacuzzi in back (though they may or may not be filled) and hammocks in the front courtyard.

Hotel Orca (☎ 252-0233, Quito ☎ 02-256-4565; s/d about $60/80) Just around the corner from the end of the *malecón*, the Orca offers peaceful sunset views from the rooftop patio, however the rooms are basic and it caters mostly to big groups.

Casa Iguana Mar y Sol (☎ 252-1788; www.sancristobalbb.com; r from $100;) Everything in this hotel, just outside of town towards Playa Mann, is marvelously handcrafted from the railings to the iguana carved into the front door. Each room is a large boutique-quality suite with surprising flourishes, the ground-floor lounge/bar/breakfast area is as stylish as a Soho hotel, and the rooftop deck/bar is ideal for a sundowner.

EATING

For better or worse, there aren't many restaurants catering to tourists in Baquerizo Moreno – most are informal spots with a few tables on the street and close early on Sundays. Women sell *chuzos* (thinly sliced steak grilled on a stick) along Alsacio Northia, near the school in the evenings.

Budget

Restaurant Barracuda (Villamil & Darwin) and **Patagonia Café & Bar** (Av Charles Darwin) are similar places on or just off the *malecón* serving inexpensive *almuerzos* ($2.50) and simple seafood and meat dishes throughout the day. **Restaurante Bambú** (Hernández & Villamil) does pizza ($3) as well as the basics. **Restaurant Opuntia** (Armada Nacional; mains $4) serves juicy rotisserie chicken in a garden setting. For outdoor weekend barbeque fare, try **Rokas y Kactus** (☎ 252-0236; José Flores & García Moreno) just up the hill south of town.

Mockingbird Café (Española & Hernández; mains $2.50), one of the few places open on Sundays, serves salads, burgers and excellent French toast. The largest, best-stocked grocery is **Galamarket** (José Flores), at the top of a hill southeast of the town center.

Midrange

Calypso Restaurant (Av Charles Darwin; mains $5-14) A more sophisticated menu than its décor would suggest, the Calypso does good seafood dishes as well as burgers, pizzas and salads. An informal place right on the patio at the western end of the *malecón,* it's equally good for a coffee, juice or delicious slice of chocolate cake.

La Playa (Av de la Armada Nacional; mains $6) Foreign groups are the name of the game at this waterfront restaurant to the west of town, just in front of the entrance to the naval zone. It has outdoor seating, and more importantly, good ceviche ($7), seafood and pizzas.

Miconia (Av Charles Darwin; mains $6-15) Occupying the second-floor of the hotel of the same name (left), this restaurant offers a wide range of international standards like pizza and pasta as well as local meat and seafood dishes. Prices are higher than at restaurants catering to locals, but the harbor views and large portions are worth it.

Miramar Restaurant (mains $6-15; 6-11pm) The only place in town with gastronomic ambitions, the Miramar does relatively virtuosic versions of Ecuadorian meat and seafood specialties (fish in coconut sauce $9) and better-than-average pasta dishes. The large, open-air second-floor dining room has a row of balcony seating with stools overlooking Playa Barrio Frío, and a small patch of sand. It's a good thing the views are so bucolic, since service can move as slowly as the sea lions below.

DRINKING & ENTERTAINMENT

Every Friday night on the *malecón*, between Wolf and Villamil, locals put on a show of folkloric and modern music, including school children with Shakira-like ambition. Arriving and departing boat passengers congregate at **Café Casa Blanca** (Av Charles Darwin), which has a few snacks but is primarily good for a coffee, beer or juice. **Cabaña El Grande** (Jose de Villamil; drinks $0.90-1.50), known for its array of *batidos* (fruit shakes), has a wall mural of nearby Leon Dormido (Kicker Rock).

Bar Arrecife (García Moreno) is the place for karaoke filled evenings. Downstairs is a typical bar, while the open-air, upstairs patio is a less-claustrophobic place to base yourself for the night. The rustic **Polos Café & Bar** (Av 12 de Febrero) is sometimes turned into a discotheque but always does good caipirinhas. **Rosita** (Ignacio Hernandez & Teodoro Wolf), an outdoor place with a vaguely nautical theme, serves food but is best visited for drinks at night. **Bar Iguana Rock** (José Flores & Quito), a good hang out for the college-age crowd, has a pool table and even gets an off-island band or two.

GETTING THERE & AWAY

Air

The airport is half a kilometer from town – a five-minute walk or a $1 taxi ride (taxis are white pickup cabs). For information on flights to Guayaquil and Quito, see p352. Regardless of the airline, you should try to check your luggage at least two hours in advance; you can always easily return to town to spend your final hours in the islands more comfortably.

Aerogal (☎ 252-1117; www.aerogal.com.ec) At the airport.

EMETEBE (☎ 252-0036; www.emetebe.com.ec) At the airport; flies within the islands.

TAME (☎ 252-1089; www.tame.com.ec; cnr Av Charles Darwin & Quito; 8am-noon & 2-5pm Mon, Tue & Thu, 9am-noon Sat) Office in town and at the airport.

Boat

Small speedboats head to Santa Cruz ($30, two to 2½ hours, 6 or 7am) and occasionally to Floreana and Isabela. See p367) for booking information.

GETTING AROUND

To reach the farming center of El Progreso, 8km into the highlands, hire a taxi $2 (one-way). From here, you can hire a vehicle ($20), walk or hitchhike for the final 10km ride to the visitor site of El Junco Lagoon. Some taxi drivers are licensed to give tours of the lagoon.

In Puerto Baquerizo Moreno, pick-up truck **taxis** (Cooperative de Transporte Terrestre; ☎ 252-0477) hang out along the *malecón* and have fixed round-trip rates to island destinations, but don't always stick to them. They'll take you to La Lobería ($6), El Progreso, El Junco Lagoon ($18), La Galapaguera ($80) and Puerto Chino ($30).

ISLA SAN SALVADOR (SANTIAGO OR JAMES)

Once a hideout for British buccaneers and one of the stops on Darwin's itinerary, Isla Santiago, whose little-used official name is San Salvador, is the fourth-largest of the islands. It's a frequent stop on boat tours because there are several interesting visitor sites and its terrain of rough lava fields is an example of the island's challenging beauty.

One of the most popular sites in all the islands is **Puerto Egas**, on James Bay on the west side of Santiago, and named after Dario Egas, the owner of a salt mine on the island that was once, as a result of presidential patronage, the only producer of salt in all the country. Here, there is a long, flat, black-lava shoreline where eroded shapes form lava pools, caves and inlets that house a great variety of wildlife. This is a great place to see colonies of marine iguanas basking in the sun. The tide pools contain hundreds of red Sally Lightfoot crabs, which attract hunting herons of all the commonly found species.

The inlets are favorite haunts of the Galápagos fur seals, and this is a great opportunity to snorkel with the surprisingly agile animals as well as many species of tropical fish, moray eels, sharks and octopuses.

Behind the black-lava shoreline is **Sugarloaf Volcano**, which can be reached via a 2km path. Lava lizards, Darwin's finches and Galápagos doves are often seen on this path. It peters out near the top of the 395m summit, but from here, the views are stupendous. There is an extinct crater in which feral goats are often seen (wild goats are a major problem on Santiago), and Galápagos hawks often hover a few meters above the top of the volcano. North of the volcano is a crater where the salt mine used to be; its remains can be visited by walking along a 3km trail from the coast.

At the north end of James Bay, about 5km from Puerto Egas, is the brown-sand **Espumilla Beach**, which can be reached with a wet landing. The swimming is good here, and by the small lagoon behind the beach you can see various wading birds including, at times, flamingos. A 2km trail leads inland through transitional vegetation where there are various finches and the Galápagos flycatcher.

At the northwestern end of Santiago, another site that is normally visited by boat is **Buccaneer Cove**, so called because it was a popular place for 17th- and 18th-century buccaneers to careen their vessels. The cliffs and pinnacles, which are used as nesting areas by several species of seabirds, are the main attraction these days.

Sullivan Bay is on Santiago's east coast. Here, a huge, black, century-old lava flow has solidified into a sheet that reaches to the edge of the sea. A dry landing enables visitors to step onto the flow and follow a trail of white posts in a 2km circuit on the lava. You can see uneroded volcanic formations such as pahoehoe lava, lava bubbles and tree-trunk molds in the surface. This site is of particular interest to those interested in volcanology or geology.

AROUND ISLA SAN SALVADOR

Isla Bartolomé

Panoramic views and frisky penguins make this tiny island just off Sullivan Bay a common stop for boat tours. A path from a jetty (for a dry landing) leads up to the windwhipped 114m summit of the island, where the dramatic views make it de rigueur for group photos. This trail leads through a wild and unearthly looking lava landscape, where a wooden boardwalk and stairs have been built to aid visitors and to protect the trail from erosion.

The other visitor site is a small, sandy beach in a cove (wet landing), from where you can don your snorkel gear and swim after the speedy Galápagos penguins that frequent this cove. Marine turtles and a gaudy variety of tropical fish are also frequently seen.

The best way to photograph the penguins is by taking a *panga* ride close to the rocks on either side of the cove, particularly around the aptly named Pinnacle Rock, to the right of the cove from the seaward side. You can often get within a few meters of these fascinating birds – the closest point to Puerto Ayora where you can do so. Other penguin colonies are on the western side of Isabela.

From the beach, a 100m trail leads across the narrowest part of Bartolomé to another sandy beach on the opposite side of the island. Marine turtles may nest here between January and March.

Sombrero Chino

This tiny island, a fairly recent volcanic cone, just off the southeastern tip of Santiago is less than a quarter of 1 sq km in size. The accuracy of its descriptive name, translated as 'Chinese Hat,' is best appreciated from the north. There is a small sea-lion cove on the north shore, where you can anchor and land at the visitor site. Opposite Sombrero Chino, on the rocky shoreline of nearby Santiago, penguins are often seen.

A 400m trail goes around the cove, where there's snorkeling and swimming opportunities, and through a sea-lion colony. Marine iguanas scurry everywhere.

Isla Rábida (Jervis)

This approximately 5-sq-km island, also known as Jervis, lies 5km south of Santiago. There is a wet landing onto a comparatively dark red beach, where sea lions haul out and pelicans nest, one of the best places to see such nesting.

Behind the beach, there is a saltwater lagoon where flamingos and white-cheeked pintails are sometimes seen. This lagoon is also the site of **a sea-lion colony**, where the *solteros* (lone males), deposed by the dominant bull, while away their days in bachelor ignominy.

There is a 750m trail with good views of the island's 367m volcanic peak, which is covered with palo santo trees. At the end of the trail there is a great snorkeling spot.

ISLA ISABELA (ALBEMARLE)

Isabela is the largest island in the archipelago at 4588 sq km, but despite its size and imposing skyline of mostly-still-active volcanoes, it's the delicate sights like frigates flying as high as the clouds or penguins making their way tentatively along the cliffs that reward visitors.

It's a relatively recent island and consists of a chain of five fairly young and intermittently active volcanoes, including Volcán Sierra Negra, which erupted in late 2005 sending up a 20km-high smoke column; Puerto Villamil, 22km to the south, and nearby wildlife were not in danger. One of the island's volcanoes, Volcán Wolf, is the highest point in the Galápagos at 1707m (some sources claim 1646m). There is also one small, older volcano, Volcán Ecuador (610m).

Volcán Alcedo (1097m) has the largest tortoise population in the Galápagos, however more than 50,000 feral goats also call it home, threatening to out-compete the tortoises for the limited food stuffs available. The campaign to preserve the tortoise population on Alcedo is a joint venture between the Charles Darwin Research Station and the Galápagos National Park Service.

Although Isabela's volcanoes dominate the westward view during passages to the western part of Santa Cruz, the island itself is not frequently visited by smaller boats because most of the best visitor sites are on the west side of the island, reached only after a long passage (over 200km) from Santa Cruz.

Visitor Sites

As you'd expect from an island that occupies over 58% of the Galápagos' land mass, Isabela has many visitor sites. One of these is the summit of **Volcán Alcedo**, famous for its 7km-wide caldera and steaming fumaroles. Hundreds of giant tortoises can be seen here, especially from June to December, and juvenile hawks soar on thermal updrafts. The view is fantastic. Permits are required to hike this long, steep and waterless trail and to camp near the summit (two days required).

A few kilometers north of the landing for Alcedo is **Punta García**, which consists mainly of very rough *aa* lava, a sharp, jagged lava; there are no proper trails, but you can land. This is one of the few places where you can see the endemic flightless cormorant without having to take the long passage around to the west side (sightings are not guaranteed).

At Isabela's northern tip is **Punta Albemarle**, which was a US radar base during WWII. There are no trails, and the site is known for the flightless cormorants, which normally are not found further to the east. Further west are several points where flightless cormorants, Galápagos penguins and other seabirds can be seen, but there are no visitor sites. You must view the birds from your boat.

At the west end of the northern arm of Isabela is the small, old Volcán Ecuador, which comes down almost to the sea. **Punta Vicente Roca**, at the volcano's base, is a rocky point with a good snorkeling and diving area, but there is no official landing site.

The first official visitor-landing site on the western side of Isabela is **Punta Tortuga**, a mangrove-surrounded beach at the base of Volcán Darwin (1280m). Although there is no trail, you can land on the beach and explore the mangroves for the mangrove finch, present here but not always easy to see. This finch is found only on Islas Isabela and Fernandina.

Just south of the point is **Tagus Cove**, where early sailors frequently anchored and scratched the names of their vessels into the cliffs around the cove. It's a strange sight to behold graffiti, the oldest from 1836, in an otherwise pristine environment next to where sea lions lazily roam.

A dry landing deposits you at the beginning of a 2km-long trail that brings you past a postcard-perfect saltwater lagoon, twice the salinity of the ocean, called **Darwin Lake**; it's a tuff cone, like a chimney from the main volcano. Here the trail leads to the lower lava slopes of Volcán Darwin, where various volcanic formations and stunning views of surrounding slopes can be observed. There are some steep sections on this trail. A *panga* ride along the cliffs will enable you to see the historical graffiti and various seabirds, usually including Galápagos penguins and flightless cormorants. There are snorkeling opportunities in the cove.

Urbina Bay lies around the middle of the western shore of Isabela and is a flat area formed by an uplift from the sea in 1954. Evidence of the uplift includes a coral reef on the land. Flightless cormorants, pelicans, giant tortoises and land and marine iguanas can be observed on land, and rays and turtles can be seen in the bay. A wet landing onto a beach brings you to a 1km trail that leads to the corals. There is a good view of Volcán Alcedo.

Near where the western shoreline of Isabela bends sharply toward the lower arm of the island, there is a visitor site that's known for its marine life. **Elizabeth Bay** is best visited by a *panga* ride, as there are no landing sites. Marine turtles and rays can usually be seen in the water, and various seabirds and shorebirds are often present. Islas Mariela are at the entrance of the bay and are frequented by penguins.

West of Elizabeth Bay is **Punta Moreno**. You can make a dry landing on to a lava flow, where there are some brackish pools. Flamingos, white-cheeked pintails and common gallinules are sometimes seen, and various pioneer plants and insects are found in the area.

On the southeastern corner of Isabela, there is the small village of Puerto Villamil. Behind and to the west of the village is the **Villamil Lagoon**, a site known for its marine iguanas and migrant birds, especially waders – more than 20 species have been reported here. A trail a little over a kilometer long begins as a wooden boardwalk over the lagoon passes through mangroves and dense vegetation, eventually ending in the **Crianza de Tortugas** (Giant Tortoise Breeding Center). Volunteers here can explain the work being done to help restore the population of this species on Isabela. Pickups from town ($1) can drop you at the entrance on the road to the highlands; finding one back is difficult.

Also west of Puerto Villamil is **Muro de las Lágrimas** (Wall of Tears), a 100m-long wall of lava rocks built by convicts under harsh and abusive conditions. The penal colony closed in 1959 but the wall stands as a monument to an infamous chapter in the island's history. Only a five-minute boat ride or so from town is **Las Tintoreras**, a small volcanic island with marine iguanas, boobies and other birdlife; nearby and in the bay around **Concha de Perla** is excellent **snorkeling**. Rays, marine turtles, the occasional white-tip reef shark and penguins can be seen, and it's especially fun to swim through the narrow fissures in the rocks, like underwater hallways decorated with plant and coral life. Islote Tortuga and islotes Cuatro Hermanos are **dive sites** within range from Puerto Villamil. There are a few good **surf breaks** for experienced surfers near town.

To the northwest near the tiny settlement of Santo Tomás lies the massive **Volcán Sierra Negra** (1490m), which erupted in late 2005. An 8km trail leads around the east side of the volcano to some active fumaroles. It is possible to walk all the way around the caldera, but the trail peters out. You should carry all your food and water or hire horses. Galápagos hawks, short-eared owls, finches and flycatchers are among the birds commonly seen on this trip. The summit is often foggy (especially during the June-to-December *garúa* season) and it is easy to get lost. There are spectacular views from nearby Volcán Chico, a subcrater where you can see more fumaroles. Trucks or jeeps can be rented for the 18km ride from Puerto Villamil ($40 round-trip) to the village of Santo Tomás; from here it's a further 9km up a steep trail to the rim of the volcano – horses can be hired in the village ($10, one hour).

Halfway up the slope is **Campo Duro** (☎ 252-9358, refugiodetortugasgigantes.com; per person $60), a full-service campsite run by the Red Mangrove Inn in Puerto Ayora (p359). Rates include transport to and from Puerto Villamil.

Puerto Villamil (Albemarle)

☎ 05 / pop 2000

More than any other settlement in the Galápagos, Puerto Villamil, also known as Albemarle, embodies the archetypal end of the road. In a good way, the kind that lures weary city folks to pick up and move halfway around the world. Backed by a lagoon where flamingos and marine iguanas live and situated on a beautiful white-sand beach, it's a sleepy little village of sandy roads; a handful of pastel-colored second homes line the road from the pier to town. For sights and activities accessible from town, see p371.

Undoubtedly, when General José Villamil moved here in 1832 with hopes of organizing a model community made up mostly of whalers, he found the location as beguiling as today's visitors do. Unfortunately, the draftees' peaceful inclinations proved to be more utopian than real and ended up destroying the colony. Villamil later introduced cows, horses and donkeys, which quickly reproduced, threatening the island's delicate ecosystem.

INFORMATION

You can change traveler's checks at Gram Money – bring US cash. A local bank has an ATM but foreign cards aren't accepted. There is a Pacifictel office on Calle Escalecias. There are four or so places in town to access the internet including **Easy Net** (Los Cactus & Escalecias; ☑ 8:30am-12:30pm & 3-6:30pm Mon-Fri, 8:30am-4:30pm Sat) and **El Rincon de Isabela** (Piquero & Cormorant), all charging around $2 per hour. A few *lavanderías* do wash and dry including **Papita's** on Av Anotonio Gil. Contact **Isabela Dive Center** (☎ 252-9418; www.isabeladive center.com; Calle Escalecia & Av Antonio Gil) to book diving trips.

SLEEPING & EATING

Hostería Isabela del Mar (☎ 252-9030; www.hoste riaisabela.com.ec; r per person $20) Really two hotels in one, the Isabela del Mar also includes rooms in another building called Hotel Ballena Azul, which serves good food. Some rooms have shared and some private bathrooms; ask for an ocean view.

Wooden House (☎ 252-8484; www.thewoodenhouse hotel.com; per person $30; 🐾 💻) Located off the dusty road between the pier and town, this meticulously maintained, all-wood home is one of the best places to base yourself. Besides the tastefully decorated, cozy rooms, there's an outdoor lounge area/restaurant/bar and a little pool in the front-yard garden.

ourpick La Casa Marita (☎ 252-9301; www.casa maritagalapagos.com; s/d/ste from $43/73/85) Close to the beach with sea views, each uniquely decorated room at the Marita has its own color scheme as well as hot showers and kitchenettes. There's a Jacuzzi, bar, library and hammocks in the garden.

Hotel Albemarle (☎ 252-9489; www.hotelalbemarle .com; r $150; 🐾 💻) Occupying a prime stretch of beachfront property in the center of town, this new two-story Mediterranean style villa is the most luxurious in Puerto Villamil. It has stylish, stone, boutique-style bathrooms and high ceilings with modern conveniences like minifridges and cable TV. Glass-paneled doors lead to balconies with ocean views. Breakfast included.

On the beach at the western edge of town is the fairly disheveled **Caleta Iguana** (Casa Rosada; ☎ 09-145-4819; r $35). One image – burlap sacks as ceiling decoration – sum up some of the bizarre aesthetic choices. **Pensión La Jungla** (☎ 252-9348; r $10), a charming mess of a place on the road heading north to the Crianza de Tortugas, is one of the cheapest options.

There are several restaurants serving seafood located on the central square on Av Antonio Gill, between Las Fragatas and 16 de Marzo, including **La Choza** (mains $5) and the more refined **El Encanto de la Pepa** (mains $7). Behind the square, at the end of a pier running out from the town beach, is **Sea Lion Bar**, a good place for sunset drinks.

GETTING THERE & AWAY

Air

Three times a week, **EMETEBE** (☎ 252-9155; www .emetebe.com.ec) flies from Baltra to San Cristóbal, Isabela and Baltra. Each leg is around $100 (plus $15 departure tax); luggage in excess of 9kg is charged. Its office is at the airport 3km north of town. See p352 for more information. The Isabela stop may be canceled if there aren't enough passengers.

Boat

There are daily 6am boats to Santa Cruz ($30, two hours, 6am) from Puerto Villamil. From Santa Cruz, boats leave at 2pm. Tickets can be purchased at the dock or from **Transmartisa** (☎ 252-9053; cnr Av Antonio Gil & Las Fragatas), attached to the EMETEBE office. The majority of people landing at the passenger pier east of town have to pay a $5 fee.

Expensive group charters are also available.

GETTING AROUND

Buses to/from Villamil to Santo Tomás and further into the highlands leave at 7am and noon, returning two hours later. Twin-cab trucks can be rented at other times – call **Cooperativa Sierra Negra** (☎ 252-9147); the fare for the airport is $2.

ISLA FERNANDINA (NARBOROUGH)

Even by Galápagos' standards, Fernandina is unique. It's home to thousands of lethargic marine iguanas, and for the volcanically minded, it's the island you'll most likely witness an eruption, with the most recent in May 2005. At 642 sq km, Fernandina is the third-largest, and the westernmost and youngest, of the main islands. Unlike other parts of the Galápagos, no introduced species have taken root here.

The one visitor site at **Punta Espinoza**, just across from Tagus Cove on Isabela, is a memorable one. Marine iguanas, too many to count, can be seen sunning themselves on the black-lava formations, a dramatic sight that looks like a museum diorama on dinosaurs come to life. Flightless cormorants nest nearby, hawks soar overhead and Galápagos penguins, turtles and sea lions sometimes frolic in an admirable display of multispecies tolerance in the lagoon near the landing.

A dry landing brings you to two trails: a 250m trail to the point and a 750m trail to recently formed lava fields. Here you can see various pioneer plants, such as the *Brachycereus* cactus as well as *pahoehoe* and *aa* lava formations. Several movies, most famously *Master and Commander,* filmed scenes here in front of a now-iconic white-mangrove tree.

SOUTHERN ISLANDS

Isla Santa María (Floreana or Charles)

This, the sixth-largest of the islands, is known as much for the tragic history of its first residents as for its intensely pink flamingos and snorkeling sites.

VISITOR SITES

From the village of Puerto Velasco Ibarra, a road runs inland for a few kilometers to **Asilo de la Paz**, an official visitor site. It is an all-day hike there and back – you can hire a guide. There are no taxis. Here you can see the endemic medium tree finch, which exists only on Floreana. Early settlers once lived in the nearby caves.

There are three visitor sites on the north coast of Floreana. Most groups spend several perfunctory minutes at **Post Office Bay**, where there's a few gone-to-seed barrels surrounded by scraps of wood sticking out every which way covered in graffiti. A functioning mailbox for American and British whalers beginning in the late 18th-century, these days it's tourists who leave postcards hoping they will find their way like a message in a bottle. Well, it's more prosaic than that; visitors are asked to grab a few to post when they return to their home countries. About 300m behind the barrel is a **lava cave** that can be descended with the aid of a short rope and flashlight. The path is slippery and involves sloshing through some chilly water. Nearby is a pleasant swimming beach and the remains of a canning factory; a wet landing is necessary.

Also reached with a wet landing is **Punta Cormorant**, a greenish beach (green because it contains crystals of the mineral olivine) where sea lions play and the swimming and snorkeling are good. A 400m trail leads up and over an isthmus to a white-sand beach where turtles sometimes lay their eggs. The beach is also good for swimming, but beware of stingrays and procreating turtles.

Between the two beaches you'll find a lagoon where several dozen flamingos are normally seen. This is also a good place to watch for other wading birds such as black-necked stilts, oystercatchers, willets and whimbrels. You must stop at the wooden rail on the edge of the lagoon – be sure to bring binoculars and your longest zoom lens, otherwise the flamingos will just be indistinct blurs on the horizon. White-cheeked pintail ducks are often seen in the lagoon and Galápagos hawks wheel overhead. It's an especially dramatic tableau when the dark shadows, cast from the setting sun, suggest a stillness that has lasted for eons.

One of the most outstanding marine sites in all the Galápagos is the **Devil's Crown**, a ragged semicircle of rocks poking up out of the ocean a few hundred meters from Punta Cormorant. A strong current sweeps snorkelers briskly past thousands of bright tropical fish, a small coral formation, sea lions, marine turtles and the occasional shark. A *panga* ride around the semi-submerged volcanic cone will give views of red-billed tropicbirds, pelicans, herons and lava gulls nesting on the rocks.

PUERTO VELASCO IBARRA

This tiny port, the only settlement on Isla Santa María (Floreana), is set on a black-sand beach on a sheltered bay. Sea lions and flamingos almost outnumber the 150-or-so human residents. The highlands are accessed by a road, though it sees little traffic other than that of the foot variety.

The descendants of the Wittmers run the modern-looking **Hostal Wittmer** (☎ 05-252-9506; s/d/tr $30/50/70), which also doubles as the best eatery and information and guide center. Most of the beachfront rooms are in a small, white two-story building and have private balconies; meals can be provided.

Another option, the **Red Mangrove Floreana Lodge** (☎ 252-6564; r $120), is a collection of tidy little cabins set out on black-lava rock a few minutes from town. Often occupied by groups on tours run out of the Red Mangrove Inn in Puerto Ayora (p359), it's a peaceful refuge from civilization.

Boats between Floreana and Santa Cruz can be arranged at travel agencies in Puerto Ayora.

CSI: FLOREANA

After the departure of Patrick Watkins, the first known resident in all the archipelago, Floreana was turned into an Ecuadorian penal colony. Then in the 1930s, three groups of German settlers arrived and strange stories have been told about them ever since.

The most colorful of the settlers was a baroness who arrived with three lovers. Another settler, Dr Friedrich Ritter, an eccentric who had all of his teeth removed before arriving to avoid having dental problems, was accompanied by his mistress. The third group was the Wittmers, a young couple from Cologne.

Despite their common nationality, there was a great deal of friction among the groups, and one by one the settlers died under mysterious circumstances. The baroness and one of her lovers simply disappeared, while another lover died in a boating accident. The vegetarian Dr Ritter died of food poisoning after eating chicken. The only ones to survive were the Wittmers, with Margaret Wittmer the last to die, in 2000 at the age of 95. Her children and grandchildren run a small hotel and restaurant in Puerto Velasco Ibarra.

Although several books and articles have been written about the strange happenings on Floreana (including one by Margaret Wittmer herself), no one is really sure of the truth.

Isla Española (Hood)

Certainly one of the more dramatically beautiful of all the islands in the Galápagos, the 61-sq-km Española is also the most southerly in the archipelago. Because it's somewhat outlying (about 90km southeast of Santa Cruz), captains of some of the smaller boats may be reluctant to go this far. Española is especially worth visiting from late March to December, because it has the only colony of the waved albatross, one of the Galápagos' most spectacular seabirds. The *Opuntia* cactus and giant tortoise population, virtually extinct in the 1960s due to introduced goats and hunting, has rebounded thanks to an aggressive restoration program – tortoises rely on the cacti for food, water and protection.

A wet landing at **Punta Suárez**, on the western end of the island, leads to a rocky 2km-long trail that takes visitors through masked and blue-footed booby colonies, a beach full of marine iguanas and, maybe most uniquely, a waved albatross colony (late March to early December, when much of the world's albatross population comes here to breed). Even at a few months old, these enormous birds are spectacular to behold, their long, curved yellow beak, fluffy molting hair and aware eyes make them seem more vulnerable than they are. Equally breathtaking are the views from the wave-battered cliffs to the south; blow holes in the rocky shore below shoot water high into the air and seabirds, especially the red-billed tropicbirds, perform their aerial acrobatics and their more clumsy take offs and landings.

Other birds to look out for are the Hood mockingbird (found nowhere else), swallow-tailed gulls and oystercatchers. There are three species of finches: large cactus, small ground, and warbler – all part of the Darwin's finch family that may hop along after you hoping to get at some of your fresh water. The large cactus finch is found on few other islands.

Reached with a wet landing at the northeast end of Isla Española is **Gardner Bay**, a beautiful white-sand beach with good swimming and a large sea-lion colony. It's a little like walking through a mine field, albeit one that moves occasionally, and it's a good idea to give the large male bulls a wide berth lest they interpret your curiosity as a challenge to their dominance. Marine iguanas and Sally Lightfoot crabs can be found on the rocks at the eastern end of the beach. An island a short distance offshore provides good, but sometimes rough, snorkeling and scuba diving – there's one rock that often has white-tipped reef sharks basking under it, and hammerheads, marine turtles, rays, sea stars and red-lip bat fish are often seen.

NORTHERN ISLANDS

Isla Genovesa (Tower)

Whatever you call it, Isla Genovesa or Tower Island or even Booby Island, lovers of the sometimes goofy- and cuddly-looking booby won't want to miss this. Watch your feet, since it's quite easy to miss a fluffy little baby booby or a camouflaged iguana while scanning the horizon for sperm whales passing in the distance or the hard-to-sight Galápagos owl.

The northeastern most of the Galápagos Islands, Tower covers only 14 sq km and is the only regularly visited island that lies entirely north of the equator (the northernmost part of Isabela pokes above the line), and so is often an opportunity for a little shipboard humorous advice to 'hold tight as we pass over the bump.'

As it is an outlying island, Tower Island is infrequently included on shorter itineraries. It is the best place to see a red-footed booby colony, and it provides visitors with the opportunity to visit colonies of great frigate birds, red-billed tropicbirds, swallow-tailed gulls, Nazca boobies and many thousands of storm petrels. Other bird attractions include Galápagos doves and short-eared owls. Both sea lions and fur seals are present, and there's the chance to snorkel with groups of hammerhead sharks. The island is fairly flat and round, with a large, almost landlocked cove named Darwin Bay on the south side.

There are two visitor sites, both on Darwin Bay. **Prince Philip's Steps** (also called El Barranco) is on the eastern arm of the bay and can be reached with a dry landing. A steep and rocky path leads to the top of 25m-high cliffs, and nesting red-footed and masked boobies are sometimes found right on the narrow path.

At the top of the cliffs, the 1km-long trail leads inland, past dry-forest vegetation and various seabird colonies to a cracked expanse of lava, where thousands of storm petrels make their nests and wheel overhead. Short-eared owls are sometimes seen here.

The second visitor site, **Darwin Bay Beach**, is a coral beach reached by a wet landing. There is a 750m trail along the beach that passes through red-footed booby colonies, several tide pools and ends at a viewpoint over the cliffs. A pleasant *panga* ride along here, often followed by playful sea lions, gives a good view of birds nesting above.

Islas Marchena (Bindloe) & Pinta (Abington)

Isla Marchena, at 130 sq km, is the seventh-largest island in the archipelago and the largest to have no official visitor sites. There are some good scuba-diving sites, however, so you may get to see the island up close if on a dive trip. The 343m-high volcano in the middle of the island was very active during 1991 – ask your guide about its current degree of activity.

Isla Pinta is the original home of the tortoise Lonesome George (p353). It's also the ninth-largest of the Galápagos Islands, and is further north than any of the bigger islands. There are landing sites, but the island has no visitor sites, and researchers require a permit to visit.

Isla Wolf (Wenman) & Isla Darwin (Culpepper)

The northernmost islands are the twin islands of Isla Wolf and Isla Darwin, about 100km northwest of the rest of the archipelago and very seldom visited, except on scuba-diving trips (no snorkeling at either). Both have nearly vertical cliffs that make landing difficult, and frigates, boobies, tropicbirds and gulls nest on these islands by the thousands. Isla Darwin was first visited in 1964, when a helicopter expedition landed on the summit.

Directory

CONTENTS

ACCOMMODATIONS

Ecuador has a wide range of accommodations, from wooden shacks in the mangroves to high-end jungle lodges in the Amazon, lovely haciendas in the Andes to traveler-friendly hostels and pleasant family-run guesthouses crisscrossing the country.

Nearly every town of any size has a hotel, but unless you stick to the most touristy destinations, you'll have to tolerate the occasional saggy bed, lousy shower or noisy neighbor – all part of the equatorial experience.

Most hotel rooms have a private bathroom, and reviews throughout this book assume so unless shared bathrooms are specified. Hot water is hardest to come by along the coast and in the Oriente, where most locals might call you crazy for wanting it in the first place. In the highlands, you can assume that water is hot unless noted otherwise in our review.

It's fairly easy to rock into town and find a bed for the night. The rare exception is during major fiestas or on the night before market day.

PRACTICALITIES

- Ecuador uses 110V AC, 60Hz (the same as in North America). Plugs have two flat prongs, as in North America.
- Ecuador uses the metric system for weights and measures.
- In Ecuadorian addresses, the term 's/n' refers to *'sin numero'* (without number), meaning the address has no street number.
- Quito's two biggest newspapers are El Comercio (www.elcomercio.com) and the more liberal Hoy (www.hoy.com.ec). Guayaquil's papers are El Telégrafo (www.telegrafo.com.ec) and El Universo (www.eluniverso.com). Ecuador's best-known news magazine is Vistazo (www.vistazo.com). International newspapers, including a locally published edition of the *Miami Herald,* can be found in Quito (p77).
- Ecuador uses VHS NTSC video format (the same as North America).

B&Bs

Bed-and-breakfasts are a tried-and-true concept in Ecuador and are especially popular in tourist destinations such as Quito, Baños, Cuenca and Otavalo. Once you're out in the countryside, there's a fine line between B&Bs and *hosterías* (small hotels; see p378).

Camping

Camping is allowed on the grounds of a few rural hotels, in the countryside and most national parks. There are no campgrounds in towns. The constant availability of cheap hotels makes them superfluous. There are

BOOK YOUR STAY ONLINE

For more accommodation reviews and recommendations by Lonely Planet authors, check out the online booking service at www.lonelyplanet.com/hotels. You'll find the true, insider low-down on the best places to stay. Reviews are thorough and independent. Best of all, you can book online.

climbers' *refugios* (mountain refuges) on some of the major mountains, in some national parks, but you need to bring a sleeping bag.

Haciendas & Hosterías

The Ecuadorian highlands have some fabulous haciendas (historic family ranches that have been refurbished to accept tourists). They usually fall into the top-end price bracket, but the price may include home-cooked meals and activities such as horseback riding or fishing. The best-known haciendas are in the northern and central highlands.

Hosterías are similar but often smaller, and more intimate. *Hosterías* regularly have rates that include full board and/or activities.

Homestays

Spanish-language schools can often arrange homestays, allowing travelers to stay overnight, eat meals and interact with a local family. You may want to 'try out' your family for a week before committing for a long period. Occasionally (though not often), families are in it only for the money, giving a less than warm experience. Homestays are mostly available in Quito and Cuenca and are difficult to find elsewhere.

In some rural communities, where there are no hotels, you can ask around and often find a local family willing to let you spend the night. This happens only in the most off-the-beaten-track places, and you should always offer payment (though it may not be accepted).

Hostels

Ecuador has a limited hostel system, though some places – such as Quito – are packed with hostels. The cheapest hostels start at around $6 per person in dorms. They run the range from saggy, dark and decrepit to cheery, traveler enclaves.

Hotels

Budget hotels are the cheapest option for accommodations. Although rooms are usually basic, with just a bed and four walls, they can nevertheless be well looked after, very clean and excellent value. They can also be good places to meet other travelers. Prices in this category range from about $8 to $16 per person. The cheapest hotels have communal bathrooms, but you can often find rooms with a private bathroom for not much more.

Midrange hotels, on the whole, are Ecuador's best bargains. They usually offer a bit more charm and more amenities – cable TV, reliably hot water and a better location – than their budget cousins.

Top-end hotels are found in only the larger cities. They generally offer a bit more luxury – spacious or heritage rooms, great views, top-notch service and the like.

No matter where you stay, make sure to always peek at a room before committing.

Lodges

Ecolodges and jungle lodges provide a fantastic way to experience Ecuador. They're almost exclusively the haunt of foreigners, but often offer the chance to interact with the wildlife. Lodges are most popular in the Oriente and in the cloud forests of the western Andean slopes, and are often the only way to really experience these unique ecosystems. The lodges in the Oriente are generally only available as part of a three- to five-day package, but this usually includes meals and activities. The lodge will arrange any river or jungle transportation, but you may have to get to the nearest departure town on your own.

Prices

Throughout this book, accommodations are grouped by the following categories when a town offers numerous choices: budget (up to $20 per double), midrange ($20 to $75 per double) and top end (over $75 per double). Throughout the book, accommodation choices are listed in budget order from cheapest to most expensive double room.

Room rates are highest throughout Ecuador around Christmas and New Year's Eve, around Semana Santa (Easter week) and during July and August. They also peak during local fiestas. Hotels in resort destinations, particularly along the coast, sometimes charge higher rates (and certainly draw bigger crowds) on weekends. Hotels are required to charge 12% sales tax (called IVA), though it's often already included in the hotel's quoted rate; prices quoted in this book include this tax where possible. Better hotels often tack on an additional 10% service charge, so be sure to check whether the rate you're quoted includes this.

Accommodations are most expensive in Quito, Cuenca and Guayaquil, but there are still scores of cheap, traveler-friendly places to choose from. The main exception is the Galápagos, where there are few rock-bottom hotels.

Most hotels charge per person.

Reservations

Most hotels accept reservations without you having to cough up your credit-card number. If you haven't prepaid, however, always confirm your reservation if you're arriving late in the day, to avoid it being given to someone else. Pricier hotels may request prepayment.

BUSINESS HOURS

Reviews found throughout this book provide opening hours when they differ from the following standard hours.

Banks open at 8am and close between 2pm and 4pm Monday to Friday (though money-changing services usually stop around 2pm). Andinatel, Pacifictel and Etapa telephone call centers are almost invariably open 8am to 10pm daily. Post offices are generally open 8am to 6pm Monday through Friday and 8am to 1pm Saturday in major cities. In smaller towns they'll close for lunch.

In Quito and Guayaquil, most stores and businesses of interest to tourists stay open from 9am to 7pm Monday through Friday, usually with an hour off for lunch (around 1pm). Government offices and businesses such as Amex are open from about 9am to 5:30pm Monday to Friday, also with an hour off for lunch around 1pm. In smaller towns, especially in the hotter lowlands, lunch breaks of two hours are not uncommon. On Saturday, many stores and some businesses are open from 9am to noon. Stores in major shopping malls are open between 8am and 10pm daily.

Restaurant are generally open noon to 3pm and 6pm to 9pm. Complete hours are given in reviews in this book only when they differ from these times. Bars usually open around 5pm and close between midnight and 2am.

CHILDREN

Foreigners traveling with children are still a curiosity in Ecuador (especially if they are gringos), and a crying or laughing child at your side can quickly break down barriers between you and locals. Parents will likely be met with extra, and extra-friendly, attention. As throughout most of the world, people in Ecuador love children. Lonely Planet's *Travel with Children* is an excellent resource.

Practicalities

Children pay full fare on buses if they occupy a seat, but they often ride for free if they sit on a parent's lap. The fare for children under 12 years is halved for domestic flights (and they get a seat), while infants under two cost 10% of the fare (but they don't get a seat). In hotels, the general rule is simply to bargain. The charge for children should never be as much as that for an adult, but whether they stay for half-price or free is open to discussion.

While kids' meals are not normally offered in restaurants, it is perfectly acceptable to order a meal to split between two children or an adult and a child.

Changing facilities are rarities in all but the best restaurants. Breast-feeding is acceptable in public. Formula foods can be difficult to come by outside the large big-city supermarkets, but disposable diapers are sold at most markets throughout the country.

Safety seats are generally hard to come by in rental cars (be sure to arrange one ahead of time), and in taxis they're unheard of. This is, after all, a country where a family of four can blaze across town on a motorcycle.

Sights & Activities

Ecuador is not a country that's big on fun parks, children's rides and organized spectacles for kids. That said, there's plenty of real-world excitement here, whether it's tramping through rainforest, canoeing down a river or playing in the waves.

Whale-watching is a must while in Puerto López (p307). Older children are likely to enjoy the snorkeling and animal-watching in the Galápagos (p342). Quito (p95) has a healthy number of activities that the young ones will enjoy, including a reptile zoo, a theme park and several good museums.

CLIMATE CHARTS

The following climate charts are handy for planning, but for specifics on the best time to visit Ecuador, see p14.

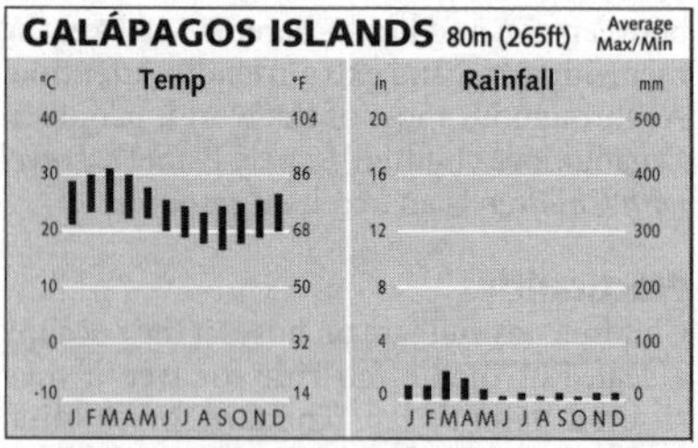

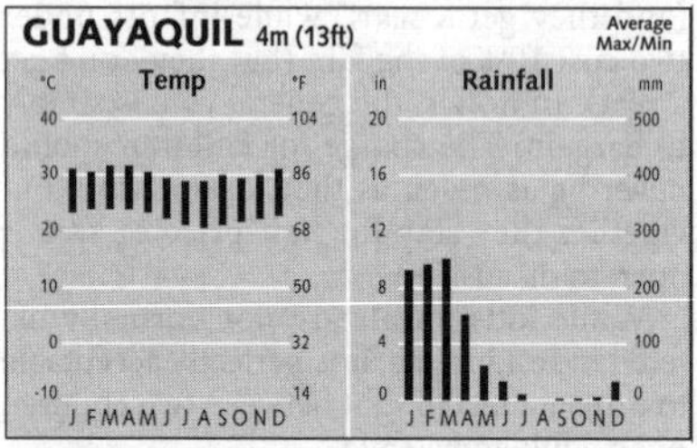

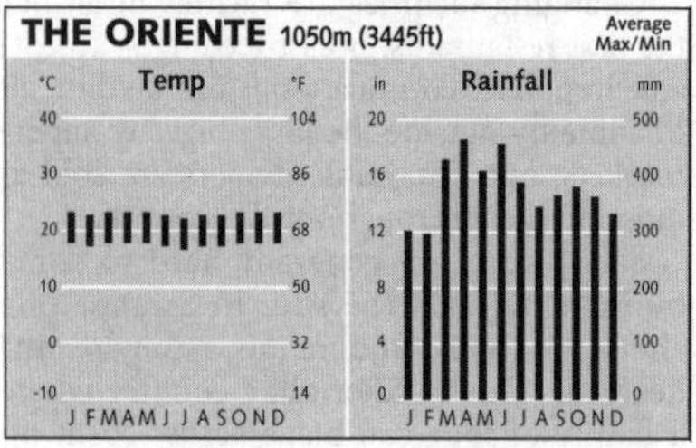

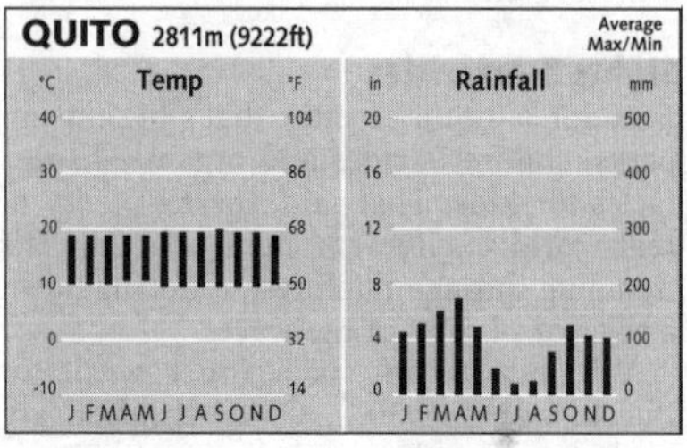

COURSES

Ecuador is one of the best places to study Spanish in South America. Ecuadorian Spanish is clear and precise, and similar to Mexican and Central American Spanish, and rates are cheap. Quito (p95) and Cuenca (p205) are the best places to study, and both have a plethora of language schools. Expect to pay between $6 and $10 per hour for private lessons. Accommodations with local families can be arranged. There are also schools in Baños (p176) and Otavalo (p125) if you want a more small-town experience.

Dance schools in Quito (see p94) offer private lessons in salsa and other Latin dances at prices unheard of in North America and Europe.

CUSTOMS

Each traveler is able to import 1L of spirits, 300 cigarettes and an unspecified 'reasonable' amount of perfume – all items are duty-free. There is no problem bringing in the usual personal belongings, but if you plan on bringing in something that might not be considered a 'usual personal belonging,' you should check with an Ecuadorian consulate.

Pre-Columbian artifacts and endangered-animal products (including mounted butterflies and beetles) are not allowed to be taken out of Ecuador or imported into most other countries.

DANGERS & ANNOYANCES

The purpose of this section is not to scare you. Just remember: *most crimes and accidents can be avoided by using common sense.* Ecuador is a safe and wonderful country for travel. No matter where you travel, it's wise to get some travel insurance; see p383 for more information.

Drowning & Shipwreck

Nasty stuff. Much of the coast suffers from riptides, especially during the highest tides and biggest waves. Some beaches use flags – red indicates dangerous conditions, while yellow indicates that it's OK to swim. Many beaches don't have flags, however, so be aware of riptides.

Most boats in the Galápagos are shipshape, but captains don't always make the best decisions. In 2005 a tourist cruiser was hit by a freak wave in bad weather and immediately sunk, sending the boat and everyone's belongings to the bottom. Out of sheer luck, no one was injured, but few were fully compensated for what they lost. Consider planning your Galápagos visit outside the foul-weather season (see the boxed text, p349).

Drugs

Imbibing illegal drugs such as marijuana and cocaine can either land you in jail, land your money in the hands of a thief, or worse. Unless you are willing to take these risks, avoid illegal drugs.

Lonely Planet has received a couple of letters from travelers who were unwittingly drugged and robbed after accepting food from a stranger.

Robbery

Every year or so, you hear of long-distance, nighttime bus robberies. Night buses are simply held up at a road block and robbed by a group of armed men. It happens to one bus in many thousands, so don't get too paranoid if your schedule demands a night bus. However day buses are best. One particular area known to have night bus robberies is the province of Guayas, in the area surrounding Guayaquil.

If you are driving a car in Ecuador, never park it unattended. Never leave valuables in sight in the car – even attended cars will have their windows smashed by hit-and-run merchants.

Make sure to never leave your gear unattended in a mountain hut while you are out hiking. Some huts, such as those on Cotopaxi or Chimborazo, have guardians and a place to lock up your gear when you climb, and these are relatively safe.

Rucu Pichincha (p93), near Quito, and Lagunas de Mojanda (p129), near Otavalo, were once plagued by armed robbers, but both places have become safer over the last few years. South American Explorers in Quito (p388) is the best place for up-to-date information on issues such as this is.

On the off chance you are robbed, you should file a police report as soon as possible. This is a requirement for any insurance claim, although it is unlikely that the police will be able to recover the property. Normally only the main police station in a town will deal with this.

Scams

Be wary of false or crooked police. Plainclothes 'policemen' may produce official-looking documents, but always treat these with suspicion, or simply walk away with a smile and a shrug. On the other hand, a uniformed official who asks to see your passport in broad daylight in the middle of a busy street is probably just doing their job.

Theft

If travelers had to confess their top five stresses, one would surely be Backpack Separation Anxiety (BSA). It's most commonly experienced when travelers are required to place their backpacks in a bus's luggage compartment or overhead rack. Aside from craning your neck at every stop until it snaps, there's little you can do to prevent it being stolen. But rest assured – for the most part, the bag-checker is on your side and knows whose bags are whose. Definitely keep your eye on it (or carry a pack small enough to bring on the bus), but don't worry yourself silly. Bag theft occurs, but not very often. Some people buy a grain sack in the market and pack their bag in it so it will blend in with the cargo.

Armed robbery is rare in Ecuador, although parts of Quito and some coastal areas are dangerous. Specific information is given in the appropriate regional chapters of this book.

Sneak theft is more common, and you should always watch your back (and back pockets) in busy bus stations, on crowded city buses and in bustling markets. All of these places are worked by bag-slashers and pickpockets. But you can avoid playing victim to them by being smart.

Carrying your wallet or passport in a back pocket is advertising. But also avoid lifting your shirt and whipping out your money pouch in public. Instead carry a wallet with a small amount of spending money in your front pocket and keep the important stuff hidden in your money pouch beneath your clothes.

Leaving money in the hotel safe deposit boxes is usually reliable, but make sure that it is in a sealed, taped envelope. A few readers have reported a loss of money from deposit boxes in the cheaper hotels. Theft from hotel rooms happens only on those rare occasions when Bad Worker and Careless Tourist (who leaves valuables in the open) cross paths.

Trouble Spots

Due to the armed conflict in neighboring Colombia, areas along the Colombian border (particularly in the northern Oriente) can be dangerous. Tours into the Oriente are almost invariably safe, but there have been a few isolated incidents of armed robbery in which no one was hurt. Lago Agrio (p236) is dodgy once you leave the main drag.

DISCOUNT CARDS

Generally, student cards are less useful in Ecuador than in European countries. Aside from reduced museum entrance fees (which can add up), the only substantial discount is 15% off high-season flights to the Galápagos. The **International Student Identity Card** (ISIC; www.isic.org) is generally accepted only when issued from the traveler's home country and presented in combination with a valid student ID card.

EMBASSIES & CONSULATES

It's important to realize what your own embassy can and can't do to help you if you get into trouble. Generally speaking, it won't be much help in emergencies if the trouble you're in is remotely your own fault. Remember that you are bound by the laws of the country you are in.

In genuine emergencies, you might get some assistance from your embassy, but only if other channels have been exhausted. If you need to get home urgently, a free ticket home is exceedingly unlikely – the embassy would expect you to have insurance. If all your money and documents are stolen, it might assist you with getting a new passport, but a loan for onward travel would be out of the question.

Embassies & Consulates in Ecuador

Many countries have embassies in Quito, and consulates in Quito or Guayaquil and in other provincial capitals or border towns. Hours are short and change regularly, so it's a good idea to call ahead. New Zealand does not have an embassy or consulate in Ecuador.

Australia (☎ 04-601-7529; ausconsulate@unidas.com.ec; Rocafuerte 510, 2nd fl, Guayaquil)

Canada Guayaquil (☎ 04-229-6895; cnr Avs Joaquin Orranita & Juan Tanca Marengo); Quito (☎ 02-245-5499; www.canadainternational.gc.ca/ecuador-equateur; cnr Av Amazonas 4153 & Unión de Periodistas)

Colombia Guayaquil (☎ 04-263-0674/5; www.consuladodecolombiagye.com; Francisco de Orellana, World Trade Center, Tower B, 11th fl); Lago Agrio (Map p237; ☎ 06-283-0084; Av Quito 1-52); Quito (☎ 02-222-2486; Av Colón 1133 & Amazonas, 7th fl); Tulcán (Map p143; ☎ 06-298-0559; Av Manabi 58-087)

France Guayaquil (☎ 04-232-8442; cnr José Mascote 909 & Hurtado); Quito (☎ 02-252-6361; cnr Leonidas Plaza 107 & Av Patria)

Germany Guayaquil (☎ 04-220-6867/8; cnr Avs Las Monjas &CJ Arosemena, Km 2.5, Edificio Berlin); Quito (Map p82; ☎ 02-297-0821; Naciones Unidas E10-44 at República de El Salvador, Edificio Citiplaza, 12th fl)

Ireland (☎ 2-245-1577; cnr Antonio de Ulloa 2651 & Rumipamba, Quito)

Netherlands (Map pp88-9; ☎ 02-222-9229; www.embajadadeholanda.com; cnr Av 12 de Octubre 1942 & Cordero, World Trade Center, Tower 1, 1st fl, Quito)

Peru Guayaquil (☎ 04-228-114; conperu@gye.satnet.net; Av Francisco de Orellana 501); Loja (Map p216; ☎ 07-257-9068; Sucre 10-56); Machala (☎ 07-930-680; cnr Bolívar & Colón); Quito (☎ 02-246-8410; embpeecu@uio.satnet.net; cnr Republica de El Salvador 495 & Irlanda)

UK Guayaquil (☎ 04-256-0400; cnr Córdova 623 & Padre Solano); Quito (Map p82; ☎ 02-297-0800; http://ukinecuador.fco.gov.uk/en; cnr Naciones Unidas & República de El Salvador, Edificio Citiplaza, 14th fl)

USA Guayaquil (☎ 04-232-3570; http://guayaquil.usconsulate.gov; cnr 9 de Octubre & García Moreno); Quito (☎ 02-398-5000; http://ecuador.usembassy.gov; cnr Av Avigiras E12-170 & Eloy Alfaro)

FOOD

For a mouthwatering idea of all the food you can eat while traveling in Ecuador, see p45. In the Eating sections throughout this book, restaurants are listed by price from least to most expensive. Our categories are subdivided based on the average price of a main course: budget (under $6), midrange ($6 to $12), top end (above $12).

GAY & LESBIAN TRAVELERS

Same-sex couples traveling in Ecuador should be wary of showing affection when in public. All same-sex civil unions were recently enshrined in the new 2008 constitution, and for most Ecuadorians gay rights remains a nonissue in a political context. But homosexuality was technically illegal until 1998, and antigay bias still exists. As in most Latin American countries, sexuality is more stereotyped than it is in Europe or North America, with the man playing a dominant macho role and the woman tagging along with that. This attitude spills over into the perception of homosexuality. A straight-acting macho man will seldom be considered gay, even if he is, while an effeminate man, regardless of his sexual orientation, may be called a *maricón*, a mildly derogatory term for a homosexual man.

Several fiestas in Ecuador have parades with men cross-dressing as women. This is all meant in fun, rather than as an open acceptance of sexual alternatives, but it does provide the public at large (both gay and straight) a popular cultural situation in which to enjoy themselves in an accepting environment. On New Year's Eve, puppets representing the old year are burned at midnight. Meanwhile, men dressed as women (posing as the puppets' widows) walk the streets, asking passersby for spare change that will later be used for the year-end party. More entertaining still, Latacunga's incredible Mamá Negra (see the boxed text, p158) festival, in late September, features cross-dressing men brandishing whips!

The best website about gay Quito is the incredibly detailed **Gay Guide to Quito** (http://gayquitoec.tripod.com). Also check out **Gay Ecuador** (www.gayecuador.com). There is a community center for lesbian, gay, bisexual and transsexual people, as well as an AIDS-activist organization called **FEDAEPS** (☎ 02-222-3298; www.fedaeps.org; cnr Baquerizo Moreno 166 & Tamayo, Quito). It's open to the public on Thursday at 3pm; gay and lesbian literature is available, and there are often discussions held at 6:30pm.

Zenith Travel (☎ 02-252-9993; www.galapagosgay.com; cnr Juan Leon Mera 453 & Roca, Edificio Chiriboga No 202, Quito) specializes in gay and lesbian tours.

HOLIDAYS

On major holidays, banks, offices and other services close. Transportation gets crowded, so buy bus tickets in advance. Major holidays are sometimes celebrated for several days around the actual date. If an official public holiday falls on a weekend, offices may be closed on the nearest Friday or Monday. If an official holiday falls midweek, it may be moved to the nearest Friday or Monday to create a long weekend.

New Year's Day January 1.
Epiphany January 6.
Semana Santa (Easter Week) March/April.
Labor Day May 1.
Battle of Pichincha May 24. This honors the decisive battle of independence from Spain in 1822.
Simón Bolívar's Birthday July 24.
Quito Independence Day August 10.
Guayaquil Independence Day October 9. This combines with the October 12 national holiday and is an important festival in Guayaquil.
Columbus Day/Día de la Raza October 12.
All Saints' Day November 1.
Day of the Dead (All Souls' Day) November 2. Celebrated by flower-laying ceremonies in cemeteries, it's especially colorful in rural areas, where entire Indian families show up at cemeteries to eat, drink and leave offerings in memory of the departed.
Cuenca Independence Day November 3. Combines with the national holidays of November 1 and 2 to give Cuenca its most important fiesta of the year.
Christmas Eve December 24.
Christmas Day December 25.

See p18 for details of festivals and events around the country.

INSURANCE

In addition to health insurance (see p403) and car insurance (see p399), a policy that protects baggage and valuables, such as cameras and camcorders, is a good idea. Keep your insurance records separate from other possessions in case you have to make a claim.

Worldwide travel insurance is available at www.lonelyplanet.com/travel_services. You can buy, extend and claim online anytime – even if you're already on the road.

INTERNET ACCESS

Internet cafés are widespread in Ecuador, with USB ports and reasonably fast connections that cost around $1 an hour. Many hotels have a computer or two for guest use, with prices varying wildly. Accommodations options in this book that have a computer for internet access are labeled with the 💻 symbol.

Wi-fi is not commonly available, though a few top-end hotels do offer wireless (sometimes available only in the lobby) or in-room cable modem connections. For internet resources, see p16.

LEGAL MATTERS

Drug penalties in Ecuador for possession of even small amounts of illegal drugs are much stricter than those in the USA or Europe. Defendants often spend many months in jail before they are brought to trial, and if convicted (as is usually the case), they can expect several years in jail.

Businesspeople should be aware that a legal dispute that may be of a civil nature in their home country may be handled as a criminal proceeding in Ecuador. This may mean that you are not allowed to leave Ecuador while your dispute is being settled, and that it could possibly lead to your arrest and jailing until the case is settled.

Drivers should carry their passport, as well as their driver's license. In the event of an accident, unless it's extremely minor, the vehicles should stay where they are until the police arrive and make a report. This is essential for all insurance claims. If the accident results in injury and you are unhurt, you should take the victim to obtain medical help, particularly in the case of a pedestrian accident. You are legally responsible for a pedestrian's injuries and will be jailed unless you pay, even if the accident was not your fault. Drive defensively.

MAPS

Anyone planning serious hikes or backcountry walking should visit the Instituto Geográfico Militar (IGM) in Quito (see p76). It publishes excellent topographical maps of the entire country, ranging from a 1:1,000,000 single-sheet map of Ecuador to 1:50,000 regional sheets. Best part – they cost only $2 each. Few city maps are published anywhere and (not to toot anyone's horn) you'll often find the ones in this book the most useful.

The blue-cover Nelson Gómez *Guía Vial del Ecuador* is a pocketbook size, countrywide road map available at most bookstores in Quito, Cuenca and Guayaquil. Another good country map available internationally is the 1:1,000,000 single sheet published by **International Travel Maps & Books** (ITMB; www.itm b.com).

MONEY

Ecuador's official currency is the US dollar. If you're not traveling from the USA, consider bringing a small supply of US dollars with you on your trip in case you have trouble exchanging currency from your home country. Western Union offices are in most big cities.

For exchange rates, see this book's inside front cover. For an idea of what things cost, see p14.

ATMs

ATMs are the easiest way of getting cash. They're found in most cities and even in smaller towns, though they are occasionally out of order. Make sure you have a four-digit Personal Identification Number (PIN); many Ecuadorian ATMs don't recognize longer ones. Bancos del Pacífico and Bancos del Pichincha have MasterCard/Cirrus ATMs. Bancos de Guayaquil and Bancos La Provisora have Visa/Plus ATMs.

Cash

US dollars are the official currency; they are identical to those issued in the USA. Coins of one, five, 10, 25 and 50 cents are identical in shape, size and color as their US equivalents, but bear images of famous Ecuadorians. Both US and Ecuadorian coins are used in Ecuador. The $1 'Sacajawea' coin is widely used.

The biggest problem when it comes to cash is finding change. It can be hard to cash a $20 bill even in big cities. No one ever has *sueltos* (literally 'loose ones,' meaning 'change'), so change your bills when you can. Forget about changing a $50 or $100 bill outside a bank.

Credit Cards

Credit cards are great as backup. Visa, MasterCard and Diners Club are the most widely accepted cards. First-class restaurants, hotels, souvenir shops and travel agencies usually accept MasterCard or Visa. Small hotels, restaurants and stores don't. Even if an establishment has a credit-card sticker in the window, don't assume that credit cards are accepted. In Ecuador, merchants accepting credit cards will often add between 4% and 10% to the bill. Paying cash is often better value.

Moneychangers

It is best to change money in the major cities of Quito, Guayaquil and Cuenca, where rates are best. Because banks have limited hours (see p379), *casas de cambio* (currency-exchange bureaus) are sometimes the only option for changing money. They are usually open 9am to 6pm Monday to Friday and until at least noon on Saturday. They're credible places, though the exchange rate might be a percentage point or so lower than that given by banks.

Euros, Peruvian pesos and Colombian *nuevos soles* are the easiest currencies to exchange in Ecuador.

Tipping

Better restaurants add a 12% tax and a 10% service charge to the bill. If the service has been satisfactory, add another 5% for the waiter. Cheaper places don't include a tax or service charge. To tip your server, do so directly – don't just leave the money on the table.

Tip porters at the airport about $0.25 per bag and bellboys at a first-class hotel about $1 per bag. Taxi drivers are not normally tipped, but you can leave them the small change from a metered ride.

Guides are usually paid low wages, and tips are greatly appreciated. If you go on a guided tour, a tip is expected. If you are in a group, tip a top-notch guide about $5 per person per day. Tip the driver about half that. If you hire a private guide, tip about $10 per day.

If you are going on a long tour that involves guides, cooks and crew (eg the Galápagos Islands), tip about $25 to $50 per client per week, and distribute among all the personnel.

Traveler's Checks

Relying on traveler's checks in Ecuador is a big mistake. Very few banks will cash them, and even top-end resorts are increasingly refusing to accept them. It's much more useful to have a supply of US cash and an ATM card (plus a back-up ATM card just in case).

PHOTOGRAPHY

Bring everything you think you'll need, as camera gear is expensive in Ecuador. Standard films are available in most towns, but Quito, Cuenca and Guayaquil are the only places you'll find speeds other than ASA 200 or 400.

The bright equatorial sun washes out photos and exaggerates shadows. Try to shoot using a polarizing lens, and shoot in the morning and afternoon. For digital photographers, most internet cafés have at least one computer with USB ports and a CD burner. Your best bet (if you can afford it) is to buy a portable hard drive.

Lonely Planet's *Travel Photography* book is packed with useful tips.

Photographing People

The Ecuadorian people make wonderful subjects for photos. From an indigenous child to the handsomely uniformed presidential guard, the possibilities of 'people pictures' are endless. However, most people resent having a camera thrust in their faces, and people in markets will often proudly turn their backs on pushy photographers. Ask for permission with a smile or a joke, and if this is refused, don't become offended. Some people believe that bad luck can be brought upon them by the eye of the camera. Others are just fed up with seeing their pictures used in books, magazines and postcards; somebody is making money at their expense. Sometimes a 'tip' is asked. Be aware and sensitive of people's feelings.

POST

Ecuador's postal service is reliable. Allow one to two weeks for a letter or package to reach its destination. A postcard or letter up to 20g costs $1.25 to North America, $2 to Europe and $2.25 to the rest of the world.

Courier services including FedEx, DHL and UPS are readily available in sizable towns, but the service is costly.

You can receive mail in Ecuador using the post office's *lista de correos* (general delivery). Mail sent to the post office is filed alphabetically. Instruct your correspondents to address letters clearly (capitalizing your last name) and in the following manner:

Johanna SMITH (surname capitalized)
Lista de Correos
Correo Central
Quito (or town and province of your choice)
Ecuador

Receiving small packages is usually no problem. If the package weighs more than 2kg, however, you will have to go to customs to retrieve it and perhaps pay duty tax.

SHOPPING

Leave plenty of extra space (or plan to bring back an extra bag), as the shopping in Ecuador is outstanding. Handicrafts, warm wooly sweaters and weavings are just a few of the attractive and wild (see the boxed text, p386) items for sale. Going to village markets is a great way to buy directly from local artisans, but if you can't make it out of town, Quito and other main cities offer a fair assortment at prices not much higher. If you only have time for just one big shopping expedition, the Saturday market at Otavalo (p122) is the one to hit (hint: it's one of the largest markets in South America). Many other markets are colorful events for locals rather than tourists.

Bags

As well as bags made from two small weavings stitched together, you can buy *shigras* – shoulder bags made from agave fiber – that are strong, colorful and eminently practical. They come in a variety of sizes and are expandable. The best places to look for them are the markets in Latacunga and Riobamba. Agave fiber is also used to make macramé bags.

BIZARRE BUYS

Sure, you can dazzle friends and family back home with the classic Ecuadorian wool sweater (like they've never seen *that* before), or a panama hat (you'll never wear it) or a goofy set of coasters (getting better). But why not bring home something a wee bit…different. Here are a few ideas for the alternative shopping spree.

- Banana press – This wooden handpress used to make *patacones* (flattened fried plantain slices) is available at most supermarkets.
- Virgin Mary gearshift handle – A bright-green plastic shifter knob, complete with a floating Virgin Mary inside. Who's gonna call you a bad driver with the Madonna at your side? Check small auto parts stores and highland markets.
- San Pedro cactus-seed crucifix – Definitely one you won't find at home: a crucifix made with the pearly seeds of the San Pedro cactus (sorry, only the cactus itself is psychoactive). Often sold in stores outside churches; try the ones in front of Basílica del Voto Nacional (p81).
- Salacious ceramics – Keep your eyes peeled for the replicas of pre-Hispanic ceramic figurines engaged in various versions of 'mating rituals.'
- Espíritu del Ecuador – It might look like a tacky miniature of the equator monument, but it's full of Ecuador's sweet liqueur. Delicious over ice cream. Available in liquor stores.
- Shrunken head – OK, so it's not a real shrunken head, but it stinks like one. Made from sheep-skin, these are morbid enough to frighten small children. Find them at crafts stores in Quito.
- Pilsener T-shirt – You can't go home without supporting Ecuador's national beer. Available at Kallari café (p107) in Quito.
- Fire water – A bottle of Zhumir or Cristal will put the zing in your friends back home (and make them believe your stories). Available at liquor stores.
- Polaroid picture – Even in the digital age, nothing replaces the Polaroid picture, snapped for $2 a pop by the old photographers on Plaza Grande, Quito (p80).

Bargaining

In markets and smaller stores, bargaining is acceptable, indeed expected, and you can sometimes lower the original price by 20% to 40%. Other times (and tourists find this happens in Otavalo) a vender won't budge an inch. In 'tourist stores' in Quito, prices are usually fixed.

Clothing

Woolen goods, particularly sweaters, are popular and are often made of a pleasantly coarse homespun wool. Otavalo is great for sweaters, scarves, hats, gloves and vests. In the central highlands, Salinas (p184) is a great place to pick up a wool sweater. In both Otavalo and Salinas, the price of a thick sweater will begin around $15, depending on size and quality; fashionable boutique sweaters, like those sold at Galería Latina in Quito (p110) can fetch $50. Wool is also spun into a much finer and tighter textile for making ponchos: indigenous ponchos from Otavalo and the Riobamba area are among the best.

Hand-embroidered clothes are also attractive, but it's worth getting them from a reputable shop; otherwise they may shrink or run. Cotton blouses, shirts, skirts, dresses and shawls are available.

Panama hats are another unique Ecuadorian product – and cost a fraction of the price you'd pay back home. The finest hats are found in Quito, Cuenca, Sígsig (near Cuenca; see p213) and Montecristi (on the Pacific coast; see p300). Also see the boxed text, p201.

Jewelry

Ecuador isn't famous for gemstones, but it has some good silverwork. Chordeleg (p212), near Cuenca, has beautifully filigreed items. The Amazon area produces necklaces made from nuts, seeds and other rainforest products.

Leather

Cotacachi (p131), located north of Otavalo, and Quisapincha (p171), situated near Ambato, are both famous centers for leatherwork. Items range from jackets and luggage to wide-brimmed hats to coin purses. Prices are extremely cheap (especially in Quisapincha, where you can pick up a jacket for about $35), but quality varies, so examine items carefully.

Other Items

Baskets made of straw, reeds or agave fibers are common everywhere. Onyx (a pale, translucent quartz with parallel layers of different colors) is carved into chess sets and other objects. Miniature blowpipes modeled after those used by indigenous groups from the Amazon are also popular, and you'll find plenty of other choices as well.

Tree Products

Ecuador's most important woodworking center is San Antonio de Ibarra (p135), where you'll find everything from utilitarian bowls, salad utensils, chess sets and candlesticks to ornately decorative crucifixes, statues and wall plaques. Again, the prices are low, but quality varies. Colorful balsa-wood birds carved into all sizes are extremely popular. They're made in the Oriente and sold throughout Quito. Carvings from the tagua nut (which resembles ivory) are common souvenirs.

Weavings

Woolen weavings are beautiful and range from square-foot pieces that can be sewn together to make throw cushions or shoulder bags, to weavings large enough to be used as floor rugs or wall hangings. Otavalo has a huge selection of mediocre-quality but very colorful weavings. The village of Salasaca (p171) is famous for its weavings. You'll see plenty of the same patterns at stores throughout Ecuador, but for something really distinctive, drop by the Folklore Olga Fisch (p110) in Quito. It's pricey, but worth it.

SOLO TRAVELERS

Traveling alone can be one of the most rewarding experiences in life. You're far more likely to meet locals and fellow travelers – which is really what travel's all about, isn't it? – without the crutch of companionship. Mind you, it can get lonely at times, and it's certainly nice to have a mate to watch your bags or go to the bar with you, but the benefits of solo travel can outweigh companionship in numerous ways.

If you do get lonely, Ecuador has an abundance of traveler-oriented hotels that make hooking up with other travelers easy. On the financial side, midrange and budget hotels often charge per person, which means you won't spend much more than you would while traveling with others.

Women traveling anywhere are inherently at greater risk than are men traveling alone. But countless women travel alone safely in Ecuador every day. For more information for women travelers, see p390.

TELEPHONE

For important nationwide numbers see the inside front cover of this book. Telephone service is readily available throughout Ecuador and is operated, depending on where you are, by one of three regional companies: Andinatel (mainly in the highlands and Oriente), Pacifictel (mainly in the coastal lowlands) and Etapa (in Cuenca). These companies operate *centros de llamadas* (telephone call centers) in many towns.

Public street phones are also common. Some use phonecards, which are sold in convenient places such as newsagents. Others accept only coins. All but the most basic hotels will allow you to make local city calls.

International calls from an Andinatel, Pacifictel or Etapa office are as cheap as $0.35 per minute to the USA and $0.45 to the UK and Australia. Rates are 20% cheaper on Sunday and after 7pm on all other days. Internet cafés provide even cheaper 'net-to-phone' services.

Hotels that provide international phone connections very often surcharge extremely heavily. Collect (reverse-charge) calls are possible to a few countries that have reciprocal agreements with Ecuador; these agreements vary from year to year, so ask at the nearest telephone office.

All telephone numbers in Ecuador have seven digits, and the first digit – except for cellular phone numbers – is always a '2.' If someone gives you a six-digit number (which happens often), simply put a '2' in front of it.

Cell Phones

Cellular telephone numbers in Ecuador are always preceded by ☎ 09. As far as bringing your own phone, only GSM cell phones operating at 850MHz (GSM 850) function in Ecuador. A triband GSM cellular will not currently work in Ecuador. This is a rapidly changing field and you can stay up to date by checking www.kropla.com and www.gsmworld.com.

Phone Codes

Two-digit area codes beginning with '0' are used throughout Ecuador; these are provided beneath each destination heading in this book. Area codes are not dialed if calling from within that area code, unless dialing from a cellular phone.

Ecuador's country code is ☎ 593. To call a number in Ecuador from abroad, call your international access code, Ecuador's country code, the area code *without* the 0, and the seven-digit local telephone number.

Phonecards

International calling cards from your country don't work well in Ecuador, because the local telephone companies don't make any money from them and are reluctant to use them. Buy local cards instead; some have instructions in English.

TIME

The Ecuadorian mainland is five hours behind Greenwich Mean Time, and the Galápagos are six hours behind. Mainland time here is equivalent to Eastern Standard Time in North America. When it's noon in Quito, it's noon in New York, 5pm in London and 4am (daylight-saving time) in Melbourne. Because of Ecuador's location on the equator, days and nights are of equal length year-round, and there is no daylight-saving time.

TOILETS

As throughout South America, Ecuadorian plumbing has very low pressure, and putting toilet paper into the bowl is a serious no-no anywhere except in the fanciest hotels. Always put your used toilet paper in the basket (it's better than a clogged and overflowing toilet!). A well-run cheap hotel will ensure that the receptacle is emptied and the toilet cleaned daily.

Public toilets are limited mainly to bus terminals, airports and restaurants. Lavatories are called *servicios higiénicos* and are usually marked 'SS.HH.' You can simply ask to use the *baño* (bathroom) in a restaurant. Toilet paper is rarely available, so the experienced traveler always carries a personal supply. Remember 'M' on the door means *mujeres* (women) not 'men.' Men's toilets are signed with an 'H' for *hombres* (men) or a 'C' for *caballeros* (gentlemen).

TOURIST INFORMATION

Ecuador's system of government-run tourist offices is hit or miss, but is getting better. Tourist information in Quito and Cuenca is excellent.

The government-run **Ministerio de Turismo** (www.vivecuador.com) is responsible for tourist information at the national level. Many towns have some form of municipal or provincial tourist office. The quality of information you'll get depends entirely on the enthusiasm of the person behind the desk. Most of the time, the staff is good at answering the majority of questions.

An excellent resource, especially once you've arrived in Ecuador, is **South American Explorers** (SAE; Map pp88-9; ☎ 02-222-5228; www.saexplorers.org; cnr Jorge Washington 311 & Leonidas Plaza Gutiérrez, Quito; 🕑 9:30am-5pm Mon-Wed & Fri, to 6pm Thu, to noon Sat), a member-supported nonprofit organization with clubhouses in Quito; Lima and Cuzco in Peru; Buenos Aires; and a head office in Ithaca, New York. The clubhouses function as information centers for travelers, adventurers, researchers etc, and provide a wealth of advice about traveling in Latin America.

Annual SAE membership is $60/50 per individual/student. Membership includes the use of all clubhouses, plus quarterly issues of the informative *South American Explorer* magazine (members from countries outside the USA must add $10 for postage). The Quito clubhouse has the following services: a lending library; maps; an outstanding compilation of trip reports left by other travelers; storage of luggage; storage of mail addressed to you at the club; relaxing reading and TV rooms; current advice about travel conditions; volunteer information; a book exchange; a notice board; extra activities, such as Thursday-night talks and comedy nights; and many other services.

Services for nonmembers are limited to the purchase of useful information sheets. Paid-up members can stay all day.

TRAVELERS WITH DISABILITIES

Unfortunately, Ecuador's infrastructure for disabled travelers is virtually nonexistent. Wheelchair ramps are few and far between, and sidewalks are often badly potholed and cracked. Bathrooms and toilets are often too small for wheelchairs. Signs in Braille or telephones for the hearing impaired are practically unheard of.

Nevertheless, Ecuadorians with disabilities get around, mainly through the help of others. It's not particularly unusual to see travelers with disabilities being carried onto a bus, for example. Buses are (legally) supposed to carry travelers with disabilities for free. Local city buses, which are already overcrowded, won't do that, but long-distance city buses sometimes do. Travelers with disabilities are also eligible for 50% discounts on domestic airfares.

When it comes to hotels, the only truly accessible rooms are found at the international chain hotels in Quito and Guayaquil.

VISAS

Most travelers entering Ecuador as tourists, including citizens of Australia, New Zealand, Japan, the EU, Canada and the USA, do not require visas. Upon entry, they will be issued a T-3 embarkation card valid for 90 days. Sixty-day stamps are rarely given, but double-check if you're going to be in the country for a while. Residents of most Central American and some Asian countries require visas.

All travelers entering as diplomats, students, laborers, religious workers, businesspeople, volunteers and cultural-exchange visitors require nonimmigrant visas. Various immigrant visas are also available.

Obtaining a visa is time-consuming, so commence the process as far ahead of your visit as possible. Visas enable holders to apply for a *censo* (temporary-residence card) and pay resident prices in national parks, as well as on trains and planes. Visas must be obtained from an Ecuadorian embassy and cannot be arranged within Ecuador. See p382 for a partial list of Ecuadorian embassies.

All (nontourist) visa holders must register at the **Dirección General de Extranjería** (☎ 02-223-1022/3; cnr 10 de Agosto & General Murgeón, Edificio Autorepuestos, 4th fl; 🕑 8am-1pm Mon-Fri) in Quito within 30 days of arrival in Ecuador. If visa holders wish to leave the country and return, they need a *salida* (exit) form from the Jefatura Provincial de Migración (see right), which can be used for multiple exits and re-entries. Visa holders who apply for residency need to get an exit permit from the immigration authorities in Quito before they leave the country.

Stay Extensions

Embarkation card extensions can be obtained from the **Jefatura Provincial de Migración** (Map p82; ☎ 02-224-7510; Isla Seymour 1152 near Río Coca, Quito). On top of the original 90 days, you can obtain a 90-day extension (for a grand total of 180 days). To get an extension, go to the Jefatura Provincial de Migración before your initial 90 days expire. If you overstay your visa, even by a day, you will be fined $200.

VOLUNTEERING

Numerous organizations look for the services of volunteers, however the vast majority require at least a minimal grasp of Spanish, a minimum commitment of several weeks or months, as well as fees (anywhere from $10 per day to $300 per month) to cover the costs of room and board. Volunteers can work in conservation programs, help street kids, teach, build nature trails, construct websites, do medical or agricultural work – the possibilities are endless. Many jungle lodges also accept volunteers for long-term stays. To keep your volunteer costs down, your best bet is to look when you get to Ecuador. Plenty of places need volunteers who only have their hard work to offer.

South American Explorers (see opposite) in Quito has a volunteer section where current offerings are posted. The clubhouse itself often needs volunteers. The classifieds section on **Ecuador Explorer** (www.ecuadorexplorer.com) has a long list of organizations seeking volunteers.

Organizations in Ecuador that often need volunteers:

AmaZOOnico (☎ 09-414-3395; www.amazoonico.org) Accepts volunteers for the animal rehabilitation sector.

Andean Bear Conservation Project (www.andeanbear.org; volunteers per month $600) An organization that trains volunteers as bear trackers.

Bosque Nublado Santa Lucia (www.santa-lucia.org, www.santaluciaecuador.com) Community-based ecotourism project in the cloud forests of northwest Ecuador. It regularly contracts volunteers to work in reforestation, trail maintenance, construction, teaching English and more.

FEVI (Fund for Intercultural Education & Community Volunteer Service; www.fevi.org) This Ecuadorian nonprofit organization places volunteers in communities throughout Ecuador. FEVI works with children, the elderly, women's groups and indigenous communities, so it's good for those seeking a cultural-exchange experience.

Fundación Natura (www.fnatura.org) Important Ecuadorian nongovernment organization (NGO) that regularly hires Spanish-speaking volunteers to work in research, reforestation and more.

Jatun Sacha Foundation (www.jatunsacha.org) Offers volunteer positions in plant conservation, reserve maintenance, environmental education, community service, agroforestry and other fields at one of 10 biological stations.
Junto con los Niños (www.juconi.org.ec) Excellent organization that works with street kids in the slum areas of Guayaquil. One-month minimum preferred.
Merazonia (☎ 03-279-0030; www.merazonia.org) Based in the central highlands – a refuge for injured animals, which welcomes volunteers. See p180 for more information.
New Era Galápagos Foundation (www.neweragalapagos.org) Unique nonprofit offering volunteerships focused on community empowerment and sustainable tourism in the Galápagos. Volunteers live and work on Isla San Cristóbal.
Rainforest Concern (www.rainforestconcern.org) British nonprofit organization offering paid but very affordable volunteer positions in forest environments in Ecuador.
Reserva Biológica Los Cedros (www.reservaloscedros.org) This biological reserve in the cloud forests of the western Andean slopes often needs volunteers. One month minimum. Also see p134.
Río Muchacho Organic Farm (www.riomuchacho.com) Coastal ecotourism project offering one-month apprenticeships in organic agriculture with volunteer opportunities. Also see p291.
Yanapuma Foundation (Map p90; ☎ 02-254-6709; www.yanapuma.org; Veintimilla E8-125, 2nd fl, Quito) Offers a number of ways for volunteers to get involved: teaching English, building houses in remote communities, helping with reforestation projects or taking part in coastal clean-ups. Stop by its Quito headquarters and language school (p95) for more information.

WOMEN TRAVELERS

Generally, women travelers will find Ecuador safe and pleasant, despite the fact that machismo is alive and well. Ecuadorian men often make flirtatious comments and whistle at single women, both Ecuadorian and foreigners. Really, it's just sport – a sort of hormonal babbling among groups of guys – and the best strategy is to ignore them.

Women who speak Spanish find that it is easier to deal with persistent questions from men, which generally follow the classic: 'Where are you from?' 'How old are you?' 'Are you married?'. If you're not interested in conversation, consider beginning your response with 'My husband…' even if it's fiction. Sometimes this is all it takes. If the come-ons get really bad, a firm '*¡No, me molestes!*' ('Don't bother me!') should do the trick. In general, don't let comments on how pretty you are get under your skin, unless they are rude. Either say 'Thank you,' or ignore them.

On the coast, come-ons are more predatory, and solo female travelers should take precautions such as staying away from bars and discos where they'll obviously get hit on, opting for taxis over walking etc. Racy conversation with a guy, while it may be ironic or humorous, is not common here, and a man will probably assume you're after one thing.

There have been stories about foreign women being put into a compromising position with a guide or boss at a volunteer organization. In the rare chance this happens to you, report the person to the organization and any parent organization. The SAE (p388) will take reports and maintains a list of problem companies or tour groups. Most licensed guides in Ecuador, however, have a high level of professionalism. Lonely Planet has received warnings in the past from women who were molested while on organized tours. If you're traveling solo, it's essential to do some research before committing to a tour: find out who's leading the tour, what other tourists will be on the outing and so on. Women-only travel groups or guides are available in a few situations.

Very occasional reports have been received of women being harassed by hotel owners or peeked at through bathroom windows that won't close, but this seems a rarity. Try to rent a room with a secure lock and throw a towel over the bathroom window if it won't close.

WORK

Ecuador has 10% unemployment and 43% underemployment, so finding work isn't easy. Officially, you need a worker's visa to be allowed to work in Ecuador. Aside from the occasional position at a tourist lodge or expat bar, there is little opportunity for paid work. The one exception is teaching English.

Most paid English-teaching job openings are in Quito and Guayaquil. Schools sometimes advertise for teachers on the bulletin boards of hotels and restaurants. Pay is just enough to live on unless you've acquired a full-time position from home. If you have a bona-fide teaching credential, so much the better. Schools such as the American School in Quito will often hire teachers of mathematics, biology and other subjects, and may help you get a work visa. They also pay much better than the language schools. Check ads in local hotels and newspapers. One of the best online English-teaching resources, complete with job boards, is **Dave's ESL Café** (www.eslcafé.com).

Transportation

CONTENTS

GETTING THERE & AWAY

ENTERING THE COUNTRY

Entering the country is straightforward, and border officials, especially at the airports, efficiently whisk you through. At land borders, officers may take a little more time examining your passport, if only to kill a little time. Officially, you need proof of onward travel and evidence of sufficient funds for your stay, but this is rarely – if ever – asked for. Proof of $20 per day or a credit card is usually evidence of sufficient funds.

THINGS CHANGE...

The information in this chapter is particularly vulnerable to change. Check directly with the airline or a travel agent to make sure you understand how a fare (and ticket you may buy) works and be aware of the security requirements for international travel. Shop carefully. The details given in this chapter should be regarded as pointers and are not a substitute for your own careful, up-to-date research.

However, international airlines flying to Quito may require a round-trip or onward ticket or a residence visa before they let you on the plane; you should be prepared for this possibility, though it's unlikely. Though not law, you may be required to show proof of vaccination against yellow fever if you are entering Ecuador from an infected area.

Flights, tours and rail tickets can all be booked online at www.lonelyplanet.com/travel_services.

Passport

All nationals entering as tourists need a passport that is valid for at least six months after arrival. You are legally required to have your passport on you at all times. Many people carry only a copy when they're hanging around a town, though this is not an officially acceptable form of ID. Never travel without your passport. For visa requirements, see p389.

AIR

Airports & Airlines

About 20km east of Quito, a new international airport is scheduled to open in late 2010. Check www.quitoairport.com for the latest details.

Currently, two major international airports serve Ecuador: Quito's **Aeropuerto Mariscal Sucre** (UIO; ☎ 02-294-4900; www.quitoairport.com; Av Amazonas at Av de la Prensa) and Guayaquil's **Aeropuerto José Joaquín de Olmedo** (GYE; ☎ 04-216-9000; www.tagsa.aero; Av de las Américas s/n).

TAME (www.tame.com.ec) and **Aerogal** (www.aerogal.com.ec) are Ecuador's main airlines, but offer limited international flights. See p395 for details.

The following international airlines serve Ecuador. Unless otherwise noted, the telephone numbers given are for Quito offices.

Aeropostal Alas de Venezuela (airline code VH; ☎ 02-226-4392; www.aeropostal.com; hub Caracas, Venezuela)
Air Europa (airline code UX; ☎ 02-256-7646; www.aireuropa.com; hub Madrid, Spain)
Air France (airline code AF; ☎ 02-222-4818; www.airfrance.com; hub Paris, France)
American Airlines (airline code AA; ☎ 02-299-5000; www.aa.com; hubs Dallas, TX & Chicago, IL, USA)

Avianca (airline code AV; ☎ 02-330-1379; www.avianca.com; hub Bogotá, Colombia)
Continental Airlines (airline code CO; ☎ 02-225-0905; www.continental.com; hub Houston, TX & Newark, NJ, USA)
Copa (airline code CM; ☎ 02-227-3082; www.copaair.com; hub Panama City, Panama)
Iberia (airline code IB; ☎ 02-256 6009; www.iberia.com; hub Madrid, Spain)
KLM (airline code KL; ☎ 02-396-6728; www.klm.com; hub Amsterdam, Holland)
LAN Airlines (airline code LA; ☎ 1800-10-1075; www.lanchile.com; hub Santiago, Chile)
Lufthansa (airline code LH; ☎ 02-254-1300, 250-8396; www.lufthansa.com; hub Cologne, Germany)
Santa Bárbara Airlines (airline code S3; ☎ 380-0082; www.sbairlines.com; hub Caracas, Venezuela)
TACA (airline code TA; ☎ 1800-00-8222; www.taca.com; hub San Salvador, El Salvador)

Tickets

Ticket prices are highest during tourist high seasons: mid-June through early September, and December through mid-January. Working with a travel agent that deals specifically in Latin American travel is always an advantage.

INTERCONTINENTAL (RTW) TICKETS

Some of the best deals for travelers visiting many countries on different continents are Round-the-World (RTW) tickets. Itineraries from the USA, Europe or Australia can include five or more layovers including Quito. Similar 'Circle Pacific' fares allow excursions between Australasia and South America. Another option is putting together your own ticket with two or three stops and a round-trip from another country. If you work with a travel agent, it might work out cheaper than a RTW ticket.

Fares for RTW and Circle Pacific tickets can vary widely, but to get an idea, shop around at the following websites:

Airbrokers (www.airbrokers.com) US based.
Airtreks (www.airtreks.com) US based.
Oneworld (www.oneworld.com) Alliance between nine airlines that offer circle and RTW tickets. Quito is on the list of destination cities for its 'Visit South America' ticket.
Roundtheworldflights.com (www.roundtheworldflights.com) UK based.
Star Alliance (www.staralliance.com) Airline alliance that allows you to build your own RTW ticket.

Australia

There is no real choice of routes between Australia and South America, and there are certainly no bargain fares available. The two most straightforward options are: fly Qantas or Air New Zealand to Los Angeles (USA) and fly from there to Quito; or fly Aerolíneas Argentinas to Buenos Aires, from where there are direct flights to Quito. Another alternative is flying Qantas to Santiago, Chile and connecting with a LanChile flight north to Ecuador.

Some of the cheapest tickets are available through **STA Travel** (☎ 1300 733 035; www.statravel.com.au) and **Flight Centre** (☎ 133 133; www.flightcentre.com.au), both of which have dozens of offices in the country. For online bookings, try www.travel.com.au.

Canada

Air Canada, American Airlines and United fly from Toronto or Montreal via New York or Miami to Guayaquil or Quito. The most direct flights (one stop only) are with Air Canada via Miami or with Continental via Houston, Texas. Flights from Montreal via New York also stop in Miami before continuing to Quito.

Travel Cuts (☎ 800-667-2887; www.travelcuts.com) is Canada's national student travel agency. For online bookings try www.expedia.ca and www.travelocity.ca.

Continental Europe

There are few direct flights from Europe to Ecuador; most involve a change of plane and airline in Miami or Houston, or in a South American capital other than Quito. Iberia, Air Europa, and LAN Airlines (LanChile/LanEcuador) all fly nonstop to Quito or Guayaquil from Madrid. There are no other nonstop flights from Continental Europe.

The following travel agencies are good possibilities for bargain fares from Continental Europe.

FRANCE

Anyway (☎ 08 92 89 38 92; www.anyway.fr)
Lastminute (☎ 08 92 70 50 00; www.lastminute.fr)
Nouvelles Frontiéres (☎ 08 25 00 07 47; www.nouvelles-frontieres.fr)

DEPARTURE TAX

All passengers flying out of Ecuador on international flights must pay a departure tax, $45 from Quito and $28 from Guayaquil, which is not included in ticket prices and must be paid in cash at the airport. Short cross-border hops, such as Tulcán–Cali (Colombia), are not taxed.

OTU Voyages (www.otu.fr) Specializes in student and youth travelers.
Voyageurs du Monde (☎ 01 40 15 11 15; www.vdm.com)

GERMANY
Expedia (www.expedia.de)
Just Travel (☎ 089 747 3330; www.justtravel.de)
Lastminute (☎ 01805 284 366; www.lastminute.de)
STA Travel (☎ 01805 456 422; www.statravel.de) For travelers under the age of 26.

ITALY
Viaggi (☎ 06 462 0431; www.cts.it) specializes in student and youth travel.

NETHERLANDS
Airfair (☎ 020 620 5121; www.airf air.nl)

Latin America
There are loads of flights from Quito or Guayaquil to South American countries including Colombia (Bogotá, Cali and Cartagena), Argentina (Buenos Aires), Venezuela (Caracas), Bolivia (La Paz), Peru (Lima), Chile (Santiago), and Brazil (Sao Paulo and Rio de Janeiro). There are also direct flights to Mexico City, Panama City and Havana, Cuba.

New Zealand
As with Australia, there are no direct routes to Ecuador from New Zealand. Your best bets are flying Air New Zealand to Los Angeles (USA), or Aerolíneas Argentinas to Buenos Aires, and connecting from either to Quito. Qantas also flies from Auckland to Santiago, Chile, where you can connect with a LanChile flight to Ecuador.

Both **Flight Centre** (☎ 0800 243 544; www.flightcentre.co.nz) and **STA Travel** (☎ 0508 782 872; www.statravel.co.nz) have branches throughout the country. For online bookings try www.travel.co.nz.

UK & Ireland
There are no direct flights from the UK or Ireland to Ecuador. Fares from London are often cheaper than those from other European cities, even though your flight route may take you from London through a European city.

Discount air travel is big business in London. Advertisements for many travel agencies can be found in the travel pages of the weekend broadsheet newspapers, in *Time Out*, the *Evening Standard* and in the free online magazine *TNT* (www.tntmagazine.com).

Recommended travel agencies in the UK include the following:
Bridge the World (☎ 0870 444 7474; www.b-t-w.co.uk)
Flightbookers (☎ 0870 814 4001; www.ebookers.com)
Flight Centre (☎ 0870 890 8099; www.flightcentre.co.uk)
North-South Travel (☎ 01245 608 291; www.northsouthtravel.co.uk) Donates part of its profit to projects in the developing world.
Quest Travel (☎ 0870 442 3542; www.questtravel.com)
STA Travel (☎ 0870 160 0599; www.statravel.co.uk) For travelers under the age of 26.
Trailfinders (www.trailfinders.co.uk)
Travel Bag (☎ 0870 890 1456; www.travelbag.co.uk)

USA
From the USA, you can get a direct flight nonstop to Quito or Guayaquil from the gateways of New York, Houston and Miami. American Airlines and Continental are the main US carriers, and some Latin American airlines, especially LanChile/LanEcuador and Grupo TACA fly to Ecuador, in the case of the latter via Central America. Flights from other cities or with any of the other airlines require an aircraft change in the US gateways listed earlier or in another Latin American capital.

Latin American travel specialist **eXito Travel** (☎ 800-655-4053; www.exitotravel.com) offers excellent fares.

The following are recommended for online bookings:
Cheap Tickets (www.cheaptickets.com)
Expedia (www.expedia.com)
Lowestfare.com (www.lowestfare.com)
Orbitz (www.orbitz.com)
STA Travel (www.sta.com) Best for travelers under 26.
Travelocity (www.travelocity.com)

LAND
If you live in the Americas, it is possible to travel overland by bus. However, if you want to start from North or Central America, the Panamericana (Pan-American Highway) stops in Panama and begins again in Colombia, leaving a 200km roadless section of jungle known as the Darien Gap. The Darien Gap remains extremely dangerous owing to banditry and drug-related problems, especially on the Colombian side, so you are advised *not* to try to cross it.

Most overland travelers fly over the Darien Gap or hire on as a crew member on a private yacht that will sail from Panama to Colombia.

Once in South America, it is relatively straightforward to travel by public bus from the neighboring Andean countries.

Border Crossings

Peru and Colombia are the only countries sharing borders with Ecuador. If you are entering or leaving Ecuador, border formalities are straightforward if your documents are in order. No taxes are levied on tourists when entering or exiting overland.

If you're leaving the country and have lost your embarkation card (see p389), you should be able to get a free replacement at the border, assuming the stamp in your passport has not expired. If your documents aren't in order, one of two things might happen. If you've overstayed the allowed time, you'll have to pay a hefty fine or you will be sent back to Quito. If you don't have an *entrada* (entrance) stamp, you will also be sent back.

COLOMBIA

The main border crossing to Colombia is via Tulcán (p144) in the northern highlands, currently the only safe place to cross into Colombia. The border crossing north of Lago Agrio (p238) in the Oriente is unsafe due to smuggling and conflict in Colombia.

PERU

There are three important border posts connecting Ecuador and Peru; all are safe. The Huaquillas crossing (p339), south of Machala, gets almost 100% of the international traffic between the two countries. A second crossing at Macará is increasingly popular because it's more relaxed than the Huaquillas crossing, and the journey from Loja (p214) in the southern highlands is beautiful. Direct buses run between Loja and Piura, Peru (eight hours) via Macará and wait for you at the border while you take care of formalities; it's easy. The least-used crossing is La Balsa at Zumba (p226), south of Vilcabamba (p223), a remote and interesting crossing that gets little traffic. People often hang out in Vilcabamba for a few days before heading to Zumba and Peru.

A fourth crossing is by river via the outpost of Nuevo Rocafuerte (p248) on the Río Napo in the Oriente, a long journey rarely undertaken by foreigners – but it's possible.

Bus

Bussing into Ecuador from Colombia or Peru is straightforward and usually requires walking across one of the earlier mentioned international borders and catching another bus once you're across. Some international bus companies offer direct, long-haul services from major cities such as Lima and Bogotá.

Car & Motorcycle

Driving a private vehicle into Ecuador can be a huge hassle, depending largely upon the mood of the official who stops you at the border. To bring your car into Ecuador, you are officially required to have a Carnet de Passage en Douane (CPD), an internationally recognized customs document that allows you to temporarily 'import' a vehicle into Ecuador without paying an import tax. The document is issued through an automobile club in the country where the car is registered, and you are strongly advised to obtain one well in advance. Motorcycles seem to present fewer hassles at the border.

RIVER

Since the 1998 peace treaty was signed with Peru, it has been possible to travel down the Río Napo from Ecuador to Peru, joining the Amazon near Iquitos. The border facilities are minimal, and the boats doing the journey are infrequent, but it is possible to do the trip – see p248. It is also geographically possible to travel down Río Putumayo into Colombia and Peru, but this is a dangerous region because of drug smuggling and terrorism, and is not recommended.

SEA

Very few cruise ships use Guayaquil as a port of call as they head down the Pacific coast of South America. Occasionally you can find a ship going to Guayaquil, Ecuador's main port, although this is a very unusual way to arrive in Ecuador; it's certainly cheaper and more convenient to fly.

A few cargo lines will carry passengers, though it usually costs more than flying. If you're determined to get here by freighter, you can start your research online at the **Internet Guide to Freighter Travel** (www.geocities.com/freighterman.geo/mainmenu.html).

It is possible to arrive in Ecuador on your own sailing boat, or if you don't happen to have one, as a crew member. In Ecuador,

Salinas is the port most frequented by international yachts. For further information, read the *World Cruising Handbook* by Jimmy Cornell.

GETTING AROUND

Ecuador has an efficient transportation system, and because of its small size you can usually get anywhere and everywhere fairly quickly and easily.

AIR

Airlines in Ecuador

Ecuador's most important domestic airline is TAME, followed by Aerogal and Icaro. In addition to domestic flights, TAME flies twice weekly between Guayaquil and Manaos (Manaus), Brazil and operates daily flights from Tulcán to Cali, Colombia. TAME also had plans to operate daily flights between Lima, Peru and Guayaquil. Aerogal flies to Bogotá, Colombia, from both Quito and Guayaquil. It also flies Quito to Medellín, and Quito to Miami. All three Ecuadorian airlines enjoy safety records on par with most world airlines, although some of the planes look a little old.

With the exception of flying to the Galápagos Islands, internal flights are generally fairly cheap, rarely exceeding $80 for a one-way ticket. All mainland flights are under an hour and often provide you with incredible views over the Andes. There is a two-tier pricing system on flights to and from the Oriente and to/from the Galápagos, on which foreigners pay more than Ecuadorians.

If you can't get a ticket, go to the airport early and get on a waiting list – passengers often don't show up. If you do have a reservation, reconfirm your flight 72 hours in advance.

Flights to most destinations originate in Quito or Guayaquil only. Detailed flight information is given under the appropriate cities throughout this book. The following are Ecuador's three passenger airlines with their reservation numbers in Quito:

Aerogal (☎ 1800-237-6425; www.aerogal.com.ec) Serves Quito, Guayaquil, Cuenca, Isla Baltra (Galápagos), Isla San Cristóbal (Galápagos), Manta, plus Bogotá (Colombia), Medellín (Colombia), and Miami (USA).

Icaro (☎ 02-330-1484; www.icaro.aero) Serves Quito, Guayaquil, Manta and Coca.

TAME (☎ 02-396-6300; www.tame.com.ec) Serves Coca, Cuenca, Esmeraldas, Isla Baltra (Galápagos), Isla San Cristóbal (Galápagos), Guayaquil, Lago Agrio, Loja, Macas, Manta, Portoviejo, Quito, Tulcán, plus Cali (Colombia) and Manaos (Brazil).

BICYCLE

Each year a handful of cyclists attempt to ride from Alaska to Argentina, or any number of shorter long-distance rides, and manage to get through Ecuador just fine, despite the fact that road rules are few, bike lanes are nonexistent and roads are poor. Cycling in the Andes is strenuous, not only because of hill climbs but because of the altitudes. Mountain bikes are recommended, as road bikes don't stand up to the poor road quality.

Bike shops are scarce outside of Quito, and those that do exist usually have a very limited selection of parts. Bring all important spare parts and tools from home. For mountain-biking destinations in Ecuador, see p64. The country's best mountain bike tour operators are in Quito (p93) and Riobamba (p189).

Hire

Renting bikes has only recently become an option in Ecuador, and is mainly for short tours, mostly from Quito, Riobamba and Cuenca. The main exception is the Andean town of Baños (p172) which has a nicely paved ride nearby and is therefore full of mountain bike rentals.

Purchase

Bicycles are extremely expensive in Ecuador, and outside of Quito or Guayaquil it is difficult to find anything even approaching a quality bike. Used bikes are hard to come by.

BOAT

Boat transportation is common in Ecuador and can be divided into several types.

Canoe

The most common boat is the motorized canoe, which acts as a water taxi or bus along the major rivers of the Oriente (especially on the Río Napo) and parts of the northern coast. Most people experience this novel form of transport during a tour in the Amazon, as motorized canoes are often the only way to a rainforest lodge.

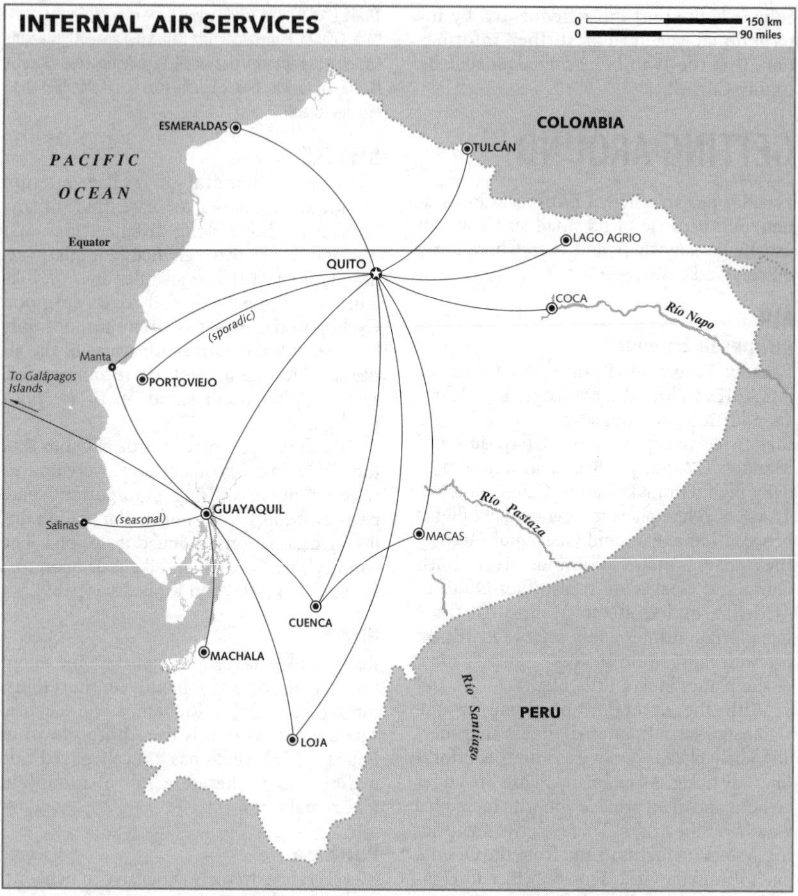

These canoes often carry as many as three-dozen passengers. Generally, they're long in shape and short on comfort. Seating is normally on hard, low wooden benches which accommodate two people each. Luggage is stashed forward under a tarpaulin, so carry hand baggage containing essentials for the journey. The most important piece of advice: *bring seat padding*. A folded sweater or towel will make a world of difference on the trip.

Pelting rain and glaring sun are major hazards, and an umbrella is an excellent defense against both. Bring suntan lotion or wear long sleeves, long pants and a sun hat – people have been literally unable to walk because of second-degree burns on their legs after six hours of exposure to the tropical sun. When the sun disappears or when the rain begins, it can get chilly, so bring a light jacket.

Insect repellent is useful during stops along the river. Bottled water and something to snack on will complete your hand baggage.

Once you're off the main branch of a river, you may have to navigate smaller tributaries in a paddled (or motorized) dugout canoe, one of the most divine modes of transportation because it moves along stealthily and silently. Tours from a jungle lodge usually involve paddled dugout canoes.

Private Yacht

The idea of sailing your own yacht around the Galápagos might sound splendid, but to do so, you need a license, and licenses are all limited to Galápagos boats. If you arrive at the islands in your own boat, you will have to moor it in Puerto Ayora and hire one of the local boats to take you around. The Ecuadorian authorities give transit permits of seven days for sailors on their own boats. Longer stays may be possible if you are moored and not sailing.

Other Boats

In the Galápagos, you have a choice of traveling in anything from a small sailboat to a cruise ship complete with air-conditioned cabins and private bathrooms. Passenger ferries run infrequently between the islands, offering the cheapest means of interisland transport. Only folks traveling around the islands independently (ie not on a cruise) need consider these (see p353).

In addition to the dugout canoes of the Oriente, one cruise ship, *Amazon Manatee Explorer,* makes relatively luxurious passages down Río Napo (see p96).

Finally, some rivers are crossed by ferries that vary from a paddled dugout taking one passenger at a time to a car ferry capable of moving half-a-dozen vehicles. These are sometimes makeshift transportation to replace a bridge that has been washed out, is being repaired or is still in the planning stages.

BUS

In terms of scope and affordability, Ecuador's bus system is impressive to say the least. Buses are the primary means of transport for most Ecuadorians, guaranteed to just about anywhere. They can be exciting, cramped, comfy, smelly, fun, scary, sociable and grueling, depending on your state of mind, where you're going and who's driving.

In terms of safety – sure, you're safer at home. To avoid mincing words, the majority of Ecuadorian bus drivers are maniacs: they pass on blind turns, they ride the air brakes till they smoke, they hit the gas going downhill and they race other buses for fun. But to their credit, most are amazingly skillful drivers. If they get too crazy, people on the bus start to complain, which can either settle the driver down or piss him off and make him drive faster. Overall, buses are a wonderful experience, and more often than not you're in good hands.

Most major cities have a main *terminal terrestre* (bus terminal), although some towns have a host of private terminals – and you'll have to go to the right one to catch the bus going where you need to go. Most stations are within walking distance or a short cab ride from the town's center. Smaller towns are occasionally served by passing buses, in which case you have to walk from the highway into town, usually only a short walk since only the smallest towns lack terminals.

If traveling lightly, take your luggage inside the bus with you; if it has to go on top or in a luggage compartment, pack it in garbage bags in case of rain. The luggage compartment is sometimes filthy or leaky, so using a protective sack is a good idea (though not crucial if rain is out of the question). Many locals use grain sacks as luggage; you can buy them for a few cents in general stores or markets and toss your bag inside it. For information on luggage theft, see p381.

On average, bus journeys cost about $1 per hour of travel. Remember to always have your passport handy when you're going anywhere by bus, as they are sometimes stopped for checks. This is especially true in the Oriente.

Classes

There are rarely classes to choose from – whatever's available is the class you ride. Most *autobuses* (buses) are nondescript passenger buses (as opposed to school-type buses), and they rarely have a bathroom on board unless they're traveling over about four hours. Some of the long-haul rides between large cities have air-conditioned buses with on-board toilets, but they are few and far between. When a bus does have a bathroom, you usually have to ask the driver's assistant for the key. If a bus doesn't have a toilet, and you're not going to make it to the next stop without your bowels exploding, simply put a panicked look on your face and tell the driver, *'necesito orinar'* ('I need to urinate'). He'll know to stop and let you out – it's not a big deal.

Long-Distance Buses

These usually stop for a 20-minute meal break at the appropriate times. The food in terminal restaurants may be somewhat basic, so if you're a picky eater you should bring food with you.

On remote routes, full buses allow passengers to travel on the roof. This can be fun, with great views but minimal comfort and a certain amount of danger involved – watch your head with oncoming obstacles!

Reservations & Schedules

Most bus companies have scheduled departure times, but these change often and may not always be adhered to. If a bus is full, it might leave early. Conversely, an almost empty bus may spend half an hour *dando vueltas* (driving around), with the driver's assistant yelling out of the door in the hope of attracting more passengers. The upside is, you'll carry these songlike hollers *(¡Saquisilí, Saquisilí, venga venga Saquisilí!)* home like souvenirs and hear them in your mind for years to come.

The larger terminals often have traveler information booths that can advise you about routes, fares and times.

For rides over four hours, you can usually purchase a ticket up to eight days in advance. Tickets must be purchased in person at the bus terminal. Except on weekends and during vacations, you'll rarely have trouble getting a ticket but it never hurts to buy one a day in advance or arrive an hour or two early. Doing so also allows you to score a better seat. The suspension at the back of a bus is usually far worse than anywhere else, so try to avoid the back rows altogether. Anyone over 180cm (6ft) should buy tickets in advance and ask for a seat with *mucho espacio* (lots of space), usually toward the front.

Bus companies with frequent departures (twice an hour or more) usually only sell tickets for the next departure.

CAR & MOTORCYCLE

Driving a car or motorcycle in Ecuador definitely has its challenges. The main north–south artery, the one you'll surely drive if you do any driving at all, is the Panamericana. This international highway, one of the world's most famous roads, passes through Ecuador and is fairly well surfaced but not without its potholes, blind turns, and insanely fast bus and truck drivers. It's quite an experience, to say the least.

Automobile Associations

Ecuador's automobile association is **Aneta** (☎ 1800-556-677; Quito ☎ 02-250-4961; www.aneta.org.ec), which offers a few member services

DRIVING DISTANCES (KM)

	Ambato	Bahía de Caráquez	Baños	Cuenca	Esmeraldas	Guayaquil	Huaquillas	Ibarra	Loja	Macará	Macas	Manta	Otavalo	Quito	Riobamba	Tena
Bahía de Caráquez	406															
Baños	40	446														
Cuenca	306	530	309													
Esmeraldas	390	392	430	667												
Guayaquil	288	280	288	235	472											
Huaquillas	440	533	445	242	670	253										
Ibarra	251	455	291	557	433	535	693									
Loja	511	695	514	205	832	415	233	762								
Macará	701	682	704	395	819	402	195	952	190							
Macas	230	642	190	231	620	432	473	479	436	626						
Manta	404	120	444	446	442	196	449	505	611	598	628					
Otavalo	231	435	271	537	413	515	673	20	742	932	459	485				
Quito	136	340	176	442	318	420	578	115	647	837	366	390	95			
Riobamba	52	464	55	254	442	233	390	303	459	649	245	456	283	188		
Tena	180	586	140	449	497	428	585	271	598	788	208	584	251	186	195	
Tulcán	376	580	416	682	558	660	818	125	887	1077	604	630	145	240	428	396

to members of foreign automobile clubs including Canadian and US AAA members. It provides 24-hour roadside assistance to Aneta members.

Bring Your Own Vehicle

Unless your visit to Ecuador is part of a longer multicountry or continent-wide road trip, it's hardly worth shipping your own vehicle to Ecuador. The cost is high, and unless you choose to container your vehicle, theft of items from inside the car is a serious problem. Containerless Ro-Ro (roll on, roll off) shipping is not recommended.

Driver's License

An international driver's license is not officially required to drive in Ecuador, but it can be beneficial as a familiar document to the officer who has never seen, say, a Nebraska state driver's license.

You are required to have a driver's license from your home country and a passport whenever you're driving. The international driver's license can also come in handy when renting a car.

Fuel & Spare Parts

There are two octane ratings for gasoline in Ecuador: 'Extra' (82 octane) and 'Super' (92 octane). Gasoline is sold by the gallon and costs about $1.50 per gallon for Extra and about $2 per gallon for Super; note that the latter is not always available in rural areas. Dirty diesel is available throughout the country. Depending on your vehicle, spare parts can be difficult to come by outside the main urban areas.

Hire

Few people rent cars in Ecuador, mainly because public transport makes getting around so easy. To get to really out-of-the-way places, however, a rental car can come in handy. Most of the international car rental companies, including **Avis** (www.avis.com), **Budget** (www.budget.com), **Hertz** (www.hertz.com) and **Localiza** (www.localiza.com.ec), have outlets in Ecuador, but it is difficult to find any agency outside of Guayaquil, Quito or Cuenca.

To rent a car you must be 25 years old and have a credit card, a valid driver's license and a passport. Occasionally a company will rent to someone between 21 and 25 years old, though it may require a higher deposit. Typical rates start at around $40 per day for a compact car, but can go over $100 for a 4WD vehicle (high clearance can be a life saver during ventures off the beaten track). It's well worth shopping around for the best price. As you do, be sure to ask if the quoted rate includes *seguro* (insurance), *kilometraje libre* (unlimited kilometers) and IVA (tax) – most likely it won't.

As with renting a car anywhere, make sure existing damage to the vehicle is noted on the rental form. Be absolutely certain that there's a spare tire (with air!) and a jack. Rental cars are targets for thieves, so don't leave your car parked with bags or other valuables in sight. When leaving your car for any period, especially overnight, park it in a guarded lot.

Motorcycle rental is hard to find in Ecuador. One of the only options is Baños (p172) where 250cc Enduro-type motorcycles are available for about $10 per hour or $40 per day. Riders with their own machines will find an endless amount of information at www.horizonsunlimited.com.

Some international rental agencies will make reservations for you from your home country.

Insurance

Car-rental companies offer insurance policies on their vehicles but they can carry a hefty deductible – anywhere between $1000 and $3500, depending on the company – so be sure you read the fine print. Even if an accident is not your fault, you will likely be responsible for the deductible in the event of a collision.

Road Hazards

Hazards in Ecuador include potholes, blind turns and, most obvious of all, bus and truck drivers who pass other buses and trucks at seemingly impossible moments. Always be alert for stopped vehicles, sudden road blocks and occasional livestock on the road. Signage in Ecuador is poor.

Road Rules

Ecuadorians drive on the right side of the road. Lanes, however, especially on the Panamericana, are a loose interpretation of the driver. In essence, the Panamericana has three lanes: one goes one direction, a second goes the opposite direction, and a hazily defined no-man's land between the two serves as a de facto passing lane. As you can imagine, this middle lane offers plenty of nerve-racking games of chicken and chance. You should be extremely cautious when overtaking other vehicles.

Road signs and traffic lights should always be obeyed even though they only seem symbolic to Ecuadorian drivers. To that end, even if a light is green, look both directions before entering a junction.

Military checkpoints are common along the Panamericana, so be certain to have all your papers in order to avoid hassle.

HITCHHIKING

Hitchhiking is never entirely safe in any country, and we don't recommend it. Travelers who decide to hitchhike should understand that they are taking a small but potentially serious risk. People who do choose to hitchhike will be safer if they travel in pairs and let someone know where they are planning to go.

Hitching is not very practical in Ecuador for three reasons: there are few private cars, public transportation is relatively cheap and trucks are used as public transportation in remote areas, so trying to hitch a free ride on one is the same as trying to hitch a free ride on a bus. Many drivers of *any* vehicle will pick you up but will also expect payment, usually minimal.

LOCAL TRANSPORTATION

Bus

Local buses are usually slow and crowded, but they are also very cheap. You can get around most towns for $0.20 to $0.25. Local buses often travel to nearby villages, and riding along is a good, inexpensive way to see the area.

Outside of Quito, the concept of a fixed bus stop is pretty much nonexistent. Buses stop (or at least come to a slow roll) when people flag them down. When you want to get off a local bus, yell '*¡Baja!*,' which means 'Down!' (as in 'the passenger is getting down'). Another favorite way of getting the driver to stop is by yelling '*¡Gracias!*' ('Thank you!'), which is unmistakably polite.

Taxi

Ecuadorian taxis come in a variety of shapes and sizes, but they are all yellow. Most taxis have a lit 'taxi' sign on top or a 'taxi' sticker in the windshield. Taxis often belong to cooperatives, with the name and telephone number printed on the door.

Always ask the fare beforehand, or you'll be overcharged more often than not. Meters are rarely seen, except in Quito where they are obligatory. For variations on the use of the taxi meter in Quito, see p113. A long ride in a large city such as Quito or Guayaquil shouldn't go over $4. The minimum fare nearly everywhere is $1, and will be required to pay $1 in Quito even if the meter only says $0.80. Fares from international airports (Quito and Guayaquil) can be exorbitantly high if you're not careful. See p113 and p334 for tips on how to avoid getting burned. On weekends and at night, fares are always about 25% to 50% higher. Taxis can be hard to flag down during rush hours.

You can hire a taxi for a day for about $40 to $60. Hiring a taxi for a few days is comparable to renting a car, except that you don't have to drive. But you will have to pay for the driver's food and room. Some tour companies in Quito rent 4WD vehicles with experienced drivers.

In less urban areas, you're also likely to see *ecotaxis* (a three-wheeled bicycle with a small covered carriage in back that fits two people) as well as *taxis ecológicos* (motorcycle taxis with a two-seater carriage in back).

Trucks

In certain towns, especially in rural areas where there are many dirt roads, pickup trucks act as taxis. If you need to get to a national park, a climbers' refuge or a trailhead from a town, often the best way to do so is hiring a pickup, which is usually as easy as asking around.

TOURS

Whether you can stomach the idea or not, there are a great many places in Ecuador that are accessible only by taking an organized tour. This is not necessarily a bad thing – in fact, you end up learning a lot from a good guide – and a tour may be small – with just two or three people.

If you're short on time, the best place to organize a tour is Quito. A plethora of operators for every budget offer trips including Galápagos cruises, climbing and hiking tours, horseback riding, jungle tours, mountain-biking tours, hacienda tours and more.

Tour costs vary tremendously depending on what your requirements are. The cheapest camping jungle tour can be as low as $40 per person per day, while the most expensive lodges can crest $200 per person per night including all meals and tours. Climbs of the volcanoes average about $160 per person for a two-day climb. Galápagos boat cruises range from $800 to over $3000 per week excluding air fare, taxes and entrance fees. Day tours out of Quito range from $25 to $80 per person per day.

See p349 and p234 for general information on tours in those areas. For a list of operators in Quito, see p96.

TRAIN

Ecuador's rail system is now extremely limited and consists primarily of two tourist trains. The most famous is the dramatic descent from Alausí along La Nariz del Diablo (The Devil's Nose; see the boxed text, p193), a spectacular section of train track that was one of the world's greatest feats of railroad engineering. The second is the weekend train excursion between Quito and the Area Nacional de Recreación El Boliche, near Cotopaxi (see p113). Passengers are allowed to ride on the roof of some cars, and these are very popular trips.

Reservations are generally not necessary for the El Boliche run. For the Devil's Nose ride, you can buy your tickets a day in advance from the train station in Riobamba. There's only one class – roof class; well, you can ride inside if you really want.

TRUCKS (RANCHERAS & CHIVAS)

In remote areas, trucks often double as buses. Sometimes these are large, flatbed trucks with a tin roof, open wooden sides and uncomfortable wooden-plank seats. These curious-looking 'buses' are called *rancheras* or *chivas,* and are seen on the coast and in the Oriente. If you get an outside seat, they're actually a blast – provided you're not going *too* far, of course.

In the remote parts of the highlands, *camionetas* (ordinary trucks or pickups) are used to carry passengers; you just climb in the back. If the weather is good, you get fabulous views and the refreshing sensation of Andean wind in your face. If the weather is bad, you hunker down beneath a tarpaulin with the other passengers. These rides are certainly far from comfortable, but can be a good time nonetheless.

Payment for these rides is usually determined by the driver and is a standard fare depending on the distance. You can ask other passengers how much they are paying; usually you'll find that the trucks double as buses and charge almost as much.

Health

David Goldberg, MD

CONTENTS

Your health depends on your predeparture preparations, your daily health care while traveling and how you handle any medical problem that does develop. While the potential dangers can seem quite frightening, in reality, few travelers experience anything more than an upset stomach.

BEFORE YOU GO

Make sure you're healthy before traveling. If going on a long trip, make sure your teeth are OK. If you wear glasses, take a spare pair and your prescription.

If you require a particular medication, take an adequate supply, as it may not be available locally. Know the generic name, as well as the brand, to make getting replacements easier. To avoid problems, have a legible prescription or letter from your doctor to show that you legally use the medication.

INSURANCE

Make sure that you have adequate health insurance. See p383.

RECOMMENDED VACCINATIONS

Plan ahead for getting your vaccinations: some require several injections, and some vaccinations should not be given together or should be avoided during pregnancy and by people with allergies – discuss this with your doctor at least six weeks before travel. Be aware that there is often a greater risk of disease for children and pregnant women.

MEDICAL CHECKLIST

Give some thought to a medical kit for your trip, particularly if you're going far off the beaten track.

It's not necessary to take every remedy for every illness you might contract during your trip. Ecuadorian pharmacies stock all kinds of drugs, and medication can be cheaper here than in other countries. Almost everything is sold over the counter. Be sure to check expiry dates.

- acetaminophen (Tylenol) or aspirin
- acetazolamide (Diamox; to help with altitude sickness)
- adhesive or paper tape
- antibacterial ointment (eg Bactroban; for cuts and abrasions)
- antibiotics
- antidiarrheal drugs (eg loperamide)
- antihistamines (for hay fever and allergic reactions)
- anti-inflammatory drugs (eg ibuprofen)
- bandages, gauze
- DEET-containing insect repellent for the skin
- iodine tablets (for water purification)
- oral rehydration salts
- permethrin-containing insect spray for clothing, tents and bed nets
- pocketknife
- scissors, safety pins, tweezers
- steroid cream or cortisone (for poison ivy and other allergic rashes)
- sunblock
- syringes and sterile needles
- thermometer

IN TRANSIT

DEEP VEIN THROMBOSIS (DVT)

Blood clots may form in the legs (deep vein thrombosis) during long plane flights, chiefly because of prolonged immobility. Though most blood clots are reabsorbed uneventfully, some may break off and travel through the blood vessels to the lungs, where they could cause life-threatening complications.

The chief symptom of DVT is swelling or pain of the foot, ankle or calf, usually but not always on just one side. When a blood clot travels to the lungs, it may cause chest pain and some difficulties in breathing.

To prevent the development of DVT on long flights you should walk about the cabin, perform isometric compressions of the leg muscles (ie contract the leg muscles while sitting), drink plenty of fluids and avoid alcohol.

JET LAG & MOTION SICKNESS

Jet lag is commonly experienced when crossing more than five time zones and usually results in insomnia, fatigue, malaise or nausea. To avoid jet lag make sure to drink plenty of fluids (nonalcoholic) and eat light meals. Upon arrival, be sure to get exposure to natural sunlight and readjust your schedule (for meals, sleep etc) as soon as possible.

Antihistamines such as dimenhydrinate (Dramamine) and meclizine (Antivert, Bonine) are usually the first choice for treating motion sickness. Their main side effect is drowsiness. Ginger is a good herbal alternative, which works like a charm for some people.

IN ECUADOR

AVAILABILITY & COST OF HEALTH CARE

Medical care is available in major cities, but may be difficult to find in rural areas. Most doctors and hospitals will expect payment in cash, regardless of whether you have travel health insurance. If you develop a life-threatening medical problem, you'll want to be evacuated to a country with state-of-the-art medical care. Since this may cost tens of thousands of dollars, be sure you have insurance to cover this before you depart. Pharmacies in Ecuador are known as *farmacias*.

> **THE MAN SAYS...**
>
> It's usually a good idea to consult your government's travel health website before departure (if one is available):
>
> - **Australia** (www.smarttraveller.gov.au)
> - **Canada** (www.travelhealth.gc.ca)
> - **UK** (www.nhs.uk/LiveWell/TravelHealth)
> - **USA** (www.cdc.gov/travel)

INFECTIOUS DISEASES

Cholera

This is the worst of the watery diarrheas, and medical help should be sought. Outbreaks of cholera are generally widely reported, so you can avoid problem areas. Fluid replacement is the most vital treatment – the risk of dehydration is severe, as you may lose up to 20L a day. If there is a delay in getting to a hospital, then begin taking tetracycline. The adult dose is 250mg four times daily. Tetracycline is not recommended for children under the age of nine or for pregnant women. Tetracycline may help shorten the illness, but adequate fluids are required to save lives.

Dengue Fever

This viral disease is transmitted by mosquitoes and is fast becoming one of the top public-health problems in the tropical world. Unlike the malaria mosquito, the *Aedes aegypti* mosquito, which transmits the dengue virus, is most active during the day and is found mainly in urban areas, in and around human dwellings.

Signs and symptoms of dengue fever include a sudden onset of high fever, headache, joint and muscle pains (hence its old name, 'breakbone fever'), and nausea and vomiting. A rash of small red spots sometimes appears three to four days after the onset of fever. In the early phase of illness, dengue fever may be mistaken for other infectious diseases, including malaria and influenza. You should seek medical attention as soon as possible if you think you may be infected.

Hepatitis A

Hepatitis A is the second most common travel-related infection (after traveler's diarrhea). It's a viral infection of the liver that's usually acquired by ingestion of contaminated water, food or ice, as well as through direct contact with infected persons. The illness occurs throughout the world, but the incidence

RECOMMENDED VACCINATIONS

Although no vaccines are legally mandated, a number are strongly recommended:

Vaccine	Recommended for	Dosage	Side effects
chickenpox	travelers who've never had chickenpox	2 doses 1 month apart	fever; mild case of chickenpox
hepatitis A	all travelers	1 dose before trip; booster 6-12 months	soreness at injection site; headaches or body aches later
hepatitis B	long-term travelers in close contact with the local population	3 doses over a 6-month period	soreness at injection site; low-grade fever
measles	travelers born after 1956 who've had only 1 measles vaccination	1 dose	fever; rash; joint pains; allergic reactions
rabies	travelers who may have contact with animals & may not have access to medical care	3 doses over 3-4 weeks	soreness at injection site; headaches; body aches
tetanus-diphtheria	all travelers who haven't had booster within 10 years	1 dose lasts 10 years	soreness at injection site
typhoid	all travelers	4 capsules by mouth, 1 taken every other day	abdominal pain; nausea; rash
yellow fever	all travelers	1 dose lasts 10 years	headaches; body aches; severe reactions are rare

is higher in developing nations. Symptoms may include fever, malaise, jaundice, nausea, vomiting and abdominal pain. Most cases resolve without complications, though hepatitis A occasionally causes severe liver damage. There is no treatment.

The vaccine for hepatitis A is safe and highly effective. If you get a booster six to 12 months later, it lasts for at least 10 years. Because the safety of hepatitis A vaccine has not been established for pregnant women or children under age two, they should instead be given a gamma globulin injection.

Hepatitis B

Hepatitis B is a liver infection that occurs worldwide but is more common in developing nations. Unlike hepatitis A, the disease is usually acquired by sexual contact or by exposure to infected blood, generally through blood transfusions or contaminated needles. The vaccine is recommended only for long-term travelers (on the road more than six months) who expect to live in rural areas or have close physical contact with the local population.

Hepatitis B vaccine is safe and highly effective. However, a total of three injections are necessary to establish full immunity. Several countries added hepatitis B vaccine to the list of routine childhood immunizations in the 1980s, so many young adults are already protected.

HIV & AIDS

Infection with the human immunodeficiency virus (HIV) may lead to acquired immune deficiency syndrome (AIDS), which is a fatal disease. Any exposure to contaminated blood, blood products or body fluids may put the individual at risk. The disease is often transmitted through sexual contact or dirty needles – vaccinations, acupuncture, tattooing and body piercing can be potentially as dangerous as intravenous drug use. HIV/AIDS can also be spread through infected blood transfusions; Ecuador's best clinics screen their blood supply. If you do need an injection, ask to see the syringe unwrapped in front of you, or take a needle and syringe pack with you.

Leishmaniasis

This is a group of parasitic diseases transmitted by sandflies. Cutaneous leishmaniasis affects the skin tissue, causing ulceration and disfigurement, and visceral leishmaniasis affects the internal organs. Seek medical advice, as laboratory testing is required for diagnosis and correct treatment. Avoiding sandfly bites is the best precaution. Bites are usually painless but itchy. Cover up and use insect repellant.

Malaria

Malaria is transmitted by mosquito bites, usually between dusk and dawn. The main symptom is high-spiking fevers, often accompanied by chills, sweats, headache, body aches, weakness, vomiting or diarrhea. Severe cases may involve the central nervous system and lead to seizures, confusion, coma and death.

Taking malaria pills is recommended for all rural areas below 1500m. Risk is highest along the northernmost coast and in the northern Oriente. There is no malaria risk in the highlands.

There is a choice of three malaria pills, all of which work about equally well. Mefloquine (Lariam) is taken once weekly, starting one to two weeks before arrival and continuing through the trip and for four weeks after return. A percentage of people develop neuropsychiatric side effects, which may range from mild to severe. Atovaquone/proguanil (Malarone) is a newly approved combination pill taken once daily with food, starting two days before arrival and continuing through the trip and for seven days after departure. Side effects are typically mild. Doxycycline is a third option, but may cause an exaggerated sunburn reaction.

In general, Malarone seems to cause fewer side effects than mefloquine and is becoming more popular. The chief disadvantage is that it has to be taken daily.

Protecting yourself against mosquito bites is just as important as taking malaria pills, since none of the pills is 100% effective.

If you do not have access to medical care while traveling, you should bring along additional pills for emergency self-treatment, which you should take if you can't reach a doctor and you develop symptoms that suggest malaria, such as high-spiking fevers. One option is to take four tablets of Malarone once daily for three days. Do not use Malarone for treatment if you're already taking it for prevention.

If you develop a fever after returning home, see a physician, as malaria symptoms may not occur for months.

Rabies

This viral infection is fatal. Many animals (dogs, cats, bats and monkeys etc) can be infected, and it is their saliva that is infectious. Any bite, scratch or even lick from an animal should be cleaned immediately and thoroughly. Scrub with soap and running water, and then apply alcohol or iodine solution. Medical help should be sought promptly to receive a course of injections to prevent the onset of symptoms and/or death.

Sexually Transmitted Diseases

Sexual contact with an infected partner can result in you contracting a number of diseases. While abstinence is the only 100%-effective prevention, the use of condoms lessens the risk of infection considerably.

The most common sexually transmitted diseases are gonorrhea and syphilis, which in men first appear as sores, blisters or rashes around the genitals and a discharge or pain when urinating. Symptoms may be less marked or not present at all in women. Syphilis symptoms eventually disappear, but the disease continues and may cause severe problems in later years. Gonorrhea and syphilis are treatable with antibiotics.

Tetanus

This disease is caused by a germ that lives in soil and in the feces of horses and other animals. It enters the body via breaks in the skin. The first symptom may be discomfort in swallowing, or a stiffening of the jaw and neck; this is followed by painful convulsions of the jaw and whole body. The disease can be fatal. It can be prevented by vaccination.

Typhoid

A dangerous gut infection, typhoid fever is caused by contaminated water and food. Medical help must be sought.

In its early stages, sufferers may feel they have a bad cold or flu on the way, as initial symptoms are a headache, body aches and a fever that rises a little each day until it is around 40°C (104°F) or more. The victim's pulse is often slow relative to the degree of fever present – unlike a normal fever, during which the pulse increases. There may also be vomiting, abdominal pain, diarrhea or constipation.

In the second week, the high fever and slow pulse continue, and a few pink spots may appear on the body; trembling, delirium, weakness, weight loss and dehydration may occur. Complications such as pneumonia or perforated bowel may occur.

FOLK REMEDIES

Problem	Treatment
altitude sickness	gingko
jet lag	melatonin
mosquito bite prevention	oil of eucalyptus
motion sickness	ginger

Typhus

This is spread by ticks, mites and lice. It begins as a severe cold followed by a fever, chills, headaches, muscle pains and a body rash. There is often a large and painful sore at the site of the bite, and nearby lymph nodes become swollen and painful.

Yellow Fever

This viral disease is endemic in South America and is transmitted by mosquitoes. The initial symptoms are fever, headache, abdominal pain and vomiting. Seek medical care urgently and drink lots of fluids.

TRAVELER'S DIARRHEA

To prevent diarrhea, avoid tap water unless it has been boiled, filtered or chemically disinfected (iodine tablets); only eat fresh fruits or vegetables if cooked or peeled; be wary of dairy products that might contain unpasteurized milk; and be highly selective when eating food from street vendors.

If you develop diarrhea, be sure to drink plenty of fluids, preferably an oral rehydration solution containing lots of salt and sugar. A few loose stools don't require treatment but, if you have more than four or five stools a day, you should start taking an antibiotic (usually a quinolone drug) and an antidiarrheal agent (such as loperamide). If diarrhea is bloody or persists for more than 72 hours or is accompanied by fever, shaking chills or severe abdominal pain you should seek medical attention.

ENVIRONMENTAL HAZARDS

Altitude Sickness

Altitude sickness may develop in travelers who ascend rapidly to altitudes greater than 2500m, including those flying directly to Quito. Being physically fit does not in any way lessen your risk of altitude sickness. Symptoms may include headaches, nausea, vomiting, dizziness, malaise, insomnia and loss of appetite. Severe cases may be complicated by fluid in the lungs (high-altitude pulmonary edema) or swelling of the brain (high-altitude cerebral edema). Most deaths are caused by high-altitude pulmonary edema.

The standard medication to prevent altitude sickness is a mild diuretic called acetazolamide (Diamox), which should be started 24 hours before ascent and continued for 48 hours after arrival at altitude. Possible side effects include increased urination, numbness, tingling, nausea, drowsiness, nearsightedness and temporary impotence. For those who cannot tolerate acetazolamide, most physicians prescribe dexamethasone, which is a type of steroid. A natural alternative is gingko, which some people find quite helpful. The usual dosage is 100mg twice daily.

To lessen the chance of getting altitude sickness, you should also be sure to ascend gradually or by increments to higher altitudes, avoid overexertion, eat light meals and avoid alcohol.

If you or any of your companions show any symptoms of altitude sickness, you should be sure not to ascend to a higher altitude until the symptoms have cleared. If the symptoms become worse, immediately descend to a lower altitude. Acetazolamide and dexamethasone may be used to treat altitude sickness as well as prevent it.

Hypothermia

If you are hiking at high altitudes, be prepared. Symptoms of hypothermia are exhaustion, numb skin (particularly in the toes and fingers), shivering, slurred speech, irrational or violent behavior, lethargy, stumbling, dizzy spells, muscle cramps and violent bursts of energy. To treat mild hypothermia, first get the victim out of the wind and/or rain, remove their clothing if it is wet and replace it with dry, warm clothing. Give them hot liquids – not alcohol – and some high-energy, easily digestible food. Do not rub the victims instead, allow them to slowly warm themselves.

Parasites

Intestinal worms are most common in rural, tropical areas. Some worms, such as tapeworms, may be ingested by eating food such as undercooked meat, and some, such as hookworms, enter through your skin. Infestations may not show up for some time, and although they are generally not serious, if left untreated some can cause severe health problems later.

Consider having a stool test when you return home to check for these.

You should always check all over your body if you have been walking through a potentially tick-infested area, as ticks can cause skin infections and other, more serious, diseases.

Snakes

Ecuador has more than 200 species of snake, of which the majority are nonvenomous. Travelers are unlikely to encounter snakes.

To minimize your chances of being bitten, always wear boots, socks and long trousers when walking through undergrowth where snakes may be present. Don't put your hands into holes and crevices, and be careful when collecting firewood.

Snakebites do not cause instantaneous death, and antivenins are usually available. Immediately wrap the bitten limb tightly, as you would for a sprained ankle, and then attach a splint to immobilize it. Keep the victim still and seek medical help, bringing the dead snake, if possible, for identification. Don't attempt to catch the snake if there is a possibility of being bitten again. Tourniquets and sucking out the poison are now comprehensively discredited.

Water & Sun

The number one rule is *be careful drinking the water*. If you don't know for certain that the water is safe, assume the worst. Take care with fruit juice, particularly if water may have been added. Tea or coffee should also be OK, since the water should have been boiled. At altitudes greater than 2000m (6500ft), boil water for three minutes. Another option is to disinfect water with iodine pills.

In the tropics or at high altitudes you can get sunburned surprisingly quickly, even through cloud cover. Use sunblock, a hat and a barrier cream for your nose and lips. Calamine lotion or a commercial after-sun preparation are good for mild sunburn. Protect your eyes with good-quality sunglasses, particularly if you will be near water, sand or snow.

TRAVELING WITH CHILDREN

Travel with Children by Cathy Lanigan includes advice on travel health for younger children.

WOMEN'S HEALTH

Antibiotic use, synthetic underwear, sweating and contraceptive pills can lead to fungal vaginal infections when traveling in hot climates. Maintaining good personal hygiene, and wearing loose-fitting clothes and cotton underwear will help to prevent these.

Women who are pregnant need to take special care on the road. Most miscarriages occur during the first three months of pregnancy, so this is the most risky time to travel. The last three months should also be spent within reasonable reach of good medical care because serious problems can develop at this stage. Pregnant women should avoid all unnecessary medication, but vaccinations and malarial prophylactics should still be taken when possible.

Birth-control pills are readily available at pharmacies throughout Ecuador.

Tampons are harder to come by than pads (which are readily available), so bring your preferred brand from home if you use the former.

Language

CONTENTS

In Ecuador, as in most of Latin America, the official language is Spanish. However, travelers to the region will encounter a mix of other European tongues, indigenous languages and colorful dialects.

Most indigenous groups are bilingual, with Quichua (known as Quechua in Peru) being their mother tongue and Spanish their second language. There are also several small lowland groups that speak their own languages. The Quichua spoken in Ecuador is quite different from that spoken in Peru and Bolivia, so it can be difficult for highland natives from these countries to communicate easily. It's rare to encounter indigenous people who understand no Spanish at all, although they certainly exist in the more remote communities.

The basic elements of Spanish are easy to pick up, and a month-long language course taken before departure can go a long way toward facilitating communication and comfort on the road. Travelers who make the effort to learn a few basic phrases and pleasantries are met with enthusiasm and appreciation.

PHRASEBOOKS & DICTIONARIES

Lonely Planet's compact *Latin American Spanish Phrasebook* is an excellent addition to your backpack. Another useful resource is the University of Chicago's *Spanish–English, English–Spanish Dictionary* – with its small size, light weight and thorough entries, it's ideal for use when traveling. Upon your departure it can also make a welcome gift for any newfound friends.

Lonely Planet's *Quechua Phrasebook* is based on the Cuzco variety of the language (southern Quechua), but can still be useful in getting your basic message across, and any attempts to speak Quichua in Ecuador will be greatly appreciated. See the Quichua box above for a few Quichua basics.

QUICHUA

The following list of words and phrases is obviously minimal, but it could be useful in areas where Ecuadorian Quichua is spoken. Pronounce them as you would a Spanish word. An apostrophe represents a glottal stop, which is the 'nonsound' that occurs in the middle of 'uh-oh.'

Hello.	*Napaykullayki.*
Please.	*Allichu.*
Thank you.	*Yusulipayki.*
Yes/No.	*Ari/Mana.*
How do you say ...?	*Imainata nincha chaita ...?*
It is called ...	*Chaipa'g sutin'ha ...*
Please repeat.	*Ua'manta niway.*
How much?	*Maik'ata'g?*
father	*tayta*
food	*mikiuy*
mother	*mama*
river	*mayu*
snowy peak	*riti-orko*
water	*yacu*

1	*u'*
2	*iskai*
3	*quinsa*
4	*tahua*
5	*phiska*
6	*so'gta*
7	*khanchis*
8	*pusa'g*
9	*iskon*
10	*chunca*

ECUADORIAN SPANISH

The Spanish of Ecuador sounds different from the Spanish of Spain and it includes regional vocabulary, much of which is derived from indigenous languages. Throughout Latin America, the Spanish language is referred to as *castellano* more often than *español.* Unlike in Spain, the plural of the familiar 'you' *(tú)* is *ustedes* rather than *vosotros;* the latter term will sound quaint and archaic in the Americas. In addition, the letters **c** and **z** are never lisped in Latin America; attempts to do so could provoke amusement or even contempt.

PRONUNCIATION

Pronunciation of Spanish is not difficult. Many Spanish sounds are similar to their English counterparts, and the relationship between pronunciation and spelling is clear and consistent. Unless otherwise indicated, the English examples below take standard American pronunciation.

Vowels & Diphthongs

a	as in 'father'
e	as in 'met'
i	as the 'i' in 'police'
o	as in British English 'hot'
u	as the 'u' in 'rude'
ai	as in 'aisle'
au	as the 'ow' in 'how'
ei	as in 'vein'
ia	as the 'ya' in 'yard'
ie	as the 'ye' in 'yes'
oi	as in 'coin'
ua	as the 'wa' in 'wash'
ue	as the 'we' in 'well'

Consonants

Spanish consonants are generally the same as in English, with the exception of those listed below.

The consonants **ch**, **ll** and **ñ** are generally considered distinct letters, but in dictionaries **ch** and **ll** are now often listed alphabetically under **c** and **l** respectively. The letter **ñ** still has a separate entry in alphabetical listings (after **n**).

b	similar to English 'b,' but softer; referred to as 'b larga'
c	as in 'celery' before **e** and **i**; elsewhere as the 'k' in 'king'
ch	as in 'choose'
d	as in 'dog'; between vowels and after **l** or **n**, it's closer to the 'th' in 'this'
g	as in 'go'; as the 'ch' in the Scottish *loch* before **e** and **i** ('kh' in our pronunciation guides)
h	invariably silent
j	as the 'ch' in the Scottish *loch* ('kh' in our pronunciation guides)
ll	as the 'y' in 'yellow'
ñ	as the 'ni' in 'onion'
r	as in 'run,' but strongly rolled
rr	very strongly rolled
v	similar to English 'b,' but softer; referred to as 'b corta'
x	usually pronounced as **j** above; as in 'taxi' in some instances
z	as the 's' in 'sun'

Word Stress

In general, words ending in vowels or the letters **n** or **s** are stressed on the second-last syllable, while those with other endings have stress on the last syllable. Thus *vaca* (cow) and *caballos* (horses) are both stressed on the next-to-last syllable, while *ciudad* (city) and *infeliz* (unhappy) are stressed on the last syllable.

Written accents generally indicate words that don't follow the rules above, eg *sótano* (basement), *América* and *porción* (portion).

GENDER & PLURALS

Spanish nouns are either masculine or feminine, and there are ways to help determine gender (there are of course some exceptions). Feminine nouns generally end with **-a** or with the groups **-ción**, **-sión** or **-dad**. Other endings typically signify a masculine noun. Endings for adjectives also change to agree with the gender of the noun they modify (masculine/feminine singular **-o**/**-a**). Where both masculine and feminine forms are included in this language guide, they are separated by a slash, with the masculine form given first, eg *perdido/a* (lost).

If a noun or adjective ends in a vowel, the plural is formed by adding **s** to the end. If it ends in a consonant, the plural is formed by adding **es** to the end.

ACCOMMODATIONS

Are there any rooms available?

¿Hay habitaciones libres? ai a·bee·ta·*syo*·nes *lee*·bres

MAKING A RESERVATION
(for phone or written requests)

To ...	*A ...*
From ...	*De ...*
Date	*Fecha*
I'd like to book ...	*Quisiera reservar ...*
in the name of ...	*en nombre de ...*
for the nights of ...	*para las noches del ...*
credit card ...	*tarjeta de crédito ...*
number	*número*
expiry date	*fecha de vencimiento*
Please confirm ...	*Puede confirmar ...*
availability	*la disponibilidad*
price	*el precio*

I'm looking for ...
Estoy buscando ... es·*toy* boos·*kan*·do ...
Where is ...?
¿Dónde hay ...? *don*·de ai ...
a hotel
un hotel oon o·*tel*
a boarding house
una pensión *oo*·na pen·*syon*
a youth hostel
un albergue juvenil oon al·*ber*·ge khoo·ve·*neel*

I'd like a ... room.	*Quisiera una habitación ...*	kee·*sye*·ra *oo*·na a·bee·ta·*syon* ...
double	*doble*	*do*·ble
single	*individual*	een·dee·bee·*dwal*
twin	*con dos camas*	kon dos *ka*·mas
How much is it per ...?	*¿Cuánto cuesta por ...?*	*kwan*·to *kwes*·ta por ...
night	*noche*	*no*·che
person	*persona*	per·*so*·na
week	*semana*	se·*ma*·na
private/shared bathroom	*baño privado/ compartido*	*ba*·nyo pree·*va*·do/ kom·par·*tee*·do
full board	*pensión completa*	pen·*syon* kom·*ple*·ta
too expensive	*demasiado caro*	de·ma·*sya*·do *ka*·ro
cheaper	*más económico*	mas e·ko·*no*·mee·ko
discount	*descuento*	des·*kwen*·to

May I see the room?
¿Puedo ver la habitación? *pwe*·do ver la a·bee·ta·*syon*
Does it include breakfast?
¿Incluye el desayuno? een·*kloo*·ye el de·sa·*yoo*·no
I don't like it.
No me gusta. no me *goos*·ta
It's fine. I'll take it.
OK. La alquilo. o·*kay* la al·*kee*·lo
I'm leaving now.
Me voy ahora. me voy a·o·ra

CONVERSATION & ESSENTIALS

Hello.	*Hola.*	*o*·la
Good morning.	*Buenos días.*	*bwe*·nos *dee*·as
Good afternoon.	*Buenas tardes.*	*bwe*·nas *tar*·des
Good evening/ night.	*Buenas noches.*	*bwe*·nas *no*·ches
Bye/See you soon.	*Hasta luego.*	*as*·ta *lwe*·go
Goodbye.	*Adios.*	a·*dyos*
Yes.	*Sí.*	see
No.	*No.*	no
Please.	*Por favor.*	por fa·*vor*
Thank you.	*Gracias.*	*gra*·syas
Many thanks.	*Muchas gracias.*	*moo*·chas *gra*·syas
You're welcome.	*De nada.*	de *na*·da
Pardon me.	*Perdón.*	per·*don*
Excuse me. (used when asking permission)	*Permiso.*	per·*mee*·so
Forgive me. (used when apologizing)	*Disculpe.*	dees·*kool*·pe

How are things?
¿Qué tal? ke tal
What's your name?
¿Cómo se llama? (pol) *ko*·mo se *ya*·ma
¿Cómo te llamas? (inf) *ko*·mo te *ya*·mas
My name is ...
Me llamo ... me *ya*·mo ...
It's a pleasure to meet you.
Mucho gusto. *moo*·cho *goos*·to
The pleasure is mine.
El gusto es mío. el *goos*·to es *mee*·o
Where are you from?
¿De dónde es? (pol) de *don*·de es
¿De dónde eres? (inf) de *don*·de *e*·res
I'm from ...
Soy de ... soy de ...
Where are you staying?
¿Dónde está alojado/a? (pol) *don*·de es·*ta* a·lo·*kha*·do/a
¿Dónde estás alojado/a? (inf) *don*·de es·*tas* a·lo·*kha*·do/a
May I take a photo?
¿Puedo sacar una foto? *pwe*·do sa·*kar* *oo*·na *fo*·to

DIRECTIONS

How do I get to ...?
¿Cómo puedo llegar a ...? *ko*·mo *pwe*·do ye·*gar* a ...
Is it far?
¿Está lejos? es·*ta* *le*·khos

EMERGENCIES

Help!	*¡Socorro!*	so·*ko*·ro
Fire!	*¡Fuego!*	*fwe*·go
Go away!	*¡Déjeme!*	*de*·khe·me
Get lost!	*¡Váyase!*	*va*·ya·se
Call ...!	*¡Llame a ...!*	*ya*·me a ...
an ambulance	*una ambulancia*	*oo*·na am·boo·*lan*·sya
a doctor	*un médico*	oon *me*·dee·ko
the police	*la policía*	la po·lee·*see*·a

It's an emergency.
Es una emergencia. es *oo*·na e·mer·*khen*·sya

Could you help me, please?
¿Me puede ayudar, por favor? me *pwe*·de a·yoo·*dar* por fa·*vor*

I'm lost.
Estoy perdido/a. es·*toy* per·*dee*·do/a

Where are the toilets?
¿Dónde están los baños? *don*·de es·*tan* los *ba*·nyos

Go straight ahead.
Siga derecho. *see*·ga de·*re*·cho

Turn left.
Voltée a la izquierda. vol·*te*·e a la ees·*kyer*·da

Turn right.
Voltée a la derecha. vol·*te*·e a la de·*re*·cha

Can you show me (on the map)?
¿Me lo podría indicar (en el mapa)? me lo po·*dree*·a een·dee·*kar* (en el *ma*·pa)

north	*norte*	*nor*·te
south	*sur*	soor
east	*este*	*es*·te
west	*oeste*	o·*es*·te
here	*aquí*	a·*kee*
there	*allí*	a·*yee*
avenue	*avenida*	a·ve·*nee*·da
block	*cuadra*	*kwa*·dra
street	*calle*	*ka*·ye

HEALTH

I'm sick.
Estoy enfermo/a. es·*toy* en·*fer*·mo/a

I need a doctor.
Necesito un médico. ne·se·*see*·to oon *me*·dee·ko

Where's the hospital?
¿Dónde está el hospital? *don*·de es·*ta* el os·pee·*tal*

I'm pregnant.
Estoy embarazada. es·*toy* em·ba·ra·*sa*·da

I've been vaccinated.
Estoy vacunado/a. es·*toy* va·koo·*na*·do/a

I'm ...	*Soy ...*	soy ...
asthmatic	*asmático/a*	as·*ma*·tee·ko/a
diabetic	*diabético/a*	dee·ya·*be*·tee·ko/a
epileptic	*epiléptico/a*	e·pee·*lep*·tee·ko/a
I'm allergic to ...	*Soy alérgico/a a ...*	soy a·*ler*·khee·ko/a a ...
antibiotics	*los antibióticos*	los an·tee·*byo*·tee·kos
nuts	*las frutas secas*	las *froo*·tas *se*·kas
penicillin	*la penicilina*	la pe·nee·see·*lee*·na
I have ...	*Tengo ...*	*ten*·go ...
a cough	*tos*	tos
diarrhea	*diarrea*	dya·*re*·a
a headache	*un dolor de cabeza*	oon do·*lor* de ka·*be*·sa
nausea	*náusea*	*now*·se·a

LANGUAGE DIFFICULTIES

Do you speak (English)?
¿Habla/Hablas (inglés)? *a*·bla/*a*·blas (een·*gles*) (pol/inf)

Does anyone here speak English?
¿Hay alguien que hable inglés? ai *al*·gyen ke *a*·ble een·*gles*

I (don't) understand.
(No) Entiendo. (no) en·*tyen*·do

How do you say ...?
¿Cómo se dice ...? *ko*·mo se *dee*·se ...

What does ... mean?
¿Qué quiere decir ...? ke *kye*·re de·*seer* ...

Could you please ...?	*¿Puede ..., por favor?*	*pwe*·de ... por fa·*vor*
repeat that	*repetirlo*	re·pe·*teer*·lo
speak more slowly	*hablar más despacio*	a·*blar* mas des·*pa*·syo
write it down	*escribirlo*	es·kree·*beer*·lo

NUMBERS

0	*cero*	*se*·ro
1	*uno/a*	*oo*·no/a
2	*dos*	dos
3	*tres*	tres
4	*cuatro*	*kwa*·tro
5	*cinco*	*seen*·ko
6	*seis*	seys
7	*siete*	*sye*·te
8	*ocho*	*o*·cho
9	*nueve*	*nwe*·ve
10	*diez*	dyes
11	*once*	*on*·se
12	*doce*	*do*·se
13	*trece*	*tre*·se
14	*catorce*	ka·*tor*·se

SIGNS

Entrada	Entrance
Salida	Exit
Abierto	Open
Cerrado	Closed
Prohibido	Prohibited
Comisaría	Police Station
Servicios/Baños	Toilets
Hombres/Varones	Men
Mujeres/Damas	Women

15	*quince*	keen·se
16	*dieciséis*	dye·see·*seys*
17	*diecisiete*	dye·see·*sye*·te
18	*dieciocho*	dye·see·*o*·cho
19	*diecinueve*	dye·see·*nwe*·ve
20	*veinte*	*vayn*·te
21	*veintiuno*	vayn·tee·*oo*·no
30	*treinta*	*trayn*·ta
31	*treinta y uno*	*trayn*·tai *oo*·no
40	*cuarenta*	kwa·*ren*·ta
50	*cincuenta*	seen·*kwen*·ta
60	*sesenta*	se·*sen*·ta
70	*setenta*	se·*ten*·ta
80	*ochenta*	o·*chen*·ta
90	*noventa*	no·*ven*·ta
100	*cien*	syen
200	*doscientos*	do·*syen*·tos
1000	*mil*	meel

SHOPPING & SERVICES

I'm looking for (the) ...	*Estoy buscando ...*	es·*toy* boos·*kan*·do ...
ATM	*el cajero automático*	el ka·*khe*·ro ow·to·*ma*·tee·ko
bank	*el banco*	el *ban*·ko
bookstore	*la librería*	la lee·bre·*ree*·a
embassy	*la embajada*	la em·ba·*kha*·da
exchange office	*la casa de cambio*	la *ka*·sa de *kam*·byo
general store	*la tienda*	la *tyen*·da
laundry	*la lavandería*	la la·van·de·*ree*·a
market	*el mercado*	el mer·*ka*·do
pharmacy	*la farmacia/ la droguería*	la far·*ma*·sya/ la dro·ge·*ree*·a
post office	*los correos*	los ko·*re*·os
supermarket	*el supermercado*	el soo·per·mer·*ka*·do
tourist office	*la oficina de turismo*	la o·fee·*see*·na de too·*rees*·mo

I'd like to buy ...
Quisiera comprar ... kee·*sye*·ra kom·*prar* ...

I'm just looking.
Sólo estoy mirando. so·lo es·*toy* mee·*ran*·do
May I look at it?
¿Puedo mirarlo? *pwe*·do mee·*rar*·lo
How much is it?
¿Cuánto cuesta? *kwan*·to *kwes*·ta
I don't like it.
No me gusta. no me *goos*·ta
That's too expensive for me.
Es demasiado caro para mí. es de·ma·*sya*·do *ka*·ro *pa*·ra mee
Could you lower the price?
¿Podría bajar un poco el precio? po·*dree*·a ba·*khar* oon *po*·ko el *pre*·syo
I'll take it.
Lo llevo. lo *ye*·vo

less	*menos*	*me*·nos
more	*más*	mas
large	*grande*	*gran*·de
small	*pequeño*	pe·*ke*·nyo

Do you accept ...?	*¿Aceptan ...?*	a·*sep*·tan ...
credit cards	*tarjetas de crédito*	tar·*khe*·tas de *kre*·dee·to
traveler's checks	*cheques de viajero*	*che*·kes de vya·*khe*·ro

What time does it open/close?
¿A qué hora abre/cierra? a ke *o*·ra *a*·bre/*sye*·ra
I want to change some money/traveler's checks.
Quiero cambiar dinero/ cheques de viajero. *kye*·ro kam·*byar* dee·*ne*·ro/ *che*·kes de vya·*khe*·ro
What's the exchange rate?
¿Cuál es el tipo de cambio? kwal es el *tee*·po de *kam*·byo
I want to call ...
Quiero llamar a ... *kye*·ro ya·*mar* a ...

airmail	*correo aéreo*	ko·*re*·o a·*e*·re·o
letter	*carta*	*kar*·ta
registered mail	*certificado*	ser·tee·fee·*ka*·do
stamps	*estampillas*	es·tam·*pee*·yas

TIME & DATES

What time is it?	*¿Qué hora es?*	ke *o*·ra es
It's (one) o'clock.	*Es la (una).*	es la (*oo*·na)
It's (seven) o'clock.	*Son las (siete).*	son las (*sye*·te)

half-past two	*dos y media*	dos ee *me*·dya
midnight	*medianoche*	me·dya·*no*·che
noon	*mediodía*	me·dyo·*dee*·a
now	*ahora*	a·*o*·ra

LANGUAGE

today	*hoy*	oy
tonight	*esta noche*	*es*·ta *no*·che
tomorrow	*mañana*	ma·*nya*·na
yesterday	*ayer*	a·*yer*

Monday	*lunes*	*loo*·nes
Tuesday	*martes*	*mar*·tes
Wednesday	*miércoles*	*myer*·ko·les
Thursday	*jueves*	*khwe*·ves
Friday	*viernes*	*vyer*·nes
Saturday	*sábado*	*sa*·ba·do
Sunday	*domingo*	do·*meen*·go

January	*enero*	e·*ne*·ro
February	*febrero*	fe·*bre*·ro
March	*marzo*	*mar*·so
April	*abril*	a·*breel*
May	*mayo*	*ma*·yo
June	*junio*	*khoo*·nyo
July	*julio*	*khoo*·lyo
August	*agosto*	a·*gos*·to
September	*septiembre*	sep·*tyem*·bre
October	*octubre*	ok·*too*·bre
November	*noviembre*	no·*vyem*·bre
December	*diciembre*	dee·*syem*·bre

TRANSPORTATION

Public Transportation

What time does ... leave/ arrive?	*¿A qué hora ... sale/llega?*	a ke *o*·ra ... *sa*·le/*ye*·ga
the bus	*el autobus*	el ow·to·*boos*
the plane	*el avión*	el a·*vyon*
the ship	*el barco*	el *bar*·ko

airport	*el aeropuerto*	el a·e·ro·*pwer*·to
bus station	*terminal terrestre*	ter·mee·*nal* te·*res*·tre
bus stop	*la parada de autobuses*	la pa·*ra*·da de ow·to·*boo*·ses
luggage check room	*guardería/ equipaje*	gwar·de·*ree*·a/ e·kee·*pa*·khe
ticket office	*la boletería*	la bo·le·te·*ree*·a

I'd like a ticket to ...
Quiero un boleto a ... — *kye*·ro oon bo·*le*·to a ...

What's the fare to ...?
¿Cuánto cuesta hasta ...? — *kwan*·to *kwes*·ta *as*·ta ...

student's (fare)	*de estudiante*	de es·too·*dyan*·te
1st class	*ejecutivo*	e·khe·ku·*tee*·vo
one-way	*ida*	*ee*·da
return	*ida y vuelta*	*ee*·da ee *vwel*·ta
taxi	*taxi*	*tak*·see

ROAD SIGNS

Acceso	Entrance
Aparcamiento	Parking
Ceda el Paso	Give Way
Despacio	Slow
Dirección Única	One-Way
Mantenga Su Derecha	Keep to the Right
No Adelantar/No Rebase	No Passing
Peaje	Toll
Peligro	Danger
Prohibido Aparcar/ No Estacionar	No Parking
Prohibido el Paso	No Entry
Pare	Stop
Salida de Autopista	Exit Freeway

Private Transportation

pickup (truck)	*camioneta*	ka·myo·*ne*·ta
truck	*camión*	ka·*myon*
hitchhike	*hacer dedo*	a·*ser de*·do

I'd like to hire a/an ...	*Quisiera alquilar ...*	kee·*sye*·ra al·kee·*lar* ...
bicycle	*una bicicleta*	*oo*·na bee·see·*kle*·ta
car	*un auto/ un coche*	oon *ow*·to/ oon *ko*·che
4WD	*un todo terreno*	oon *to*·do te·*re*·no
motorbike	*una moto*	*oo*·na *mo*·to

Is this the road to ...?
¿Se va a ... por esta carretera? — se va a ... por *es*·ta ka·re·*te*·ra

Where's a gas/petrol station?
¿Dónde hay una gasolinera? — *don*·de ai *oo*·na ga·so·lee·*ne*·ra

Please fill it up.
Lleno, por favor. — *ye*·no por fa·*vor*

I'd like (10) gallons.
Quiero (diez) galones. — *kye*·ro (dyes) ga·*lo*·nes

diesel	*diesel*	*dee*·sel
gas/petrol	*gasolina*	ga·so·*lee*·na
unleaded	*gasolina sin plomo*	ga·so·*lee*·na seen *plo*·mo

(How long) Can I park here?
¿(Por cuánto tiempo) Puedo aparcar aquí? — (por *kwan*·to *tyem*·po) *pwe*·do a·par·*kar* a·*kee*

Where do I pay?
¿Dónde se paga? — *don*·de se *pa*·ga

I need a mechanic.
Necesito un mecánico. — ne·se·*see*·to oon me·*ka*·nee·ko

The car has broken down in ...
El coche se ha averiado en ... — el *ko*·che se a a·ve·*rya*·do en ...

The motorbike won't start.
No arranca la moto. — no a·*ran*·ka la *mo*·to

I have a flat tire.
Tengo un pinchazo. — *ten*·go oon peen·*cha*·so

I've run out of gas/petrol.
Me quedé sin gasolina. — me ke·*de* seen ga·so·*lee*·na

I've had an accident.
Tuve un accidente. — *too*·ve oon ak·see·*den*·te

TRAVEL WITH CHILDREN

I need ...
Necesito ... — ne·se·*see*·to ...

Do you have ...?
¿Hay ...? — ai ...

a car baby seat
un asiento de seguridad para bebés
oon a·*syen*·to de se·goo·ree·*da* *pa*·ra be·*bes*

a child-minding service
un servicio de cuidado de niños
oon ser·*vee*·syo de kwee·*da*·do de *nee*·nyos

a children's menu
una carta infantil
oo·na *kar*·ta een·fan·*teel*

a day nursery
una guardería
oo·na gwar·de·*ree*·a

(disposable) diapers/nappies
pañales (de usar y tirar)
pa·*nya*·les (de oo·*sar* ee tee·*rar*)

a/an (English-speaking) babysitter
una niñera (que habla inglesa)
oo·na nee·*nye*·ra (ke *a*·bla een·*gle*·sa)

infant formula (milk)
leche en polvo para bebés
le·che en *pol*·vo *pa*·ra be·*bes*

a high chair
una trona
oo·na *tro*·na

a potty (toddler's portable toilet)
una pelela
oo·na pe·*le*·la

a stroller
un cochecito
oon ko·che·*see*·to

Do you mind if I breastfeed here?
¿Le molesta que dé de pecho aquí? — le mo·*les*·ta ke *de* de *pe*·cho a·*kee*

Are children allowed?
¿Se admiten niños? — se ad·*mee*·ten *nee*·nyos

Also available from Lonely Planet:
Latin American Spanish Phrasebook

Glossary

For help translating eating- and drinking-related words and phrases, see p51.

abrazo – backslapping hug exchanged between men
AGAR – Asociación de Guías de Aguas Rapidas del Ecuador (Ecuadorian White-Water Guides Association)
aguardiente – sugarcane alcohol
ASEGUIM – Asociación Ecuatoriana de Guías de Montaña (Ecuadorian Mountain Guides Association)

balneario – literally 'spa', but any place where you can swim or soak

cabaña – cabin, found both on the coast and in the Oriente
camioneta – pickup or light truck
campesino – peasant
capitanía – port captain
casa de cambio – currency-exchange bureau
centro comercial – shopping center; often abbreviated to 'CC'
chifa – Chinese restaurant
chiva – open-sided bus, or truck mounted with uncomfortably narrow bench seats; also called *ranchera*
colectivo – shared taxi
comedore – cheap restaurant
comida típica – typical Ecuadorian cuisine
costeño – person from the coast
cuencano – person from Cuenca
curandero – medicine man

ejecutivo – 1st class, on buses

folklórica – traditional Andean folk music

guayaquileño – person from Guayaquil

hostal – small and reasonably priced hotel; not a youth hostel
hostería – small hotel, which tends to be a midpriced country inn; often, but not always, found in rural areas

IGM – Instituto Geográfico Militar, the Ecuadorian government agency that produces topographic and other maps
indígena – indigenous person

lavandería – laundry

malecón – waterfront
mestizo – person of mixed indigenous and Spanish descent
migraciones – immigration offices

otavaleño – person from Otavalo

paja toquilla – straw from the *toquilla* (a small palm), used in crafts and hat making
Panamericana – Pan-American Hwy, which is the main route joining Latin American countries to one another; known as the Interamericana in some countries
panga – small boat used to ferry passengers, especially in the Galápagos Islands, but also on the rivers and lakes of the Oriente and along the coast
páramo – high-altitude Andean grasslands of Ecuador, which continue north into Colombia with relicts in the highest parts of Costa Rica
parque nacional – national park
pasillo – Ecuador's national music
peña – bar or club featuring live folkloric music
playa – beach
puente – bridge

quinta – fine house or villa found in the countryside
quiteño – person from Quito

ranchera – see *chiva*
refugio – simple mountain shelters for spending the night
residencial – cheap hotel

salsoteca – (also *salsateca*) nightclub where dancing to salsa music is the main attraction
serranos – people from the highlands
servicio – service charge
shigra – small string bag

tagua nut – from a palm tree grown in local forest; the 'nuts' are actually hard seeds, which are carved into a variety of ornaments
terminal terrestre – central bus terminal for many different companies
tzantza – shrunken head

The Authors

REGIS ST LOUIS **Coordinating Author, Quito, North Coast & Lowlands**

After Regis' first journey to the Andes in 1999, he returned home, sold all his belongings and set off on a classic journey across South America. Since then he's returned numerous times to travel the continent, logging thousands of miles on dodgy jungle and mountain roads, and he's learned to speak Spanish and Portuguese. Ecuador never fails to captivate Regis, and he spent his most recent trip exploring the rarely visited jungle towns of the north coast. Regis is the coordinating author of *South America on a Shoestring*, and he has contributed to more than a dozen Lonely Planet guides. His work has appeared in the *Chicago Tribune* and the *Los Angeles Times*, among other publications. He lives in New York City.

LUCY BURNINGHAM **Northern Highlands, The Oriente**

Lucy first explored Ecuador in 2004 between magazine-editor jobs – the trip that inspired her freelance career. She gladly returned for Lonely Planet, an opportunity to befriend a pair of rubber boots and eat copious quantities of highland fruits. As an independent journalist with a master's degree in nonfiction writing, she has written for a variety of publications, including the *New York Times*, *Imbibe* and *Men's Journal*. When she's not pursuing stories at home or abroad, Lucy enjoys wearing out running shoes and sampling the beers of Portland, Oregon, where she lives with her husband and their fleet of bicycles.

AIMÉE DOWL **Central Highlands, Southern Highlands**

By canoe, plane, bicycle, horse, 4WD or her own two feet, Aimée Dowl has set down in every one of Ecuador's 24 provinces. These journeys have taken her along the Inca Trail, into tiny indigenous communities, up glaciered Andean volcanoes, over precarious avalanches, and into the wettest jungles on earth. From her high-altitude home in Quito, Aimée works as a freelance travel and culture writer, and her articles have appeared in the *New York Times*, *Viajes*, *Ms.* magazine and *BBC History*.

LONELY PLANET AUTHORS

Why is our travel information the best in the world? It's simple: our authors are passionate, dedicated travelers. They don't take freebies in exchange for positive coverage so you can be sure the advice you're given is impartial. They travel widely to all the popular spots, and off the beaten track. They don't research using just the internet or phone. They discover new places not included in any other guidebook. They personally visit thousands of hotels, restaurants, palaces, trails, galleries, temples and more. They speak with dozens of locals every day to make sure you get the kind of insider knowledge only a local could tell you. They take pride in getting all the details right, and in telling it how it is. Think you can do it? Find out how at **lonelyplanet.com**.

MICHAEL GROSBERG

South Coast, Galápagos Islands

After a childhood spent stateside in the Washington, DC area and with a valuable philosophy degree in hand, Michael has had many careers, from business on a small Pacific island to journalism and NGO work in South Africa. He returned to New York City (NYC) for graduate school in comparative literature focusing on Latin America, and spent a summer teaching in Quito and traveling through much of Ecuador. After a few years of teaching literature and writing in several NYC colleges he's since been back to Ecuador and other countries in the region for pleasure and for other Lonely Planet assignments.

CONTRIBUTING AUTHOR

Dr David Goldberg MD wrote the Health chapter. David completed his training in internal medicine and infectious diseases at Columbia-Presbyterian Medical Center in New York City, where he has also served as voluntary faculty. At present he is an infectious-diseases specialist in Scarsdale, New York State, and the editor-in-chief of the website MDTravelHealth.com.

Behind the Scenes

THIS BOOK

This is the 8th edition of *Ecuador & the Galápagos Islands*. Regis St Louis served as coordinating author, writing all of the front and back chapters as well as the Quito and North Coast & Lowlands chapters. Lucy Burningham covered the Northern Highlands and Oriente chapters. Aimée Dowl researched and wrote the Central Highlands and Southern Highlands chapters. Michael Grosberg covered the South Coast and Galápagos Islands chapters. Dr David Goldberg MD contributed the Health chapter. The previous edition of this book was written by Danny Palmerlee, Michael Grosberg and Carolyn McCarthy. Danny Palmerlee and Rob Rachowiecki wrote the 6th edition, and Rob Rachowiecki wrote the first five editions. This guidebook was commissioned in Lonely Planet's Oakland office, and produced by the following:

Commissioning Editors Jay Cooke, Catherine Craddock, Kathleen Munnelly
Coordinating Editor Penelope Goodes
Coordinating Cartographer Bonnie Wintler
Coordinating Layout Designers Nicholas Colicchia, Indra Kilfoyle
Managing Editor Imogen Bannister
Managing Cartographers Shahara Ahmed, Alison Lyall
Managing Layout Designer Sally Darmody
Assisting Editors Judith Bamber, Rebecca Chau, Kate Evans, Kim Hutchins, Simon Sellars
Assisting Cartographers Ross Butler, Corey Hutchison, Andy Rojas, Andrew Smith, Tom Webster
Cover Designer Jane Hart
Project Manager Fabrice Rocher
Language Content Coordinator Quentin Frayne, Branislava Vladisavljevic
Thanks to Jessica Boland, David Connolly, Chris Girdler, Brice Gosnell, Martin Heng, Glenn van der Knijff, Raphael Richards

THANKS

REGIS ST LOUIS

At Lonely Planet, I'd like to thank hardworking in-house staff, especially Kathleen Munnelly for her tireless dedication. On the road, I'd like to thank Silvia Freire for a fascinating tour in Quito; Santiago and friends at the Blue House; Ruby, Gabi and Shanti at Casa de Amigos in Same; Rick and Holly in Quito; Natalia and Viviana for nightlife tips in Manta; and Tony at Cafecito for insight into the best of Quito. Big thanks to Esto es Eso stars Max and Luís for a fine interview (and a fun night) at Ananké. Heartfelt thanks to Cassandra and Magdalena, for their continued love

THE LONELY PLANET STORY

Fresh from an epic journey across Europe, Asia and Australia in 1972, Tony and Maureen Wheeler sat at their kitchen table stapling together notes. The first Lonely Planet guidebook, *Across Asia on the Cheap,* was born.

Travelers snapped up the guides. Inspired by their success, the Wheelers began publishing books to Southeast Asia, India and beyond. Demand was prodigious, and the Wheelers expanded the business rapidly to keep up. Over the years, Lonely Planet extended its coverage to every country and into the virtual world via lonelyplanet.com and the Thorn Tree message board.

As Lonely Planet became a globally loved brand, Tony and Maureen received several offers for the company. But it wasn't until 2007 that they found a partner whom they trusted to remain true to the company's principles of traveling widely, treading lightly and giving sustainably. In October of that year, BBC Worldwide acquired a 75% share in the company, pledging to uphold Lonely Planet's commitment to independent travel, trustworthy advice and editorial independence.

Today, Lonely Planet has offices in Melbourne, London and Oakland, with over 500 staff members and 300 authors. Tony and Maureen are still actively involved with Lonely Planet. They're traveling more often than ever, and they're devoting their spare time to charitable projects. And the company is still driven by the philosophy of *Across Asia on the Cheap*: 'All you've got to do is decide to go and the hardest part is over. So go!'

and support throughout the exciting Lonely Planet journey.

LUCY BURNINGHAM

I couldn't have done it without my husband Tony, who supports me during all my adventures, especially this one, just three weeks after our wedding. Thanks to Tom and Mariela in Mindo, Jairon Garzon, William in Ibarra, Gary Dent and his family, all the guides along the Rio Napo, especially Juan at Sani, Deon Duncan, Sophie Mather, Rachel Bagley, my fellow Portland LPers, coauthor Aimée Dowl and editor Kathleen Munnelly. Thanks to all the strangers I met on the road, who treated me with much kindness and hospitality, and my friends and family for their constant encouragement.

AIMÉE DOWL

Many thanks to the pioneers on the Quilotoa loop, Michelle and Andy; Catherine and Boudewijn in Zamora; Rebecca and Doug in Baños; Lou Jost, Paul J Greenfield and other scientists and conservationists who schooled me; to David Moscoso and Esteban Pozo in Ambato for a wonderful day; Mark Thurber for trail advice; and the Divino Boy, who never ceased to be there, arms outstretched. *Un montó'n de agradecimientos* to Ruti Vela, an Ecuadorian lady who taught me Spanish years ago and then became a friend – I wouldn't know much without you. To Derek Kverno, my partner in all things and intrepid navigator of broken roads, thanks for keeping us safe and amused, from the Smooth Neck of the Moon to the Devil's Nose! *¡Pite y pase, mi amor!* To the people of Ecuador, who adopted a new constitution during the research of this book, thanks for your wonderful example of hope and belief in a better future.

MICHAEL GROSBERG

Gracias go out to fellow Galápagos boat passengers Kevin Wiggen, Dylan, Louise, Kim and Odette for keeping things fun and their bravery in the face of mediocre buffet food; to Maria Antonieta Rueda for her knowledge and experience of the islands and helping ensure my plans went smoothly; to Edgardo for sharing a harrowing drive along southern Ecuador's roadways; to the easygoing group of surfers in Montañita who encouraged a beginner; to my niece, the Sashmeister and nephew Nono, who I promised stuffed-animal penguins, and to Rebecca Tessler for her continued courage and inspiration.

OUR READERS

Many thanks to the travelers who used the last edition and wrote to us with helpful hints, useful advice and interesting anecdotes:

Dino 1993 **A** Nelleke Aben, Jorgen Abrahamsson, Fredy Alfaro, Mary Jo Allen, Chris Andrews, Suzie Anon Y Garcia **B** Eleni Bachlava, Joel Baehr, Walter Baer, Marie-Kristin Baier, Patrick Barnett, Tina Barrett, Andre Barthelemy, Mandy Bartok, Mary Belvoir, Simon Berglund, Matthew Bertrand, Nicole Beyeler, Melanie Bieger, Jan Joost Bierhoff, Kathleen Bird, Iain Bisset, Stig Arve Bjånesøy, Jane Blackmore, Andrea Blaser, Jessica Blick, Peter Blincowe, Ken Blum, Carlos Bolaños, Tad Boniecki, John Bowen, Jerry Brooks, Susan Brown, Françoise Brown, Kat Brown, Ian Brownlee, Kerstin Brueckner, Gonda Bruijn, Julie Burley **C** Julian Callaghan, Ms Canicolai, Robert Capelli, Olivier Carron, Diane Caulkett, David Childs, Larisa Clarke, Jean Colvin, Tom Connell, Alicia Cooperman, Dan Coplan, Karina Cote, Benjamin Craigen, Janet And John Croft **D** Laura Dalby, Inbal Danan, Stuart Davis, Simon De Baat, Reinout De Bock, Nellie De Coloma, Ruud De Dood, Hans De Schryver, Paul De Vries, Benjamin Deissler, Manuel Denner, Tom Derks, Megan Dickie, Debra Dipple, David Doyon, Derek Drager, Steve Dretz, Lee Dubs, Anne Durston **E** Roland Ehrat, Lesley Elphick, William English, Monica Esgueva, Renato Espinoza, Carmen Estermann, Judy Evans **F** Cyril Faivre, Joos Feenstra, Marvin Feldman, Jennifer Fleetwood, Gary Fogelman, Luisa Frescura, Vaz Frigerio, Sharon Fueller **G** Sarah Gannon, Ronald Garconius, Angela Gehrels, Richard George, Pierre-Rudolf Gerlach, Anna Grady, Janna Graeger, Martina Grahl,

SEND US YOUR FEEDBACK

We love to hear from travelers – your comments keep us on our toes and help make our books better. Our well-traveled team reads every word on what you loved or loathed about this book. Although we cannot reply individually to postal submissions, we always guarantee that your feedback goes straight to the appropriate authors, in time for the next edition. Each person who sends us information is thanked in the next edition – and the most useful submissions are rewarded with a free book.

To send us your updates – and find out about Lonely Planet events, newsletters and travel news – visit our award-winning website: **lonelyplanet.com/contact**.

Note: we may edit, reproduce and incorporate your comments in Lonely Planet products such as guidebooks, websites and digital products, so let us know if you don't want your comments reproduced or your name acknowledged. For a copy of our privacy policy visit lonelyplanet.com/privacy.

Paul Gunn **H** Peter Haberfeld, David Hagen, Taylor Hahn, Imke Hahn, Amy Halls, Yuki Haruyama, Craig Hauger, Laura Heckman, Jessica Heiler, Anna Helms, Gregor Henneka, Chris Henrion, Joanne Heraty, Manuel Hernandez Macias, Tom Hogan, Grainne Holohan, Eric Von Horstman, Michael Howard, Jess Hugi, Mollie Hull, Marion Hunger, Maria Hurtado **I** Sindy Irmscher **J** Shelley Jackson, Frank Jansen, Juan Carlos Jaramillo, Karen Jescavage-Bernard **K** Sonia Kasten, Janine Kelso, T J Kemoly, Denis Kennedy, John Key, Yvonne Kiener, Sarah Koch **L** Suzi Lancaster, Daniel Lang, Gjert Langseth, Beatrice Lemucchi, Matan Levinson, Lynne Lichtenstein, Jorgen Lindeborg, Stephanie Lindinger, Jorge Lombeida, Sanna Lonqvist, Cathal Loughney, James Lucas **M** Heidi Maki, Andy May, Fiona Mcgarry, Malcolm Mckinnon, Isaac Menashe, Carolin Meyer, Viekko Miettiueup, Aaron Mills, Astley Milne, Lucre Minondo, Laurel Mitchell, Liliane Mollet, Juno Moore, Umberto Morelli, Michele Morris, Fernando Moscoso, Peter Mosmans, Julia Mueller, Subir Mukerjee, Roberto Muller, Tom Munro, Thomas Muse, Daniel Musikant **N** Mark Nassutti, Matt Nawrocki, Emma Naylor, Shirley Nelson, Steve Newsome, Colette Nichol, Martin Nielsen, Henning Nilsen, Thomasina Nolan, Chieko Nomura, Kath Norgrove, Alissa Nostas **O** Robineau Ophélie, Diana Ordonez, Luciano Orlievsky, James Ovenden **P** Elisa Pardini, Montse Pejuan, Itai Peleg, Aidee Perez, Antonio Perrone, Helen Peter, Rochelle Pincini, William Platt, Luis Ponte Díaz, Ineke Pos, Claude-Eric Poulin, Joanna Priestley, Jeff Pugh **Q** Brian Quinn **R** Mordechai Rabfogel, Laura Raymond-Audet, Tamryn Renwick, Jacson Javier Rivadeneira Zapata, Karen Robacker, Elliot Roberts, Jessica Roberts, Greg Roberts, William Robertson, Lisa Robles, James Rodriguez, Rebecca Rose, Rebecca Rowse **S** Flavio Samaniego, Hilary Sanders, Jan Saunder, Tom Saunders, Linda Schilz, Gisela Schmidtlein, Rosemarie Scholler, Philip Scholte, Peter Schramm, Anne-Marie Schulze, Iris Schwarz, Theodore Scott, Barbara Scrope, Lior Sela, Todd Seliga, Carol Severino, Stephen Shaw, Maureen Shea, Kelsey Sheridan, Dahmay Shiday, Timothy Silvers, Henry Skaggs, Judith Skelton-Green, Charlotte Skrubbeltrang Madsen, Luke Smith, Kate Smith, Diana Spehn, SJ Srinivas, Lisa Stachura, Kate Stalker, Laura Stevens, Jan Van Der Stoep, Laurie Strong, Celina Su, Helga Svendsen, Jesse Swanhuyser, Anna Szwed **T** Leonie Ten Hove, Michel Tessier, Amish Thakkar, Anita Thamm, Mirko Thulke, Arie Tijssen **U** Wiebke Ullmann, Luca Urech **V** Bert Van Ishoven, Janniek Van Wijk, Catiane Vander Kelen, Carla Vank, Ray Vansickle, Nick Vasey, An Vleugels **W** Phoebe Walker, Clinton Watkins, Luke Weatherill, Lynn Weddle, Tom Weiss, David Werier, Tara White, Lisa Whitworth, Tony Whyte, Gerrit Wijns, Shane Wilson, Petra Winkel, Michelle Wright, Keith Wright, Jonathan Wrobel, Victoria Wymark **Y** Suzanne Yin

ACKNOWLEDGMENTS

Many thanks to the following for the use of their content:

Globe on title page ©Mountain High Maps 1993 Digital Wisdom, Inc.

Internal photographs by Lonely Planet Images, and by Chris Beall p72 (#2); Jeff Greenberg p68 (#1); Ralph Hopkins p66 (#1, #2, #3), p69 (#4), p71 (#3); Richard l'Anson p66 (#4), p68 (#2), p70 (#1, #2); Paul Kennedy p65; Ernest Manewal p69 (#3), p71 (#4); Wes Walker p72 (#1);

All images are the copyright of the photographers unless otherwise indicated. Many of the images in this guide are available for licensing from Lonely Planet Images: www.lonelyplanetimages.com.

Index

A

B

C

000 Map pages
000 Photograph pages

INDEX

D

INDEX

INDEX

000 Map pages
000 Photograph pages

N

000 Map pages
000 Photograph pages

INDEX

INDEX

000 Map pages
000 Photograph pages

GREENDEX

Sustainable travel is still a new concept in Ecuador, but one that's growing fast.

Our authors have highlighted the following places that contribute to sustainable tourism in Ecuador, whether it's by using alternative energy, supporting local and indigenous communities, or helping to preserve Ecuador's environment.

You can help us improve this list by sending your recommendations to talk2us@lonelyplanet.com.au. To find out more about sustainable tourism at Lonely Planet, head to www.lonelyplanet.com/responsibletravel.

MAP LEGEND
ROUTES

Tollway	Mall/Steps
Freeway	Tunnel
Primary	Pedestrian Overpass
Secondary	Walking Tour
Tertiary	Walking Tour Detour
Lane	Walking Trail
Under Construction	Walking Path
Unsealed Road	Track
One-Way Street	

TRANSPORT

Ferry	Rail
Metro	Rail (Underground)
Bus Route	Electric Bus

HYDROGRAPHY

River, Creek	Canal
Intermittent River	Water
Swamp	Lake (Dry)
Mangrove	Lake (Salt)
Reef	Mudflats

BOUNDARIES

International	Regional, Suburb
State, Provincial	Ancient Wall
Disputed	Cliff
Marine Park	

AREA FEATURES

Airport	Land
Area of Interest	Mall/Market
Beach, Desert	Park
Building	Reservation
Campus	Rocks
Cemetery, Christian	Sports
Forest	Urban

POPULATION

○ CAPITAL (NATIONAL)	◉ CAPITAL (STATE)
● Large City	● Medium City
○ Small City	○ Town, Village

SYMBOLS

Sights/Activities
- Beach
- Bodysurfing
- Canoeing, Kayaking
- Castle, Fortress
- Christian
- Diving, Snorkeling
- Monument
- Museum, Gallery
- Point of Interest
- Pool
- Ruin
- Snorkeling
- Surfing, Surf Beach
- Trail Head
- Zoo, Bird Sanctuary

Eating
- Eating

Drinking
- Drinking
- Café

Entertainment
- Entertainment

Shopping
- Shopping

Sleeping
- Sleeping
- Camping

Transport
- Airport, Airfield
- Border Crossing
- Bus Station
- Cycling, Bicycle Path
- General Transport
- Parking Area
- Gas Station
- Taxi Rank

Information
- Bank, ATM
- Embassy/Consulate
- Hospital, Medical
- Information
- Internet Facilities
- Police Station
- Post Office, GPO
- Telephone
- Toilets

Geographic
- Lighthouse
- Lookout
- Mountain, Volcano
- National Park
-) (Pass, Canyon
- Picnic Area
- River Flow
- Shelter, Hut
- Waterfall

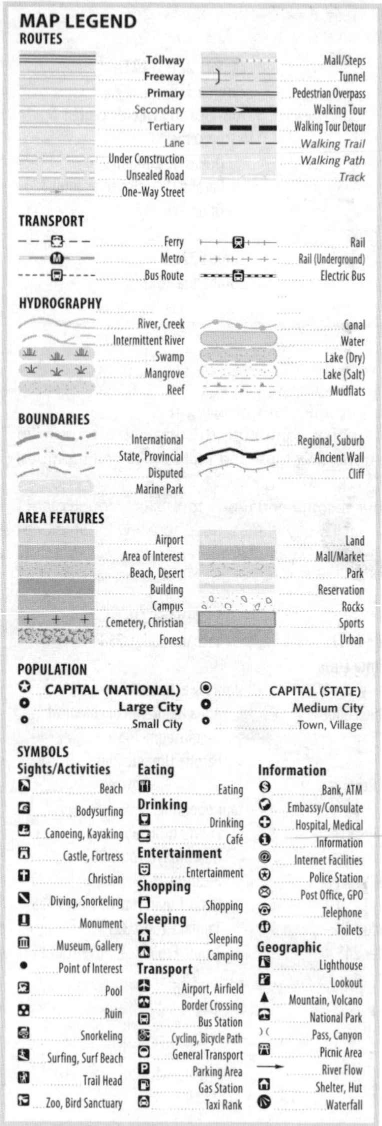

LONELY PLANET OFFICES

Australia
Head Office
Locked Bag 1, Footscray, Victoria 3011
☎ 03 8379 8000, fax 03 8379 8111
talk2us@lonelyplanet.com.au

USA
150 Linden St, Oakland, CA 94607
☎ 510 250 6400, toll free 800 275 8555
fax 510 893 8572
info@lonelyplanet.com

UK
2nd fl, 186 City Rd,
London EC1V 2NT
☎ 020 7106 2100, fax 020 7106 2101
go@lonelyplanet.co.uk

Published by Lonely Planet Publications Pty Ltd
ABN 36 005 607 983

© Lonely Planet Publications Pty Ltd 2009

© photographers as indicated 2009

Cover photograph: Lava lizard sitting on marine iguana on black lava rocks on Isla Fernandina, Galápagos Islands, Ecuador, Paul Souders/Aurora Photos. Many of the images in this guide are available for licensing from Lonely Planet Images: www.lonelyplanetimages.com.

Printed by Toppan Security Printing Pte. Ltd., Singapore.

Mixed Sources
Product group from well-managed forests and other controlled sources
www.fsc.org Cert no. SGS-COC-005002
© 1996 Forest Stewardship Council

FSC